Property and Human Rights

Property and Human Rights

Florence Wagman Roisman
INDIANA UNIVERSITY ROBERT H. MCKINNEY SCHOOL OF LAW

CAROLINA ACADEMIC PRESS
Durham, North Carolina

ISBN 978-0-89089-352-4
LCCN 2007008480

Carolina Academic Press
700 Kent Street
Durham, North Carolina 27701
Telephone: (919) 489-7486
Fax: (919) 493-5668
www.cap-press.com

2024 Printing

For Abram, Christa, Rachel, Jason, B.J., Cassandra, Madeline, Henry, Grace and Michael, in the hope that Cassie, Madeline, Henry, Grace, Michael, and others of their generation will come to maturity in a much more just and peaceful world.

Summary of Contents

Contents

Introduction and Acknowledgments

Property and Human Rights (PHR) is designed to be used either independently or with any Property casebook to enhance consideration of issues of racism, poverty, international human rights, other forms of discrimination and segregation, and related issues.

I am grateful to Ms. Mary Ruth Deer for years of meticulous assistance and to a series of research assistants who have helped to put this material into publishable condition. Among the research assistants are Katie Orton, Janis Sims, Andrea Bonds, Vicki Déak, Monica Doerr, Marissa Florio, Paul Jefferson, Tami Hart, April Meade, Steve LeClere, Ravinder Deol, Victoria Leigh, Aida Ramirez, and Christopher Pottratz. I am especially grateful to Aida Ramirez for preparing the indices. I appreciate very much the support that the Indiana University Robert H. McKinney School of Law always has provided for me.

Many deletions have been made; often, these are not indicated by ellipses or asterisks. Although I have tried to eliminate all errors, it is not likely that I have succeeded. I apologize for any mistakes, and hope that readers will inform me of these so that I may correct them in future editions.

Florence Wagman Roisman
William F. Harvey Professor of Law
Indiana University Robert H. McKinney School of Law
Chancellor's Professor
froisman@iupui.edu
March 21, 2012

Permissions

Excerpts from the following are reprinted with permission:

A Dream Denied: The Criminalization of Homelessness in U.S. Cities. A Report by the National Coalition for the Homeless and the National Law Center on Homelessness and Poverty (2006).

Charles Abrams, Forbidden Neighbors: A Study of Prejudice in Housing (Harper Collins 1955).

Gwendolyn Brooks, The Ballad of Rudolph Reed, from Blacks (Third World Press 1991).

Toi Derricotte, The Black Notebooks: An Interior Journey (W.W. Norton & Co. 1997).

D.E. Fehrenbacher, Dred Scott Case: Its Significance in American Law and Politics (Oxford University Press 2001).

Jonathan L. Entin, Defeasible Fees, State Action, and the Legacy of Massive Resistance, 34 Wm. & Mary L. Rev. 769 (1993).

Maria Foscarinis, Brad Paul, Brucke Porter, and Andrew Scherer, The Human Right to Housing: Making the Case in U.S. Advocacy, 38 Clearinghouse Rev. J. of Pov. L. and Policy 97 (2004).

Lorraine Hansberry, A Raisin In The Sun (Vintage 1958).

Lorraine Hansberry, To Be Young, Gifted and Black (Vintage 1969).

Helen Hershkoff, Transforming Legal Theory in the Light of Practice: The Judicial Application of Social and Economic Rights in the Developing World (Cambridge University Press 2008).

Langston Hughes, Harlem (2), from The Collected Poems of Langston Hughes (Random House 1994).

Kenneth T. Jackson, The Suburban Home as the Answer to Middle-Class Hopes and Fears, from Crabgrass Frontier: The Suburbanization of The United States (Oxford University Press 1985).

Martin Luther King, Jr., I See the Promised Land, in A Testament of Hope: The Essential Writings of Martin Luther King, Jr. (Harper Press 1968).

Melvin Oliver and Thomas Shapiro, Black Wealth/White Wealth: A New Perspective on Racial Inequality (Routledge 1995).

Spencer Overton, Racial Disparities and the Political Function of Property, 49 UCLA L. Rev. 1553 (2002).

J.D. Shelley, I Ain't Moving Nowhere! In Peter Irons, The Courage of Their Convictions (Free Press 1988).

J. Mills Thornton III, Dividing Lines: Municipal Politics and the Struggle for Civil Rights in Montgomery, Birmingham, and Selma (University of Alabama Press 2002).

Clement E. Vose, Caucasians Only: The Supreme Court, the NAACP, and the Restrictive Covenant Cases (University of Calif. Press 1959).

Property and Human Rights

I

The Nature of Property

Dred Scott, Plaintiff in Error v. John F. A. Sandford
60 U.S. 393 (1856)

Mr. Blair and Mr. G.F. Curtis for plaintiff. Mr. Geyer and Mr. Johnson for the defendant.

The counsel filed the following agreed statement of facts, viz:

> In the year 1834, the plaintiff was a negro slave belonging to Dr. Emerson, who was a surgeon in the army of the United States. In that year, 1834, said Dr. Emerson took the plaintiff from the State of Missouri to the military post at Rock Island, in the State of Illinois, and held him there as a slave until the month of April or May, 1836. At the time last mentioned, said Dr. Emerson removed the plaintiff from said military post at Rock Island to the military post at Fort Snelling, situate on the west bank of the Mississippi river, in the Territory known as Upper Louisiana, acquired by the United States of France, and situated north of the latitude of thirty-six degrees thirty minutes north, and north of the State of Missouri. Said Dr. Emerson held the plaintiff in slavery at said Fort Snelling, from said last-mentioned date until the year 1838.

> In the year 1835, Harriet, who is named in the second count of the plaintiff's declaration, was the negro slave of Major Taliaferro, who belonged to the army of the United States. In that year, 1835, said Major Taliaferro took said Harriet to said Fort Snelling, a military post, situated as hereinbefore stated, and kept her there as a slave until the year 1836, and then sold and delivered her as a slave at said Fort Snelling unto the said Dr. Emerson hereinbefore named. Said Dr. Emerson held said Harriet in slavery at said Fort Snelling until the year 1838.

> In the year 1836, the plaintiff and said Harriet at said Fort Snelling, with the consent of said Dr. Emerson, who then claimed to be their master and owner, intermarried, and took each other for husband and wife. Eliza and Lizzie, named in the third count of the plaintiff's declaration, are the fruit of that marriage. Eliza is about fourteen years old, and was born on board the steamboat Gipsey, north of the north line of the State of Missouri, and upon the river Mississippi. Lizzie is about seven years old, and was born in the State of Missouri, at the military post called Jefferson Barracks.

> In the year 1838, said Dr. Emerson removed the plaintiff and said Harriet and their said daughter Eliza, from said Fort Snelling to the State of Missouri, where they have ever since resided.

> Before the commencement of this suit, said Dr. Emerson sold and conveyed the plaintiff, said Harriet, Eliza, and Lizzie, to the defendant, as slaves, and the defendant has ever since claimed to hold them and each of them as slaves.

3

Mr. Chief Justice Taney delivered the opinion of the court.*

There are two leading questions presented by the record:

1. Had the Circuit Court of the United States jurisdiction to hear and determine the case between these parties? And

2. If it had jurisdiction, is the judgment it has given erroneous or not?

The plaintiff in error, who was also the plaintiff in the court case below, was, with his wife and children, held as slaves by the defendant, in the State of Missouri; and he brought this action in the Circuit Court of the United States for that district, to assert the title of himself and his family to freedom.

The declaration is in the form usually adopted in the State to try questions of this description, and contains the averment necessary to give the court jurisdiction; that he and the defendant are citizens of different States; that is, that he is a citizen of Missouri, and the defendant [a] citizen of New York.

The defendant pleaded in abatement to the jurisdiction of the court, that the plaintiff was not a citizen of the State of Missouri, as alleged in his declaration, being a negro of African descent, whose ancestors were of pure African blood, and who were brought into this country and sold as slaves. [The lower court ruled for defendant on the merits.].... Whereupon the plaintiff brought this writ of error.

[First, the Chief Justice considered whether the question of jurisdiction was properly before the Court, and concluded that it was.] * * *

The question is simply this: Can a negro, whose ancestors were imported into this country, and sold as slaves, become a member of the political community formed and brought into existence by the Constitution of the United States, and as such become entitled to all the rights, and privileges, and immunities, guarantied by that instrument to the citizen? One of which rights is the privilege of suing in a court of the United States in the cases specified in the Constitution.

It will be observed, that the plea applies to that class of persons only whose ancestors were negroes of the African race, and imported into this country, and sold and held as slaves. The only matter in issue before the court, therefore, is, whether the descendants of such slaves, when they shall be emancipated, or who are born of parents who had become free before their birth, are citizens of a State, in the sense in which the word citizen is used in the Constitution of the United States. And this being the only matter in dispute on the pleadings, the court must be understood as speaking in this opinion of that class only, that is, of those persons who are the descendants of Africans who were imported into this country, and sold as slaves.

The situation of this population was altogether unlike that of the Indian race. The latter, it is true, formed no part of the colonial communities, and never amalgamated with them in social connections or in government. But although they were uncivilized, they were yet a free and independent people, associated together in nations or tribes, and governed by their own laws. Many of these political communities were situated in territories to which the white race claimed the ultimate right of dominion. But that claim was acknowledged to be subject to the right of the Indians to occupy it as long as they thought proper, and neither the English nor colonial Governments claimed or exercised any dominion over the tribe or nation by whom it was occupied, nor claimed

---

* Editor's Note: Justices Wayne, Catron, Daniel, Nelson, Grier, and Campbell concurred. Justices McLean and Curtis dissented. Their opinions are omitted.

the right to the possession of the territory, until the tribe or nation consented to cede it. These Indian Governments were regarded and treated as foreign Governments, as much so as if an ocean had separated the red man from the white; and their freedom has constantly been acknowledged, from the time of the first emigration to the English colonies to the present day, by the different Governments which succeeded each other. Treaties have been negotiated with them, and their alliance sought for in war; and the people who compose these Indian political communities have always been treated as foreigners not living under our Government. It is true that the course of events has brought the Indian tribes within the limits of the United States under subjection to the white race; and it has been found necessary, for their sake as well as our own, to regard them as in a state of pupilage, and to legislate to a certain extent over them and the territory they occupy. But they may, without doubt, like the subjects of any other foreign Government, be naturalized by the authority of Congress, and become citizens of a State, and of the United States; and if an individual should leave his nation or tribe, and take up his abode among the white population, he would be entitled to all the rights and privileges which would belong to an emigrant from any other foreign people. . . .

The words "people of the United States" and "citizens" are synonymous terms, and mean the same thing. They both describe the political body who, according to our republican institutions, form the sovereignty, and who hold the power and conduct the Government through their representatives. They are what we familiarly call the "sovereign people," and every citizen is one of this people, and a constituent member of this sovereignty. The question before us is, whether the class of persons described in the plea in abatement compose a portion of this people, and are constituent members of this sovereignty? We think they are not, and that they are not included, and were not intended to be included, under the word "citizens" in the Constitution, and can therefore claim none of the rights and privileges which that instrument provides for and secures to citizens of the United States. On the contrary, they were at that time considered as a subordinate and inferior class of beings, who had been subjugated by the dominant race, and, whether emancipated or not, yet remained subject to their authority, and had no rights or privileges but such as those who held the power and the Government might choose to grant them.

It is not the province of the court to decide upon the justice or injustice, the policy or impolicy, of these laws. The decision of that question belonged to the political or law-making power; to those who formed the sovereignty and framed the Constitution. The duty of the court is, to interpret the instrument they have framed, with the best lights we can obtain on the subject, and to administer it as we find it, according to its true intent and meaning when it was adopted.

In discussing this question, we must not confound the rights of citizenship which a State may confer within its own limits, and the rights of citizenship as a member of the Union. It does not by any means follow, because he has all the rights and privileges of a citizen of a State, that he must be a citizen of the United States. He may have all of the rights and privileges of the citizen of a State, and yet not be entitled to the rights and privileges of a citizen in any other State. For, previous to the adoption of the Constitution of the United States, every State had the undoubted right to confer on whomsoever it pleased the character of citizen, and to endow him with all its rights. But this character of course was confined to the boundaries of the State, and gave him no rights or privileges in other States beyond those secured to him by the laws of nations and the comity of States. Nor have the several States surrendered the power of conferring these rights and privileges by adopting the Constitution of the United States. Each State may still confer them upon an alien, or any one it thinks proper, or upon any class or description of persons; yet he would not be a citizen in the sense in which that word is used in the Constitution of the United States, nor entitled to sue as such in one of its courts, nor to the privileges and immunities of a citizen in the other States. The rights which he would acquire would be restricted to the State which gave them. The Constitution has conferred on Congress the right to establish an uniform rule of naturalization, and this right is evidently exclusive, and has always been held by this court to be so. Consequently, no State, since the adoption of the Constitution, can b[y] naturalizing an alien invest him with the rights and privileges secured to a citizen of a State under the Federal Government, although, so far as the State alone was concerned, he would undoubtedly be entitled to the rights of a citizen, and clothed with all the rights and immunities which the Constitution and laws of the State attached to that character.

It is very clear, therefore, that no State can, by any act or law of its own, passed since the adoption of the Constitution, introduce a new member into the political community created by the Constitution of the United States. It cannot make him a member of this community by making him a member of its own. And for the same reason it cannot introduce any person, or description of persons, who were not intended to be embraced in this new political family, which the Constitution brought into existence, but were intended to be excluded from it.

The question then arises, whether the provisions of the Constitution, in relation to the personal rights and privileges to which the citizen of a State should be entitled, embraced the negro African race, at that time in this country, or who might afterwards be imported, who had then or should afterwards be made free in any State; and to put it in the power of a single State to make him a citizen of the United States, and endue him with the full rights of citizenship in every other State without their consent? Does the Constitution of the United States act upon him whenever he shall be made free under the laws of a State, and raised there to the rank of a citizen, and immediately clothe him with all the privileges of a citizen in every other State, and in its own courts?

The court think the affirmative of these propositions cannot be maintained. And if it cannot, the plaintiff in error could not be a citizen of the State of Missouri, within the meaning of the Constitution of the United States, and, consequently, was not entitled to sue in its courts.

It is true, every person, and every class and description of persons, who were at the time of the adoption of the Constitution recognized as citizens in the several States, became also citizens of this new political body; but none other; it was formed by them, and for them and their posterity, but for no one else. And the personal rights and privileges guarantied to citizens of this new sovereignty were intended to embrace those only who were then members of the several State communities, or who should afterwards by birthright or otherwise become members, according to the provisions of the Constitution and the principles on which it was founded. It was the union of those who were at that time members of distinct and separate political communities into one political family, whose power, for certain specified purposes, was to extend over the whole territory of the United States. And it gave to each citizen rights and privileges outside of his State which he did not before possess, and placed him in every other State upon a perfect equality with its own citizens as to rights of person and rights of property; it made him a citizen of the United States.

It becomes necessary, therefore, to determine who were citizens of the several States when the Constitution was adopted. And in order to do this, we must recur to the Governments and institutions of the thirteen colonies, when they separated from Great Britain and formed new sovereignties, and took their places in the family of independent nations. We must inquire who, at that time, were recognized as the people or citizens of a State, whose rights and liberties had been outraged by the English Government; and who declared their independence, and assumed the powers of Government to defend their rights by force of arms.

In the opinion of the court, the legislation and histories of the times, and the language used in the Declaration of Independence, show, that neither the class of persons who had been imported as slaves, nor their descendants, whether they had become free or not, were then acknowledged as a part of the people, nor intended to be included in the general words used in that memorable instrument.

It is difficult at this day to realize the state of public opinion in relation to that unfortunate race, which prevailed in the civilized and enlightened portions of the world at the time of the Declaration of Independence, and when the Constitution of the United States was framed and adopted. But the public history of every European nation displays it in a manner too plain to be mistaken.

They had for more than a century before been regarded as beings of an inferior order, and altogether unfit to associate with the white race, either in social or political relations; and so far inferior, that they had no rights which the white man was bound to respect; and that the negro might justly and lawfully be reduced to slavery for his benefit. He was bought and sold, and treated as an ordinary article of merchandise and traffic, whenever a profit could be made by it. This opinion was at that time fixed and universal in the civilized portion of the white race. It was regarded as an axiom in morals as well as in politics, which no one thought of disputing, or supposed to be open to dispute; and men in every grade and position in society daily and habitually acted upon it in their private pursuits, as well as in matters of public concern, without doubting for a moment the correctness of this opinion.

And in no nation was this opinion more firmly fixed or more uniformly acted upon than by the English Government and English people. They not only seized them on the coast of Africa, and sold them or held them in slavery for their own use; but they took them as ordinary articles of merchandise to every country where they could make a profit on them, and were far more extensively engaged in this commerce than any other nation in the world.

The opinion thus entertained and acted upon in England was naturally impressed upon the colonies they founded on this side of the Atlantic. And, accordingly, a negro of the African race was regarded by them as an article of property, and held, and bought and sold as such, in every one of the thirteen colonies which united in the Declaration of Independence, and afterwards formed the Constitution of the United States. The slaves were more or less numerous in the different colonies, as slave labor was found more or less profitable. But no one seems to have doubted the correctness of the prevailing opinion of the time.

The legislation of the different colonies furnishes positive and indisputable proof of this fact. * * *

We refer to these historical facts for the purpose of showing the fixed opinions concerning that race, upon which the statesmen of that day spoke and acted. It is necessary to do this, in order to determine whether the general terms used in the Constitution of the United States, as to the rights of man and the rights of the people, was intended to include them, or to give to them or their posterity the benefit of any of its provisions.

The language of the Declaration of Independence is equally conclusive:

It begins by declaring that, "when in the course of human events it becomes necessary for one people to dissolve the political bands which have connected them with another, and to assume among the powers of the earth the separate and equal station to
which the laws of nature and nature's God entitle them, a decent respect for the opinions of mankind requires that they should declare the causes which impel them to the
separation."

It then proceeds to say: "We hold these truths to be self-evident: that all men are created equal; that they are endowed by their Creator with certain unalienable rights; that
among them is life, liberty, and the pursuit of happiness; that to secure these rights,
Governments are instituted, deriving their just powers from the consent of the governed."

The general words above quoted would seem to embrace the whole human family,
and if they were used in a similar instrument at this day would be so understood. But it
is too clear for dispute, that the enslaved African race were not intended to be included,
and formed no part of the people who framed and adopted this declaration; for if the
language, as understood in that day, would embrace them, the conduct of the distinguished men who framed the Declaration of Independence would have been utterly and
flagrantly inconsistent with the principles they asserted; and instead of the sympathy of
mankind, to which they so confidently appealed, they would have deserved and received universal rebuke and reprobation.

Yet the men who framed this declaration were great men—high in literary acquire-
ments—high in their sense of honor, and incapable of asserting principles inconsistent
with those on which they were acting. They perfectly understood the meaning of the
language they used, and how it would be understood by others; and they knew that it
would not in any part of the civilized world be supposed to embrace the negro race,
which, by common consent, had been excluded from civilized Governments and the
family of nations, and doomed to slavery. They spoke and acted according to the then
established doctrines and principles, and in the ordinary language of the day, and no
one misunderstood them. The unhappy black race were separated from the white by in-
delible marks, and laws long before established, and were never thought of or spoken of
except as property, and when the claims of the owner or the profit of the trader were
supposed to need protection.

This state of public opinion had undergone no change when the Constitution was
adopted, as is equally evident from its provisions and language.

The brief preamble sets forth by whom it was formed, for what purposes, and for
whose benefit and protection. It declares that it is formed by the *people* of the United
States; that is to say, by those who were members of the different political communities
in the several States; and its great object is declared to be to secure the blessings of liberty to themselves and their posterity. It speaks in general terms of the *people* of the
United States, and of *citizens* of the several States, when it is providing for the exercise
of the powers granted or the privileges secured to the citizen. It does not define what
description of persons are intended to be included under these terms, or who shall be
regarded as a citizen and one of the people. It uses them as terms so well understood,
that no further description or definition was necessary.

But there are two clauses in the Constitution which point directly and specifically to
the negro race as a separate class of persons, and show clearly that they were not regarded as a portion of the people or citizens of the Government then formed.

One of these clauses reserves to each of the thirteen States the right to import slaves until the year 1808, if it thinks proper. And the importation which it thus sanctions was unquestionably of persons of the race of which we are speaking, as the traffic in slaves in the United States had always been confined to them. And by the other provision the States pledge themselves to each other to maintain the right of property of the master, by delivering up to him any slave who may have escaped from his service, and be found within their respective territories. By the first above-mentioned clause, therefore, the right to purchase and hold this property is directly sanctioned and authorized for twenty years by the people who framed the Constitution. And by the second, they pledge themselves to maintain and uphold the right of the master in the manner specified, as long as the Government they then formed should endure. And these two provisions show, conclusively, that neither the description of persons therein referred to, no[r] their descendants, were embraced in any of the other provisions of the Constitution; for certainly these two clauses were not intended to confer on them or their posterity the blessings of liberty, or any of the personal rights so carefully provided for the citizen.

No one of that race had ever migrated to the United States voluntarily; all of them had been brought here as articles of merchandise. The number that had been emancipated at that time were but few in comparison with those held in slavery; and they were identified in the public mind with the race to which they belonged, and regarded as a part of the slave population rather than the free. It is obvious that they were not even in the minds of the framers of the Constitution when they were conferring special rights and privileges upon the citizens of a State in every other part of the Union.

Indeed, when we look to the condition of this race in the several States at the time, it is impossible to believe that these rights and privileges were intended to be extended to them. * * *

Neither was it used with any reference to the African race imported into or born in this country; because Congress had no power to naturalize them, and therefore there was no necessity for using particular words to exclude them. * * *

And upon a full and careful consideration of the subject, the court is of opinion, that, upon the facts stated in the plea in abatement, Dred Scott was not a citizen of Missouri within the meaning of the Constitution of the United States, and not entitled as such to sue in its courts; and, consequently, that the Circuit Court had no jurisdiction of the case, and that the judgment on the plea in abatement is erroneous. * * *

We proceed to examine the [substantive] question.

The act of Congress, upon which the plaintiff relies, declares that slavery and involuntary servitude, except as a punishment for crime, shall be forever prohibited in all that part of the territory ceded by France, under the name of Louisiana, which lies north of thirty-six degrees thirty minutes north latitude, and not included within the limits of Missouri. And the difficulty which meets us at the threshold of this part of the inquiry is, whether Congress was authorized to pass this law under any of the powers granted to it by the Constitution; for if the authority is not given by that instrument, it is the duty of this court to declare it void and inoperative, and incapable of conferring freedom upon any one who is held as a slave under the laws of any one of the States. * * *

But the power of Congress over the person or property of a citizen can never be a mere discretionary power under our Constitution and form of Government. The powers of the Government and the rights and privileges of the citizen are regulated and plainly defined by the Constitution itself. * * *

These powers, and others, in relation to rights of person, which it is not necessary here to enumerate, are, in express and positive terms, denied to the General Government; and the rights of private property have been guarded with equal care. Thus the rights of property are united with the rights of person, and placed on the same ground by the fifth amendment to the Constitution, which provides that no person shall be deprived of life, liberty, and property, without due process of law. And an act of Congress which deprives a citizen of the United States of his liberty or property, merely because he came himself or brought his property into a particular Territory of the United States, and who had committed no offence against the laws, could hardly be dignified with the name of due process of law. * * *

The powers over person and property of which we speak are not only not granted to Congress, but are in express terms denied, and they are forbidden to exercise them. And this prohibition is not confined to the States, but the words are general, and extend to the whole territory over which the Constitution gives it power to legislate, including those portions of it remaining under Territorial Government, as well as that covered by States. It is a total absence of power everywhere within the dominion of the United States, and places the citizens of a Territory, so far as these rights are concerned, on the same footing with citizens of the States, and guards them as firmly and plainly against any inroads which the General Government might attempt, under the plea of implied or incidental powers. And if Congress itself cannot do this—if it is beyond the powers conferred on the Federal Government—it will be admitted, we presume, that it could not authorize a Territorial Government to exercise them. It could confer no power on any local Government, established by its authority, to violate the provisions of the Constitution.

It seems, however, to be supposed, that there is a difference between property in a slave and other property, and that different rules may be applied to it in expounding the Constitution of the United States. And the laws and usages of nations, and the writings of eminent jurists upon the relation of master and slave and their mutual rights and duties, and the powers which Governments may exercise over it, have been dwelt upon in the argument.

But in considering the question before us, it must be borne in mind that there is no law of nations standing between the people of the United States and their Government, and interfering with their relation to each other. The powers of the Government, and the rights of the citizen under it, are positive and practical regulations plainly written down. The people of the United States have delegated to it certain enumerated powers, and forbidden it to exercise others. It has no power over the person or property of a citizen but what the citizens of the United States have granted. And no laws or usages of other nations, or reasoning of statesmen or jurists upon the relations of master and slave, can enlarge the powers of the Government, or take from the citizens the rights they have reserved. And if the Constitution recognizes the right of property of the master in a slave, and makes no distinction between that description of property and other property owned by a citizen, no tribunal, acting under the authority of the United States, whether it be legislative, executive, or judicial, has a right to draw such a distinction, or deny to it the benefit of the provisions and guarantees which have been provided for the protection of private property against the encroachments of the Government.

Now, as we have already said in an earlier part of this opinion, upon a different point, the right of property in a slave is distinctly and expressly affirmed in the Constitution. The right to traffic in it, like an ordinary article of merchandise and property, was guaranteed to the citizens of the United States, in every State that might desire it, for twenty years. And the Government in express terms is pledged to protect it in all future time, if the slave escapes from his owner. This is done in plain words—too plain to be misunderstood. And no word can be found in the Constitution which gives Congress a greater power over slave property, or which entitles property of that kind to less protection than property of any other description. The only power conferred is the power coupled with the duty of guarding and protecting the owner in his rights.

Upon these considerations, it is the opinion of the court that the act of Congress which prohibited a citizen from holding and owning property of this kind in the territory of the United States north of the line therein mentioned, is not warranted by the Constitution, and is therefore void; and that neither Dred Scott himself, nor any of his family, were made free by being carried into this territory; even if they had been carried there by the owner, with the intention of becoming a permanent resident.

Notes

1. With respect to Chief Justice Taney's interpretation of the Declaration of Independence, compare the view of Abraham Lincoln, who said that the authors of the Declaration meant

> simply to declare the *right* so that the *enforcement* of it might follow as fast as the circumstances should permit. They meant to set up a standard maxim for free men which should be familiar to all, and revered by all; constantly looked to, and constantly labored for, and even though never perfectly attained, constantly approximated and thereby constantly spreading and deepening its influence, and augmenting the happiness and value of life to all people of all colors everywhere.*

2. From Don E. Fehrenbacher, The Dred Scott Case: Its Significance in American Law and Politics 380–81 (Oxford U. Press 1978) (emphasis and numbering of statements in Chief Justice Taney's opinion in original):

> [1] Now, as we have already said in an earlier part of this opinion, upon a different point, the right of property in a slave is distinctly and expressly affirmed in the Constitution. [2] The right to traffic in it, like an ordinary article of merchandise and property, was guarantied to the citizens of the United States, in every State that might desire it, for twenty years. [3] And the Government in express terms is pledged to protect it in all future time, if the slave escapes from his owner. [4] This is done in plain words—too plain to be misunderstood. [5] And no word can be found in the Constitution which gives Congress a greater power over slave property, or which entitles property of that kind to less protection than the property of any other description. [6] The only power conferred is the power coupled with the duty of guarding and protecting the owner in his rights.

Since the Constitution uses neither the word "slavery" nor the word "property" in connection with Negroes, the first sentence is manifestly untrue. Whatever implications may have been understood by the framers, nothing is *expressly* affirmed about slavery as a property right. The second and third sentences constitute the whole of Taney's proof

---

* Lincoln-Douglas Debates: The First Complete, Unexpurgated Text (Henry Holzer, ed. 1993) 344–45, quoted in Pauline Maier, American Scripture: Making the Declaration of Independence 205–06 (Vintage Books 1997).

for his assertion in sentence number one, and both are stated in misleading terms. The Constitution permitted, but did not guarantee, continuation of the African slave trade for twenty years. Even this temporary immunity applied only to the original thirteen states. Hence, insofar as the slave-trade clause did recognize a "right of property" in slaves, it likewise acknowledged the power of Congress to extinguish that right, eventually in the original states and immediately in the rest of the national domain. As for the fugitive-slave clause, it appears in the section of the Constitution devoted to interstate comity and from its text alone could have been interpreted as an obligation laid solely on the individual states (as with the rendition of fugitives from justice). There is no express "pledge" of assistance from the central government in the recovery of fugitive slaves. If the clause required such intervention, it did so only by implication. The fourth sentence, coming after emphatic use of the words "express" and "expressly," is one of those superfluous reiterations that weaken credibility. It exemplifies Taney's habit of strengthening a dubious argument by declaring it to be an incontestable argument. The fifth sentence, restating the principle of the unexceptionalness and equality of slave property, seems incompatible with the fugitive-slave and slave-trade clauses, which, if they treat slaves as property, treat them as a unique and specially favored kind of property. The sixth sentence may or may not have been intended merely as an elaboration of sentence number three, on the fugitive-slave clause, but the effect of its broad phrasing was to endorse subsequent southern demands for a comprehensive federal slave code in the territories.

Together, the fifth and sixth sentences of this summary paragraph constituted a return to the strict-construction approach with which Taney had begun his discussion of the Missouri Compromise restriction. After affirming that slaves were recognized as property by the Constitution, he did not, as one might expect, invoke the due-process clause in defense of property rights against congressional interference. Instead, he contented himself with holding that Congress had been delegated no power to treat property in slaves differently from other property. This is not the broad construction of the negative or restraining clauses of the Constitution with which we associate later use of the due-process clause. Nevertheless, he was now ready to make his historic pronouncement:

> Upon these considerations, it is the opinion of the court that the Act of Congress which prohibited a citizen from holding and owning property of this kind in the territory of the United States north of the line therein mentioned, is not warranted by the Constitution, and is therefore void; and that neither Dred Scott himself, nor any of his family, were made free by being carried into this territory; even if they had been carried there by the owner, with the intention of becoming a permanent resident.*

Newman v. Sathyavaglswaran

287 F.3d 786 (9th Cir. 2002), cert. denied, 537 U.S. 1029 (2002)

Bill Colovos, Southgate, MI, for the plaintiffs-appellants.

Cheryl A. Orr, Musick, Peeler & Garrett LLP, Los Angeles, CA; Aaron M. Peck, Arter & Hadden LLP, Los Angeles, CA, for the defendants-appellees.

---

* This final clause was Taney's only reference to the important question of whether Dred Scott's half-dozen years in free territory constituted "temporary" or "permanent" residence. Taney, by implication took the view that it was temporary, ignoring a long tradition of southern jurisprudence to the contrary.... [This footnote is Professor Fehrenbacher's.]

Before Browning, Fernandez, and Fisher, Circuit Judges. Dissent by Judge Fernandez.
Fisher, Circuit Judge.

Parents, whose deceased children's corneas were removed by the Los Angeles County Coroner's office without notice or consent, brought this 42 U.S.C. § 1983 action alleging a taking of their property without due process of law. The complaint was dismissed by the district court for a failure to state a claim upon which relief could be granted. We must decide whether the longstanding recognition in the law of California, paralleled by our national common law, that next of kin have the exclusive right to possess the bodies of their deceased family members creates a property interest, the deprivation of which must be accorded due process of law under the Fourteenth Amendment of the United States Constitution. We hold that it does. The parents were not required to exhaust post deprivation procedures prior to bringing this suit. Thus, we hold that they properly stated a claim under § 1983.

I. Factual and Procedural Background

In reviewing the district court's dismissal of the complaint under Rule 12(b)(6), "we must 'take as true all allegations of material fact stated in the complaint and construe them in the light most favorable to the nonmoving party.'" Robert Newman and Barbara Obarski (the parents) each had children, Richard Newman and Kenneth Obarski respectively, who died in Los Angeles County in October 1997. Following their deaths, the Office of the Coroner for the County of Los Angeles (the coroner) obtained possession of the bodies of the children and, under procedures adopted pursuant to California Government Code § 27491.47 as it then existed,[1] removed the corneas from those bodies without the knowledge of the parents and without an attempt to notify them and request consent. The parents became aware of the coroner's actions in September 1999 and subsequently filed this § 1983 action alleging a deprivation of their property without due process of law in violation of the Fourteenth Amendment.[2]

The coroner filed a Rule 12(b)(6) motion to dismiss, arguing that the parents could not have a property interest in their deceased children's corneas. The coroner also argued that to the extent the parents did have due process rights, they were required to exhaust state post-deprivation remedies prior to bringing suit. The district court granted the motion to dismiss.... We review de novo to assess whether "it appears beyond doubt that the plaintiff[s] can prove no set of facts in support of [their] claim which would entitle [them] to relief." Conley v. Gibson, 355 U.S. 41, 45-46 (1957).

II. Property Interests in Dead Bodies

The Fourteenth Amendment prohibits states from "depriv[ing] any person of life, liberty, or property, without due process of law." U.S. Const. amend. XIV, § 1. At the threshold, a claim under § 1983 for an unconstitutional deprivation of property must

---

1. California Government Code § 27491.47(a) stated:

Notwithstanding any other provision of law, the coroner may, in the course of an autopsy, remove and release or authorize the removal and release of corneal eye tissue from a body within the coroner's custody, if ... [t]he coroner has no knowledge of objection to the removal....

2. 42 U.S.C. § 1983 states, in relevant part:

Every person who, under color of any statute, ordinance, regulation, custom, or usage, of any State or Territory or the District of Columbia, subjects, or causes to be subjected, any citizen of the United States or other person within the jurisdiction thereof to the deprivation of any rights, privileges, or immunities secured by the Constitution and laws, shall be liable to the party injured in an action at law, suit in equity, or other proper proceeding for redress....

show (1) a deprivation (2) of property (3) under color of state law. If these elements are met, the question becomes whether the state afforded constitutionally adequate process for the deprivation. Here, it is uncontested that the coroner's action was a deprivation under color of state law. The coroner argues, however, that the dismissal of the parents' complaint was proper because they could not have a property interest in their children's corneas.

Since Rochin v. California, 342 U.S. 165 (1952), the Supreme Court repeatedly has affirmed that "the right of every individual to the possession and control of his own person, free from all restraint or interference of others" is "so rooted in the traditions and conscience of our people" as to be ranked as one of the fundamental liberties protected by the "substantive" component of the Due Process Clause. This liberty, the Court has "strongly suggested," extends to the personal decisions about "how to best protect dignity and independence at the end of life." Washington v. Glucksberg, 521 U.S. 702, 716, 720 (1997); Cruzan v. Missouri Dep't of Health, 497 U.S. 261, 302, 305 (1990) (Brennan, J. dissenting) (expressing the view that a right "to choose to die with dignity" flows from "[t]he right ... to determine what shall be done with one's own body, [which] *is* deeply rooted in this Nation's traditions ... and is securely grounded in the earliest common law"). The Court has not had occasion to address whether the rights of possession and control of one's own body, the most "sacred" and "carefully guarded" of all rights in the common law, are property interests protected by the Due Process Clause. Nor has it addressed what Due Process protections are applicable to the rights of next of kin to possess and control the bodies of their deceased relatives.

"[T]he property interests protected by procedural due process extend well beyond actual ownership of real estate, chattels, or money." Board of Regents v. Roth, 408 U.S. 564, 571–72 (1972).[3] "The Fourteenth Amendment's procedural protection of property is a safeguard of the security of interests that a person has already acquired[.]" Id. at 576.[4] These property interests "are not created by the Constitution[;] ... they are created and their dimensions are defined by existing rules or understandings that stem from an independent source such as state law[.]" Id. at 577. Thus, the first step of our analysis is to analyze the history of rules and understandings of our nation with respect to the possession and protection of the bodies of the dead.

A. History of Common Law Interests in Dead Bodies

Duties to protect the dignity of the human body after its death are deeply rooted in our nation's history. In a valuable history of the subject, the Supreme Court of Rhode Island recounted:

> By the civil law of ancient Rome, the charge of burial was first upon the person to whom it was delegated by the deceased; second, upon the *scripti haeredes* (to whom the property was given), and if none, then upon the *haeredes legitimi* or *cognati* in order.... The heirs might be compelled to comply with the provi-

---

3. See Morton J. Horwitz, The Transformation of American Law: 1870–1960 145 (1992) (describing the transformation of the concept of property after the Civil War away from "the prevailing emphasis in traditional law ... on a 'physicalist' definition of property derived from land").

4. See Arthur Linton Corbin, Taxation of Seats on the Stock Exchange, 31 Yale L.J. 429, 429 (1922) ("Our concept of property has shifted.... '[P]roperty' has ceased to describe any res, or object of sense, at all, and has become merely a bundle of legal relations — rights, powers, privileges, immunities.")

sions of the will in regard to burial. And the Pontifical College had the power of providing for the burial of those who had no place of burial in their own right.

Pierce v. Proprietors of Swan Point Cemetery, 10 R.I. 227, 235–36, 1872 WL 3575 (1872) (citations omitted).

In 17th century England, and in much of Europe, duties to bury the dead and protect the dignified disposition of the body, described as flowing from a *"right of burial, ...* a person's *right* to be buried,"* id. at 238–39; accord In re Johnsons's Estate, 169 Misc. 215, 7 N.Y.S.2d 81, 84 (N.Y.Surr.Ct.1938) (explaining that in 17th century England, "[a] man had a right to the decent interment of his own body in expectation of the day of resurrection"),[5] were borne primarily by churches, which had a duty to bury the bodies of those residing in their parishes. Pierce, 10 R.I. at 236. These duties, and the explanation of their genesis in the rights of the dead, carried over into New England colonial practice where "[i]n many parts ... the parish system prevailed, and every family was considered to have a right of burial in the churchyard of the parish in which they lived." Id. at 235.

The Roman practice of including duties to protect the body of the dead in civil law had no parallel in the early English common law because burials were matters of ecclesiastical cognizance. Id. Thus, Blackstone explained that "though the heir has a property [interest] in the monuments and escutcheons of his ancestors, yet he has none in their bodies or ashes; nor can he bring any suit or action against such as indecently, at least, if not injuriously, violate and disturb their remains, when dead and buried." Bessemer Land & Improvement Co. v. Jenkins, 111 Ala. 135, 18 So. 565, 567 (1895) (quoting 1 Bl. Comm. 429); see also In re Johnson's Estate, 7 N.Y.S.2d at 83 (discussing Lord Coke's assertion that "buriall of the cadaver ... is nullius in bonis, and belongs to ecclesiastical cognisance").

A change in the common law in England can be traced to the 1840 case of Rex v. Stewart, 12 AD. & E. 773 (1840). In that case, the socially recognized right of the dead to a dignified disposition, previously enforced only through ecclesiastical courts, was interpreted as creating enforceable common law duties. The question before the court was whether the hospital in which "a pauper" died or the parish in which she was to be buried was under a duty to carry the body to the grave. The court expressed "extreme difficulty in placing ... any legal foundation" for either rule, but stated it was unwilling to discharge the case "considering how long the practice had prevailed, and been sanctioned, of burying such persons at the expense of the parish, and the general consequences of holding that such practice ha[d] no warrant in law." It stated the premises that, under long-standing tradition, "[e]very person ... has a right to Christian bur-

---

5. The logical relationship between rights and duties has been the subject of considerable academic examination. Wesley Hohfeld famously described rights and duties as "jural correlatives" — different aspects of the same legal relation. See Wesley Hohfeld, Some Fundamental Legal Conceptions as Applied in Judicial Reasoning, 23 Yale L.J. 16 (1913); see also Joseph William Singer, The Legal Rights Debate in Analytical Jurisprudence from Bentham to Hohfeld, 1982 Wis. L.Rev. 975; Arthur Corbin, Jural Relations and Their Classification, 30 Yale L.J. 226 (1921). Oliver Wendell Holmes described rights as "intellectual constructs used to describe the consequences of legal obligations. As he puts it [in The Common Law (1881)], 'legal duties are logically antecedent to legal rights.'" Horowitz, supra at 138. Holmes' description appears particularly apt in respect to the law regarding dead bodies where duties to provide burial were recognized as flowing from a right of the dead, even though "strictly speaking, ... a dead man cannot be said to have rights." Pierce, 10 R.I. at 239.

ial ... that implies the right to be carried from the place where his body lies to the parish cemetery" and "bodies ... carried in a state of naked exposure to the grave [ ] would be a real offence to the living, as well as an apparent indignity to the dead." From these traditional understandings, the court concluded that "[t]he feelings and interests of the living require" that "the common law cast [ ] on some one the duty of carrying to the grave, decently covered, the dead body of any person dying in such a state of indigence as to leave no funds for that purpose." That duty, it held, was imposed on "the individual under whose roof a poor person dies ... : he cannot keep him unburied, nor do any thing which prevents Christian burial: he cannot therefore cast him out, so as to expose the body to violation, or to offend the feelings or endanger the health of the living: and for the same reason, he cannot carry him uncovered to the grave."

Many early American courts adopted Blackstone's description of the common law, holding that "a dead body is not the subject of property right." The duty to protect the body by providing a burial was often described as flowing from the "universal ... right of sepulture," rather than from a concept of property law. As cases involving unauthorized mutilation and disposition of bodies increased toward the end of the 19th century, paralleling the rise in demand for human cadavers in medical science and use of cremation as an alternative to burial, courts began to recognize an exclusive right of the next of kin to possess and control the disposition of the bodies of their dead relatives, the violation of which was actionable at law. Thus, in holding that a city council could not "seize upon existing private burial grounds, make them public, and exclude the proprietors from their management," the Supreme Court of Indiana commented that "the burial of the dead can [not] ... be taken out of the hands of the relatives thereof" because "we lay down the proposition, that the bodies of the dead belong to the surviving relations, in the order of inheritance, as property, and that they have the right to dispose of them as such, within restrictions analogous to those by which the disposition of other property may be regulated." Bogert v. City of Indianapolis, 13 Ind. 134, 136, 138 (1859).[6] Over a decade later, the Rhode Island Supreme Court described the nation's common law as bestowing upon next of kin "a duty [towards the dead], and we may also say a right, to protect from violation; and a duty on the part of others to abstain from violation"; a dead body "may therefore be considered as a sort of *quasi* property." Pierce, 10 R.I. at 238.

---

6. Bogert attributed the rule that dead bodies "belong to the surviving relations ... as property" to a report by the Honorable Samuel B. Ruggles, special master to the State Supreme Court of New York, 4 Bradford's Surrogate 503, 503–532 (1856). Ruggles was appointed to analyze the legal implications of relocating some graves to complete the widening of Beekman street. He "submitted the following conclusion[s], as justly deducible from the fact, that no ecclesiastical element existed in the jurisprudence of the state of New York":

  1. That neither a corpse, nor its burial, is legally subject, in any way, to ecclesiastical cognizance, nor to sacerdotal power of any kind.
  2. That the right to bury a corpse and to preserve its remains, is a legal right, which the Courts of law will recognize and protect.
  3. That such right, in the absence of any testamentary disposition, belongs exclusively to the next of kin.
  4. That the right to protect the remains, includes the right to preserve them by separate burial, to select the place of sepulture, and to change it at pleasure.
  5. That if the place of burial be taken for public use, the next of kin may claim to be indemnified for the expense of removing and suitably reinterring their remains.

Bogert, 13 Ind. at 140 n. 1.

B. Interests in Dead Bodies in California Law

In 1872, the same year Pierce was decided, California enacted Penal Code § 292, imposing a legal duty on next of kin to bury the deceased. In 1899, the California Supreme Court held that duty required recognition of exclusive rights of possession, control and disposition vesting in those with the duty. O'Donnel v. Slack, 123 Cal. 285, 55 P. 906, 907 (1899). These rights, it explained, were by law "protected, and for a violation of which [next of kin] are entitled to indemnification."

At issue in O'Donnel was a probate court's order that a third party "stranger in blood" be charged with removing O'Donnel's body to his desired grave in Ireland. His wife, who was too sick to move the body immediately, objected that only she had the right to accompany the body and refused to consent to anyone else being given that charge. Relying heavily on the reasoning of Pierce, the California Supreme Court explained:

> The duty of the burial of the dead is made an express legal obligation [by Penal Code § 292]; but aside from the obligation, there is a right, well defined and universally recognized, that in disposing of the body of deceased the last sad offices belong of right to the next of kin.... This right had its origin in sentiment, in affection for the dead, in religious belief in some form of future life. It therefore early became a subject of cognizance by the ecclesiastical courts. But, while thus having its origin in affection and religious sentiment, it soon came to be recognized as a strictly legal right; and the next of kin, while not, in the full proprietary sense, 'owning' the body of the deceased, have property rights in the body....

The court annulled the order of the probate court, holding the next of kin's rights of possession and control of the body exclusive of others.

One year later, in Enos v. Snyder, 131 Cal. 68, 63 P. 170 (1900), the California Supreme Court upheld the interests of next of kin in relation to dead bodies. In that case, Mr. Enos had directed in his will that his burial be "'according to the wishes and directions of Mrs. R.J. Snyder,'" with whom he was living when he died. His wife and daughter, as next of kin, sued Snyder for possession and control of the body for its disposition. Thus was raised the question: "did the respondents, as next of kin, have the right to the possession of the body of the deceased for the purpose of burying it, as against the appellants, who claim that right under the will?" The court resolved the question in favor of the next of kin. In doing so, it held: "in the absence of statutory provisions, there is no property in a dead body, that it is not part of the estate of the deceased person, and that a man cannot by will dispose of that which after his death will be his corpse."

The holding of Enos that a person cannot by will dispose of his corpse was abrogated by statute. The explanation that "there is no property in a dead body" has been modified by most courts addressing the subject. Following O'Donnel and Pierce, California courts commonly use the term "quasi property" to describe the rights of next of kin to the body of the deceased.

In 1931, the exclusive rights of possession, control and disposition of the corpse recognized in O'Donnel, together with the duty previously contained in Penal Code § 292, were codified in Health and Safety Code § 7100.[7] California has at all times recognized

---

7. At the time relevant to this case, the statute read:
The right to control the disposition of the remains of a deceased person, unless other directions have been given by the decedent, vests in, and the duty of interment and the liability for the reasonable cost of interment of such remains devolves upon the following in the order named:
(a) The surviving spouse.

these rights as exclusive of others. Thus civil litigants have no right to demand an autopsy, and friends of the deceased have no right to attend the burial over the objection
of next of kin. Violation of the correlative duty of others to refrain from disturbing the
body is subject to an action for "tortious interference with a right to dispose of a decedent's remains."

C. The Right to Transfer Body Parts

The first successful transplantation of a kidney in 1954 led to an expansion of the
rights of next of kin to the bodies of the dead. In 1968, the National Conference of
Commissioners on Uniform State Laws approved the Uniform Anatomical Gift Act
(UAGA), adopted by California the same year, which grants next of kin the right to
transfer the parts of bodies in their possession to others for medical or research purposes. Cal. Health & Safety Code § 7150 et seq. The right to transfer is limited. The California UAGA prohibits any person from "knowingly, for valuable consideration, pur-
chas[ing] or sell[ing] a part for transplantation, therapy, or reconditioning, if removal
of the part is intended to occur after the death of the decedent," Cal. Health & Safety
Code § 7155, as does federal law, 42 U.S.C. § 274e (prohibiting the "transfer [of] any
human organ for valuable consideration");[8] cf. Finley v. Atl. Transport Co., 220 N.Y.
249, 115 N.E. 715, 717 (1917) ("[T]here is no right of property in a dead body ... as
understood in the commercial sense."); Larson v. Chase, 47 Minn. 307, 50 N.W. 238,
239 (1891) ("[A] dead body is not property in the common commercial sense of that
term[.]").

In the 1970s and 1980s, medical science improvements and the related demand for
transplant organs prompted governments to search for new ways to increase the supply
of organs for donation. See National Organ Transplant Act, Pub.L. No. 98-507, 98 Stat
2339 (1984) (establishing Task Force on Organ Transplantation and the Organ Procurement and Transplantation Network); S.Rep. No. 98-382, at 2–4 (1984), reprinted in
1984 U.S.C.C.A.N. 3975, 3976–78 (discussing "major advances ... in the science of
human organ transplantation," and the "need[ ] ... to encourage organ donation" to
meet a supply "far short" of demand). Many perceived as a hindrance to the supply of
needed organs the rule implicit in the UAGA that donations could be effected only if
consent was received from the decedent or next of kin. Erik S. Jaffe, "She's Got Bette
Davis['s] Eyes": Assessing the Nonconsensual Removal of Cadaver Organs Under the
Takings and Due Process Clauses, 90 Colum. L.Rev. 528, 535 (1990); cf. S. Rep. 98-382
at 2 (discussing estimates that "organs are ... recovered from fewer than 15 percent" of
people who die under circumstances that make them suitable donors). In response,
some states passed "presumed consent" laws that allow the taking and transfer of body
parts by a coroner without the consent of next of kin as long as no objection to the re-

---

(b) The surviving child or children of the decedent.
(c) The surviving parent or parents of the decedent.
(d) The person or persons respectively in the next degrees of kindred in the order named by the
laws of California as entitled to succeed to the estate of the decedent.
(e) The public administrator when the deceased has sufficient assets.
8. One commentator has argued that the "the very existence of a law forbidding commercial
alienation of organs paradoxically portrays the human body as 'an article of commerce' that lies
within the purview of congressional power and would otherwise be subject to sale on the market."
Radhika Rao, Property, Privacy, and the Human Body, 80 B.U. L.Rev. 359, 376 (2000).

moval is known. Jaffe, supra at 535–36.[9] California Government Code § 27491.47, enacted in 1983, was such a law.[10]

III. Due Process Analysis

"[T]o provide California non-profit eye banks with an adequate supply of corneal tissue," S. Com. Rep. SB 21 (Cal.1983), § 27491.47(a) authorized the coroner to "remove and release or authorize the removal and release of corneal eye tissue from a body within the coroner's custody" without any effort to notify and obtain the consent of next of kin "if … [t]he coroner has no knowledge of objection to the removal." The law also provided that the coroner or any person acting upon his or her request "shall [not] incur civil liability for such removal in an action brought by any person who did not object prior to the removal … nor be subject to criminal prosecution." § 27491.47(b).[11]

In analyzing whether the implementation of that law by the coroner deprived the parents of property, we define property as "the group of rights inhering in the citizen's relation to the physical thing, as the right to possess, use and dispose of it…. In other words, it deals with what lawyers term the individual's 'interest' in the thing in question." United States v. General Motors Corp., 323 U.S. 373, 378 (1945); accord Phillips v. Washington Legal Found., 524 U.S. 156, 167–68 (1998); cf. Perry v. Sindermann, 408 U.S. 593, 601 (1972) (explaining that "'property' denotes a broad range of interests"). "To have a property interest … a person clearly must have more than an abstract need or desire" for the thing in question, "[h]e must, instead, have a legitimate claim of entitlement to it…. It is a purpose of the constitutional right to a hearing to provide an opportunity for a person to vindicate those claims." Roth, 408 U.S. at 577.

In two decisions the Sixth Circuit, the only federal circuit to address the issue until now, held that the interests of next of kin in dead bodies recognized in Michigan and Ohio allowed next of kin to bring § 1983 actions challenging implementation of cornea removal statutes similar to California's. Whaley v. County of Tuscola, 58 F.3d 1111 (6th Cir. 1995) (Michigan); Brotherton v. Cleveland, 923 F.2d 477 (6th Cir. 1991) (Ohio). The Sixth Circuit noted that courts in each state had recognized a right of next of kin to possess the body for burial and a claim by next of kin against others who disturb the body. Those common law rights, combined with the statutory right to control the disposition of the body recognized in each state's adoption of the UAGA, was held to be

---

9. Other laws, including the 1987 version of the UAGA, authorize the taking of body parts without consent only where a reasonable effort has been made to locate the next of kin and obtain consent to the transfer. Jaffe, supra at 536–537. The majority of states adhere to the original version of the UAGA, which requires consent from the donee or next of kin for any transfer of organs. Id. at 538.

10. In 1998, § 27491.47(a)(2) was amended to require that the coroner obtain written or telephonic consent of the next of kin prior to removing corneas. The Committee Report accompanying that change in law argued that "existing law governing corneal tissue removal does not adequately reflect the importance of obtaining the consent of a decedent's next-of-kin…. [A]natomical gifts are … 'gifts' and … the removal of corneal tissue without the consent of a decedent's next-of-kin violates the legally recognized principle that … an individual's right to make or decline to make an anatomical gift [is] passed on to the next-of-kin." S. Com. Rep. S.B. 1403 (1998).

11. For body parts other than corneas, California adopted the 1987 version of the UAGA authorizing transfer when no knowledge of objection is known and after "[a] reasonable effort has been made to locate and inform [next of kin] of their option to make, or object to making, an anatomical gift." Cal. Health & Safety Code § 7151.5(a)(2).

sufficient to create in next of kin a property interest in the corneas of their deceased relatives that could not be taken without due process of law.

The supreme courts of Florida and Georgia, however, have held that similar legal interests of next of kin in the possession of the body of a deceased family member, recognized as "quasi property" rights in each state, are "not ... of constitutional dimension." Georgia Lions Eye Bank, Inc. v. Lavant, 255 Ga. 60, 335 S.E.2d 127, 128 (1985); State v. Powell, 497 So.2d 1188, 1191 (Fla.1986) (commenting that "[a]ll authorities generally agree that the next of kin have no property right in the remains of a decedent"). The Florida Supreme Court recently rejected the broad implications of the reasoning in Powell, distinguishing that decision as turning on a balance between the public health interest in cornea donation and the "'infinitesimally small intrusion'" of their removal. Crocker v. Pleasant, 778 So.2d 978, 985, 988 (Fla.2001) (allowing a § 1983 action to go forward for interference with the right of next of kin to possess the body of their son because "in Florida there is a legitimate claim of entitlement by the next of kin to possession of the remains of a decedent for burial or other lawful disposition").

We agree with the reasoning of the Sixth Circuit and believe that reasoning is applicable here. Under traditional common law principles, serving a duty to protect the dignity of the human body in its final disposition that is deeply rooted in our legal history and social traditions, the parents had exclusive and legitimate claims of entitlement to possess, control, dispose and prevent the violation of the corneas and other parts of the bodies of their deceased children. With California's adoption of the UAGA, Cal. Health and Safety Code § 7151.5, it statutorily recognized other important rights of the parents in relation to the bodies of their deceased children—the right to transfer body parts and refuse to allow their transfer. These are all important components of the group of rights by which property is defined, each of which carried with it the power to exclude others from its exercise, "traditionally ... one of the most treasured strands in an owner's bundle of property rights." Loretto v. Teleprompter Manhattan CATV Corp., 458 U.S. 419, 435–436 (1982); see Thomas W. Merrill, Property and the Right To Exclude, 77 Neb. L.Rev. 730, 740–752 (1998) (discussing the "primacy of the right to exclude"); Jeremy Bentham, The Limits of Jurisprudence Defined 164 (Charles Warren Everett ed., 1945) (stating that "[t]o give a man a property" interest in a thing, there must be "a mandate prohibiting persons at large from meddling with it"). Thus, we hold that the parents had property interests in the corneas of their deceased children protected by the Due Process Clause of the Fourteenth Amendment.

Our holding is not affected by California's labeling of the interests of the next of kin as "quasi property," a term with little meaningful legal significance.[13] "Although the underlying substantive interest is created by 'an independent source such as state law,' federal constitutional law determines whether that interest rises to the level of a 'legitimate claim or [sic] entitlement' protected by the Due Process Clause." Memphis Light, Gas and Water Div. v. Craft, 436 U.S. 1, 9 (1978). As the Sixth Circuit correctly recounted in Whaley and Brotherton, the identification of property interests under constitutional

---

13. The Supreme Court has used the term to identify a property interest only once. In International News Service v. Associated Press, 248 U.S. 215, 236–242 (1918) the majority held that news "must be regarded as quasi property," the taking of which without consent constitutes the basis for an unfair competition action. The Court's label did not affect the holding of the case. There is no entry for "quasi property" in Black's Law Dictionary (6th Ed. 1990) or Ballentine's Law Dictionary (3d ed. 1969), although each contains entries for "quasi contract." The only examples of "quasi property" listed under the entry in Words and Phrases are news, citing International News Service, and dead bodies. 35A Words and Phrases 487 (1965); see id. (2000 cumulative supp.).

law turns on the substance of the interest recognized, not the name given that interest by the state. See Whaley, 58 F.3d at 1114 (explaining that courts must "look beyond the law's nomenclature and to its substance"); Brotherton, 923 F.2d at 482 (holding that rights of next of kin in Ohio "form a substantial interest in the dead body, regardless of Ohio's classification of that interest"). Thus[,] in Brotherton, the interests created by Ohio law were recognized as constitutionally protected property interests despite Ohio courts['] not characterizing the rights of next of kin to dead bodies as "quasi-property right[s]," as have "a majority of the courts confronted with the issue." Similarly, in Whaley, the court recognized that next of kin in Michigan possessed constitutionally protected property rights to the corneas of deceased relatives even though "Michigan has repeatedly emphasized" that recovery for violation of the rights of next of kin "'is not for the damage to the corpse as property.'" Our holding similarly turns on the substance of the rights California recognizes, not on the label given to them.

Nor does the fact that California forbids the trade of body parts for profit mean that next of kin lack a property interest in them. The Supreme Court has "never held that a physical item is not 'property' simply because it lacks a positive economic or market value." Phillips [v. Washington Legal Found.], 524 U.S. 156, 169; cf. Int'l News Service v. Assoc. Press, 248 U.S. 215, 246 (1918) (Holmes, J. dissenting) ("Property, a creation of law, does not arise from value....").

Because the property interests of next of kin to dead bodies are firmly entrenched in the "background principles of property law," based on values and understandings contained in our legal history dating from the Roman Empire, California may not be free to alter them with exceptions that lack "a firm basis in traditional property principles." Phillips, 524 U.S. at 165–68 (holding that state could legislatively exempt income only trusts and community property from long established rule that interest follows principle [sic] because those exceptions "have a historical pedigree"); accord[,] Washington Legal Found. v. Legal Found. of Washington, 271 F.3d 835, 852–53 (9th Cir.2001) (en banc); Schneider, 151 F.3d at 1200–01; cf. PruneYard Shopping Center v. Robins, 447 U.S. 74, 93–94 (1980) (Marshall, J. concurring) ("[T]here are limits on governmental authority to abolish 'core' common-law rights.").[14] We need not, however, decide whether California has transgressed basic property principles with enactment of §27491.47 because that statute did not extinguish California's legal recognition of the property interests of the parents to the corneas of their deceased children. It allowed the removal of corneas only if "the coroner has no knowledge of objection," a provision that implicitly acknowledges the ongoing property interests of next of kin.[15]

The effect of §27491.47 was to remove a procedure—notice and request for consent prior to the deprivation—and a remedy—the opportunity to seek redress for the deprivation in California's courts. A state may not evade due process analysis by defining "'[p]roperty'... by the procedures provided for its deprivation." Cleveland Bd. of Educ.

---

14. Of course, states may choose between multiple legal rules that are consistent with the basic principles of the common law "at the will, or even the whim, of the legislature." Munn v. Illinois, 94 U.S. 113, 134 (1876); accord Duke Power Co. v. Carolina Envtl. Study Group, Inc., 438 U.S. 59, 88 n. 32 (1978) ("Our cases have clearly established that '[a] person has no property, no vested interest, in any rule of the common law.'").

15. In this respect, §27491.47(a) differs from California law governing the state's duty to conduct autopsies to determine the cause of death which may be performed contrary to the wishes of the individual or next of kin. See Cal. Govt. Code §27491; Huntly v. Zurich Gen. Accident & Liab. Ins. Co., 100 Cal.App. 201, 280 P. 163 (1929) (holding next of kin have no right to prohibit state from performing invasive autopsy to determine cause of death).

v. Loudermill, 470 U.S. 532, 541 (1985). "While the legislature may elect not to confer a property interest … it may not constitutionally authorize the deprivation of such an interest, once conferred, without appropriate procedural safeguards." Id. With § 27491.47, California eliminated procedural safeguards but retained the interest.

When the coroner removed the corneas from the bodies of the parents' deceased children and transferred them to others, the parents could no longer possess, control, dispose or prevent the violation of those parts of their children's bodies. To borrow a metaphor used when the government physically occupies property, the coroner did not merely "take a single 'strand' from the 'bundle' of property rights: it chop[ped] through the bundle, taking a slice of every strand." Loretto, 458 U.S. at 435. This was a deprivation of the most certain variety.

At bottom, "[p]roperty rights serve human values. They are recognized to that end, and are limited by it." State v. Shack, 58 N.J. 297, 277 A.2d 369, 372 (1971). The property rights that California affords to next of kin to the body of their deceased relatives serve the premium value our society has historically placed on protecting the dignity of the human body in its final disposition. California infringed the dignity of the bodies of the children when it extracted the corneas from those bodies without the consent of the parents. The process of law was due the parents for this deprivation of their rights.

IV. Postdeprivation Process

The scope of the process of law that was due the parents is not a question that we can answer based on the pleadings alone. This question must be addressed in future proceedings.

The coroner's argument that, as a matter of law, postdeprivation process is sufficient and the parents should therefore be required to exhaust postdeprivation procedures must fail. "[T]he State may not finally destroy a property interest without first giving the putative owner an opportunity to present his claim of entitlement." Logan v. Zimmerman Brush Co., 455 U.S. 422, 434 (1982). The timing of a hearing depends upon the accommodation of competing interests including the importance of the private interests, the length or finality of the deprivation and the magnitude of governmental interest. Id.; Mathews v. Eldridge, 424 U.S. 319, 335 (1976). But, absent "extraordinary situations," Boddie v. Connecticut, 401 U.S. 371, 379 (1971), such as "'the necessity of quick action by the State or the impracticality of providing any predeprivation process.'" the deprivation of property resulting from an established state procedure does not meet due process requirements without a predeprivation hearing. Logan, 455 U.S. at 436 (quoting Parratt, 451 U.S. at 539); accord[,] Hudson v. Palmer, 468 U.S. 517, 532 (1984) ("[P]ostdeprivation remedies do not satisfy due process where a deprivation of property is caused by conduct pursuant to established state procedure, rather than random and unauthorized action."). The coroner's removal of corneas was in accordance with the state procedures established by § 27491.47(a). Whether extraordinary situations justify the failure of the coroner to afford a predeprivation hearing turns on issues of fact that cannot be properly examined at this stage of the litigation.

We do not hold that California lacks significant interests in obtaining corneas or other organs of the deceased in order to contribute to the lives of the living. Courts are required to evaluate carefully the state's interests in deciding what process must be due the holders of property interests for their deprivation. An interest so central to the state's core police powers as improving the health of its citizens is certainly one that must be considered seriously in determining what process the parents were due. See

Cruzan, 497 U.S. at 262 (explaining that states have an "unqualified interest in the preservation of human life"). But our Constitution requires the government to assert its interests and subject them to scrutiny when it invades the rights of its subjects.[17] Accordingly, we reverse the district court's dismissal of the parents' complaint and remand for proceedings in which the government's justification for its deprivation of parents' interests may be fully aired and appropriately scrutinized.

The dismissal of the parents' § 1983 claim is reversed and remanded for further proceedings.

Fernandez, Circuit Judge, Dissenting:

I dissent because I do not believe that the asthenic legal interest in a decedent's body, which California confers upon relatives and others, should be treated as a puissant giant for federal constitutional purposes.

To begin with, it has always been true in California that absent a statute "there is no property in a dead body." For that reason, no action for conversion will lie against someone who is said to have damaged or taken a part of the body. To the extent that any right exists, it is, in general, merely a right to possession. That right exists solely "for the limited purpose of determining who shall have its custody for burial."

Of course, any civilized state desires that the bodies of its deceased members be disposed of in an appropriate way, on grounds of decency, consideration for others, and pragmatism. And it should be done with reasonable haste and without undue acrimony.

California's statutory scheme reflects all of that. It decidedly does not confer a property right upon anyone. Assuming that a decedent has not made his own arrangements for disposal of his own earthly remains, the state makes sure that somebody else will both do so and pay for it. To that end, California has provided that "[t]he right to control the disposition of the remains of a deceased person ... vests in, and the duty of disposition and the liability for the reasonable cost of disposition of the remains devolves upon," a list of individuals. Cal. Health & Safety Code § 7100(a). Thus, this so-called right is actually in the nature of a duty and expense designed to assure that the remains will not simply be left about, but will be quickly interred. And the state has created something like a table of intestate succession for the purpose of assuring that the right and duty land firmly on a defined group. First comes the person who has a power of attorney for healthcare. Cal. Health & Safety Code § 7100(a)(1). Then comes the spouse. Id. at (a)(2). Then adult children, then parents, then next of kin. Id. at (a)(3)–(5). At the end is the public administrator, but he only gets the so-called right if there are "sufficient assets" to allow him to discharge his duty. Id. at (a)(6). This somewhat remarkable list surely shows just how peculiar it is to dub what we are dealing with a constitutionally protected property right. Is not it interesting that the holder of a power of attorney comes before the closest relatives, and equally interesting to see that the public administrator may wind up with the "right?" Or is it essentially a duty?

---

17. It has been said in another context that establishing "a culture of justification—a culture in which every exercise of power is expected to be justified"—lies at the heart of the establishment of constitutional bills of rights. Etienne Mureinik, A Bridge to Where? Introducing the Interim Bill of Rights, 10 S. Afr. J. Hum. Rts. 31, 32 (1994); Pharm. Mfr. Ass'n in re: ex parte application of the President of the Republic of South Africa, 2000(2) SA 674, para 85 n. 107(CC) (describing holding that executive action is subject to rationality review as an "an incident of the 'culture of justification' described by Mureinik").

I rather think that it is really a duty rather than a right, and because a duty in one person must mean that a right is lodged in someone else, it seems pellucid that the state holds the right to demand that someone on the list bear the burden of disposing of the deceased's remains; it then makes it possible for that person to do so by also giving him the right to do so.[2] Again, that hardly looks like the kind of interest that United States Constitution was designed to protect.

This leads, I think, to a fairly simple proposition: when the state sees to it that the duty, with its necessarily associated right, devolves upon a person, it can constitutionally limit that duty and the right that goes with it. And that is precisely what California did when it declared that the coroner can, in the course of an autopsy, release corneal eye tissue if he "has no knowledge of objection to the removal and release of corneal tissue having been made by the decedent or any other person specified in Section 7151.5 of the Health and Safety Code." Cal. Gov't Code § 27491.47(a) (1983). In that respect, it should be noted that the people referred to in § 7151.5 are not precisely the same as the people referred to in § 7100(a). The so-called right to consent, therefore, does not follow the so-called duty, and right, to see to interment. This, again, demonstrates just how asthenic the right conferred by § 7100(a) really is.

Nobody who has had the misfortune of having his loved ones die can fail to be moved by the prospect that somebody else will treat the loved one's former earthly vessel with disrespect. That feeling does not, however, demonstrate that California has conferred a constitutionally protected property right upon family members. In fact, it has not; it has merely given them enough of a right to allow them to fulfill their duty, and it has limited that in a number of ways. One of those ways has to do with corneal tissue. As to that, the duty may not devolve, and concomitantly the right will be neither necessary nor constitutionally protected.

Thus, I respectfully dissent.

Town of Castle Rock, Colorado v. Gonzales
545 U.S. 748 (2005)

John C. Eastman argued the cause for petitioner.

John P. Elwood argued the cause for the United States, as amicus curiae, by special leave of court.

Brian J. Reichel argued the cause for respondents.

Scalia, J., delivered the opinion of the Court, in which Rehnquist, C. J., and O'Connor, Kennedy, Souter, Thomas, and Breyer, JJ., joined. Souter, J., filed a concurring opinion, in which Breyer, J., joined. Stevens, J., filed a dissenting opinion, in which Ginsburg, J., joined.

Justice Scalia delivered the opinion of the Court.

We decide in this case whether an individual who has obtained a state-law restraining order has a constitutionally protected property interest in having the police enforce the restraining order when they have probable cause to believe it has been violated.

---

2. The correlative duty is for others not to interfere with this subsidiary right to inter the decedent and incur an expense.

I.

The horrible facts of this case are contained in the complaint. (Because the case comes to us on appeal from a dismissal of the complaint, we assume its allegations are true.) Respondent alleges that petitioner, the town of Castle Rock, Colorado, violated the Due Process Clause of the Fourteenth Amendment to the United States Constitution when its police officers, acting pursuant to official policy or custom, failed to respond properly to her repeated reports that her estranged husband was violating the terms of a restraining order.

The restraining order had been issued by a state trial court several weeks earlier in conjunction with respondent's divorce proceedings. The original form order, issued on May 21, 1999, and served on respondent's husband on June 4, 1999, commanded him not to "molest or disturb the peace of [respondent] or of any child," and to remain at least 100 yards from the family home at all times. The bottom of the pre-printed form noted that the reverse side contained "IMPORTANT NOTICES FOR RESTRAINED PARTIES AND LAW ENFORCEMENT OFFICIALS." The preprinted text on the back of the form included the following "WARNING":

> **A KNOWING VIOLATION OF A RESTRAINING ORDER IS A CRIME.... A** VIOLATION WILL ALSO CONSTITUTE CONTEMPT OF COURT. **YOU MAY BE ARRESTED** WITHOUT NOTICE IF A LAW ENFORCEMENT OFFICER HAS PROBABLE CAUSE TO BELIEVE THAT YOU HAVE KNOWINGLY VIOLATED THIS ORDER.

The preprinted text on the back of the form also included a "NOTICE TO LAW ENFORCEMENT OFFICIALS," which read in part:

> YOU SHALL USE EVERY REASONABLE MEANS TO ENFORCE THIS RESTRAINING ORDER. YOU SHALL ARREST, OR, IF AN ARREST WOULD BE IMPRACTICAL UNDER THE CIRCUMSTANCES, SEEK A WARRANT FOR THE ARREST OF THE RESTRAINED PERSON WHEN YOU HAVE INFORMATION AMOUNTING TO PROBABLE CAUSE THAT THE RESTRAINED PERSON HAS VIOLATED OR ATTEMPTED TO VIOLATE ANY PROVISION OF THIS ORDER AND THE RESTRAINED PERSON HAS BEEN PROPERLY SERVED WITH A COPY OF THIS ORDER OR HAS RECEIVED ACTUAL NOTICE OF THE EXISTENCE OF THIS ORDER.

On June 4, 1999, the state trial court modified the terms of the restraining order and made it permanent. The modified order gave respondent's husband the right to spend time with his three daughters (ages 10, 9, and 7) on alternate weekends, for two weeks during the summer, and, "'upon reasonable notice,'" for a mid-week dinner visit "'arranged by the parties'"; the modified order also allowed him to visit the home to collect the children for such "parenting time."

According to the complaint, at about 5 or 5:30 p.m. on Tuesday, June 22, 1999, respondent's husband took the three daughters while they were playing outside the family home. No advance arrangements had been made for him to see the daughters that evening. When respondent noticed the children were missing, she suspected her husband had taken them. At about 7:30 p.m., she called the Castle Rock Police Department, which dispatched two officers. The complaint continues: "When [the officers] arrived..., she showed them a copy of the TRO and requested that it be enforced and the three children be returned to her immediately. [The officers] stated that there was nothing they could do about the TRO and suggested that [respondent] call the Police Department again if the three children did not return home by 10:00 p.m."

At approximately 8:30 p.m., respondent talked to her husband on his cellular telephone. He told her "he had the three children [at an] amusement park in Denver." She called the police again and asked them to "have someone check for" her husband or his vehicle at the amusement park and "put out an [all points bulletin]" for her husband, but the officer with whom she spoke "refused to do so," again telling her to "wait until 10:00 p.m. and see if "her husband returned the girls."

At approximately 10:10 p.m., respondent called the police and said her children were still missing, but she was now told to wait until midnight. She called at midnight and told the dispatcher her children were still missing. She went to her husband's apartment and, finding nobody there, called the police at 12:10 a.m.; she was told to wait for an officer to arrive. When none came, she went to the police station at 12:50 a.m. and submitted an incident report. The officer who took the report "made no reasonable effort to enforce the TRO or locate the three children. Instead, he went to dinner."

At approximately 3:20 a.m., respondent's husband arrived at the police station and opened fire with a semiautomatic handgun he had purchased earlier that evening. Police shot back, killing him. Inside the cab of his pickup truck, they found the bodies of all three daughters, whom he had already murdered.

On the basis of the foregoing factual allegations, respondent brought an action under Rev. Stat. § 1979, 42 U.S.C. § 1983, claiming that the town violated the Due Process Clause because its police department had "an official policy or custom of failing to respond properly to complaints of restraining order violations" and "tolerated the non-enforcement of restraining orders by its police officers." The complaint also alleged that the town's actions "were taken either willfully, recklessly or with such gross negligence as to indicate wanton disregard and deliberate indifference to" respondent's civil rights.

Before answering the complaint, the defendants filed a motion to dismiss under Federal Rule of Civil Procedure 12(b)(6). The District Court granted the motion, concluding that, whether construed as making a substantive due process or procedural due process claim, respondent's complaint failed to state a claim upon which relief could be granted.

A panel of the Court of Appeals affirmed the rejection of a substantive due process claim, but found that respondent had alleged a cognizable procedural due process claim. On rehearing en banc, a divided court reached the same disposition, concluding that respondent had a "protected property interest in the enforcement of the terms of her restraining order" and that the town had deprived her of due process because "the police never 'heard' nor seriously entertained her request to enforce and protect her interests in the restraining order."

II.

The Fourteenth Amendment to the United States Constitution provides that a State shall not "deprive any person of life, liberty, or property, without due process of law." In 42 U.S.C. § 1983, Congress has created a federal cause of action for "the deprivation of any rights, privileges, or immunities secured by the Constitution and laws." Respondent claims the benefit of this provision on the ground that she had a property interest in police enforcement of the restraining order against her husband; and that the town deprived her of this property without due process by having a policy that tolerated nonenforcement of restraining orders.

As the Court of Appeals recognized, we left a similar question unanswered in De-Shaney v. Winnebago County Dep't of Social Servs., 489 U.S. 189 (1989), another case with "undeniably tragic" facts: Local child-protection officials had failed to protect a young boy from beatings by his father that left him severely brain damaged. We held that the so-called "substantive" component of the Due Process Clause does not "require the State to protect the life, liberty, and property of its citizens against invasion by private actors." We noted, however, that the petitioner had not properly preserved the argument that—and we thus "declined to consider" whether—state "child protection statutes gave [him] an 'entitlement' to receive protective services in accordance with the terms of the statute, an entitlement which would enjoy due process protection."

The procedural component of the Due Process Clause does not protect everything that might be described as a "benefit": "To have a property interest in a benefit, a person clearly must have more than an abstract need or desire" and "more than a unilateral expectation of it. He must, instead, have a legitimate claim of entitlement to it." Board of Regents of State Colleges v. Roth, 408 U.S. 564 (1972). Such entitlements are "'of course, ... not created by the Constitution. Rather, they are created and their dimensions are defined by existing rules or understandings that stem from an independent source such as state law.'" Paul v. Davis, 424 U.S. 693, 709 (1976) (quoting Roth); see also Phillips v. Washington Legal Foundation, 524 U.S. 156, 164 (1998).

A.

Our cases recognize that a benefit is not a protected entitlement if government officials may grant or deny it in their discretion. The Court of Appeals in this case determined that Colorado law created an entitlement to enforcement of the restraining order because the "court-issued restraining order ... specifically dictated that its terms must be enforced" and a "state statute commanded" enforcement of the order when certain objective conditions were met (probable cause to believe that the order had been violated and that the object of the order had received notice of its existence). Respondent contends that we are obliged "to give deference to the Tenth Circuit's analysis of Colorado law on" whether she had an entitlement to enforcement of the restraining order.

We will not, of course, defer to the Tenth Circuit on the ultimate issue: whether what Colorado law has given respondent constitutes a property interest for purposes of the Fourteenth Amendment. That determination, despite its state-law underpinnings, is ultimately one of federal constitutional law. "Although the underlying substantive interest is created by 'an independent source such as state law,' *federal constitutional law* determines whether that interest rises to the level of a 'legitimate claim of entitlement' protected by the Due Process Clause." Memphis Light, Gas & Water Div. v. Craft, 436 U.S. 1, 9 1978) (emphasis added) (quoting Roth, supra, at 577). Resolution of the federal issue begins, however, with a determination of what it is that state law provides. In the context of the present case, the central state-law question is whether Colorado law gave respondent a right to police enforcement of the restraining order. It is on this point that respondent's call for deference to the Tenth Circuit is relevant.

We have said that a "presumption of deference [is] given the views of a federal court as to the law of a State within its jurisdiction." Phillips, supra, at 167. That presumption can be overcome, however, see Leavitt v. Jane L., 518 U.S. 137(1996) (per curiam), and we think deference inappropriate here. The Tenth Circuit's opinion, which reversed the Colorado District Judge, did not draw upon a deep well of state-specific expertise, but consisted primarily of quoting language from the restraining order, the statutory text, and a state-legislative-hearing transcript. These texts, moreover, say nothing distinctive to Colorado, but use mandatory language that (as we shall discuss) appears in many state and federal statutes. As for case law: the only state-law cases about restraining orders that the Court of Appeals relied upon were decisions of Federal District Courts in Ohio and Pennsylvania and state courts in New Jersey, Oregon, and Tennessee. Moreover, if we were simply to accept the Court of Appeals' conclusion, we would necessarily have to decide conclusively a federal constitutional question (i.e., whether such an entitlement constituted property under the Due Process Clause and, if so, whether petitioner's customs or policies provided too little process to protect it). We proceed, then, to our own analysis of whether Colorado law gave respondent a right to enforcement of the restraining order.

B.

The critical language in the restraining order came not from any part of the order itself (which was signed by the state-court trial judge and directed to the restrained party, respondent's husband), but from the preprinted notice to law-enforcement personnel that appeared on the back of the order. That notice effectively restated the statutory provision describing "peace officers' duties" related to the crime of violation of a restraining order. At the time of the conduct at issue in this case, that provision read as follows:

(a) Whenever a restraining order is issued, the protected person shall be provided with a copy of such order. *A peace officer shall use every reasonable means to enforce a restraining order.*

(b) *A peace officer shall arrest, or, if an arrest would be impractical under the circumstances, seek a warrant for the arrest of a restrained person* when the peace officer has information amounting to probable cause that:

(I) The restrained person has violated or attempted to violate any provision of a restraining order; and

(II) The restrained person has been properly served with a copy of the restraining order or the restrained person has received actual notice of the existence and substance of such order.

(c) In making the probable cause determination described in paragraph (b) of this subsection (3), a peace officer shall assume that the information received from the registry is accurate. *A peace officer shall enforce a valid restraining order whether or not there is a record of the restraining order in the registry.* Colo. Rev. Stat. § 18-6-803.5(3) (Lexis 1999) (emphases added).

The Court of Appeals concluded that this statutory provision—especially taken in conjunction with a statement from its legislative history,[6] and with another statute re-

---

6. The Court of Appeals quoted one lawmaker's description of how the bill "'would really attack the domestic violence problems'":

"'[T]he entire criminal justice system must act in a consistent manner, which does not now occur. The police must make probable cause arrests. The prosecutors must prosecute every case. Judges must apply appropriate sentences, and probation officers must monitor their probationers closely. And the offender needs to be sentenced to offender-specific therapy.

"'[T]he entire system must send the same message ... [that] violence is criminal. And so we hope that House Bill 1253 starts us down this road.'" 366 F.3d at 1107 (quoting Tr. of Colorado House Judiciary Hearings on House Bill 1253, Feb. 15, 1994) (emphasis deleted).

stricting criminal and civil liability for officers making arrests[7] — established the Colorado Legislature's clear intent "to alter the fact that the police were not enforcing domestic abuse retraining orders," and thus its intent "that the recipient of a domestic abuse restraining order have an entitlement to its enforcement." Any other result, it said, "would render domestic abuse restraining orders utterly valueless."

This last statement is sheer hyperbole. Whether or not respondent had a right to enforce the restraining order, it rendered certain otherwise lawful conduct by her husband both criminal and in contempt of court. See §§ 18-6-803.5(2)(a), (7). The creation of grounds on which he could be arrested, criminally prosecuted, and held in contempt was hardly "valueless" — even if the prospect of those sanctions ultimately failed to prevent him from committing three murders and a suicide.

We do not believe that these provisions of Colorado law truly made enforcement of restraining orders *mandatory*. A well established tradition of police discretion has long coexisted with apparently mandatory arrest statutes.

"In each and every state there are long-standing statutes that, by their terms, seem to preclude nonenforcement by the police.... However, for a number of reasons, including their legislative history, insufficient resources, and sheer physical impossibility, it has been recognized that such statutes cannot be interpreted literally.... They clearly do not mean that a police officer may not lawfully decline to make an arrest. As to third parties in these states, the full-enforcement statutes simply have no effect, and their significance is further diminished." 1 ABA Standards for Criminal Justice 1-4.5, commentary, pp. 1-124 to 1-125 (2d ed. 1980) (footnotes omitted).

The deep-rooted nature of law-enforcement discretion, even in the presence of seemingly mandatory legislative commands, is illustrated by Chicago v. Morales, 527 U.S. 41 (1999), which involved an ordinance that said a police officer "'shall order'" persons to disperse in certain circumstances. This Court rejected out of hand the possibility that "the mandatory language of the ordinance ... afforded the police *no* discretion." It is, the Court proclaimed, simply "common sense that *all* police officers must use some discretion in deciding when and where to enforce city ordinances." Ibid. (emphasis added).

Against that backdrop, a true mandate of police action would require some stronger indication from the Colorado Legislature than "shall use every reasonable means to enforce a restraining order" (or even "shall arrest ... or ... seek a warrant"), §§ 18-6-803.5(3)(a), (b). That language is not perceptibly more mandatory than the Colorado statute which has long told municipal chiefs of police that they "shall pursue and arrest any person fleeing from justice in any part of the state" and that they "shall apprehend any person in the act of committing any offense ... and, forthwith and without any warrant, bring such person before a ... competent authority for examination and trial." Colo. Rev. Stat. § 31-4-112 (Lexis 2004). It is hard to imagine that a Colorado peace officer would not have some discretion to determine that — despite probable cause to believe a restraining order has been violated — the circumstances of the violation or the competing duties of that officer or his agency counsel decisively against enforcement in a particular instance.[8] The practical necessity for discretion is particularly apparent in a

---

7. Under Colo. Rev. Stat. § 18-6-803.5(5) (Lexis 1999), "[a] peace officer arresting a person for violating a restraining order or otherwise enforcing a restraining order" was not to be held civilly or criminally liable unless he acted "in bad faith and with malice" or violated "rules adopted by the Colorado supreme court."

8. Respondent in fact concedes that an officer may "properly" decide not to enforce a restraining order when the officer deems "a technical violation" too "immaterial" to justify arrest. Respondent

case such as this one, where the suspected violator is not actually present and his whereabouts are unknown.

The dissent correctly points out that, in the specific context of domestic violence,
mandatory-arrest statutes have been found in some States to be more mandatory than
traditional mandatory-arrest statutes. The Colorado statute mandating arrest for a domestic-violence offense is different from but related to the one at issue here, and it includes similar though not identical phrasing. See Colo. Rev. Stat. § 18-6-803.6(1) (Lexis
1999) ("When a peace officer determines that there is probable cause to believe that a
crime or offense involving domestic violence ... has been committed, the officer shall,
without undue delay, arrest the person suspected of its commission ..."). Even in the
domestic-violence context, however, it is unclear how the mandatory-arrest paradigm
applies to cases in which the offender is not present to be arrested. As the dissent explains, much of the impetus for mandatory-arrest statutes and policies derived from the
idea that it is better for police officers to arrest the aggressor in a domestic-violence incident than to attempt to mediate the dispute or merely to ask the offender to leave the
scene. Those other options are only available, of course, when the offender is present at
the scene.

As one of the cases cited by the dissent recognized, "there will be situations when no
arrest is possible, *such as when the alleged abuser is not in the home*"(emphasis added).
That case held that Washington's mandatory-arrest statute required an arrest only in
"cases where the offender is on the scene," and that it "did not create an on-going
mandatory duty to conduct an investigation" to locate the offender. Colorado's restrain-
ing-order statute appears to contemplate a similar distinction, providing that when arrest is "impractical"—which was likely the case when the whereabouts of respondent's
husband were unknown—the officers' statutory duty is to "seek a warrant" rather than
"arrest."

Respondent does not specify the precise means of enforcement that the Colorado re-
straining-order statute assertedly mandated—whether her interest lay in having police
arrest her husband, having them seek a warrant for his arrest, or having them "use every
reasonable means, up to and including arrest, to enforce the order's terms,"[9] Such indeterminacy is not the hallmark of a duty that is mandatory. Nor can someone be safely
deemed "entitled" to something when the identity of the alleged entitlement is vague.
The dissent, after suggesting various formulations of the entitlement in question,[10] ultimately contends that the obligations under the statute were quite precise: either make
an arrest or (if that is impractical) seek an arrest warrant. The problem with this is that
the seeking of an arrest warrant would be an entitlement to nothing but procedure—

explains this as a determination that there is no probable cause. Brief for Respondent 28. We think,
however, that a determination of no probable cause to believe a violation has occurred is quite different from a determination that the violation is too insignificant to pursue.

9. Respondent characterizes her entitlement in various ways ("'entitlement' to receive protective
services"); ("interest in police enforcement action"); ("specific government benefit" consisting of
"the government service of enforcing the objective terms of the court order protecting her and her
children against her abusive husband"); ("[T]he restraining order here mandated the arrest of Mr.
Gonzales under specified circumstances, or at a minimum required the use of reasonable means to
enforce the order").

10. ("[E]ntitlement to police protection"); ("entitlement to mandatory individual protection by
the local police force"); ("a right to police assistance"); ("a citizen's interest in the government's
commitment to provide police enforcement in certain defined circumstances"); ("respondent's
property interest in the enforcement of her restraining order"); (the "service" of "protection from
her husband"); ("interest in the enforcement of the restraining order").

which we have held inadequate even to support standing, see Lujan v. Defenders of Wildlife, 504 U.S. 555 (1992); much less can it be the basis for a property interest. After the warrant is sought, it remains within the discretion of a judge whether to grant it, and after it is granted, it remains within the discretion of the police whether and when to execute it.[11] Respondent would have been assured nothing but the seeking of a warrant. This is not the sort of "entitlement" out of which a property interest is created.

Even if the statute could be said to have made enforcement of restraining orders "mandatory" because of the domestic-violence context of the underlying statute, that would not necessarily mean that state law gave *respondent* an entitlement to *enforcement* of the mandate. Making the actions of government employees obligatory can serve various legitimate ends other than the conferral of a benefit on a specific class of people. See, e.g., Sandin v. Conner, 515 U.S. 472, 482 (1995) (finding no constitutionally protected liberty interest in prison regulations phrased in mandatory terms, in part because "such guidelines are not set forth solely to benefit the prisoner"). The serving of public rather than private ends is the normal course of the criminal law because criminal acts, "besides the injury [they do] to individuals, ... strike at the very being of society; which cannot possibly subsist, where actions of this sort are suffered to escape with impunity." 4 W. Blackstone, Commentaries on the Laws of England 5 (1769). This principle underlies, for example, a Colorado district attorney's discretion to prosecute a domestic assault, even though the victim withdraws her charge.

Respondent's alleged interest stems only from a State's *statutory* scheme—from a restraining order that was authorized by and tracked precisely the statute on which the Court of Appeals relied. She does not assert that she has any common-law or contractual entitlement to enforcement. If she was given a statutory entitlement, we would expect to see some indication of that in the statute itself. Although Colorado's statute spoke of "protected persons" such as respondent, it did so in connection with matters other than a right to enforcement. It said that a "protected person shall be provided with a copy of [a restraining] order" when it is issued, § 18-6-803.5(3)(a); that a law enforcement agency "shall make all reasonable efforts to contact the protected party upon the arrest of the restrained person," § 18-6-803.5(3)(d); and that the agency "shall give [to the protected person] a copy" of the report it submits to the court that issued the order, § 18-6-803.5(3)(e). Perhaps most importantly, the statute spoke directly to the protected person's power to "initiate contempt proceedings against the restrained person if the order [was] issued in a civil action or request the prosecuting attorney to initiate contempt proceedings if the order [was] issued in a criminal action." § 18-6-803.5(7). The protected person's express power to "initiate" civil contempt proceedings contrasts tellingly with the mere ability to "request" initiation of criminal contempt proceedings—and even more dramatically with the complete silence about any power to "request" (much less demand) that an arrest be made.

The creation of a personal entitlement to something as vague and novel as enforcement of restraining orders cannot "simply go without saying." (Stevens, J., dissenting). We conclude that Colorado has not created such an entitlement.

C.

Even if we were to think otherwise concerning the creation of an entitlement by Colorado, it is by no means clear that an individual entitlement to enforcement of a re-

---

11. The dissent asserts that the police would lack discretion in the execution of this warrant, but cites no statute mandating immediate execution. The general Colorado statute governing arrest provides that police "may arrest" when they possess a warrant "commanding" arrest.

straining order could constitute a "property" interest for purposes of the Due Process Clause. Such a right would not, of course, resemble any traditional conception of property. Although that alone does not disqualify it from due process protection, as Roth and its progeny show, the right to have a restraining order enforced does not "have some ascertainable monetary value," as even our "Roth-type property-as-entitlement" cases have implicitly required. Merrill, *The Landscape of Constitutional Property*, 86 Va. L. Rev. 885, 964 (2000).[12] Perhaps most radically, the alleged property interest here arises *incidentally*, not out of some new species of government benefit or service, but out of a function that government actors have always performed—to wit, arresting people who they have probable cause to believe have committed a criminal offense.[13]

The indirect nature of a benefit was fatal to the due process claim of the nursing-home residents in O'Bannon v. Town Court Nursing Center, 447 U.S. 773 (1980). We held that, while the withdrawal of "direct benefits" (financial payments under Medicaid for certain medical services) triggered due process protections, the same was not true for the "indirect benefits" conferred on Medicaid patients when the Government enforced "minimum standards of care" for nursing-home facilities. "An indirect and incidental result of the Government's enforcement action ... does not amount to a deprivation of any interest in life, liberty, or property." In this case, as in O'Bannon, "the simple distinction between government action that directly affects a citizen's legal rights ... and action that is directed against a third party and affects the citizen only indirectly or incidentally, provides a sufficient answer to" respondent's reliance on cases that found government-provided services to be entitlements. The O'Bannon Court expressly noted, that the distinction between direct and indirect benefits distinguished Memphis Light Gas & Water Div. v. Craft, one of the government-services cases on which the dissent relies.

III.

We conclude, therefore, that respondent did not, for purposes of the Due Process Clause, have a property interest in police enforcement of the restraining order against her husband. It is accordingly unnecessary to address the Court of Appeals' determination that the town's custom or policy prevented the police from giving her due process when they deprived her of that alleged interest.

In light of today's decision and that in DeShaney, the benefit that a third party may receive from having someone else arrested for a crime generally does not trigger protections under the Due Process Clause, neither in its procedural nor in its "substantive" manifestations. This result reflects our continuing reluctance to treat the Fourteenth

---

12. The dissent suggests that the interest in having a restraining order enforced does have an ascertainable monetary value, because one may "contract with a private security firm ... to provide protection" for one's family. That is, of course, not as precise as the analogy between public and private schooling that the dissent invokes. Respondent probably could have hired a private firm to guard her house, to prevent her husband from coming onto the property, and perhaps even to search for her husband after she discovered that her children were missing. Her alleged entitlement here, however, does not consist in an abstract right to "protection," but (according to the dissent) in enforcement of her restraining order through the arrest of her husband, or the seeking of a warrant for his arrest, after she gave the police probable cause to believe the restraining order had been violated. A private person would not have the power to arrest under those circumstances because the crime would not have occurred in his presence.

13. In other contexts, we have explained that "a private citizen lacks a judicially cognizable interest in the prosecution or nonprosecution of another." Linda R. S. v. Richard D., 410 U.S. 614, 619 (1973).

Amendment as "'a font of tort law,'" but it does not mean States are powerless to provide victims with personally enforceable remedies. Although the framers of the Fourteenth Amendment and the Civil Rights Act of 1871, 17 Stat. 13 (the original source of §1983), did not create a system by which police departments are generally held financially accountable for crimes that better policing might have prevented, the people of Colorado are free to craft such a system under state law.[15]

The state cases cited by the dissent that afford a cause of action for police failure to enforce restraining orders, vindicate state common-law or statutory tort claims — not procedural due process claims under the Federal Constitution.

[Omitted: Concurrence by Justice Souter, with whom Justice Breyer joins.]

Justice Stevens, with whom Justice Ginsburg joins, dissenting.

The issue presented to us is much narrower than is suggested by the far-ranging arguments of the parties and their amici. Neither the tragic facts of the case, nor the importance of according proper deference to law enforcement professionals, should divert our attention from that issue. That issue is whether the restraining order entered by the Colorado trial court on June 4, 1999, created a "property" interest that is protected from arbitrary deprivation by the Due Process Clause of the Fourteenth Amendment.

It is perfectly clear, on the one hand, that neither the Federal Constitution itself, nor any federal statute, granted respondent or her children any individual entitlement to police protection. Nor, I assume, does any Colorado statute create any such entitlement for the ordinary citizen. On the other hand, it is equally clear that federal law imposes no impediment to the creation of such an entitlement by Colorado law. Respondent certainly could have entered into a contract with a private security firm, obligating the firm to provide protection to respondent's family; respondent's interest in such a contract would unquestionably constitute "property" within the meaning of the Due Process Clause. If a Colorado statute enacted for her benefit, or a valid order entered by a Colorado judge, created the functional equivalent of such a private contract by granting respondent an entitlement to mandatory individual protection by the local police force, that state-created right would also qualify as "property" entitled to constitutional protection.

I do not understand the majority to rule out the foregoing propositions, although it does express doubts. Moreover, the majority does not contest that if respondent did have a cognizable property interest in this case, the deprivation of that interest violated due process. As the Court notes, respondent has alleged that she presented the police with a copy of the restraining order issued by the Colorado court and requested that it be enforced. In response, she contends, the officers effectively ignored her. If these allegations are true, a federal statute, Rev. Stat. §1979, 42 U.S.C. §1983, provides her with a remedy against the petitioner, even if Colorado law does not.

The central question in this case is therefore whether, as a matter of Colorado law, respondent had a right to police assistance comparable to the right she would have possessed to any other service the government or a private firm might have undertaken to provide.

---

15. In Colorado, the general statutory immunity for government employees does not apply when "the act or omission causing ... injury was willful and wanton." Colo. Rev. Stat. §24-10-118(2)(a) (Lexis 1999). Respondent's complaint does allege that the police officers' actions "were taken either willfully, recklessly or with such gross negligence as to indicate wanton disregard and deliberate indifference to" her civil rights.

There was a time when our tradition of judicial restraint would have led this Court to defer to the judgment of more qualified tribunals in seeking the correct answer to that difficult question of Colorado law. Unfortunately, although the majority properly identifies the "central state-law question" in this case as "whether Colorado law gave respondent a right to police enforcement of the restraining order," it has chosen to ignore our settled practice by providing its *own* answer to that question. Before identifying the flaws in the Court's ruling on the merits, I shall briefly comment on our past practice.

I.

The majority's decision to plunge ahead with its own analysis of Colorado law imprudently departs from this Court's longstanding policy of paying "deference [to] the views of a federal court as to the law of a State within its jurisdiction." This policy is not only efficient, but it reflects "our belief that district courts and courts of appeal are better schooled in and more able to interpret the laws of their respective States." Accordingly, we have declined to show deference only in rare cases in which the court of appeal's resolution of state law was "clearly wrong" or otherwise seriously deficient.

Unfortunately, the Court does not even attempt to demonstrate that the six-judge en banc majority was "clearly wrong" in its interpretation of Colorado's domestic restraining order statute; nor could such a showing be made. For it is certainly *plausible* to construe "*shall* use every reasonable means to enforce a restraining order" and "*shall* arrest," Colo. Rev. Stat. §§ 18-6-803.5(3)(a)–(b) (Lexis 1999) (emphases added), as conveying mandatory directives to the police, particularly when the same statute, at other times, tellingly employs different language that suggests police discretion, see § 18-6-803.5(6)(a) ("A peace officer *is authorized to* use every reasonable means to protect ..."; "Such peace officer *may* transport ..." (emphases added)). Moreover, unlike today's decision, the Court of Appeals was attentive to the legislative history of the statute, focusing on a statement by the statute's sponsor in the Colorado House, which it took to "emphasize the importance of the police's mandatory enforcement of domestic restraining orders." Far from overlooking the traditional presumption of police discretion, then, the Court of Appeals' diligent analysis of the statute's text, purpose, and history led it to conclude that the Colorado Legislature intended precisely to abrogate that presumption in the specific context of domestic restraining orders. That conclusion is eminently reasonable and, I believe, worthy of our deference.

II.

Even if the Court had good reason to doubt the Court of Appeals' determination of state law, it would, in my judgment, be a far wiser course to certify the question to the Colorado Supreme Court. Powerful considerations support certification in this case. First, principles of federalism and comity favor giving a State's high court the opportunity to answer important questions of state law, particularly when those questions implicate uniquely local matters such as law enforcement and might well require the weighing of policy considerations for their correct resolution. Second, by certifying a potentially dispositive state-law issue, the Court would adhere to its wise policy of avoiding the unnecessary adjudication of difficult questions of constitutional law. Third, certification would promote both judicial economy and fairness to the parties. After all, the Colorado Supreme Court is the ultimate authority on the meaning of Colorado law, and if in later litigation it should disagree with this Court's provisional state-law holding, our efforts will have been wasted and respondent will have been deprived of the opportunity to have her claims heard under the authoritative view of Colorado law. The unique facts of this case only serve to emphasize the importance of employing a procedure that will provide the correct answer to the central question of state law.

III.

Three flaws in the Court's rather superficial analysis of the merits highlight the unwisdom of its decision to answer the state-law question *de novo*. First, the Court places undue weight on the various statutes throughout the country that seemingly mandate police enforcement but are generally understood to preserve police discretion. As a result, the Court gives short shrift to the unique case of "mandatory arrest" statutes in the domestic violence context; States passed a wave of these statutes in the 1980's and 1990's with the unmistakable goal of eliminating police discretion in this area. Second, the Court's formalistic analysis fails to take seriously the fact that the Colorado statute at issue in this case was enacted for the benefit of the narrow class of persons who are beneficiaries of domestic restraining orders, and that the order at issue in this case was specifically intended to provide protection to respondent and her children. Finally, the Court is simply wrong to assert that a citizen's interest in the government's commitment to provide police enforcement in certain defined circumstances does not resemble any "traditional conception of property"; in fact, a citizen's property interest in such a commitment is just as concrete and worthy of protection as her interest in any other important service the government or a private firm has undertaken to provide.

In 1994, the Colorado General Assembly passed omnibus legislation targeting domestic violence. The part of the legislation at issue in this case mandates enforcement of a domestic restraining order upon probable cause of a violation, §18-6-803.5(3), while another part directs that police officers "shall, without undue delay, arrest" a suspect upon "probable cause to believe that a crime or offense of domestic violence has been committed," §18-6-803.6(1). In adopting this legislation, the Colorado General Assembly joined a nationwide movement of States that took aim at the crisis of police under-enforcement in the domestic violence sphere by implementing "mandatory arrest" statutes. The crisis of underenforcement had various causes, not least of which was the perception by police departments and police officers that domestic violence was a private, "family" matter and that arrest was to be used as a last resort. Sack, *Battered Women and the State: The Struggle for the Future of Domestic Violence Policy*, 2004 Wis. L. Rev. 1657, 1662–1663 (hereinafter Sack); id., at 1663 ("Because these cases were considered noncriminal, police assigned domestic violence calls low priority and often did not respond to them for several hours or ignored them altogether"). In response to these realities, and emboldened by a well-known 1984 experiment by the Minneapolis police department,[8] "many states enacted mandatory arrest statutes under which a police officer must arrest an abuser when the officer has probable cause to believe that a domestic assault has occurred or that a protection order has been violated." *Develop-*

---

8. See Sack 1669 ("The movement to strengthen arrest policies was bolstered in 1984 by the publication of the results of a study on mandatory arrest in domestic violence cases that had been conducted in Minneapolis. In this study, police handled randomly assigned domestic violence offenders by using one of three different responses: arresting the offender, mediating the dispute or requiring the offender to leave the house for eight hours. The study concluded that in comparison with the other two responses, arrest had a significantly greater impact on reducing domestic violence recidivism. The findings from the Minneapolis study were used by the U.S. Attorney General in a report issued in 1984 that recommended, among other things, arrest in domestic violence cases as the standard law enforcement response"); see also Zorza, The Criminal Law of Misdemeanor Domestic Violence, 1970–1990, 83 J. Crim. L. & C. 46, 63–65 (1992) (tracing history of mandatory arrest laws and noting that the first such law was implemented by Oregon in 1977).

ments in the Law: Legal Responses to Domestic Violence, 106 Harv. L. Rev. 1528, 1537 (1993). The purpose of these statutes was precisely to "counter police resistance to arrests in domestic violence cases by removing or restricting police officer discretion; mandatory arrest policies would increase police response and reduce batterer recidivism." Sack 1670.

Given the specific purpose of these statutes, there can be no doubt that the Colorado Legislature used the term "shall" advisedly in its domestic restraining order statute. While "shall" is probably best read to mean "may" in other Colorado statutes that seemingly mandate enforcement, cf. Colo. Rev. Stat. §31-4-112 (Lexis 2004) (police "*shall suppress* all riots, disturbances or breaches of the peace, *shall apprehend* all disorderly persons in the city ..." (emphases added)), it is clear that the elimination of police discretion was integral to Colorado and its fellow States' solution to the problem of underenforcement in domestic violence cases.[10] Since the text of Colorado's statute perfectly captures this legislative purpose, it is hard to imagine what the Court has in mind when it insists on "some stronger indication from the Colorado Legislature."

While Colorado case law does not speak to the question, it is instructive that other state courts interpreting their analogous statutes have not only held that they eliminate the police's traditional discretion to refuse enforcement, but have also recognized that they create rights enforceable against the police under state law. For example, in Nearing v. Weaver, 295 Ore. 702, 670 P.2d 137 (1983) (en banc), the court held that although the common law of negligence did not support a suit against the police for failing to enforce a domestic restraining order, the statute's mandatory directive formed the basis for the suit because it was "a specific duty imposed by statute for the benefit of individuals previously identified by judicial order.[11] In Matthews v. Pickett County, 996 S.W.2d 162 (Tenn. 1999) (on certification to the Sixth Circuit), the court confirmed that the statute mandated arrest for violations of domestic restraining orders, and it held that the "public duty" defense to a negligence action was unavailable to the defendant police officers because the restraining order had created a "special duty" to protect the plaintiff. Id., at 165. See also Campbell v. Campbell, 294 N. J. Super. 18, 24, 682 A.2d 272, 274 (1996) (domestic restraining order statute "allows no discretion" with regard to arrest; "the duty imposed on the police officer is ministerial"); Donaldson v.

---

10. See Note, *Mandatory Arrest: A Step Toward Eradicating Domestic Violence, But is It Enough?* 1996 U. Ill. L. Rev. 533, 542, 544–546 (describing the problems that attend a discretionary arrest regime: "Even when probable cause is present, police officers still frequently try to calm the parties and act as mediators.... Three studies found the arrest rate to range between 3% and 10% when the decision to arrest is left to police discretion. Another study found that the police made arrests in only 13% of the cases where the victim had visible injuries.... Police officers often employ irrelevant criteria such as the 'reason' for the abuse or the severity of the victim's injuries in making their decision to arrest.... Some [officers] may feel strongly that police should not interfere in family arguments or lovers' quarrels. Such attitudes make police much more likely to investigate intent and provocation, and consider them as mitigating factors, in responding to domestic violence calls than in other types of cases"); see also Walsh, *The Mandatory Arrest Law: Police Reaction*, 16 Pace L. Rev. 97, 98 (1995). Cf. Sack 1671–1672 ("Mandatory arrest policies have significantly increased the number of arrests of batterers for domestic violence crimes.... In New York City, from 1993, the time the mandatory arrest policy was instituted, to 1999, felony domestic violence arrests increased 33%, misdemeanor domestic violence arrests rose 114%, and arrests for violation of orders of protection were up 76%" (footnotes omitted)).

11. The Oregon Supreme Court noted that the "widespread refusal or failure of police officers to remove persons involved in episodes of domestic violence was presented to the legislature as the main reason for tightening the law so as to require enforcement of restraining orders by mandatory arrest and custody." Nearing, 295 Ore., at 709, 670 P. 2d, at 142.

Seattle, 65 Wn. App. 661, 670, 831 P.2d 1098, 1103 (1992) ("Generally, where an officer has legal grounds to make an arrest he has considerable discretion to do so. In regard to domestic violence, the rule is the reverse. If the officer has the legal grounds to arrest pursuant to the statute, he has a mandatory duty to make the arrest"). To what extent the Colorado Supreme Court would agree with the views of these courts is, of course, an open question, but it does seem rather brazen for the majority to assume that the Colorado Supreme Court would repudiate this consistent line of persuasive authority from other States.

Indeed, the Court fails to come to terms with the wave of domestic violence statutes that provides the crucial context for understanding Colorado's law. The Court concedes that, "in the specific context of domestic violence, mandatory-arrest statutes have been found in some States to be more mandatory than traditional mandatory-arrest statutes," but that is a serious understatement. The difference is not a matter of degree, but of kind. Before this wave of statutes, the legal rule was one of discretion; as the Court shows, the "traditional," general mandatory arrest statutes have always been understood to be "mandatory" in name only. The innovation of the domestic violence statutes was to make police enforcement, not "more mandatory," but simply *mandatory*. If, as the Court says, the existence of a protected "entitlement" turns on whether "government officials may grant or deny it in their discretion," the new mandatory statutes undeniably create an entitlement to police enforcement of restraining orders.

Perhaps recognizing this point, the Court glosses over the dispositive question — whether the police enjoyed discretion to deny enforcement — and focuses on a different question — which "precise means of enforcement," were called for in this case. But that question is a red herring. The statute directs that, upon probable cause of a violation, "a peace officer shall arrest, or, if an arrest would be impractical under the circumstances, seek a warrant for the arrest of a restrained person." Colo. Rev. Stat. § 18-6-803.5(3)(b) (Lexis 1999). Regardless of whether the enforcement called for in this case was arrest or the seeking of an arrest warrant (the answer to that question probably changed over the course of the night as the respondent gave the police more information about the husband's whereabouts), the crucial point is that, under the statute, the police were *required* to provide enforcement; *they lacked the discretion to do nothing*.[12] The Court suggests that the fact that "enforcement" may encompass different acts infects any entitlement to enforcement with "indeterminacy." But this objection is also unfounded. Our cases have never required the object of an entitlement to be some mechanistic, unitary thing. Suppose a State entitled every citizen whose income was under a certain level to receive health care at a state clinic. The provision of health care is not a unitary thing — doctors and administrators must decide what tests are called for and what procedures are required, and these decisions often involve difficult applications of judg-

---

12. Under the Court's reading of the statute, a police officer with probable cause is mandated to seek an arrest warrant if arrest is "impractical under the circumstances," but then enjoys unfettered discretion in deciding whether to *execute* that warrant. This is an unlikely reading given that the statute was motivated by a profound distrust of police discretion in the domestic violence context and motivated by a desire to improve the protection given to holders of domestic restraining orders. We do not have the benefit of an authoritative construction of Colorado law, but I would think that if an estranged husband harassed his wife in violation of a restraining order, and then absconded after she called the police, the statute would not only obligate the police to seek an arrest warrant, but also obligate them to execute it by making an arrest. In any event, under respondent's allegations, by the time the police were informed of the husband's whereabouts, an arrest was practical and, under the statute's terms, mandatory.

ment. But it could not credibly be said that a citizen lacks an entitlement to health care simply because the content of that entitlement is not the same in every given situation. Similarly, the enforcement of a restraining order is not some amorphous, indeterminate thing. Under the statute, if the police have probable cause that a violation has occurred, enforcement consists of either making an immediate arrest or seeking a warrant and then executing an arrest — traditional, well-defined tasks that law enforcement officers perform every day.[13]

The Court similarly errs in speculating that the Colorado Legislature may have mandated police enforcement of restraining orders for "various legitimate ends other than the conferral of a benefit on a specific class of people," ante, at 15; see also ibid. (noting that the "serving of public rather than private ends is the normal course of the criminal law"). While the Court's concern would have some bite were we faced with a broadly drawn statute directing, for example, that the police "*shall suppress* all riots," there is little doubt that the statute at issue in this case conferred a benefit "on a specific class of people" — namely, recipients of domestic restraining orders. Here, respondent applied for and was granted a restraining order from a Colorado trial judge, who found a risk of "irreparable injury" and found that "physical or emotional harm" would result if the husband were not excluded from the family home.[14] As noted earlier, the restraining order required that the husband not "molest or disturb" the peace of respondent and the daughters, and it ordered (with limited exceptions) that the husband stay at least 100 yards away from the family home. It also directed the police to "use every reasonable means to enforce this ... order," and to arrest or seek a warrant upon probable cause of a violation. Under the terms of the statute, when the order issued, respondent and her

---

13. The Court wonders "how the mandatory-arrest paradigm applies to cases in which the offender is not present to be arrested." Again, questions as to the *scope* of the obligation to provide enforcement are far afield from the key issue — whether there exists an entitlement to enforcement. In any event, the Court's speculations are off-base. First, this is not a case like *Donaldson* v. *Seattle*, 65 Wn. App. 661, 831 P.2d 1098 (1992), in which the restrained person violated the order and then left the scene. Here, not only did the husband violate the restraining order by coming within 100 yards of the family home, but he continued to violate the order while his abduction of the daughters persisted. This is because the restraining order prohibited him from "molesting or disturbing the peace" of the daughters. Because the "scene" of the violation was wherever the husband was currently holding the daughters, this case does not implicate the question of an officer's duties to arrest a person who has left the scene and is no longer in violation of the restraining order. Second, to the extent that arresting the husband was initially "impractical under the circumstances" because his whereabouts were unknown, the Colorado statute (unlike some other States' statutes) expressly addressed that situation — it *required* the police to seek an arrest warrant. Third, the Court is wrong to suggest that this case falls outside the core situation that these types of statutes were meant to address. One of the well-known cases that contributed to the passage of these statutes involved facts similar to this case. See Sorichetti v. New York City, 65 N. Y. 2d 461, 467, 482 N.E.2d 70, 74, 492 N.Y.S.2d 591 (1985) (police officers at police station essentially ignored a mother's pleas for enforcement of a restraining order against an estranged husband who made threats about their 6-year-old daughter; hours later, as the mother persisted in her pleas, the daughter was found mutilated, her father having attacked her with a fork and a knife and attempted to saw off her leg); Note, 1996 U. Ill. L. Rev., at 539 (noting Sorichetti in the development of mandatory arrest statutes); see also Sack 1663 (citing the police's failure to respond to domestic violence calls as an impetus behind mandatory arrest statutes). It would be singularly odd to suppose that in passing its sweeping omnibus domestic violence legislation, the Colorado Legislature did not mean to require enforcement in the case of an abduction of children in violation of a restraining order.

14. The order also stated: "If you violate this order thinking that the other party or child named in this order has given you permission, you are wrong, and can be arrested and prosecuted. The terms of this order cannot be changed by agreement of the other party or the child(ren)[;] only the court can change this order."

daughters became "'protected persons.'" § 18-6-803.5(1.5)(a) ("'Protected person' means the person or persons identified in the restraining order as the person or persons for whose benefit the restraining order was issued").[15] The statute criminalized the knowing violation of the restraining order, § 18-6-803.5(1), and, as already discussed, the statute (as well as the order itself) mandated police enforcement, §§ 18-6-803.5(3)(a)–(b).[16]

Because the statute's guarantee of police enforcement is triggered by, and operates only in reference to, a judge's granting of a restraining order in favor of an identified "'protected person,'" there is simply no room to suggest that such a person has received merely an "'incidental'" or "'indirect'" benefit. As one state court put it, domestic restraining order statutes "identify with precision when, to whom, and under what circumstances police protection must be afforded. The legislative purpose in requiring the police to enforce individual restraining orders clearly is to protect the named persons for whose protection the order is issued, not to protect the community at large by general law enforcement activity." Nearing, 295 Ore., at 712, 670 P. 2d, at 143. Not only does the Court's doubt about whether Colorado's statute created an entitlement in a protected person fail to take seriously the purpose and nature of restraining orders, but it fails to account for the decisions by other state courts, that recognize that such statutes and restraining orders create individual rights to police action.

IV.

Given that Colorado law has quite clearly eliminated the police's discretion to deny enforcement, respondent is correct that she had much more than a "unilateral expectation" that the restraining order would be enforced; rather, she had a "legitimate claim of entitlement" to enforcement. Roth, 408 U.S., at 577. Recognizing respondent's property interest in the enforcement of her restraining order is fully consistent with our precedent. This Court has "made clear that the property interests protected by procedural due process extend well beyond actual ownership of real estate, chattels, or money." Id., at 571–572. The "types of interests protected as 'property' are varied and, as often as not, intangible, 'relating to the whole domain of social and economic fact.'" Logan v. Zimmerman Brush Co., 455 U.S. 422 (1982); see also Perry v. Sindermann, 408 U.S. 593, 601 (1972) ("'Property' interests subject to procedural due process protection are not limited by a few rigid, technical forms. Rather, 'property' denotes a broad range of interests that are secured by 'existing rules or understandings'"). Thus, our cases have found "property" interests in a number of state-conferred benefits and services, including welfare benefits, Goldberg v. Kelly, 397 U.S. 254 (1970); disability benefits, Mathews

---

15. A concern for the "'protected person'" pervades the statute. For example, the statute provides that a "peace officer may transport, or obtain transportation for, the alleged victim to shelter. Upon the request of the protected person, the peace officer may also transport the minor child of the protected person, who is not an emancipated minor, to the same shelter...." § 18-6-803.5(6)(a).

16. I find it neither surprising nor telling that the statute requires the restraining order to contain, "in capital letters and bold print," a "notice" informing protected persons that they can demand or request, respectively, civil and criminal contempt proceedings. § 18-6-803.5(7). While the legislature may have thought that these legal remedies were not popularly understood, a person's right to "demand" or "request" police enforcement of a restraining order simply goes without saying given the nature of the order and its language. Indeed, for a holder of a restraining order who has read the order's emphatic language, it would likely come as quite a shock to learn that she has no right to demand enforcement in the event of a violation. To suggest that a protected person has no such right would posit a lacuna between a protected person's rights and an officer's duties—a result that would be hard to reconcile with the Colorado Legislature's dual goals of putting an end to police indifference and empowering potential victims of domestic abuse.

v. Eldridge, 424 U.S. 319 (1976); public education, Goss v. Lopez, 419 U.S. 565 (1975); utility services, Memphis Light, Gas & Water Div. v. Craft, 436 U.S. 1 (1978); government employment, Cleveland Bd. of Ed. v. Loudermill, 470 U.S. 532 (1985); as well as in other entitlements that defy easy categorization, see, e.g., Bell v. Burson, 402 U.S. 535 (1971) (due process requires fair procedures before a driver's license may be revoked pending the adjudication of an accident claim); Logan, 455 U.S., at 431 (due process prohibits the arbitrary denial of a person's interest in adjudicating a claim before a state commission).

Police enforcement of a restraining order is a government service that is no less concrete and no less valuable than other government services, such as education. The relative novelty of recognizing this type of property interest is explained by the relative novelty of the domestic violence statutes creating a mandatory arrest duty; before this innovation, the unfettered discretion that characterized police enforcement defeated any citizen's "legitimate claim of entitlement" to this service. Novel or not, respondent's claim finds strong support in the principles that underlie our due process jurisprudence. In this case, Colorado law *guaranteed* the provision of a certain service, in certain defined circumstances, to a certain class of beneficiaries, and respondent reasonably relied on that guarantee. As we observed in Roth, "it is a purpose of the ancient institution of property to protect those claims upon which people rely in their daily lives, reliance that must not be arbitrarily undermined." Surely, if respondent had contracted with a private security firm to provide her and her daughters with protection from her husband, it would be apparent that she possessed a property interest in such a contract. Here, Colorado undertook a comparable obligation, and respondent—with restraining order in hand—justifiably relied on that undertaking. Respondent's claim of entitlement to this promised service is no less legitimate than the other claims our cases have upheld, and no less concrete than a hypothetical agreement with a private firm.[19] The fact that it is based on a statutory enactment and a judicial order entered for her special protection, rather than on a formal contract, does not provide a principled basis for refusing to consider it "property" worthy of constitutional protection.

Justice Souter also errs in suggesting that respondent cannot have a property interest in enforcement because she would not be authorized to instruct the police to refrain from enforcement in the event of a violation. The right to insist on the provision of a service is separate from the right to refuse the service. For example, compulsory attendance laws deny minors the right to refuse to attend school. Nevertheless, we have recognized that minors have a property interest in public education and that school offi-

---

19. As the analogy to a private security contract demonstrates, a person's interest in police enforcement has "'some ascertainable monetary value,'" ante, at 17. Cf. Merrill, *The Landscape of Constitutional Property*, 86 Va. L. Rev. 885, 964, n. 289 (2000) (remarking, with regard to the property interest recognized in Goss v. Lopez, 419 U.S. 565 (1975), that "any parent who has contemplated sending their children to private schools knows that public schooling has a monetary value"). And while the analogy to a private security contract need not be precise to be useful, I would point out that the Court is likely incorrect in stating that private security guards could not have arrested the husband under the circumstances. Because the husband's ongoing abduction of the daughters would constitute a knowing violation of the restraining order, and therefore a crime under the statute, see § 18-6-803.5(1), a private person who was at the scene and aware of the circumstances of the abduction would have authority to arrest. See § 16-3-201 ("A person who is not a peace officer may arrest another person when any crime has been or is being committed by the arrested person in the presence of the person making the arrest"). Our cases, of course, have never recognized any requirement that a property interest possess "'some ascertainable monetary value.'" Regardless, I would assume that respondent would have paid the police to arrest her husband if that had been possible; at the very least, the entitlement has a monetary value in that sense.

cials must therefore follow fair procedures when they seek to deprive minors of this valuable benefit through suspension. See Goss, 419 U.S. 565. In the end, Justice Souter overlooks the core purpose of procedural due process—ensuring that a citizen's reasonable reliance is not frustrated by arbitrary government action.

V.

Because respondent had a property interest in the enforcement of the restraining order, state officials could not deprive her of that interest without observing fair procedures. Her description of the police behavior in this case and the department's callous policy of failing to respond properly to reports of restraining order violations clearly alleges a due process violation. At the very least, due process requires that the relevant state decisionmaker *listen* to the claimant and then *apply the relevant criteria* in reaching his decision.[22] The failure to observe these minimal procedural safeguards creates an unacceptable risk of arbitrary and "erroneous deprivations," Mathews, 424 U.S., at 335. According to respondent's complaint—which we must construe liberally at this early stage in the litigation—the process she was afforded by the police constituted nothing more than a "'sham or a pretense.'" Joint Anti-Fascist Refugee Comm. v. McGrath, 341 U.S. 123, 164 (1951) (Frankfurter, J., concurring).

Accordingly, I respectfully dissent.

Note Re: Town of Castle Rock v. Gonzales

With Castle Rock v. Gonzales, we can contrast the "dramatic" and "widely-noted" decision of the South African Constitutional Court in Carmichele v. Minister of Safety and Security.[1] Ms. Carmichele had suffered a vicious attack by a man who had been convicted of indecent assault on one woman and then charged with attempted rape and murder of another woman; while awaiting trial on the attempted rape and murder charges, the defendant was allowed to remain free despite many indications to police and prosecutors that he posed a substantial danger to other women. A police officer told the prosecutor "that there was no reason to deny ... bail and recommended that [the assailant] be released on warning"; the prosecutor did not give the magistrate any information about the assailant's previous conviction, "nor did he oppose ... release on his own recognisance." While the assailant enjoyed his unconditional release, he attacked Ms. Carmichele. Her suit claimed that the police and prosecutors had violated a duty owed to her when they did not seek to prevent the assailant from remaining free while awaiting trial.

---

22. See Fuentes v. Shevin, 407 U.S. 67 (1972) ("When a person has an opportunity to speak up in his own defense, and *when the State must listen to what he has to say*, substantively unfair and simply mistaken deprivations of property interests can be prevented" (emphasis added)); Bell v. Burson, 402 U.S. 535, 542 (1971) ("It is a proposition which hardly seems to need explication that a hearing which excludes consideration of an element essential to the decision whether licenses of the nature here involved shall be suspended does not meet [the] standard [of due process]"); Goldberg v. Kelly, 397 U.S. 254, 271 (1970) ("The decisionmaker's conclusion as to a recipient's eligibility must rest solely on the legal rules and evidence adduced at the hearing"). ("Of course, an impartial decision maker is essential").

1. Carmichelle v. Minister of Safety and Security and Minister of Justice and Constitutional Development, Constitutional Court of South Africa, Case 2001 (10) BCLR 995 (CC), 2001 SACLR LEXIS 64. The decision is called "dramatic" in Daniel Visser, *Cultural Forces in the Making of Mixed Legal Systems*, 78 Tul. L. Rev. 41, 67 (2003); it is said to be "widely-noted" in Frank I. Michelman, *The Bill of Rights, the Common Law, and the Freedom-Friendly State*, 58 U. Miami L. Rev. 401, 408 (2003).

Both the trial court and the Supreme Court of Appeal decided that Ms. Carmichele had no cause of action because neither the police nor the prosecutors owed her a legal duty to protect her from this assault. The Constitutional Court reversed these judgments, relying on the South African Constitution's requirement that all courts "develop the common law" so as to promote the "spirit, purport and objects of the Bill of Rights."[2] In particular, the court relied upon the provisions of the South African Bill of Rights that "entrench ... the rights to life, human dignity[,] and freedom and security of the person."

The court referred to the U.S. Supreme Court's decision in DeShaney v. Winnebago County Dept. of Social Services, and cited Justice Brennan's observation, in dissent, that "The Court's baseline is the absence of positive rights in the Constitution and a concomitant suspicion of any claim that seems to depend on such rights."[3] The South African Constitutional Court said that the provisions of the South African Constitution and those of the European Convention on Human Rights "point in the opposite direction," requiring affirmative action by the government to protect these interests. The court also cited a recent decision of the House of Lords upholding a "claim against a local authority for the negligent failure to safeguard the welfare of a minor...." The court said that "constitutional obligations are now placed on the state to respect, protect, promote and fulfil the rights in the Bill of Rights and, in particular, the right of women to have their safety and security protected."[4] The court held that the police in South Africa had a positive obligation to protect women "from the threat of sexual violence." Also, the court said, "South Africa also has a duty under international law to prohibit all gender-based discrimination that has the effect or purpose of impairing the enjoyment by women of fundamental rights and freedoms and to take reasonable appropriate measures to prevent the violation of those rights."[5] This duty derives from the Convention on the Elimination of All Forms of Discrimination Against Women, ratified by South Africa in December 1995. The court held that the case should be referred back to the High Court so that it might proceed to try the question whether the police and the prosecutor had violated their duties to the complainant.

Goldberg v. Kelly
397 U.S. 254 (1970)

John J. Loflin, Jr., argued the cause for appellant. With him on the briefs were J. Lee Rankin and Stanley Buchsbaum.

Lee A. Albert argued the cause for appellees. With him on the brief were Robert Borsody, Martin Garbus, and David Diamond.*

Before Chief Justice Burger and Justices Black, Douglas, Harlan, Brennan, Stewart, White, Marshall, and Blackmun. Chief Justice Burger and Justice Black dissented.

---

2. Section 39(2) of the Constitution provides that: "When interpreting any legislation, and when developing the common law or customary law, every court, tribunal or forum must promote the spirit, purport and objects of the Bill of Rights." Although this case had been brought while the Interim Constitution was in effect, the Constitutional Court held that the provisions of the permanent Constitution controlled.

3. Citing DeShaney v. Winnebago County Dept. of Social Services, 489 U.S. 189, 204 (1988) (Brennan, J., dissenting).

4. Carmichelle, at 66.

5. Id. at 83.

* Briefs amici curiae were filed by Solicitor General Griswold, Assistant Attorney General Ruckelshaus, and Robert V. Zener for the United States, and by Victor G. Rosenblum and Daniel Wm. Fessler for the National Institute for Education in Law and Poverty.

Mr. Justice Brennan delivered the opinion of the Court.

The question for decision is whether a State that terminates public assistance payments to a particular recipient without affording him the opportunity for an evidentiary hearing prior to termination denies the recipient procedural due process in violation of the Due Process Clause of the Fourteenth Amendment.

This action was brought in the District Court for the Southern District of New York by residents of New York City receiving financial aid under the federally assisted program of Aid to Families with Dependent Children (AFDC)** or under New York State's general Home Relief program. Their complaint alleged that the New York State and New York City officials administering these programs terminated, or were about to terminate, such aid without prior notice and hearing, thereby denying them due process of law.[2] At the time the suits were filed there was no requirement of prior notice or hearing of any kind before termination of financial aid. However, the State and city adopted procedures for notice and hearing after the suits were brought, and the plaintiffs, appellees here, then challenged the constitutional adequacy of those procedures.

The State Commissioner of Social Services amended the State Department of Social Services' Official Regulations to require that local social services officials proposing to discontinue or suspend a recipient's financial aid do so according to a procedure that conforms to either subdivision (a) or subdivision (b) of §351.26 of the regulations as amended.[3] The City of New York elected to promulgate a local procedure according to

---

** Editor's Note: The AFDC program was replaced by Temporary Assistance to Needy Families (TANF) by the Personal Responsibility and Work Opportunity Reconciliation Act of 1996, P.L. 104-193, 110 Stat. 2181, 42 U.S.C. §601 note. Section 601(b) specifies that "This part shall not be interpreted to entitle any individual or family to assistance under any state program funded under the part."

2. Two suits were brought and consolidated in the District Court. The named plaintiffs were 20 in number, including intervenors. Fourteen had been or were about to be cut off from AFDC, and six from Home Relief. During the course of this litigation most, though not all, of the plaintiffs either received a "fair hearing" or were restored to the rolls without a hearing. However, even in many of the cases where payments have been resumed, the underlying questions of eligibility that resulted in the bringing of this suit have not been resolved. For example, Mrs. Altagracia Guzman alleged that she was in danger of losing AFDC payments for failure to cooperate with the City Department of Social Services in suing her estranged husband. She contended that the departmental policy requiring such cooperation was inapplicable to the facts of her case. The record shows that payments to Mrs. Guzman have not been terminated, but there is no indication that the basic dispute over her duty to cooperate has been resolved, or that the alleged danger of termination has been removed. Home Relief payments to Juan DeJesus were terminated because he refused to accept counseling and rehabilitation for drug addiction. Mr. DeJesus maintains that he does not use drugs. His payments were restored the day after his complaint was filed. But there is nothing in the record to indicate that the underlying factual dispute in his case has been settled.

3. The adoption in February 1968 and the amendment in April of Regulation §351.26 coincided with or followed several revisions by the Department of Health, Education, and Welfare of its regulations implementing 42 U.S.C. §602(a)(4), which is the provision of the Social Security Act that requires a State to afford a "fair hearing" to any recipient of aid under a federally assisted program before termination of his aid becomes final. This requirement is satisfied by a post-termination "fair hearing" under regulations presently in effect. A new HEW regulation, now scheduled to take effect in July 1970, would require continuation of AFDC payments until the final decision after a "fair hearing" and would give recipients a right to appointed counsel at "fair hearings." Another recent regulation now in effect requires a local agency administering AFDC to give "advance notice of questions it has about an individual's eligibility so that a recipient has an opportunity to discuss his situation before receiving formal written notice of reduction in payment or termination of assistance." This case presents no issue of the validity or construction of the federal regulations. It is only subdivision (b) of §351.26 of the New York State regulations and implementing procedure 68-18 of

subdivision (b). That subdivision, so far as here pertinent, provides that the local procedure must include the giving of notice to the recipient of the reasons for a proposed discontinuance or suspension at least seven days prior to its effective date, with notice also that upon request the recipient may have the proposal reviewed by a local welfare official holding a position superior to that of the supervisor who approved the proposed discontinuance or suspension, and, further, that the recipient may submit, for purposes of the review, a written statement to demonstrate why his grant should not be discontinued or suspended. The decision by the reviewing official whether to discontinue or suspend aid must be made expeditiously, with written notice of the decision to the recipient. The section further expressly provides that "(a)ssistance shall not be discontinued or suspended prior to the date such notice of decision is sent to the recipient and his representative, if any, or prior to the proposed effective date of discontinuance or suspension, whichever occurs later."

Pursuant to subdivision (b), the New York City Department of Social Services promulgated Procedure No. 68-18. A caseworker who has doubts about the recipient's continued eligibility must first discuss them with the recipient. If the caseworker concludes that the recipient is no longer eligible, he recommends termination of aid to a unit supervisor. If the latter concurs, he sends the recipient a letter stating the reasons for proposing to terminate aid and notifying him that within seven days he may request that a higher official review the record, and may support the request with a written statement prepared personally or with the aid of an attorney or other person. If the reviewing official affirms the determination of ineligibility, aid is stopped immediately and the recipient is informed by letter of the reasons for the action. Appellees' challenge to this procedure emphasizes the absence of any provisions for the personal appearance of the recipient before the reviewing official, for oral presentation of evidence, and for confrontation and cross-examination of adverse witnesses. However, the letter does inform the recipient that he may request a post-termination "fair hearing." This is a proceeding before an independent state hearing officer at which the recipient may appear personally, offer oral evidence, confront and cross-examine the witnesses against him, and have a record made of the hearing. If the recipient prevails at the "fair hearing" he is paid all funds erroneously withheld. A recipient whose aid is not restored by a "fair hearing" decision may have judicial review. The recipient is so notified.

I.

The constitutional issue to be decided, therefore, is the narrow one whether the Due Process Clause requires that the recipient be afforded an evidentiary hearing *before* the termination of benefits. The District Court held that only a pre-termination evidentiary hearing would satisfy the constitutional command, and rejected the argument of the state and city officials that the combination of the post-termination "fair hearing" with the informal pre-termination review disposed of all due process claims. The court said:

New York City that pose the constitutional question before us. Even assuming that the constitutional question might be avoided in the context of AFDC by construction of the Social Security Act or of the present federal regulations thereunder, or by waiting for the new regulations to become effective, the question must be faced and decided in the context of New York's Home Relief program, to which the procedures also apply.

[Editor's Note: In 1979, Congress passed the Department of Education Organization Act, Pub. L. 90-88, 93 Stat. 671 as amended, 20 U.S.C. §3411 (1979). It split the Department of Health, Education, and Welfare (HEW) into two separate entities: the Department of Health and Human Services (HHS) and the Department of Education.]

"While post-termination review is relevant, there is one overpowering fact which controls here. By hypothesis, a welfare recipient is destitute, without funds or assets.... Suffice it to say that to cut off a welfare recipient in the face of ... 'brutal need' without a prior hearing of some sort is unconscionable, unless overwhelming considerations justify it." The court rejected the argument that the need to protect the public's tax revenues supplied the requisite "overwhelming consideration." "Against the justified desire to protect public funds must be weighed the individual's overpowering need in this unique situation not to be wrongfully deprived of assistance.... While the problem of additional expense must be kept in mind, it does not justify denying a hearing meeting the ordinary standards of due process. Under all the circumstances, we hold that due process requires an adequate hearing before termination of welfare benefits, and the fact that there is a later constitutionally fair proceeding does not alter the result." Although state officials were party defendants in the action, only the Commissioner of Social Services of the City of New York appealed.... We affirm.

Appellant does not contend that procedural due process is not applicable to the termination of welfare benefits. Such benefits are a matter of statutory entitlement for persons qualified to receive them.[8] Their termination involves state action that adjudicates important rights. The constitutional challenge cannot be answered by an argument that public assistance benefits are "a 'privilege' and not a 'right.'" Relevant constitutional restraints apply as much to the withdrawal of public assistance benefits as to disqualification for unemployment compensation, Sherbert v. Verner, 374 U.S. 398 (1963); or to denial of a tax exemption, Speiser v. Randall, 357 U.S. 513 (1958); or to discharge from public employment, Slochower v. Board of Higher Education, 350 U.S. 551 (1956). The extent to which procedural due process must be afforded the recipient is influenced by the extent to which he may be "condemned to suffer grievous loss," and depends upon whether the recipient's interest in avoiding that loss outweighs the governmental interest in summary adjudication. Accordingly, as we said in Cafeteria & Restaurant Workers Union, etc. v. McElroy, 367 U.S. 886, 895 (1961), "consideration of what procedures due process may require under any given set of circumstances must begin with a determination of the precise nature of the government function involved as well as of the private interest that has been affected by governmental action."

It is true, of course, that some governmental benefits may be administratively terminated without affording the recipient a pre-termination evidentiary hearing. But we agree with the District Court that when welfare is discontinued, only a pre-termination evidentiary hearing provides the recipient with procedural due process. For qualified

---

8. It may be realistic today to regard welfare entitlements as more like "property" than a "gratuity." Much of the existing wealth in this country takes the form of rights that do not fall within traditional common-law concepts of property. It has been aptly noted that

> (s)ociety today is built around entitlement. The automobile dealer has his franchise, the doctor and lawyer their professional licenses, the worker his union membership, contract, and pension rights, the executive his contract and stock options; all are devices to aid security and independence. Many of the most important of these entitlements now flow from government: subsidies to farmers and businessmen, routes for airlines and channels for television stations; long term contracts for defense, space, and education; social security pensions for individuals. Such sources of security, whether private or public, are no longer regarded as luxuries or gratuities; to the recipients they are essentials, fully deserved, and in no sense a form of charity. It is only the poor whose entitlements, although recognized by public policy, have not been effectively enforced. Reich, Individual Rights and Social Welfare: The Emerging Legal Issues, 74 Yale L.J. 1245, 1255 (1965). See also Reich, The New Property, 73 Yale L.J. 733 (1964).

recipients, welfare provides the means to obtain essential food, clothing, housing, and medical care. Thus the crucial factor in this context—a factor not present in the case of the blacklisted government contractor, the discharged government employee, the taxpayer denied a tax exemption, or virtually anyone else whose governmental entitlements are ended—is that termination of aid pending resolution of a controversy over eligibility may deprive an *eligible* recipient of the very means by which to live while he waits. Since he lacks independent resources, his situation becomes immediately desperate. His need to concentrate upon finding the means for daily subsistence, in turn, adversely affects his ability to seek redress from the welfare bureaucracy.

Moreover, important governmental interests are promoted by affording recipients a pre-termination evidentiary hearing. From its founding the Nation's basic commitment has been to foster the dignity and well-being of all persons within its borders. We have come to recognize that forces not within the control of the poor contribute to their poverty. This perception, against the background of our traditions, has significantly influenced the development of the contemporary public assistance system. Welfare, by meeting the basic demands of subsistence, can help bring within the reach of the poor the same opportunities that are available to others to participate meaningfully in the life of the community. At the same time, welfare guards against the societal malaise that may flow from a widespread sense of unjustified frustration and insecurity. Public assistance, then, is not mere charity, but a means to "promote the general Welfare, and secure the Blessings of Liberty to ourselves and our Posterity." The same governmental interests that counsel the provision of welfare, counsel as well its uninterrupted provision to those eligible to receive it; pre-termination evidentiary hearings are indispensable to that end.

Appellant does not challenge the force of these considerations but argues that they are outweighed by countervailing governmental interests in conserving fiscal and administrative resources. These interests, the argument goes, justify the delay of any evidentiary hearing until after discontinuance of the grants. Summary adjudication protects the public fisc by stopping payments promptly upon discovery of reason to believe that a recipient is no longer eligible. Since most terminations are accepted without challenge, summary adjudication also conserves both the fisc and administrative time and energy by reducing the number of evidentiary hearings actually held.

We agree with the District Court, however, that these governmental interests are not overriding in the welfare context. The requirement of a prior hearing doubtless involves some greater expense, and the benefits paid to ineligible recipients pending decision at the hearing probably cannot be recouped, since these recipients are likely to be judgment-proof. But the State is not without weapons to minimize these increased costs. Much of the drain on fiscal and administrative resources can be reduced by developing procedures for prompt pre-termination hearings and by skillful use of personnel and facilities. Indeed, the very provision for a post-termination evidentiary hearing in New York's Home Relief program is itself cogent evidence that the State recognizes the primacy of the public interest in correct eligibility determinations and therefore in the provision of procedural safeguards. Thus, the interest of the eligible recipient in uninterrupted receipt of public assistance, coupled with the State's interest that his payments not be erroneously terminated, clearly outweighs the State's competing concern to prevent any increase in its fiscal and administrative burdens. As the District Court correctly concluded, "(t)he stakes are simply too high for the welfare recipient, and the possibility for honest error or irritable misjudgment too great, to allow termination of aid without giving the recipient a chance, if he so desires, to be fully informed of the case against him so that he may contest its basis and produce evidence in rebuttal."

II.

We also agree with the District Court, however, that the pre-termination hearing need not take the form of a judicial or quasi-judicial trial. We bear in mind that the statutory "fair hearing" will provide the recipient with a full administrative review.[14] Accordingly, the pre-termination hearing has one function only: to produce an initial determination of the validity of the welfare department's grounds for discontinuance of payments in order to protect a recipient against an erroneous termination of his benefits. Thus, a complete record and a comprehensive opinion, which would serve primarily to facilitate judicial review and to guide future decisions, need not be provided at the pre-termination stage. We recognize, too, that both welfare authorities and recipients have an interest in relatively speedy resolution of questions of eligibility, that they are used to dealing with one another informally, and that some welfare departments have very burdensome caseloads. These considerations justify the limitation of the pre-termination hearing to minimum procedural safeguards, adapted to the particular characteristics of welfare recipients, and to the limited nature of the controversies to be resolved. We wish to add that we, no less than the dissenters, recognize the importance of not imposing upon the States or the Federal Government in this developing field of law any procedural requirements beyond those demanded by rudimentary due process.

[margin handwritten note: basic principles]

"The fundamental requisite of due process of law is the opportunity to be heard." The hearing must be "at a meaningful time and in a meaningful manner." In the present context these principles require that a recipient have timely and adequate notice detailing the reasons for a proposed termination, and an effective opportunity to defend by confronting any adverse witnesses and by presenting his own arguments and evidence orally. These rights are important in cases such as those before us, where recipients have challenged proposed terminations as resting on incorrect or misleading factual premises or on misapplication of rules or policies to the facts of particular cases.

We are not prepared to say that the seven-day notice currently provided by New York City is constitutionally insufficient per se, although there may be cases where fairness would require that a longer time be given. Nor do we see any constitutional deficiency in the content or form of the notice. New York employs both a letter and a personal conference with a caseworker to inform a recipient of the precise questions raised about his continued eligibility. Evidently the recipient is told the legal and factual bases for the Department's doubts. This combination is probably the most effective method of communicating with recipients.

The city's procedures presently do not permit recipients to appear personally with or without counsel before the official who finally determines continued eligibility. Thus a recipient is not permitted to present evidence to that official orally, or to confront or cross-examine adverse witnesses. These omissions are fatal to the constitutional adequacy of the procedures.

The opportunity to be heard must be tailored to the capacities and circumstances of those who are to be heard. It is not enough that a welfare recipient may present his position to the decision maker in writing or second-hand through his caseworker. Written submissions are an unrealistic option for most recipients, who lack the educational attainment necessary to write effectively and who cannot obtain professional as-

---

14. Due process does not, of course, require two hearings. If, for example, a State simply wishes to continue benefits until after a "fair" hearing there will be no need for a preliminary hearing.

sistance. Moreover, written submissions do not afford the flexibility of oral presenta-
tions; they do not permit the recipient to mold his argument to the issues the decision
maker appears to regard as important. Particularly where credibility and veracity are
at issue, as they must be in many termination proceedings, written submissions are a
wholly unsatisfactory basis for decision. The second-hand presentation to the decisionmaker by the caseworker has its own deficiencies; since the caseworker usually
gathers the facts upon which the charge of ineligibility rests, the presentation of the
recipient's side of the controversy cannot safely be left to him. Therefore a recipient
must be allowed to state his position orally. Informal procedures will suffice; in this
context due process does not require a particular order of proof or mode of offering
evidence.

In almost every setting where important decisions turn on questions of fact, due
process requires an opportunity to confront and cross-examine adverse witnesses.
What we said in Greene v. McElroy, 360 U.S. 474, 496–497 (1959), is particularly pertinent here:

> Certain principles have remained relatively immutable in our jurisprudence.
> One of these is that where governmental action seriously injures an individual,
> and the reasonableness of the action depends on fact findings, the evidence
> used to prove the Government's case must be disclosed to the individual so that
> he has an opportunity to show that it is untrue. While this is important in the
> case of documentary evidence, it is even more important where the evidence
> consists of the testimony of individuals whose memory might be faulty or who,
> in fact, might be perjurers or persons motivated by malice, vindictiveness, in-
> tolerance, prejudice, or jealousy. We have formalized these protections in the
> requirements of confrontation and cross-examination. They have ancient
> roots. They find expression in the Sixth Amendment.... This Court has been
> zealous to protect these rights from erosion. It has spoken out not only in
> criminal cases, ... but also in all types of cases where administrative ... actions
> were under scrutiny.

Welfare recipients must ... be given an opportunity to confront and cross-examine
the witnesses relied on by the department.

"The right to be heard would be, in many cases, of little avail if it did not comprehend the right to be heard by counsel." Powell v. Alabama, 287 U.S. 45, 68–69 (1932).
We do not say that counsel must be provided at the pre-termination hearing, but only
that the recipient must be allowed to retain an attorney if he so desires. Counsel can
help delineate the issues, present the factual contentions in an orderly manner, conduct
cross-examination, and generally safeguard the interests of the recipient. We do not an-
ticipate that this assistance will unduly prolong or otherwise encumber the hearing....

Finally, the decisionmaker's conclusion as to a recipient's eligibility must rest solely
on the legal rules and evidence adduced at the hearing. To demonstrate compliance
with this elementary requirement, the decision maker should state the reasons for his
determination and indicate the evidence he relied on, though his statement need not
amount to a full opinion or even formal findings of fact and conclusions of law. And, of
course, an impartial decision maker is essential. We agree with the District Court that
prior involvement in some aspects of a case will not necessarily bar a welfare official
from acting as a decision maker. He should not, however, have participated in making
the determination under review.

Affirmed.

Washington Legal Clinic for the Homeless v. Barry
107 F.3d 32 (D.C. Cir. 1997)

Donna M. Murasky, Assistant Corporation Counsel, argued the cause for appellant. With her on the brief were Charles F.C. Ruff, Corporation Counsel, and Charles L. Reischel, Deputy Corporation Counsel. Edward E. Schwab, Assistant Corporation Counsel, entered an appearance.

Katherine D. McManus argued the cause for appellees. With her on the brief were Peder A. Garske and Martin F. Cunniff. Mark D. Wegener entered an appearance.

Before Wald, [Douglas] Ginsburg, and Tatel, Circuit Judges.

Tatel, Circuit Judge.

The central question in this case is whether District of Columbia law creates a constitutionally protected entitlement to emergency family shelter. Although D.C. law establishes objective eligibility criteria for homeless families seeking shelter, for a combination of reasons we hold that homeless families lack an expectation of shelter sufficient to create a property right: the city does not provide enough shelter to meet the needs of all eligible families, it leaves allocation of limited shelter space among eligible families to the unfettered discretion of city administrators, and nothing in District law prohibits administrators from allocating space in such a way that not all eligible families receive shelter. Indeed, the city administered the family shelter program just that way at the time this suit was filed. We thus reverse the district court's due process ruling. We agree with the district court, however, that the city's policy allowing certain advocates for the homeless to visit the Shelter Office waiting room only on Wednesday mornings and Tuesday and Friday afternoons violates the First Amendment.

I.

In 1984, District of Columbia voters approved an initiative known as the District of Columbia Right to Overnight Shelter Act, guaranteeing to "all persons in the District ... the right to adequate overnight shelter." D.C. Code Ann. § 3-601 (1988 Repl.). Three years later, the City Council enacted the Emergency Shelter Services for Families Reform Amendment Act, authorizing creation of a temporary shelter program for eligible homeless families. Known as the Family Shelter Act, it required the Mayor to "claim federal financial participation to the extent allowable by law for housing assistance and services to homeless families with minor children."

After several lawsuits against the city for failing properly to administer its emergency shelter programs produced huge contempt fines, the City Council, citing an "explosion" in costs associated with shelter programs, moved to "limit specifically and define clearly the obligation of the District of Columbia" under the Overnight Shelter and Family Shelter Acts. To accomplish this goal, the City Council amended both Acts to provide that nothing in either "shall be construed to create an entitlement in any homeless person or family to overnight shelter."

Under the District's family shelter program, families are eligible for shelter if they are homeless; if they can pay for shelter or, if not, if they receive vocational training or perform community service in exchange for shelter; and if they have not occupied emergency family shelter within the previous twelve months. ... [T]he Overnight Shelter Act and District of Columbia Department of Human Services implementing regulations establish additional eligibility criteria for families seeking shelter, including that applicants must be current on city taxes, must not have been evicted or expelled from temporary family housing or emergency shelter for drug-related reasons, and must not have been evicted from public housing for failing to accept employment or training or for nonpayment of rent. Shelter applicants must "provide any information requested by the intake worker that is necessary to establish" their eligibility for emergency shelter, unless the information is not "reasonably available." D.C. Mun. Regs. tit. 29, § 2503. Requested information may include eviction or foreclosure notices, income statements, social security numbers for each family member seeking shelter, and a statement of the reasons the family needs shelter, itself encompassing eighteen subcategories of information. * * *

Because the city lacks space to accommodate all families seeking shelter, and because neither the Overnight Shelter Act nor its implementing regulations direct the Shelter Office how to allocate available shelter, the Office has developed its own system for allocating shelter space among eligible families. Under current procedures, when a homeless family first applies for shelter, the Shelter Office screens the family to determine preliminarily whether the family meets the three basic statutory eligibility requirements. If no eligibility problems appear, the family is placed on a waiting list, assigned a number, and given a "document checklist" identifying the documents needed to verify eligibility. The family is instructed to call the Shelter Office each day to learn whether its number has been reached. Wait-list numbers are usually reached one to two months after families file their initial applications for "emergency" shelter. During this waiting period, about half of the applicant families drop out of the process. When a family's wait-list number is reached, the Shelter Office reviews any additional documentation supplied by the family and makes a final eligibility determination. Families declared eligible then receive shelter.

Homeless families ruled ineligible for emergency shelter may obtain administrative review within the Shelter Office or a hearing before the District's Office of Fair Hearings. Almost all families appealing adverse eligibility determinations are represented by counsel, and the great majority of cases appealed to the Office of Fair Hearings are resolved informally and quickly. Unsuccessful applicants may appeal to the District of Columbia Court of Appeals.

The Washington Legal Clinic for the Homeless ... and several homeless or recently homeless mothers ... filed this suit in 1993, alleging that the city was violating federal and D.C. law and the Fifth Amendment's due process and equal protection guarantees by imposing upon applicants unnecessary and burdensome documentation requirements and by failing to afford disappointed applicants timely hearings.

Relying on the First Amendment, the complaint also challenged District policy limiting Clinic staff access to the Shelter Office waiting room. Although the policy allows advocates having pre-existing relationships with shelter applicants to be in the waiting room whenever open, the policy limits advocates without clients, i.e., "unsolicited advocates," to one at a time and only on Wednesday mornings and Tuesday and Friday afternoons.

Shortly after the suit was filed, the district court scheduled a hearing on plaintiffs' request for a preliminary injunction to halt alleged violations of a federal emergency assistance program in which the District participated. On the eve of the hearing, the city withdrew from the program. When the district court then denied preliminary injunctive relief as moot, plaintiffs amended their complaint, adding a request for a declaratory judgment that by opting out of federal assistance for the family shelter program, the District had violated D.C. Code Ann. § 3-206.3(a), which requires the Mayor to seek federal financial assistance for housing and supplemental services to homeless families.

Over the next three years, the district court rendered the decisions at issue in this appeal. First, declaring the Shelter Office waiting room a nonpublic forum and finding that the city had offered no reasonable grounds for restricting access to the waiting room to only three periods per week, the court ruled that this portion of the District's access policy violated the First Amendment. * * *

Next, the district court ruled that by opting out of federal funding for the city's emergency shelter services, the Mayor had violated D.C. Code Ann. § 3-206.3(a). * * *

Third, the district court ruled that plaintiffs had a constitutionally protected right to emergency shelter. [T]he court held that two aspects of the District's documentation requirements—the city's failure to define "reasonably available" documentation and to coordinate with other DHS offices to assemble documentation—violated plaintiffs' due process rights. The court also ordered the city to develop swifter appeal procedures. * * *

II.

Before addressing the district court's due process ruling, we emphasize what is at stake in this case and what is not. The quantity of emergency shelter available to homeless families is not at issue. The District does not attempt to supply shelter to all eligible families, nor does the Clinic seek the creation of additional shelter space. Because the city's emergency family shelters operate at capacity, a fact counsel for the District confirmed at oral argument, this case is not about available beds going empty while homeless families pursue Kafkaesque application procedures.... The sole question before us is whether D.C. laws and regulations governing the city's emergency family shelter program create a constitutionally protected property interest in shelter, which in turn would require that the District's allocation and appeal procedures satisfy due process standards.

We begin with familiar principles. The Fifth Amendment's Due Process Clause prohibits the District of Columbia from depriving persons of "property, without due process of law." Individuals are entitled to due process, however, only if they have a constitutionally protected property interest. Board of Regents v. Roth, 408 U.S. 564, 569 (1972). To have a property interest in a government benefit, "a person clearly must have more than an abstract need or desire for [the benefit]. He must have more than a unilateral expectation of it. He must, instead, have a legitimate claim of entitlement to it." Roth, 408 U.S. at 577. Entitlements derive from "an independent source such as state law," i.e., statutes or regulations "that secure certain benefits and that support claims of entitlement to those benefits."

To determine whether a particular statute creates a constitutionally protected property interest, we ask whether the statute or implementing regulations place "substantive limitations on official discretion." Statutes or regulations limit official discretion if they contain "'explicitly mandatory language,' i.e., specific directives to the decisionmaker that if the regulations' substantive predicates are present, a particular outcome must follow." Kentucky Dep't of Corrections v. Thompson, 490 U.S. 454, 463 (1989). In Goldberg v. Kelly (1970), for example, the Supreme Court held that because persons meeting state AFDC eligibility standards automatically qualified for benefits, eligible individuals had a protected property interest in the receipt of the benefits. Where, however, the legislature leaves final determination of which eligible individuals receive benefits to the "unfettered discretion" of administrators, no constitutionally protected property interest exists. Roth, 408 U.S. at 567; see Eidson v. Pierce, 745 F.2d 453, 462 (7th Cir.1984) (where landlord participating in federal housing subsidy program has discretion to judge whether an eligible applicant is "otherwise acceptable," no property interest in housing subsidy).

Applying these principles, we ask whether homeless families meeting the statutory qualifications for shelter are entitled to receive it. If so, as in Goldberg, eligible families would have a constitutionally protected property interest in shelter. But if not entitled to shelter because administrators have discretion to choose among otherwise eligible families, they would have no constitutionally protected interest.

As the Clinic observes, the eligibility standards set forth in the Overnight Shelter Act and its regulations are "fact based, objective criteria ... [which] do not involve intangible assessments or discretionary factors." If all families meeting these criteria received shelter, we would agree with the district court and our dissenting colleague that applicants have a constitutionally protected entitlement to shelter. But that is not this case.

All parties agree and the City Council has recognized that the District has insufficient resources to provide shelter for all eligible families. Indeed, the supply of emergency shelter has dropped precipitously, from 495 spaces in late 1994 to only 139 in May 1995. Moreover, neither District statutes nor implementing regulations set forth standards or procedures for allocating scarce shelter space among eligible families. The city has left that matter to the discretion of the Shelter Office. When appellants filed this lawsuit, for example, the Shelter Office used a first-come, first-served system for allocating emergency shelter. Homeless families camped out overnight outside the Shelter Office attempting, often fruitlessly, to secure priority in the application process. Families found eligible for shelter on one day but turned away for lack of space returned to square one the next morning, competing for priority with other rejected families as well as with families entirely new to the process. Under this system, not all eligible families received shelter. As in Thompson, although the "substantive predicates" conferring eligibility might be present, a "particular outcome" might not follow.

In early 1994, the Shelter Office abandoned the first-come, first-served system, replacing it with the wait-list procedures currently in effect. Now, all eligible families remaining on the waiting list eventually receive shelter. If this procedure were mandated by statute or regulation, eligible homeless families might well have a constitutionally protected entitlement to shelter, even though delay between application and shelter would almost always occur.

But D.C. law does not mandate the wait-list system. Like the pre-1994, first-come, first-served system, the wait-list procedures are informal office policy and nothing in governing statutes or regulations prohibits the Shelter Office from again changing its allocation procedures. The Shelter Office could return to the first-come, first-served daily system; it could give priority to families with infants or disabled children; or it could select applicant families at random from a rolling eligibility list. Under the first and third options, some eligible families—those whose names were not called—would never receive shelter, at least as long as shelter supplies remain limited. Under the second option, families having neither infant nor disabled children might or might not receive shelter. As these examples illustrate, the Shelter Office is free to adopt an allocation system under which not all eligible families receive emergency shelter. Indeed, the District candidly acknowledges its "indifferen[ce] to which families, among those eligible for shelter, actually receive it." Under these circumstances, we hold that eligible homeless families lack the "legitimate claim of entitlement" necessary to create a constitutionally protected property right. Roth, 408 U.S. at 577.

secured in possession

future interest in land (property)

a provision that renders an agreement void under certain conditions possible

Relying on traditional property law and citing for illustration contingent remainders, vested remainders subject to defeasance, and executory interests, the dissent argues that a property right can exist even though eligible families might not receive shelter. In the realm of real property law, it is certainly true that improbability of vesting will not defeat a contingent future interest in property. The question in this case, however, is not whether eligible families have a legally enforceable future interest in emergency shelter, but whether they have a constitutionally enforceable property right to emergency shelter. The common law of real property, where uncertainty of future vesting merely reduces the value of property, does not answer that question. Instead, we must look to principles of due process, where the uncertainty of shelter due to the exercise of administrative discretion prevents the creation of a constitutionally protected entitlement. The Supreme Court recognized a constitutionally protected property right in Goldberg because administrators had no discretion in the allocation of AFDC benefits—all statutorily eligible individuals automatically received benefits....

making informed decisions based on data while being open to new ideas

Pointing to procedures available to eligible families denied shelter, the dissent argues that the Shelter Office has insufficient discretion to defeat a constitutionally protected property right. Acting on behalf of its clients, the Clinic regularly uses those procedures, often successfully, to challenge administrative determinations of ineligibility. Such procedures, however, do not restrict the discretion the City Council has left to administrators to select the method of allocating scarce shelter space among eligible families, and it is the presence of *that* discretion which precludes a finding of an entitlement to emergency shelter. That eligible families reaching the top of the wait-list now receive shelter is of no constitutional significance because the Shelter Office can change its procedures tomorrow. The dissent views this as an "extreme notion," but the notion is not ours. The District has chosen to leave just this kind of discretion in the hands of its administrators.

We agree with the dissent that in certain circumstances property rights may arise from administrative "rules or understandings." Roth, 408 U.S. at 577; Perry v. Sindermann, 408 U.S. 593, 599–601 (1972). Equally clear[ly], however, administrative actions may not create property rights where that result would "contravene the intent of the legislature." Here, the City Council's intent is plain: "Nothing in this chapter shall be construed to create an entitlement in any homeless person or family to emergency shelter...." D.C. Code §3-206.9(a). While we doubt that blanket "no-entitlement" disclaimers can by themselves strip entitlements from individuals in the face of statutes or regulations unequivocally conferring them, the District's "no-entitlement" disclaimer reinforces our conclusion that District of Columbia law, by leaving allocation of limited shelter among eligible families to administrative discretion, creates no constitutionally protected entitlement to emergency shelter. Moreover, outside the employment context, we have found no decision of the Supreme Court or of this Circuit holding that administrative rules or understandings existing wholly apart from legislation or regulations may create a property interest. We are not surprised by the lack of such decisions. In the absence of special circumstances neither alleged nor present in this case, such as where reliance on administrative action creates contractual responsibilities, obligations enforceable against the public fisc, i.e., entitlements, may arise only from the people acting through their legislators, not from administrative fiat.

[The First Amendment discussion is omitted.]

Wald, Circuit Judge, dissenting in part.

I part from the majority on the issue of whether families eligible for emergency shelter under the District's laws and regulations have a "property interest" which triggers some form of procedural protection under the Fifth Amendment Due Process Clause. I agree with the district court that families who meet the threshold eligibility requirements of the statute and whose place on the waiting list has been reached are entitled to some modicum of procedural due process by virtue of the statutory mandate of the program, and the Shelter Office's policy and practice in the administration of the program. Thus I respectfully dissent from that portion of the majority opinion finding no entitlement worthy of procedural protection.

In Board of Regents v. Roth, 408 U.S. 564 (1972), the Supreme Court defined the parameters of Fifth Amendment "property interests" to incorporate the fundamental tenets of the "ancient institution of property." According to these enduring principles, a person has no "property" interest in a thing simply because he has an "abstract need or desire for it," or a "unilateral expectation of it." Rather, he must have a "legitimate claim of entitlement to it," a claim based on some "rule[ ] or understanding [ ]" that "secures" the benefit for the claimant and supports his claim of entitlement. Thus it is common ground that a statute declaring that people meeting certain eligibility criteria will receive a government benefit secures the benefit for those people, just as a blanket of common law rules secures more traditional forms of private property for individuals. And correlatively the fact that only those who meet specified criteria are entitled to the benefit does not mean that due process doesn't enter the picture until eligibility has been conclusively proved, since this approach would deny the very procedures needed to demonstrate that a property interest exists in the first place. [Roth, 408 U.S. at 577] ("[T]he welfare recipients in Goldberg v. Kelly ... had not yet shown that they were, in fact, within the statutory terms of eligibility. But we held that they had a right to a hearing at which they might attempt to do so.")

The Roth Court's distinction between "abstract needs or desires" or "unilateral expectations," on the one hand, and "legitimate claims of entitlement" on the other, mirrors the old common law distinction between "bare expectancies," which are not recognized as legitimate property, and future interests, which are. See Lewis M. Simes & Allan F. Smith, The Law of Future Interests § 391 (2d ed. 1956) (distinguishing future interests from "bare expectancies"); 1 American Law of Property § 4.1 (A. James Casner ed., 1st ed.1952). The clearest example of the former is an apparent or presumptive heir who has a "unilateral expectation" of inheriting; this bare expectancy is like a fish that one hopes to catch, or a bird in the bush — it is not property. The concept of property exists to "protect those claims upon which people rely in their daily lives," Roth, 408 U.S. at 577, not to enable people to claim "ownership" of whatever they think they deserve. On the other hand traditional property law readily acknowledges that, if there is some formal statement or understanding establishing that a person can expect a benefit in the future provided that specified contingencies are satisfied, that person does have a property interest — specifically, a future interest — in the benefit, even if the specified contingencies may never occur. Although the privilege of possession or enjoyment is deferred for the holder of a future interest, it is "of the essence" that such an interest "is property which now exists." See 1 American Law of Property § 4.1, at 405. Examples of such future interests are contingent remainders, vested remainders subject to complete

---

2. Contingent remainders are remainders (future interests in someone other than the transferor or his successor in interest that take effect at the termination of a prior estate) that are subject to some condition precedent other than the termination of all prior estates. See American Law of Property §§ 4.25, 4.36. Thus if A conveys property "to B for life, and if C survives B and lives to attain the age of twenty-one, then to C and his heirs," C has a contingent remainder. See id. at § 4.36.

defeasance,[3] and most executory interests[4] where the right of actual possession is subject to conditions which may or may not occur. Although the holder of such a future interest may realistically have a smaller probability of ever gaining possession of the benefit than the holder of a "bare expectancy," the former's interest receives higher priority in the eyes of the law because unlike the latter's it is not merely subjective or "unilateral," but the product of a joint agreement with the present owner.

Applying these bedrock principles of property law to the facts of this dispute,[5] I find myself in disagreement with the majority's unequivocal statement that "eligible homeless families lack the 'legitimate claim of entitlement' necessary to create a constitutionally protected property right." I believe that under the Family Shelter Act as implemented by the Shelter Office, eligible homeless families[6] have precisely the sort of future interest in emergency shelter that our legal traditions have long regarded as a legitimate property interest. The statute and regulations defining the program and specifying the criteria for eligibility secure the benefit for eligible families, even though they include a contingency which is not certain to occur in the case of any individual eligible family— the availability of emergency shelter to meet their need. To pursue the analysis a bit further: If, in a given year, the District were to fund the emergency shelter program fully enough to reach all eligible families, then no one suggests that each eligible family would not receive emergency shelter regardless of the degree of discretion accorded to the Shelter Office over the intake procedure. In short, the administering agency does not have discretion to deny emergency shelter to eligible families. If, as is the case now, the amount of shelter available regularly falls short of the need, many statutorily-eligible families must wait until their interests ripen into rights of present possession, just as holders of other future interests wait for specified contingencies to occur such that they may take possession of more traditional forms of property. As with almost any government largesse or "new property," there is the additional understanding that the government may by legislation eliminate the benefit program entirely in the interim. In Goldberg, however, the Supreme Court implicitly held that this inherent power of government to repeal or modify legislative programs does not preclude a potential gov-

3. Vested remainders subject to complete defeasance are remainders that are vested (i.e., that become a present estate whenever and however the preceding estates terminate) and that are subject to termination on conditions that may occur before, at, or after the termination of the prior estates. See id. §4.35. If O conveys property "to A for life, remainder to B and his heirs, but if B die without leaving any children him surviving, then to C and his heirs," B has a vested remainder subject to complete defeasance. See id.

4. Executory interests are future interests in a transferee that cut off another's vested interest immediately upon the occurrence of a specified condition or event. See id. §4.53. If A conveys property "to B and his heirs, but if B die without leaving children him surviving, then to C and his heirs," C has an executory interest. See id. §4.55.

5. The majority makes the unsupported assertion that these principles, however forceful they may be "[i]n the realm of real property law," have no place in the inquiry into whether a "property interest" protected by the Constitution exits. But the Constitution extends due process protection to deprivations of "property," an institution which is, and always has been, defined and given substance by real property law. The Supreme Court recognized this in Roth, explicitly incorporating "the ancient institution of property" into its discussion of the parameters of protected "property" interests.

6. To be eligible under the applicable statutory and regulatory provisions, families must be homeless, must be willing to pay for shelter if able or to accept vocational training or perform community services in exchange for shelter if unable, must not have occupied emergency family shelter within the previous twelve months, must be current on city taxes, must not have been evicted or expelled from temporary family housing or emergency shelter for drug-related reasons, and must not have been evicted from public housing for failing to accept employment or training without good cause, or for nonpayment of rent.

ernment benefit from constituting an entitlement that triggers due process protections while the program is in effect. See Goldberg, 397 U.S. at 262 ("[welfare benefits] are a matter of statutory entitlement for persons qualified to receive them.") (citing Charles A. Reich, The New Property, 73 Yale L.J. 733 (1964)).

It is extremely important, then, in any due process entitlement analysis to distinguish between the uncertainty of public shelter stock, which makes the eligible families' interest in the shelter a contingent future interest, and whatever discretion has been delegated to the Shelter Office to decide the *priority* in which individual eligible families will be assigned available shelter. The majority suggests that the Shelter Office's discretion in determining the intake priority for eligible families is utterly unconstrained, such that intake workers may simply choose their favorite eligible family whenever a unit becomes available. But the majority's premise that the Shelter Office enjoys such "unfettered discretion" is in fact impossible to reconcile with the regulations governing the administration of the shelter program. These regulations set out in detail the eligibility criteria and specify that *these criteria shall constitute the grounds for the denial of shelter*. Other than those denied shelter based on the unavailability of housing resulting from funding limitations any applicant family denied shelter is entitled to notice, "both oral[ ] and in writing," of the reasons for the denial — "including reference to the law or regulations supporting the action." The applicant family may request a "Fair Hearing," and may include in the request information that may be pertinent to the denial. At the hearing, the applicant family is entitled to present testimony, witnesses or other evidence, to cross-examine the District's witnesses, and to be represented by counsel. When the hearing examiner issues a decision, she must put it in writing, being careful to include findings of fact "based exclusively on evidence presented at the hearing," and conclusions of law supported by appropriate citations. Families that fail to secure a favorable result from the Fair Hearing may appeal the final adverse decision to the District of Columbia Court of Appeals. If, as the majority postulates, an eligible family that reached the top of the waitlist could be passed over for the next available unit pursuant to the Shelter Office's inscrutable whim or "unfettered discretion," this extensive set of procedures would be the cruellest of shams. If the Shelter Office had no "law or regulations" to cite in support of its decision to deny them shelter, what earthly purpose would the "Fair Hearing" procedures and review by the District of Columbia Court of Appeals serve? In short, it is beyond my ken that the District painstakingly drafted the blueprints for such an intricate structure of procedural protections built atop the quicksand of "unfettered discretion."[8]

Even if the Shelter Office does have some degree of discretion to determine what system of intake priorities it will use, that sort of administrative discretion is fundamentally and qualitatively different from "unfettered discretion" to determine whether eligible families will receive shelter *regardless of its availability*. I do not read the statute and regulations to accord the Shelter Office any, let alone "unfettered," discretion of the latter type. Other courts have identified this distinction as relevant in determining the existence of entitlements to due process procedures. In Eidson v. Pierce, 745 F.2d 453 (7th Cir. 1984), the Seventh Circuit ruled that holders of federal housing subsidies had no property interest in particular private housing units because the owners of those units

---

8. Thus I obviously disagree with the majority's assertion that the intake procedures which the Shelter Office institutes exist "wholly apart" from any law or regulation. Far from being "wholly apart" from the regulations, the implementation of an intake procedure constraining "unfettered discretion" is the linchpin without which these regulations would be rendered completely ineffectual.

had complete discretion to turn away individual subsidy-holders for any reason or for no reason at all, even when the subsidy-holders had stellar credit and references and an apartment stood empty. The Shelter Office, in our case, has no such absolute power to turn away eligible applicants. While the Office presumably could change (and has in fact changed) from a first-come-first-served to a waitlist system, and perhaps could change again to give priority to different specific characteristics of needy families, the fact remains that if at any point in time there is an available unit for an eligible family, the Shelter Office is without authority to turn that family away. See D.C. Mun. Regs. tit. 29, §2503 (1992). ("At the time of initial application for … temporary family housing services … the Department shall inform the applicant that he or she is required to provide documentation of eligibility … The Department shall verify that an applicant is homeless … The Department shall provide an applicant family determined eligible for temporary family housing a written referral to a designated temporary family housing facility.").

Indeed, Eidson specifically noted the quintessential difference between programs that distribute scarce benefits according to unfettered discretion and programs whereunder such benefits are distributed according to preset eligibility criteria. Referring to their earlier decision in Davis v. Ball Memorial Hospital Ass'n, 640 F.2d 30 (7th Cir. 1980), the Eidson court distinguished the indigent hospital care program at issue in Davis by observing that "[i]f the patient established facts showing his or her eligibility, and if the hospital had not yet met its financial obligations for the year, then the patient was entitled to the benefits" under the hospital's first-come-first-served intake system. Thus "a hearing in Davis could establish entitlement," while a hearing for subsidy-holders turned away by private landlords could not. Similarly in our case, if shelter is available and under the existing allocation system no other eligible applicant family has a higher priority, some form of due process procedure would have the practical consequence of ensuring that an eligible applicant family would receive the shelter.

The unfortunate reality that the number of eligible families currently exceeds the number of available shelter units does indeed prevent many eligible families from receiving shelter, but by itself the improbability that a future interest in property will ever vest has never turned cognizable property interests into noncognizable "bare expectations." For example, the holder of a future interest which trails behind a series of prior life interests may, as a practical matter, have scant chance of ever coming into possession of the property, but he nonetheless holds a legally recognizable interest in the property. Similarly, individual eligible families may have little chance of receiving shelter, but this is essentially a function of the project's limited funding. One need only conjure up a situation in which available shelter units outnumber eligible applicants to realize that the Shelter Office's discretionary allocative power is not of the sort that removes the applicants' claims from the realm of property interests. Vandermark v. Housing Auth. of York, 663 F.2d 436 (3rd Cir. 1981) (applicants for housing subsidy "certificates" have a property interest in the certificates).

Accordingly, because the interests of eligible families fall squarely within the realm of interests traditionally recognized under the common law of property, families have a right to some due process protection in the intake procedure which determines their eligibility; that right is "triggered" by the nature of the District's shelter program itself, and by the regulations implementing the program.

Furthermore, the Supreme Court recognized in Perry v. Sindermann, 408 U.S. 593 (1972), overruled on other grounds by Rust v. Sullivan, 500 U.S. 173 (1991), that traditional notions of property do not, by excluding "mere subjective 'expectancies,'" preclude individuals from claiming a property interest in a benefit based on the "policies and practices" of the institution controlling the distribution of the benefit. Institutional "policies and practices" that may create procedural entitlements need not be enshrined in any statute, rule, or regulation; in fact they need not even be written down. See Perry, 408 U.S. at 602 ("There may be an unwritten 'common law' in a particular university that certain employees shall have the equivalent of tenure."). But in fact, the Waiting List policy *is* "written down"; it is incorporated into a form that the Shelter Office distributes to all applicant families who have passed a preliminary eligibility determination, that tells them where they are on the waiting list. What a travesty it would be if the Shelter Office could distribute such Waiting List placements and then blatantly ignore them in handing out shelter to the most impoverished segment of our community. No one has suggested that such a practice would comply with the statute and regulations governing the administration of the shelter program.

Nor can I agree that the Shelter Office's current Waitlist Policy is incapable of giving rise to an entitlement because "the Shelter Office can change its procedures tomorrow." The same of course could have been said of the alleged "common law" tenure system at issue in Perry, which the Court thought might well be entrenched enough to create reasonable expectations deserving of due process protection. Institutional policies or patterns of official action may spawn entitlements while they are in effect; it is their pervasive penetration into the day-to-day practice of an institution and the expectations these practices raise in affected constituencies which is determinative.

When an alleged property interest is based in an institution's policy or practice, rather than in a statute or regulation, a claim of entitlement may sometimes depend on the individual's own status with regard to the relevant policy or practice. For example, the teacher claiming an entitlement to tenure in Perry premised his claim both on the "common law" tenure system that he alleged had been followed by the university and on the fact that he had been teaching in the institution long enough for his tenure interest to have "vested" under that unwritten system. Similarly, it might be argued that any entitlement created by the waitlist policy currently in effect does not "vest" until a family has reached a certain status vis-a-vis the waitlist such that specific shelter is available to them if they meet eligibility requirements. But even if that were true, eligible families would minimally have a property interest of the Perry variety which "vests" at the point that they reach the top of the waitlist and a unit becomes available for their occupancy. Because the Shelter Office's current policy and practice is to conduct a final eligibility determination for a family only when a unit becomes available and that family is at the top of the waitlist, families that have ascended to that pinnacle and can demonstrate their eligibility clearly have a "legitimate claim of entitlement" to the available unit. Indeed the existence of an appeal procedure to control denials of shelter following such determinations attests to the District's acknowledgment that such families have a reasonable expectation of shelter. See D.C. Mun. Regs. tit. 29, § 2511.1 (1992) ("Any applicant … who is aggrieved by the Department's decision to deny … temporary family housing … has a right to a fair hearing from the Department's Office of Fair Hearings, except [if the denial is based on the unavailability of shelter resulting from funding limitations].").[11]

---

11. I do agree with the majority that the statute's disclaimer, "[n]othing in this chapter shall be construed to create an entitlement in any homeless person or family to emergency shelter…." D.C. Code Ann. § 3-609, does not by itself control the due process determination. To the extent that this provision could be read as the City Council's attempt to require this court to construe the Fifth Amendment in a particular way, it is of course without effect. See Marbury v. Madison, 5 U.S. (1 Cranch) 137, 177 (1803) ("It is emphatically the province and duty of the judicial department to say

Finally, it is useful to reiterate that the "entitlement" we are debating here is a far cry from any right to emergency shelter "on demand"; it is nothing more than an *interest* in shelter which I find sufficiently substantial to implicate the constitutional requirement of regularized procedures in the allocation of what shelter is available to eligible families. The majority seems peculiarly taken with what I regard as an extreme notion— that the statute and implementing regulations permit the Shelter Office on a whim or caprice to disclaim all statements it has made to applicant families regarding their priority for receiving shelter pursuant to an intake system that has been in place for months, and perhaps even years, and either announce with no notice or formal procedure a new "allocation scheme for the day," or just choose their favorite families to receive the available shelter units. Nothing I can find in the relevant legislation, regulations, or public statements put out by the Shelter Office suggests the existence of any such "unfettered discretion." In fact, the regulations mandate the opposite conclusion, explicitly requiring the Shelter Office to deny shelter only to those found ineligible under the law or those for whom no shelter is available.

Because I believe that families at the head of the waiting list who are found eligible for emergency shelter have a constitutionally-protected property interest in available shelter which is deserving of procedural due process protection, I would proceed to the issue of whether the District's present intake procedures satisfy these strictures.[12] On this due process issue, I respectfully dissent from the majority opinion.

---

what the law is."). Rather, the disclaimer is more naturally read as the District's answer to an applicant family's argument that the failure to provide enough shelter to reach all eligible families violates the terms of the statute. This is the construction that the District itself has placed upon this provision, by implementing it in the form of a regulation stating that "[e]ligibility for temporary housing ... does not entitle a homeless person to shelter...." D.C. Mun. Regs. tit. 29, §2500.3 (1992). (Because I concede that the statute does not require the District to provide a quantity of shelter sufficient to reach all eligible families, I am certainly not suggesting that eligible families hold an "obligation [ ] enforceable against the public fisc.") Furthermore, a Perry-type entitlement would not violate the terms of the statutory disclaimer, because such entitlements spring from institutional policies and practices, rather than from the statute alone. The disclaimer only seeks to prevent anything "in the chapter" from being construed as creating an entitlement to shelter.

12. In brief, I would affirm the district court's holding that the failure to define criteria established which documents are to be considered "reasonably available," and the essentially arbitrary nature of the appeals process, violate the requirements of due process.

II

The Historical Development of Civil Rights Principles in the United States

A. Racial Zoning

In Re Lee Sing

43 F. 359 (N.D. CA 1890)

Thos. D. Riordan, for petitioners.

John I. Humphreys, for the City.

Sawyer, J.

The petitioners are under arrest for the violation of order No. 2190, commonly called the "Bingham Ordinance," requiring all Chinese inhabitants to remove from the portion of the city heretofore occupied by them, outside the city and county, or to another designated part of the city and county.*

[The court quoted §1 of the 14th Amendment; what is now 42 U.S.C. §1981(a); the Supremacy Clause of the Constitution; and] Article 6 of the Burlingame treaty with

---

* Editor's Note: The Bingham Resolution was enacted pursuant to the 1879 California constitution and an 1880 state law that authorized cities to remove people or set aside prescribed portions of the city for their residence. Defending the Bingham Resolution, counsel for the city "analogized it to an immigration law excluding paupers, lepers, and known criminals from landing on a nation's shores." Charles J. McClain, In Search of Equality: The Chinese Struggle Against Discrimination in Nineteenth-Century America 229 (U. CA Press 1994). Charles J. McClain wrote that the City's written defense

> ... deserves some brief discussion inasmuch as it represents undoubtedly one of the more appalling statements of racial bigotry in Western legal history. Among its allegations: that the Chinese were as a race criminal, vicious, and immoral; that they were all incorrigible perjurers; that they abandoned their sick in the street to die; that their occupation of property anywhere decreased the value of surrounding property; that their presence in any number anywhere was offensive to the senses and dangerous to the morals of other races; and that these racial and national characteristics could only be made tolerable if they were removed from the center of town to a remote area where they would have less contact with other races.

The area designated for the Chinese "had by previous legislation been set aside for slaughter houses, tallow factories, hog factories and other businesses thought to be prejudicial to the public health or comfort." Id. at 224.

China, [which] provides that Chinese subjects, visiting or residing in the United States, shall enjoy the same privileges, immunities and exemptions, in respect to travel or residence, as may there be enjoyed by the citizens or subjects of the most favored nation. * * *

The discrimination against Chinese, and the gross inequality of the operation of this ordinance upon Chinese, as compared with others, in violation of the constitutional, treaty, and statutory provisions cited, are so manifest upon its face, that I am unable to comprehend how this discrimination and inequality of operation, and the consequent violation of the express provisions of the constitution, treaties and statutes of the United States, can fail to be apparent to the mind of every intelligent person, be he lawyer or layman.

The ordinance is not aimed at any particular vice, or any particular unwholesome or immoral occupation, or practice, but it declares it "to be unlawful for any Chinese to locate, reside or carry on business within the limits of the city and county of San Francisco, except in that district of said city and county hereinafter provided for their location."

It further provides that "within sixty days after the passage of this ordinance all Chinese now located, residing or carrying on business within the limits of said city and county of San Francisco, shall either remove without the limits of said city and county of San Francisco, or remove and locate within the district of the city and county of San Francisco, herein provided for their location." And again, section 4 provides that "any Chinese residing, locating, or carrying on business within the limits of the city and county, contrary to the provisions of this order, shall be deemed guilty of a misdemeanor, and upon conviction thereof, shall be punished by imprisonment in the county jail for a term not exceeding six months.["] Upon what other people are these requirements, disabilities and punishments imposed? Upon none.

The obvious purpose of this order, is, to forcibly drive out a whole community of twenty-odd thousand people, old and young, male and female, citizens of the United States, born on the soil, and foreigners of the Chinese race, moral and immoral, good, bad, and indifferent, and without respect to circumstances or conditions, from a whole section of the city which they have inhabited, and in which they have carried on all kinds of business appropriate to a city, mercantile, manufacturing, and otherwise, for more than 40 years. Many of them were born there, in their own houses, and are citizens of the United States, entitled to all the rights, and privileges under the constitution and laws of the United States, that are lawfully enjoyed by any other citizen of the United States. They all, without distinction or exception, are to leave their homes and property, occupied for nearly half a century, and go, either out of the city and county, or to a section with prescribed limits, within the city and county, not owned by them, or by the city. This, besides being discriminating, against the Chinese, and unequal in its operation as between them and all others, is simply an arbitrary confiscation of their homes and property, a depriving them of it, without due process or any process of law. And what little there would be left after abandoning their homes, and various places of business would again be confiscated in compulsorily buying lands in the only place assigned to them, and which they do not own, upon such exorbitant terms as the present owners with the advantage given them would certainly impose. It must be that or nothing. There would be no room for freedom of action, in buying again. They would be compelled to take any lands, upon any terms, arbitrarily imposed, or get outside the city and county of San Francisco.

That this ordinance is a direct violation, of, not only, the express provisions of the constitution of the United States, in several particulars, but also of the express provisions of our several treaties with China, and of the statutes of the United States, is so obvious, that I shall not waste more time, or words in discussing the matter. To any reasonably intelligent and well-balanced mind, discussion or argument would be wholly unnecessary and superfluous. To those minds, which are so constituted, that the invalidity of this ordinance is not apparent upon inspection, and comparison with the provisions of the constitution, treaties and laws cited, discussion or argument would be useless. The authority to pass this order is not within any legitimate police power of the state.

Let the order be adjudged to be void, as being in direct conflict with the constitution, treaties, and statutes, of the United States, and let the petitioners be discharged.

Buchanan v. Warley
245 U.S. 60 (1917)

Mr. Clayton B. Blakey and Mr. Moorfield Storey, with whom Mr. Harold S. Davis was on the briefs, for plaintiff in error.

Mr. Pendleton Beckley and Mr. Stuart Chevalier, both of Louisville, Ky., for defendant in error.

Before Chief Justice White and Justices McKenna, Holmes, Day, Van Devanter, Pitney, McReynolds, Brandeis, and Clarke.*

Mr. Justice Day delivered the opinion of the Court.

Buchanan brought an action for the specific performance of a contract for the sale of certain real estate situated in the City of Louisville. The offer in writing to purchase the property contained a proviso:

> It is understood that I am purchasing the above property for the purpose of having erected thereon a house which I propose to make my residence, and it is a distinct part of this agreement that I shall not be required to accept a deed to the above property or to pay for said property unless I have the right under the laws of the State of Kentucky and the City of Louisville to occupy said property as a residence.

This offer was accepted by the plaintiff.

To the action for specific performance the defendant by way of answer set up the condition above set forth, that he is a colored person, and that on the block of which the lot in controversy is a part there are ten residences, eight of which at the time of the making of the contract were occupied by white people, and only two (those nearest the

---

* Mr. S. S. Field, by leave of court, filed a brief on behalf of the Mayor and City Council of Baltimore as amicus curiae.

Mr. W. Ashbie Hawkins, by leave of court, filed a brief on behalf of the Baltimore Branch of the National Association for the Advancement of Colored People as amicus curiae.

Mr. Frederick W. Lehmann and Mr. Wells H. Blodgett, by leave of court, filed a brief as amici curiae.

Mr. Alfred E. Cohen, by leave of court, filed a brief as amicus curiae.

Mr. Chilton Atkinson, by leave of court, filed a brief on behalf of the United Welfare Association of St. Louis as amicus curiae.

Mr. H. R. Pollard, by leave of court, filed a brief on behalf of the City of Richmond, Virginia, as amicus curiae.

Mr. Wells H. Blodgett, Mr. Charles Nagel, Mr. James A. Seddon, Mr. Selden P. Spencer, Mr. Sidney F. Andrews, Mr. W. L. Sturdevant, Mr. Percy Werner, Mr. Everett W. Pattison and Mr. Joseph Wheless, by leave of court, filed a brief as amici curiae.

lot in question) were occupied by colored people, and that under and by virtue of the ordinance of the city of Louisville, approved May 11, 1914, he would not be allowed to occupy the lot as a place of residence.

In reply to this answer the plaintiff set up, among other things, that the ordinance was in conflict with the Fourteenth Amendment to the Constitution of the United States, and hence no defense to the action for specific performance of the contract.

In the court of original jurisdiction in Kentucky, and in the Court of Appeals of that State, the case was made to turn upon the constitutional validity of the ordinance. The Court of Appeals of Kentucky held the ordinance valid and of itself a complete defense to the action.

The title of the ordinance is:

> An ordinance to prevent conflict and ill-feeling between the white and colored races in the City of Louisville, and to preserve the public peace and promote the general welfare by making reasonable provisions requiring, as far as practicable, the use of separate blocks for residences, places of abode and places of assembly by white and colored people respectively.

By the first section of the ordinance it is made unlawful for any colored person to move into and occupy as a residence, place of abode, or to establish and maintain as a place of public assembly any house upon any block upon which a greater number of houses are occupied as residences, places of abode, or places of public assembly by white people than are occupied as residences, places of abode, or places of public assembly by colored people.

Section 2 provides that it shall be unlawful for any white person to move into and occupy as a residence, place of abode, or to establish and maintain as a place of public assembly any house upon any block upon which a greater number of houses are occupied as residences, places of abode or places of public assembly by colored people than are occupied as residences, places of abode or places of public assembly by white people.

Section 4 provides that nothing in the ordinance shall affect the location of residences, places of abode or places of assembly made previous to its approval; that nothing contained therein shall be construed so as to prevent the occupancy of residences, places of abode or places of assembly by white or colored servants or employees of occupants of such residences, places of abode or places of public assembly on the block on which they are so employed, and that nothing therein contained shall be construed to prevent any person who, at the date of the passage of the ordinance, shall have acquired or possessed the right to occupy any building as a residence, place of abode or place of assembly from exercising such a right; that nothing contained in the ordinance shall prevent the owner of any building, who when the ordinance became effective, leased, rented, or occupied it as a residence, place of abode or place of public assembly for colored persons, from continuing to rent, lease or occupy such residence, place of abode or place of assembly for such persons, if the owner shall so desire; but if such house should, after the passage of the ordinance, be at any time leased, rented or occupied as a residence, place of abode or place of assembly for white persons, it shall not thereafter be used for colored persons, if such occupation would then be a violation of section one of the ordinance; that nothing contained in the ordinance shall prevent the owner of any building, who when the ordinance became effective leased, rented or occupied it as a residence, place of abode, or place of assembly for white persons from continuing to rent, lease or occupy such residence, place of abode or place of assembly for such purpose, if the owner shall so desire, but if such house should, after the passage of the ordinance, be at any time leased, rented or occupied as a residence, place of abode or place of assembly for colored persons, then it shall not thereafter be used for white persons, if such occupation would then be a violation of section two thereof. * * *

The objection is made that this writ of error should be dismissed because the alleged denial of constitutional rights involves only the rights of colored persons, and the plaintiff in error is a white person. This court has frequently held that while an unconstitutional act is no law, attacks upon the validity of laws can only be entertained when made by those whose rights are directly affected by the law or ordinance in question. Only such persons, it has been settled, can be heard to attack the constitutionality of the law or ordinance. But this case does not run counter to that principle.

The property here involved was sold by the plaintiff in error, a white man, on the terms stated, to a colored man; the action for specific performance was entertained in the court below, and in both courts the plaintiff's right to have the contract enforced was denied solely because of the effect of the ordinance making it illegal for a colored person to occupy the lot sold. But for the ordinance the state courts would have enforced the contract, and the defendant would have been compelled to pay the purchase price and take a conveyance of the premises. The right of the plaintiff in error to sell his property was directly involved and necessarily impaired because it was held in effect that he could not sell the lot to a person of color who was willing and ready to acquire the property, and had obligated himself to take it. This case does not come within the class wherein this court has held that where one seeks to avoid the enforcement of a law or ordinance he must present a grievance of his own, and not rest the attack upon the alleged violation of another's rights. In this case the property rights of the plaintiff in error are directly and necessarily involved.

We pass then to a consideration of the case upon its merits. This ordinance prevents the occupancy of a lot in the City of Louisville by a person of color in a block where the greater number of residences are occupied by white persons; where such a majority exists colored persons are excluded. This interdiction is based wholly upon color; simply that and nothing more. In effect, premises situated as are those in question in the so-called white block are effectively debarred from sale to persons of color, because if sold they cannot be occupied by the purchaser nor by him sold to another of the same color.

This drastic measure is sought to be justified under the authority of the State in the exercise of the police power. It is said such legislation tends to promote the public peace by preventing racial conflicts; that it tends to maintain racial purity; that it prevents the deterioration of property owned and occupied by white people, which deterioration, it is contended, is sure to follow the occupancy of adjacent premises by persons of color.

The authority of the State to pass laws in the exercise of the police power, having for their object the promotion of the public health, safety and welfare is very broad as has been affirmed in numerous and recent decisions of this court. Furthermore, the exercise of this power, embracing nearly all legislation of a local character, is not to be interfered with by the courts where it is within the scope of legislative authority and the means adopted reasonably tend to accomplish a lawful purpose. But it is equally well established that the police power, broad as it is, cannot justify the passage of a law or ordinance which runs counter to the limitations of the Federal Constitution; that principle has been so frequently affirmed in this court that we need not stop to cite the cases.

The Federal Constitution and laws passed within its authority are by the express terms of that instrument made the supreme law of the land. The Fourteenth Amendment protects life, liberty, and property from invasion by the States without due process of law. Property is more than the mere thing which a person owns. It is elementary that it includes the right to acquire, use, and dispose of it. The Constitution protects these essential attributes of property. Property consists of the free use, enjoyment, and disposal of a person's acquisitions without control or diminution save by the law of the land. 1 Blackstone's Commentaries (Cooley's Ed.), 127.

True it is that dominion over property springing from ownership is not absolute and unqualified. The disposition and use of property may be controlled in the exercise of the police power in the interest of the public health, convenience, or welfare. Harmful occupations may be controlled and regulated. Legitimate business may also be regulated in the interest of the public. Certain uses of property may be confined to portions of the municipality other than the resident district, such as livery stables, brickyards and the like, because of the impairment of the health and comfort of the occupants of neighboring property. Many illustrations might be given from the decisions of this court, and other courts, of this principle, but these cases do not touch the one at bar.

The concrete question here is: May the occupancy, and, necessarily, the purchase and sale of property of which occupancy is an incident, be inhibited by the States, or by one of its municipalities, solely because of the color of the proposed occupant of the premises? That one may dispose of his property, subject only to the control of lawful enactments curtailing that right in the public interest, must be conceded. The question now presented makes it pertinent to enquire into the constitutional right of the white man to sell his property to a colored man, having in view the legal status of the purchaser and occupant.

Following the Civil War certain amendments to the Federal Constitution were adopted, which have become an integral part of that instrument, equally binding upon all the States and fixing certain fundamental rights which all are bound to respect. The Thirteenth Amendment abolished slavery in the United States and in all places subject to their jurisdiction, and gave Congress power to enforce the Amendment by appropriate legislation. The Fourteenth Amendment made all persons born or naturalized in the United States citizens of the United States and of the States in which they reside, and provided that no State shall make or enforce any law which shall abridge the privileges or immunities of citizens of the United States, and that no State shall deprive any person of life, liberty, or property without due process of law, nor deny to any person the equal protection of the laws.

The effect of these Amendments was first dealt with by this court in The Slaughter House Cases. The reasons for the adoption of the Amendments were elaborately considered by a court familiar with the times in which the necessity for the Amendments arose and with the circumstances which impelled their adoption. In that case Mr. Justice Miller, who spoke for the majority, pointed out that the colored race, having been freed from slavery by the Thirteenth Amendment, was raised to the dignity of citizenship and equality of civil rights by the Fourteenth Amendment, and the States were prohibited from abridging the privileges and immunities of such citizens, or depriving any person of life, liberty, or property without due process of law. While a principal purpose of the latter Amendment was to protect persons of color, the broad language used was deemed sufficient to protect all persons, white or black, against discriminatory legislation by the States. This is now the settled law. In many of the cases since arising the question of color has not been involved and the cases have been decided upon alleged violations of civil or property rights irrespective of the race or color of the complainant. In The Slaughter House Cases it was recognized that the chief inducement to the passage of the Amendment was the desire to extend federal protection to the recently emancipated race from unfriendly and discriminating legislation by the States. * * *

In giving legislative aid to these constitutional provisions Congress enacted in 1866 that:

All citizens of the United States shall have the same right in every State and Territory, as is enjoyed by white citizens thereof to inherit, purchase, lease, sell, hold, and convey real and personal property.

And in 1870:

All persons within the jurisdiction of the United States shall have the same right in every State and Territory to make and enforce contracts, to sue, be parties, give evidence, and to the full and equal benefit of all laws and proceedings for the security of persons and property as is enjoyed by white citizens, and shall be subject to like punishment, pains, penalties, taxes, licenses and exactions of every kind, and no other.

In the face of these constitutional and statutory provisions, can a white man be denied, consistently with due process of law, the right to dispose of his property to a purchaser by prohibiting the occupation of it for the sole reason that the purchaser is a person of color intending to occupy the premises as a place of residence?

The statute of 1866, originally passed under sanction of the Thirteenth Amendment and practically reenacted after the adoption of the Fourteenth Amendment, expressly provided that all citizens of the United States in any State shall have the same right to purchase property as is enjoyed by white citizens. Colored persons are citizens of the United States and have the right to purchase property and enjoy and use the same without laws discriminating against them solely on account of color. These enactments did not deal with the social rights of men, but with those fundamental rights in property which it was intended to secure upon the same terms to citizens of every race and color. Civil Rights Cases. The Fourteenth Amendment and these statutes enacted in furtherance of its purpose operate to qualify and entitle a colored man to acquire property without state legislation discriminating against him solely because of color.

The defendant in error insists that Plessy v. Ferguson is controlling in principle in favor of the judgment of the court below. In that case this court held that a provision of a statute of Louisiana requiring railway companies carrying passengers to provide in their coaches equal but separate accommodations for the white and colored races did not run counter to the provisions of the Fourteenth Amendment. It is to be observed that in that case there was no attempt to deprive persons of color of transportation in the coaches of the public carrier, and the express requirements were for equal though separate accommodations for the white and colored races. In Plessy v. Ferguson, classification of accommodation was permitted upon the basis of equality for both races.

In the Berea College Case, a state statute was sustained in the courts of Kentucky, which, while permitting the education of white persons and negroes in different localities by the same incorporated institution, prohibited their attendance at the same place, and in this court the judgment of the Court of Appeals of Kentucky was affirmed solely upon the reserved authority of the legislature of Kentucky to alter, amend, or repeal charters of its own corporations, and the question here involved was neither discussed nor decided.

In Carey v. City of Atlanta, the Supreme Court of Georgia, holding an ordinance, similar in principle to the one herein involved, to be invalid, dealt with Plessy v. Ferguson, and The Berea College Case, in language so apposite that we quote a portion of it:

> In each instance the complaining person was afforded the opportunity to ride, or to attend institutions of learning, or afforded the thing of whatever nature to which in the particular case he was entitled. The most that was done was to require him as a member of a class to conform with reasonable rules in regard to the separation of the races. In none of them was he denied the right to use, control, or dispose of his property, as in this case. Property of a person, whether as a member of a class or as an individual, cannot be taken without due process of law....

> The effect of the ordinance under consideration was not merely to regulate a business or the like, but was to destroy the right of the individual to acquire, enjoy, and dispose of his property. Being of this character, it was void as being opposed to the due-process clause of the constitution.

That there exists a serious and difficult problem arising from a feeling of race hostility which the law is powerless to control, and to which it must give a measure of consideration, may be freely admitted. But its solution cannot be promoted by depriving citizens of their constitutional rights and privileges.

As we have seen, this court has held laws valid which separated the races on the basis of equal accommodations in public conveyances, and courts of high authority have held enactments lawful which provide for separation in the public schools of white and colored pupils where equal privileges are given. But in view of the rights secured by the Fourteenth Amendment to the Federal Constitution such legislation must have its limitations, and cannot be sustained where the exercise of authority exceeds the restraints of the Constitution. We think these limitations are exceeded in laws and ordinances of the character now before us.

It is the purpose of such enactments, and, it is frankly avowed it will be their ultimate effect, to require by law, at least in residential districts, the compulsory separation of the races on account of color. Such action is said to be essential to the maintenance of the purity of the races, although it is to be noted in the ordinance under consideration that the employment of colored servants in white families is permitted, and nearby residences of colored persons not coming within the blocks, as defined in the ordinance, are not prohibited.

The case presented does not deal with an attempt to prohibit the amalgamation of the races. The right which the ordinance annulled was the civil right of a white man to dispose of his property if he saw fit to do so to a person of color and of a colored person to make such disposition to a white person.

It is urged that this proposed segregation will promote the public peace by preventing race conflicts. Desirable as this is, and important as is the preservation of the public peace, this aim cannot be accomplished by laws or ordinances which deny rights created or protected by the Federal Constitution.

It is said that such acquisitions by colored persons depreciate property owned in the neighborhood by white persons. But property may be acquired by undesirable white neighbors or put to disagreeable though lawful uses with like results.

We think this attempt to prevent the alienation of the property in question to a person of color was not a legitimate exercise of the police power of the State, and is in direct violation of the fundamental law enacted in the Fourteenth Amendment of the Constitution preventing state interference with property rights except by due process of law. That being the case, the ordinance cannot stand.

City of Birmingham v. Monk

185 F.2d 859 (5th Cir. 1950), cert. denied, 341 U.S. 940 (1951)

Horace C. Wilkinson, Special Counsel for City of Birmingham, Thomas E. Huey, Jr., Asst. City Atty., Birmingham, Ala., for appellants.

Thurgood Marshall, New York City, Arthur D. Shores, Peter A. Hall, and David H. Hood, Jr., all of Birmingham, Ala., for appellees.

Before McCord, Borah, and Russell, Circuit Judges.

Borah, Circuit Judge.

This is an appeal from a final judgment in an action brought by Mary Means Monk and several other Negro citizens of the United States, residents of the City of Birmingham, Alabama [challenging parts of] the basic zoning law of the City [which] make it unlawful for a Negro to occupy property for residential purposes in an area zoned A-1 or white residential, or for a white person to occupy property for residential purposes in an area zoned B-1 or Negro residential. * * *

The important question presented by this appeal is whether or not the zoning laws and supplemental ordinance in question constitute a legitimate exercise of the police power of the State or are unconstitutional and void as violative of the Fourteenth Amendment to the Constitution of the United States.

The property rights of plaintiffs are here directly involved. The rights created by the first section of the Fourteenth Amendment are, by its terms, guaranteed to the individual. The rights established are personal rights. One of the basic objectives sought to be effectuated by the framers of the Fourteenth Amendment was freedom from discrimination by the States and their municipalities in the enjoyment of property rights. The Fourteenth Amendment prevents State interference with property rights save by due process of law and "property is more than the mere thing which a person owns"[;] it includes the right to use, acquire and dispose of it and more specifically the right to residential occupancy for lawful purposes without discriminatory restriction. It is true, as urged by appellants, that the State and its municipalities in the exercise of those police powers that were reserved at the time of the adoption of the Constitution has wide discretion in determining its own public policy and what means are necessary for its own protection and properly to promote the safety, peace, public health, convenience and good order of its people. But it is equally true that the police power, however broad and extensive, is not above the Constitution. When it speaks its voice must be heeded and it is the obligation of this court so to declare. But we need not labor the point for the precise question presented here is foreclosed by the decisions of the courts, both Federal and State. Buchanan v. Warley, 245 U.S. 60; Tyler v. Harmon, 273 U.S. 668; City of Richmond v. Dean, 37 F.2d 712 [(4 Cir.)], affirmed 281 U.S. 704 [(1930)]; Shelley v. Kraemer, 334 U.S. 1; and the Courts of Georgia, Maryland, North Carolina, Oklahoma, Texas, and Virginia have also declared similar statutes invalid as being in contravention of the Fourteenth Amendment. Glover v. City of Atlanta, 96 S.E. 562 [(1918)];

Jackson v. State, 103 A. 910 [(1918)]; Clinard v. City of Winston-Salem, 6 S.E.2d 867 [(1940)]; Allen v. Oklahoma City, 52 [P].2d 1054 [(1936)]; Liberty Annex Corp. v. City of Dallas, 289 S.W. 1067 [(1927)]; Irvine v. City of Clifton Forge, 97 S.E. 310 [(1918)].
* * *

We find no merit in appellant's further contention that the court below erred in excluding certain evidence of a social and economic character. This evidence was irrelevant and immaterial to the issue of constitutionality.

There being no error, it follows that the decree below must be and it is

Affirmed.

Rehearing denied.

Russell, Circuit Judge (dissenting).

The proposition that State law or ordinances are generally unenforceable when their operation is contrary to the Federal Constitution of course can not be disputed. However it is not true that every limitation or restriction of such a right is in all events subject to be struck down without determination of the law and facts then obtaining and giving rise to the enactment. In this case, the finding of the City Commission in its ordinance of August, 1949, which supplemented the general zoning ordinance of Birmingham of 1926, that in the prevailing situation "breaches of the peace, riots, destruction of property and life," which neither the City nor other law enforcement officers could prevent, would follow attempts to violate the zoning restrictions, was entitled to some consideration. Even if the ordinance with such findings was nevertheless prima facie invalid upon constitutional grounds, the enactment should not have been destroyed unless and until the Court found that no sufficient danger was present to justify the dire apprehension of the Commission or to support its enactment. The Court could not judicially know, contrary to the findings of the legislative body, whether conditions in Birmingham were as declared by such body, though it is to be hoped that such findings were and are exaggerated. However, if the findings were established by evidence, declining to enjoin the enforcement of the ordinance would only give primacy to true general welfare over private rights, resulting from a determination of whose right should be subordinated, at least for the time being. To properly appraise the situation the Court should have heard the evidence offered in support of the legislative determination. Constitutionality may, and frequently does, depend upon particular circumstances. I disapprove the holding implying that whatever the danger to the public welfare, it must be suffered and endured when opposed by the assertion of a constitutional right to use one's property without restriction. I do not understand Buchanan v. Warley to require such a holding.

Other constitutional rights have been restricted because of the circumstances in which they were sought to be exercised. There comes to mind Mr. Justice Holmes' oft repeated utterance in Schenck v. U.S., 249 U.S. 47 [(1919)], "The most stringent protection of free speech would not protect a man in falsely shouting fire in a theatre and causing a panic," and the principle of clear and present danger announced following it. Vested property rights (also constitutionally protected) have been forced to yield to zoning ordinances which were determined not arbitrary or unreasonable. Hadacheck v. Sebastian, 239 U.S. 394; Pierce Oil Corp. v. City of Hope, 248 U.S. 498.

If the legislative finding that an emergency existed was to be overlooked or disregarded, the city should have been allowed to introduce evidence of the true situation.

Thereupon the Court could have determined the foundation and extent of danger and adjudged accordingly.

J. Mills Thornton III, Dividing Lines: Municipal Politics and the Struggle for Civil Rights in Montgomery, Birmingham, and Selma
(U. Alabama Press 2002), pp. 158–64

II. The Rise and Fall of the Racial Moderates, 1946–1956

Zoning came to Birmingham in 1915. In 1917 the U.S. Supreme Court declared unconstitutional a 1914 Louisville, Kentucky, ordinance that forbade blacks to purchase property in white sections of the city. New Orleans, Louisiana, then sought to circumvent this decision by adopting an ordinance that permitted blacks to own property in any part of the city, but forbade them to use the property for residential purposes in specified areas. In 1926, Birmingham's newly elected city commission, with its Klan-endorsed majority, amended the city's zoning ordinance to include a racial zoning provision patterned after that of New Orleans. In the meantime, the New Orleans ordinance had come under legal attack, and in 1927 the Supreme Court summarily declared it too unconstitutional. But the Birmingham provision remained on the books. It delineated three small black residential sections, totaling just 15 percent of the city's land area, though blacks were nearly 40 percent of the population. Blacks, however, initially paid little attention to the racial zoning ordnance, because the vast majority of them did not live in residential areas at all; they lived in company houses near the mines and mills, in sections zoned industrial and therefore without racial designation. Few blacks in the late 1920s and 1930s were sufficiently well off to be homeowners. This situation changed rapidly during World War II. In the first place, as we have seen, during the Depression the corporations began to close company housing. Then during the war years, the city's population exploded upward. Between 1940 and 1950 the total population increased by more than 20 percent and the black population by some 30 percent. Birmingham's factories operated at capacity under the stimulus of war production, and the demand for labor in all sectors of the economy was enormous, attracting workers to the city from rural areas. The availability of mortgage financing guarantees from the Federal Housing Administration and the Veterans Administration, added to these other factors, suddenly and sharply increased the demand for black homes.

One of the three sections in which blacks were legally permitted to reside was Smithfield, in northwest Birmingham. Smithfield was a well-to-do black neighborhood, but in 1938 the city had erected a large black public housing project there, absorbing land previously available for private residences and pushing the black middle class toward the northwestern edge of the enclave. As a result of this decision, and the more general developments just discussed, by 1945 the pressure on Smithfield's northern racial border had become intense. Smithfield adjoined two middle-class white neighborhoods, Graymont and College Hills. But separating the black and white districts was North Smithfield, an area nominally zoned for whites but in fact very sparsely settled, because its proximity to the black enclave had made whites reluctant to purchase there. In practice, then, North Smithfield served as a buffer zone segregating the races. But its vacant lots infuriated the many blacks who now had the money to buy or build a home, but were unable to obtain one zoned for their race when only blocks away, land was going begging. And white realtors, unable to sell to white purchasers, were consequently willing to sell to the eager blacks, who under the city ordinance could legally own but could not live on the land.

Events in early 1946 pushed blacks into action. In the spring the Birmingham Zoning Board recommended that an area near Titusville be rezoned to permit the construction of additional black housing, but in April the city commission refused to permit the change. In July the Birmingham Housing Authority evicted a number of black tenants from its Smithfield and Southtown public housing projects because their incomes were too high to qualify for continued residence, but because of the severe limitations on black housing created by racial zoning, the tenants could find no new accommodations and were left homeless. They appealed to the city commission but found Mayor Green and Commissioner Connor entirely unsympathetic. In August, Birmingham's NAACP branch undertook to sponsor a federal court suit, filed in the name of Mrs. Alice Allen, an administrator at the black Miles College, which sought to have the racial zoning ordinance declared unconstitutional. In September a white real estate developer filed a similar suit against suburban Tarrant City's ordinance that forbade any blacks to buy or own property there. In October, ruling from the bench, U.S. District Judge Clarence Mullins declared the Tarrant City ordinance unconstitutional. At the same time, Arthur Shores, representing the NAACP, filed a companion suit to Mrs. Allen's in behalf of Samuel Matthews, an iron ore miner who had built a home on the edge of North Smithfield on land he thought was zoned for blacks, but who then was denied an occupancy permit when building inspectors said that it was in fact outside the black area.

In the meantime, these events had led to the revival of the Ku Klux Klan, effectively dormant in the city since the early years of the Depression. In March crosses were burned in various sections of Birmingham, and in July the Klan formally incorporated itself, under the leadership of retired physician Dr. Elihu P. Pruitt, roofing contractor W. Hugh Morris, and salesman Robert S. Gulledge. In January 1947 it sent warning letters to the officers of the NAACP branch, demanding that the suits against the radical zoning ordinance be withdrawn. Later that month, Shores did withdraw Mrs. Allen's suit, on technical grounds, but he pressed Samuel Matthews's. In June Judge Mullins dismissed the Matthews suit when testimony revealed that Matthews had never formally applied for an occupancy permit because building inspectors had told him he could not get one. But in dismissing the suit, Judge Mullins commented that the racial zoning provision was clearly unconstitutional. Matthews thereupon applied for the occupancy permit, it was denied on racial grounds, and Shores refiled the suit. On August 4, 1947, Judge Mullins entered an injunction ordering building inspectors to grant Matthews a certificate of occupancy. On the night of August 18, the Klan responded by bombing Matthews's new home; it was completely destroyed. This was the first of the dozen racial bombings that by 1951 had gained for North Smithfield the unenviable nickname "Dynamite Hill."

Other events in this period intensified the violent emotions surrounding the engagement in Smithfield. The adoption in November 1946 of the Boswell Amendment, strengthening the state constitution's disfranchising provisions, produced, as we have seen, a federal court confrontation that resulted in March 1949 in the U.S. Supreme Court's declaring the amendment unconstitutional. But the state legislature then struck back with a second amendment, ratified by a very narrow margin in December 1951, that introduced a written voter qualification questionnaire; the new questionnaire, in increasingly stringent versions, restricted registration until 1965. These racially charged suffrage debates took place in the midst of the bitter political contests generated by the Dixiecrat revolt of 1948 and the ultimately successful efforts of the national party loyalists, led by U.S. senators Lister Hill and John Sparkman, to recapture control of the state Democratic Executive Committee in 1950. And all of these struggles were reflected in the activities of the newly revivified Ku Klux Klan. In June 1948 a group of hooded Klansmen invaded Camp Fletcher, the black Girl Scout camp just outside the city, to forbid the continuation of a training session in which two white Scout leaders were instructing a group of black camp counselors. The two white women were ordered to leave Birmingham. A year later, in June 1949, a Klan mob flogged a middle-aged white woman whom they accused of operating a house of ill repute. In a separate incident at the same time, they beat a white restaurant owner and organized a boycott of his restaurant because the establishment served both races, though in segregated sections. In July, whites cut the cables supporting the broadcasting tower of what was to be Birmingham's first black radio station; they thus sent the tower crashing to the ground and delayed the station's debut for a month. In September, Klansmen beat and terrorized two black families in Tuscaloosa who owed money to a white loan shark. By that time the Klan in Jefferson County was estimated to have some sixty-five hundred members, up from only seven hundred at its revival three years before.

It was in this context that the battle of Smithfield escalated. Judge Mullins, in the course of granting Samuel Matthews's injunction, had given his opinion that Birmingham's residential segregation ordinance was unconstitutional, but Matthews's suit was not a class action, the injunction ordered only that Matthews be given an occupancy permit, and the decision was unreported. Nevertheless, armed with Judge Mullins's opinion, blacks now with increasing frequency pressed city officials to open North Smithfield to them. For this purpose they formed the Birmingham Property Owners' Protective Association, headed by the executive secretary of the Negro Tuberculosis Association, Robert F. Coar, and realtor Wilbur H. Hollins. But on the other side, to insist that the races remain divided, their white neighbors rallied to the Graymont-College Hills Civic Association, headed by Colonel Horace B. Hansen, a retired army officer, and Olin H. Horton, personnel manager of an insurance company, who in later years would become a leader of the segregationist American States' Rights Association. Commissioner James Morgan, who supervised the building inspectors and the zoning board, struggled to find a compromise that would satisfy each group. He met with committees of the two residential associations and urged them to accept the creation of a park as a buffer between the neighborhoods. The two groups were open to the plan, but they could not agree on the size and location of the buffer zone. By the spring of 1949, the negotiations reached an impasse and the bombing resumed. On the night of March 25, three North Smithfield homes that had been purchased by blacks were bombed. In May, Klansman Robert Chambliss intimidated a black family into fleeing a home they had just occupied, and other blacks in the area received threatening telephone calls. In July a bomb was found at another black home and disarmed, but in August that home and another one were damaged by bombs thrown from a car.

As the violence continued, Commissioner Morgan rather desperately pressed his compromise plan. At a public hearing on it, both he and Mayor Green essentially conceded that it was unconstitutional, but Mayor Green said, "Sometimes you have to go beyond the letter of the law of man to meet situations like this." In an attempt to persuade the contending forces to reach a settlement, Morgan appointed a committee of blacks led by wealthy insurance executive Arthur G. Gaston, attorney Arthur Shores, and restaurant owner Robert L. Williams and a committee of whites headed by banker A. Key Foster and including former Klansman and Democratic Party leader Ben Ray and the United Mine Workers executive William Mitch. Federal authorities privately warned Morgan that he could face prosecution if the city attempted to enforce racial zoning. As a result, though police and building inspectors continued to threaten and harass blacks who moved into North Smithfield, officials took no steps to remove them. Segregationists denounced this timidity. "We want action, even if we lose," former police officer C.E. Henderson told the commission in July. Klansmen seemed to have felt that enforcement of segregation was being left up to them. In the meantime, activists in the NAACP denounced the willingness of more moderate blacks to compromise. The branch's most aggressive leader, its executive secretary, Emory O. Jackson, the editor of the *Birmingham World*, resigned his NAACP office in July in protest against the irresolution and conservatism of other prominent blacks. Under this pressure from the militant of both races, Morgan's middle ground gave way. The NAACP refused to renounce the possibility of further legal action, and Commissioner Connor voted against the ordinance creating the buffer zone, thus killing it because changes in zoning required the city commission's unanimous consent. In August Connor proposed a new city ordinance, drafted by his friend James Simpson, that made it a crime for any person to move into an area historically occupied by another race. Simpson believed that what a city could not legally require under its zoning authority, it could nevertheless compel as an exercise of its police power, to keep the public peace. In September the commission enacted the proposal. At the same time, Arthur Shores, finally abandoning the negotiations, turned to the courts to settle the dispute. In August he filed a suit in state court for Mrs. Mary Means Monk, the owner of a lot in North Smithfield, to force the city to issue her a building permit. And when Circuit Judge J. Edgar Bowron dismissed the petition, on the grounds that Mrs. Monk had not yet exhausted all her administrative remedies, in September Shores filed a class action in federal court in behalf of Mrs. Monk and fourteen other black property owners, seeking a formal declaration that both racial zoning and Connor's new criminal ordinance were unconstitutional.

In early December 1949, Commissioner Connor declared his candidacy for governor of Alabama on a platform of saving white supremacy; he denounced the Monk suit as a joint scheme of the NAACP and the national Democratic Party and pledged that, if elected, he would order President Harry Truman "to keep his filthy hands out of our affairs." In mid-December the suit came to trial before Judge Clarence Mullins. To present its case the city had hired the violently Negrophobic former Klan leader Horace Wilkinson, who sought to justify the ordinance by presenting evidence of blacks' moral inferiority and of the economic losses that neighborhood integration could bring to whites. But Judge Mullins would have none of it. Ruling from the bench immediately at the conclusion of the trial, he entered a permanent injunction against the enforcement of residential segregation in Birmingham. The city appealed to the Fifth Circuit.

Following Judge Mullins's ruling, the bombings—which had been suspended in August when Connor offered his tough new ordinance and the city began fighting the black initiative in court—resumed. In mid-April 1950 the recently constructed Smithfield home of black dentist Dr. Joel Boykins was bombed and destroyed. Later that month another black home, which had been bombed in August 1949 and then repaired and resold, was bombed again. Following this bombing, Olin H. Horton of the Graymont-College Hills Civic Association told reporters grimly that the association was determined that North Center Street, where the home was located, would remain a racial dividing line. Robert Chambliss, the Klansman identified in the intimidation of the black family in May 1949, was detained by police in connection with this latest bombing, but he was released at the end of the month. Some weeks thereafter an office building under construction at a point where racial neighborhoods abutted was bombed.

A Fifth Circuit panel heard arguments in the *Monk* case in October, and on December 20, 1950, in an opinion by Judge Wayne G. Borah, it sustained Judge Mullins's decision. Judge Robert L. Russell, a brother of Georgia's U.S. senator Richard Russell, however, filed a bitter dissent. The court, he claimed, was elevating private property rights over the general peace and welfare. On December 21, Mrs. Monk's newly constructed home was bombed and badly damaged. Six persons were in the house at the time of the explosion and narrowly escaped death. The following May the two Center Street homes that had been bombed in August 1949, one of which had been bombed again in April 1950, fell victim to arson and were burned to the ground after a six-hour fire. But thereafter the Smithfield violence ended until 1956, with a single exception in May 1954.

The reasons for the suspension of the Smithfield bombings are twofold. The first of these is that the blacks involved began to take steps to fight back. It had been clear from the beginning that the response of Connor's police to these offenses had been insouciant at best. Officers made virtually no effort to discover the culprits. Later testimony indicated that this inactivity was in accord with Connor's own attitudes. Certainly Connor's adamant hostility to any weakening of racial zoning was well known. Black leaders therefore quickly came to the conclusion that they would have to circumvent the police to end the terror. In their first effort to do so, in the summer of 1949, they hired a white private detective, Herbert Browne, to try to find out the identity of the bombers. But police, learning of this initiative in mid-August, promptly put a stop to it by arresting Browne for doing business without a license. Thereafter blacks turned to the racially moderate Governor James Folsom and the state highway patrol. At the end of August the highway patrol began providing protection in North Smithfield, and as we have seen, the bombing then stopped until the following April. When the violence resumed, Governor Folsom met in May 1950 with a black Smithfield delegation consisting of the Protective Association's Coar and Hollins, attorney Arthur Shores, *World* editor Emory Jackson, and civil rights activist the Reverend James L. Ware. Following this meeting, Folsom offered a reward for information leading to the apprehension of the bombers and ordered his three state investigators to enter the case. And on June 25, Folsom traveled to Birmingham to denounce racial prejudice in an address to more than a thousand blacks at the Sixteenth Street Baptist Church. But without the cooperation of the Birmingham police, the state investigators were unable to make any progress, and the posting of permanent highway patrol guards in the area was impossible given the many demands on the force. However, the cold war, intensified just at this time by the outbreak of fighting in Korea, adventitiously supplied Smithfield's blacks with a more permanent solution. They applied to federal authorities to organize a civil defense unit for their neighborhood. They thus gained helmets, armbands, and badges — and, most importantly, official sanction and justification for maintaining a paramilitary organization. Beginning apparently in early 1951, following the bombing of Mrs. Monk's home, for the next fifteen or more years the fifty-member Smithfield District Civil Defense Reserve Police patrolled every night, initially under the command of letter carrier Robert F. Walker and later of postal maintenance worker James E. Lay. At first their efforts were focused on Smithfield itself, but as Klan violence spread to other areas after 1956 the civil defense unit extended its coverage as well. By 1963 it was assisting in providing security for five black sections of the city.

B. Racially Restrictive Covenants

Shelley v. Kraemer
334 U.S. 1 (1948)

George L. Vaughn and Herman Willer argued the cause and filed a brief for petitioners in No. 72. Earl Susman was also of counsel.

Thurgood Marshall and Loren Miller argued the cause for petitioners in No. 87. With them on the brief were Willis M. Graves, Francis Dent, William H. Hastie, Charles H. Houston, George M. Johnson, William R. Ming, Jr., James Nabrit, Jr., Marian Wynn Perry, Spottswood W. Robinson, III, Andrew Weinberger and Ruth Weyand.*

By special leave of Court, Solicitor General Perlman argued the cause for the United States, as amicus curiae, supporting petitioners. With him on the brief was Attorney General Clark.

Gerald L. Seegers argued the cause for respondents in No. 72. With him on the brief was Walter H. Pollmann. Benjamin F. York was also of counsel.

Henry Gilligan and James A. Crooks argued the cause and filed a brief for respondents in No. 87. Lloyd T. Chockley was also of counsel.**

Before Chief Justice Vinson and Justices Black, Frankfurter, Douglas, Murphy, and Burton; Justices Reed, Jackson, and Rutledge took no part in the consideration or decision of this case.***

Mr. Chief Justice Vinson delivered the opinion of the Court.

These cases present for our consideration questions relating to the validity of court enforcement of private agreements, generally described as restrictive covenants, which

---

* Briefs of amici curiae supporting petitioners were filed by Perry W. Howard for the Civil Liberties Department, Grand Lodge of Elks, I. B. P. O. E. W.; Isaac Pacht, Irving Hill and Clore Warne; Robert McC. Marsh and Eugene Blanc, Jr. for the Protestant Council of New York City; Herbert S. Thatcher and Robert A. Wilson for the American Federation of Labor; Julius L. Goldstein for the Non-Sectarian Anti-Nazi League to Champion Human Rights, Inc.; Melville J. France for the General Council of Congregational Christian Churches et al.; Robert W. Kenny, O. John Rogge and Mozart G. Ratner for the National Lawyers Guild; Lee Pressman, Eugene Cotton, Frank Donner, John J. Abt, Leon M. Despres, M. H. Goldstein, Isadore Katz, David Rein, Samuel L. Rothbard, Harry Sacher, William Standard and Lindsay P. Walden for the Congress of Industrial Organizations et al.; Phineas Indritz, Irving R. M. Panzer and Richard A. Solomon for the American Veterans Committee; William Maslow, Shad Polier, Joseph B. Robison, Byron S. Miller and William Strong for the American Jewish Congress; Joseph M. Proskauer and Jacob Grumet for the American Jewish Committee et al.; William Strong for the American Indian Citizens League of California, Inc.; Francis M. Dent, Walter M. Nelson, Eugene H. Buder, Victor B. Harris, Luther Ely Smith and Harold I. Kahen for the American Civil Liberties Union; Earl B. Dickerson, Richard E. Westbrooks and Loring B. Moore for the National Bar Association; Alger Hiss, Joseph M. Proskauer and Victor Elting for the American Association for the United Nations; and Edward C. Park and Frank B. Frederick for the American Unitarian Association.

** Briefs of amici curiae supporting respondents were filed by Roger J. Whiteford and John J. Wilson for the National Association of Real Estate Boards; Ray C. Eberhard and Elisabeth Eberhard Zeigler for the Arlington Heights Property Owners Association et al.; and Thomas F. Cadwalader and Carlyle Barton for the Mount Royal Protective Association, Inc.

*** Editor's Note: Justices Reed, Jackson, and Rutledge did not participate, "reportedly because each of them owned property which was covered by a restrictive covenant." C. Herman Pritchett, Civil Liberties and the Vinson Court 142 (U. Chicago Press 1954); see also Clement E. Vose, Caucasians Only: The Supreme Court, the NAACP, and the Restrictive Covenant Cases 9–10 (U. CA

have as their purpose the exclusion of persons of designated race or color from the ownership or occupancy of real property. Basic constitutional issues of obvious importance have been raised.

The first of these cases comes to this Court on certiorari to the Supreme Court of Missouri. On February 16, 1911, thirty out of a total of thirty-nine owners of property fronting both sides of Labadie Avenue between Taylor Avenue and Cora Avenue in the city of St. Louis, signed an agreement, which was subsequently recorded, providing in part:

> ... the said property is hereby restricted to the use and occupancy for the term of Fifty (50) years from this date, so that it shall be a condition all the time and whether recited and referred to as [sic] not in subsequent conveyances and shall attach to the land, as a condition precedent to the sale of the same, that hereafter no part of said property or any portion thereof shall be, for said term of Fifty-years, occupied by any person not of the Caucasian race, it being intended hereby to restrict the use of said property for said period of time against the occupancy as owners or tenants of any portion of said property for resident or other purpose by people of the Negro or Mongolian Race.

The entire district described in the agreement included fifty-seven parcels of land. The thirty owners who signed the agreement held title to forty-seven parcels, including the particular parcel involved in this case. At the time the agreement was signed, five of the parcels in the district were owned by Negroes. One of those had been occupied by Negro families since 1882, nearly thirty years before the restrictive agreement was executed. The trial court found that owners of seven out of nine homes on the south side of Labadie Avenue, within the restricted district and "in the immediate vicinity" of the premises in question, had failed to sign the restrictive agreement in 1911. At the time this action was brought, four of the premises were occupied by Negroes, and had been so occupied for periods ranging from twenty-three to sixty-three years. A fifth parcel had been occupied by Negroes until a year before this suit was instituted.

On August 11, 1945, pursuant to a contract of sale, petitioners Shelley, who are Negroes, for valuable consideration received from one Fitzgerald a warranty deed to the parcel in question. The trial court found that petitioners had no actual knowledge of the restrictive agreement at the time of the purchase.

On October 9, 1945, respondents, as owners of other property subject to the terms of the restrictive covenant, brought suit in Circuit Court of the city of St. Louis praying that petitioners Shelley be restrained from taking possession of the property and that judgment be entered divesting title out of petitioners Shelley and revesting title in the immediate grantor or in such other person as the court should direct. The trial court denied the requested relief on the ground that the restrictive agreement, upon which respondents based their action, had never become final and complete because it was the intention of the parties to that agreement that it was not to become effective until signed by all property owners in the district, and signatures of all the owners had never been obtained.

The Supreme Court of Missouri sitting en banc reversed and directed the trial court to grant the relief for which respondents had prayed. That court held the agreement effective and concluded that enforcement of its provisions violated no rights guaranteed to petitioners by the Federal Constitution. At the time the court rendered its decision,

Press 1959); Francis A. Allen, *Remembering Shelley v. Kraemer: Of Public and Private Worlds*, 67 Wash. U. L.Q. 709, 721 (1989).

petitioners were occupying the property in question. [The discussion of the Michigan cases is omitted.]

I.

Whether the equal protection clause of the Fourteenth Amendment inhibits judicial enforcement by state courts of restrictive covenants based on race or color is a question which this Court has not heretofore been called upon to consider. Only two cases have been decided by this Court which in any way have involved the enforcement of such agreements. The first of these was the case of Corrigan v. Buckley, 271 U.S. 323 (1926). There, suit was brought in the courts of the District of Columbia to enjoin a threatened violation of certain restrictive covenants relating to lands situated in the city of Washington. Relief was granted, and the case was brought here on appeal. It is apparent that that case, which had originated in the federal courts and involved the enforcement of covenants on land located in the District of Columbia, could present no issues under the Fourteenth Amendment; for that Amendment by its terms applies only to the States. Nor was the question of the validity of court enforcement of the restrictive covenants under the Fifth Amendment properly before the Court, as the opinion of this Court specifically recognizes. The only constitutional issue which the appellants had raised in the lower courts, and hence the only constitutional issue before this Court on appeal, was the validity of the covenant agreements as such. This Court concluded that since the inhibitions of the constitutional provisions invoked apply only to governmental action, as contrasted to action of private individuals, there was no showing that the covenants, which were simply agreements between private property owners, were invalid. Accordingly, the appeal was dismissed for want of a substantial question. Nothing in the opinion of this Court, therefore, may properly be regarded as an adjudication on the merits of the constitutional issues presented by these cases, which raise the question of the validity, not of the private agreements as such, but of the judicial enforcement of those agreements.

The second of the cases involving racial restrictive covenants was Hansberry v. Lee, 311 U.S. 32 (1940). In that case, petitioners, white property owners, were enjoined by the state courts from violating the terms of a restrictive agreement. The state Supreme Court had held petitioners bound by an earlier judicial determination, in litigation in which petitioners were not parties, upholding the validity of the restrictive agreement, although, in fact, the agreement had not been signed by the number of owners necessary to make it effective under state law. This Court reversed the judgment of the state Supreme Court upon the ground that petitioners had been denied due process of law in being held estopped to challenge the validity of the agreement on the theory, accepted by the state court, that the earlier litigation, in which petitioners did not participate, was in the nature of a class suit. In arriving at its result, this Court did not reach the issues presented by the cases now under consideration.

It is well, at the outset, to scrutinize the terms of the restrictive agreements involved in these cases. In the Missouri case, the covenant declares that no part of the affected property shall be "occupied by any person not of the Caucasian race, it being intended hereby to restrict the use of said property ... against the occupancy as owners or tenants of any portion of said property for resident or other purpose by people of the Negro or Mongolian Race." Not only does the restriction seek to proscribe use and occupancy of the affected properties by members of the excluded class, but as construed by the Missouri courts, the agreement requires that title of any person who uses his property in violation of the restriction shall be divested. The restriction of the covenant in the Michigan case seeks to bar occupancy by persons of the excluded class. It provides that "This property shall not be used or occupied by any person or persons except those of the Caucasian race."

It should be observed that these covenants do not seek to proscribe any particular use of the affected properties. Use of the properties for residential occupancy, as such, is not forbidden. The restrictions of these agreements, rather, are directed toward a designated class of persons and seek to determine who may and who may not own or make use of the properties for residential purposes. The excluded class is defined wholly in terms of race or color, "simply that and nothing more."

It cannot be doubted that among the civil rights intended to be protected from discriminatory state action by the Fourteenth Amendment are the rights to acquire, enjoy, own and dispose of property. Equality in the enjoyment of property rights was regarded by the framers of that Amendment as an essential pre-condition to the realization of other basic civil rights and liberties which the Amendment was intended to guarantee.[7] Thus, § 1978 of the Revised Statutes, derived from § 1 of the Civil Rights Act of 1866 which was enacted by Congress while the Fourteenth Amendment was also under consideration,[8] provides:

> All citizens of the United States shall have the same right, in every State and Territory, as is enjoyed by white citizens thereof to inherit, purchase, lease, sell, hold, and convey real and personal property.

This Court has given specific recognition to the same principle. Buchanan v. Warley, 245 U.S. 60 (1917).

It is likewise clear that restrictions on the right of occupancy of the sort sought to be created by the private agreements in these cases could not be squared with the requirements of the Fourteenth Amendment if imposed by state statute or local ordinance. We do not understand respondents to urge the contrary. In the case of Buchanan v. Warley a unanimous Court declared unconstitutional the provisions of a city ordinance which denied to colored persons the right to occupy houses in blocks in which the greater number of houses were occupied by white persons, and imposed similar restrictions on white persons with respect to blocks in which the greater number of houses were occupied by colored persons....

In Harmon v. Tyler, 273 U.S. 668 (1927), a unanimous court, on the authority of Buchanan v. Warley, declared invalid an ordinance which forbade any Negro to establish a home on any property in a white community or any white person to establish a home in a Negro community, "except on the written consent of a majority of the persons of the opposite race inhabiting such community or portion of the City to be affected."

The precise question before this Court in both the Buchanan and Harmon cases, involved the rights of white sellers to dispose of their properties free from restrictions as to potential purchasers based on considerations of race or color. But that such legislation is also offensive to the rights of those desiring to acquire and occupy property and barred on grounds of race or color is clear, not only from the language of the opinion in

---

7. Slaughter-House Cases, 16 Wall. 36 (1873).

8. In Oyama v. California, 332 U.S. 633 (1948), the section of the Civil Rights Act herein considered is described as the federal statute, "enacted before the Fourteenth Amendment but vindicated by it." The Civil Rights Act of 1866 was reenacted in § 18 of the Act of May 31, 1870, subsequent to the adoption of the Fourteenth Amendment. [Editor's note: this is now codified as 42 U.S.C. § 1982.]

Buchanan v. Warley, but from this Court's disposition of the case of Richmond v. Deans, 281 U.S. 704 (1930). There, a Negro, barred from the occupancy of certain property by the terms of an ordinance similar to that in the Buchanan case, sought injunctive relief in the federal courts to enjoin the enforcement of the ordinance on the grounds that its provisions violated the terms of the Fourteenth Amendment. Such relief was granted, and this Court affirmed, finding the citation of Buchanan v. Warley and Harmon v. Tyler sufficient to support its judgment.

But the present cases, unlike those just discussed, do not involve action by state legislatures or city councils. Here the particular patterns of discrimination and the areas in which the restrictions are to operate, are determined, in the first instance, by the terms of agreements among private individuals. Participation of the State consists in the enforcement of the restrictions so defined. The crucial issue with which we are here confronted is whether this distinction removes these cases from the operation of the prohibitory provisions of the Fourteenth Amendment.

Since the decision of this Court in the Civil Rights Cases, 109 U.S. 3 (1883), the principle has become firmly embedded in our constitutional law that the action inhibited by the first section of the Fourteenth Amendment is only such action as may fairly be said to be that of the States. That Amendment erects no shield against merely private conduct, however discriminatory or wrongful.

We conclude, therefore, that the restrictive agreements standing alone cannot be regarded as a violation of any rights guaranteed to petitioners by the Fourteenth Amendment. So long as the purposes of those agreements are effectuated by voluntary adherence to their terms, it would appear clear that there has been no action by the State and the provisions of the Amendment have not been violated.

But here there was more. These are cases in which the purposes of the agreements were secured only by judicial enforcement by state courts of the restrictive terms of the agreements. The respondents urge that judicial enforcement of private agreements does not amount to state action; or, in any event, the participation of the State is so attenuated in character as not to amount to state action within the meaning of the Fourteenth Amendment. Finally, it is suggested, even if the States in these cases may be deemed to have acted in the constitutional sense, their action did not deprive petitioners of rights guaranteed by the Fourteenth Amendment. We move to a consideration of these matters.

II.

That the action of state courts and of judicial officers in their official capacities is to be regarded as action of the State within the meaning of the Fourteenth Amendment, is a proposition which has long been established by decisions of this Court. That principle was given expression in the earliest cases involving the construction of the terms of the Fourteenth Amendment.... In the Civil Rights Cases, this Court pointed out that the Amendment makes void "State action of every kind" which is inconsistent with the guaranties therein contained, and extends to manifestations of "State authority in the shape of laws, customs, or judicial or executive proceedings."

Similar expressions, giving specific recognition to the fact that judicial action is to be regarded as action of the State for the purposes of the Fourteenth Amendment, are to be found in numerous cases which have been more recently decided....

One of the earliest applications of the prohibitions contained in the Fourteenth Amendment to action of state judicial officials occurred in cases in which Negroes had been excluded from jury service in criminal prosecutions by reason of their race or color. These cases demonstrate, also, the early recognition by this Court that state action in violation of the Amendment's provisions is equally repugnant to the constitutional commands whether directed by state statute or taken by a judicial official in the absence of statute. Thus, in Strauder v. West Virginia, 100 U.S. 303 (1880), this Court declared invalid a state statute restricting jury service to white persons as amounting to a denial of the equal protection of the laws to the colored defendant in that case. In the same volume of the reports, the Court in Ex parte Virginia, [100 U.S. 339 (1880),] held that a similar discrimination imposed by the action of a state judge denied rights protected by the Amendment, despite the fact that the language of the state statute relating to jury service contained no such restrictions.

The action of state courts in imposing penalties or depriving parties of other substantive rights without providing adequate notice and opportunity to defend, has, of course, long been regarded as a denial of the due process of law guaranteed by the Fourteenth Amendment. Brinkerhoff-Faris Trust & Savings Co. v. Hill[, 281 U.S. 673 (1930)]; Cf. Pennoyer v. Neff, 95 U.S. 714 (1878).

In numerous cases, this Court has reversed criminal convictions in state courts for failure of those courts to provide the essential ingredients of a fair hearing. Thus it has been held that convictions obtained in state courts under the domination of a mob are void. Convictions obtained by coerced confessions, by the use of perjured testimony known by the prosecution to be such, or without the effective assistance of counsel, have also been held to be exertions of state authority in conflict with the fundamental rights protected by the Fourteenth Amendment.

But the examples of state judicial action which have been held by this Court to violate the Amendment's commands are not restricted to situations in which the judicial proceedings were found in some manner to be procedurally unfair. It has been recognized that the action of state courts in enforcing a substantive common-law rule formulated by those courts, may result in the denial of rights guaranteed by the Fourteenth Amendment, even though the judicial proceedings in such cases may have been in complete accord with the most rigorous conceptions of procedural due process.[19] Thus, in American Federation of Labor v. Swing, 312 U.S. 321 (1941), enforcement by state courts of the common-law policy of the State, which resulted in the restraining of peaceful picketing, was held to be state action of the sort prohibited by the Amendment's guaranties of freedom of discussion. In Cantwell v. Connecticut, 310 U.S. 296 (1940), a conviction in a state court of the common-law crime of breach of the peace was, under the circumstances of the case, found to be a violation of the Amendment's commands relating to freedom of religion. In Bridges v. California, 314 U.S. 252 (1941), enforcement of the state's common-law rule relating to contempts by publication was held to be state action inconsistent with the prohibitions of the Fourteenth Amendment.

The short of the matter is that from the time of the adoption of the Fourteenth Amendment until the present, it has been the consistent ruling of this Court that the action of the States to which the Amendment has reference, includes action of state courts and state judicial officials. Although, in construing the terms of the Fourteenth Amendment, differences have from time to time been expressed as to whether particular types of state action may be said to offend the Amendment's prohibitory provi-

---

19. In applying the rule of Erie R. Co. v. Tompkins, 304 U.S. 64 (1938), it is clear that the common-law rules enunciated by state courts in judicial opinions are to be regarded as a part of the law of the State.

sions, it has never been suggested that state court action is immunized from the operation of those provisions simply because the act is that of the judicial branch of the state government.

III.

Against this background of judicial construction, extending over a period of some three-quarters of a century, we are called upon to consider whether enforcement by state courts of the restrictive agreements in these cases may be deemed to be the acts of those States; and, if so, whether that action has denied these petitioners the equal protection of the laws which the Amendment was intended to insure.

We have no doubt that there has been state action in these cases in the full and complete sense of the phrase. The undisputed facts disclose that petitioners were willing purchasers of properties upon which they desired to establish homes. The owners of the properties were willing sellers; and contracts of sale were accordingly consummated. It is clear that but for the active intervention of the state courts, supported by the full panoply of state power, petitioners would have been free to occupy the properties in question without restraint.

These are not cases, as has been suggested, in which the States have merely abstained from action, leaving private individuals free to impose such discriminations as they see fit. Rather, these are cases in which the States have made available to such individuals the full coercive power of government to deny to petitioners, on the grounds of race or color, the enjoyment of property rights in premises which petitioners are willing and financially able to acquire and which the grantors are willing to sell. The difference between judicial enforcement and nonenforcement of the restrictive covenants is the difference to petitioners between being denied rights of property available to other members of the community and being accorded full enjoyment of those rights on an equal footing.

The enforcement of the restrictive agreements by the state courts in these cases was directed pursuant to the common-law policy of the States as formulated by those courts in earlier decisions. In the Missouri case, enforcement of the covenant was directed in the first instance by the highest court of the State after the trial court had determined the agreement to be invalid for want of the requisite number of signatures. In the Michigan case, the order of enforcement by the trial court was affirmed by the highest state court. The judicial action in each case bears the clear and unmistakable imprimatur of the State. We have noted that previous decisions of this Court have established the proposition that judicial action is not immunized from the operation of the Fourteenth Amendment simply because it is taken pursuant to the state's common-law policy. Nor is the Amendment ineffective simply because the particular pattern of discrimination, which the State has enforced, was defined initially by the terms of a private agreement. State action, as that phrase is understood for the purposes of the Fourteenth Amendment, refers to exertions of state power in all forms. And when the effect of that action is to deny rights subject to the protection of the Fourteenth Amendment, it is the obligation of this Court to enforce the constitutional commands.

We hold that in granting judicial enforcement of the restrictive agreements in these cases, the States have denied petitioners the equal protection of the laws and that, therefore, the action of the state courts cannot stand. We have noted that freedom from discrimination by the States in the enjoyment of property rights was among the basic objectives sought to be effectuated by the framers of the Fourteenth Amendment. That such discrimination has occurred in these cases is clear. Because of the race or color of these petitioners they have been denied rights of ownership or occupancy enjoyed as a matter of course by other citizens of different race or color. The Fourteenth Amendment declares "that all persons, whether colored or white, shall stand equal before the laws of the States, and, in regard to the colored race, for whose protection the amendment was primarily designed, that no discrimination shall be made against them by law because of their color."[26] Strauder v. West Virginia, at 307.

Only recently this Court has had occasion to declare that a state law which denied equal enjoyment of property rights to a designated class of citizens of specified race and ancestry, was not a legitimate exercise of the state's police power but violated the guaranty of the equal protection of the laws. Oyama v. California. Nor may the discriminations imposed by the state courts in these cases be justified as proper exertions of state police power. Cf. Buchanan v. Warley.

Respondents urge, however, that since the state courts stand ready to enforce restrictive covenants excluding white persons from the ownership or occupancy of property covered by such agreements, enforcement of covenants excluding colored persons may not be deemed a denial of equal protection of the laws to the colored persons who are thereby affected.[28] This contention does not bear scrutiny. The parties have directed our attention to no case in which a court, state or federal, has been called upon to enforce a covenant excluding members of the white majority from ownership or occupancy of real property on grounds of race or color. But there are more fundamental considerations. The rights created by the first section of the Fourteenth Amendment are, by its terms, guaranteed to the individual. The rights established are personal rights. It is, therefore, no answer to these petitioners to say that the courts may also be induced to deny white persons rights of ownership and occupancy on grounds of race or color. Equal protection of the laws is not achieved through indiscriminate imposition of inequalities.

Nor do we find merit in the suggestion that property owners who are parties to these agreements are denied equal protection of the laws if denied access to the courts to enforce the terms of restrictive covenants and to assert property rights which the state courts have held to be created by such agreements. The Constitution confers upon no individual the right to demand action by the State which results in the denial of equal protection of the laws to other individuals. And it would appear beyond question that the power of the State to create and enforce property interests must be exercised within the boundaries defined by the Fourteenth Amendment. Cf. Marsh v. Alabama, 326 U.S. 501 (1946).

The problem of defining the scope of the restrictions which the Federal Constitution imposes upon exertions of power by the States has given rise to many of the most persistent and fundamental issues which this Court has been called upon to consider. That problem was foremost in the minds of the framers of the Constitution, and since that

---

26. Restrictive agreements of the sort involved in these case have been used to exclude other than Negroes from the ownership or occupancy of real property. We are informed that such agreements have been directed against Indians, Jews, Chinese, Japanese, Mexicans, Hawaiians, Puerto Ricans, and Filipinos, among others.

28. It should be observed that the restrictions relating to residential occupancy contained in ordinances involved in the Buchanan, Harmon and Deans cases, cited supra, and declared by this Court to be inconsistent with the requirements of the Fourteenth Amendment, applied equally to white persons and Negroes.

early day, has arisen in a multitude of forms. The task of determining whether the action of a State offends constitutional provisions is one which may not be undertaken lightly. Where, however, it is clear that the action of the State violates the terms of the fundamental charter, it is the obligation of this Court so to declare.

The historical context in which the Fourteenth Amendment became a part of the Constitution should not be forgotten. Whatever else the framers sought to achieve, it is clear that the matter of primary concern was the establishment of equality in the enjoyment of basic civil and political rights and the preservation of those rights from discriminatory action on the part of the States based on considerations of race or color. Seventy-five years ago this Court announced that the provisions of the Amendment are to be construed with this fundamental purpose in mind.[30] Upon full consideration, we have concluded that in these cases the States have acted to deny petitioners the equal protection of the laws guaranteed by the Fourteenth Amendment. Having so decided, we find it unnecessary to consider whether petitioners have also been deprived of property without due process of law or denied privileges and immunities of citizens of the United States.

Note

"'This house is going to be sold to whites only,' said the owner.... 'It's not for colored.'"

According to the New York Times, reporting on court documents, this statement was made to an African American woman shopping for a home in Richmond, Virginia in 2002. See Motoko Rich, Restrictive Covenants Stubbornly Stay on the Books, New York Times, April 20, 2005, at D1, reporting on a conversation "three years ago." The Times reports that the owner "later testified before the Virginia Fair Housing Board that he believed a clause in his deed prohibited him from selling to 'any person not of the Caucasian race.'" He also testified that "his neighbors told him the area was zoned 'for whites only.'"

Hurd v. Hodge
334 U.S. 24 (1948)

Charles H. Houston and Phineas Indritz argued the cause for petitioners. With them on the brief was Spottswood W. Robinson, III.*

---

30. Slaughter-House Cases, 16 Wall. 36, 81 (1873); Strauder v. West Virginia, 100 U.S. 303 (1880). See Flack, The Adoption of the Fourteenth Amendment.

* Briefs of amici curiae supporting petitioners were filed by A. L. Wirin, Saburo Kido and Fred Okrand for the Japanese American Citizens League; Robert W. Kenny, O. John Rogge and Mozart G. Ratner for the National Lawyers Guild; Lee Pressman, Eugene Cotton, Frank Donner, John J. Abt, Leon M. Despres, M. H. Goldstein, Isadore Katz, David Rein, Samuel L. Rothbard, Harry Sacher, William Standard and Lindsay P. Walden for the Congress of Industrial Organizations et al.; Phineas Indritz, Irving R. M. Panzer and Richard A. Solomon for the American Veterans Committee; William Maslow, Shad Polier, Joseph B. Robison, Byron S. Miller and William Strong for the American Jewish Congress; Joseph M. Proskauer and Jacob Grumet for the American Jewish Committee et al.; William Strong for the American Indian Citizens League of California, Inc.; Francis M. Dent, Walter M. Nelson, Eugene H. Buder, Victor B. Harris, Luther Ely Smith and Harold I. Kahen for the American Civil Liberties Union; Herbert S. Thatcher and Robert A. Wilson for the American Federation of Labor; Earl B. Dickerson, Richard E. Westbrooks and Loring B. Moore for the National Bar Association; Alger Hiss, Joseph M. Proskauer and Victor Elting for the American Association for the United Nations; and Edward C. Park and Frank B. Frederick for the American Unitarian Association.

By special leave of Court, Solicitor General Perlman argued the cause for the United States, as amicus curiae, supporting petitioners. With him on the brief was Attorney General Clark.

Henry Gilligan and James A. Crooks argued the cause and filed a brief for respondents.**

Before Chief Justice Vinson and Justices Black, Frankfurter, Douglas, Murphy, and Burton; Justices Reed, Jackson, and Rutledge took no part in the consideration or decision of this case.***

Mr. Chief Justice Vinson delivered the opinion of the Court.

These are companion cases to Shelley v. Kraemer and McGhee v. Sipes.

In 1906, twenty of thirty-one lots in the 100 block of Bryant Street, Northwest, in the City of Washington, were sold subject to the following covenant:

> ... that said lot shall never be rented, leased, sold, transferred or conveyed unto any Negro or colored person, under a penalty of Two Thousand Dollars ($2,000), which shall be a lien against said property.

Prior to the sales which gave rise to these cases, the twenty lots which are subject to the covenants were at all times owned and occupied by white persons, except for a brief period when three of the houses were occupied by Negroes who were eventually induced to move without legal action. The remaining eleven lots in the same block, however, are not subject to a restrictive agreement and, as found by the District Court, were occupied by Negroes for the twenty years prior to the institution of this litigation.

Whether judicial enforcement of racial restrictive agreements by the federal courts of the District of Columbia violates the Fifth Amendment has never been adjudicated by this Court. In Corrigan v. Buckley, 1926, an appeal was taken to this Court from a judgment of the United States Court of Appeals for the District of Columbia which had affirmed an order of the lower court granting enforcement to a restrictive covenant. But as was pointed out in our opinion in Shelley v. Kraemer, the only constitutional issue which had been raised in the lower courts in the Corrigan case, and, consequently, the only constitutional question before this Court on appeal, related to the validity of the private agreements as such. Nothing in the opinion of this Court in that case, therefore, may properly be regarded as an adjudication of the issue presented by petitioners in this case which concerns, not the validity of the restrictive agreements standing alone, but the validity of court enforcement of the restrictive covenants under the due process clause of the Fifth Amendment.

This Court has declared invalid municipal ordinances restricting occupancy in designated areas to persons of specified race and color as denying rights of white sellers and Negro purchasers of property, guaranteed by the due process clause of the Fourteenth Amendment. Buchanan v. Warley, 245 U.S. 60 (1917); Harmon v. Tyler, 273 U.S. 668 (1927); City of Richmond v. Deans, 281 U.S. 704 (1930). Petitioners urge that judicial enforcement of the restrictive covenants by courts of the District of Columbia should likewise be held to deny rights of white sellers and Negro purchasers of property, guaranteed by the due process clause of the Fifth Amendment. Petitioners point out that this Court in Hirabayashi v. United States, 320 U.S. 81, 100 (1943), reached its decision in a case in which issues under the Fifth Amendment were presented, on the assumption

---

** Briefs of amici curiae supporting respondents were filed by E. Hilton Jackson and John W. Jackson for the Federation of Citizens Associations of the District of Columbia et al.; and Thomas F. Cadwalader and Carlyle Barton for the Mount Royal Protective Association, Inc.

*** See note ***, Shelley v. Kraemer, supra.

that "racial discriminations are in most circumstances irrelevant and therefore prohibited. ..." And see Korematsu v. United States, 323 U.S. 214, 216 (1944).

Upon full consideration, however, we have found it unnecessary to resolve the constitutional issue which petitioners advance; for we have concluded that judicial enforcement of restrictive covenants by the courts of the District of Columbia is improper for other reasons hereinafter stated.

Section 1978 of the Revised Statutes, derived from § 1 of the Civil Rights Act of 1866, provides:

> All citizens of the United States shall have the same right, in every State and Territory, as is enjoyed by white citizens thereof to inherit, purchase, lease, sell, hold, and convey real and personal property.*

All the petitioners in these cases, as found by the District Court, are citizens of the United States. We have no doubt that, for the purposes of this section, the District of Columbia is included within the phrase "every State and Territory." Nor can there be doubt of the constitutional power of Congress to enact such legislation with reference to the District of Columbia.

We may start with the proposition that the statute does not invalidate private restrictive agreements so long as the purposes of those agreements are achieved by the parties through voluntary adherence to the terms. The action toward which the provisions of the statute under consideration is directed is governmental action. ...

In considering whether judicial enforcement of restrictive covenants is the kind of governmental action which the first section of the Civil Rights Act of 1866 was intended to prohibit, reference must be made to the scope and purposes of the Fourteenth Amendment; for that statute and the Amendment were closely related both in inception and in the objectives which Congress sought to achieve.

Both the Civil Rights Act of 1866 and the joint resolution which was later adopted as the Fourteenth Amendment were passed in the first session of the Thirty-Ninth Congress. Frequent references to the Civil Rights Act are to be found in the record of the legislative debates on the adoption of the Amendment. It is clear that in many significant respects the statute and the Amendment were expressions of the same general congressional policy. Indeed, as the legislative debates reveal, one of the primary purposes of many members of Congress in supporting the adoption of the Fourteenth Amendment was to incorporate the guaranties of the Civil Rights Act of 1866 in the organic law of the land. Others supported the adoption of the Amendment in order to eliminate doubt as to the constitutional validity of the Civil Rights Act as applied to the States.

The close relationship between § 1 of the Civil Rights Act and the Fourteenth Amendment was given specific recognition by this Court in Buchanan v. Warley. There, the Court observed that, not only through the operation of the Fourteenth Amendment, but also by virtue of the "statutes enacted in furtherance of its purpose," including the provisions here considered, a colored man is granted the right to acquire property free from interference by discriminatory state legislation. In Shelley v. Kraemer, we have held that the Fourteenth Amendment also forbids such discrimination where imposed by state courts in the enforcement of restrictive covenants. That holding is clearly indicative of the construction to be given to the relevant provisions of the Civil Rights Act in their application to the Courts of the District of Columbia.

---

* Editor's Note: This is now 42 U.S.C. § 1982.

Moreover, the explicit language employed by Congress to effectuate its purposes leaves no doubt that judicial enforcement of the restrictive covenants by the courts of the District of Columbia is prohibited by the Civil Rights Act. That statute, by its terms, requires that all citizens of the United States shall have the same right "as is enjoyed by white citizens ... to inherit, purchase, lease, sell, hold, and convey real and personal property." That the Negro petitioners have been denied that right by virtue of the action of the federal courts of the District is clear. The Negro petitioners entered into contracts of sale with willing sellers for the purchase of properties upon which they desired to establish homes. Solely because of their race and color they are confronted with orders of court divesting their titles in the properties and ordering that the premises be vacated. White sellers, one of whom is a petitioner here, have been enjoined from selling the properties to any Negro or colored person. Under such circumstances, to suggest that the Negro petitioners have been accorded the same rights as white citizens to purchase, hold, and convey real property is to reject the plain meaning of language. We hold that the action of the District Court directed against the Negro purchasers and the white sellers denies rights intended by Congress to be protected by the Civil Rights Act and that, consequently, the action cannot stand.

But even in the absence of the statute, there are other considerations which would indicate that enforcement of restrictive covenants in these cases is judicial action contrary to the public policy of the United States, and as such should be corrected by this Court in the exercise of its supervisory powers over the courts of the District of Columbia. The power of the federal courts to enforce the terms of private agreements is at all times exercised subject to the restrictions and limitations of the public policy of the United States as manifested in the Constitution, treaties, federal statutes, and applicable legal precedents. Where the enforcement of private agreements would be violative of that policy, it is the obligation of courts to refrain from such exertions of judicial power.

We are here concerned with action of federal courts of such a nature that if taken by the courts of a State would violate the prohibitory provisions of the Fourteenth Amendment. Shelley v. Kraemer. It is not consistent with the public policy of the United States to permit federal courts in the Nation's capital to exercise general equitable powers to compel action denied the state courts where such state action has been held to be violative of the guaranty of the equal protection of the laws. We cannot presume that the public policy of the United States manifests a lesser concern for the protection of such basic rights against discriminatory action of federal courts than against such action taken by the courts of the States.

Clement E. Vose, Caucasians Only: The Supreme Court, the NAACP, and the Restrictive Covenant Cases
(U. CA Press 1959), pp. 82–90

The Plaintiffs: Mrs. Hodge and Her Neighbors

At the trial which began before Judge F. Dickinson Letts on October 9, 1945, Lena M. Hodge agreed, when referred to as "the big chief" around her neighborhood, that she seemed "to have been looking after the place for more than twenty years." She and her husband purchased their house at 136 Bryant Street in 1909 as the area was just being developed. One of the first things that the agent for Middaugh & Shannon showed the Hodges, she reported, was the "covenant that was in the deed to the house, which of course we liked." But they did not inquire whether restrictive covenants covered houses in the surrounding area, although they desired to live in a neighborhood where all the people were white. Through the passing years adjacent streets became occupied by Negroes. Adams Street immediately back of her own house became colored, and areas to the east and west of the one-hundred block of Bryant Street also changed. She could do nothing about that, for as she said, "I felt that I had enough to think about and fight for on my own street. I felt that somebody over there could take the reins over there and fight that out." So in her own block, made up of twenty houses, Mrs. Hodge was the leader who took over from Middaugh & Shannon the task of keeping the neighborhood white. She was asked the following questions at the trial:

Q. … just how did you go about taking hold of this matter in connection with the whole community when the matter of the enforcement of the covenant in your block came up?

A. You mean now, or earlier?

Q. Any time.

A. Well, I don't know, it is just one of those things. I got into it, I guess, and the different ones, as soon as they would hear or know of a colored person moving, they always called me and I just simply assumed the responsibility, I guess, because they wanted me to.

Q. Did you get in touch with any of the people in the community, citizens associations, or executive committee of owners?

A. I did earlier and later, too.

Q. Did they cooperate with the people on your block?

A. They certainly did.

Q. Are the plaintiffs, knowing the cost, and others in the block, helping to take care of expenses of this suit?

A. Certainly.

At the time of the trial the neighbors had contributed $85, which had been turned over to the Executive Committee of Owners of the North Capitol Citizens Association to pay the retaining fee. Three families not in the case had contributed. However, the main burden of the case was on the shoulders of Mrs. Hodge and the other plaintiffs. The others had moved to Bryant Street more recently than the Hodges. Constantino and Mary Marchegiani had purchased their house in 1930 and were now renting it, having moved to Maryland themselves. Balduino and Margaret Giancola obtained their house in 1936, and Pasquale and Victoria DeRita acquired theirs in 1940. All had been emigrants from Italy, and the DeRitas were not yet citizens. None had seen Negroes before leaving Italy and claimed no difficulty in their limited relations with colored people since coming to the United States. But all of them supported the covenant and could agree with Mrs. Giancola, their most articulate representative, when she told Urciolo that "we feel bitter towards you for coming in and breaking up our block. We were very peaceful and harmonious there and we feel that you bought the property just to transact it over to colored people and we don't like it."

The plaintiffs' deep antipathy against Negroes was expressed by Mrs. Hodge. It was not a person's skin color but his race which she found intolerable. The defense attorney, Charles Houston[,] brought out the feelings of Mrs. Hodge in cross examination.

Q. … Now, suppose, Mrs. Hodge, it was a very, very, light negro, say 99 percent so-called white blood …

A. It would still be a negro, I think.

Q. And it would not make any difference?

A. No.

Q. If you got a person in the block who was supposed to be white and that person was undesirable, in the sense of untidy or something like that, you couldn't do anything about it?

A. No, certainly we couldn't.

Q. And you would prefer that untidy white person to a negro, no matter how educated or cultured?

A. As long as they are white, I would prefer them.

Q. No negro, no matter how, or whether he might be Senator or Congressman, it would not make any difference to you?

A. It wouldn't make any difference.

Q. Even if the white man just came from jail, you would prefer him?

A. Because he is white and I am white.

Her husband, Frederic Hodge, agreed with this expression of affinity for Caucasians. He said that the reason the movement of Negroes into sections near the Bryant Street neighborhood had not affected "the sociability of the neighborhood" was that the Negroes "stay by theirselves and white folks stay by theirselves."

These were the people to be protected by the enforcement of the restrictive covenants, and the following is the official complaint made by them to the United States District Court for the District of Columbia in the case of *Hodge v. Hurd*. The occupancy of houses on Bryant Street by Negroes, they said,

> ... will be injurious, depreciative and absolutely ruinous of the real estate owned by the plaintiffs, and will be harmful, detrimental and subversive of the peace of mind, comfort and property rights and interests of plaintiffs and of other property owners, and said neighborhood will become depreciative in value, and undesirable as a neighborhood wherein white people may live; that the continued occupancy and/or ownership by the defendants, Hurd, or any person or persons of the Negro race or blood, will constitute a continuing wrong and injury that is irreparable, and is incapable of ascertainment and compensation in damages, and the only adequate remedy is by way of injunction.

The Negroes' Defense

Charles Houston for the defense planned to dispute every possible assumption entertained by the white property owners. This strategy was dictated by Houston's conviction that the courtroom was an educational forum. Because he was smarting under the loss of *Mays v. Burgess* in the same court, Houston was determined to take every opportunity to raise doubts about the soundness of court enforcement of restrictive covenants. The plaintiffs drew the issues narrowly and assumed the outcome: The covenants existed, they were valid; Negroes had violated them; the court should enjoin the Negroes from ownership and occupancy. Houston broadened these issues and added new ones. As the trial opened he boldly denied that the plaintiffs were white, that it was a white neighborhood, and questioned whether the covenant was a valid instrument.

> We deny that all the defendants are colored. We say there has been a change of neighborhood. We say that the covenant is unenforceable, that an injunction

should not issue because the object of the injunction could not be obtained, and that the purposes of the covenant can no longer be achieved.

In a separate tactic, Houston charged that the assigned judge, F. Dickinson Letts, had a personal prejudice and bias against the defendants and should be disqualified. The claim was based on the fact that Judge Letts lived in premises in northwest Washington covered by a racial restrictive covenant. Judge Letts declined to excuse himself, explaining that he was merely a "tenant by the month" of the house in question and did not know of the existence of the covenant. The Court of Appeals for the District of Columbia Circuit in a *per curiam*, or unsigned opinion, ruled that the refusal of Judge Letts to disqualify himself "was entirely proper." The question to be determined, the court explained, was whether the defense had asserted facts "from which a sane and reasonable mind might fairly infer personal bias or prejudice on the part of a judge." It was held to be a "far-fetched conclusion" that the existence of a restrictive covenant "for which he is neither responsible or accountable" would "under any circumstances" create in Judge Letts' mind a personal prejudice against the defendants in this trial.

One of the basic defenses employed by Houston was that James Hurd was an American Indian. It seemed a dubious contention from the start, and Hurd's own testimony that he was a Mohawk Indian from the Smokey [sic] Mountains of North Carolina added little credence to it. But he explained away the implied admission of being a Negro made in his letter to Gilligan in which he had agreed to move. Hurd stated that Ryan, the person from whom he had purchased the house, had drafted the letter and that he signed it at work, when he was too busy to read it. The question of his automobile driver's license came up, for his own license showed that he had marked an "x" in the square for colored. But Hurd could point out that there was no space for Indian, so he had no recourse but to mark white or colored, neither of which were [sic] really applicable. Mrs. Hodge testified that Hurd had personally told her that he and his wife were Negroes. He had agreed to move originally, he said, because he was very nervous and high strung, and had always run away from trouble, but that the difficulty of finding another place militated against actually moving, in this instance. He had been constantly buffeted by questions about race. By now, his resentment had become acute. As Hurd put it, "Everytime you turn around, someone is asking your color.... You get tired of those things."

Frederic Hodge testified that Hurd "looked to me like a Negro, therefore I presumed he was a Negro." When called upon to define what was Negro about Hurd's features, he replied, "I would say the nose for one thing." The nostrils were the distinguishing features, he said. Hodge admitted that Hurd had rather straight hair, which was not a Negroid characteristic. The other plaintiffs did not discuss Hurd's racial features, but did venture to define the meaning of race. Mrs. Hodge asserted that Negroes could be distinguished from whites. "There is always a look with regard to their eyes and nose that would give them away, as a rule." She had no specific test for telling colored people; "simply, you see they are colored, as a rule, you know." Mrs. Giancola never confused Assyrians, Turks, or Arabs with Negroes, because even though these people may be dark, "there is something about them that brings out the fact that they are of white blood." The plaintiffs agreed that they could be wrong, but all of them with Mrs. Hodge made clear that they had never been wrong yet.

The testimony on defining race by the experts called by the defense contrast with that of the plaintiffs. The views of Monseigneur John M. Cooper, head of the Department of Anthropology at Catholic University, were those of a scholar dealing with a highly complex and difficult problem about which most knowledge was tentative. Dr. Cooper was asked this question:

Q. Could one make sure by any simply visible physical traits, such as fingernails, eyes, lips, nose, that a given light skinned individual thought to be partly negroid, is actually so?

A. None of these ordinary criteria are reliable. A highly frizzly hair is a very important criterion, but you get that occasionally even in causcasoids. One recent case has been reported in Norway of a family, typically blonde Nordics in which, however, there is a distinct kinky, grizzly hair. We do not know the cause of that. In most cases, highly kinky hair would be a very strong indication, but not absolutely infallible. These other criteria, such as the stripe in the fingernail, or coloring of the fingernail are not reliable.

He agreed that there were no reliable tests for making a distinction between the races, and that social concepts enter very largely into the problem.

A professor of bacteriology at the medical school of George Washington University, Dr. Leland W. Paar, was asked if there was any test by blood specimens by which could be ascertained the race to which a group of heterogeneous people belonged. He answered that he did not know of any blood test or any other test that fell within the field of medicine. Thus the experts stressed the difficulty of telling the difference between members of various races. It was a personal or social matter which could not be corroborated by scientific means.

Another theme in the defense strategy was to probe into the feelings aroused in the plaintiff by the presence of Negroes in their neighborhood. Houston kept asking them what it was about the Negro that made him undesirable. Mrs. Hodge, for example, admitted the fact that it was no special action on the part of a colored person that alarmed her. Thus if she were ignorant of one's race, there would be no objection. Houston then posed this query:

Q. … although she had not changed a bit in her conduct or anything, if later you heard she was a negro, you would object?

A. I certainly would.

Q. Although she would be the same one and you would object, and on appearance you can't tell whether she is white or colored?

A. I would object until I found out.

Q. It is the label of "negro"?

A. Not entirely, it is the color — yes, the label.

Q. It can't be the color, because you can't tell whether that lady is white or colored.

A. Yes.

Q. So it is the label?

A. Yes.

At this point Urciolo entered the colloquy.

Q. Mrs. Hodge, in other words, if I am labeled negro and I want to move into one of those houses you would ask that I be put out?

A. I would.

Pinpointing the actual objection to the proximity of Negroes proved difficult for the plaintiffs, who at times seemed almost to have turned into witnesses for the defense. Thus, Mr. Hodge testified that he had no trouble with the Negroes in the area, and that the occupancy of nearby covenanted houses by the Hurds, Savages, Rowes, and Stewarts, had not disturbed his peace of mind a bit. Since, in addition to being emotionally content over the new state of affairs, he had not moved out of his house, he was asked what disturbed him so far as the Hurd occupancy was concerned.

A. Well, Mr. Houston, I feel this way—as far as the colored coming in, I have nothing against them having their home, but it does, in a way take away from the—well you might say the sociability of the white people in the neighborhood, that is, in our block. That is the only reason that I can give.

Even though it was shown that neighborhood peace had always been maintained, that the few children there of whatever race played together, and that on the whole all including the plaintiffs had customarily stayed to themselves, Hodge insisted that sociability within in the block would be affected by the Negroes' presence. If a person was not known to be Negro, it would make no difference, Houston discovered through cross-examination. What then would be the result if this person was found to be a Negro, even though he stayed by himself? Hodge repeated that this would affect the sociability. How? He couldn't say, but it would "in a general way."

In addition to attacking the foundations of the plaintiffs' racial and social ideas, the defense attorneys also disputed the claim that the occupancy of the covenanted property by Negroes would be "injurious, depreciative, and absolutely ruinous of the real estate" in the neighborhood. Some of the plaintiffs did not understand the meaning of the clause. Mr. Marchegiani could only answer, when asked to explain how property would depreciate because of Negroes' presence, that it would depreciate "in every way." Mrs. DeRita came though cross-examination even more poorly.

As might be expected, Mrs. Hodge did the best job of explaining the reasons for the decline in property values. Although her statements were not based on evidence but on personal observation, it was her considered belief that if colored people entered an area, the value of all house nearby would be depreciated. She thought that in most cases the homes of Negroes "are not kept up as well; the majority understand, I am saying,—as possibly my house is, and naturally if houses are not kept up, I would say the market value would go down, and of course, if that went down, mine naturally would have to go down, I would think." However, she agreed that some Negroes kept up their homes well. Even the Hurd house at 116 Bryant Street she agreed was "being kept up very nicely." Mrs. Hodge was then asked by Houston whether depreciation would follow when neat Negroes moved into a neighborhood:

A. Well, if property was sold to Negroes, as I think the property would depreciate in value, as far as having them further occupied by white persons is concerned.

Hodge said that she did not believe that a white person would buy it after other property in the area had been sold to Negroes. "I wouldn't be able to dispose of my property to advantage unless I sold to a negro." She would not say, however, that the property could be sold to a Negro for what it was worth.

The defense presented the testimonies of Urciolo, a rent-control official, and a Negro real-estate dealer to support the claim that the value of real estate was higher as Negroes moved into an area. Urciolo's statement that Negroes pay from 30 to 40 percent more both for rents and sales of property in the Washington area than do whites for comparable dwellings was corroborated by these disinterested authorities. This fact was closely related to the limited availability of housing for Negroes. Because of restrictions, both legal and tacit, the supply of housing for Negroes was small; but the continually increasing population of Negroes made the demand great. It was a simple case of supply and demand. The defense therefore appeared to have scored in its effort to show that property appreciated as the real estate changed from a white to a Negro market.

The scarcity of housing for Negroes had another result besides increasing the prices they were forced to pay; it was no easy task for Negroes to find a place to live at all, whether or not they had the money. All Negro defendants, it was shown, had moved to Bryant Street only after they had been forced to move out of their last abode. They claimed to have looked far and wide for housing and taken the Bryant Street places only after the most exhaustive search. Although one witness, a social welfare board consultant, said that the housing shortage prevailed among whites as well, most testimony supported the claim that it was more serious for Negroes. Upon this basis the defense attorneys argued that the difficulty for Negroes in the circumstances was so serious that under the doctrine of balancing equities the covenants should not be enforced.

One more defense was made for the Negroes who had purchased homes on Bryant Street. Houston said that conditions had changed considerably since the restrictive covenants had been placed in the deeds about 1906, and the entry of Negroes was but the final chapter in the progression of a neighborhood. Thus he tried to establish that Negroes were now closer to the Hodges than the Hurd house. When he sought Mrs. Hodge's answer to the question of whether the injunction would be of any use unless the Negroes in the surrounding area were diminished, the opposing attorney Gilligan objected, and the court sustained the objection. Houston then stated his design:

> I want to put my objection in the record on the ground that a court of equity or a court exercising an equity jurisdiction will not do a vain thing and if the defense can establish, out of the plaintiff's own mouth, on cross-examination that it would be futile to issue the injunction, I say the question is a proper question and should be allowed, sir.

Lorraine Hansberry, To Be Young, Gifted, and Black
(Vintage 1969), pp. 20–21

April 23, 1964

To the Editor,
The New York Times:

… My father was typical of a generation of Negroes who believed that the "American way" could successfully be made to work to democratize the United States. Thus, twenty-five years ago, he spent a small personal fortune, his considerable talents, and many years of his life fighting, in association with NAACP attorneys, Chicago's "restrictive covenants" in one of this nation's ugliest ghettoes.

That fight also required that our family occupy the disputed property in a hellishly hostile "white neighborhood" in which, literally, howling mobs surrounded our house. One of their missiles almost took the life of the then eight-year-old signer of this letter. My memories of this "correct" way of fighting white supremacy in America include being spat at, cursed and pummeled in the daily trek to and from school. And I also remember my desperate and courageous mother, patrolling our house all night with a loaded German luger, doggedly guarding her four children, while my father fought the respectable part of the battle in the Washington court.

The fact that my father and the NAACP "won" a Supreme Court decision, in a now famous case which bears his name in the lawbooks, is—ironically—the sort of "progress" our satisfied friends allude to when they presume to deride the more radical means of struggle. The cost, in emotional turmoil, time and money, which led to my father's early death as a permanently embittered exile in a foreign country when he saw that after such sacrificial efforts the Negroes of Chicago were as ghetto-locked as ever, does not seem to figure in their calculations.

That is the reality that I am faced with when I now read that some Negroes my own age and younger say that we must now lie down in the streets, tie up traffic, do whatever we can—take to the hills with guns if necessary—and fight back. Fatuous people remark these days on our "bitterness." Why, of course we are bitter. The entire situation suggests that the nation be reminded of the too little noted final lines of Langston Hughes' mighty poem:

> What happens to a dream deferred?
> Does it dry up
> Like a raisin in the sun?
> Or fester like a sore—
> And then run?
> Does it stink like rotten meat?
> Or crust and sugar over—
> Like a syrupy sweet?
>
> Maybe it just sags
> Like a heavy load.
>
> *Or does it explode?*

Sincerely,
Lorraine Hansberry

Lorraine Hansberry, *A Raisin in the Sun*, in A Raisin in the Sun and the Sign in Sidney Brustein's Window
(Vintage 1958, 1959, 1966, 1984, 1987), pp. 113–119

(BENEATHA *goes to the door and opens it as* WALTER *and* RUTH *go on with the clowning.* BENEATHA *is somewhat surprised to see a quiet-looking middle-aged white man in a business suit holding his hat and a briefcase in his hand and consulting a small piece of paper*)

MAN Uh—how do you do, miss. I am looking for a Mrs.—(*He looks at the slip of paper*) Mrs. Lena Younger? (*He stops short, struck dumb at the sight of the oblivious* WALTER *and* RUTH)

BENEATHA (*Smoothing her hair with slight embarrassment*) Oh—yes, that's my mother. Excuse me (*She closes the door and turns to quiet the other two*) Ruth! Brother! (*Enunciating precisely but soundlessly: "There's a white man at the door!" They stop dancing,* RUTH *cuts off the phonograph,* BENEATHA *opens the door. The man casts a curious quick glance at all of them*) Uh—come in please.

MAN (*Coming in*) Thank you.

BENEATHA My mother isn't here just now. Is it business?

MAN Yes ... well, of a sort.

WALTER (*Freely, the Man of the House*) Have a seat. I'm Mrs. Younger's son. I look after most of her business matters.

(RUTH *and* BENEATHA *exchange amused glances*)

MAN (*Regarding* WALTER, *and sitting*) Well—my name is Karl Lindner ...

WALTER (*Stretching out his hand*) Walter Younger. This is my wife—(RUTH *nods politely*)—and my sister.

LINDNER How do you do.

WALTER (*Amiably, as he sits himself easily on a chair, leaning forward on his knees with interest and looking expectantly into the newcomer's face*) What can we do for you, Mr. Lindner!

LINDNER (*Some minor shuffling of the hat and briefcase on his knees*) Well—I am a representative of the Clybourne Park Improvement Association—

WALTER (*Pointing*) Why don't you sit your things on the floor?

LINDNER Oh—yes. Thank you. (*He slides the briefcase and hat under the chair*) And as I was saying—I am from the Clybourne Park Improvement Association and we have had it brought to our attention at the last meeting that you people—or at least your mother—has bought a piece of residential property at—(*He digs for the slip of paper again*)—four o six Clybourne Street ...

WALTER That's right. Care for something to drink? Ruth, get Mr. Lindner a beer.

LINDNER (*Upset for some reason*) Oh—no, really. I mean thank you very much, but no thank you.

RUTH (*Innocently*) Some coffee?

LINDNER Thank you, noting at all.

(BENEATHA *is watching the man carefully*)

LINDNER Well, I don't know how much you folks know about our organization (*He is a gentle man; thoughtful and somewhat labored in his manner*) It is one of these community organizations set up to look after—oh, you know, things like block upkeep and special projects and we also have what we call our New Neighbors Orientation Committee ...

BENEATHA (*Drily*) Yes—and what do they do?

LINDNER (*Turning a little to her and then returning the main force to* WALTER) Well—it's what you might call a sort of welcoming committee, I guess. I mean they, we—I'm the chairman of the committee—go around and see the new people who move into the neighborhood and sort of give them the lowdown on the way we do things out in Clybourne Park.

BENEATHA (*With appreciation of the two meanings, which escape* RUTH *and* WALTER) Uh-huh.

LINDNER And we also have the category of what the association calls—(*He looks elsewhere*)—uh—special community problem ...

BENEATHA Yes—and what are some of those?

WALTER Girl, let the man talk.

LINDNER (*With understated relief*) Thank you. I would sort of like to explain this thing in my own way. I mean I want to explain to you in a certain way.

WALTER Go ahead.

LINDNER Yes. Well. I'm going to try to get this right to the point. I'm sure we'll all appreciate that in the long run.

BENEATHA Yes.

RUTH (*Still innocently*) Would you like another chair—you don't look comfortable.

LINDNER (*More frustrated than annoyed*) No, thank you very much. Please. Well—to get right to the point I—(*A great breath and he is off at last*) I am sure you people must be aware of some of the incidents which have happened in various parts of the city when colored people have moved into certain areas—(BENEATHA *exhales heavily and starts tossing a piece of fruit up and down in the air*) Well—because we have what I think is going to be a unique type of organization in American community life—not only do we deplore that kind of thing—but we are trying to do something about it. (BE-NEATHA *stops tossing and turns with a new and quizzical interest to the man*) We feel—(*gaining confidence in his mission because of the interest in the faces of the people he is talking to*)—We feel that most of the trouble in this world, when you come right down to it—(*He hits his knee for emphasis*)—most of the trouble exists because people just don't sit down and talk to each other.

RUTH (*Nodding as she might in church, pleased with the remark*) You can say that again, mister.

LINDNER (*More encouraged by such affirmation*) That we don't try hard enough in this world to understand the other fellow's problem. The other guy's point of view.

RUTH Now that's right.

(BENEATHA *and* WALTER *merely watch and listen with genuine interest*)

LINDNER Yes—that's the way we feel out in Clybourne Park. And that's why I was elected to come here this afternoon and talk to you people. Friendly like, you know, the way people should talk to each other and see if we couldn't find some way to work this thing out. As I say, the whole business is a matter of *caring* about the other fellow. Anybody can see that you are a nice family of folks, hard working and honest I'm sure. (BENEATHA *frowns slightly, quizzically, her head tilted regarding him*) Today everybody knows what it means to be on the outside of *something*. And of course, there is always somebody who is out to take advantage of people who don't always understand.

WALTER What do you mean?

LINDNER Well—you see our community is made of people who've worked hard as the dickens for years to build up that little community. They're not rich and fancy people; just hard-working, honest people who don't really have much but those little homes and a dream of the kind of community they want to raise their children in. Now, I don't say we are perfect and there is a lot wrong in some of the things they want. But you've got to admit that a man, right or wrong, has the right to want to have the neighborhood he lives in a certain kind of way. And at the moment the overwhelming majority of our people out there feel that people get along better, take more of a common interest in the life of the community, when they share a common background. I want you to believe me when I tell you that race prejudice simply doesn't enter into it. It is a matter of the people of Clybourne Park believing, rightly or wrongly, as I say, that for the happiness of all concerned that our Negro families are happier when they live in their *own* communities.

BENEATHA (*With a grand and bitter gesture*) This, friends, is the Welcoming Committee!

WALTER (*Dumfounded, looking at LINDNER*) Is this what you came marching all the way over here to tell us?

LINDNER Well, now we've been having a fine conversation. I hope you'll hear me all the way through.

WALTER (*Tightly*) Go ahead, man.

LINDNER You see—in the face of all the things I have said, we are prepared to make your family a very generous offer …

BENEATHA Thirty pieces and not a coin less!

WALTER Yeah?

LINDNER (*Putting on his glasses and drawing a form out of the briefcase*) Our association is prepared through the collective effort of our people, to buy the house from you at a financial gain to your family.

RUTH Lord have mercy, ain't this the living gall!

WALTER All right, you through?

LINDNER Well, I want to give you the exact terms of the financial arrangement—

WALTER We don't want to hear no exact terms of no arrangements. I want to know if you got any more to tell us 'bout getting together?

LINDNER (*Taking off his glasses*) Well—I don't suppose that you feel …

WALTER Never mind how I feel—you got any more to say 'bout how people ought to sit down and talk to each other? … Get out of my house, man.

(*He turns his back and walks to the door*)

LINDNER (*Looking around at the hostile faces and reaching and assembling his hat and briefcase*) Well—I don't understand why you people are reacting this way. What do you think you are going to gain by moving into a neighborhood where you just aren't wanted and where some elements—well—people can get awful worked up when they feel that their whole way of life and everything they've worked for is threatened.

WALTER Get out.

LINDNER (*At the door, holding a small card*) Well—I'm sorry it went like this.

WALTER Get out.

LINDNER (*Almost sadly regarding* WALTER) You just can't force people to change their hearts, son.

(*He turns and put his card on a table and exits.* WALTER *pushes the door to with stinging hatred, and stands looking at it.* RUTH *just sits and* BENEATHA *just stands. They say nothing.* MAMA *and* TRAVIS *enter*)

Brief for United States as amicus curiae supporting petitioners in Shelley v. Kraemer, 334 U.S. 1 (1948)

* * *

International Agreements

The Charter of the United Nations, approved as a treaty by the Senate on July 28, 1945, provides in its preamble, among other things, that:

> We the people of the United Nations, determined … to reaffirm faith in fundamental human rights, in the dignity and worth of the human person, in the equal rights of men and women … and to promote social progress and better

standards of life in larger freedom, and for these ends to practice tolerance ... have resolved to combine our efforts to accomplish these aims.

In Article 55 of the Charter, the United Nations agree to promote "universal respect for, and observance of, human rights and fundamental freedoms for all without distinction as to race, sex, language, or religion."

By Article 56, "All Members pledge themselves to take joint and separate action in co-operation with the Organization for the achievement of the purposes set forth in Article 55."

The United Nations General Assembly, on November 19, 1946, adopted the following resolution:

> The General Assembly declares that it is in the higher interests of Humanity to put an immediate end to religious and so-called racial persecutions and discrimination, and calls on the Governments and responsible authorities to conform both to the letter and to the spirit of the Charter of the United Nations, and to take the most prompt and energetic steps to that end.

At the Inter-American Conference on Problems of War and Peace held at Mexico City in 1945, at which the Act of Chapultepec of March, 1945 was agreed upon, the United States Delegation submitted a draft resolution, which was later adopted by the Conference, entitled "Economic Charter of the Americas." The following statement appears in this resolution:

> "The fundamental economic aspiration of the peoples of the Americas, in common with peoples everywhere, is to be able to exercise effectively their natural right to live decently...."

Another resolution adopted by the Conference provides:

> Whereas: World peace cannot be consolidated until men are able to exercise their basic rights without distinction as to race or religion, The Inter-American Conference on Problems of War and Peace resolves:
>
> 1.   To reaffirm the principle, recognized by all the American States, of equality of rights and opportunities for all men, regardless of race or religion.
>
> 2.   To recommend that the Governments of the American Republics, without jeopardizing freedom of expression, either oral or written, make every effort to prevent in their respective countries all acts which may provoke discrimination among individuals because of race or religion.

At the conclusion of this Conference, the Secretary of State issued a statement in which he said:

> ... in the Declaration of Mexico and in other resolutions, we have rededicated ourselves at this Conference to American principles of humanity and to raising the standards of living of our peoples, so that all men and women in these republics may live decently in peace, in liberty, and in security. That is the ultimate objective of the program for social and economic co-operation which has been agreed upon at Mexico City.

A particularly pertinent statement, also in the form of a Resolution, was made at and adopted by The English International Conference of American States at Lima, Peru, in 1938. This Resolution, approved by the Conference on December 23, 1938, reads:

The Republics represented at the Eighth International Conference of American States declare:

1. That, in accordance with the fundamental principle of equality before the Law, any persecution on account of racial or religious motives which makes it impossible for a group of human beings to live decently, is contrary to the political and juridical systems of America.

2. That the democratic conception of the State guarantees to all individuals the conditions essential for carrying on their legitimate activities with self respect.

3. That they will always apply these principles of human solidarity.

Mr. J.D. Shelley, *I Ain't Moving Nowhere!*, in Peter Irons, The Courage of Their Convictions
(Free Press 1988), pp. 73–79

I was born in Starkville, Mississippi, on Christmas Day in 1907. My folks worked on farms around there; they worked for white people. They named me J.D., but the initials don't stand for nothing. People call me J.D. or some people call me Shelley. Me and my wife, Ethel, got married on December 14, 1923. I wasn't quite sixteen and she was younger than me.

I been working all my life. When I was down South, I did sawmill work, railroad, construction, all like that. In Mississippi I did mostly construction work; just before I left they was building a highway in Starkville and I worked on that. After they completed that then I started doing construction work at the A & M college; they was building houses out there. That's where I was working when I left and came here to St. Louis.

There is a lot of reasons I left Mississippi and come up here. One of them is what happened to a colored girl that got in trouble with white people and the police. We was living in a place right out from the city that was owned by a white preacher who built some houses and rented to colored. My wife was working for these white people and she was going to quit and they asked her did she know anybody she could get to work there. She said, yes, she knowed a girl name of Sister Hon; she going to see her. So she sent this kid up there and before long this white lady claimed that she taken some jewelry from her.

So this particular Sunday my wife had went to church with the kids, but they come home after Sunday school. And the police come to the house that Sister Hon live in and we was all looking in it. The police they take Sister Hon away, and I told her father, who didn't say nothing, I say, Man, you let them take your kid, whyn't you go with your kid? And he say no. So they take Sister Hon up there to the lady's house and they beat her, they beat that child with a hose and then they brought her over to the colored quarter and throwed her in a ditch. And my kids come from church and they saw her, and they come running to the house and say, Dad, they done beat Sister Hon and she cain't walk.

I jumped up and got Hannah, another colored lady, and we tried to get the men and they wouldn't go. So Hannah said, Me and you get her, J.D. And we went up and got that child, she beat so bad she couldn't sit. And I said, It's time for me to leave here now. 'Cause, if they beat my kids like that, these white folks have to *lynch* me down here, so I'm going to leave. And I left, and come to St. Louis. That was in the fall of '39.

When I first come to St. Louis, my wife and kids they stayed in Mississippi and I stayed here for a year. When I first came here I was only making $17 a week. I was working at a medical place where they made pills, and I was paying $12 a month rent at that time. It was cheap; I didn't have to pay much for nothing. White people here was prejudiced against colored at that time. When I came to St. Louis, they had places like the Fox Theater, no colored could go there; and the baseball diamond up on Sportsman's Park, they don't allow no colored in there at one time. When they did open up Sportsman's Park for colored, onliest place they could sit was in the bleachers. That changed after the war. Down in South St. Louis, there's places now you can't go if you're colored.

After I was here for a year, I went back down to Mississippi and came back with my wife and kids. The first place I rented was on Francis Avenue and I moved from there to North 9th St. My wife was working at a baby-care company and during the war I was working out at the small-arms bullet plant, out on Goodfellow. They had women operating the machines that make bullets. The mechanics, they were all men, and they had to fix the machines when they broke down. The colored men, they had to fix the colored girls' machines; the white men, they fixed the white.

Some of the colored mechanics, they complained about this, they figure they should fix whatever machine is broke. So they had a meeting at the Kiel Auditorium downtown, which was called by the union. A union man come from up north somewhere, and the man say we got a war and colored is over there fighting for this country. And he say, There's got to be a change made; we going to fix it where the colored man going to be the mechanic on the machine for the white girl and the white men for the colored. And one white man get up and says he would rather work with a dog than work with a nigger. And they told him, You just have to work with a dog; if you want to stay out there you going to be a mechanic on the colored girls' machine. So they changed that.

With me having so many kids, they put me in 4F during the war. I had six kids, and it was hard fitting us all in the places we was living during the war. At that time it was hard for you to find a place when you had children, so every place we'd go they didn't want us. We had been wanting to buy us a house, but we thought we better save up some money while we was both working. I told my wife, I tell you what we'll do. My check is more than yours, and we'll just save my check and we'll use your check to take care of the family and the household.

So we had some money saved up, and I wanted to buy a new car. My wife says, J.D., no! We got these kids and it's hard for us to find a place. What we'll do, we'll take what money we got and buy us a home. And when we get it straight and I'm still working, then we'll buy us a car. I told her we couldn't pay for no home and she said we pay rent, so we can make the payments on a house.

I talked to my supervisor the next day when I got to work and he say, Shelley, you know what? Your wife is right. So I came home and told her, Well, we'll just go ahead and find a place. This was just about when the war was over in Japan. Ethel went to the Church of God in Christ and her pastor, Elder Robert Bishop, he was also in real estate. So we went and talked to him and he said, Yeah, I know a place on Labadie that's for sale. It's got two apartments, so you can rent one out. So we went and looked at it and decided we would buy it. The price of the house was five thousand, seven hundred.

The day we supposed to move, I got a fellow with a truck to move me. That evening when I got off work, I was riding the bus, and I got off at Cora. That's about two blocks from where my house was on Labadie. At that time, the police were walking the beat. This one police, he come up and he ask me what was my name and I told him,

J.D. Shelley. He ask me what was I doing out here, and I told him I'm going home. He say, Home? Where you live? I say, 4600 Labadie. He say, Labadie? I say, I just moved; my family just moved today. I had a fellow to move me. I didn't take off from work, I just hired this fellow to move me. So the police, he followed me all the way to the house. He stopped on the sidewalk, and I went on up the steps and got my key out of my pocket and went on in the house. So he left. Later on, it was just a few days later, I come home one evening and my wife, she says, J.D., we got to go to court. I said, Court for what? She say, This supposed to be a restricted area, no colored on this side of Taylor Avenue. We're not supposed to be living out here. A man just came here and gave me a summons when I got back from work. He'll be back to give you one. He got one for you too.

Around about seven o'clock the doorbell rang and I went to the door, and this man say, Are you Shelley? I say, yes. He say, I got some papers here for you. I say, Papers? For what? He say, It's just some papers. You going to take them? I say, I ain't going to take no papers unless you tell me what it's for. And he say, Mr. Shelley, I'm trying to help you. I say, I still ain't going to take no papers unless you tell me what's the papers for. Just like that. So he threw the papers down on the floor and walked on out.

So I didn't have to go to court, because if you don't receive a summons in your hand, you don't got to go to court. But my wife had to go to court. Elder Bishop, he got lawyer Vaughn. George Vaughn was his name; he was a colored lawyer. I didn't know him, but I guess he was Elder Bishop's lawyer. A couple of weeks after this man come around with the papers, Ethel went to court. When we bought the house, there was a family living downstairs; he was a street-car motorman. When he saw the sign says the property was sold, he moved. So that's why I got to move in downstairs. The family that was living upstairs, they was renting from the real-estate agent and they stayed for a while. This man and his wife upstairs, they had to go to court too, and the judge wanted to know, how did we treat them. This white lady that lived upstairs, she say, They seem just like when the white were living downstairs. When I go down to the basement to wash, Miz Shelley, she come down and we laugh and talk. And she say, They treat us nice. We don't have no trouble.

What they say in court was that this was supposed to be a restricted area, no colored live on this side of Taylor Avenue. That's one or two blocks from where my house was on Labadie. This Jack Kraemer that sued us, he didn't even *own* no property on this block. I never even seen him around here. Nobody who lived on this block never say they want us to move. They say in court that they had restrictions on all the property on Labadie since 1911. I guess Elder Bishop knowed it, but I didn't know that when we bought the house. It was hard for me to hear a lot of what the judge and the lawyers say in court. You know how they do, they talk but you couldn't hear what they be saying.

I liked that house on Labadie. There was white on this side of me, and white on that side, and all the way down. I knowed all of them, and they treated us nice. None of the white never did say nothing about us living here. My supervisor say, Shelley, you might have to move, man. I says, Man, I ain't moving nowhere. Long as they don't mess with my kids. I ain't worried about them messing with me, but they better not mess with my kids. My kids was teenagers then.

There was some white boys that messed with my little daughter. She went to the store down on the corner and they messed with my daughter and throwed something at her, and my boy went out there and beat them. After that, the kids was all right. The white kids played with my kids, and their parents would have to come to the house sometimes to get them to come home.

After I moved out here, other colored started to buy and they started throwing stink bombs in their house. Every time they'd buy a house, they'd have trouble. They throw bricks in their window. But they never did bother me. My wife, she was going to church and praying. I'd go, but I wasn't like she was.

After the first time we went to court, the lawyers took the case up to the Supreme Court. They was having meetings at the churches about the case; the lawyers and all would be there. Lawyer Vaughn would talk, and this other lawyer, Mr. Willer, he would talk too. That was the Supreme lawyer. They'd be white there, and colored, and they'd be talking about this, and what it meant to colored to be able to buy a house where you wanted, long as you could afford it. They'd ask me questions, what did I think about it and I'd just tell them my opinion about it.

Lawyer Vaughn, he come to the house one night, he always come by and talk, and one night he say, Mr. Shelley, you know, I ain't never had a case this hard. This case getting on my nerves. This white lawyer, Mr. Willer, he was real nice, he come to the house a couple of times. But we still hadn't won the case. I didn't know whether we were going to win the case or not.

When they took it to the Supreme Court they passed a decision, they say it don't make no difference, white or colored, long as they was able to buy property, anywhere in the United States. When I got home that evening, my wife was sitting on the front porch reading the paper that says we won the case. That night, the photographer come, and we was sitting on the couch, with the kids sitting betwixt us, and some on the floor, and they had it in the newspaper.

When we won the case, we didn't sleep that night. People was calling me from overseas, congratulating me. Say they heard it on the news, they saw it in the paper. People called from everywhere. Every time we'd hang up, the phone rings.

We lived in that house on Labadie for maybe ten years. Then we moved over here to St. Louis Avenue, about two blocks, so we could have more room in the house. I sold that house on Labadie two years after I bought this house. People left owing two months rent, wouldn't pay, so I just got mad and sold it. I got nine-five when I sold it. I kept on working in construction long as I could, and my kids and their kids were all working too. Right now, I got five great-great-grandchildren. Ethel passed on September 15, 1984. We was married sixty years, and when we had our anniversary they had a big ceremony over to the church.

This neighborhood is almost all colored now. There was this one time, this was quite a few years after we won this case, I was down there at the tavern on the corner. And this boy says, J.D. Shelley, you the one that caused us to be out here. A friend of mine was sitting there and he say, What you say? What you talking about? And this boy say, J.D., he's the first colored that bought out here. He made it possible for us. I ain't kidding you, Johnny. And Johnny say, I'll bet you five dollars. I say, Johnny, don't bet him no five dollars, because you going to *lose!* They had me holding the money. So this boy went up to his house and got this book and brought it back and he says, Now you read for yourself. And that book told about our case and it say that J.D. Shelley, he was the first one.

The way I see it, it was a good thing that we done this case. When all this happened, when I bought the property, I didn't think there was going to be anything about it. But I knowed it was important. We was the first ones to live where they said colored can't live.

C. Federal Housing Programs

Kenneth T. Jackson, Crabgrass Frontier:
The Suburbanization of the United States
(Oxford U. Press 1985), pp. 190–91, 209, 213–14, 215–16, 217

[T]here are many ways in which government largesse can affect where people live. For example, the federal tax code encourages businesses to abandon old structures before their useful life is at an end by permitting greater tax benefits for new construction than for the improvement of existing buildings. Thus, the government subsidizes an acceleration in the rate at which economic activity is dispersed to new locations. Similarly, Roger Lotchin has recently begun important research on the significance of defense spending to the growth of Sunbelt cities since 1920. Military expenditures have meanwhile worked to the detriment of other areas. Estimates were common in the late 1970s that Washington was annually collecting between $6 billion and $11 billion more in the New York area than it was returning in expenditures, and the gap widened during the Reagan years as even large proportions of the national budget was devoted to defense.

On the urban-suburban level, the potential for federal influence is also enormous. For example, the Federal Highway Act of 1916 and the Interstate Highway Act of 1956 moved the government toward a transportation policy emphasizing and benefiting the road, the truck, and the private motorcar. In conjunction with cheap fuel and mass-produced automobiles, the urban expressways led to lower marginal transport costs and greatly stimulated deconcentration. Equally important to most families is the incentive to detached-home living provided by the deduction of mortgage interest and real-estate taxes from their gross income. Even the reimbursement formulas for water-line and sewer construction have had an impact on the spatial patterns of metropolitan areas.

The purpose of this chapter is to look at the impact of federal housing policies on how and where Americans live. More specifically, I seek to determine whether the results of such policies were foreseen by a government anxious to use its power and resources for the social control of ethnic and racial minorities. Has the American government been as benevolent—or at least as neutral—as its defenders have claimed?[8] * * *

The Federal Housing Administration

As late as November 19, 1948, Assistant FHA Commissioner W. J. Lockwood could write that FHA "has never insured a housing project of mixed occupancy" because of the expectation that "such projects would probably in a short period of time become all-Negro or all-white."

Occasionally, FHA decisions were particularly bizarre and capricious. In the late 1930s, for example, as Detroit grew outward, white families began to settle near a black enclave adjacent to Eight Mile Road. By 1940 the blacks were surrounded, but neither

---

8. For a conspiratorial view of the state, see Peter Marcuse, "The Myth of the Benevolent State: Notes Toward a Theory of Housing Conflict" (Discussion paper, Division of Urban Planning, Columbia University, 1978). [Editor's Note: See Peter Marcuse, *Housing Policy and the Myth of the Benevolent State*, in Critical Perspectives on Housing 148 (Rachel Bratt, Chester Hartman, & Ann Meyerson, eds., Temple U. Press 1986).]

they nor the whites could get FHA insurance because of the proximity of an "inharmonious" racial group. So in 1941 an enterprising white developer built a concrete wall between the white and black areas. The FHA appraisers then took another look and approved mortgages on the white properties. . . .

But FHA also helped to turn the building industry against the minority and inner-city housing market, and its policies supported the income and racial segregation of suburbia. For perhaps the first time, the federal government embraced the discriminatory attitudes of the marketplace. Previously, prejudices were personalized and individualized; FHA exhorted segregation and enshrined it as public policy. Whole areas of cities were declared ineligible for loan guarantees; as late as 1966, for example, FHA did not have a mortgage on a single home in Camden or Paterson, New Jersey, both declining industrial cities. This withdrawal of financing often resulted in an inability to sell houses in a neighborhood, so that vacant units often stood empty for months, producing a steep decline in value.

Despite the fact that the government's leading housing agency openly exhorted segregation throughout the first thirty years of its operation, very few voices were raised against FHA red-lining practices. Between 1943 and 1945, Harland Bartholomew and Associates, the nation's leading urban planning firm, prepared a master plan for Dallas. Criticizing FHA for building "nearly all housing" in the suburbs, the company argued that "this policy has hastened the process of urban decentralization immeasurably." In 1955 Columbia Professor Charles Abrams pointed a much stronger accusatory finger at FHA for discriminatory practices. Writing in 1955, the famed urban planner said:

> A government offering such bounty to builders and lenders could have required compliance with a nondiscrimination policy. Or the agency could at least have pursued a course of evasion, or hidden behind the screen of local autonomy. Instead, FHA adopted a racial policy that could well have been culled from the Nuremberg laws. From its inception FHA set itself up as the protector of the all white neighborhood. It sent its agents into the field to keep Negroes and other minorities from buying houses in white neighborhoods.[68] * * *

From the perspective of the suburbs, but not most cities, the system worked remarkably well from 1933 until the late 1960s. As returning World War II veterans sought homes to raise their families, the government financed large tracts of houses on the periphery. Thus, the main beneficiary of the $119 billion in FHA mortgage insurance issued in the first four decades of FHA operation was suburbia, where almost half of all housing could claim FHA or VA financing in the 1950s and 1960s. And as the percentage of families who were homeowners increased from 44 percent in 1934 to 63 percent in 1972, the American suburb was transformed from an affluent preserve into the normal expectation of the middle class. . . .

Federal housing policies were also not the *sine qua non* in the mushrooming of the suburbs. Mortgage insurance obviously made it easier for families to secure their dream houses, but the dominant residential drift in American cities had been toward the periphery for at least a century before the New Deal, and there is no reason to as-

---

68. Mel Scott, American City Planning Since 1890 (Berkeley, 1968), 401; and Charles Abrams, Forbidden Neighbors: A Study of Prejudice in Housing (New York, 1955), 229–35.

sume that the suburban trend would not have continued in the absence of direct federal assistance.

The lasting damage done by the national government was that it put its seal of approval on ethnic and racial discrimination and developed policies which had the result of the practical abandonment of large sections of older, industrial cities.

Levitt and Sons v. Division Against Discrimination in State Department of Education
31 N.J. 514, 158 A.2d 177 (Supreme Court of New Jersey 1960), app. dis., 363 U.S. 418 (1960)

Mr. Harold E. Kohn, of the Philadelphia Bar, argued the cause for the plaintiffs-appellants (Messrs. Pitney, Hardin & Ward, attorneys for plaintiff-appellant Levitt and Sons, Incorporated; Mr. Sidney S. Jaffe, attorney for plaintiff-appellant Green Fields Farm, Inc.; Messrs. William P. Reiss and Clyde A. Szuch, on the brief).

Mr. David D. Furman, Attorney General of New Jersey, argued the cause for the defendant-respondent Division Against Discrimination in the State Department of Education (Mr. Lee A. Holley, Deputy Attorney General, of counsel).

Mr. Julius Wildstein argued the cause for all individual defendants-respondents (Messrs. Kapelsohn, Lerner, Leuchter & Reitman, and Emerson L. Darnell, attorneys for defendant-respondent Willie R. James; Messrs. Herbert H. Tate and Jerome C. Eisenberg, attorneys for defendant-respondent Franklin D. Todd; Mr. Julius Wildstein, attorney for defendant-respondent Yuther Gardner, and of counsel for all other individual defendants-respondents; Messrs. Julius Wildstein and Joseph B. Robison, of the New York Bar, and Mrs. Ruth Blumrosen of the Michigan Bar, on the brief).

For affirmance — Justices Burling, Jacobs, Francis, Proctor, Hall and Schettino. For reversal — None. The opinion of the court was delivered by Burling, J.

Burling, J.

The plaintiff Levitt and Sons, Incorporated ... is the developer of a single home housing project called Levittown, located in Levittown Township, Burlington County, New Jersey. The plaintiff Green Fields, Inc.... is the developer of a similar project called Green Fields Village located in West Deptford Township, Gloucester County, New Jersey. Defendants Todd and James allegedly were rejected by Levitt as purchasers of houses in Levittown because of their color; both are Negroes. Defendant Gardner, also a Negro, allegedly was rejected by Green Fields as a purchaser of a house in Green Field Village because of his color. All three, Todd, James and Gardner, filed individual complaints with the New Jersey Division Against Discrimination [(DAD)] charging the plaintiffs with refusals to sell to the individual defendants in violation of the New Jersey Law Against Discrimination.... Findings of probable cause for the complaints were made by the DAD and attempts at conciliation were unsuccessful....

... Levitt and Green Fields instituted independent suits challenging the jurisdiction of the DAD to hear the discrimination complaints and attacking the constitutionality of the New Jersey Law Against Discrimination....

Levitt's single home housing project, Levittown, in which approximately 2,000 houses have been built to the present time, will contain 16,000 houses when completed, according to original plans. Green Fields' project, Green Fields Village, comprises approximately 550 houses.... Both projects have been planned and constructed in order that they might qualify for purchase money loans insured by the Federal Housing Administration (FHA), a process which requires attention to the desired end from the very earliest beginnings of the development.

Before construction has begun, a housing project developer who seeks to have FHA insured loans available to purchasers of his houses must contact an FHA office in the region in which the project will be located to obtain FHA approval of the site selected for the project. Once a site approval is given, the developer will submit detailed subdivision information to the FHA office, on a form prepared by the FHA, together with certain exhibits, such as a topographic map, photographs, detailed development plan and like items; frequently these are amended or completely revised to accord with suggestions made by the FHA. When the subdivision information and exhibits are satisfactory to the FHA, that agency issues a subdivision report, giving FHA requirements concerning street layouts, curb and sidewalk specifications, utilities, drainage, open spaces, lot improvements and similar matters. House plans are submitted to determine if they meet FHA requirements; the FHA architectural section will often recommend changes in these plans. Upon receiving the subdivision report, the developer arranges with an FHA-approved lending institution to submit individual applications for commitments for FHA insurance on any loan which [will] be made by the institutions. These individual applications are reviewed by the architectural, valuation and mortgage credit sections in addition to the Chief Underwriter's office, after which commitments are issued to the approved lending institution covering the individual properties contemplated in the application. These commitments take various forms. One is a conditional commitment, an agreement between the FHA and the approved lending institution that, subject to the conditions stated in the commitment and subject to the approved lending institution's submitting a proposed purchaser whose qualifications are satisfactory to the FHA, a loan made to finance the purchase of the property in question will be insured. Another form of commitment is an "Operative-Builder Firm Commitment," which differs from a conditional commitment primarily in that the former also contemplates loans being made directly to the developer, prior to sale, if requested.

Once the commitment is issued, the developer may commence construction. As construction progresses, the developer or the approved lending institution through which the FHA commitment was made arranges for an FHA inspection. Normally three such inspections are made during the course of construction. In some larger developments, such as Levittown, an FHA inspector is stationed at the project. Often the inspector or other FHA personnel will meet with the developer to discuss problems that have arisen during construction affecting compliance with FHA requirements. As the houses are sold by the developer to purchasers interested in obtaining an FHA insured mortgage loan, an application for approval of the purchaser is submitted to the FHA by the approved lending institution to whom the conditional commitment was made. If the qualifications of the purchaser are satisfactory to the FHA, an individual firm commitment is issued to the approved lending institution in the name of the purchaser. After title is closed, the approved lending institution submits the mortgage bond to the FHA along with copies of the bond, the mortgage and the original commitment. When these are approved, the FHA endorses the bond for insurance, which comprises the contract between the FHA and the lender.

Having received conditional commitments, the developer advertises the availability of FHA financing to purchasers. By using FHA insured loans, a purchaser needs only a 3% downpayment on a principal sum of up to $13,500, 15% on the difference between $13,500 and $16,000, and 30% on the difference between $16,000 and $20,000. The term of the loan may be as long as 30 years. Conventional financing often involves downpayments of 20% to 25% and frequently will be limited to terms of 20 to 25 years. Thus it is apparent that FHA financing is a large factor in stimulating home buying, since the low down payment opens the home market to persons who have accumulated only small savings and the extended term of the loan allows home ownership to be achieved by payments from income by a much larger proportion than would ordinarily be the case. Concerning the importance of FHA approval to the large housing project developer, Robert A. Budd, president of Green Fields, stated on his deposition that such approval "is the basics (sic) on which to go on." William Levitt, president of Levitt, stated before the House Subcommittee on Housing of the Committee on Banking and Currency of the Eighty-Fifth Congress that "We are 100 percent dependent on Government. Whether this is right or wrong it is a fact." Only a very small percentage of the buyers of homes in Levittown and Green Fields Village financed their purchase other than with federally insured loans.

II.

First to be determined is whether the DAD has jurisdiction under the Law Against Discrimination, N.J.S.A. 18:25-1 et seq., to entertain the complaints brought by the individual defendants against the plaintiffs. There are two questions here. The first is whether the plaintiffs' developments are "publicly assisted housing accommodation" as that phrase is used in section 4 of the Law Against Discrimination and amplified by section 5(k) of that statute. The second is, if plaintiffs' developments are within the classification, whether the statute gives the DAD jurisdiction to hear or act on complaints claiming discrimination with respect thereto.

A.

The statute plainly includes, as publicly assisted housing, housing projects such as those here involved as to which, at the time of the discrimination, an FHA insured loan is committed. And the public assistance demonstrated by the federal insurance of such loans is much the same, under the circumstances of this case, as that demonstrated by an FHA commitment to insure housing loans. Just as ownership of housing and its concomitant benefits attributable to an FHA insured loan is said by the statute to be publicly assisted, by the same reasoning the advantages which accrue to the developers in question from the FHA commitments are plainly the result of public assistance. The very existence of the development can be attributed to the FHA commitment. The mass market opened by FHA and other government insured purchase money housing loans accounts for the prospect of sufficient buyers to purchase the housing in question. Without such a mass market, it is inconceivable that the developments would have been built; the number of prospective purchasers with adequate savings accumulated to make the downpayment required by conventional financing and with sufficient income to meet from their income the payments on a conventionally financed debt would not warrant the mass housing construction in evidence today. Thus the very fact that there are houses with which to discriminate in the development in question is primarily attributable to public assistance. We need not here decide what are the outer limits of the term "publicly assisted housing accommodation." Suffice it to say that the public assistance rendered the housing here in question places it within the definition of that term as used in N.J.S.A. 18:25-4....

B.

[The court upheld the jurisdiction of DAD and rejected plaintiffs' five other arguments.]

Gautreaux v. Chicago Housing Authority

503 F.2d 930 (7th Cir. 1974),
aff'd *sub nom*. Hills v. Gautreaux, 425 U.S. 284 (1976)

Alexander Polikoff and Milton I. Shadur, Chicago, IL, for Dorothy Gautreaux, et al.

Patrick W. O'Brien and Watson B. Tucker, Chicago, Ill., for Chicago Housing Authority.*

Carla A. Hills, Asst. Atty. Gen., Anthony J. Steinmeyer, Atty. Dept. of Justice, Washington D.C., James R. Thompson, U.S. Atty., Gary L. Starkman, Asst. U.S. Atty., Chicago, Ill. for Department of Housing and Urban Development.

Before Clark, Associate Justice,** Cummings and Tone, Circuit Judges. Tone, Circuit Judge, dissenting.

Mr. Justice Clark.

Appellants, black tenants in and applicants for public housing, brought these consolidated cases separately in 1966 against the Chicago Housing Authority (CHA) and the Secretary of Housing and Urban Development (HUD) respectively, charging that CHA had intentionally violated 42 U.S.C.A. §1981 and §1982 in maintaining existing patterns of residential separation of races by its tenant assignment and site selection procedures, contrary to the Equal Protection Clause of the Fourteenth Amendment; and that HUD had "assisted in the carrying on ... of racially discriminatory public housing system within the City of Chicago" in violation of the Fifth Amendment. Appellants sought an injunction against CHA restraining such practices and requiring CHA to remedy past effects of its unconstitutional site-selection and tenant-assignment procedures by building any future public housing units in predominantly white areas. This appeal grows out of the decision of the district court on remand for a determination of appropriate relief pursuant to separate findings that both CHA and HUD were responsible for de jure segregation in the public housing program in Chicago. In 1969 the District Court found with the appellants on the merits and since that time has devoted its efforts to effectuating this ruling. After some four years of hearings, several judgment orders and four appeals, the District Court on the last remand called on the parties to propose a "comprehensive plan" to remedy past effects of the public housing segregation indulged in by CHA and HUD, including "alternatives which are not confined in their scope to the geographic boundary of the City of Chicago." HUD proposed, and the District Court, after an evidentiary hearing, ordered a plan under which HUD would "cooperate" with CHA in the latter's efforts to increase the supply of public housing units but eliminated any relief not confined to the geographic boundary of the City of Chicago and refused to impose any specific affirmative obligations upon HUD beyond its "best efforts." 363 F. Supp. 690 (1973). The appellants contend that a metropolitan area remedial plan including housing in suburban areas, as well as those within the limits of Chicago, is necessary to remedy the past effects of said unconstitutional public housing segregation policy and attain that racial balance required by the Fourteenth Amendment. Given the eight years tortuous course of these cases, together with the

---

* Editor's Note: The Federal Reporter incorrectly lists Messrs. Polikoft and Shadur as counsel for the Chicago Housing Authority. In fact, they represented the plaintiff class. Their co-counsel were Chuck Markels, Bernard Weisberg, and Merrill Freed. See Alexander Polikoff, Waiting for Gautreaux: A Story of Segregation, Housing, and The Black Ghetto 5, 25–26 (Northwestern U. Press 2006).

** Associate Justice Tom C. Clark of the Supreme Court of the United States (Ret.) is sitting by designation.

findings and judgment orders of the District Court and the opinions of this Court (now numbering five) we believe the relief granted is not only much too little but also much too late in the proceedings. In effect, appellants, having won the battle back in 1969, have now lost the war. We are fully aware of the many difficult and sensitive problems that the cases have presented to the able District Judge and we applaud the care, meticulous attention and the judicious manner in which he has approached them. With his orders being ignored and frustrated as they were, he kept his cool and courageously called the hand of the recalcitrant. Perhaps in the opinion on remand on the third appeal, 457 F.2d 124 (7th Cir. 1972), the repetition of a statement … in the second appeal, 448 F.2d 731 that: "It may well be that the District Judge, in his wise discretion, will conclude that little equitable relief above the entry of a declaratory judgement and a simple 'best efforts' clause, will be necessary …" led the beleaguered District Judge to limit any plan to the boundaries of the City of Chicago and the "best efforts" of CHA and HUD. This is to be regretted and we trust that upon remand the matter will be expedited to the end that the segregated public housing system which has resulted from the action of CHA and HUD will be disestablished, and the deficiency in the supply of dwelling units will be corrected as rapidly as possible and in the manner indicated in this opinion.

We shall not burden this opinion with the details of the eight-year delay that has thus far deprived the appellants of the fruits of the District Court's judgment entered on July 1, 1969. In addition the unconstitutional action of CHA had stripped thousands of residents of the City of Chicago of their Fifth and Fourteenth Amendment rights for a score of years. Indeed, anyone reading the various opinions of the District Court and of this Court quickly discovers a callousness on the part of the appellees towards the rights of the black, underprivileged citizens of Chicago that is beyond comprehension. As far back as 1954, the District Court found that CHA had continuously refused to permit black families to reside in four public housing projects built before 1944; and that as far back as 1954 CHA had imposed a black quota on the four projects to the end that at the beginning of 1968 black tenants only occupied between 1 percent to 7 percent of the 1,654 units in the projects. The non-white population of Chicago at that time was 34.4 percent. In 64 public housing sites, having 30,848 units (other than the four above mentioned), the tenants were 99 percent black. All during this period Illinois law required that CHA secure prior approval of new sites for public housing from the City Council of the City of Chicago, but the District Court found that CHA set up a preclearance arrangement under which the alderman in whose ward a site was proposed would receive an informal request from CHA for clearance. The alderman, the Court found, to whom sites in the white neighborhoods were submitted, vetoed the sites and the City Council rejected 99½ percent of the units proposed for white sites while only 10 percent were refused in black areas. Moreover, the Court found that during this period about 90 percent of the waiting list of some 13,000 applicants to CHA for occupancy in its projects were black. These findings were neither challenged nor appealed. Furthermore, as early as July 1, 1969, a judgment order was entered herein, requiring CHA to build 700 new housing units in predominantly white areas and requiring 75 percent of all future units built by CHA to be constructed in such areas. This judgment also ran against the City Council of the City of Chicago (not then a party) on the basis of notice. Finally, CHA was directed by the District Court to "affirmatively administer its public housing system … to the end of disestablishing the segregated public housing system which has resulted from CHA's unconstitutional site selection and tenant assignment procedures … [and] use its best efforts to increase the supply of Dwelling Units as rapidly as possible …". 304 F.Supp. 736 (1969). No appeal was taken from this judgment.

Appellants and the District Court waited patiently for a year and a half but CHA submitted no sites for family dwellings to the City Council. The appellants contacted CHA and were advised that CHA had no intention to submit sites prior to the Chicago mayoralty election of April, 1971. The parties then asked for and were given informal hearings, so as to prevent publicity, and finally the District Court modified its "best efforts" provision in the July 1, 1969 judgment order so as to affirmatively require CHA to submit sites for no fewer than 1500 units to the City Council for approval on or before September 20, 1970. This order was appealed by CHA and affirmed.

Meanwhile, in the separate suit against HUD filed simultaneously with the one against CHA (and now consolidated), the District Court had dismissed all four counts. On appeal this Court held that HUD had violated the due process clause of the Fifth Amendment and reversed with directions to enter a summary judgment for the appellants. This Court found that HUD had approved and funded family housing sites chosen by CHA in black areas of Chicago. HUD's explanation was "it was better to fund a segregated housing system" than deny housing altogether. This Court found that in the sixteen years (1950–1966) HUD spent nearly $350 million on such projects "in a manner which perpetuated a racially discriminatory housing system in Chicago"; that its excuse of community and local government resistance has not been accepted as viable and that this Court was "unable to avoid the conclusion that the Secretary's past actions constituted racial discriminatory conduct in their own right." Gautreaux v. Romney, 448 F.2d 731 (7th Cir. 1971).

During the progress of this litigation, HUD was conferring with the City of Chicago concerning grants under the Model Cities Program (established by the Demonstration Cities and Metropolitan Development Act of 1966, 42 U.S.C. § 3301 et seq.). A $38 million grant was made for the calendar year 1970. However, for the 1971 calendar year HUD required a "letter of intention" signed by the Mayor of Chicago, the Chairman of CHA and the Regional Administrator of HUD, indicating how Chicago's large housing deficiency would be met. Under this letter CHA was to acquire sites for 1700 units within a specified timetable. HUD approved $26 million and had released $12 million when the opinion in Romney came down. Appellants then sought an injunction from the District Court restraining further payments by HUD under the Model Cities Program unless and until sites in predominantly white areas for 700 dwelling units had been certified to the City Council for approval (at the time only 288 had been approved). The District Court granted this relief but on appeal the order was reversed. 457 F.2d 124 (7th Cir. 1972). On remand the District Court entered a summary judgment against HUD, consolidated the cases and entered an order calling for each of the parties to file suggestions for a "comprehensive plan" to remedy the past effects of the public housing segregation, including "alternatives which are not confined in their scope to the geographic boundary of the City of Chicago.

HUD proposed a "best efforts" judgment order under which it would "cooperate" with CHA in the latter's efforts to increase the supply of housing units in accordance with the earlier judgment order against CHA and reported in 304 F. Supp. 736. Its proposed relief was confined to the geographic boundaries of the City of Chicago. Its "best thinking" was that the letter of intention previously mentioned and signed by the Mayor, the Regional Administrator of HUD and CHA should be carried out. This letter only covered the matter of the relocation housing deficiency of 4300 units and did not spell out any "comprehensive plan to remedy the past effects". Appellants' proposed plan provided a mechanism by which CHA could supply remedial housing in suburban areas as well as within Chicago and required HUD to administer its programs affirmatively to ensure that the order was carried out. At the hearing the appellants introduced evidence of the need for a metropolitan plan and the unreliability of HUD's "best efforts". HUD offered evidence of the lack of funds then available and CHA offered no evidence. On December 8, 1972, Bradley v. Milliken, 484 F.2d 215 (6th Cir. 197[3]) came down, holding that a remedial plan involving suburban school districts in the metropolitan area of Detroit was necessary to disestablish existing segregation. Appellants then requested a "Bradley plan" order. [T]he District Court sustained the HUD proposal and this appeal resulted.*

2. A Metropolitan Plan is Necessary and Equitable

After careful consideration and reflection we are obliged to conclude that on the record here it is necessary and equitable that any remedial plan to be effective must be on a suburban or metropolitan area basis. This could entail additional time but not under proper management since the intra-city portion of the plan may proceed without any further delay. In the meanwhile the suburban or metropolitan phases of the plan can be perfected (new parties, if necessary, etc.) and effectuated without delaying or interfering with the intracity phase of the comprehensive plan. There are only five housing authorities (in addition to CHA) involved, and while voluntary cooperation is not indicated, a Court order directing that those not volunteering were to be made parties might help. On the record here we are not able to discuss—much less pass upon—the validity of any specific metropolitan plan. We leave that for the district court on remand.

Our decision in regard to the necessity and equity of suburban or metropolitan area action is predicated on the following:

The equitable factors which prevented metropolitan relief in Milliken v. Bradley are simply not present here. There is no deeply rooted tradition of local control of public housing; rather, public housing is a federally supervised program with early roots in federal statutes. See 42 U.S.C. §1401 et seq.; Gautreaux v. Romney, 448 F.2d 731, 737–740 (7th Cir. 1971). There has been a federal statutory commitment to non-discrimination in housing for more than a century, 42 U.S.C. §1982, and the Secretary of HUD is directed to administer housing programs "in a manner affirmatively to further the policies" of non-discrimination, 42 U.S.C. §3608(d)(5). In short, federal involvement is pervasive.

Similarly, the administrative problems of building public housing outside Chicago are not remotely comparable to the problems of daily bussing thousands of children to schools in other districts run by other local governments. CHA and HUD can build housing much like any other landowner, and whatever problems arise would be insignificant compared to restructuring school systems as proposed in Milliken v. Bradley.

In Milliken v. Bradley, the Chief Justice emphasized that there was no evidence of discrimination by the suburban school districts affected. Here, although the record was not made with the Supreme Court's Milliken opinions in mind, there is evidence of suburban discrimination. Plaintiff's Exhibit 11 indicates that of twelve suburban public housing projects, ten were located in or adjacent to overwhelmingly black census tracts. And although the case was not limited to public housing, it is not irrelevant that we recently took judicial notice of widespread residential segregation "in Chicago and its en-

---

* Editor's Note: Before this case reached the Seventh Circuit, the U.S. Supreme Court reversed the Sixth Circuit's decision. The Supreme Court rejected an interdistrict remedy in Milliken v. Bradley, 418 U.S. 717 (1974).

virons." Clark v. Universal Builders, Inc., 501 F.2d 324[, 335] (7th. Cir. 1974). We went on to hold that a prima facie showing had been made that this segregation had discriminatory effects throughout the metropolitan area.

Finally, the possibility of metropolitan relief has been under consideration for a long time in this case. While they disagree as to what relief the District Court should order, the parties are in agreement that the metropolitan area is a single relevant locality for low rent housing purposes and that a city-only remedy will not work. * * *

In addition to CHA's and HUD's strong, positive statements as to the necessity for a metropolitan plan here, the appellants also offered the testimony of a recognized demographer who estimated that a continuance of present trends in black and white census tracts would lead to at least a 30 percent black occupancy in every census tract in Chicago by the year 2000. The District Judge himself added support to this thesis; however his prediction was 1984:

> Existing patterns of racial separation must be reversed if there is to be a chance of averting the desperately intensifying division of Whites and Negroes in Chicago. On the basis of present trends of Negro residential concentration and of Negro migration into and White migration out of the central city, the President's Commission on Civil Disorders estimates that Chicago will be 50% Negro by 1984. By 1984 it may be too late to heal racial divisions. (296 F. Supp. 907, 915).

If this prediction comes true it will mean that there will be no "general Public Housing Area" left in Chicago on which CHA could build desegregated public housing. In the ten-year period 1960–1970 the population of the City of Chicago declined by 183,000 people, a decrease of 505,000 whites and an increase of 322,000 blacks. The expert demographer further testified that by providing desegregated housing opportunities in the suburban areas, the rate of white exodus from the city would diminish. There was no testimony to the contrary. In fact "White flight" has brought on the same condition in most of our metropolitan cities, such as Indianapolis, Indiana. See United States v. Board of School Commissioners, 332 F. Supp. 655, 676 ([S.D.Ind.] 1971); also as to Atlanta, Georgia, Calhoun v. Cook, 332 F. Supp. 804, 805 ([N.D.Ga.] 1971). Like conditions—but aggravated—exist in Washington, D.C. and Cleveland, Ohio.

The realities of "White flight" to the suburbs and the inevitability of "resegregation" by rebuilding the ghettos as CHA and HUD were doing in Chicago must therefore be considered in drawing a comprehensive plan. The trial judge back in 1969 ordered scattered-site, low-rise housing—despite much criticism—but the experts now agree that such requirements are mandatory. His warning that "By 1984 it may be too late to heal racial divisions[,]" rather than a cliché, is a solemn warning as to the interaction of "White flight" and "black concentration". It is the most serious domestic problem facing America today. As Assistant Secretary Simmons further advises:

> As Whites have left the cities, jobs have left with them. After 1960, three-fifths of all new industrial plants constructed in this country were outside of central cities. In some cases as much as 85% of all new industrial plants located outside central cities were inaccessible to Blacks and other minorities who swelled ghetto populations.

These words also convey a solemn warning, i.e., we must not sentence our poor, our underprivileged, our minorities to the jobless slums of the ghettos and thereby forever trap them in the vicious cycle of poverty which can only lead them to lives of crime and violence.

By way of concluding, we have carefully read the records in these cases and find no evidence that the suburban or metropolitan area should not be included in a comprehensive plan. All of the parties, the Government officials, the documentary evidence, the sole expert and the decided cases agree that a suburban or metropolitan area plan is the *sine qua non* of an effective remedy. In fact the Judge himself recognized its importance in his original judgment order by authorizing housing units to be provided in suburban Cook County on a voluntary basis. See 304 F. Supp. at 739. Furthermore, in his order of December 23, 1971, calling for the preparation by the parties of a "comprehensive plan", he wisely included the following paragraph:

> 3.   In the preparation of such plan or plans, the parties are requested to provide the Court with as broad a range of alternatives as seem to the parties feasible as a partial or complete remedy for such past effects, including, if the parties deem it necessary or appropriate to provide full relief, alternatives which are not confined in their scope to the geographic boundary of the City of Chicago.

In light of all these considerations we can but conclude that the District Court's finding as to not including in a comprehensive plan of relief areas outside the City of Chicago, i.e., the suburban or metropolitan area, was clearly erroneous.

3. Action on Remand

The judgment order of September 11, 1973, is reversed and the causes are remanded for further consideration in the light of this opinion, to wit: the adoption of a comprehensive metropolitan area plan that will not only disestablish the segregated public housing system in the City of Chicago which has resulted from CHA's and HUD's unconstitutional site selection and tenant assignment procedures but will increase the supply of dwelling units as rapidly as possible.

[The dissenting opinion of Judge Tone is omitted.]

On Rehearing

Mr. Justice Clark.

On rehearing, we reaffirm our view that the trial judge should not have refused to "consider the propriety of metropolitan area relief." His conclusion that the only factual basis for plaintiffs' request was the opinion of an urbanologist ignores much of the record and, in particular, the statements of the parties themselves to the effect that "only metropolitan-wide solutions will do."

The requested relief does not go "far beyond the issues of this case," as the trial judge suggests. Rather, it is reasonable to conclude from the record that defendants' discriminatory site selection within the City of Chicago may well have fostered racial paranoia and encouraged the "white flight" phenomenon which has exacerbated the problems of achieving integration to such an extent that intra-city relief alone will not suffice to remedy the constitutional injuries. The extra-city impact of defendants' intra-city discrimination appears to be profound and far-reaching and has affected the housing patterns of hundreds of thousands of people throughout the Chicago metropolitan region.

It is in this sense, we believe, that the Supreme Court requires a showing that "there has been a constitutional violation within one district that produces a significant segregative effect in another district." Milliken v. Bradley, 418 U.S. at 745. We therefore reaffirm our remanding of this case for additional evidence and for further consideration of the issue of metropolitan area relief in light of this opinion and that of the Supreme Court in Milliken v. Bradley. In the meantime, intra-city relief should proceed apace without further delay.

A majority of the judges in regular active service not having requested that a vote be taken on the suggestion for an en banc rehearing, and a majority of the panel having voted to deny a rehearing,

It is ordered that the petition of the appellees for a rehearing in the above-entitled appeal be, and the same is hereby denied.

Tone, Circuit Judge, adheres to his prior dissent.

D. The Civil Rights Act of 1964

Heart of Atlanta Motel, Inc. v. United States
379 U.S. 241 (1964)

Moreton Rolleston, Jr., argued the cause and filed a brief for appellant.*

Solicitor General Cox argued the cause for the United States. With him on the brief were Assistant Attorney General [Burke] Marshall, Philip B. Heymann, and Harold H. Greene.**

Before Chief Justice Warren and Justices Black, Douglas, Clark, Harlan, Brennan, Stewart, White, and Goldberg.

Mr. Justice Clark delivered the opinion of the Court.

This is a declaratory judgment action, attacking the constitutionality of Title II of the Civil Rights Act of 1964.

1. The Factual Background and Contentions of the Parties.

Appellant owns and operates the Heart of Atlanta Motel which has 216 rooms available to transient guests. The motel is located on Courtland Street, two blocks from downtown Peachtree Street. It is readily accessible to interstate highways 75 and 85 and state highways 23 and 41. Appellant solicits patronage from outside the State of Georgia through various national advertising media, including magazines of national circulation; it maintains over 50 billboards and highway signs within the State, soliciting patronage for the motel; it accepts convention trade from outside Georgia and approximately 75% of its registered guests are from out of State. Prior to passage of the Act the

---

* Briefs of amici curiae, urging reversal, were filed by James W. Kynes, Attorney General of Florida, and Fred M. Burns and Joseph C. Jacobs, Assistant Attorneys General, for the State of Florida; and Robert Y. Button, Attorney General of Virginia, and Frederick T. Gray, Special Assistant Attorney General, for the Commonwealth of Virginia.

** Briefs of amici curiae, urging affirmance, were filed by Thomas C. Lynch, Attorney General of California, Charles E. Corker and Dan Kaufmann, Assistant Attorneys General, and Charles B. McKesson and Jerold L. Perry, Deputy Attorneys General, for the State of California; Edward W. Brooke, Attorney General of Massachusetts, for the Commonwealth of Massachusetts; and Louis J. Lefkowitz, Attorney General of New York, Samuel A. Hirshowitz, First Assistant Attorney General, and Shirley Adelson Siegel, Assistant Attorney General, for the State of New York.

motel had followed a practice of refusing to rent rooms to Negroes, and it alleged that it intended to continue to do so. In an effort to perpetuate that policy this suit was filed.

The appellant contends that Congress in passing this Act exceeded its power to regulate commerce under Art. I, §8, cl. 3, of the Constitution of the United States; that the Act violates the Fifth Amendment because appellant is deprived of the right to choose its customers and operate its business as it wishes, resulting in a taking of its liberty and property without due process of law and a taking of its property without just compensation; and, finally, that by requiring appellant to rent available rooms to Negroes against its will, Congress is subjecting it to involuntary servitude in contravention of the Thirteenth Amendment. * * *

2. The History of the Act.

Congress first evidenced its interest in civil rights legislation in the Civil Rights or Enforcement Act of April 9, 1866. There followed four Acts, with a fifth, the Civil Rights Act of March 1, 1875, culminating the series. In 1883 this Court struck down the public accommodations sections of the 1875 Act in the Civil Rights Cases, 109 U.S. 3. No major legislation in this field had been enacted by Congress for 82 years when the Civil Rights Act of 1957 became law. It was followed by the Civil Rights Act of 1960. Three years later, on June 19, 1963, the late President Kennedy called for civil rights legislation in a message to Congress to which he attached a proposed bill. Its stated purpose was

> to promote the general welfare by eliminating discrimination based on race, color, religion, or national origin in … public accommodations through the exercise by Congress of the powers conferred upon it … to enforce the provisions of the fourteenth and fifteenth amendments, to regulate commerce among the several States, and to make laws necessary and proper to execute the powers conferred upon it by the Constitution.

Bills were introduced in each House of the Congress, embodying the President's suggestion. However, it was not until July 2, 1964, upon the recommendation of President Johnson, that the Civil Rights Act of 1964, here under attack, was finally passed.

After extended hearings each of these bills was favorably reported to its respective house.… Although each bill originally incorporated extensive findings of fact these were eliminated from the bills as they were reported. The House passed its bill in January 1964 and sent it to the Senate. Through a bipartisan coalition of Senators Humphrey and Dirksen, together with other Senators, a substitute was worked out in informal conferences. This substitute was adopted by the Senate and sent to the House where it was adopted without change. This expedited procedure prevented the usual report on the substitute bill in the Senate as well as a Conference Committee report ordinarily filed in such matters. Our only frame of reference as to the legislative history of the Act is, therefore, the hearings, reports and debates on the respective bills in each house.

The Act as finally adopted was most comprehensive, undertaking to prevent through peaceful and voluntary settlement discrimination in voting, as well as in places of accommodation and public facilities, federally secured programs and in employment. Since Title II is the only portion under attack here, we confine our consideration to those public accommodation provisions.

3. Title II of the Act.

This Title is divided into seven sections beginning with §201(a) which provides that:

All persons shall be entitled to the full and equal enjoyment of the goods, services, facilities, privileges, advantages, and accommodations of any place of public accommodation, as defined in this section, without discrimination or segregation on the ground of race, color, religion, or national origin.

There are listed in § 201(b) four classes of business establishments, each of which "serves the public" and "is a place of public accommodation" within the meaning of § 201(a) "if its operations affect commerce, or if discrimination or segregation by it is supported by State action." The covered establishments are:

(1) any inn, hotel, motel, or other establishment which provides lodging to transient guests, other than an establishment located within a building which contains not more than five rooms for rent or hire and which is actually occupied by the proprietor of such establishment as his residence;

(2) any restaurant, cafeteria ... [not here involved];

(3) any motion picture house ... [not here involved];

(4) any establishment ... which is physically located within the premises of any establishment otherwise covered by this subsection, or ... within the premises of which is physically located any such covered establishment ... [not here involved].

Section 201(c) defines the phrase "affect commerce" as applied to the above establishments. It first declares that "any inn, hotel, motel, or other establishment which provides lodging to transient guests" affects commerce per se. Restaurants, cafeterias, etc., in class two affect commerce only if they serve or offer to serve interstate travelers or if a substantial portion of the food which they serve or products which they sell have "moved in commerce." Motion picture houses and other places listed in class three affect commerce if they customarily present films, performances, etc., "which move in commerce." And the establishments listed in class four affect commerce if they are within, or include within their own premises, an establishment "the operations of which affect commerce." Private clubs are excepted under certain conditions.

Section 201(d) declares that "discrimination or segregation" is supported by state action when carried on under color of any law, statute, ordinance, regulation or any custom or usage required or enforced by officials of the State or any of its subdivisions.

In addition, § 202 affirmatively declares that all persons "shall be entitled to be free, at any establishment or place, from discrimination or segregation of any kind on the ground of race, color, religion, or national origin, if such discrimination or segregation is or purports to be required by any law, statute, ordinance, regulation, rule, or order of a State or any agency or political subdivision thereof."

Finally, § 203 prohibits the withholding or denial, etc., of any right or privilege secured by § 201 and 202 or the intimidation, threatening or coercion of any person with the purpose of interfering with any such right or the punishing, etc., of any person for exercising or attempting to exercise any such right.

The remaining sections of the Title are remedial ones for violations of any of the previous sections. Remedies are limited to civil actions for preventive relief. The Attorney General may bring suit where he has "reasonable cause to believe that any person or group of persons is engaged in a pattern or practice of resistance to the full enjoyment of any of the rights secured by this title, and that the pattern or practice is of such a nature and is intended to deny the full exercise of the rights herein described...." § 206(a).

A person aggrieved may bring suit, in which the Attorney General may be permitted to intervene.

4. Application of Title II to Heart of Atlanta Motel.

It is admitted that the operation of the motel brings it within the provisions of §201(a) of the Act and that appellant refused to provide lodging for transient Negroes because of their race or color and that it intends to continue that policy unless restrained.

The sole question posed is, therefore, the constitutionality of the Civil Rights Act of 1964 as applied to these facts. The legislative history of the Act indicates that Congress based the Act on §5 and the Equal Protection Clause of the Fourteenth Amendment as well as its power to regulate interstate commerce under Art. I, §8, cl. 3, of the Constitution.

The Senate Commerce Committee made it quite clear that the fundamental object of Title II was to vindicate "the deprivation of personal dignity that surely accompanies denials of equal access to public establishments." At the same time, however, it noted that such an objective has been and could be readily achieved "by congressional action based on the commerce power of the Constitution." Our study of the legislative record, made in the light of prior cases, has brought us to the conclusion that Congress possessed ample power in this regard, and we have therefore not considered the other grounds relied upon. This is not to say that the remaining authority upon which it acted was not adequate, a question upon which we do not pass, but merely that since the commerce power is sufficient for our decision here we have considered it alone. Nor is §§201(d) or 202, having to do with state action, involved here and we do not pass upon either of those sections.

5. The Civil Rights Cases, 109 U.S. 3 (1883), and their Application.

In light of our ground for decision, it might be well at the outset to discuss the Civil Rights Cases, which declared provisions of the Civil Rights Act of 1875 unconstitutional. We think that decision inapposite, and without precedential value in determining the constitutionality of the present Act. Unlike Title II of the present legislation, the 1875 Act broadly proscribed discrimination in "inns, public conveyances on land or water, theaters, and other places of public amusement," without limiting the categories of affected businesses to those impinging upon interstate commerce. In contrast, the applicability of Title II is carefully limited to enterprises having a direct and substantial relation to the interstate flow of goods and people, except where state action is involved. Further, the fact that certain kinds of businesses may not in 1875 have been sufficiently involved in interstate commerce to warrant bringing them within the ambit of the commerce power is not necessarily dispositive of the same question today. Our populace had not reached its present mobility, nor were facilities, goods and services circulating as readily in interstate commerce as they are today. Although the principles which we apply today are those first formulated by Chief Justice Marshall in Gibbons v. Ogden, 9 Wheat. 1 (1824), the conditions of transportation and commerce have changed dramatically, and we must apply those principles to the present state of commerce. The sheer increase in volume of interstate traffic alone would give discriminatory practices which inhibit travel a far larger impact upon the Nation's commerce than such practices had on the economy of another day. Finally, there is language in the Civil Rights Cases which indicates that the Court did not fully consider whether the 1875 Act could be sustained as an exercise of the commerce power. Though the Court observed that "no one will contend that the power to pass it was contained in the Constitution before the adoption of the last three amendments [Thirteenth, Fourteenth, and Fifteenth]," the Court went on specifically to note that the Act was not "conceived" in terms of the commerce power and expressly pointed out:

> Of course, these remarks [as to lack of congressional power] do not apply to those cases in which Congress is clothed with direct and plenary powers of legislation over the whole subject, accompanied with an express or implied denial of such power to the States, as in the regulation of commerce with foreign nations, among the several States, and with the Indian tribes.... In these cases Congress has power to pass laws for regulating the subjects specified in every detail, and the conduct and transactions of individuals in respect thereof.

Since the commerce power was not relied on by the Government and was without support in the record it is understandable that the Court narrowed its inquiry and excluded the Commerce Clause as a possible source of power. In any event, it is clear that such a limitation renders the opinion devoid of authority for the proposition that the Commerce Clause gives no power to Congress to regulate discriminatory practices now found substantially to affect interstate commerce.

We, therefore, conclude that the Civil Rights Cases have no relevance to the basis of decision here where the Act explicitly relies upon the commerce power, and where the record is filled with testimony of obstructions and restraints resulting from the discriminations found to be existing. We now pass to that phase of the case.

6. The Basis of Congressional Action.

While the Act as adopted carried no congressional findings the record of its passage through each house is replete with evidence of the burdens that discrimination by race or color places upon interstate commerce [citing hearings before Congressional committees]. This testimony included the fact that our people have become increasingly mobile with millions of people of all races traveling from State to State; that Negroes in particular have been the subject of discrimination in transient accommodations, having to travel great distances to secure the same; that often they have been unable to obtain accommodations and have had to call upon friends to put them up overnight[,] and that these conditions had become so acute as to require the listing of available lodging for Negroes in a special guidebook which was itself "dramatic testimony to the difficulties" Negroes encounter in travel. These exclusionary practices were found to be nationwide, the Under Secretary of Commerce testifying that there is "no question that this discrimination in the North still exists to a large degree" and in the West and Midwest as well. This testimony indicated a qualitative as well as quantitative effect on interstate travel by Negroes. The former was the obvious impairment of the Negro traveler's pleasure and convenience that resulted when he continually was uncertain of finding lodging. As for the latter, there was evidence that this uncertainty stemming from racial discrimination had the effect of discouraging travel on the part of a substantial portion of the Negro community. This was the conclusion not only of the Under Secretary of Commerce but also of the Administrator of the Federal Aviation Agency who wrote the Chairman of the Senate Commerce Committee that it was his "belief that air commerce is adversely affected by the denial to a substantial segment of the traveling public of adequate and desegregated public accommodations." We shall not burden this opinion with further details since the voluminous testimony presents overwhelming evidence that discrimination by hotels and motels impedes interstate travel.

7. The Power of Congress Over Interstate Travel.

The power of Congress to deal with these obstructions depends on the meaning of the Commerce Clause. Its meaning was first enunciated 140 years ago by the great Chief Justice John Marshall in Gibbons v. Ogden, 9 Wheat. 1 (1824), in these words:

> The subject to be regulated is commerce; and ... to ascertain the extent of the power, it becomes necessary to settle the meaning of the word. The counsel for the appellee would limit it to traffic, to buying and selling, or the interchange of commodities ... but it is something more: it is intercourse ... between nations, and parts of nations, in all its branches, and is regulated by prescribing rules for carrying on that intercourse....

> To what commerce does this power extend? The constitution informs us, to commerce 'with foreign nations, and among the several States, and with the Indian tribes.'

> It has, we believe, been universally admitted, that these words comprehend every species of commercial intercourse.... No sort of trade can be carried on ... to which this power does not extend....

> The subject to which the power is next applied, is to commerce 'among the several States.' The word 'among' means intermingled....

> ... It may very properly be restricted to that commerce which concerns more States than one.... The genius and character of the whole government seem to be, that its action is to be applied to all the ... internal concerns [of the Nation] which affect the States generally; but not to those which are completely within a particular State, which do not affect other States, and with which it is not necessary to interfere, for the purpose of executing some of the general powers of the government....

> We are now arrived at the inquiry — What is this power?

> It is the power to regulate; that is, to prescribe the rule by which commerce is to be governed. This power, like all others vested in Congress, is complete in itself, may be exercised to its utmost extent, and acknowledges no limitations, other than are prescribed in the constitution.... If, as has always been understood, the sovereignty of Congress ... is plenary as to those objects [specified in the Constitution], the power over commerce ... is vested in Congress as absolutely as it would be in a single government, having in its constitution the same restrictions on the exercise of the power as are found in the constitution of the United States. The wisdom and the discretion of Congress, their identity with the people, and the influence which their constituents possess at elections, are, in this, as in many other instances, as that, for example, of declaring war, the sole restraints on which they have relied, to secure them from its abuse. They are the restraints on which the people must often rely solely, in all representative governments.

In short, the determinative test of the exercise of power by the Congress under the Commerce Clause is simply whether the activity sought to be regulated is "commerce which concerns more States than one" and has a real and substantial relation to the national interest. Let us now turn to this facet of the problem.

That the "intercourse" of which the Chief Justice spoke included the movement of persons through more States than one was settled as early as 1849, in the Passenger Cases, 7 How. 283, where Mr. Justice McLean stated: "That the transportation of passengers is a part of commerce is not now an open question." Again in 1913 Mr. Justice McKenna, speaking for the Court, said: "Commerce among the States, we have said, consists of intercourse and traffic between their citizens, and includes the transportation of persons and property." And only four years later in 1917 in Caminetti v. United States, 242 U.S. 470, Mr. Justice Day held for the Court:

> The transportation of passengers in interstate commerce, it has long been settled, is within the regulatory power of Congress, under the commerce clause of the Constitution, and the authority of Congress to keep the channels of interstate commerce free from immoral and injurious uses has been frequently sustained, and is no longer open to question.

Nor does it make any difference whether the transportation is commercial in character. In Morgan v. Virginia, 328 U.S. 373 (1946), Mr. Justice Reed observed as to the modern movement of persons among the States:

> The recent changes in transportation brought about by the coming of automobiles [do] not seem of great significance in the problem. People of all races travel today more extensively than in 1878 when this Court first passed upon state regulation of racial segregation in commerce. [It but] emphasizes the soundness of this Court's early conclusion in Hall v. DeCuir, 95 U.S. 485.

The same interest in protecting interstate commerce which led Congress to deal with segregation in interstate carriers and the white-slave traffic has prompted it to extend the exercise of its power to gambling; to criminal enterprises, to deceptive practices in the sale of products; to fraudulent security transactions; to misbranding of drugs; to wages and hours; to members of labor unions; to crop control; to discrimination against shippers; to the protection of small business from injurious price cutting; to resale price maintenance; to professional football; and to racial discrimination by owners and managers of terminal restaurants, Boynton v. Virginia, 364 U.S. 454 (1960).

That Congress was legislating against moral wrongs in many of these areas rendered its enactments no less valid. In framing Title II of this Act Congress was also dealing with what it considered a moral problem. But that fact does not detract from the overwhelming evidence of the disruptive effect that racial discrimination has had on commercial intercourse. It was this burden which empowered Congress to enact appropriate legislation, and, given this basis for the exercise of its power, Congress was not restricted by the fact that the particular obstruction to interstate commerce with which it was dealing was also deemed a moral and social wrong.

It is said that the operation of the motel here is of a purely local character. But, assuming this to be true, "if it is interstate commerce that feels the pinch, it does not matter how local the operation which applies the squeeze." As Chief Justice Stone put it in United States v. Darby [312 U.S. 100, 118 (1941)]:

> The power of Congress over interstate commerce is not confined to the regulation of commerce among the states. It extends to those activities intrastate which so affect interstate commerce or the exercise of the power of Congress over it as to make regulation of them appropriate means to the attainment of a legitimate end, the exercise of the granted power of Congress to regulate interstate commerce. See McCulloch v. Maryland, 4 Wheat. 316, 421.

Thus the power of Congress to promote interstate commerce also includes the power to regulate the local incidents thereof, including local activities in both the States of origin and destination, which might have a substantial and harmful effect upon that commerce. One need only examine the evidence which we have discussed above to see that Congress may—as it has—prohibit racial discrimination by motels serving travelers, however "local" their operations may appear.

Nor does the Act deprive appellant of liberty or property under the Fifth Amendment. The commerce power invoked here by the Congress is a specific and plenary one authorized by the Constitution itself. The only questions are: (1) whether Congress had a rational basis for finding that racial discrimination by motels affected commerce, and (2) if it had such a basis, whether the means it selected to eliminate that evil are reasonable and appropriate. If they are, appellant has no "right" to select its guests as it sees fit, free from governmental regulation.

There is nothing novel about such legislation. Thirty-two States now have it on their books either by statute or executive order and many cities provide such regulation. Some of these Acts go back fourscore years. It has been repeatedly held by this Court that such laws do not violate the Due Process Clause of the Fourteenth Amendment. Perhaps the first such holding was in the Civil Rights Cases themselves, where Mr. Justice Bradley for the Court inferentially found that innkeepers, "by the laws of all the States, so far as we are aware, are bound, to the extent of their facilities, to furnish proper accommodation to all unobjectionable persons who in good faith apply for them."

As we have pointed out, 32 States now have such provisions and no case has been cited to us where the attack on a state statute has been successful, either in federal or state courts. Indeed, in some cases the Due Process and Equal Protection Clause objections have been specifically discarded in this Court. As a result the constitutionality of such state statutes stands unquestioned. "The authority of the Federal Government over interstate commerce does not differ," it was held in United States v. Rock Royal Co-op., Inc., 307 U.S. 533[, 569–70] (1939), "in extent or character from that retained by the states over intrastate commerce."

It is doubtful if in the long run appellant will suffer economic loss as a result of the Act. Experience is to the contrary where discrimination is completely obliterated as to all public accommodations. But whether this be true or not is of no consequence since this Court has specifically held that the fact that a "member of the class which is regulated may suffer economic losses not shared by others ... has never been a barrier" to such legislation. Bowles v. Willingham [321 U.S. 503, 518 (1944)]. Likewise in a long line of cases this Court has rejected the claim that the prohibition of racial discrimination in public accommodations interferes with personal liberty. See District of Columbia v. John R. Thompson Co., 346 U.S. 100 (1953), and cases there cited, where we concluded that Congress had delegated law-making power to the District of Columbia "as broad as the police power of a state" which included the power to adopt "a law prohibiting discriminations against Negroes by the owners and managers of restaurants in the District of Columbia." Neither do we find any merit in the claim that the Act is a taking of property without just compensation. The cases are to the contrary.

We find no merit in the remainder of appellant's contentions, including that of "involuntary servitude." As we have seen, 32 States prohibit racial discrimination in public accommodations. These laws but codify the common-law innkeeper rule which long predated the Thirteenth Amendment. It is difficult to believe that the Amendment was intended to abrogate this principle. Indeed, the opinion of the Court in the Civil Rights Cases is to the contrary as we have seen, it having noted with approval the laws of "all the States" prohibiting discrimination. We could not say that the requirements of the Act in this regard are in any way "akin to African slavery."

We, therefore, conclude that the action of the Congress in the adoption of the Act as applied here to a motel which concededly serves interstate travelers is within the power granted it by the Commerce Clause of the Constitution, as interpreted by this Court for 140 years. It may be argued that Congress could have pursued other methods to eliminate the obstructions it found in interstate commerce caused by racial discrimination. But this is a matter of policy that rests entirely with the Congress not with the courts. How obstructions in commerce may be removed—what means are to be employed—is within the sound and exclusive discretion of the Congress. It is subject only to one caveat—that the means chosen by it must be reasonably adapted to the end permitted by the Constitution. We cannot say that its choice here was not so adapted. The Constitution requires no more.

Mr. Justice Douglas, concurring.

[Mr. Justice Douglas concurred, but would have rested the decision on the Fourteenth Amendment. He quoted from the Senate Report]:

Does the owner of private property devoted to use as a public establishment enjoy a property right to refuse to deal with any member of the public because of that member's race, religion, or national origin? As noted previously, the English common law answered this question in the negative. It reasoned that one who employed his private property for purposes of commercial gain by offering goods or services to the public must stick to his bargain. It is to be remembered that the right of the private property owner to serve or sell to whom he pleased was never claimed when laws were enacted prohibiting the private property owner from dealing with persons of a particular race. Nor were such laws ever struck down as an infringement upon this supposed right of the property owner.

But there are stronger and more persuasive reasons for not allowing concepts of private property to defeat public accommodations legislation. The institution of private property exists for the purpose of enhancing the individual freedom and liberty of human beings. This institution assures that the individual need not be at the mercy of others, including government, in order to earn a livelihood and prosper from his individual efforts. Private property provides the individual with something of value that will serve him well in obtaining what he desires or requires in his daily life.

Is this time honored means to freedom and liberty now to be twisted so as to defeat individual freedom and liberty? Certainly denial of a right to discriminate or segregate by race or religion would not weaken the attributes of private property that make it an effective means of obtaining individual freedom. In fact, in order to assure that the institution of private property serves the end of individual freedom and liberty it has been restricted in many instances. The most striking example of this is the abolition of slavery. Slaves were treated as items of private property, yet surely no man dedicated to the cause of individual freedom could contend that individual freedom and liberty suffered by emancipation of the slaves.

There is not any question that ordinary zoning laws place far greater restrictions upon the rights of private property owners than would public accommodations legislation. Zoning laws tell the owner of private property to what type of business his property may be devoted, what structures he may erect upon that property, and even whether he may devote his private property to any business purpose whatsoever. Such laws and regulations restricting private property are necessary so that human beings may develop their communities in a reasonable and peaceful manner. Surely the presence of such restrictions does not detract from the role of private property in securing individual liberty and freedom.

Nor can it be reasonably argued that racial or religious discrimination is a vital factor in the ability of private property to constitute an effective vehicle for assuring personal freedom. The pledge of this Nation is to secure freedom for every individual; that pledge will be furthered by elimination of such practices.

Katzenbach v. McClung
379 U.S. 294 (1964)

Solicitor General Cox argued the cause for appellants. With him on the brief were Assistant Attorney General [Burke] Marshall, Ralph S. Spritzer, Philip B. Heymann, Harold H. Greene, and Gerald P. Choppin.*

Robert McDavid Smith argued the cause for appellees. With him on the briefs was William G. Somerville.**

Before Chief Justice Warren and Justices Black, Douglas, Clark, Harlan, Brennan, Stewart, White, and Goldberg.

Mr. Justice Clark delivered the opinion of the Court.

This case was argued with Heart of Atlanta Motel v. United States, decided this date, in which we upheld the constitutional validity of Title II of the Civil Rights Act of 1964 against an attack by hotels, motels, and like establishments. This complaint for injunctive relief against appellants attacks the constitutionality of the Act as applied to a restaurant. The case was heard by a three-judge United States District Court and an injunction was issued restraining appellants from enforcing the Act against the restaurant.* * *

2. The Facts.

Ollie's Barbecue is a family-owned restaurant in Birmingham, Alabama, specializing in barbecued meats and homemade pies, with a seating capacity of 220 customers. It is located on a state highway 11 blocks from an interstate one and a somewhat greater distance from railroad and bus stations. The restaurant caters to a family and white-collar trade with a take-out service for Negroes. It employs 36 persons, two-thirds of whom are Negroes.

In the 12 months preceding the passage of the Act, the restaurant purchased locally approximately $150,000 worth of food, $69,683 or 46% of which was meat that it bought from a local supplier who had procured it from outside the State. The District Court expressly found that a substantial portion of the food served in the restaurant had moved in interstate commerce. The restaurant has refused to serve Negroes in its dining accommodations since its original opening in 1927, and since July 2, 1964, it has been operating in violation of the Act. The court below concluded that if it were required to serve Negroes it would lose a substantial amount of business.

---

* Jack Greenberg, Constance Baker Motley, James M. Nabrit, III, and Charles L. Black, Jr., filed a brief for the NAACP Legal Defense and Educational Fund, Inc., as amicus curiae, urging reversal.

** T. W. Bruton, Attorney General of North Carolina, and Ralph Moody, Deputy Attorney General, filed a brief for the State of North Carolina, as amicus curiae, urging affirmance.

On the merits, the District Court held that the Act could not be applied under the Fourteenth Amendment because it was conceded that the State of Alabama was not involved in the refusal of the restaurant to serve Negroes. It was also admitted that the Thirteenth Amendment was authority neither for validating nor for invalidating the Act. As to the Commerce Clause, the court found that it was "an express grant of power to Congress to regulate interstate commerce, which consists of the movement of persons, goods or information from one state to another"; and it found that the clause was also a grant of power "to regulate intrastate activities, but only to the extent that action on its part is necessary or appropriate to the effective execution of its expressly granted power to regulate interstate commerce." There must be, it said, a close and substantial relation between local activities and interstate commerce which requires control of the former in the protection of the latter. The court concluded, however, that the Congress, rather than finding facts sufficient to meet this rule, had legislated a conclusive presumption that a restaurant affects interstate commerce if it serves or offers to serve interstate travelers or if a substantial portion of the food which it serves has moved in commerce. This, the court held, it could not do because there was no demonstrable connection between food purchased in interstate commerce and sold in a restaurant and the conclusion of Congress that discrimination in the restaurant would affect that commerce.

The basic holding in Heart of Atlanta Motel answers many of the contentions made by the appellees.[1] There we outlined the overall purpose and operations plan of Title II and found it a valid exercise of the power to regulate interstate commerce insofar as it requires hotels and motels to serve transients without regard to their race or color. In this case we consider its application to restaurants which serve food a substantial portion of which has moved in commerce.

3. The Act As Applied.

Section 201(a) of Title II commands that all persons shall be entitled to the full and equal enjoyment of the goods and services of any place of public accommodation without discrimination or segregation on the ground of race, color, religion, or national origin; and §201(b) defines establishments as places of public accommodation if their operations affect commerce or segregation by them is supported by state action. Sections 201(b)(2) and (c) place any "restaurant … principally engaged in selling food for consumption on the premises" under the Act "if … it serves or offers to serve interstate travelers or a substantial portion of the food which it serves … has moved in commerce."

Ollie's Barbecue admits that it is covered by these provisions of the Act. The Government makes no contention that the discrimination at the restaurant was supported by the State of Alabama. There is no claim that interstate travelers frequented the restaurant. The sole question, therefore, narrows down to whether Title II, as applied to a restaurant annually receiving about $70,000 worth of food which has moved in commerce, is a valid exercise of the power of Congress. The Government has contended that Congress had ample basis upon which to find that racial discrimination at restaurants which receive from out of state a substantial portion of the food served does, in fact, impose commercial burdens of national magnitude upon interstate commerce. The appellees' major argument is directed to this premise. They urge that no such basis existed. It is to that question that we now turn.

---

1. That decision disposes of the challenges that the appellees base on the Fifth, Ninth, Tenth, and Thirteenth Amendments, and on the Civil Rights Cases, 109 U.S. 3 (1883).

4. The Congressional Hearings.

As we noted in Heart of Atlanta Motel, both Houses of Congress conducted prolonged hearings on the Act. And, as we said there, while no formal findings were made, which of course are not necessary, it is well that we make mention of the testimony at these hearings the better to understand the problem before Congress and determine whether the Act is a reasonable and appropriate means toward its solution. The record is replete with testimony of the burdens placed on interstate commerce by racial discrimination in restaurants. A comparison of per capita spending by Negroes in restaurants, theaters, and like establishments indicated less spending, after discounting income differences, in areas where discrimination is widely practiced. This condition, which was especially aggravated in the South, was attributed in the testimony of the Under Secretary of Commerce to racial segregation. See Hearings before the Senate Committee on Commerce on S. 1732, 88th Cong., 1st Sess., 695. This diminutive spending springing from a refusal to serve Negroes and their total loss as customers has, regardless of the absence of direct evidence, a close connection to interstate commerce. The fewer customers a restaurant enjoys the less food it sells and consequently the less it buys. S. Rep. No. 872, 88th Cong., 2d Sess., at 19; Senate Commerce Committee Hearings, at 207. In addition, the Attorney General testified that this type of discrimination imposed "an artificial restriction on the market" and interfered with the flow of merchandise. Id., at 18–19; also, on this point, see testimony of Senator Magnuson, 110 Cong. Rec. 7402–7403. In addition, there were many references to discriminatory situations causing wide unrest and having a depressant effect on general business conditions in the respective communities.

Moreover there was an impressive array of testimony that discrimination in restaurants had a direct and highly restrictive effect upon interstate travel by Negroes. This resulted, it was said, because discriminatory practices prevent Negroes from buying prepared food served on the premises while on a trip, except in isolated and unkempt restaurants and under most unsatisfactory and often unpleasant conditions. This obviously discourages travel and obstructs interstate commerce for one can hardly travel without eating. Likewise, it was said, that discrimination deterred professional, as well as skilled, people from moving into areas where such practices occurred and thereby caused industry to be reluctant to establish there.

We believe that this testimony afforded ample basis for the conclusion that established restaurants in such areas sold less interstate goods because of the discrimination, that interstate travel was obstructed directly by it, that business in general suffered and that many new businesses refrained from establishing there as a result of it. Hence the District Court was in error in concluding that there was no connection between discrimination and the movement of interstate commerce. The court's conclusion that such a connection is outside "common experience" flies in the face of stubborn fact.

It goes without saying that, viewed in isolation, the volume of food purchased by Ollie's Barbecue from sources supplied from out of state was insignificant when compared with the total foodstuffs moving in commerce. But, as our late Brother Jackson said for the Court in Wickard v. Filburn, 317 U.S. 111 (1942):

> That appellee's own contribution to the demand for wheat may be trivial by itself is not enough to remove him from the scope of federal regulation where, as here, his contribution, taken together with that of many others similarly situated, is far from trivial.

We noted in Heart of Atlanta Motel that a number of witnesses attested to the fact that racial discrimination was not merely a state or regional problem but was one of nationwide scope. Against this background, we must conclude that while the focus of the legislation was on the individual restaurant's relation to interstate commerce, Congress appropriately considered the importance of that connection with the knowledge that the discrimination was but "representative of many others throughout the country, the total incidence of which if left unchecked may well become far-reaching in its harm to commerce." Polish National Alliance of U.S. v. National Labor Relations Board, 322 U.S. 643, 648 (1944).

With this situation spreading as the record shows, Congress was not required to await the total dislocation of commerce. As was said in Consolidated Edison Co. of New York v. National Labor Relations Board, 305 U.S. 197 (1938):

> But it cannot be maintained that the exertion of federal power must await the disruption of that commerce. Congress was entitled to provide reasonable preventive measures and that was the object of the National Labor Relations Act.

5. The Power of Congress to Regulate Local Activities.

Article I, §8, cl. 3, confers upon Congress the power "to regulate Commerce ... among the several States" and Clause 18 of the same Article grants it the power "to make all Laws which shall be necessary and proper for carrying into Execution the foregoing Powers...." This grant, as we have pointed out in Heart of Atlanta Motel, "extends to those activities intrastate which so affect interstate commerce, or the exertion of the power of Congress over it, as to make regulation of them appropriate means to the attainment of a legitimate end, the effective execution of the granted power to regulate interstate commerce." Much is said about a restaurant business being local but "even if appellee's activity be local and though it may not be regarded as commerce, it may still, whatever its nature, be reached by Congress if it exerts a substantial economic effect on interstate commerce...." Wickard v. Filburn, supra, at 125. The activities that are beyond the reach of Congress are "those which are completely within a particular State, which do not affect other States, and with which it is not necessary to interfere, for the purpose of executing some of the general powers of the government." Gibbons v. Ogden, 9 Wheat. 1, 195 (1824). This rule is as good today as it was when Chief Justice Marshall laid it down almost a century and a half ago.

This Court has held time and again that this power extends to activities of retail establishments, including restaurants, which directly or indirectly burden or obstruct interstate commerce. We have detailed the cases in Heart of Atlanta Motel, and will not repeat them here.

Nor are the cases holding that interstate commerce ends when goods come to rest in the State of destination apposite here. That line of cases has been applied with reference to state taxation or regulation but not in the field of federal regulation.

The appellees contend that Congress has arbitrarily created a conclusive presumption that all restaurants meeting the criteria set out in the Act "affect commerce." Stated another way, they object to the omission of a provision for a case-by-case determination—judicial or administrative—that racial discrimination in a particular restaurant affects commerce.

But Congress' action in framing this Act was not unprecedented. In United States v. Darby, 312 U.S. 100 (1941), this Court held constitutional the Fair Labor Standards Act of 1938. There Congress determined that the payment of substandard wages to employees engaged in the production of goods for commerce, while not itself commerce, so inhibited it as to be subject to federal regulation. The appellees in that case argued, as do the appellees here, that the Act was invalid because it included no provision for an independent inquiry regarding the effect on commerce of substandard wages in a particular business. But the Court rejected the argument, observing that:

> [S]ometimes Congress itself has said that a particular activity affects the commerce, as it did in the present Act, the Safety Appliance Act … and the Railway Labor Act.… In passing on the validity of legislation of the class last mentioned the only function of courts is to determine whether the particular activity regulated or prohibited is within the reach of the federal power.

Here, as there, Congress has determined for itself that refusals of service to Negroes have imposed burdens both upon the interstate flow of food and upon the movement of products generally. Of course, the mere fact that Congress has said when particular activity shall be deemed to affect commerce does not preclude further examination by this Court. But where we find that the legislators, in light of the facts and testimony before them, have a rational basis for finding a chosen regulatory scheme necessary to the protection of commerce, our investigation is at an end. The only remaining question — one answered in the affirmative by the court below — is whether the particular restaurant either serves or offers to serve interstate travelers or serves food a substantial portion of which has moved in interstate commerce.

The appellees urge that Congress, in passing the Fair Labor Standards Act and the National Labor Relations Act, made specific findings which were embodied in those statutes. Here, of course, Congress had included no formal findings. But their absence is not fatal to the validity of the statute, see United States v. Carolene Products Co., 304 U.S. 144, 152 (1938), for the evidence presented at the hearings fully indicated the nature and effect of the burdens on commerce which Congress meant to alleviate.

Confronted as we are with the facts laid before Congress, we must conclude that it had a rational basis for finding that racial discrimination in restaurants had a direct and adverse effect on the free flow of interstate commerce. Insofar as the sections of the Act here relevant are concerned, §§ 201(b)(2) and (c), Congress prohibited discrimination only in those establishments having a close tie to interstate commerce, i.e., those, like the McClungs', serving food that has come from out of the State. We think in so doing that Congress acted well within its power to protect and foster commerce in extending the coverage of Title II only to those restaurants offering to serve interstate travelers or serving food, a substantial portion of which has moved in interstate commerce.

The absence of direct evidence connecting discriminatory restaurant service with the flow of interstate food, a factor on which the appellees place much reliance, is not, given the evidence as to the effect of such practices on other aspects of commerce, a crucial matter.

The power of Congress in this field is broad and sweeping; where it keeps within its sphere and violates no express constitutional limitation it has been the rule of this Court, going back almost to the founding days of the Republic, not to interfere. The Civil Rights Act of 1964, as here applied, we find to be plainly appropriate in the resolution of what the Congress found to be a national commercial problem of the first magnitude. We find it in no violation of any express limitations of the Constitution and we therefore declare it valid.

The judgment is therefore reversed.

E. The Civil Rights Act of 1968 and the Reinvigoration of the Civil Rights Act of 1866

Jones v. Mayer
392 U.S. 409 (1968)

Samuel H. Liberman, St. Louis, Mo., for petitioners.

Israel Treiman, St. Louis, Mo., for respondents.

Attorney General Ramsey Clark for the United States, as amicus curiae, by special leave of Court.

Before Chief Justice Warren and Justices Black, Douglas, Harlan, Brennan, Stewart, White, Fortas, and Marshall.

Mr. Justice Stewart delivered the opinion of the Court.

In this case we are called upon to determine the scope and the constitutionality of an Act of Congress, 42 U.S.C. § 1982, which provides that:

> All citizens of the United States shall have the same right, in every State and Territory, as is enjoyed by white citizens thereof to inherit, purchase, lease, sell, hold, and convey real and personal property.

On September 2, 1965, the petitioners filed a complaint in the District Court for the Eastern District of Missouri, alleging that the respondents had refused to sell them a home in the Paddock Woods community of St. Louis County for the sole reason that petitioner Joseph Lee Jones is a Negro.... The District Court sustained the respondents' motion to dismiss the complaint, and the Court of Appeals for the Eighth Circuit affirmed, concluding that § 1982 applies only to state action and does not reach private refusals to sell. [W]e reverse the judgment of the Court of Appeals. We hold that § 1982 bars *all* racial discrimination, private as well as public, in the sale or rental of property, and that the statute, thus construed, is a valid exercise of the power of Congress to enforce the Thirteenth Amendment.[5]

I.

At the outset, it is important to make clear precisely what this case does *not* involve. Whatever else it may be, 42 U.S.C. § 1982 is not a comprehensive open housing law. In sharp contrast to the Fair Housing Title (Title VIII) of the Civil Rights Act of 1968, the statute in this case deals only with racial discrimination and does not address itself to discrimination on grounds of religion or national origin. It does not deal specifically with discrimination in the provision of services or facilities in connection with the sale or rental of a dwelling. It does not prohibit advertising or other representations that indicate discriminatory preferences. It does not refer explicitly to discrimination in financing arrangements or in the provision of brokerage services.[10] It does not empower a

---

5. Because we have concluded that the discrimination alleged in the petitioners' complaint violated a federal statute that Congress had the power to enact under the Thirteenth Amendment, we find it unnecessary to decide whether that discrimination also violated the Equal Protection Clause of the Fourteenth Amendment.

10. Contrast § 806. In noting that 42 U.S.C. § 1982 differs from the Civil Rights Act of 1968 in not dealing explicitly and exhaustively with such matters, we intimate no view upon the question whether ancillary services or facilities of this sort might in some situations constitute "property" as

federal administrative agency to assist aggrieved parties. It makes no provision for intervention by the Attorney General. And, although it can be enforced by injunction, it contains no provision expressly authorizing a federal court to order the payment of damages.

Thus, although § 1982 contains none of the exemptions that Congress included in the Civil Rights Act of 1968, it would be a serious mistake to suppose that § 1982 in any way diminishes the significance of the law recently enacted by Congress. Indeed, the Senate Subcommittee on Housing and Urban Affairs was informed in hearings held after the Court of Appeals had rendered its decision in this case that § 1982 might well be "a presently valid federal statutory ban against discrimination by private persons in the sale or lease of real property." The Subcommittee was told, however, that even if this Court should so construe § 1982, the existence of that statute would not "eliminate the need for congressional action" to spell out "responsibility on the part of the federal government to enforce the rights it protects." The point was made that, in light of the many difficulties confronted by private litigants seeking to enforce such rights on their own, "legislation is needed to establish federal machinery for enforcement of the rights guaranteed under Section 1982 of Title 42 even if the plaintiffs in Jones v. Alfred H. Mayer Company should prevail in the United States Supreme Court."

On April 10, 1968, Representative Kelly of New York focused the attention of the House upon the present case and its possible significance. She described the background of this litigation, recited the text of § 1982, and then added:

> When the Attorney General was asked in court about the effect of the old law [§ 1982] as compared with the pending legislation which is being considered on the House floor today, he said that the scope was somewhat different, the remedies and procedures were different, and that the new law was still quite necessary.

Later the same day, the House passed the Civil Rights Act of 1968. Its enactment had no effect upon § 1982 and no effect upon this litigation, but it underscored the vast differences between, on the one hand, a general statute applicable only to racial discrimination in the rental and sale of property and enforceable only by private parties acting on their own initiative, and, on the other hand, a detailed housing law, applicable to a broad range of discriminatory practices and enforceable by a complete arsenal of federal authority. Having noted these differences, we turn to a consideration of § 1982 itself.

II.

This Court last had occasion to consider the scope of 42 U.S.C. § 1982 in 1948, in Hurd v. Hodge.* It is true that a dictum in Hurd v. Hodge characterized Corrigan v. Buckley [(1926)] as having "held" that "the action toward which the provisions of the statute ... [are] directed is governmental action." But no such statement appears in the Corrigan opinion, and a careful examination of Corrigan reveals that it cannot be read as authority for the proposition attributed to it in Hurd. In Corrigan, suits had been brought to enjoin a threatened violation of certain restrictive covenants in the District of Columbia. The courts of the District had granted relief.... As the opinion in Corri-

---

that term is employed in § 1982. Nor do we intimate any view upon the extent to which discrimination in the provision of such services might be barred by 42 U.S.C. § 1981....

* Editor's Note: Recall that Hurd v. Hodge was a companion case to Shelley v. Kraemer. Hurd v. Hodge arose in the District of Columbia, and therefore could not be resolved on the basis of the Equal Protection Clause.

gan specifically recognized, no claim that the covenants could not validly be *enforced* against the appellants had been raised in the lower courts, and no such claim was properly before this Court. The only question presented for decision was whether the restrictive covenants *themselves* violated the Fifth, Thirteenth, and Fourteenth Amendments, and §§ 1977, 1978, and 1979 of the Revised Statutes (now 42 U.S.C. §§ 1981, 1982, and 1983). Addressing itself to that narrow question, the Court said that none of the provisions relied upon by the appellants prohibited private individuals from "enter[ing] into ... [contracts] in respect to the control and disposition of their own property." Nor, added the Court, had the appellants even *claimed* that the provisions in question "had, in and of themselves, ... [the] effect" of prohibiting such contracts.

Even if Corrigan should be regarded as an adjudication that 42 U.S.C. § 1982 (then § 1978 of the Revised Statutes) does not prohibit private individuals from *agreeing* not to sell their property to Negroes, Corrigan would *not* settle the question whether § 1982 prohibits an *actual refusal to sell* to a Negro. Moreover, since the appellants in Corrigan had not even argued in this Court that the statute prohibited private agreements of the sort there involved, it would be a mistake to treat the Corrigan decision as a considered judgment even on that narrow issue.

III.

We begin with the language of the statute itself. In plain and unambiguous terms, § 1982 grants to all citizens, without regard to race or color, "the same right" to purchase and lease property "as is enjoyed by white citizens." As the Court of Appeals in this case evidently recognized, that right can be impaired as effectively by "those who place property on the market" as by the State itself. For, even if the State and its agents lend no support to those who wish to exclude persons from their communities on racial grounds, the fact remains that, whenever property "is placed on the market for whites only, whites have a right denied to Negroes." So long as a Negro citizen who wants to buy or rent a home can be turned away simply because he is not white, he cannot be said to enjoy "the *same* right ... as is enjoyed by white citizens ... to ... purchase [and] lease ... real and personal property."

On its face, therefore, § 1982 appears to prohibit *all* discrimination against Negroes in the sale or rental of property—discrimination by private owners as well as discrimination by public authorities. Indeed, even the respondents seem to concede that, if § 1982 "means what it says"—to use the words of the respondents' brief—then it must encompass every racially motivated refusal to sell or rent and cannot be confined to officially sanctioned segregation in housing. Stressing what they consider to be the revolutionary implications of so literal a reading of § 1982, the respondents argue that Congress cannot possibly have intended any such result. Our examination of the relevant history, however, persuades us that Congress meant exactly what it said.

IV.

In its original form, 42 U.S.C. § 1982 was part of § 1 of the Civil Rights Act of 1866. That section was cast in sweeping terms:

> *Be it enacted by the Senate and House of Representatives of the United States of America in Congress assembled,* that all persons born in the United States and not subject to any foreign power, ... are hereby declared to be citizens of the United States; and such citizens, of every race and color, without regard to any previous condition of slavery or involuntary servitude, ... shall have the same

right, in every State and Territory in the United States, to make and enforce contracts, to sue, be parties, and give evidence, to inherit, purchase, lease, sell, hold, and convey real and personal property, and to full and equal benefit of all laws and proceedings for the security of person and property, as is enjoyed by white citizens, and shall be subject to like punishment, pains, and penalties, and to none other, any law, statute, ordinance, regulation, or custom, to the contrary notwithstanding.

The crucial language for our purposes was that which guaranteed all citizens "the same right, in every State and Territory in the United States, ... to inherit, purchase, lease, sell, hold, and convey real and personal property ... as is enjoyed by white citizens...." To the Congress that passed the Civil Rights Act of 1866, it was clear that the right to do these things might be infringed not only by "State or local law" but also by "custom or prejudice."[30] Thus, when Congress provided in § 1 of the Civil Rights Act that the right to purchase and lease property was to be enjoyed equally throughout the United States by Negro and white citizens alike, it plainly meant to secure that right against interference from any source whatever, whether governmental or private.

Indeed, if § 1 had been intended to grant nothing more than an immunity from *governmental* interference, then much of § 2 would have made no sense at all. For that section, which provided fines and prison terms for certain individuals who deprived others of rights "secured or protected" by § 1, was carefully drafted to exempt private violations of § 1 from the criminal sanctions it imposed. There would, of course, have been no private violations to exempt if the only "right" granted by § 1 had been a right to be free of discrimination by public officials. Hence the structure of the 1866 Act, as well as its language, points to the conclusion urged by the petitioners in this case — that § 1 was meant to prohibit *all* racially motivated deprivations of the rights enumerated in the statute, although only those deprivations perpetrated "under color of law" were to be criminally punishable under § 2.

In attempting to demonstrate the contrary, the respondents rely heavily upon the fact that the Congress which approved the 1866 statute wished to eradicate the recently enacted Black Codes — laws which had saddled Negroes with "onerous disabilities and burdens, and curtailed their rights ... to such an extent that their freedom was of little value...." Slaughter-House Cases. The respondents suggest that the only evil Congress sought to eliminate was that of racially discriminatory laws in the former Confederate States. But the Civil Rights Act was drafted to apply throughout the country, and its language was far broader than would have been necessary to strike down discriminatory statutes.

---

30. Several weeks before the House began its debate on the Civil Rights Act of 1866, Congress had passed a bill (S. 60) to enlarge the powers of the Freedmen's Bureau (created by Act of March 3, 1865) by extending military jurisdiction over certain areas in the South where, "in consequence of any State or local law, ... *custom*, or *prejudice*, any of the civil rights ... belonging to white persons (including the right ... to inherit, purchase, lease, sell, hold, and convey real and personal property ...) are refused or denied to negroes ... on account of race, color, or any previous condition of slavery or involuntary servitude...." Both Houses had passed S. 60 and although the Senate had failed to override the President's veto the bill was nonetheless significant for its recognition that the "right to purchase" was a right that could be "refused or denied" by "custom or prejudice" as well as by "State or local law." Of course an "abrogation of civil rights made 'in consequence of ... custom, or prejudice' might as easily be perpetrated by private individuals or by unofficial community activity as by state officers armed with statute or ordinance." J. TenBroek, Equal Under Law 179 (1965 ed.).

That broad language, we are asked to believe, was a mere slip of the legislative pen. We disagree. For the same Congress that wanted to do away with the Black Codes *also* had before it an imposing body of evidence pointing to the mistreatment of Negroes by private individuals and unofficial groups, mistreatment unrelated to any hostile state legislation. "Accounts in newspapers North and South, Freedmen's Bureau and other official documents, private reports and correspondence were all adduced" to show that "private outrage and atrocity" were "daily inflicted on freedmen...." The congressional debates are replete with references to private injustices against Negroes — references to white employers who refused to pay their Negro workers, white planters who agreed among themselves not to hire freed slaves without the permission of their former masters, white citizens who assaulted Negroes or who combined to drive them out of their communities.

Indeed, one of the most comprehensive studies then before Congress stressed the prevalence of private hostility toward Negroes and the need to protect them from the resulting persecution and discrimination. The report noted the existence of laws virtually prohibiting Negroes from owning or renting property in certain towns, but described such laws as "mere isolated cases," representing "the local outcroppings of a spirit ... found to prevail everywhere" — a spirit expressed, for example, by lawless acts of brutality directed against Negroes who traveled to areas where they were not wanted. The report concluded that, even if anti-Negro legislation were "repealed in all the States lately in rebellion," equal treatment for the Negro would not yet be secured.

In this setting, it would have been strange indeed if Congress had viewed its task as encompassing merely the nullification of racist laws in the former rebel States. That the Congress which assembled in the Nation's capital in December 1865 in fact had a broader vision of the task before it became clear early in the session, when three proposals to invalidate discriminatory state statutes were rejected as "too narrowly conceived." From the outset it seemed clear, at least to Senator Trumbull of Illinois, Chairman of the Judiciary Committee, that stronger legislation might prove necessary. After Senator Wilson of Massachusetts had introduced his bill to strike down all racially discriminatory laws in the South, Senator Trumbull said this:

> I reported from the Judiciary Committee the second section of the [Thirteenth Amendment] for the very purpose of conferring upon Congress authority to see that the first section was carried out in good faith ... and I hold that under that second section Congress will have the authority, when the constitutional amendment is adopted, *not only to pass the bill of the Senator from Massachusetts, but a bill that will be much more efficient to protect the freedman in his rights....* And, sir, when the constitutional amendment shall have been adopted, if the information from the South be that the men whose liberties are secured by it are deprived of the privilege to go and come when they please, *to buy and sell when they please,* to make contracts and enforce contracts, I give notice that, if no one else does, I shall introduce a bill and urge its passage through Congress that will secure to those men every one of these rights: they would not be freemen without them. *It is idle to say that a man is free who cannot go and come at pleasure, who cannot buy and sell, who cannot enforce his rights....* [So] when the constitutional amendment is adopted I trust we may pass a bill, if the action of the people in the southern States should make it necessary, that will be *much more sweeping and efficient than the bill under consideration.*

Five days later, on December 18, 1865, the Secretary of State officially certified the ratification of the Thirteenth Amendment. The next day Senator Trumbull again rose to speak. He had decided, he said, that the "more sweeping and efficient" bill of which he had spoken previously ought to be enacted "at an early day for the purpose of quieting apprehensions in the minds of many friends of freedom lest by local legislation *or a prevailing public sentiment* in some of the States persons of the African race should continue to be oppressed and in fact deprived of their freedom...."

On January 5, 1866, Senator Trumbull introduced the bill he had in mind—the bill which later became the Civil Rights Act of 1866. He described its objectives in terms that belie any attempt to read it narrowly:

> Mr. President, I regard the bill to which the attention of the Senate is now called as the most important measure that has been under its consideration since the adoption of the constitutional amendment abolishing slavery. That amendment declared that all persons in the United States should be free. This measure is intended to give effect to that declaration and secure to all persons within the United States practical freedom. There is very little importance in the general declaration of abstract truths and principles unless they can be carried into effect, unless the persons who are to be affected by them have some means of availing themselves of their benefits.

Of course, Senator Trumbull's bill would, as he pointed out, "destroy all [the] discriminations" embodied in the Black Codes, but it would do more: It would affirmatively secure for all men, whatever their race or color, what the Senator called the "great fundamental rights":

> The right to acquire property, the right to go and come at pleasure, the right to enforce rights in the courts, to make contracts, and to inherit and dispose of property.

As to those basic civil rights, the Senator said, the bill would "break down *all* discrimination between black men and white men."

That the bill would indeed have so sweeping an effect was seen as its great virtue by its friends and as its great danger by its enemies but was disputed by none. Opponents of the bill charged that it would not only regulate state laws but would directly "determine the persons who [would] enjoy ... property within the States," threatening the ability of white citizens "to determine who [would] be members of [their] communit[ies]...." The bill's advocates did not deny the accuracy of those characterizations. Instead, they defended the propriety of employing federal authority to deal with "the white man ... [who] would invoke the power of local prejudice" against the Negro. Thus, when the Senate passed the Civil Rights Act on February 2, 1866, it did so fully aware of the breadth of the measure it had approved.

In the House, as in the Senate, much was said about eliminating the infamous Black Codes. But, like the Senate, the House was moved by a larger objective—that of giving real content to the freedom guaranteed by the Thirteenth Amendment. Representative Thayer of Pennsylvania put it this way:

> When I voted for the amendment to abolish slavery ... I did not suppose that I was offering ... a mere paper guarantee. And when I voted for the second section of the amendment, I felt ... certain that I had ... given to Congress ability to protect ... the rights which the first section gave....

> The bill which now engages the attention of the House has for its object to carry out and guaranty the reality of that great measure. It is to give to it practical effect and force. It is to prevent that great measure from remaining a dead

letter upon the constitutional page of this country.... The events of the last four years ... have changed [a] large class of people ... from a condition of slavery to that of freedom. *The practical question now to be decided is whether they shall be in fact freemen. It is whether they shall have the benefit of this great charter of liberty* given to them by the American people.

Representative Cook of Illinois thought that, without appropriate federal legislation, any "combination of men in [a] neighborhood [could] prevent [a Negro] from having any chance" to enjoy those benefits. To Congressman Cook and others like him, it seemed evident that, with respect to basic civil rights — including the "right to ... purchase, lease, sell, hold, and convey ... property," Congress must provide that "there ... be *no* discrimination" on grounds of race or color.

It thus appears that, when the House passed the Civil Rights Act on March 13, 1866, it did so on the same assumption that had prevailed in the Senate: It too believed that it was approving a comprehensive statute forbidding *all* racial discrimination affecting the basic civil rights enumerated in the Act.

President Andrew Johnson vetoed the Act on March 27, and in the brief congressional debate that followed, his supporters characterized its reach in all-embracing terms. One stressed the fact that § 1 would confer "the right ... to purchase ... real estate ... without any qualification and without any restriction whatever...." Another predicted, as a corollary, that the Act would preclude preferential treatment for white persons in the rental of hotel rooms and in the sale of church pews. Those observations elicited no reply. On April 6 the Senate, and on April 9 the House, overrode the President's veto by the requisite majorities, and the Civil Rights Act of 1866 became law.

In light of the concerns that led Congress to adopt it and the contents of the debates that preceded its passage, it is clear that the Act was designed to do just what its terms suggest: to prohibit all racial discrimination, whether or not under color of law, with respect to the rights enumerated therein — including the right to purchase or lease property.

Nor was the scope of the 1866 Act altered when it was re-enacted in 1870, some two years after the ratification of the Fourteenth Amendment. It is quite true that some members of Congress supported the Fourteenth Amendment "in order to eliminate doubt as to the constitutional validity of the Civil Rights Act as applied to the States." Hurd v. Hodge. But it certainly does not follow that the adoption of the Fourteenth Amendment or the subsequent readoption of the Civil Rights Act were meant somehow to *limit* its application to state action. The legislative history furnishes not the slightest factual basis for any such speculation, and the conditions prevailing in 1870 make it highly implausible. For by that time most, if not all, of the former Confederate States, then under the control of "reconstructed" legislatures, had formally repudiated racial discrimination, and the focus of congressional concern had clearly shifted from hostile statutes to the activities of groups like the Ku Klux Klan, operating wholly outside the law.

Against this background, it would obviously make no sense to assume, without any historical support whatever, that Congress made a silent decision in 1870 to exempt private discrimination from the operation of the Civil Rights Act of 1866. "The cardinal rule is that repeals by implication are not favored." All Congress said in 1870 was that the 1866 law "is hereby re-enacted." That is all Congress meant.

V.

The remaining question is whether Congress has power under the Constitution to do what § 1982 purports to do: to prohibit all racial discrimination, private and public, in the sale and rental of property. Our starting point is the Thirteenth Amendment, for it was pursuant to that constitutional provision that Congress originally enacted what is now § 1982. The Amendment consists of two parts. Section 1 states:

> Neither slavery nor involuntary servitude, except as a punishment for crime whereof the party shall have been duly convicted, shall exist within the United States, or any place subject to their jurisdiction.

Section 2 provides:

> Congress shall have power to enforce this article by appropriate legislation.

As its text reveals, the Thirteenth Amendment "is not a mere prohibition of State laws establishing or upholding slavery, but an absolute declaration that slavery or involuntary servitude shall not exist in any part of the United States." Civil Rights Cases. It has never been doubted, therefore, "that the power vested in Congress to enforce the article by appropriate legislation," includes the power to enact laws "direct and primary, operating upon the acts of individuals, whether sanctioned by State legislation or not."[74]

Thus, the fact that § 1982 operates upon the unofficial acts of private individuals, whether or not sanctioned by state law, presents no constitutional problem. If Congress has power under the Thirteenth Amendment to eradicate conditions that prevent Negroes from buying and renting property because of their race or color, then no federal statute calculated to achieve that objective can be thought to exceed the constitutional power of Congress simply because it reaches beyond state action to regulate the conduct of private individuals. The constitutional question in this case, therefore, comes to this: Does the authority of Congress to enforce the Thirteenth Amendment "by appropriate legislation" include the power to eliminate all racial barriers to the acquisition of real and personal property? We think the answer to that question is plainly yes.

"By its own unaided force and effect," the Thirteenth Amendment "abolished slavery, and established universal freedom." Civil Rights Cases. Whether or not the Amendment *itself* did any more than that—a question not involved in this case—it is at least clear that the Enabling Clause of that Amendment empowered Congress to do much more. For that clause clothed "Congress with power to pass *all laws necessary and proper for abolishing all badges and incidents of slavery in the United States.*" [Civil Rights Cases, 109 U.S. 3.]

Those who opposed passage of the Civil Rights Act of 1866 argued in effect that the Thirteenth Amendment merely authorized Congress to dissolve the legal bond by which the Negro slave was held to his master. Yet many had earlier opposed the Thirteenth Amendment on the very ground that it would give Congress virtually unlimited power to enact laws for the protection of Negroes in every State. And the majority leaders in Congress—who were, after all, the authors of the Thirteenth Amendment—had no doubt that its Enabling Clause contemplated the sort of positive legislation that was embodied in the 1866 Civil Rights Act. Their chief spokesman, Senator Trumbull of Illinois, the Chairman of the Judiciary Committee, had brought the Thirteenth Amendment to the floor of the Senate in 1864. In defending the constitutionality of the 1866 Act, he argued that, if the narrower construction of the Enabling Clause were correct, then

---

74. So it was, for example, that this Court unanimously upheld the power of Congress under the Thirteenth Amendment to make it a crime for one individual to compel another to work in order to discharge a debt. Clyatt v. United States, 197 U.S. 207.

The trumpet of freedom that we have been blowing throughout the land has given an "uncertain sound," and the promised freedom is a delusion. Such was not the intention of Congress, which proposed the constitutional amendment, nor is such the fair meaning of the amendment itself.... I have no doubt that under this provision ... we may destroy all these discriminations in civil rights against the black man; and if we cannot, our constitutional amendment amounts to nothing. It was for that purpose that the second clause of that amendment was adopted, which says that Congress shall have authority, by appropriate legislation, to carry into effect the article prohibiting slavery. Who is to decide what that appropriate legislation is to be? The Congress of the United States; and it is for Congress to adopt such appropriate legislation as it may think proper, so that it be a means to accomplish the end.

Surely Senator Trumbull was right. Surely Congress has the power under the Thirteenth Amendment rationally to determine what are the badges and the incidents of slavery, and the authority to translate that determination into effective legislation. Nor can we say that the determination Congress has made is an irrational one. For this Court recognized long ago that, whatever else they may have encompassed, the badges and incidents of slavery—its "burdens and disabilities"—included restraints upon "those fundamental rights which are the essence of civil freedom, namely, the same right ... to inherit, purchase, lease, sell and convey property, as is enjoyed by white citizens." Civil Rights Cases.[78] Just as the Black Codes, enacted after the Civil War to restrict the free exercise of those rights, were substitutes for the slave system, so the exclusion of Negroes from white communities became a substitute for the Black Codes. And when racial discrimination herds men into ghettos and makes their ability to buy property turn on the color of their skin, then it too is a relic of slavery.

Negro citizens, North and South, who saw in the Thirteenth Amendment a promise of freedom—freedom to "go and come at pleasure" and to "buy and sell when they please"—would be left with "a mere paper guarantee" if Congress were powerless to assure that a dollar in the hands of a Negro will purchase the same thing as a dollar in the hands of a white man. At the very least, the freedom that Congress is empowered to secure under the Thirteenth Amendment includes the freedom to buy whatever a white man can buy, the right to live wherever a white man can live. If Congress cannot say

---

78. The Court did conclude in the Civil Rights Cases that "the act of ... the owner of the inn, the public conveyance or place of amusement, refusing ... accommodation" cannot be "justly regarded as imposing any badge of slavery or servitude upon the applicant." 109 U.S., at 24. "It would be running the slavery argument into the ground," the Court thought, "to make it apply to every act of discrimination which a person may see fit to make as to the guests he will entertain, or as to the people he will take into his coach or cab or car, or admit to his concert or theatre, or deal with in other matters of intercourse or business." Mr. Justice Harlan dissented, expressing the view that "such discrimination practised by corporations and individuals in the exercise of their public or quasi-public functions is a badge of servitude the imposition of which Congress may prevent under its power, by appropriate legislation, to enforce the Thirteenth Amendment."

Whatever the present validity of the position taken by the majority on that issue—a question rendered largely academic by Title II of the Civil Rights Act of 1964 (see Heart of Atlanta Motel v. United States, 379 U.S. 241; Katzenbach v. McClung, 379 U.S. 294)—we note that the entire Court agreed upon at least one proposition: The Thirteenth Amendment authorizes Congress not only to outlaw all forms of slavery and involuntary servitude but also to eradicate the last vestiges and incidents of a society half slave and half free, by securing to all citizens, of every race and color, "the same right to make and enforce contracts, to sue, be parties, give evidence, and to inherit, purchase, lease, sell and convey property, as is enjoyed by white citizens." 109 U.S., at 22. Cf. id., at 35 (dissenting opinion).

that being a free man means at least this much, then the Thirteenth Amendment made a promise the Nation cannot keep.

Representative Wilson of Iowa was the floor manager in the House for the Civil Rights Act of 1866. In urging that Congress had ample authority to pass the pending bill, he recalled the celebrated words of Chief Justice Marshall in McCulloch v. Maryland, 4 Wheat. 316:

> Let the end be legitimate, let it be within the scope of the constitution, and all means which are appropriate, which are plainly adapted to that end, which are not prohibited, but consist with the letter and spirit of the constitution, are constitutional.

"The end is legitimate," the Congressman said, "because it is defined by the Constitution itself. The end is the maintenance of freedom.... A man who enjoys the civil rights mentioned in this bill cannot be reduced to slavery.... This settles the appropriateness of this measure, and that settles its constitutionality."

We agree. The judgment is reversed.

[Justice Douglas's concurring opinion is omitted, as is the dissent of Justice Harlan, in which Justice White concurred.]

42 U.S.C. §§ 1981, 1982, and 1983

§1981. Equal Rights Under The Law

(a) Statement of equal rights*

All persons within the jurisdiction of the United States shall have the same right in every State and Territory to make and enforce contracts, to sue, be parties, give evidence, and to the full and equal benefit of all laws and proceedings for the security of persons and property as is enjoyed by white citizens, and shall be subject to like punishment, pains, penalties, taxes, licenses, and exactions of every kind, and to no other.

(b) Definition [added by the Civil Rights Act of 1991]

For purposes of this section, the term "make and enforce contracts" includes the making, performance, modification, and termination of contracts, and the enjoyment of all benefits, privileges, terms, and conditions of the contractual relationship.

(c) Protection against impairment [added by the Civil Rights Act of 1991]

The rights protected by this section are protected against impairment by nongovernmental discrimination and impairment under color of State law.

§1982. Property rights of citizens

All citizens of the United States shall have the same right, in every State and Territory, as is enjoyed by white citizens thereof to inherit, purchase, lease, sell, hold, and convey real and personal property.

---

* Editor's Note: Until the Civil Rights Act of 1991, §1981 was what is now §1981(a). In the 1991 Act, Congress added subsections (b) and (c) and designated what had been §1981 as §1981(a). Civil Rights Act of 1991, R.S. §1977A, Nov. 21, 1991, P.L. 102-166, Title I, §101, 105 Stat. 1071.

§ 1983. Civil action for deprivation of rights

Every person who, under color of any statute, ordinance, regulation, custom, or usage, of any State or Territory or the District of Columbia, subjects, or causes to be subjected, any citizen of the United States or other person within the jurisdiction thereof to the deprivation of any rights, privileges, or immunities secured by the Constitution and laws, shall be liable to the party injured in an action at law, suit in equity, or other proper proceeding for redress, except that in any action brought against a judicial officer for an act or omission taken in such officer's judicial capacity, injunctive relief shall not be granted unless a declaratory decree was violated or declaratory relief was unavailable. For the purposes of this section, any Act of Congress applicable exclusively to the District of Columbia shall be considered to be a statute of the District of Columbia [P.L. 96-170, 93 Stat. 1284 (1979)].

Title VIII of the Civil Rights Act of 1968

Pub. L. 90-284, 82 Stat. 81 (1968) as amended, 42 U.S.C. §§ 3601–3639 (2008).

§ 3601. Declaration of policy

It is the policy of the United States to provide, within constitutional limitations, for fair housing throughout the United States.

§ 3602. Definitions

As used in this title— ...

(b) "Dwelling" means any building, structure, or portion thereof which is occupied as, or designed or intended for occupancy as, a residence by one or more families, and any vacant land which is offered for sale or lease for the construction or location thereon of any such building, structure, or portion thereof.

(c) "Family" includes a single individual.

(e) "To rent" includes to lease, to sublease, to let and otherwise to grant for a consideration the right to occupy premises not owned by the occupant.

(f) "Discriminatory housing practice" means an act that is unlawful under section 804, 805, 806, or 818....

(h) "Handicap" means, with respect to a person—

  (1) a physical or mental impairment which substantially limits one or more of such person's major life activities,

  (2) a record of having such an impairment, or

  (3) being regarded as having such an impairment, but such term does not include current, illegal use of or addiction to a controlled substance (as defined in section 102 of the Controlled Substances Act (21 U.S.C. 802)).

(i) "Aggrieved person" includes any person who—

  (1) claims to have been injured by a discriminatory housing practice; or

  (2) believe that such person will be injured by a discriminatory housing practice that is about to occur.

(k) "Familial status" means one or more individuals (who have not attained the age of 18 years) being domiciled with—

   (1) a parent or another person having legal custody of such individual or individuals; or

   (2) the designee of such parent or other person having such custody, with the written permission of such parent or other person.

The protections afforded against discrimination on the basis of familial status shall apply to any person who is pregnant or is in the process of securing legal custody of any individual who has not attained the age of 18 years.

§ 3603(b)

(b) Exemptions. Nothing in section 804 [3604] (other than subsection (c)) shall apply to—

   (1) any single-family house sold or rented by an owner: Provided, That such private individual owner does not own more than three such single-family houses at any one time: Provided further, That in the case of the sale of any such single-family house by a private individual owner not residing in such house at the time of such sale or who was not the most recent resident of such house prior to such sale, the exemption granted by this subsection shall apply only with respect to one such sale within any twenty-four month period: Provided further, That such bona fide private individual owner does not own any interest in, nor is there owned or reserved on his behalf, under any express or voluntary agreement, title to or any right to all or a portion of the proceeds from the sale or rental of, more than three such single-family houses at any one time:

   Provided further, That after December 31, 1969, the sale or rental of any such single-family house shall be excepted from the application of this title only if such house is sold or rented

   (A) without the use in any manner of the sales or rental facilities or the sales or rental services of any real estate broker, agent, or salesman, or of such facilities or services of any person in the business of selling or renting dwellings, or of any employee or agent of any such broker, agent, salesman, or person and

   (B) without the publication, posting or mailing, after notice, of any advertisement or written notice in violation of section 804(c) of this title; but nothing in this proviso shall prohibit the use of attorneys, escrow agents, abstractors, title companies, and other such professional assistance as necessary to perfect or transfer the title, or

   (2) rooms or units in dwellings containing living quarters occupied or intended to be occupied by no more than four families living independently of each other, if the owner actually maintains and occupies one of such living quarters as his residence.

§ 3604 Discrimination in the sale or rental of housing and other prohibited practices

As made applicable by section 803 [3603] and except as exempted by sections 803(b) [3603(b)] and 807 [3607], it shall be unlawful—

(a) To refuse to sell or rent after the making of a bona fide offer, or to refuse to negotiate for the sale or rental of, or otherwise make unavailable or deny, a dwelling to any person because of race, color, religion, sex, familial status, or national origin.

(b) To discriminate against any person in the terms, conditions, or privileges of sale or rental of a dwelling, or in the provision of services or facilities in connection therewith, because of race, color, religion, sex, familial status, or national origin.

(c) To make, print, or publish, or cause to be made, printed, or published any notice, statement, or advertisement, with respect to the sale or rental of a dwelling that indicates any preference, limitation, or discrimination based on race, color, religion, sex, handicap, familial status, or national origin, or an intention to make any such preference, limitation, or discrimination.

(d) To represent to any person because of race, color, religion, sex, handicap, familial status, or national origin that any dwelling is not available for inspection, sale, or rental when such dwelling is in fact so available.

(e) For profit, to induce or attempt to induce any person to sell or rent any dwelling by representations regarding the entry or prospective entry into the neighborhood of a person or persons of a particular race, color, religion, sex, handicap, familial status, or national origin.

(f) (1) To discriminate in the sale or rental, or to otherwise make unavailable or deny, a dwelling to any buyer or renter because of a handicap of—

   (A) that buyer or renter,

   (B) a person residing in or intending to reside in that dwelling after it is so sold, rented, or made available; or

   (C) any person associated with that buyer or renter.

   (2) To discriminate against any person in the terms, conditions, or privileges of sale or rental of a dwelling, or in the provision of services or facilities in connection with such dwelling, because of a handicap of—

   (A) that person; or

   (B) a person residing in or intending to reside in that dwelling after it is so sold, rented, or made available; or

   (C) any person associated with that person.

   (3) For purposes of this subsection, discrimination includes—

   (A) a refusal to permit, at the expense of the handicapped person, reasonable modifications of existing premises occupied or to be occupied by such person if such modifications may be necessary to afford such person full enjoyment of the premises except that, in the case of a rental, the landlord may where it is reasonable to do so condition permission for a modification on the renter agreeing to restore the interior of the premises to the condition that existed before the modification, reasonable wear and tear excepted.[;]

   (B) a refusal to make reasonable accommodations in rules, policies, practices, or services, when such accommodations may be necessary to afford such person equal opportunity to use and enjoy a dwelling; or

   (C) in connection with the design and construction of covered multifamily dwellings for first occupancy after the date that is 30 months after the date of enactment of the Fair Housing Amendments Act of 1988 [enacted Sept. 13, 1988], a failure to design and construct those dwellings in such a manner that—

(i)   the public use and common use portions of such dwellings are readily accessible to and usable by handicapped persons;

(ii) all the doors designed to allow passage into and within all premises within such dwellings are sufficiently wide to allow passage by handicapped persons in wheelchairs; and

(iii) all premises within such dwellings contain the following features of adaptive design:

    (I)   an accessible route into and through the dwelling;

    (II)   light switches, electrical outlets, thermostats, and other environmental controls in accessible locations;

    (III) reinforcements in bathroom walls to allow later installation of grab bars; and

    (IV)   usable kitchens and bathrooms such that an individual in a wheelchair can maneuver about the space....

(7) As used in this subsection, the term "covered multifamily dwellings" means—

(A) buildings consisting of 4 or more units if such buildings have one or more elevators; and

(B) ground floor units in other buildings consisting of 4 or more units.

(8) Nothing in this title shall be construed to invalidate or limit any law of a State or political subdivision of a State, or other jurisdiction in which this title shall be effective, that requires dwellings to be designed and constructed in a manner that affords handicapped persons greater access than is required by this title.

(9) Nothing in this subsection requires that a dwelling be made available to an individual whose tenancy would constitute a direct threat to the health or safety of other individuals or whose tenancy would result in substantial physical damage to the property of others.

§ 3605. Discrimination in residential real estate-related transactions

(a) In general. It shall be unlawful for any person or other entity whose business includes engaging in residential real estate-related transactions to discriminate against any person in making available such a transaction, or in the terms or conditions of such a transaction, because of race, color, religion, sex, handicap, familial status, or national origin.

(b) Definition. As used in this section, the term "residential real estate-related transaction" means any of the following:

(1) The making or purchasing of loans or providing other financial assistance—

(A) for purchasing, constructing, improving, repairing, or maintaining a dwelling; or

(B) secured by residential real estate.

(2) The selling, brokering, or appraising of residential real property.

(c) Appraisal exemption. Nothing in this title prohibits a person engaged in the business of furnishing appraisals of real property to take into consideration factors other than race, color, religion, national origin, sex, handicap, or familial status.

§ 3606. Discrimination in the provision of brokerage services

After December 31, 1968, it shall be unlawful to deny any person access to or membership or participation in any multiple-listing service, real estate brokers' organization or other service, organization, or facility relating to the business of selling or renting dwellings, or to discriminate against him in the terms or conditions of such access, membership, or participation, on account of race, color, religion, sex, handicap, familial status, or national origin.

§ 3607. Religious organization or private club exemption

(a) Nothing in this title shall prohibit a religious organization, association, or society, or any nonprofit institution or organization operated, supervised or controlled by or in conjunction with a religious organization, association, or society, from limiting the sale, rental or occupancy of dwellings which it owns or operates for other than a commercial purpose to persons of the same religion, or from giving preference to such persons, unless membership in such religion is restricted on account of race, color, or national origin. Nor shall anything in this subchapter prohibit a private club not in fact open to the public, which as an incident to its primary purpose or purposes provides lodgings which it owns or operates for other than a commercial purpose, from limiting the rental or occupancy of such lodgings to its members or from giving preference to its members.

(b) (1) Nothing in this subchapter limits the applicability of any reasonable local, State, or Federal restrictions regarding the maximum number of occupants permitted to occupy a dwelling. Nor does any provision in this subchapter regarding familial status apply with respect to housing for older persons.

(2) As used in this section, "housing for older persons" means housing—

(A) provided under any State or Federal program that the Secretary determines is specifically designed and operated to assist elderly persons (as defined in the State or Federal program); or

(B) intended for, and solely occupied by, persons 62 years of age or older; or

(C) intended and operated for occupancy by persons 55 years of age or older, and—

(i) at least 80 percent of the occupied units are occupied by at least one person who is 55 years of age or older;

(ii) the housing facility or community publishes and adheres to policies and procedures that demonstrate the intent required under this subparagraph; and

(iii) the housing facility or community complies with rules issued by the Secretary for verification of occupancy, which shall—

(I) provide for verification by reliable surveys and affidavits; and

(II) include examples of the types of policies and procedures relevant to a determination of compliance with the requirement of clause (ii). Such surveys and affidavits shall be admissible in administrative and judicial proceedings for the purposes of such verification.

(3) Housing shall not fail to meet the requirements for housing for older persons by reason of:

    (A) persons residing in such housing as of September 13, 1988, who do not meet the age requirements of subsections (2)(B) or (C): Provided, That new occupants of such housing meet the age requirements of subsections (2)(B) or (C); or

    (B) unoccupied units: Provided, That such units are reserved for occupancy by persons who meet the age requirements of subsections (2)(B) or (C).

(4) Nothing in this subchapter prohibits conduct against a person because such person has been convicted by any court of competent jurisdiction of the illegal manufacture or distribution of a controlled substance as defined in section 802 of Title 21.

(5) (A) A person shall not be held personally liable for monetary damages for a violation of this subchapter if such person reasonably relied, in good faith, on the application of the exemption under this subsection relating to housing for older persons.

    (B) For the purposes of this paragraph, a person may only show good faith reliance on the application of the exemption by showing that—

        (i) such person has no actual knowledge that the facility or community is not, or will not be, eligible for such exemption; and

        (ii) the facility or community has stated formally, in writing, that the facility or community complies with the requirements for such exemption.

§ 3608. Administration....

(d) Cooperation of Secretary and executive departments and agencies in administration of housing and urban development programs and activities to further fair housing purposes

All executive departments and agencies shall administer their programs and activities relating to housing and urban development (including any Federal agency having regulatory or supervisory authority over financial institutions) in a manner affirmatively to further the purposes of this subchapter and shall cooperate with the Secretary to further such purposes.

(e) Functions of Secretary

The Secretary of Housing and Urban Development shall—...

(5) administer the programs and activities relating to housing and urban development in a manner affirmatively to further the policies of this subchapter; and

(6) annually report to the Congress, and make available to the public, data on the race, color, religion, sex, national origin, age, handicap, and family characteristics of persons and households who are applicants for, participants in, or beneficiaries or potential beneficiaries of, programs administered by the Department to the extent such characteristics are within the coverage of the provisions of law and Executive orders referred to in subsection (f) of this section which apply to such programs (and in order to develop the data to be included and made available to the public under this subsection, the Secretary shall, without regard to any other provision of law, collect such information relating to those characteristics as the Secretary determines to be necessary or appropriate).

§ 3610. Administrative enforcement; preliminary matters

(a) Complaints and answers

   (1) (A) (i)   An aggrieved person may, not later than one year after an alleged discriminatory housing practice has occurred or terminated, file a complaint with the Secretary alleging such discriminatory housing practice. The Secretary, on the Secretary's own initiative, may also file such a complaint.

§ 3612. Enforcement by Secretary

(a) Election of judicial determination

When a charge is filed under section 3610 of this title, a complainant, a respondent, or an aggrieved person on whose behalf the complaint was filed, may elect to have the claims asserted in that charge decided in a civil action under subsection (o) of this section in lieu of a hearing under subsection (b) of this section. The election must be made not later than 20 days after the receipt by the electing person of service under section 3610(h) of this title or, in the case of the Secretary, not later than 20 days after such service. The person making such election shall give notice of doing so to the Secretary and to all other complainants and respondents to whom the charge relates.

b)   Administrative law judge hearing in absence of election

If an election is not made under subsection (a) of this section with respect to a charge filed under section 3610 of this title, the Secretary shall provide an opportunity for a hearing on the record with respect to a charge issued under section 3610 of this title. The Secretary shall delegate the conduct of a hearing under this section to an administrative law judge appointed under section 3105 of Title 5. The administrative law judge shall conduct the hearing at a place in the vicinity in which the discriminatory housing practice is alleged to have occurred or to be about to occur.

§ 3613. Enforcement by private persons

(a) Civil action

   (1) (A) An aggrieved person may commence a civil action in an appropriate United States district court or State court not later than 2 years after the occurrence or the termination of an alleged discriminatory housing practice, or the breach of a conciliation agreement entered into under this subchapter, whichever occurs last, to obtain appropriate relief with respect to such discriminatory housing practice or breach. ....

   (2) An aggrieved person may commence a civil action under this subsection whether or not a complaint has been filed under section 3610(a) of this title and without regard to the status of any such complaint, but if the Secretary or a State or local agency has obtained a conciliation agreement with the consent of an aggrieved person, no action may be filed under this subsection by such aggrieved person with respect to the alleged discriminatory housing practice which forms the basis for such complaint except for the purpose of enforcing the terms of such an agreement.

   (3) An aggrieved person may not commence a civil action under this subsection with respect to an alleged discriminatory housing practice which forms the basis of a charge issued by the Secretary if an administrative law judge has commenced a hearing on the record under this subchapter with respect to such charge.

(b) Appointment of attorney by court

Upon application by a person alleging a discriminatory housing practice or a person against whom such a practice is alleged, the court may—

(1) appoint an attorney for such person; or

(2) authorize the commencement or continuation of a civil action under subsection (a) of this section without the payment of fees, costs, or security, if in the opinion of the court such person is financially unable to bear the costs of such action.

(c) Relief which may be granted

(1) In a civil action under subsection (a) of this section, if the court finds that a discriminatory housing practice has occurred or is about to occur, the court may award to the plaintiff actual and punitive damages, and subject to subsection (d) of this section, may grant as relief, as the court deems appropriate, any permanent or temporary injunction, temporary restraining order, or other order (including an order enjoining the defendant from engaging in such practice or ordering such affirmative action as may be appropriate).

(2) In a civil action under subsection (a) of this section, the court, in its discretion, may allow the prevailing party, other than the United States, a reasonable attorney's fee and costs. The United States shall be liable for such fees and costs to the same extent as a private person.

(d) Effect on certain sales, encumbrances, and rentals

Relief granted under this section shall not affect any contract, sale, encumbrance, or lease consummated before the granting of such relief and involving a bona fide purchaser, encumbrancer, or tenant, without actual notice of the filing of a complaint with the Secretary or civil action under this subchapter.

(e) Intervention by Attorney General

Upon timely application, the Attorney General may intervene in such civil action, if the Attorney General certifies that the case is of general public importance. Upon such intervention the Attorney General may obtain such relief as would be available to the Attorney General under section 3614(e) of this title in a civil action to which such section applies.

§ 3614. Enforcement by Attorney General

(a) Pattern or practice cases

Whenever the Attorney General has reasonable cause to believe that any person or group of persons is engaged in a pattern or practice of resistance to the full enjoyment of any of the rights granted by this subchapter, or that any group of persons has been denied any of the rights granted by this subchapter and such denial raises an issue of general public importance, the Attorney General may commence a civil action in any appropriate United States district court.

(b) On referral of discriminatory housing practice or conciliation agreement for enforcement

(1) (A) The Attorney General may commence a civil action in any appropriate United States district court for appropriate relief with respect to a discriminatory housing practice referred to the Attorney General by the Secretary under section 3610(g) of this title.

§ 3615. Effect on State laws

Nothing in this subchapter shall be construed to invalidate or limit any law of a State or political subdivision of a State, or of any other jurisdiction in which this subchapter shall be effective, that grants, guarantees, or protects the same rights as are granted by this subchapter; but any law of a State, a political subdivision, or other such jurisdiction that purports to require or permit any action that would be a discriminatory housing practice under this subchapter shall to that extent be invalid.

§ 3617. Interference, coercion, or intimidation

It shall be unlawful to coerce, intimidate, threaten, or interfere with any person in the exercise of enjoyment of, or on account of his having exercise or enjoyment, or on account of his having aided or encouraged any other person in the exercise or enjoyment of, any right granted or protected by section 3603, 3604, 3605, or 3606 of this title.

§ 3631. Violations; penalties

Whoever, whether or not acting under color of law, by force or threat of force willfully injures, intimidates or interferes with, or attempts to injure, intimidate or interfere with—

(a) any person because of his race, color, religion, sex, handicap (as such term is defined in section 3602 of this title), familial status (as such term is defined in section 3602 of this title), or national origin and because he is or has been selling, purchasing, renting, financing, occupying, or contracting or negotiating for the sale, purchase, rental, financing or occupation of any dwelling, or applying for or participating in any service, organization, or facility relating to the business of selling or renting dwellings; or

(b) any person because he is or has been, or in order to intimidate such person or any other person or any class of persons from—

    (1) participating, without discrimination on account of race, color, religion, sex, handicap (as such term is defined in section 3602 of this title), familial status (as such term is defined in section 3602 of this title), or national origin, in any of the activities, services, organizations or facilities described in subsection (a) of this section; or

    (2) affording another person or class of persons opportunity or protection so to participate; or

(c) any citizen because he is or has been, or in order to discourage such citizen or any other citizen from lawfully aiding or encouraging other persons to participate, without discrimination on account of race, color, religion, sex, handicap (as such term is defined in section 3602 of this title), familial status (as such term is defined in section 3602 of this title), or national origin, in any of the activities, services, organizations or facilities described in subsection (a) of this section, or participating lawfully in speech or peaceful assembly opposing any denial of the opportunity to so participate—

shall be fined under Title 18 or imprisoned not more than one year, or both; and if bodily injury results from the acts committed in violation of this section or if such acts include the use, attempted use, or threatened use of a dangerous weapon, explosives, or fire shall be fined under Title 18 or imprisoned not more than ten years, or both; and if death results from the acts committed in violation of this section or if such acts include kidnapping or an attempt to kidnap, aggravated sexual abuse or an attempt to commit aggravated sexual abuse, or an attempt to kill, shall be fined under Title 18 or imprisoned for any term of years or for life, or both.

Timeline with Respect to Jones v. Mayer and the Enactment of Title VIII

1957	First municipal fair housing legislation enacted—in New York City.
1965	Riots in Watts and elsewhere.
	Chicago Freedom Movement
1966	President Johnson sends fair housing legislation to Congress. House passes bill; filibuster prevents Senate action.
1967	Riots
1967	Administration sends to Congress civil rights legislation that includes fair housing. House passes bill that does not include housing provisions.
Early 1968	On Senate floor, Brooke-Mondale fair housing amendment is replaced by Dirksen amendment, which is the subject of a filibuster.
March 1, 1968	Kerner Commission Report issued.
March 4, 1968	Senate votes cloture on the filibuster blocking the Dirksen amendment.
March 11, 1968	Senate passes fair housing bill (71-20).
April 1–2, 1968	Jones v. Mayer argued in the U.S. Supreme Court.
April 4, 1968	Dr. King assassinated.
	Riots*
April 5, 1968	U.S. Supreme Court holds first conference on *Jones v. Mazer*.

---

* Editor's Note: The riots of 1965–1968 are summarized in Christopher Bonastia, Knocking on the Door: The Federal Government's Attempt to Desegregate the Suburbs 77 (Princeton U. Press 2006):

Beginning in 1965, the nation endured three consecutive summers of deadly urban riots. In August of that year, a police stop of a drunk driver in the Watts section of Los Angeles escalated into six days of chaos that left thirty-four dead, nine hundred injured, and four thousand arrested. Several thousand local police officers were joined by fourteen thousand members of the National Guard to stop the rioting. The following summer, no single riot matched the intensity of Watts, but thirty-eight "civil disorders" across the United States resulted in seven deaths, four hundred injuries, three thousand arrests, and $5 million of property burned or looted. The summer of 1967 saw more violence in the streets, culminating in the July riot in Detroit, which claimed forty-three lives and left hundreds injured, five thousand people without homes, and thirteen hundred buildings destroyed. In April 1968, riots broke out in 138 localities after the murder of the Reverend Martin Luther King, Jr.; forty-three people died. All told, "hostile outbursts" occurred in forty-three cities in 1966, seventy-one cities in 1967, and 106 cities in 1968, with many cities recording more than one outburst.

For a discussion of the contradictory ways in which the riots were used by opponents and proponents of fair housing legislation in 1966 and 1968, see Mara J. Sidney, *Images of Race, Class, and Markets: Rethinking the Origin of U.S. Fair Housing Policy*, 13 J. of Policy Hist. 191 (2001). For conflicting assessments of the importance of President Johnson's role in securing passage of the Fair Housing Act, see Charles M. Lamb, Housing Segregation in Suburban America since 1960: Presi-

April 10, 1968	House accepts Senate amendment (250-172).
April 11, 1968	President Johnson signs the Civil Rights Act of 1968 into law.
June 5, 1968	Robert Kennedy assassinated.
June 17, 1968	Jones v. Mayer decided.

Report of the National Advisory Commission on Civil Disorders
(The Kerner Commission, March 1, 1968), pp. 1–2

Summary of Report

Introduction

The summer of 1967 again brought racial disorders to American cities, and with them shock, fear and bewilderment to the nation.

The worst came during a two-week period in July, first in Newark and then in Detroit. Each set off a chain reaction in neighboring communities.

On July 28, 1967, the President of the United States established the Commission and directed us to answer three basic questions:

What happened?

Why did it happen?

What can be done to prevent it from happening again?

To respond to these questions, we have undertaken a broad range of studies and investigations. We have visited the riot cities; we have heard many witnesses; we have sought the counsel of experts across the country.

This is our basic conclusion: Our nation is moving toward two societies, one black, one white—separate and unequal.

Reaction to last summer's disorders has quickened the movement and deepened the division. Discrimination and segregation have long permeated much of American life; they now threaten the future of every American.

This deepening racial division is not inevitable. The movement apart can be reversed. Choice is still possible. Our principal task is to define that choice and to press for a national resolution.

To pursue our present course will involve the continuing polarization of the American community and, ultimately, the destruction of basic democratic values.

The alternative is not blind repression or capitulation to lawlessness. It is the realization of common opportunities for all within a single society.

This alternative will require a commitment to national action—compassionate, massive and sustained, backed by resources of the most powerful and the richest nation on this earth. From every American it will require new attitudes, new understanding, and, above all, new will.

---

dential and Judicial Politics (Cambridge U. Press 2005) at 51–54 (concluding that "LBJ's influence was the single most important catalyst behind the initiation and evolution of the Fair Housing Act," but noting Professor Gary Orfield's view that President Johnson "played no significant role in the process and the civil rights groups never mobilized mass support. It was basically a battle within the Senate, a battle to win the crucial Republican votes for cloture.").

The vital needs of the nation must be met; hard choices must be made, and, if necessary, new taxes enacted.

Violence cannot build a better society. Disruption and disorder nourish repression, not justice. They strike at the freedom of every citizen. The community cannot—it will not—tolerate coercion and mob rule.

Violence and destruction must be ended—in the streets of the ghetto, and in the lives of people.

Segregation and poverty have created in the racial ghetto a destructive environment totally unknown to most white Americans.

What white Americans have never fully understood—but what the Negro can never forget—is that white society is deeply implicated in the ghetto. White institutions created it, white institutions maintain it, and white society condone it.

It is time now to turn with all the purpose at our command to the major unfinished business of this nation. It is time to adopt strategies for action that will produce quick and visible progress. It is time to make good the promises of American democracy to all citizens—urban and rural, white and black, Spanish-surname, American Indian, and every minority group.

Our recommendations embrace three basic principles:

- To mount programs on a scale equal to the dimension of the problems;
- To aim these programs for high impact in the immediate future in order to close the gap between promise and performance;
- To undertake new initiatives and experiments that can change the system of failure and frustration that now dominates the ghetto and weaken our society.

These programs will require unprecedented levels of funding and performance, but they neither probe deeper nor demand more than the problems which called them forth. There can be no higher priority for national action and no higher claim on the nation's conscience.

We issue this Report now, four months before the date called for by the President. Much remains that can be learned. Continued study is essential.

As Commissioners we have worked together with a sense of the greatest urgency and have sought to compose whatever differences exist among us. Some differences remain. But the gravity of the problem and the pressing need for action are too clear to allow further delay in the issuance of this Report.

Rev. Dr. Martin Luther King, Jr., *I See the Promised Land*, in A Testament of Hope: The Essential Writings of Martin Luther King, Jr.
(James M. Washington, ed., Harper 1990), pp. 279–286

Thank you very kindly, my friends. As I listened to Ralph Abernathy in his eloquent and generous introduction and then thought about myself, I wondered who he was talking about. It's always good to have your closest friend and associate say something good about you. And Ralph is the best friend that I have in the world.

I'm delighted to see each of you here tonight in spite of a storm warning. You reveal that you are determined to go on anyhow. Something is happening in Memphis, something is happening in our world.

As you know, if I were standing at the beginning of time, with the possibility of general and panoramic view of the whole human history up to now, and the Almighty said to me, "Martin Luther King, which age would you like to live in?"—I would take my mental flight by Egypt through, or rather across the Red Sea, through the wilderness on toward the promised land. And in spite of its magnificence, I wouldn't stop there. I would move on by Greece, and take my mind to Mount Olympus. And I would see Plato, Aristotle, Socrates, Euripides and Aristophanes assembled around the Parthenon as they discussed the great and eternal issues of reality.

But I wouldn't stop there. I would go on, even to the great heyday of the Roman Empire. And I would see developments around there through various emperors and leaders. But I wouldn't stop there. I would even come up to the day of the Renaissance, and get a quick picture of all that the Renaissance did for the cultural and esthetic life of man. But I wouldn't stop there. I would even go by the way that the man for whom I'm named had his habitat. And I would watch Martin Luther as he tacked his ninety-five theses on the door at the church in Wittenberg.

But I wouldn't stop there. I would come on up even to 1863, and watch a vacillating president by the name of Abraham Lincoln finally come to the conclusion that he had to sign the Emancipation Proclamation. But I wouldn't stop there. I would even come up to the early thirties, and see a man grappling with the problems of the bankruptcy of his nation. And come with an eloquent cry that we have nothing to fear but fear itself.

But I wouldn't stop there. Strangely enough, I would turn to the Almighty, and say, "If you allow me to live just a few years in the second half of the twentieth century, I will be happy." Now that's a strange statement to make, because the world is all messed up. The nation is sick. Trouble is in the land. Confusion all around. That's a strange statement. But I know, somehow, that only when it is dark enough, can you see the stars. And I see God working in this period of the twentieth century in a way that men, in some strange way, are responding—something is happening in our world. The masses of people are rising up. And wherever they are assembled today, whether they are in Johannesburg, South Africa; Nairobi, Kenya; Accra, Ghana; New York City; Atlanta, Georgia; Jackson, Mississippi; or Memphis, Tennessee—the cry is always the same—"We want to be free."

And another reason that I'm happy to live in this period is that we have been forced to a point where we're going to have to grapple with the problems that men have been trying grapple with through history, but the demands didn't force them to do it. Survival demands that we grapple with them. Men, for years now, have been talking about war and peace. But now, no longer can they just talk about it. It is no longer a choice between violence and nonviolence in this world; it's nonviolence or nonexistence.

That is where we are today. And also in the human rights revolution, if something isn't done, and in a hurry, to bring the colored peoples of the world out of their long years of poverty, their long years of hurt and neglect, the whole world is doomed. Now, I'm just happy that God has allowed me to live in this period, to see what is unfolding. And I'm happy that he's allowed me to be in Memphis.

I can remember, I can remember when Negroes were just going around as Ralph has said, so often, scratching where they didn't itch, and laughing when they were not tickled. But that day is all over. We mean business now, and we are determined to gain our rightful place in God's world.

And that's all this whole thing is about. We aren't engaged in any negative protest and in any negative arguments with anybody. We are saying that we are determined to be men. We are determined to be people. We are saying that we are God's children. And that we don't have to live like we are forced to live.

Now, what does all of this mean in this great period of history? It means that we've got to stay together. We've got to stay together and maintain unity. You know, whenever Pharaoh wanted to prolong the period of slavery in Egypt, he had a favorite, favorite formula for doing it, What was that? He kept the slaves fighting among themselves. But whenever the slaves get together, something happens in Pharaoh's court, and he cannot hold the slaves in slavery. When the slaves get together, that's the beginning of getting out of slavery. Now let us maintain unity.

Secondly, let us keep the issues where they are. The issue is injustice. The issue is the refusal of Memphis to be fair and honest in its dealings with its public servants, who happen to be sanitation workers. Now, we've got to keep attention on that. That's always the problem with a little violence. You know what happened the other day, and the press dealt only with the window-breaking. I read the articles. They very seldom got around to mentioning the fact that one thousand, three hundred sanitation workers were on strike, and that Memphis is not being fair to them, and that Mayor Loeb is in dire need of a doctor. They didn't get around to that.

Now we're going to march again, and we've got to march again, in order to put the issue where it is supposed to be. And force everybody to see that there are thirteen hundred of God's children here suffering, sometimes going hungry, going through dark and dreary nights wondering how this thing is going to come out. For when people get caught up with that which is right and they are willing to sacrifice for it, there is no stopping point short of victory.

We aren't going to let any mace stop us. We are masters in our nonviolent movement in disarming police forces; they don't know what to do. I've seen them so often. I remember in Birmingham, Alabama, when we were in that majestic struggle there we would move out of the 16th Street Baptist Church day after day; by the hundreds we would move out. And Bull Connor would tell them to send the dogs forth and they did come; but we just went before the dogs singing, "Ain't gonna let nobody turn me around." Bull Connor next would say, "Turn the fire hoses on." And as I said to you the other night, Bull Connor didn't know history. He knew a kind of physics that somehow didn't relate to the transphysics that we knew about. And that was the fact that there was a certain kind of fire that no water could put out. And we went before the fire hoses; we had known water. If we were Baptist or some other denomination, we had been immersed. If we were Methodist, and some others, we had been sprinkled, but we knew water.

That couldn't stop us. And we just went on before the dogs and we would look at them; and we'd go on before the water hoses and we would look at it, and we'd just go on singing "Over my head I see freedom in the air." And then we would be thrown in the paddy wagons, and sometimes we were stacked in there like sardines in a can. And they would throw us in, and old Bull would say, "Take them off," and they did; and we would just go in the paddy wagon singing, "We Shall Overcome." And every now and then we'd get in the jail, and we'd see the jailers looking through the windows being moved by our prayers, and being moved by our words and our songs. And there was a power there which Bull Connor couldn't adjust to; and so we ended up transforming Bull into a steer, and we won our struggle in Birmingham.

Now we've got to go on in Memphis just like that. I call upon you to be with us Monday. Now about injunctions: We have an injunction and we're going into court tomorrow morning to fight this illegal, unconstitutional injunction. All we say to America is, "Be true to what you said on paper." If I lived in China or even Russia, or any totalitarian country, maybe I could understand the denial of certain basic First Amendment privileges, because they hadn't committed themselves to that over there. But somewhere I read of the freedom of assembly. Somewhere I read of the freedom of speech. Somewhere I read of the freedom of the press. Somewhere I read that the greatness of America is the right to protest for right. And so just as I say, we aren't going to let any injunction turn us around. We are going on.

We need all of you. And you know what's beautiful to me, is to see all of these ministers of the Gospel. It's a marvelous picture. Who is it that is supposed to articulate the longings and aspirations of the people more than the preacher? Somehow the preacher must be an Amos, and say, "Let justice roll down like waters and righteousness like a mighty stream." Somehow, the preacher must say with Jesus, "The spirit of the Lord is upon me, because he hath anointed me to deal with the problems of the poor."

And I want to commend the preachers, under the leadership of these noble men: James Lawson, one who has been in this struggle for many years; he's been to jail for struggling; but he's still going on, fighting for the rights of his people. Rev. Ralph Jackson, Billy Kiles; I could just go right on down the list, but time will not permit. But I want to thank them all. And I want you to thank them, because so often, preachers aren't concerned about anything but themselves. And I'm always happy to see a relevant ministry.

It's all right to talk about "long white robes over yonder," in all of its symbolism. But ultimately people want some suits and dresses and shoes to wear down here. It's all right to talk about "streets flowing with milk and honey," but God has commanded us to be concerned about the slums down here, and his children who can't eat three square meals a day. It's all right to talk about the new Jerusalem, but one day, God's preacher must talk about the New York, the new Atlanta, the new Philadelphia, the new Los Angeles, the new Memphis, Tennessee. This is what we have to do.

Now the other thing we'll have to do is this: Always anchor our external direct actions with the power of economic withdrawal. Now, we are poor people, individually, we are poor when you compare us with white society in America. We are poor. Never stop and forget that collectively, that means all of us together, collectively we are richer than all the nations in the world, with the exception of nine. Did you ever think about that? After you leave the United States, Soviet Russia, Great Britain, West Germany, France, and I could name the others, the Negro collectively is richer than most nations of the world. We have an annual income of more than thirty billion dollars a year, which is more than all of the exports of the United States, and more than the national budget of Canada. Did you know that? That's power right there, if we know how to pool it.

We don't have to argue with anybody. We don't have to curse and go around acting bad with our words. We don't need any bricks and bottles, we don't need any Molotov cocktails, we just need to go around to these stores, and to these massive industries in our country, and say, "God sent us by here, to say to you that you're not treating his children right. And we've come by here to ask you to make the first item on your agenda—fair treatment, where God's children are concerned. Now, if you are not prepared to do that, we do have an agenda that we must follow. And our agenda calls for withdrawing economic support from you."

And so, as a result of this, we are asking you tonight, to go out and tell your neighbors not to buy Coca-Cola in Memphis. Go by and tell them not to buy Sealtest milk. Tell them not to buy—what is the other bread?—Wonder Bread. And what is the other bread company, Jesse? Tell them not to buy Hart's bread. As Jesse Jackson had said, up to now, only the garbage men have been feeling pain; now we must kind of redistribute the pain. We are choosing these companies because they haven't been fair in their hiring policies; and we are choosing them because they can begin the process of saying, they are going to support the needs and the rights of these men who are on strike. And then they can move on downtown and tell Major Loeb to do what is right.

But not only that, we've got to strengthen black institutions. I call upon you to take your money out of the banks downtown and deposit your money in Tri-State Bank—we want a "bank-in" movement in Memphis. So go by the savings and loan association. I'm not asking you something we don't do ourselves at SCLC. Judge Hooks and others will tell you that we have an account here in the saving and loan association from the Southern Christian Leadership Conference. We're just telling you to follow what we're doing. Put your money there. You have six or seven black insurance companies in Memphis. Take out your insurance there. We want to have an "insurance-in."

Now these are some practical things we can do. We begin the process of building a greater economic base. And at the same time, we are putting pressure where it really hurts. I ask you to follow through here.

Now, let me say as I move to my conclusion that we've got to give ourselves to this struggle until the end. Nothing would be more tragic than to stop at this point, in Memphis. We've got to see it through. And when we have our march, you need to be there. Be concerned about your brother. You may not be on strike. But either we go together, or we go down together.

Let us develop a kind of dangerous unselfishness. One day a man came to Jesus; and he wanted to raise some questions about some vital matters in life. At points, he wanted to trick Jesus, and show him off base. Now that question could have easily ended up in a philosophical and theological debate. But Jesus immediately pulled that question from mid-air, and placed it on a dangerous curve between Jerusalem and Jericho. And he talked about a certain man, who fell among thieves. You remember that a Levite and a priest passed by on the other side. They didn't stop to help him. And finally a man of another race came by. He got down from his beast, decided not be compassionate by proxy. But with him, administered first aid, and helped the man in need. Jesus ended up saying, this was the good man, this was the great man, because he had the capacity to project the "I" into the "thou," and to be concerned about his brother. Now you know, we use our imagination a great deal to try to determine why the priest and the Levite didn't stop. At times we say they were busy going to church meetings—an ecclesiastical gathering—and they had to get on down to Jerusalem so they wouldn't be late for their meeting. At other times we would speculate that there was a religious law that "One who was engaged in religious ceremonials was not to touch a human body twenty-four hours before the ceremony." And every now and then we begin to wonder whether maybe they were not going down to Jerusalem, or down to Jericho, rather to organize a "Jericho Road Improvement Association." That's a possibility. Maybe they felt that it was better to deal with the problem from the causual root, rather than to get bogged down with an individual effort.

But I'm going to tell you what my imagination tells me. It's possible that these men were afraid. You see, the Jericho road is a dangerous road. I remember when Mrs. King and I were first in Jerusalem. We rented a car and drove to Jerusalem, which is about 1200 miles, or rather 1200 feet above sea level. And by the time you get down to Jericho, fifteen or twenty minutes later, you're about 2200 feet below sea level. That's a dangerous road. In the days of Jesus it came to be known as the "Bloody Pass." And you know, it's possible that the priest and the Levite looked over that man on the ground and wondered if the robbers were still around. Or it's possible that they felt that the man on the ground was merely faking. And he was acting like he had been robbed and hurt, in order to seize them over there, lure them there for quick and easy seizure. And so the first question that the Levite asked was, "If I stop to help this man, what will happen to me?" But then the Good Samaritan came by. And he reversed the question: "If I do not stop to help this man, what will happen to him?"

That's the question before you tonight. Not, "If I stop to help the sanitation workers, what will happen to all of the hours that I usually spend in my office every day and every week as a pastor?" The question is not, "If I stop to help this man in need, what will happen to me?" "If I do not stop to help the sanitation workers, what will happen to them?" That's the question.

Let us rise up tonight with a greater readiness. Let us stand with a greater determination. And let us move on in these powerful days, these days of challenge to make America what it ought to be. We have an opportunity to make America a better nation. And I want to thank God, once more, for allowing me to be here with you.

You know, several years ago, I was in New York City autographing the first book that I had written. And while sitting there autographing books, a demented black woman came up. The only question I heard from her was, "Are you Martin Luther King?"

And I was looking down writing, and said yes. And the next minute I felt something beating on my chest. Before I knew it I had been stabbed by this demented woman. I was rushed to Harlem Hospital. It was a dark Saturday afternoon. And that blade had gone through, and the X-rays revealed that the tip of the blade was on the edge of my aorta, the main artery. And once that's punctured you drown in your own blood— that's the end of you.

It came out in the *New York Times*, the next morning, that if I had sneezed, I would have died. Well, about four days later, they allowed me, after the operation, after my chest had been opened, and the blade had been taken out, to move around in the wheel chair in the hospital. They allowed me to read some of the mail that came in, and from all over the states, and the world, kind letters came in. I read a few, but one of them I will never forget. I had received one from the President and the Vice-President. I've forgotten what those telegrams said. I'd received a visit and a letter from the Governor of New York, but I've forgotten what the letter said. But there was another letter that came from a little girl, a young girl who was a student at the White Plains High School. And I looked at that letter, and I'll never forget it. It said simply, "Dear Dr. King: I am a ninth-grade student at the White Plains High School." She said, "While it should not matter, I would like to mention that I am a white girl. I read in the paper of your misfortune, and of your suffering. And I read that if you had sneezed, you would have died. And I'm simply writing you to say that I'm so happy that you didn't sneeze."

And I want to say tonight, I want to say that I am happy I didn't sneeze. Because if I had sneezed, I wouldn't have been around here in 1960, when students all over the South started sitting-in at lunch counters. And I knew that as they were sitting in, they were really standing up for the best in the American dream. And taking the whole nation back to those great walls of democracy which were dug deep by the Founding Fathers in the Declaration of Independence and the Constitution. If I had sneezed, I wouldn't have been around in 1962, when Negroes in Albany, Georgia, decided to straighten their backs up. And whenever men and women straighten their backs up, they are going somewhere, because a man can't ride your back unless it is bent. If I had sneezed, I wouldn't have been here in 1963, when the black people of Birmingham, Alabama, aroused the conscience of this nation, and brought into being the Civil Rights Bill. If I had sneezed, I wouldn't have had a chance later that year, in August, to try to tell America about a dream that I had had. If I had sneezed, I wouldn't have been down in Selma, Alabama, to see the great movement there. If I had sneezed, I wouldn't have been in Memphis to see a community rally around those brothers and sisters who are suffering. I'm so happy that I didn't sneeze.

And they were telling me, now it doesn't matter now. It really doesn't matter what happens now. I left Atlanta this morning, and as we got started on the plane, there were six of us, the pilot said over the public address system, "We are so sorry for the delay, but we have Dr. Martin Luther King on the plane. And to be sure that all of the bags were checked, and to be sure that nothing would be wrong with the plane, we had to check out everything carefully. And we've had the plane protected and guarded all night."

And then I got into Memphis. And some began to say the threats, or talk about the threats that were out there. What would happen to me from some of our sick white brothers?

Well, I don't know what will happen now. We've got some difficult days ahead. But it doesn't matter with me now. Because I've been to the mountaintop. And I don't mind. Like anybody, I would like to live a long life. Longevity has its place. But I'm not concerned about that now. I just want to do God's will. And He's allowed me to go up to the mountain. And I've looked over. And I've seen the promised land. I may not get there with you. But I want you to know tonight, that we, as a people will get to the promised land. And I'm happy, tonight. I'm not worried about anything. I'm not fearing any man. Mine eyes have seen the glory of the coming of the Lord.

Gwendolyn Brooks, *The Ballad of Rudolph Reed*, in Blacks
(Third World Press 1991)

Rudolph Reed was oaken.
His wife was oaken too.
And his two good girls and his good little man
Oakened as they grew.

"I am not hungry for berries.
I am not hungry for bread.
But hungry hungry for a house
Where at night a man in bed

"May never hear the plaster
Stir as if in pain.
May never hear the roaches
Falling like fat rain.

"Where never wife and children need
Go blinking through the gloom.
Where every room of many rooms
Will be full of room.

"Oh my home may have its east or west
Or north or south behind it.
All I know is I shall know it,
And fight for it when I find it."

It was in a street of bitter white
That he made his application.
For Rudolph Reed was oakener
Than others in the nation.

The agent's steep and steady stare
Corroded to a grin.
Why, you black old, tough old hell of a man,
Move your family in!

Nary a grin grinned Rudolph Reed,
Nary a curse cursed he,
But moved in his House. With his dark little wife,
And his dark little children three.

A neighbor would *look*, with a yawning eye
That squeezed into a slit.
But the Rudolph Reeds and the children three
Were too joyous to notice it.

For were they not firm in a home of their own
With windows everywhere
And a beautiful banistered stair
And a front yard for flowers and a back for grass?

The first night, a rock, big as two fists.
The second, a rock big as three.
But nary a curse cursed Rudolph Reed.
(Though oaken as man could be.)

The third night, a silvery ring of glass.
Patience ached to endure,
But he looked, and lo! small Mabel's blood
Was staining her gaze so pure.

Then up did rise our Rudolph Reed
And pressed the hand of his wife,
And went to the door with a thirty-four
And a beastly butcher knife.

He ran like a mad thing into the night
And the words in his mouth were stinking.
By the time he had hurt his first white man
He was no longer thinking.

By the time he had hurt his fourth white man
Rudolph Reed was dead.
His neighbors gathered and kicked his corpse.
"Nigger—" his neighbors said.

Small Mabel whimpered all night long,
For calling herself the cause.
Her oak-eyed mother did no thing
But change the bloody gauze.

Toi Derricotte, THE BLACK NOTEBOOKS: AN INTERIOR JOURNEY
(W.W. Norton & Co. 1997), pp. 31–49

On Sunday afternoons Bruce and I would drive through the small bedroom communities close to New York, blocks and blocks of stately colonials and overpowering elms, and I would imagine a kind of life, a kind of happiness—a light on in an upstairs bedroom, a tricycle turned over in a drive, a swing on a front porch barely moving, as if it were just waiting for someone to come and sit down. I began to think that that was happiness. The happiness of expectancy. Everything that had to be prepared had been prepared, and now all that was needed was for the human heart to begin beating. I wanted to be in those houses, to be those people. I wanted to go all the way, as a pilot will make up his mind on a dangerous mission that there is no turning back. There were all kinds of practical reasons why we chose Upper Montclair, but, looking back, it was love that drove me through the streets of that unsuspecting city. Love.

September

Last month, seeing an advertisement in the newspaper for a contemporary in our price range, I called an agent. "I shouldn't be telling you about this one on the phone," she said, "but there is a house I think you would be interested in. It's on an estate on Highland Avenue, and the people are very particular about who buys it."

My heart shriveled. Should I find out whom they are "particular" not to have? Should I let her think I'm white and go without Bruce to see it? When I take Bruce, we are shown entirely different neighborhoods, all-black or integrated.

I decided to act dumb. "Oh, really? That seems strange. Why isn't the house multiple-listed? What are they so careful about?"

"Well, you know, some people like to do it this way. Let me have your phone number; I'll call you back." But she never called back. So I wonder if our name is known— "That black couple looking for a house in town and the wife looks white."

This week I called another agent and played a game. "We'd like to look at the house you're describing, but we'd also like to see a house we heard about on an estate."

"Oh," she gargled, "you mean, ah, the one that came on the market this morning?"

"I don't know when it came on the market, but I *do* know it's on Highland Ave."

"I don't know if you'd be interested in that. The rooms are small, it's overgrown, overpriced, no view." She went on and on. I was still interested.

"Well," she finally agreed, "I'll see if I can get the owners on the phone and we can go and see it."

When Bruce and I got to her office, of course she hadn't gotten hold of them. "The man works at night. No one is at home."

"I'd still like to see it. Drive by on the way to the other house." She got lost! Imagine a real estate dealer getting lost in her own town!

"That's all right," I reassured her. "We can go past it on the way back."

The house she showed us, in the integrated part of town, was expensive and run-down. On the way to the "particular" house, once again she got lost. We had to direct her. Bruce said, "There it is! There it is!" It was all lit up. And she kept driving. Finally a half mile down the road (I was waiting to see if she would ever stop), I said, "Why didn't you stop at the house?"

"Oh," she stammered, "did we pass it?"

"My husband pointed it out to you."

"It's so dark, I can't find it. It's too dark tonight. I think we should come back to-morrow."

"I don't mind the dark."

"You mean you want me to turn around and go *back*?" she gasped.

When we got to the house, we sat in the car while she "checked." We could see in the front window. Two old ladies were reading the paper. She came back and said they didn't want visitors.

I felt a hopelessness descend. No matter how clever and determined I am, they can always find a way to stop me. Perhaps I should call a lawyer, sue.... But it would proba-bly take forever, and I'd need a courage and commitment that I don't feel. I decide to look for a house in another community, one where we are not yet known, and this time I'll go to the real estate agent's alone.

October

It's the overriding reality I must get through. Each time I drive down the streets and see only whites, each time I notice no blacks in the local supermarket or walking on the streets, I think, *I'm not supposed to be here.* When I go into real estate agents' offices, I put on a mask. At first they hope you are in for a quick sell. They show you houses they want to get rid of. But if you stick around, and if you are the "right kind," they show you ones just newly listed, and sometimes not even on the market. There are neighborhoods that even most white people are not supposed to be in.

I make myself likable, optimistic. I am married, a woman who belongs to a man. Sometimes I reveal I am Catholic, if it might add a feeling of connection. It is not en-tirely that I am acting. I am myself but slightly strained, like you might strain slightly in order to hear something whispered.

Yesterday an agent took me into the most lily-white neighborhood imaginable, took me right into the spotless kitchen, the dishwasher rumbling, full of the children's dishes. I opened the closets as if I were a thief, as if I were filthying them, as if I believe about myself what they believe: that I'm "passing," that my silence is a crime.

The first woman I knew about who "passed" was the bronze-haired daughter of in-surance money, one of the wealthiest black families in the United States. I remember my mother telling me stories of her white roadster, how she wrote plays and opened a theater. She had directed several of the plays in which my mother and father had acted. She went to New York to "make it" and was published in *The New York Times.* I was seven when my father went down to meet the midnight train that brought her home: people said she had confessed to her rich fiancé that she was black and he had jilted her. They dressed her in a long bronze dress, a darkened tone of her long auburn hair. She looked like Sleeping Beauty in a casket made especially for her with a glass top.

My mother told me how, when she was young, her mother used to get great pleasure when she would seat her daughter in the white part of the train and then depart, as if she were her servant. She said her mother would stand alongside the train and wave good-bye with a smile on her face, like a kid who has gotten away with the cookies. And my fa-ther told how, during the Detroit riots of 1943, when black men were being pulled off the buses and beaten to death, he used to walk down East Grand Boulevard as a dare.

Of course, we are never caught; it is absolutely inconceivable that we could go unrecognized, that we are that much like them. In fact, we are the same.

When Bruce and I first got married, I had been looking for an apartment for months. Finally, I found a building, in a nice neighborhood with a playground nearby, and a school that was integrated. I rang the bell and was relieved when the supervisor who came to the door was black. I loved the apartment. Then I became terrified. Should I tell *him* we're black? Would that make my chances of getting the apartment greater? I wondered if he would be glad to have another black family in the building, or if maybe his job was dependent on his keeping us out. I decided to be silent, to take the chance that he liked me.

When I left, sailing over the George Washington Bridge, I had my first panic attack. I thought I might drive my car right over the edge. I felt so high up there, so disconnected, so completely at my own mercy. Some part of me doesn't give a fuck about boundaries—in fact, sees the boundaries and is determined to dance over them no matter what the consequences are. I am so precarious, strung out between two precipices, that even when I get to the other side, I am still not down, still not so low I can't harm myself.

I could hardly control my car, my heart pounding, my hands sweaty on the wheel. I had to pull off the West Side Highway as soon as I could, and I went into the first place I could find, a meat-packing house. The kind white man let me use the phone to call Bruce before he took me in a big meat truck to the nearest hospital. The doctor said it was anxiety, and I should just go home and rest. For days, I was afraid to come out of my house, and even now, though I push myself to do it, every time I go over a high place, or am in a strange territory, I fear I will lose control, that something horrible and destructive will come out of me.

Each night Bruce and I don't talk about it, as if there were no cost to what I'm doing, or as if whatever the cost is I've got to pay.

March

I had told the real estate dealers that Bruce was away on a long trip—I had looked at over eighty houses!—and that I had to make a decision by myself. At night, under cover of darkness, we'd go back and circle the houses and I'd describe the insides.

In Maplewood, a nearby town in which I had looked, the real estate agent took us to the house I had seen alone the day before—a dark, sturdy Tudor—without seeming to bat an eye. However, when we got back to his office and were ready to close the deal, the head broker had intervened. "That house has been sold," he said.

Our agent looked shocked. "No it hasn't," he said stupidly. "I just checked the listing before we went out!"

"Yes it has." the other insisted.

We had called a lawyer who specializes in civil rights cases and he had not been encouraging. "These kinds of cases are hard to prove and your money will be tied up for months."

We finally decided on Upper Montclair. The houses in Essex County are comparatively cheaper than the house in Bergen County, and even though the neighborhoods aren't integrated, the schools are, since busing is in effect. Many afternoons, instead of asking—not wanting to arouse the suspicions of the real estate agents—I would sit outside the neighborhood schools at lunch hour like a pederast, counting the number of black faces. Though sometimes I'd be brave and ask. I didn't only want information; I wanted to commit a small revolutionary act—to leave the impression that the world is full of liberal white parents who want change.

When Bruce finally saw the house in Upper Montclair, he said, "It's all right. I liked the Tudor much better." I was furious. Didn't he know how hard I had tried! "Next time *you* look at eighty houses," I had burst out on the way home. At each point, even as we accomplished our goals, we didn't feel proud of ourselves and confirmed in our powers, we felt divided, muted, and out of control.

The real estate dealer in Montclair had been flustered when Bruce showed up at her office. I had hoped that, maybe, since I had purposely let it slip he is a vice president at the bank and has hundreds of people working for him (Bruce has the highest position of any black person at the bank), she would decide, as many whites have, that a person with his credentials, whose skin and hair is, in the least, indeterminate, must be something else, Spanish or Arab. But when we signed the contract, she had insisted she and her husband pick up the deposit at our apartment, though it was a half-hour drive. They want to check us out, I thought. I cleaned all day, fixed hors d'oeuvres. I opened a bottle of champagne and we toasted each other, as if we were friends.

During the months we waited for the closing, neither one of went to the house. We didn't want to rock the boat. Several times minor problems arose, and I couldn't decide whether to get very involved, to bother people, or stay out of the way.

The week before we moved in, I made a dozen trips with lamps, paintings, books. Emptied of the lady's furniture, the walls showed hand prints, rubs; the carpet was drab, muddied, there was a dinginess to the light. Had they gotten rid of a loser? A few days after, Bruce warned: "Be careful, they know more about us than you think!" A neighbor had come up to while he was out shoveling snow. "I hear you're a V.P. at the bank and a Michigan man!" Bruce hadn't told *anybody* where he worked or went to school!

Last week the people across the street gave us a cocktail party. I felt grateful, but out of place. Would I break a glass or say something unforgivable? I couldn't get over the feeling that I had to prove myself different from what I was sure almost all of them took for granted—that Bruce and I didn't know anything about wine or art and had never seen an Oriental carpet in our lives—yet at the same time, I had to be absolutely "myself," *that* was the only way I could earn their respect. I told one woman she had the most beautiful violet eyes—I found out later that she was the wife of the president of one of the largest New York brokerage houses—and she looked shocked. She avoided me the rest of the night. Was it wrong to confess love as well as hatred? Suddenly, right in the middle of urgent desire to belong, came my hatred of them and everything they stood for.

Bruce and I went our separate ways, like those black people who have learned not to sit together in the lunchroom. Sometimes I looked at him from across the room and thought, he looks so uncomfortable. It comes out in the way he spills his drink or drops some dip on his tie and then calls attention to himself: "I spilled something," he says, looking down and dabbing it with his handkerchief.

I know that way we stumble, trying so hard, how something gets blocked so that we either become hard and inflexible or so muted we can't be heard, or maybe something gets out of control, so that no matter what we do, for how long, for countless years, finally we make some mistake, something that we can't make up for, and we don't know why, can't stop ourselves, and, in the end, we are more sorry for our mistake than the ones it hurts.

April

Montclair is divided into two parts, Upper and—though not referred to as such on maps—so-called Lower. A neighbor said that a hundred years ago Upper Montclair was where the rich people lived and Lower Montclair was where the people lived who worked for them. There are lots of mansion and estates on that side of town, but even so, in a way, an invisible map has grown into the nerves and bones of the people, a reference not only to geography but to the importance of the self, who you are in relation to the other. The map is pressed into the feet of the children. The dividing line is Watchung Avenue—you're on one side or the other.

The kids are mixed in schools because of busing, but lots of white families, and some black, still try to stop it. Just because the kids are in school together doesn't mean things are better. Things seem to be worse. There is a great deal of pain when the dividing line is broken. It is like breaking the self in two. We have nothing to heal it, and no medicine to relieve the pain. We think, Break it and it will heal itself. We just don't know whether it will grow together in such a crooked way that it will never be able to be used.

We know so little—almost nothing about how the cells become part of the body—whether to root the sickness out with surgery, whether that will destroy too many healthy parts, or whether to take tiny pills, every day, for the rest of our lives, to admit we have a chronic disease that we must attend to.

I ran into a woman at the vet's today, a white woman married to a black man whose son is very, very dark. We got into a heavy conversation about Montclair, and when I told her I was black, she couldn't believe it. She wanted to know what color my parents were. I think she feels sad that her son is so dark. She said she and her husband had had a daughter, but they "lost" her (a miscarriage?). She never saw her. I guess, looking at me, she wondered what color her daughter would have been.

This woman wanted her son to have the best education, so she put him in a private school in Montclair. But there was so much prejudice, she took him out. He's now in one of the lowest sections in public school. She says he's very bright, but he told her he liked being the smartest kid in the group. He told her, "Don't worry, Mom. I don't want to ever be anything really big. I just want to get by." He's in the sixth grade.

She told me they couldn't get an apartment in Upper Montclair because of her son. When they saw her, fine, but when they saw her son, no way. She said finally they bought a house and as soon as they moved in the neighbors called the law. They had to spend ten thousand dollars on repairs right away. She said she's not running. She's not going no place. If anyone runs, it will be them. She says she doesn't make friends with anyone. Since she's married a black man, she's realized the only friends you have are your family. She says she's happy with her life. It's the other people who must be unhappy to do all these things. She's just fine.

July

This morning I put my car in the shop. The neighborhood shop. When I went to pick it up I had a conversation with the man who had worked on it. I told him I had been afraid to leave the car there at night with the keys in it. "Don't worry," he said, "You don't have to worry about stealing as long as the niggers don't move in." I couldn't believe it. I hoped I had heard him wrong. "What did you say?" I asked. He repeated the same thing without hesitation.

In the past, my anger would have swelled quickly. I would have blurted out something, hotly demanded he take my car down off the rack immediately, though he had not finished working on it, and taken off in a blaze. I love that reaction. The only feeling of power one can possibly have in a situation in which there is such a sudden feeling of powerless is to "do" something, handle the situation. When you "do" something, everything is clear. But this is the only repair shop in the city. Might I have to come back here someday in an emergency?

Blowing off steam is supposed to make you feel better. But in this situation, it *doesn't!* After responding in anger, I often feel sad, guilty, frightened, and confused. Perhaps my anger isn't just about race. Perhaps it's like those rapid-fire responses to Bruce—a way of dulling the edge of feelings that lie even deeper.

I let the tension stay in my body. I go home and sit with myself for an hour, trying to grasp the feeling—the odor of self-hatred, the biting stench of shame.

July

Last week a young woman who lives down the street came over for dinner. She's thirty, the daughter of a doctor. She lived in New York for a few years on her own, lost her job, may have had a breakdown, and came home to "get herself together."

After dinner we got into a conversation about Tall Oaks Country Club, where she is the swimming instructor. I asked her, hesitantly, but unwilling not to get this information, if blacks were allowed to join. (Everybody on our block belongs; all were told about "the club" and asked to join as soon as they moved in. We were never told or asked to join.)

"No," she said.

"You mean the people on this block who have had us over for dinner, who I have invited to my home for dinner, I can't swim in a pool with them?"

"That's the rule," she said, as if she was stating a mathematical fact. She told us about one girl, the daughter of the president of a bank, who worked on the desk at Tall Oaks. When they told her blacks couldn't join, she quit. I wondered why she told this—the swimming instructor—as if she wasn't ashamed of herself.

I remembered how once she had looked at pictures in our family album and seen my mother's house. "This is like one of the houses on Upper Mountain Avenue," she had exclaimed. "I didn't know black people had homes like this!"

I have begun therapy—with a white therapist—and when I told him about how disturbed I was by this conversation, he said he didn't believe that people were like this anymore. He said I would have to try to join to be able to tell. He told me it had something to do with how I see myself as deprived by my family, my neurosis.

Four days ago Ann called, the woman down the street, asking if my son could babysit. I like this woman. I don't know why. She has that red hair and ruddy coloring out of a Rubens painting. Easy to talk to. She and her husband are members of the club, and I couldn't resist telling her my story.

She said, "Oh, Toi, John and I wanted to invite you and Bruce to be our guests at a dinner party. I was just picking up the phone to call when Holly [a woman who lives across the street] called and said, 'Do you think that's a good idea? You better check with the Stevens [old members of the club] first.' I called George and he called a meeting of the executive committee. We met for four hours. Several of us said we would turn in our resignations unless you could come. But the majority felt it wouldn't be a good idea because you would see all the good things and want to join, and since you couldn't join, it would just hurt you and be frustrating. John and I wanted to quit. I feel very ashamed of myself, but the next summer, when I was stuck in the house with the kids and nothing to do, we started going again."

When I related this to my therapist, he said it sounded like my feelings about my mother. I see my mother as having something that she is keeping from me, some love that I can't get from her. He said that all this feeling of deprivation is really because I can't get to the sadness of living without her.

Yesterday the executive board of Poets & Writers of New Jersey met to read the poetry of a new applicant. I am a member. Right away I said to myself, "The poetry is too loose. Not precise enough. She's not ready." But soon after I recognized certain colloquialisms, settings. *She is probably black*, I thought.

I know these people are very particular about who they let in. They vote no on just about everybody. I'm usually the one who believes that seriousness is the best criterion for entrance. I got terrified. Would I have to stand up for this woman's work against all these people? How could I do so when I didn't really believe in it? Was I judging her too harshly because she is black? Was I putting myself down by judging her harshly? Could I hear her voice inside these poems? Or am I too brainwashed by the sound of Yeats, Eliot, Lowell, Plath? What was I expecting? I went foggy. If I was going to have to fight for her, I'd do it. But I prayed I wouldn't have to. She had to get in. Her voice had to have a place.

Luckily, everyone in the group said she was good. I put her poems back on the table. I didn't say anything. * * *

February

Last night we had two couples over for dinner: the Alvarezes, the first friends Bruce made when he moved to New York; and the Kings, new friends who live in this area. Charles King is the first black vice principal of one of the neighboring city's junior high schools, a position that, in many cases, has been reserved for a black man, somebody who can discipline black students without being accused of racism.

Before long we got to talking about Tall Oaks. Charles and his wife related experiences they had had. Charles had tried to buy a home in Upper Montclair about ten years ago. The night he looked at it someone burned a cross on the lawn. It shouldn't surprise me, but it *does* surprise me, that in 1968 people were still burning crosses — not down South, but way, way up North. He remembers that when he was a boy, a black kid couldn't walk down the street in the neighboring town, Glen Ridge. It was a big joke to the kids. They knew they could always save the dime carfare by walking over to Glen Ridge Avenue; the cops would pick them up and drive them to the border of Montclair.

Ray Alvarez thinks we have a good lawsuit. They can't keep us out of the club because we're black; it's illegal. He was turned on to finding a good lawyer. Bruce was hesitant. He said, "White money sticks together. They'll get back at us where it hurts — in the pocketbook." I'm sure he was thinking about his job at the bank.

After dinner I noticed that the dining room window was open. I thought back on the heated discussion we had had. How passionate we had been — angry, loud. If someone had been out walking a dog or coming home late, they would have heard us. I felt like glass. Now they would know the anger that was under that polite woman who held conversations with them over their fences about wallpaper, an enraged black woman who called them "fucking assholes!"

In bed that night, I felt unsure of my anger. Had I just been saying those things about my neighbors to fit in with the others? Is it the story of my life to try to get along with whomever I am with — not knowing who I really love, to which group belongs my true allegiance?

I remembered an incident from childhood. When I was about nine, I was passionately in love with my cousin. I thought she didn't love me as much as I loved her. One day she was very angry at our aunt and started saying things about her — they way we often talked about adults when we were angry. I didn't believe these things. My aunt had been kind to me all my life. But I felt that in order to win my cousin's love, I had to accede to the things she said — and I made up a few of my own. Suddenly my aunt opened the door. She had heard everything. My relationship with her was never the same.

I lie in bed wondering who and what I love. Who I identify with. Who I am. Suddenly a terrible fear comes over me, so real it is in my throat, in my mouth, so great it could swallow me. My neighbors had heard. They knew what I really was like and now they hated me. They would hurt me and my family. They would kill us. It was so real — the way fears can be when the defenses of the day are stripped away.

If we sued, I would be terrified. I wouldn't be able to sleep or eat. How had those people in the South during the civil rights struggle stood up? I would go mad or commit suicide — as if what they think of me were more powerful than what I think of myself. As if I could be eaten up by another's idea.

CBOCS West, Inc. v. Hedrick G. Humphries
128 S.Ct. 1951 (2008)

Michael W. Hawkins, Lebanon, TN, for petitioner.

Cynthia H. Hyndman, Chicago, IL, for respondent.

Michael W. Hawkins, Counsel of Record, Michael J. Newman, Dinsmore & Shohl LLP, Cincinnati, OH, Michael Zylstra, General Counsel and Vice President, Lebanon, TN, for Petitioner CBOCS West, Inc.

Eric Schnapper, School of Law, University of Washington, Seattle, Washington, Carolyn Shapiro, Chicago-Kent College of Law, Illinois Institute of Technology, Chicago, Illinois, Cynthia H. Hyndman, Counsel of Record, Aleeza M. Strubel, Robinson, Curley & Clayton, P.C., Chicago, Illinois, for Respondent.

Justice Breyer delivered the opinion of the Court, in which Chief Justice Roberts and Justices Stevens, Kennedy, Souter, Ginsburg, and Alito joined. Justice Thomas filed a dissenting opinion, in which Justice Scalia joined.

A longstanding civil rights law, first enacted just after the Civil War, provides that "[a]ll persons within the jurisdiction of the United States shall have the same right in every State and Territory to make and enforce contracts ... as is enjoyed by white citizens." Rev. Stat. § 1977, 42 U.S.C. § 1981(a). The basic question before us is whether the provision encompasses a complaint of retaliation against a person who has complained about a violation of another person's contract-related "right." We conclude that it does.

I.

The case before us arises out of a claim by respondent, Hedrick G. Humphries, a former assistant manager of a Cracker Barrel restaurant, that CBOCS West, Inc. (Cracker Barrel's owner) dismissed him (1) because of racial bias (Humphries is a black man) and (2) because he had complained to managers that a fellow assistant manager had dismissed another black employee, Venus Green, for race-based reasons. Humphries timely filed a charge with the Equal Employment Opportunity Commission (EEOC), pursuant to 42 U.S.C. § 2000e-5, and received a "right to sue" letter. He then filed a complaint in Federal District Court charging that CBOCS' actions violated both Title VII of the Civil Rights Act of 1964, and the older "equal contract rights" provision here at issue, § 1981. The District Court dismissed Humphries' Title VII claims for failure to pay necessary filing fees on a timely basis. It then granted CBOCS' motion for summary judgment on Humphries' two § 1981 claims.

The U.S. Court of Appeals for the Seventh Circuit upheld the District Court's grant of summary judgment in respect to his direct discrimination claim. But it ruled in Humphries' favor and remanded for a trial in respect to his § 1981 retaliation claim. In doing so, the Court of Appeals rejected CBOCS' argument that § 1981 did not encompass a claim of retaliation.

II.

The question before us is whether § 1981 encompasses retaliation claims. We conclude that it does. And because our conclusion rests in significant part upon principles of *stare decisis,* we begin by examining the pertinent interpretive history.

A.

The Court first considered a comparable question in 1969, in Sullivan v. Little Hunting Park, Inc., 396 U.S. 229. The case arose under 42 U.S.C. § 1982, a statutory provision that Congress enacted just after the Civil War, along with § 1981, to protect the rights of black citizens. The provision was similar to § 1981 except that it focused, not upon rights to make and to enforce contracts, but rights related to the ownership of property. The statute provides that "[a]ll citizens of the United States shall have the same right, in every State and Territory, as is enjoyed by white citizens thereof to inherit, purchase, lease, sell, hold, and convey real and personal property." § 1982.

Paul E. Sullivan, a white man, had rented his house to T.R. Freeman, Jr., a black man. He had also assigned Freeman a membership share in a corporation, which permitted the owner to use a private park that the corporation controlled. Because of Freeman's race, the corporation, Little Hunting Park, Inc., refused to approve the share assignment. And, when Sullivan protested, the association expelled Sullivan and took away his membership shares.

Sullivan sued Little Hunting Park, claiming that its actions violated § 1982. The Court upheld Sullivan's claim. It found that the corporation's refusal "to approve the assignment of the membership share … was clearly an interference with Freeman's [the black lessee's] right to 'lease.'" It added that Sullivan, the white lessor, "has standing to maintain this action," because, as the Court had previously said, "the white owner is at times 'the only effective adversary of the unlawful restrictive covenant." The Court noted that to permit the corporation to punish Sullivan "for trying to vindicate the rights of minorities protected by § 1982" would give "impetus to the perpetuation of racial restrictions on property." And this Court has made clear that Sullivan stands for the proposition that § 1982 encompasses retaliation claims. See Jackson v. Birmingham Bd. of Ed., 544 U.S. 167, 176 (2005) ("[I]n Sullivan we interpreted a general prohibition on racial discrimination [in § 1982] to cover retaliation against those who advocate the rights of groups protected by that prohibition").

While the Sullivan decision interpreted § 1982, our precedents have long construed §§ 1981 and 1982 similarly....

[T]he Court has construed §§ 1981 and 1982 alike because it has recognized the sister statutes' common language, origin, and purposes. Like § 1981, § 1982 traces its origin to § 1 of the Civil Rights Act of 1866. Like § 1981, § 1982 represents an immediately post-Civil War legislative effort to guarantee the then newly freed slaves the same legal rights that other citizens enjoy. Like § 1981, § 1982 uses broad language that says "[a]ll citizens of the United States shall have the same right, in every State and Territory, as is enjoyed by white citizens...." Indeed, § 1982 differs from § 1981 only in that it refers, not to the "right ... to make and enforce contracts," 42 U.S.C. § 1981(a), but to the "right ... to inherit, purchase, lease, sell, hold, and convey real and personal property," § 1982.*

In light of these precedents, it is not surprising that following Sullivan, federal appeals courts concluded, on the basis of Sullivan or its reasoning, that § 1981 encompassed retaliation claims.

B.

....

The upshot is this: (1) in 1969, Sullivan, as interpreted by Jackson, recognized that § 1982 encompasses a retaliation action; (2) this Court has long interpreted §§ 1981 and 1982 alike; (3) in 1989, Patterson, without mention of retaliation, narrowed § 1981 by excluding from its scope conduct, namely post-contract-formation conduct, where retaliation would most likely be found; but in 1991, Congress enacted legislation that superseded Patterson and explicitly defined the scope of § 1981 to include post-contract-formation conduct; and (4) since 1991, the lower courts have uniformly interpreted § 1981 as encompassing retaliation actions.

C.

Sullivan, as interpreted and relied upon by Jackson, as well as the long line of related cases where we construe §§ 1981 and 1982 similarly, lead us to conclude that the view that § 1981 encompasses retaliation claims is indeed well embedded in the law. That being so, considerations of *stare decisis* strongly support our adherence to that view. And those considerations impose a considerable burden upon those who would seek a different interpretation that would necessarily unsettle many Court precedents.

III.

In our view, CBOCS' several arguments taken separately or together, cannot justify a departure from what we have just described as the well-embedded interpretation of § 1981. First, CBOCS points to the plain text of § 1981—a text that says that "*[a]ll per-*

---

* Editor's Note: Section 1982 differs from Section 1981 also in that Section 1982 refers to "citizens" and Section 1981 refers to "persons."

sons ... shall have the same right ... to make and enforce contracts ... as is enjoyed by *white citizens.*" 42 U.S.C. § 1981(a) (emphasis added). CBOCS adds that, insofar as Humphries complains of retaliation, he is complaining of a retaliatory action that the employer would have taken against him whether he was black or white, and there is no way to construe this text to cover that kind of deprivation. Thus the text's language, CBOCS concludes, simply "does not provide for a cause of action based on retaliation." Brief for Petitioner 8.

We agree with CBOCS that the statute's language does not expressly refer to the claim of an individual (black or white) who suffers retaliation because he has tried to help a different individual, suffering direct racial discrimination, secure his § 1981 rights. But that fact alone is not sufficient to carry the day. After all, this Court has long held that the statutory text of § 1981's sister statute, § 1982, provides protection from retaliation for reasons related to the enforcement of the express statutory right.

Moreover, the Court has recently read another broadly worded civil rights statute, namely, Title IX of the Education Amendments of 1972, as including an antiretaliation remedy. Despite the fact that Title IX does not use the word "retaliation," the Court held in Jackson that the statute's language encompassed such a claim, in part because: (1) "Congress enacted Title IX just three years after Sullivan was decided"; (2) it is " 'realistic to presume that Congress was thoroughly familiar' " with Sullivan; and (3) Congress consequently " 'expected its enactment' " of Title IX " 'to be interpreted in conformity with' " Sullivan.

Regardless, the linguistic argument that CBOCS makes was apparent at the time the Court decided Sullivan. See 396 U.S., at 241 (Harlan, J., dissenting) (noting the construction of § 1982 in Jones was "in no way required by [the statute's] language"—one of the bases of Justice Harlan's dissent in Jones—and further contending that the Court in Sullivan had gone "yet beyond" Jones). And we believe it is too late in the day in effect to overturn the holding in that case (nor does CBOCS ask us to do so) on the basis of a linguistic argument that was apparent, and which the Court did not embrace at that time.

Second, CBOCS argues that Congress, in 1991 when it reenacted § 1981 with amendments, intended the reenacted statute not to cover retaliation. CBOCS rests this conclusion primarily upon the fact that Congress did not include an explicit antiretaliation provision or the word "retaliation" in the new statutory language—although Congress has included explicit antiretaliation language in other civil rights statutes.

We believe, however, that the circumstances to which CBOCS points find a far more plausible explanation in the fact that, given Sullivan and the new statutory language nullifying Patterson, there was no need for Congress to include explicit language about retaliation. After all, the 1991 amendments themselves make clear that Congress intended to supersede the result in Patterson and embrace pre-Patterson law. And pre-Patterson law included Sullivan....

IV.

We conclude that considerations of *stare decisis* strongly support our adherence to Sullivan and the long line of related cases where we interpret §§ 1981 and 1982 similarly. CBOCS' arguments do not convince us to the contrary. We consequently hold that 42 U.S.C. § 1981 encompasses claims of retaliation. The judgment of the Court of Appeals is affirmed.

F. Retrenchment — Civil Rights and Future Interests

Evans v. Abney
396 U.S. 435 (1970)

James M. Nabrit, III argued the cause for petitioners. With him on the brief were William H. Alexander, Jack Greenberg, Charles L. Black, Jr., and Anthony G. Amsterdam.

Deputy Solicitor General Claiborne, by special leave of Court, argued the cause for the United States as amicus curiae urging reversal.

Frank C. Jones argued the cause for respondents. With him on the brief was Charles M. Cork.

Before Chief Justice Burger, and Justices Black, Douglas, Harlan, Brennan, Stewart, and White. Justice Marshall took no part in the consideration or decision of this case.*

Justices Douglas and Brennan dissented.

Mr. Justice Black delivered the opinion of the Court.

Once again this Court must consider the constitutional implications of the 1911 will of United States Senator A. O. Bacon of Georgia[,] which conveyed property in trust to Senator Bacon's home city of Macon for the creation of a public park for the exclusive use of the white people of that city. As a result of our earlier decision in this case which held that the park, Baconsfield, could not continue to be operated on a racially discriminatory basis, Evans v. Newton, 382 U.S. 296 (1966), the Supreme Court of Georgia ruled that Senator Bacon's intention to provide a park for whites only had become impossible to fulfill and that accordingly the trust had failed and the parkland and other trust property had reverted by operation of Georgia law to the heirs of the Senator. Petitioners, the same Negro citizens of Macon who have sought in the courts to integrate the park, contend that this termination of the trust violates their rights to equal protection and due process under the Fourteenth Amendment....

The early background of this litigation was summarized by Mr. Justice Douglas in his opinion for the Court in Evans v. Newton:

> In 1911 United States Senator Augustus O. Bacon executed a will that de-vised to the Mayor and Council of the City of Macon, Georgia, a tract of land which, after the death of the Senator's wife and daughters, was to be used as 'a park and pleasure ground' for white people only, the Senator stat-ing in the will that while he had only the kindest feeling for the Negroes he was of the opinion that 'in their social relations the two races (white and negro) should be forever separate.' The will provided that the park should be under the control of a Board of Managers of seven persons, all of whom were to be white. The city kept the park segregated for some years but in time let Negroes use it, taking the position that the park was a public facility

---

* Editor's Note: Only eight justices participated in this decision because Justice Abe Fortas had resigned on May 14, 1969 and his replacement, Justice Harry Blackmun, was not confirmed until May 12, 1970. President Nixon had made two nominations before Justice Blackmun's, but these were not confirmed. See Stephen L. Wasby, *Harry Andrew Blackmun*, in The Oxford Companion to the Supreme Court of the United States 75–76 (Kermit L. Hall ed. 1992).

which it could not constitutionally manage and maintain on a segregated basis.

Thereupon, individual members of the Board of Managers of the park brought this suit in a state court against the City of Macon and the trustees of certain residuary beneficiaries of Senator Bacon's estate, asking that the city be removed as trustee and that the court appoint new trustees, to whom title to the park would be transferred....

Several Negro citizens of Macon intervened, alleging that the racial limitation was contrary to the laws and public policy of the United States, and asking that the court refuse to appoint private trustees. Thereafter the city resigned as trustee and amended its answer accordingly. Moreover, other heirs of Senator Bacon intervened and they and the defendants other than the city asked for reversion of the trust property to the Bacon estate in the event that the prayer of the petition were denied.

The Georgia court accepted the resignation of the city as trustee and appointed three individuals as new trustees, finding it unnecessary to pass on the other claims of the heirs. On appeal by the Negro intervenors, the Supreme Court of Georgia affirmed, holding that Senator Bacon had the right to give and bequeath his property to a limited class, that charitable trusts are subject to supervision of a court of equity, and that the power to appoint new trustees so that the purpose of the trust would not fail was clear.

The [U.S. Supreme] Court in Evans v. Newton [held] that the public character of Baconsfield "requires that it be treated as a public institution subject to the command of the Fourteenth Amendment, regardless of who now has title under state law." Thereafter, the Georgia Supreme Court interpreted this Court's reversal of its decision as requiring that Baconsfield be henceforth operated on a nondiscriminatory basis. "Under these circumstances," the state high court held, "we are of the opinion that the sole purpose for which the trust was created has become impossible of accomplishment and has been terminated." Without further elaboration of this holding, the case was remanded to the Georgia trial court to consider the motion of Guyton G. Abney and others, successor trustees of Senator Bacon's estate, for a ruling that the trust had become unenforceable and that accordingly the trust property had reverted to the Bacon estate and to certain named heirs of the Senator. The motion was opposed by petitioners and by the Attorney General of Georgia, both of whom argued that the trust should be saved by applying the cy pres doctrine to amend the terms of the will by striking the racial restrictions and opening Baconsfield to all the citizens of Macon without regard to race or color. The trial court, however, refused to apply cy pres. It held that the doctrine was inapplicable because the park's segregated, whites-only character was an essential and inseparable part of the testator's plan. Since the "sole purpose" of the trust was thus in irreconcilable conflict with the constitutional mandate expressed in our opinion in Evans v. Newton, the trial court ruled that the Baconsfield trust had failed and that the trust property had by operation of law reverted to the heirs of Senator Bacon. On appeal, the Supreme Court of Georgia affirmed.

We are of the opinion that in ruling as they did the Georgia courts did no more than apply well-settled general principles of Georgia law to determine the meaning and effect of a Georgia will. At the time Senator Bacon made his will Georgia cities and towns were, and they still are, authorized to accept devises of property for the establishment and preservation of "parks and pleasure grounds" and to hold the property thus received in charitable trust for the exclusive benefit of the class of persons named by the testator. These provisions of the Georgia Code explicitly authorized the testator to include, if he should choose, racial restrictions such as those found in Senator Bacon's will. The city accepted the trust with these restrictions in it. When this Court in Evans v. Newton held that the continued operation of Baconsfield as a segregated park was unconstitutional, the particular purpose of the Baconsfield trust as stated in the will failed under Georgia law. The question then properly before the Georgia Supreme Court was whether as a matter of state law the doctrine of cy pres should be applied to prevent the trust itself from failing. Petitioners urged that the cy pres doctrine allowed the Georgia courts to strike the racially restrictive clauses in Bacon's will so that the terms of the trust could be fulfilled without violating the Constitution.

The Georgia cy pres statutes upon which petitioners relied provide:

> When a valid charitable bequest is incapable for some reason of execution in the exact manner provided by the testator, donor, or founder, a court of equity will carry it into effect in such a way as will as nearly as possible effectuate his intention.

> A devise or bequest to a charitable use will be sustained and carried out in this State; and in all cases where there is a general intention manifested by the testator to effect a certain purpose, and the particular mode in which he directs it to be done shall fail from any cause, a court of chancery may, by approximation, effectuate the purpose in a manner most similar to that indicated by the testator.

The Georgia courts have held that the fundamental purpose of these cy pres provisions is to allow the court to carry out the general charitable intent of the testator where this intent might otherwise be thwarted by the impossibility of the particular plan or scheme provided by the testator. But this underlying logic of the cy pres doctrine implies that there is a certain class of cases in which the doctrine cannot be applied. Professor Scott in his treatise on trusts states this limitation on the doctrine of cy pres which is common to many States as follows:

> It is not true that a charitable trust never fails where it is impossible to carry out the particular purpose of the testator. In some cases ... it appears that the accomplishment of the particular purpose and only that purpose was desired by the testator and that he had no more general charitable intent and that he would presumably have preferred to have the whole trust fail if the particular purpose is impossible of accomplishment. In such a case the cy pres doctrine is not applicable.

A. Scott, The Law of Trusts § 399, p. 3085 (3d ed. 1967).

In this case, Senator Bacon provided an unusual amount of information in his will from which the Georgia courts could determine the limits of his charitable purpose. Immediately after specifying that the park should be for "the sole, perpetual and unending, use, benefit and enjoyment of the white women, white girls, white boys and white children of the City of Macon," the Senator stated that "the said property under no circumstances ... [is] to be ... at any time for any reason devoted to any other purpose or use excepting so far as herein specifically authorized." And the Senator continued:

I take occasion to say that in limiting the use and enjoyment of this property perpetually to white people, I am not influenced by any unkindness of feeling or want of consideration for the Negroes, or colored people. On the contrary I have for them the kindest feeling, and for many of them esteem and regard, while for some of them I have sincere personal affection.

I am, however, without hesitation in the opinion that in their social relations the two races ... should be forever separate and that they should not have pleasure or recreation grounds to be used or enjoyed, together and in common.

The Georgia courts, construing Senator Bacon's will as a whole, concluded from this and other language in the will that the Senator's charitable intent was not "general" but extended only to the establishment of a segregated park for the benefit of white people. The Georgia trial court found that "Senator Bacon could not have used language more clearly indicating his intent that the benefits of Baconsfield should be extended to white persons only, or more clearly indicating that this limitation was an essential and indispensable part of his plan for Baconsfield." Since racial separation was found to be an inseparable part of the testator's intent, the Georgia courts held that the State's cy pres doctrine could not be used to alter the will to permit racial integration. The Baconsfield trust was therefore held to have failed, and, under Georgia law, "[w]here a trust is expressly created, but [its] uses ... fail from any cause, a resulting trust is implied for the benefit of the grantor, or testator, or his heirs."[2] The Georgia courts concluded, in effect, that Senator Bacon would have rather had the whole trust fail than have Baconsfield integrated.

When a city park is destroyed because the Constitution requires it to be integrated, there is reason for everyone to be disheartened. We agree with petitioners that in such a case it is not enough to find that the state court's result was reached through the application of established principles of state law. No state law or act can prevail in the face of contrary federal law, and the federal courts must search out the fact and truth of any proceeding or transaction to determine if the Constitution has been violated. Here, however, the action of the Georgia Supreme Court declaring the Baconsfield trust terminated presents no violation of constitutionally protected rights, and any

---

2. Although Senator Bacon's will did not contain an express provision granting a reverter to any party should the trust fail, § 108-106(4) of the Georgia Code quoted in the text makes such an omission irrelevant under state law. At one point in the Senator's will he did grant "all remainders and reversions" to the city of Macon, but the Supreme Court of Georgia showed in its opinion that this language did not relate in any way to what should happen upon a failure of the trust but was relevant only to the initial vesting of the property in the city. The Georgia court said:

Senator Bacon devised a life estate in the trust property to his wife and two daughters, and the language pointed out by the intervenors appears in the following provision of the will: 'When my wife, Virginia Lamar Bacon and my two daughters, Mary Louise Bacon Sparks and Augusta Lamar Bacon Curry, shall all have departed this life, and immediately upon the death of the last survivor of them, it is my will that all right, title and interest in and to said property hereinbefore described and bounded, both legal and equitable, including all remainders and reversions and every estate in the same of whatsoever kind, shall thereupon vest in and belong to the Mayor and Council of the City of Macon, and to their successors forever, in trust etc.' This language concerned remainders and reversions prior to the vesting of the legal title in the City of Macon, as trustee, and not to remainders and reversions occurring because of a failure of the trust, which Senator Bacon apparently did not contemplate, and for which he made no provision.

harshness that may have resulted from the state court's decision can be attributed solely to its intention to effectuate as nearly as possible the explicit terms of Senator Bacon's will.

Petitioners first argue that the action of the Georgia court violates the United States Constitution in that it imposes a drastic "penalty," the "forfeiture" of the park, merely because of the city's compliance with the constitutional mandate expressed by this Court in Evans v. Newton. Of course, Evans v. Newton did not speak to the problem of whether Baconsfield should or could continue to operate as a park; it held only that its continued operation as a park had to be without racial discrimination. But petitioners now want to extend that holding to forbid the Georgia courts from closing Baconsfield on the ground that such a closing would penalize the city and its citizens for complying with the Constitution. We think, however, that the will of Senator Bacon and Georgia law provide all the justification necessary for imposing such a "penalty." The construction of wills is essentially a state-law question, and in this case the Georgia Supreme Court, as we read its opinion, interpreted Senator Bacon's will as embodying a preference for termination of the park rather than its integration. Given this, the Georgia court had no alternative under its relevant trust laws, which are long standing and neutral with regard to race, but to end the Baconsfield trust and return the property to the Senator's heirs.

A second argument for petitioners stresses the similarities between this case and the case in which a city holds an absolute fee simple title to a public park and then closes that park of its own accord solely to avoid the effect of a prior court order directing that the park be integrated as the Fourteenth Amendment commands. Yet, assuming arguendo that the closing of the park would in those circumstances violate the Equal Protection Clause, that case would be clearly distinguishable from the case at bar because there it is the State and not a private party which is injecting the racially discriminatory motivation. In the case at bar there is not the slightest indication that any of the Georgia judges involved were motivated by racial animus or discriminatory intent of any sort in construing and enforcing Senator Bacon's will. Nor is there any indication that Senator Bacon in drawing up his will was persuaded or induced to include racial restrictions by the fact that such restrictions were permitted by the Georgia trust statutes. On the contrary, the language of the Senator's will shows that the racial restrictions were solely the product of the testator's own full-blown social philosophy. Similarly, the situation presented in this case is also easily distinguishable from that presented in Shelley v. Kraemer, 334 U.S. 1 (1948), where we held unconstitutional state judicial action which had affirmatively enforced a private scheme of discrimination against Negroes. Here the effect of the Georgia decision eliminated all discrimination against Negroes in the park by eliminating the park itself, and the termination of the park was a loss shared equally by the white and Negro citizens of Macon since both races would have enjoyed a constitutional right of equal access to the park's facilities had it continued.

Petitioners also contend that since Senator Bacon did not expressly provide for a reverter in the event that the racial restrictions of the trust failed, no one can know with absolute certainty that the Senator would have preferred termination of the park rather than its integration, and the decision of the Georgia court therefore involved a matter of choice. It might be difficult to argue with these assertions if they stood alone, but then petitioners conclude: "Its [the court's] choice, the anti-Negro choice, violates the Fourteenth Amendment, whether it be called a 'guess,' an item in 'social philosophy,' or anything else at all." We do not understand petitioners to be contending here that the Georgia judges were motivated either consciously or unconsciously by a desire to discriminate against Negroes. In any case, there is, as noted above, absolutely nothing before this Court to support a finding of such motivation. What remains of petitioners' argument is the idea that the Georgia courts had a constitutional obligation in this case to resolve any doubt about the testator's intent in favor of preserving the trust. Thus stated, we see no merit in the argument. The only choice the Georgia courts either had or exercised in this regard was their judicial judgment in construing Bacon's will to determine his intent, and the Constitution imposes no requirement upon the Georgia courts to approach Bacon's will any differently than they would approach any will creating any charitable trust of any kind. Surely the Fourteenth Amendment is not violated where, as here, a state court operating in its judicial capacity fairly applies its normal principles of construction to determine the testator's true intent in establishing a charitable trust and then reaches a conclusion with regard to that intent which, because of the operation of neutral and nondiscriminatory state trust laws, effectively denies everyone, whites as well as Negroes, the benefits of the trust.

Another argument made by petitioners is that the decision of the Georgia courts holding that the Baconsfield trust had "failed" must rest logically on the unspoken premise that the presence or proximity of Negroes in Baconsfield would destroy the desirability of the park for whites. This argument reflects a rather fundamental misunderstanding of Georgia law. The Baconsfield trust "failed" under that law not because of any belief on the part of any living person that whites and Negroes might not enjoy being together but, rather, because Senator Bacon who died many years ago intended that the park remain forever for the exclusive use of white people.

Petitioners also advance a number of considerations of public policy in opposition to the conclusion which we have reached. In particular, they regret, as we do, the loss of the Baconsfield trust to the City of Macon, and they are concerned lest we set a precedent under which other charitable trusts will be terminated. It bears repeating that our holding today reaffirms the traditional role of the States in determining whether or not to apply their cy pres doctrines to particular trusts. Nothing we have said here prevents a state court from applying its cy pres rule in a case where the Georgia court, for example, might not apply its rule. More fundamentally, however, the loss of charitable trusts such as Baconsfield is part of the price we pay for permitting deceased persons to exercise a continuing control over assets owned by them at death. This aspect of freedom of testation, like most things, has its advantages and disadvantages. The responsibility of this Court, however, is to construe and enforce the Constitution and laws of the land as they are and not to legislate social policy on the basis of our own personal inclinations....

The judgment is affirmed.

Mr. Justice Douglas, dissenting.

Bacon's will did not leave any remainder or reversion in "Baconsfield" to his heirs. He left "all remainders and reversions and every estate in the same of whatsoever kind" to the City of Macon. He further provided that the property "under no circumstances, or by any authority whatsoever" should "be sold or alienated or disposed of, or at any time for any reason" be "devoted to any other purpose or use excepting so far as herein specifically authorized." Giving the property to the heirs, rather than reserving it for some municipal use, does therefore as much violence to Bacon's purpose as would a conversion of an "all-white" park into an "all-Negro" park.

No municipal use is of course possible where the beneficiaries are members of one race only. That was true in 1911 when Bacon made his will. Plessy v. Ferguson, 163 U.S.

537, decided in 1896, had held that while "separate" facilities could be supplied each race, those facilities had to be "equal." The concept of "equal" in this setting meant not just another park for Negroes but one equal in quality and service to that municipal facility which is furnished the whites. See Sweatt v. Painter, 339 U.S. 629 [(1950)]. It is apparent that Bacon's will projected a municipal use which at the time was not constitutionally permissible unless like accommodations were made for the Negro race.

So far as this record reveals, the day the present park was opened to whites it may, constitutionally speaking, also have been available to Negroes.

The Supreme Court of Georgia stated that the sole purpose for which the trust was created had become impossible. But it was impossible in those absolute terms even under the regime of Plessy v. Ferguson. As to cy pres, the ... Georgia court held that the doctrine of cy pres "can not be applied to establish a trust for an entirely different purpose from that intended by the testator." That, however, does not state the issue realistically. No proposal to bar use of the park by whites has ever been made, except the reversion ordered to the heirs. Continuation of the use of the property as a municipal park or for another municipal purpose carries out a larger share of Bacon's purpose than the complete destruction of such use by the decree we today affirm.

The purpose of the will was to dedicate the land for some municipal use. That is still possible. Whatever that use, Negroes will of course be admitted, for such is the constitutional command. But whites will also be admitted. Letting both races share the facility is closer to a realization of Bacon's desire than a complete destruction of the will and the abandonment of Bacon's desire that the property be used for some municipal purpose.* * *

The Georgia decision, which we today approve, can only be a gesture toward a state-sanctioned segregated way of life, now passe. It therefore should fail as the imposition of a penalty for obedience to a principle of national supremacy.

Mr. Justice Brennan, dissenting.

For almost half a century Baconsfield has been a public park. Senator Bacon's will provided that upon the death of the last survivor among his widow and two daughters title to Baconsfield would vest in the Mayor and Council of the City of Macon and their successors forever. Pursuant to the express provisions of the will, the Mayor and City Council appointed a Board of Managers to supervise the operation of the park, and from time to time these same public officials made appointments to fill vacancies on the Board. Senator Bacon also bequeathed to the city certain bonds which provided income used in the operation of the park.

The city acquired title to Baconsfield in 1920 by purchasing the interests of Senator Bacon's surviving daughter and another person who resided on the land. Some $46,000 of public money was spent over a number of years to pay the purchase price. From the outset and throughout the years the Mayor and City Council acted as trustees, Baconsfield was administered as a public park. T. Cleveland James, superintendent of city parks during this period, testified that when he first worked at Baconsfield it was a "wilderness ... nothing there but just undergrowth everywhere, one road through there and that's all, one paved road." He said there were no park facilities at that time. In the 1930's Baconsfield was transformed into a modern recreational facility by employees of the Works Progress Administration, an agency of the Federal Government. WPA did so upon the city's representation that Baconsfield was a public park. WPA employed men daily for the better part of a year in the conversion of Baconsfield to a park. WPA and Mr. James and his staff cut underbrush, cleared paths, dug ponds, built bridges and benches, planted shrubbery, and, in Mr. James' words, "just made a general park out of it." Other capital improvements were made in later years with both federal and city money. The Board of Managers also spent funds to improve and maintain the park.

Although the Board of Managers supervised operations, general maintenance of Baconsfield was the responsibility of the city's superintendent of parks. Mr. James was asked whether he treated Baconsfield about the same as other city parks. He answered, "Yes, included in my appropriation...." The extent of the city's services to Baconsfield is evident from the increase of several thousand dollars in the annual expenses incurred for maintenance by the Board of Managers after the Mayor and City Council withdrew as trustees in 1964.

The city officials withdrew after suit was brought in a Georgia court by individual members of the Board of Managers to compel the appointment of private trustees on the ground that the public officials could not enforce racial segregation of the park. The Georgia court appointed private trustees, apparently on the assumption that they would be free to enforce the racially restrictive provision in Senator Bacon's will. In Evans v. Newton, we held that the park had acquired such unalterable indicia of a public facility that for the purposes of the Equal Protection Clause it remained "public" even after the city officials were replaced as trustees by a board of private citizens. Consequently, Senator Bacon's discriminatory purpose could not be enforced by anyone. This Court accordingly reversed the Georgia court's acceptance of the city officials' resignations and its appointment of private trustees. On remand the Georgia courts held that since Senator Bacon's desire to restrict the park to the white race could not be carried out, the trust failed and the property must revert to his heirs. The Court today holds that that result and the process by which it was reached do not constitute a denial of equal protection. I respectfully dissent.

No record could present a clearer case of the closing of a public facility for the sole reason that the public authority that owns and maintains it cannot keep it segregated. This is not a case where the reasons or motives for a particular action are arguably unclear, nor is it one where a discriminatory purpose is one among other reasons, nor one where a discriminatory purpose can be found only by inference. The reasoning of the Georgia Supreme Court is simply that Senator Bacon intended Baconsfield to be a segregated public park, and because it cannot be operated as a segregated public park any longer, the park must be closed down and Baconsfield must revert to Senator Bacon's heirs. This Court agrees that this "city park is [being] destroyed because the Constitution require[s] it to be integrated...." No one has put forward any other reason why the park is reverting from the City of Macon to the heirs of Senator Bacon. It is therefore quite plain that but for the constitutional prohibition on the operation of segregated public parks, the City of Macon would continue to own and maintain Baconsfield.

I have no doubt that a public park may constitutionally be closed down because it is too expensive to run or has become superfluous, or for some other reason, strong or weak, or for no reason at all. But under the Equal Protection Clause a State may not close down a public facility solely to avoid its duty to desegregate that facility.... When it is as starkly clear as it is in this case that a public facility would remain open but for the constitutional command that it be operated on a non-segregated basis, the closing of that facility conveys an unambiguous message of community involvement in racial discrimination. Its closing for the sole and unmistakable purpose of avoiding desegregation, like its operation as a segregated park, "generates [in Negroes] a feeling of inferiority as to their status in the community that may affect their hearts and minds in a way unlikely ever to be undone." Brown v. Board of Education, 347 U.S. 483, 494 (1954). It is no answer that continuing operation as a segregated facility is a constant reminder of a public policy that stigmatizes one race, whereas its closing occurs once and is over. That difference does not provide a constitutional distinction: state involvement in discrimination is unconstitutional, however short-lived.

The Court, however, affirms the judgment of the Georgia Supreme Court on the ground that the closing of Baconsfield did not involve state action. The Court concedes that the closing of the park by the city "solely to avoid the effect of a prior court order directing that the park be integrated" would be unconstitutional. However, the Court finds that in this case it is not the State or city but "a private party which is injecting the racially discriminatory motivation." The exculpation of the State and city from responsibility for the closing of the park is simply indefensible on this record. This discriminatory closing is permeated with state action: at the time Senator Bacon wrote his will Georgia statutes expressly authorized and supported the precise kind of discrimination provided for by him; in accepting title to the park, public officials of the City of Macon entered into an arrangement vesting in private persons the power to enforce a reversion if the city should ever incur a constitutional obligation to desegregate the park; it is a *public* park that is being closed for a discriminatory reason after having been operated for nearly half a century as a segregated *public* facility; and it is a state court that is enforcing the racial restriction that keeps apparently willing parties of different races from coming together in the park. That is state action in overwhelming abundance. I need emphasize only three elements of the state action present here.

First, there is state action whenever a State enters into an arrangement that creates a private right to compel or enforce the reversion of a public facility. Whether the right is a possibility of reverter, a right of entry, an executory interest, or a contractual right, it can be created only with the consent of a public body or official, for example the official action involved in Macon's acceptance of the gift of Baconsfield. The State's involvement in the creation of such a right is also involvement in its enforcement; the State's assent to the creation of the right necessarily contemplates that the State will enforce the right if called upon to do so. Where, as in this case, the State's enforcement role conflicts with its obligation to comply with the constitutional command against racial segregation the attempted enforcement must be declared repugnant to the Fourteenth Amendment.

Moreover, a State cannot divest itself by contract of the power to perform essential governmental functions. Thus a State cannot bind itself not to operate a public park in accordance with the Equal Protection Clause, upon pain of forfeiture of the park. The decision whether or not a public facility shall be operated in compliance with the Constitution is an essentially *governmental* decision. An arrangement that purports to prevent a State from complying with the Constitution cannot be carried out. Nor can it be enforced by a reversion; a racial restriction is simply invalid when intended to bind a public body and cannot be given any effect whatever, cf. Commonwealth of Pennsylvania v. Brown, 392 F.2d 120 (C.A.3d Cir. 1968).* * *

A finding of discriminatory state action is required here on a second ground. Shelley v. Kraemer stands at least for the proposition that where parties of different races are willing to deal with one another a state court cannot keep them from doing so by enforcing a privately devised racial restriction. Nothing in the record suggests that after our decision in Evans v. Newton the City of Macon retracted its previous willingness to manage Baconsfield on a nonsegregated basis, or that the white beneficiaries of Senator Bacon's generosity were unwilling to share it with Negroes, rather than have the park revert to his heirs. Indeed, although it may be that the city would have preferred to keep the park segregated, the record suggests that, given the impossibility of that goal, the city wanted to keep the park open. The resolution by which the Mayor and Council resigned as trustees prior to the decision in Evans v. Newton reflected, not opposition to the admission of Negroes into the park, but a fear that if Negroes were admitted the park would be lost to the city. The Mayor and Council did not participate in this litigation after the decision in Evans v. Newton. However, the Attorney General of Georgia was made a party after remand from this Court, and, acting "as parens patriae in all legal matters pertaining to the administration and disposition of charitable trusts in the State of Georgia in which the rights of beneficiaries are involved," he opposed a reversion to the heirs and argued that Baconsfield should be maintained "as a park for all the citizens of the State of Georgia." Thus, so far as the record shows, this is a case of a state court's enforcement of a racial restriction to prevent willing parties from dealing with one another. The decision of the Georgia courts thus, under Shelley v. Kraemer, constitutes state action denying equal protection.

Finally, a finding of discriminatory state action is required on a third ground. In Reitman v. Mulkey, 387 U.S. 369 (1967), this Court announced the basic principle that a State acts in violation of the Equal Protection Clause when it singles out racial discrimination for particular encouragement, and thereby gives it a special preferred status in the law, even though the State does not itself impose or compel segregation. This approach to the analysis of state action was foreshadowed in Mr. Justice White's separate opinion in Evans v. Newton. There Mr. Justice White comprehensively reviewed the law of trusts as that law stood in Georgia in 1905, prior to the enactment of §§ 69-504 and 69-505 of the Georgia Code. He concluded that prior to the enactment of those statutes "it would have been extremely doubtful" whether Georgia law authorized "a trust for park purposes when a portion of the public was to be excluded from the park." Sections 69-504 and 69-505 removed this doubt by expressly permitting dedication of land to the public for use as a park open to one race only. Thereby Georgia undertook to facilitate racial restrictions as distinguished from all other kinds of restriction on access to a public park. Reitman compels the conclusion that in doing so Georgia violated the Equal Protection Clause.

In 1911, only six years after the enactment of §§ 69-504 and 69-505, Senator Bacon, a lawyer, wrote his will. When he wrote the provision creating Baconsfield as a public park open only to the white race, he was not merely expressing his own testamentary intent, but was taking advantage of the special power Georgia had conferred by §§ 69-504 and 69-505 on testators seeking to establish racially segregated public parks. As Mr. Justice White concluded in Evans v. Newton, "*the State through its regulations has become involved to such a significant extent' in bringing about the discriminatory provision in Senator Bacon's trust that the racial restriction 'must be held to reflect ... state policy and therefore to violate the Fourteenth Amendment.'*" This state-encouraged testamentary provision is the sole basis for the Georgia courts' holding that Baconsfield must revert to Senator Bacon's heirs. The Court's finding that it is not the State of Georgia but "a private party which is injecting the racially discriminatory motivation" inexcusably disregards the State's role in enacting the statute without which Senator Bacon could not have written the discriminatory provision.

This, then, is not a case of private discrimination. It is rather discrimination in which the State of Georgia is "significantly involved," and enforcement of the reverter is therefore unconstitutional.

I would reverse the judgment of the Supreme Court of Georgia.

Hermitage Methodist Homes v. Dominion Trust Co.

239 Va. 46, 387 S.E.2d 740 (Supreme Court of Virginia 1990), cert. denied, 498 U.S. 907 (1990)

R. Kenneth Wheeler (Francis M. Fenderson, Jr.; Thomas A. Cooper; Kane, Wheeler, Fenderson, Jeffries & Wolf, on briefs), for appellee Hermitage Methodist Homes of Virginia, Inc.

Judith B. Henry (Martin A. Donlan, Jr.; John William Crews; Crews & Hancock, on brief), for appellee Prince Edward School Foundation.

Thomas J. Michie, Jr. (James P. Cox, III; Michie, Hamlett, Lowry, Rasmussen & Tweel, on brief), for appellant.

Before Chief Justice Carrico and Compton, Stephenson, Russell, Whiting and Lacy, JJ., and Harrison, Retired Justice.

Compton, J.

In 1956, Jack Adams, a resident of Lynchburg, executed his will establishing the trust in question. In 1964, the testator executed a codicil to the will. In 1968, Adams died testate.... Article IV of the codicil provides that the residuum of Adams' estate be held in trust and the income therefrom be distributed pursuant to clause (a), [which] provides:

> So long as Prince Edward School Foundation, Prince Edward Co., Va., admits to any school, operated or supported by it, only members of the White Race ... my said Trustee shall pay the net income ... to the Trustees (or other governing body) of such Foundation, to be expended by them ... for the benefit of any of said schools.

The clause further provides:

> In the event that the said Foundation should cease to operate for one year, or should at any time permit to matriculate in any of the schools operated or supported by it any person who is not a member of the White Race, no further payment of income shall be made to the said Foundation; but all income accruing after such date shall be paid to the Trustees of the Miller School, situated in Albemarle County, ... so long as said School admits only members of the White Race; said income shall be expended by such Trustees ... for the payment of the expenses of maintaining and operating said School....

The clause further provides for successive gifts over first to Seven Hills School, Inc. and then to Hampden-Sydney College, in the event of the occurrence of the same contingencies. The final beneficiary of the successive gifts over is Hermitage Methodist Homes of Virginia, Inc., without the limitation of the described contingencies.

Code § 55-26 was effective when the will and codicil were executed, and at the time of the testator's death. It provided, as pertinent:

> Every gift, grant, devise or bequest which, since April second, eighteen hundred and thirty-nine, has been or at any time hereafter shall be made for literary purposes or for the education of white persons, and every gift, grant, devise or bequest which, since April tenth, eighteen hundred and sixty-five, has been or at any time hereafter shall be made for literary purposes or for the education of colored persons, and every gift, grant, devise or bequest made hereafter for charitable purposes, whether made in any case to a body corporate or

unincorporated, or to a natural person, shall be as valid as if made to or for the benefit of a certain natural person, …

In Triplett v. Trotter, 193 S.E. 514 (1937), this Court construed the statute as validating a charitable gift for the education of members from one of the two races, but not from both. In 1975, the General Assembly repealed § 55-26. In the next year, the legislature enacted the substance of former § 55-26 without the discriminatory provisions.

In 1987, appellee Dominion Trust Company filed the present suit naming as parties defendant the income beneficiaries and the Attorney General of Virginia. Asserting that it was the successor trustee of the Adams Trust, the trustee alleged that it had paid over the income to Prince Edward School Foundation since the creation of the trust. It stated that "a determinable event" as described in Article IV may have occurred with respect to the school administered by the Foundation. (Counsel represented at the bar of this Court that subsequent to creation of the trust each educational beneficiary had enrolled black students in its schools.)

The trustee sought advice and guidance on "whether the determinative event or contingency [were] legal, valid and enforceable." Therefore, the trustee asserted, it was "uncertain as to the proper income beneficiary of said trust" and asked the court to construe and interpret the will to determine the rights of the parties.* * *

Asserting that the restrictive language provides for an illegal condition subsequent, Prince Edward relies on Meek v. Fox, 88 S.E. 161 (1916), to sustain the trial court's ruling that the racially discriminatory condition is void, but the gift is valid.

The issue presented in Meek involved the proper construction of a will regarding the testator's devise to his daughter, Julia Anne. In the will, the testator devised one-third of his land to his son in fee simple. To Eliza, his only married daughter, he devised one-third of his land during her life, remainder to her heirs. The testator made the following provision for Julia Anne: "Also to my daughter, Julia Anne, I desire that she shall have her equal share laid off, also according to quality and quantity, and she shall have it forever, except she should marry, then at her death I desire that it shall revert to her legal heirs."

After the testator's death, Julia Anne married. Later, she conveyed the land devised by the above clause to one Fox and another. After Julia Anne's marriage, her brother conveyed his land to one Meek, and included in his conveyance what he claimed to be his remainder in the land devised to his sister, Julia Anne, by the foregoing clause of the will.

In the ensuing litigation brought to remove a cloud upon the title to the land devised to Julia Anne, the appellant claimed the land under the conveyance to Meek while the appellees claimed under Julia Anne. The appellees contended that a fee simple estate vested in Julia Anne under the will; that the provision in the will created a condition subsequent in general restraint on marriage; that the condition was void as against public policy; and that the subsequent marriage of Julia Anne did not divest her of the fee simple estate, but the same continued in her and was passed from her by the conveyance to Fox.

This Court agreed with the appellees and held that the devise to Julia Anne, "and she shall have it forever," transferred to her upon the testator's death a fee simple estate in the land. The Court further held that the added provision of the devise, "except she should marry, then at her death I desire that it revert to her legal heirs," was a condition subsequent and was in restraint of marriage, and void. Therefore, the Court struck the condition, "and the estate thus became absolute and free from condition."

Drawing on the rationale of Meek, Prince Edward contends that because the discriminatory condition is void, its "interest in the income from the Trust remains vested" and "a subsequent beneficiary's interest will vest only in the event that Prince Edward ceases operation of a school." We disagree.

The principle of striking the offending condition subsequent and thereby creating an absolute estate, as applied in Meek, does not control this case because the provision at issue here is not a condition subsequent. Rather, this provision is a special limitation. Further, the estate in personalty created here is defeasible subject to an executory limitation. See Daniel v. Lipscomb, 66 S.E. 850, 851–52 (1910) (estate was a fee subject to executory limitation and not determinable fee because future interest was created in third person following defeasible fee, and not possibility of reverter in grantor or his heirs).

Professor Minor explains that "special limitations are created by such words as 'while,' 'during,' 'as long as,' 'until,' etc. Thus, a grant to A *until* Z returns from abroad; to a woman *while* she remains a widow, or *during* widowhood..., to D and his heirs *as long as* Y has heirs of his body..., all these are special limitations and not conditions subsequent." 1 Minor on Real Property § 525 at 690 (Ribble ed. 1928). "Limitations differ from conditions subsequent in this: A limitation marks the *utmost time of continuance* of an estate; a condition marks some event, which, if it happens in the course of that time, is to *defeat the estate*." Id., quoted in Meek.

In the granting clauses of Adams' will, he repeatedly specified that each educational beneficiary's right to receive income extended only "so long as" the beneficiary complied with the restrictive provision. But, if an educational beneficiary violated the restrictive provision by the matriculation of a black student, that beneficiary's interest would terminate, and the gift would devolve to successive educational beneficiaries who had not violated the provision. Further, Adams makes his intent clear in clause (b) that the creation of the educational beneficiaries' rights to receive income "shall be determinable" upon the happening of the contingency and that "all rights" of those institutions, successively to receive income from the trust "shall automatically terminate." Clearly this is language of limitation and not condition.

Meek makes clear that if the provision in that case had been a limitation, although equally offensive to the public policy against restraints on marriage, the Court could not have found it void. "Hence, while an estate limited 'to A in fee, but if he attempts to alien his estate then to B in fee,' would give A an absolute estate and in fee, free from condition, because the condition is an unreasonable restraint of alienation and void, yet a limitation 'to A until he attempts to alien, and then to B,' would be a perfectly good limitation, and upon A's attempt his estate would cease and go over to B." Although it did not address the issue of what happens when a gift subject to a special limitation offends constitutional considerations, the essential nature of a limitation as described by the Court in Meek points to the decision of the issue in this case.

In the words of Minor, a limitation marks the utmost time of continuance of the estate. And, a limitation cannot be altered to extend "beyond that period without violating the terms of the devise." 88 S.E. at 162. If a condition subsequent is unlawful, a court can merely excise the offending language and leave the remaining estate intact. But, where a gift or estate subject to a limitation is unlawful, in order to cure the defect the court must terminate the entire gift or estate.

Therefore, unlike in Meek, the interests of the educational charities fail completely. And, this is not because we give effect to an invalid trust provision. Rather, we strike the entire gift to Prince Edward and the gifts to the other educational beneficiaries because the offending language cannot be stricken from the provision without changing the essential nature and quality of the estate. See Evans v. Abney, 396 U.S. 435, 444–45 (1970).

It necessarily follows from the foregoing that, while the gifts to all the beneficiaries of Adams' charitable educational trust must fail, the executory interest of Hermitage survives. Adams did not place any unconstitutional limitations upon Hermitage's interest. And, as all prior estates have been declared invalid, Hermitage has the only valid, remaining interest. The trial court erred in holding to the contrary.

Because we find that the provision is a limitation, the same final result would be reached if we found that the trust's provisions were constitutional, as we have said earlier. By the natural operation of this limitation, if it were valid, upon the matriculation of a black student into Prince Edward, the school's interest terminated. And, because as counsel have represented, the educational institutions have all admitted black students, their respective interests in the trust proceeds can never vest into possession. Hermitage would be the ultimate beneficiary since no limitations are placed on its interest.

Finally, we reject the contentions of Seven Hills School and Miller School that, once the restrictive provisions are declared invalid the cy pres doctrine should be applied and evidence taken to determine the testator's intent in view of the changed circumstances.

The doctrine is codified in Code § 55-31, which provides, as relevant:

> When any … person gives, bequeaths, … any … property in trust to or for any educational, charitable or eleemosynary purpose, the indefiniteness or uncertainty of the beneficiaries named in any instrument creating such a gift, bequest … or the indefiniteness of the purpose of the trust itself, shall not defeat any such trust and, … it shall be administered to conform as near as may be to the purpose for which created or, if impossible of performance for this purpose, for some other educational, charitable, benevolent or eleemosynary purpose.…

Here, there is no indefiniteness or uncertainty regarding the beneficiaries or purpose of the trust. Moreover, there is a valid gift over to Hermitage, as we have said, and this eliminates any need for the court to search for the testator's intent. Under these circumstances, it would be inappropriate to look beyond the four corners of the testamentary documents.

For these reasons, we will affirm the trial court's ruling that cy pres is inapplicable. We will reverse the ruling that the trust income will be paid to Prince Edward. Instead, we will enter final judgment here ordering the trustee to pay all retained trust income and future trust income to Hermitage.

Jonathan L. Entin, *Defeasible Fees, State Action, and the Legacy of Massive Resistance*
34 Wm. & Mary L. Rev. 769, 793 (1993)

The background to the creation of the Adams trust resonates deeply in modern American history. The Prince Edward School Foundation was founded in June 1955 to establish private schools for white pupils in the event that the federal courts ordered the public schools of Prince Edward County to desegregate. Such an order seemed certain because the county school board was one of the defendants in Brown v. Bd. of Educ. The order finally came in 1959. Local officials responded by shutting down the public schools. At the same time, the Foundation opened a private school known as Prince Edward Academy that enrolled almost every white student in the county. The Academy continued to enroll a large majority of the county's white pupils for some years after the Supreme Court ordered the public schools reopened on a desegregated basis in 1964.

III

International and Foreign Human Rights Law

Universal Declaration of Human Rights
(G.A. res. 217 A (III) U.N. GAOR, 3d Sess.,
Supp. No. 13, at 71, U.N. Doc. A/810 (1948)

Preamble

Whereas recognition of the inherent dignity and of the equal and inalienable rights of all members of the human family is the foundation of freedom, justice and peace in the world,

Whereas disregard and contempt for human rights have resulted in barbarous acts which have outraged the conscience of mankind, and the advent of a world in which human beings shall enjoy freedom of speech and belief and freedom from fear and want has been proclaimed as the highest aspiration of the common people,

Whereas it is essential, if man is not to be compelled to have recourse, as a last resort, to rebellion against tyranny and oppression, that human rights should be protected by the rule of law,

Whereas it is essential to promote the development of friendly relations between nations,

Whereas the peoples of the United Nations have in the Charter reaffirmed their faith in fundamental human rights, in the dignity and worth of the human person and in the equal rights of men and women and have determined to promote social progress and better standards of life in larger freedom,

Whereas Member States have pledged themselves to achieve, in co-operation with the United Nations, the promotion of universal respect for and observance of human rights and fundamental freedoms,

Whereas a common understanding of these rights and freedoms is of the greatest importance for the full realization of this pledge,

Now, therefore, The General Assembly proclaims this Universal Declaration of Human Rights as a common standard of achievement for all peoples and all nations, to the end that every individual and every organ of society, keeping this Declaration constantly in mind, shall strive by teaching and education to promote respect for these rights and freedoms and by progressive measures, national and international, to secure their universal and effective recognition and observance, both among the peoples of Member States themselves and among the peoples of territories under their jurisdiction.

Article 1

All human beings are born free and equal in dignity and rights. They are endowed with reason and conscience and should act towards one another in a spirit of brotherhood.

Article 2

Everyone is entitled to all the rights and freedoms set forth in this Declaration, without distinction of any kind, such as race, colour, sex, language, religion, political or other opinion, national or social origin, property, birth or other status. Furthermore, no distinction shall be made on the basis of the political, jurisdictional or international status of the country or territory to which a person belongs, whether it be independent, trust, non-self-governing or under any other limitation of sovereignty.

Article 3

Everyone has the right to life, liberty and security of person.

Article 4

No one shall be held in slavery or servitude; slavery and the slave trade shall be prohibited in all their forms.

Article 5

No one shall be subjected to torture or to cruel, inhuman or degrading treatment or punishment.

Article 6

Everyone has the right to recognition everywhere as a person before the law.

Article 7

All are equal before the law and are entitled without any discrimination to equal protection of the law. All are entitled to equal protection against any discrimination in violation of this Declaration and against any incitement to such discrimination.

Article 8

Everyone has the right to an effective remedy by the competent national tribunals for acts violating the fundamental rights granted him by the constitution or by law.

Article 9

No one shall be subjected to arbitrary arrest, detention or exile.

Article 10

Everyone is entitled in full equality to a fair and public hearing by an independent and impartial tribunal, in the determination of his rights and obligations and of any criminal charge against him.

Article 11

(1) Everyone charged with a penal offence has the right to be presumed innocent until proved guilty according to law in a public trial at which he has had all the guarantees necessary for his defence.

(2) No one shall be held guilty of any penal offence on account of any act or omission which did not constitute a penal offence, under national or international law, at the time when it was committed. Nor shall a heavier penalty be imposed than the one that was applicable at the time the penal offence was committed.

Article 12

No one shall be subjected to arbitrary interference with his privacy, family, home or correspondence, nor to attacks upon his honour and reputation. Everyone has the right to the protection of the law against such interference or attacks.

Article 13

(1) Everyone has the right to freedom of movement and residence within the borders of each State.

(2) Everyone has the right to leave any country, including his own, and to return to his country.

Article 14

(1) Everyone has the right to seek and to enjoy in other countries asylum from persecution.

(2) This right may not be invoked in the case of prosecutions genuinely arising from non-political crimes or from acts contrary to the purposes and principles of the United Nations.

Article 15

(1) Everyone has the right to a nationality.

(2) No one shall be arbitrarily deprived of his nationality nor denied the right to change his nationality.

Article 16

(1) Men and women of full age, without any limitation due to race, nationality or religion, have the right to marry and to found a family. They are entitled to equal rights as to marriage, during marriage and at its dissolution.

(2) Marriage shall be entered into only with the free and full consent of the intending spouses.

(3) The family is the natural and fundamental group unit of society and is entitled to protection by society and the State.

Article 17

(1) Everyone has the right to own property alone as well as in association with others.

(2) No one shall be arbitrarily deprived of his property.

Article 18

Everyone has the right to freedom of thought, conscience and religion; this right includes freedom to change his religion or belief, and freedom, either alone or in community with others and in public or private, to manifest his religion or belief in teaching, practice, worship and observance.

Article 19

Everyone has the right to freedom of opinion and expression; this right includes freedom to hold opinions without interference and to seek, receive and impart information and ideas through any media and regardless of frontiers.

Article 20

(1) Everyone has the right to freedom of peaceful assembly and association.

(2) No one may be compelled to belong to an association.

Article 21

(1) Everyone has the right to take part in the government of his country, directly or through freely chosen representatives.

(2) Everyone has the right to equal access to public service in his country.

(3) The will of the people shall be the basis of the authority of government; this will shall be expressed in periodic and genuine elections which shall be by universal and equal suffrage and shall be held by secret vote or by equivalent free voting procedures.

Article 22

Everyone, as a member of society, has the right to social security and is entitled to realization, through national effort and international co-operation and in accordance with the organization and resources of each State, of the economic, social and cultural rights indispensable for his dignity and the free development of his personality.

Article 23

(1) Everyone has the right to work, to free choice of employment, to just and favourable conditions of work and to protection against unemployment.

(2) Everyone, without any discrimination, has the right to equal pay for equal work.

(3) Everyone who works has the right to just and favourable remuneration ensuring for himself and his family an existence worthy of human dignity, and supplemented, if necessary, by other means of social protection.

(4) Everyone has the right to form and to join trade unions for the protection of his interests.

Article 24

Everyone has the right to rest and leisure, including reasonable limitation of working hours and periodic holidays with pay.

Article 25

(1) Everyone has the right to a standard of living adequate for the health and well-being of himself and of his family, including food, clothing, housing and medical care and necessary social services, and the right to security in the event of unemployment, sickness, disability, widowhood, old age or other lack of livelihood in circumstances beyond his control.

(2) Motherhood and childhood are entitled to special care and assistance. All children, whether born in or out of wedlock, shall enjoy the same social protection.

Article 26

(1) Everyone has the right to education. Education shall be free, at least in the elementary and fundamental stages. Elementary education shall be compulsory. Technical and professional education shall be made generally available and higher education shall be equally accessible to all on the basis of merit.

(2) Education shall be directed to the full development of the human personality and to the strengthening of respect for human rights and fundamental freedoms. It shall promote understanding, tolerance and friendship among all nations, racial or religious groups, and shall further the activities of the United Nations for the maintenance of peace.

(3) Parents have a prior right to choose the kind of education that shall be given to their children.

Article 27

(1) Everyone has the right freely to participate in the cultural life of the community, to enjoy the arts and to share in scientific advancement and its benefits.

(2) Everyone has the right to the protection of the moral and material interests resulting from any scientific, literary or artistic production of which he is the author.

Article 28

Everyone is entitled to a social and international order in which the rights and freedoms set forth in this Declaration can be fully realized.

Article 29

(1) Everyone has duties to the community in which alone the free and full development of his personality is possible.

(2) In the exercise of his rights and freedoms, everyone shall be subject only to such limitations as are determined by law solely for the purpose of securing due recognition and respect for the rights and freedoms of others and of meeting the just requirements of morality, public order and the general welfare in a democratic society.

(3) These rights and freedoms may in no case be exercised contrary to the purposes and principles of the United Nations.

Article 30

Nothing in this Declaration may be interpreted as implying for any State, group or person any right to engage in any activity or to perform any act aimed at the destruction of any of the rights and freedoms set forth herein.

International Covenant on Economic, Social, and Cultural Rights

G.A. res. 2200A (XXI), 21 U.N.GAOR Supp. (No. 16) at 49, U.N. Doc. A/6316 (1966), 993 U.N.T.S. 3, *entered into force* Jan. 3, 1976

Preamble

The States Parties to the present Covenant,

Considering that, in accordance with the principles proclaimed in the Charter of the United Nations, recognition of the inherent dignity and of the equal and inalienable rights of all members of the human family is the foundation of freedom, justice and peace in the world,

Recognizing that these rights derive from the inherent dignity of the human person,

Recognizing that, in accordance with the Universal Declaration of Human Rights, the ideal of free human beings enjoying freedom from fear and want can only be achieved if conditions are created whereby everyone may enjoy his economic, social and cultural rights, as well as his civil and political rights,

Considering the obligation of States under the Charter of the United Nations to promote universal respect for, and observance of, human rights and freedoms,

Realizing that the individual, having duties to other individuals and to the community to which he belongs, is under a responsibility to strive for the promotion and observance of the rights recognized in the present Covenant,

Agree upon the following articles:

Part I

Article 1

1. All peoples have the right of self-determination. By virtue of that right they freely determine their political status and freely pursue their economic, social and cultural development.

2. All peoples may, for their own ends, freely dispose of their natural wealth and resources without prejudice to any obligations arising out of international economic co-operation, based upon the principle of mutual benefit, and international law. In no case may a people be deprived of its own means of subsistence.

3. The States Parties to the present Covenant, including those having responsibility for the administration of Non-Self-Governing and Trust Territories, shall promote the realization of the right of self-determination, and shall respect that right, in conformity with the provisions of the Charter of the United Nations.

Part II

Article 2

1. Each State Party to the present Covenant undertakes to take steps, individually and through international assistance and co-operation, especially economic and technical, to the maximum of its available resources, with a view to achieving progressively the full realization of the rights recognized in the present Covenant by all appropriate means, including particularly the adoption of legislative measures.

2. The States Parties to the present Covenant undertake to guarantee that the rights enunciated in the present Covenant will be exercised without discrimination of any kind as to race, colour, sex, language, religion, political or other opinion, national or social origin, property, birth or other status.

3. Developing countries, with due regard to human rights and their national economy, may determine to what extent they would guarantee the economic rights recognized in the present Covenant to non-nationals.

Article 3

The States Parties to the present Covenant undertake to ensure the equal right of men and women to the enjoyment of all economic, social and cultural rights set forth in the present Covenant.

Article 4

The States Parties to the present Covenant recognize that, in the enjoyment of those rights provided by the State in conformity with the present Covenant, the State may subject such rights only to such limitations as are determined by law only in so far as this may be compatible with the nature of these rights and solely for the purpose of promoting the general welfare in a democratic society.

Article 5

1. Nothing in the present Covenant may be interpreted as implying for any State, group or person any right to engage in any activity or to perform any act aimed at the destruction of any of the rights or freedoms recognized herein, or at their limitation to a greater extent than is provided for in the present Covenant.

2. No restriction upon or derogation from any of the fundamental human rights recognized or existing in any country in virtue of law, conventions, regulations or custom shall be admitted on the pretext that the present Covenant does not recognize such rights or that it recognizes them to a lesser extent.

Part III

Article 6

1. The States Parties to the present Covenant recognize the right to work, which includes the right of everyone to the opportunity to gain his living by work which he freely chooses or accepts, and will take appropriate steps to safeguard this right.

2. The steps to be taken by a State Party to the present Covenant to achieve the full realization of this right shall include technical and vocational guidance and training programmes, policies and techniques to achieve steady economic, social and cultural development and full and productive employment under conditions safeguarding fundamental political and economic freedoms to the individual.

Article 7

The States Parties to the present Covenant recognize the right of everyone to the enjoyment of just and favourable conditions of work which ensure, in particular:

(a) Remuneration which provides all workers, as a minimum, with:

(i) Fair wages and equal remuneration for work of equal value without distinction of any kind, in particular women being guaranteed conditions of work not inferior to those enjoyed by men, with equal pay for equal work;

(ii) A decent living for themselves and their families in accordance with the provisions of the present Covenant;

(b) Safe and healthy working conditions;

(c) Equal opportunity for everyone to be promoted in his employment to an appropriate higher level, subject to no considerations other than those of seniority and competence;

(d) Rest, leisure and reasonable limitation of working hours and periodic holidays with pay, as well as remuneration for public holidays

Article 8

1. The States Parties to the present Covenant undertake to ensure:

(a) The right of everyone to form trade unions and join the trade union of his choice, subject only to the rules of the organization concerned, for the promotion and protection of his economic and social interests. No restrictions may be placed on the exercise of this right other than those prescribed by law and which are necessary in a democratic society in the interests of national security or public order or for the protection of the rights and freedoms of others;

(b) The right of trade unions to establish national federations or confederations and the right of the latter to form or join international trade-union organizations;

(c) The right of trade unions to function freely subject to no limitations other than those prescribed by law and which are necessary in a democratic society in the interests of national security or public order or for the protection of the rights and freedoms of others;

(d) The right to strike, provided that it is exercised in conformity with the laws of the particular country.

2. This article shall not prevent the imposition of lawful restrictions on the exercise of these rights by members of the armed forces or of the police or of the administration of the State.

3. Nothing in this article shall authorize States Parties to the International Labour Organisation Convention of 1948 concerning Freedom of Association and Protection of the Right to Organize to take legislative measures which would prejudice, or apply the law in such a manner as would prejudice, the guarantees provided for in that Convention.

Article 9

The States Parties to the present Covenant recognize the right of everyone to social security, including social insurance.

Article 10

The States Parties to the present Covenant recognize that:

1. The widest possible protection and assistance should be accorded to the family, which is the natural and fundamental group unit of society, particularly for its establishment and while it is responsible for the care and education of dependent children. Marriage must be entered into with the free consent of the intending spouses.

2. Special protections should be accorded to mothers during a reasonable period before and after childbirth. During such period working mothers should be accorded paid leave or leave with adequate social security benefits.

3. Special measures of protection and assistance should be taken on behalf of all children and young persons without any discrimination for reasons of parentage or other conditions. Children and young persons should be protected from economic and social exploitation. Their employment in work harmful to their morals or health or dangerous to life or likely to hamper their normal development should be punishable by law. States should also set age limits below which the paid employment of child labour should be prohibited and punishable by law.

Article 11

1. The States Parties to the present Covenant recognize the right of everyone to an adequate standard of living for himself and his family, including adequate food, clothing and housing, and to the continuous improvement of living conditions. The States Parties will take appropriate steps to ensure the realization of this right, recognizing to this effect the essential importance of international co-operation based on free consent.

2. The States Parties to the present Covenant, recognizing the fundamental right of everyone to be free from hunger, shall take, individually and through international co-operation, the measures, including specific programmes, which are needed:

   (a) To improve methods of production, conservation and distribution of food by making full use of technical and scientific knowledge, by disseminating knowledge of the principles of nutrition and by developing or reforming agrarian systems in such a way as to achieve the most efficient development and utilization of natural resources;

   (b) Taking into account the problems of both food-importing and food-exporting countries, to ensure an equitable distribution of world food supplies in relation to need.

Article 12

1. The States Parties to the present Covenant recognize the right of everyone to the enjoyment of the highest attainable standard of physical and mental health.

2. The steps to be taken by the States Parties to the present Covenant to achieve the full realization of this right shall include those necessary for:

   (a) The provision for the reduction of the stillbirth-rate and of infant mortality and for the healthy development of the child;

   (b) The improvement of all aspects of environmental and industrial hygiene;

   (c) The prevention, treatment and control of epidemic, endemic, occupational and other diseases;

   (d) The creation of conditions which would assure to all medical service and medical attention in the event of sickness.

Article 13

1. The States Parties to the present Covenant recognize the right of everyone to education. They agree that education shall be directed to the full development

of the human personality and the sense of its dignity, and shall strengthen the respect for human rights and fundamental freedoms. They further agree that education shall enable all persons to participate effectively in a free society, promote understanding, tolerance and friendship among all nations and all racial, ethnic or religious groups, and further the activities of the United Nations for the maintenance of peace.

2. The States Parties to the present Covenant recognize that, with a view to achieving the full realization of this right:

   (a) Primary education shall be compulsory and available free to all;

   (b) Secondary education in its different forms, including technical and vocational secondary education, shall be made generally available and accessible to all by every appropriate means, and in particular by the progressive introduction of free education;

   (c) Higher education shall be made equally accessible to all, on the basis of capacity, by every appropriate means, and in particular by the progressive introduction of free education;

   (d) Fundamental education shall be encouraged or intensified as far as possible for those persons who have not received or completed the whole period of their primary education;

   (e) The development of a system of schools at all levels shall be actively pursued, an adequate fellowship system shall be established, and the material conditions of teaching staff shall be continuously improved.

3. The States Parties to the present Covenant undertake to have respect for the liberty of parents and, when applicable, legal guardians to choose for their children schools, other than those established by the public authorities, which conform to such minimum educational standards as may be laid down or approved by the State and to ensure the religious and moral education of their children in conformity with their own convictions.

4. No part of this article shall be construed so as to interfere with the liberty of individuals and bodies to establish and direct educational institutions, subject always to the observance of the principles set forth in paragraph I of this article and to the requirement that the education given in such institutions shall conform to such minimum standards as may be laid down by the State.

Article 14

Each State Party to the present Covenant which, at the time of becoming a Party, has not been able to secure in its metropolitan territory or other territories under its jurisdiction compulsory primary education, free of charge, undertakes, within two years, to work out and adopt a detailed plan of action for the progressive implementation, within a reasonable number of years, to be fixed in the plan, of the principle of compulsory education free of charge for all.

Article 15

1. The States Parties to the present Covenant recognize the right of everyone:

   (a) To take part in cultural life;

   (b) To enjoy the benefits of scientific progress and its applications;

(c) To benefit from the protection of the moral and material interests resulting from any scientific, literary or artistic production of which he is the author.

2. The steps to be taken by the States Parties to the present Covenant to achieve the full realization of this right shall include those necessary for the conservation, the development and the diffusion of science and culture.

3. The States Parties to the present Covenant undertake to respect the freedom indispensable for scientific research and creative activity.

4. The States Parties to the present Covenant recognize the benefits to be derived from the encouragement and development of international contacts and co-operation in the scientific and cultural fields.

[Parts IV and V have been omitted.]

International Convention on the Elimination of All Forms of Racial Discrimination

Adopted and opened for signature and ratification
by General Assembly resolution 2106 (XX) of 21 December 1965
entry into force 4 January 1969, in accordance with Article 19

The States Parties to this Convention,

Considering that the Charter of the United Nations is based on the principles of the dignity and equality inherent in all human beings, and that all Member States have pledged themselves to take joint and separate action, in co-operation with the Organization, for the achievement of one of the purposes of the United Nations which is to promote and encourage universal respect for and observance of human rights and fundamental freedoms for all, without distinction as to race, sex, language or religion,

Considering that the Universal Declaration of Human Rights proclaims that all human beings are born free and equal in dignity and rights and that everyone is entitled to all the rights and freedoms set out therein, without distinction of any kind, in particular as to race, colour or national origin,

Considering that all human beings are equal before the law and are entitled to equal protection of the law against any discrimination and against any incitement to discrimination,

Considering that the United Nations has condemned colonialism and all practices of segregation and discrimination associated therewith, in whatever form and wherever they exist, and that the Declaration on the Granting of Independence to Colonial Countries and Peoples of 14 December 1960 (General Assembly resolution 1514 (XV)) has affirmed and solemnly proclaimed the necessity of bringing them to a speedy and unconditional end,

Considering that the United Nations Declaration on the Elimination of All Forms of Racial Discrimination of 20 November 1963 (General Assembly resolution 1904 (XVIII)) solemnly affirms the necessity of speedily eliminating racial discrimination throughout the world in all its forms and manifestations and of securing understanding of and respect for the dignity of the human person,

Convinced that any doctrine of superiority based on racial differentiation is scientifically false, morally condemnable, socially unjust and dangerous, and that there is no justification for racial discrimination, in theory or in practice, anywhere,

Reaffirming that discrimination between human beings on the grounds of race, colour or ethnic origin is an obstacle to friendly and peaceful relations among nations and is capable of disturbing peace and security among peoples and the harmony of persons living side by side even within one and the same State,

Convinced that the existence of racial barriers is repugnant to the ideals of any human society,

Alarmed by manifestations of racial discrimination still in evidence in some areas of the world and by governmental policies based on racial superiority or hatred, such as policies of apartheid, segregation or separation,

Resolved to adopt all necessary measures for speedily eliminating racial discrimination in all its forms and manifestations, and to prevent and combat racist doctrines and practices in order to promote understanding between races and to build an international community free from all forms of racial segregation and racial discrimination,

Bearing in mind the Convention concerning Discrimination in respect of Employment and Occupation adopted by the International Labour Organisation in 1958, and the Convention against Discrimination in Education adopted by the United Nations Educational, Scientific and Cultural Organization in 1960,

Desiring to implement the principles embodied in the United Nations Declaration on the Elimination of Al l Forms of Racial Discrimination and to secure the earliest adoption of practical measures to that end,

Have agreed as follows:

Part I

Article 1

1. In this Convention, the term "racial discrimination" shall mean any distinction, exclusion, restriction or preference based on race, colour, descent, or national or ethnic origin which has the purpose or effect of nullifying or impairing the recognition, enjoyment or exercise, on an equal footing, of human rights and fundamental freedoms in the political, economic, social, cultural or any other field of public life.

2. This Convention shall not apply to distinctions, exclusions, restrictions or preferences made by a State Party to this Convention between citizens and non-citizens.

3. Nothing in this Convention may be interpreted as affecting in any way the legal provisions of States Parties concerning nationality, citizenship or naturalization, provided that such provisions do not discriminate against any particular nationality.

4. Special measures taken for the sole purpose of securing adequate advancement of certain racial or ethnic groups or individuals requiring such protection as may be necessary in order to ensure such groups or individuals equal enjoyment or exercise of human rights and fundamental freedoms shall not be deemed racial discrimination, provided, however, that such measures do not, as a consequence, lead to the maintenance of separate rights for different racial groups and that they shall not be continued after the objectives for which they were taken have been achieved.

Article 2

1. States Parties condemn racial discrimination and undertake to pursue by all appropriate means and without delay a policy of eliminating racial discrimination in all its

forms and promoting understanding among all races, and, to this end: (a) Each State Party undertakes to engage in no act or practice of racial discrimination against persons, groups of persons or institutions and to ensure that all public authorities and public institutions, national and local, shall act in conformity with this obligation;

(b) Each State Party undertakes not to sponsor, defend or support racial discrimination by any persons or organizations;

(c) Each State Party shall take effective measures to review governmental, national and local policies, and to amend, rescind or nullify any laws and regulations which have the effect of creating or perpetuating racial discrimination wherever it exists;

(d) Each State Party shall prohibit and bring to an end, by all appropriate means, including legislation as required by circumstances, racial discrimination by any persons, group or organization;

(e) Each State Party undertakes to encourage, where appropriate, integrationist multiracial organizations and movements and other means of eliminating barriers between races, and to discourage anything which tends to strengthen racial division.

2. States Parties shall, when the circumstances so warrant, take, in the social, economic, cultural and other fields, special and concrete measures to ensure the adequate development and protection of certain racial groups or individuals belonging to them, for the purpose of guaranteeing them the full and equal enjoyment of human rights and fundamental freedoms. These measures shall in no case entail as a consequence the maintenance of unequal or separate rights for different racial groups after the objectives for which they were taken have been achieved.

Article 3

States Parties particularly condemn racial segregation and apartheid and undertake to prevent, prohibit and eradicate all practices of this nature in territories under their jurisdiction.

Article 4

States Parties condemn all propaganda and all organizations which are based on ideas or theories of superiority of one race or group of persons of one colour or ethnic origin, or which attempt to justify or promote racial hatred and discrimination in any form, and undertake to adopt immediate and positive measures designed to eradicate all incitement to, or acts of, such discrimination and, to this end, with due regard to the principles embodied in the Universal Declaration of Human Rights and the rights expressly set forth in article 5 of this Convention, inter alia:

(a) Shall declare an offence punishable by law all dissemination of ideas based on racial superiority or hatred, incitement to racial discrimination, as well as all acts of violence or incitement to such acts against any race or group of persons of another colour or ethnic origin, and also the provision of any assistance to racist activities, including the financing thereof;

(b) Shall declare illegal and prohibit organizations, and also organized and all other propaganda activities, which promote and incite racial discrimination, and shall recognize participation in such organizations or activities as an offence punishable by law;

(c) Shall not permit public authorities or public institutions, national or local, to promote or incite racial discrimination.

Article 5

In compliance with the fundamental obligations laid down in article 2 of this Convention, States Parties undertake to prohibit and to eliminate racial discrimination in all its forms and to guarantee the right of everyone, without distinction as to race, colour, or national or ethnic origin, to equality before the law, notably in the enjoyment of the following rights:

(a) The right to equal treatment before the tribunals and all other organs administering justice;

(b) The right to security of person and protection by the State against violence or bodily harm, whether inflicted by government officials or by any individual group or institution;

(c) Political rights, in particular the right to participate in elections—to vote and to stand for election—on the basis of universal and equal suffrage, to take part in the Government as well as in the conduct of public affairs at any level and to have equal access to public service;

(d) Other civil rights, in particular:

   (i)   The right to freedom of movement and residence within the border of the State;

   (ii) The right to leave any country, including one's own, and to return to one's country;

   (iii) The right to nationality;

   (iv) The right to marriage and choice of spouse;

   (v)   The right to own property alone as well as in association with others;

   (vi) The right to inherit;

   (vii) The right to freedom of thought, conscience and religion;

   (viii) The right to freedom of opinion and expression;

   (ix) The right to freedom of peaceful assembly and association;

(e) Economic, social and cultural rights, in particular:

   (i)   The rights to work, to free choice of employment, to just and favourable conditions of work, to protection against unemployment, to equal pay for equal work, to just and favourable remuneration;

   (ii) The right to form and join trade unions;

   (iii) The right to housing;

   (iv) The right to public health, medical care, social security and social services;

   (v)   The right to education and training;

   (vi) The right to equal participation in cultural activities;

(f) The right of access to any place or service intended for use by the general public, such as transport hotels, restaurants, cafes, theatres and parks.

Article 6

States Parties shall assure to everyone within their jurisdiction effective protection and remedies, through the competent national tribunals and other State institutions, against any acts of racial discrimination which violate his human rights and fundamental freedoms contrary to this Convention, as well as the right to seek from such tribunals just and adequate reparation or satisfaction for any damage suffered as a result of such discrimination.

Article 7

States Parties undertake to adopt immediate and effective measures, particularly in the fields of teaching, education, culture and information, with a view to combating prejudices which lead to racial discrimination and to promoting understanding, tolerance and friendship among nations and racial or ethnical groups, as well as to propagating the purposes and principles of the Charter of the United Nations, the Universal Declaration of Human Rights, the United Nations Declaration on the Elimination of All Forms of Racial Discrimination, and this Convention.

[Articles 8–25 have been omitted.]

International Convention on the Elimination of All Forms of Discrimination against Women

Adopted and opened for signature, ratification and accession
by General Assembly resolution 34/180 of 18 December 1979
entry into force 3 September 1981, in accordance with article 27(1)

The States Parties to the present Convention,

Noting that the Charter of the United Nations reaffirms faith in fundamental human rights, in the dignity and worth of the human person and in the equal rights of men and women,

Noting that the Universal Declaration of Human Rights affirms the principle of the inadmissibility of discrimination and proclaims that all human beings are born free and equal in dignity and rights and that everyone is entitled to all the rights and freedoms set forth therein, without distinction of any kind, including distinction based on sex,

Noting that the States Parties to the International Covenants on Human Rights have the obligation to ensure the equal rights of men and women to enjoy all economic, social, cultural, civil and political rights,

Considering the international conventions concluded under the auspices of the United Nations and the specialized agencies promoting equality of rights of men and women,

Noting also the resolutions, declarations and recommendations adopted by the United Nations and the specialized agencies promoting equality of rights of men and women,

Concerned, however, that despite these various instruments extensive discrimination against women continues to exist,

Recalling that discrimination against women violates the principles of equality of rights and respect for human dignity, is an obstacle to the participation of women, on equal terms with men, in the political, social, economic and cultural life of their countries, hampers the growth of the prosperity of society and the family and makes more difficult the full development of the potentialities of women in the service of their countries and of humanity,

Concerned that in situations of poverty women have the least access to food, health, education, training and opportunities for employment and other needs,

Convinced that the establishment of the new international economic order based on equity and justice will contribute significantly towards the promotion of equality between men and women,

Emphasizing that the eradication of apartheid, all forms of racism, racial discrimination, colonialism, neo-colonialism, aggression, foreign occupation and domination and interference in the internal affairs of States is essential to the full enjoyment of the rights of men and women,

Affirming that the strengthening of international peace and security, the relaxation of international tension, mutual co-operation among all States irrespective of their social and economic systems, general and complete disarmament, in particular nuclear disarmament under strict and effective international control, the affirmation of the principles of justice, equality and mutual benefit in relations among countries and the realization of the right of peoples under alien and colonial domination and foreign occupation to self-determination and independence, as well as respect for national sovereignty and territorial integrity, will promote social progress and development and as a consequence will contribute to the attainment of full equality between men and women,

Convinced that the full and complete development of a country, the welfare of the world and the cause of peace require the maximum participation of women on equal terms with men in all fields,

Bearing in mind the great contribution of women to the welfare of the family and to the development of society, so far not fully recognized, the social significance of maternity and the role of both parents in the family and in the upbringing of children, and aware that the role of women in procreation should not be a basis for discrimination but that the upbringing of children requires a sharing of responsibility between men and women and society as a whole,

Aware that a change in the traditional role of men as well as the role of women in society and in the family is needed to achieve full equality between men and women,

Determined to implement the principles set forth in the Declaration on the Elimination of Discrimination against Women and, for that purpose, to adopt the measures required for the elimination of such discrimination in all its forms and manifestations,

Have agreed on the following:

Part I

Article I

For the purposes of the present Convention, the term "discrimination against women" shall mean any distinction, exclusion or restriction made on the basis of sex which has the effect or purpose of impairing or nullifying the recognition, enjoyment or exercise by women, irrespective of their marital status, on a basis of equality of men and women, of human rights and fundamental freedoms in the political, economic, social, cultural, civil or any other field.

Article 2

States Parties condemn discrimination against women in all its forms, agree to pursue by all appropriate means and without delay a policy of eliminating discrimination against women and, to this end, undertake:

  (a) To embody the principle of the equality of men and women in their national constitutions or other appropriate legislation if not yet incorporated therein and to ensure, through law and other appropriate means, the practical realization of this principle;

(b) To adopt appropriate legislative and other measures, including sanctions where appropriate, prohibiting all discrimination against women;

(c) To establish legal protection of the rights of women on an equal basis with men and to ensure through competent national tribunals and other public institutions the effective protection of women against any act of discrimination;

(d) To refrain from engaging in any act or practice of discrimination against women and to ensure that public authorities and institutions shall act in conformity with this obligation;

(e) To take all appropriate measures to eliminate discrimination against women by any person, organization or enterprise;

(f) To take all appropriate measures, including legislation, to modify or abolish existing laws, regulations, customs and practices which constitute discrimination against women;

(g) To repeal all national penal provisions which constitute discrimination against women.

Article 3

States Parties shall take in all fields, in particular in the political, social, economic and cultural fields, all appropriate measures, including legislation, to ensure the full development and advancement of women, for the purpose of guaranteeing them the exercise and enjoyment of human rights and fundamental freedoms on a basis of equality with men.

Article 4

1. Adoption by States Parties of temporary special measures aimed at accelerating de facto equality between men and women shall not be considered discrimination as defined in the present Convention, but shall in no way entail as a consequence the maintenance of unequal or separate standards; these measures shall be discontinued when the objectives of equality of opportunity and treatment have been achieved.

2. Adoption by States Parties of special measures, including those measures contained in the present Convention, aimed at protecting maternity shall not be considered discriminatory.

Article 5

States Parties shall take all appropriate measures:

(a) To modify the social and cultural patterns of conduct of men and women, with a view to achieving the elimination of prejudices and customary and all other practices which are based on the idea of the inferiority or the superiority of either of the sexes or on stereotyped roles for men and women;

(b) To ensure that family education includes a proper understanding of maternity as a social function and the recognition of the common responsibility of men and women in the upbringing and development of their children, it being understood that the interest of the children is the primordial consideration in all cases. * * *

Part III

Article 10

States Parties shall take all appropriate measures to eliminate discrimination against women in order to ensure to them equal rights with men in the field of education and in particular to ensure, on a basis of equality of men and women:

(a) The same conditions for career and vocational guidance, for access to studies and for the achievement of diplomas in educational establishments of all categories in rural as well as in urban areas; this equality shall be ensured in pre-school, general, technical, professional and higher technical education, as well as in all types of vocational training;

(b) Access to the same curricula, the same examinations, teaching staff with qualifications of the same standard and school premises and equipment of the same quality;

(c) The elimination of any stereotyped concept of the roles of men and women at all levels and in all forms of education by encouraging coeducation and other types of education which will help to achieve this aim and, in particular, by the revision of textbooks and school programmes and the adaptation of teaching methods;

(d) The same opportunities to benefit from scholarships and other study grants;

(e) The same opportunities for access to programmes of continuing education, including adult and functional literacy programmes, particularly those aimed at reducing, at the earliest possible time, any gap in education existing between men and women;

(f) The reduction of female student drop-out rates and the organization of programmes for girls and women who have left school prematurely;

(g) The same opportunities to participate actively in sports and physical education;

(h) Access to specific educational information to help to ensure the health and well-being of families, including information and advice on family planning.

Article 11

1. States Parties shall take all appropriate measures to eliminate discrimination against women in the field of employment in order to ensure, on a basis of equality of men and women, the same rights, in particular:

(a) The right to work as an inalienable right of all human beings;

(b) The right to the same employment opportunities, including the application of the same criteria for selection in matters of employment;

(c) The right to free choice of profession and employment, the right to promotion, job security and all benefits and conditions of service and the right to receive vocational training and retraining, including apprenticeships, advanced vocational training and recurrent training;

(d) The right to equal remuneration, including benefits, and to equal treatment in respect of work of equal value, as well as equality of treatment in the evaluation of the quality of work;

(e) The right to social security, particularly in cases of retirement, unemployment, sickness, invalidity and old age and other incapacity to work, as well as the right to paid leave;

(f) The right to protection of health and to safety in working conditions, including the safeguarding of the function of reproduction. * * *

Article 13

States Parties shall take all appropriate measures to eliminate discrimination against women in other areas of economic and social life in order to ensure, on a basis of equality of men and women, the same rights, in particular:

(a) The right to family benefits;

(b) The right to bank loans, mortgages and other forms of financial credit;

(c) The right to participate in recreational activities, sports and all aspects of cultural life.

Article 14

1. States Parties shall take into account the particular problems faced by rural women and the significant roles which rural women play in the economic survival of their families, including their work in the non-monetized sectors of the economy, and shall take all appropriate measures to ensure the application of the provisions of the present Convention to women in rural areas.

2. States Parties shall take all appropriate measures to eliminate discrimination against women in rural areas in order to ensure, on a basis of equality of men and women, that they participate in and benefit from rural development and, in particular, shall ensure to such women the right:

(a) To participate in the elaboration and implementation of development planning at all levels;

(b) To have access to adequate health care facilities, including information, counselling and services in family planning;

(c) To benefit directly from social security programmes;

(d) To obtain all types of training and education, formal and non-formal, including that relating to functional literacy, as well as, inter alia, the benefit of all community and extension services, in order to increase their technical proficiency;

(e) To organize self-help groups and co-operatives in order to obtain equal access to economic opportunities through employment or self employment;

(f) To participate in all community activities;

(g) To have access to agricultural credit and loans, marketing facilities, appropriate technology and equal treatment in land and agrarian reform as well as in land resettlement schemes;

(h) To enjoy adequate living conditions, particularly in relation to housing, sanitation, electricity and water supply, transport and communications.

Part IV

Article 15

1. States Parties shall accord to women equality with men before the law.

2. States Parties shall accord to women, in civil matters, a legal capacity identical to that of men and the same opportunities to exercise that capacity. In particular, they shall give women equal rights to conclude contracts and to administer property and shall treat them equally in all stages of procedure in courts and tribunals.

3. States Parties agree that all contracts and all other private instruments of any kind with a legal effect which is directed at restricting the legal capacity of women shall be deemed null and void.

4. States Parties shall accord to men and women the same rights with regard to the law relating to the movement of persons and the freedom to choose their residence and domicile.

Article 16

1. States Parties shall take all appropriate measures to eliminate discrimination against women in all matters relating to marriage and family relations and in particular shall ensure, on a basis of equality of men and women:

    (a) The same right to enter into marriage;

    (b) The same right freely to choose a spouse and to enter into marriage only with their free and full consent;

    (c) The same rights and responsibilities during marriage and at its dissolution;

    (d) The same rights and responsibilities as parents, irrespective of their marital status, in matters relating to their children; in all cases the interests of the children shall be paramount;

    (e) The same rights to decide freely and responsibly on the number and spacing of their children and to have access to the information, education and means to enable them to exercise these rights;

    (f) The same rights and responsibilities with regard to guardianship, wardship, trusteeship and adoption of children, or similar institutions where these concepts exist in national legislation; in all cases the interests of the children shall be paramount;

    (g) The same personal rights as husband and wife, including the right to choose a family name, a profession and an occupation;

    (h) The same rights for both spouses in respect of the ownership, acquisition, management, administration, enjoyment and disposition of property, whether free of charge or for a valuable consideration.

2. The betrothal and the marriage of a child shall have no legal effect, and all necessary action, including legislation, shall be taken to specify a minimum age for marriage and to make the registration of marriages in an official registry compulsory.

Government of Republic of South Africa and Others
v. Grootboom and Others
2000 (11) BCLR 1169 (CC)

For the first and second appellants: JJ Gauntlett SC, A Schippers and N Bawa instructed by the State Attorney, Cape Town.

For the third and fourth appellants: JC Heunis SC and JW Olivier instructed by De Klerk & Van Gend for the third appellant and Marais Muller for the fourth appellant.

For the Respondents: P Hodes SC, I Jamie and A Musikanth instructed by Apollos Smith & Associates.

Attorney for the *amici curiae*: GM Budlender instructed the Legal Resources Centre.

Chaskalson P, Langa DP, Goldstone J, Kriegler J, Madala J, Mokgoro J, Ngcobo J, O'Regan J, Sachs J and Cameron AJ concur in the judgment of Yacoob J.

Yacoob J.

A. Introduction

The people of South Africa are committed to the attainment of social justice and the improvement of the quality of life for everyone. The Preamble to our Constitution records this commitment. The Constitution declares the founding values of our society to be "[h]uman dignity, achievement of equality and the advancement of human rights and freedoms." This case grapples with the realisation of these aspirations for it concerns the state's constitutional obligations in relation to housing: a constitutional issue of fundamental importance to the development of South Africa's new constitutional order.

The issues here remind us of the intolerable conditions under which many of our people are still living. The respondents are but a fraction of them. It is also a reminder that unless the plight of these communities is alleviated, people may be tempted to take the law into their own hands in order to escape these conditions. The case brings home the harsh reality that the Constitution's promise of dignity and equality for all remains for many a distant dream. People should not be impelled by intolerable living conditions to resort to land invasions. Self-help of this kind cannot be tolerated, for the unavailability of land suitable for housing development is a key factor in the fight against the country's housing shortage.

The group of people with whom we are concerned in these proceedings lived in appalling conditions, decided to move out and illegally occupied someone else's land. They were evicted and left homeless. The root cause of their problems is the intolerable conditions under which they were living while waiting in the queue for their turn to be allocated low-cost housing. They are the people whose constitutional rights have to be determined in this case.

Mrs Irene Grootboom and the other respondents[2] were rendered homeless as a result of their eviction from their informal homes situated on private land earmarked for formal low-cost housing. They applied to the Cape of Good Hope High Court (the High Court) for an order requiring government to provide them with adequate basic shelter or housing until they obtained permanent accommodation and were granted certain relief. The appellants were ordered to provide the respondents who were children and their parents with shelter. The judgment provisionally concluded that "tents, portable latrines and a regular supply of water (albeit transported) would constitute the bare minimum." The appellants who represent all spheres of government responsible for housing challenge the correctness of that order.

---

2. The respondents are 510 children and 390 adults.

* * *

The cause of the acute housing shortage lies in apartheid. A central feature of that policy was a system of influx control that sought to limit African occupation of urban areas. Influx control was rigorously enforced in the Western Cape, where government policy favoured the exclusion of African people in order to accord preference to the coloured community: a policy adopted in 1954 and referred to as the "coloured labour preference policy." In consequence, the provision of family housing for African people in the Cape Peninsula was frozen in 1962. This freeze was extended to other urban areas in the Western Cape in 1968. Despite the harsh application of influx control in the Western Cape, African people continued to move to the area in search of jobs. Colonial dispossession and a rigidly enforced racial distribution of land in the rural areas had dislocated the rural economy and rendered sustainable and independent African farming increasingly precarious. Given the absence of formal housing, large numbers of people moved into informal settlements throughout the Cape peninsula. The cycle of the apartheid era, therefore, was one of untenable restrictions on the movement of African people into urban areas, the inexorable tide of the rural poor to the cities, inadequate housing, resultant overcrowding, mushrooming squatter settlements, constant harassment by officials and intermittent forced removals.[7] The legacy of influx control in the Western Cape is the acute housing shortage that exists there now. Although the precise extent is uncertain, the shortage stood at more than 100,000 units in the Cape Metro at the time of the inception of the interim Constitution in 1994. Hundreds of thousands of people in need of housing occupied rudimentary informal settlements providing for minimal shelter, but little else.

Mrs Grootboom and most of the other respondents previously lived in an informal squatter settlement called Wallacedene. It lies on the edge of the municipal area of Oostenberg, which in turn is on the eastern fringe of the Cape Metro. The conditions under which most of the residents of Wallacedene lived were lamentable. A quarter of the households of Wallacedene had no income at all, and more than two thirds earned less than R500 per month. About half the population were children; all lived in shacks. They had no water, sewage or refuse removal services and only 5% of the shacks had electricity. The area is partly waterlogged and lies dangerously close to a main thoroughfare. Mrs Grootboom lived with her family and her sister's family in a shack about twenty metres square.

Many had applied for subsidised low-cost housing from the municipality and had been on the waiting list for as long as seven years. Despite numerous enquiries from the municipality no definite answer was given. Clearly it was going to be a long wait. Faced with the prospect of remaining in intolerable conditions indefinitely, the respondents began to move out of Wallacedene at the end of September 1998. They put up their shacks and shelters on vacant land that was privately owned and had been earmarked for low-cost housing. They called the land "New Rust."

They did not have the consent of the owner and on 8 December 1998 he obtained an ejectment order against them in the magistrates' court. The order was served on the occupants but they remained in occupation beyond the date by which they had been ordered to vacate. Mrs Grootboom says they had nowhere else to go: their for-

---

7. In 1985 when the coloured labour preference policy was finally abolished, it became possible for African people to acquire 99-year leasehold tenure in the Western Cape (this form of tenure had been established in the rest of the country in 1978). The following year the government abandoned its policy of influx control in its entirety.

mer sites in Wallacedene had been filled by others. The eviction proceedings were re-newed in March 1999. The respondents' attorneys in this case were appointed by the magistrate to represent them.... Negotiations resulted in the grant of an order re-quiring the occupants to vacate New Rust and authorising the sheriff to evict them and to dismantle and remove any of their structures remaining on the land on 19 May 1999. The magistrate also directed that the parties and the municipality mediate to identify alternative land for the permanent or temporary occupation of the New Rust residents.

[A]t the beginning of the cold, windy and rainy Cape winter, the respondents were forcibly evicted at the municipality's expense. This was done prematurely and inhu-manely: reminiscent of apartheid-style evictions. The respondents' homes were bull-dozed and burnt and their possessions destroyed. Many of the residents who were not there could not even salvage their personal belongings.

The respondents went and sheltered on the Wallacedene sports field under such tem-porary structures as they could muster. Within a week the winter rains started and the plastic sheeting they had erected afforded scant protection. The next day the respon-dents' attorney wrote to the municipality describing the intolerable conditions under which his clients were living and demanded that the municipality meet its constitu-tional obligations and provide temporary accommodation to the respondents.... As in-dicated above, the High Court granted relief to the respondents and the appellants now appeal against that relief.

In the remainder of this judgment, I first outline the reasoning adopted in the High Court judgment. Consideration is then given to the right of access to adequate housing in section 26 of the Constitution and the proper approach to be adopted to the applica-tion of that section. This is followed by evaluation of the housing programme adopted by the state in the light of the obligations imposed upon it by section 26. The respon-dents' claim in terms of the rights of children in section 28 of the Constitution is there-after considered. Finally, the respondents' arguments concerning the conduct of the ap-pellants towards them will be examined.

B. The Case in the High Court

Mrs Grootboom and the other respondents applied for an order directing the appel-lants forthwith to provide:

(i) adequate basic temporary shelter or housing to the respondents and their chil-dren pending their obtaining permanent accommodation;

(ii) or basic nutrition, shelter, healthcare and social services to the respondents who are children.

The respondents based their claim on two constitutional provisions. First, on section 26 of the Constitution which provides that everyone has the right of access to adequate housing. Section 26(2) imposes an obligation upon the state to take reasonable legisla-tive and other measures to ensure the progressive realisation of this right within its available resources.... The second basis for their claim was section 28(1)(c) of the Con-stitution which provides that children have the right to shelter.... [With respect to] sec-tion 26 of the Constitution ... the High Court concluded:

In short [appellants] are faced with a massive shortage in available housing and an extremely constrained budget. Furthermore in terms of the pressing de-mands and scarce resources [appellants] had implemented a housing programme in an attempt to maximise available resources to redress the housing shortage. For this reason it could not be said that [appellants] had not taken reasonable legislative and other measures within its available resources to achieve the progressive realisation of the right to have access to adequate housing.

The court rejected an argument that the right of access to adequate housing under section 26 included a minimum core entitlement to shelter in terms of which the state was obliged to provide some form of shelter pending implementation of the programme to provide adequate housing. This submission was based on the provisions of certain international instruments that are discussed later.[13]

The second part of the judgment addressed the claim of the children for shelter in terms of section 28(1)(c). The court reasoned that the parents bore the primary obligation to provide shelter for their children, but that section 28(1)(c) imposed an obligation on the state to provide that shelter if parents could not. It went on to say that the shelter to be provided according to this obligation was a significantly more rudimentary form of protection from the elements than is provided by a house and falls short of adequate housing. The court concluded that:

> an order which enforces a child's right to shelter should take account of the need of the child to be accompanied by his or her parent. Such an approach would be in accordance with the spirit and purport of section 28 as a whole.

In the result the court ordered as follows:

(2) It is declared, in terms of section 28 of the Constitution that;

    (a) the applicant children are entitled to be provided with shelter by the appropriate organ or department of state;

    (b) the applicant parents are entitled to be accommodated with their children in the aforegoing shelter; and

(c) the appropriate organ or department of state is obliged to provide the applicant children, and their accompanying parents, with such shelter until such time as the parents are able to shelter their own children;

* * *

D. The relevant constitutional provisions and their justiciability

The key constitutional provisions at issue in this case are section 26 and section 28(1)(c). Section 26 provides:

(1) Everyone has the right to have access to adequate housing.

(2) The state must take reasonable legislative and other measures, within its available resources, to achieve the progressive realisation of this right.

(3) No one may be evicted from their home, or have their home demolished, without an order of court made after considering all the relevant circumstances. No legislation may permit arbitrary evictions.

Section 28(1)(c) provides:

(1) Every child has the right—

    ...

---

13. The International Covenant on Economic, Social and Cultural Rights, and the general comments issued by the United Nations Committee on Social and Economic Rights.

(c) to basic nutrition, shelter, basic health care services and social services.

These rights need to be considered in the context of the cluster of socio-economic rights enshrined in the Constitution. They entrench the right of access to land,[15] to adequate housing and to health care, food, water and social security.[16] They also protect the rights of the child[17] and the right to education.[18]

---

15. Section 25(5) provides:

The state must take reasonable legislative and other measures, within its available resources, to foster conditions which enable citizens to gain access to land on an equitable basis.

16. Section 27 provides:

(1) Everyone has the right to have access to—
    (a) health care services, including reproductive health care;
    (b) sufficient food and water; and
    (c) social security, including, if they are unable to support themselves and their dependants, appropriate social assistance.

(2) The state must take reasonable legislative and other measures, within its available resources, to achieve the progressive realisation of each of these rights.

(3) No one may be refused emergency medical treatment.

17. Section 28 provides:

(1) Every child has the right—
    (a) to a name and a nationality from birth;
    (b) to family care or parental care, or to appropriate alternative care when removed from the family environment;
    (c) to basic nutrition, shelter, basic health care services and social services;
    (d) to be protected from maltreatment, neglect, abuse or degradation;
    (e) to be protected from exploitative labour practices;
    (f) not to be required or permitted to perform work or provide services that—
        (i) are inappropriate for a person of that child's age; or
        (ii) place at risk the child's well-being, education, physical or mental health or spiritual, moral or social development;
    (g) not to be detained except as a matter of last resort, in which case, in addition to the rights the child enjoys under sections 12 and 35, the child may be detained only for the shortest appropriate period of time, and has the right to be—
        (i) kept separately from detained person over the age of 18 years; and
        (ii) treated in a manner, and kept in conditions, that take account of the child's age;
    (h) to have a legal practitioner assigned to the child by the state, and at state expense, in civil proceedings affecting the child, if substantial injustice would otherwise result; and
    (i) not to be used directly in armed conflict, and to be protected in times of armed conflict.

(2) A child's best interests are of paramount importance in every matter concerning the child.

(3) In this section "child" means a person under the age of 18 years.

18. Section 29(1) provides:

(1) Everyone has the right—
    (a) to a basic education, including adult basic education, and
    (b) to further education, which the state, through reasonable measures, must make progressively available and accessible.

(2) Everyone has the right to receive education in the official language or languages of their choice in public education institutions where that education is reasonably practicable. In order to ensure the effective access to, and implementation of, this right, the state must consider all reasonable educational alternatives, including single medium [sic] institutions, taking into account—
    (a) equity;
    (b) practicability; and
    (c) the need to redress the results of past racially discriminatory laws and practices.

(3) Everyone has the right to establish and maintain, at their own expense, independent

While the justiciability of socio-economic rights has been the subject of considerable jurisprudential and political debate, the issue of whether socio-economic rights are justiciable at all in South Africa has been put beyond question by the text of our Constitution as construed in the Certification judgment.[20] During the certification proceedings before this Court, it was contended that they were not justiciable and should therefore not have been included in the text of the new Constitution. In response to this argument, this Court held:

> [T]hese rights are, at least to some extent, justiciable. As we have stated in the previous paragraph, many of the civil and political rights entrenched in the [constitutional text before this Court for certification in that case] will give rise to similar budgetary implications without compromising their justiciability. The fact that socio-economic rights will almost inevitably give rise to such implications does not seem to us to be a bar to their justiciability. At the very minimum, socio-economic rights can be negatively protected from improper invasion.

Socio-economic rights are expressly included in the Bill of Rights; they cannot be said to exist on paper only. Section 7(2) of the Constitution requires the state "to respect, protect, promote and fulfil the rights in the Bill of Rights" and the courts are constitutionally bound to ensure that they are protected and fulfilled. The question is therefore not whether socio-economic rights are justiciable under our Constitution, but how to enforce them in a given case....

E. Obligations imposed upon the state by section 26

i) Approach to interpretation

Like all the other rights in Chapter 2 of the Constitution (which contains the Bill of Rights), section 26 must be construed in its context. The section has been carefully crafted. It contains three subsections. The first confers a general right of access to adequate housing. The second establishes and delimits the scope of the positive obligation imposed upon the state to promote access to adequate housing and has three key elements. The state is obliged: (a) to take reasonable legislative and other measures; (b) within its available resources; (c) to achieve the progressive realisation of this right. These elements are discussed later. The third subsection provides protection against arbitrary evictions.

Interpreting a right in its context requires the consideration of two types of context. On the one hand, rights must be understood in their textual setting. This will require a consideration of Chapter 2 and the Constitution as a whole. On the other hand, rights must also be understood in their social and historical context.

Our Constitution entrenches both civil and political rights and social and economic rights. All the rights in our Bill of Rights are inter-related and mutually supporting. There can be no doubt that human dignity, freedom and equality, the foundational values of our society, are denied those who have no food, clothing or shelter. Affording socio-economic rights to all people therefore enables them to enjoy the other rights enshrined in Chapter 2. The realisation of these rights is also key to the advancement of

---

educational institutions that—
(a) do not discriminate on the basis of race;
(b) are registered with the state; and
(c) maintain standards that are of no inferior [sic] to standards at comparable public educational institutions.

20. *Ex Parte Chairperson of the Constitutional Assembly: In Re Certification of the Constitution of the Republic of South Africa, 1996* 1996 (4) SA 744; 1996 (10) BCLR 1253 (CC) at para 78.

race and gender equality and the evolution of a society in which men and women are equally able to achieve their full potential.

The right of access to adequate housing cannot be seen in isolation. There is a close relationship between it and the other socio-economic rights. Socio-economic rights must all be read together in the setting of the Constitution as a whole. The state is obliged to take positive action to meet the needs of those living in extreme conditions of poverty, homelessness or intolerable housing. Their interconnectedness needs to be taken into account in interpreting the socio-economic rights, and, in particular, in determining whether the state has met its obligations in terms of them.

Rights also need to be interpreted and understood in their social and historical context. The right to be free from unfair discrimination, for example, must be understood against our legacy of deep social inequality. The context in which the Bill of Rights is to be interpreted was described by Chaskalson P in Soobramoney:[23]

> We live in a society in which there are great disparities in wealth. Millions of people are living in deplorable conditions and in great poverty. There is a high level of unemployment, inadequate social security, and many do not have access to clean water or to adequate health services. These conditions already existed when the Constitution was adopted and a commitment to address them, and to transform our society into one in which there will be human dignity, freedom and equality, lies at the heart of our new constitutional order. For as long as these conditions continue to exist that aspiration will have a hollow ring.

ii) The relevant international law and its impact

… Section 39 of the Constitution[25] obliges a court to consider international law as a tool to interpretation of the Bill of Rights. In Makwanyane[,] Chaskalson P, in the context of section 35(1) of the interim Constitution,[26] said:

> … public international law would include non-binding as well as binding law. They may both be used under the section as tools of interpretation. International agreements and customary international law accordingly provide a framework within which [the Bill of Rights] can be evaluated and under-

---

23. *Soobramoney v Minister of Health, KwaZulu-Natal* 1998 (1) SA 765 (CC); 1997 (12) BCLR 1696 (CC) at para 8.

25. Section 39 of the Constitution provides:
    (1) When interpreting the Bill of Rights, a court, tribunal or forum—
        (a) must promote the values that underlie and open and democratic society based on human dignity, equality and freedom;
        (b) must consider international law; and
        (c) may consider foreign law.
    (2) When interpreting any legislation, and when developing the common law or customary law, every court, tribunal or forum must promote the spirit, purport and objects of the Bill of Rights.
    (3) The Bill of Rights does not deny the existence of any other rights or freedoms that are recognised or conferred by common law, customary law or legislation, to the extent that they are consistent with the Bill.

26. Section 35(1) of the interim Constitution provides:
In interpreting the provisions of this Chapter a court of law shall promote the values which underlie an open and democratic society based on freedom and equality and shall, where applicable, have regard to public international law applicable to the protection of the rights entrenched in this Chapter, and may have regard to comparable foreign case law.

stood, and for that purpose, decisions of tribunals dealing with comparable instruments, such as the United Nations Committee on Human Rights, the Inter-American Commission on Human Rights, the Inter-American Court of Human Rights, the European Commission on Human Rights, and the European Court of Human Rights, and, in appropriate cases, reports of specialised agencies such as the International Labour Organisation, may provide guidance as to the correct interpretation of particular provisions of [the Bill of Rights].

The relevant international law can be a guide to interpretation but the weight to be attached to any particular principle or rule of international law will vary. However, where the relevant principle of international law binds South Africa, it may be directly applicable.

The amici submitted that the International Covenant on Economic, Social and Cultural Rights (the Covenant)[27] is of significance in understanding the positive obligations created by the socio-economic rights in the Constitution. Article 11.1 of the Covenant provides:

The States Parties to the present Covenant recognize the right of everyone to an adequate standard of living for himself and his family, including adequate food, clothing and housing, and to the continuous improvement of living conditions. The States Parties will take appropriate steps to ensure the realization of this right, recognizing to this effect the essential importance of international co-operation based on free consent.

This Article must be read with Article 2.1 which provides:

Each State Party to the present Covenant undertakes to take steps, individually and. through international assistance and co-operation, especially economic and technical, to the maximum of its available resources, with a view to achieving progressively the full realization of the rights recognized in the present Covenant by all appropriate means, including particularly the adoption of legislative measures.

The differences between the relevant provisions of the Covenant and our Constitution are significant in determining the extent to which the provisions of the Covenant may be a guide to an interpretation of section 26. These differences, in so far as they relate to housing, are:

(a) The Covenant provides for a *right to adequate housing* while section 26 provides for the *right of access* to adequate housing.

(b) The Covenant obliges states parties to take *appropriate* steps which must include legislation while the Constitution obliges the South African state to take *reasonable* legislative and other measures.

The obligations undertaken by states parties to the Covenant are monitored by the United Nations Committee on Economic, Social and Cultural Rights (the committee).[30] The amici relied on the relevant general comments issued by the committee

---

27. The Covenant was signed by South Africa on 3 October 1994 but has as yet not been ratified.

30. The committee consists of eighteen independent experts. Its purpose is to assist the United Nations Economic and Social Council to carry out its responsibilities relating to the implementation of the Covenant. See Craven *The International Covenant on Economic, Social and Cultural Rights* (Clarendon, Oxford 1995) at 1 and 42.

concerning the interpretation and application of the Covenant, and argued that these general comments constitute a significant guide to the interpretation of section 26. In particular they argued that in interpreting this section, we should adopt an approach similar to that taken by the committee in paragraph 10 of general comment 3 issued in 1990, in which the committee found that socio-economic rights contain a minimum core:

> 10. On the basis of the extensive experience gained by the Committee, as well as by the body that preceded it, over a period of more than a decade of examining States parties' reports the Committee is of the view that minimum core obligation to ensure the satisfaction of, at the very least, minimum essential levels of each of the rights is incumbent upon every State party. Thus, for example, a State party in which any significant number of individuals is deprived of essential foodstuffs, of essential primary health care, of basic shelter and housing, or of the most basic forms of education, is prima facie, failing to discharge its obligations under the Covenant. If the Covenant were to be read in such a way as not to establish such a minimum core obligation, it would be largely deprived of its raison d'etre. By the same token, it must be noted that any assessment as to whether a State has discharged its minimum core obligation must also take account of resource constraints applying within the country concerned. Article 2(1) obligates each State party to take the necessary steps "to the maximum of its available resources". In order for a State party to be able to attribute its failure to meet at least its minimum core obligations to a lack of available resources it must demonstrate that every effort has been made to use all resources that are at its disposition in an effort to satisfy, as a matter of priority, those minimum obligations.

It is clear from this extract that the committee considers that every state party is bound to fulfil a minimum core obligation by ensuring the satisfaction of a minimum essential level of the socio-economic rights, including the right to adequate housing. Accordingly, a state in which a significant number of individuals is deprived of basic shelter and housing is regarded as prima facie in breach of its obligations under the Covenant. A state party must demonstrate that every effort has been made to use all the resources at its disposal to satisfy the minimum core of the right. However, it is to be noted that the general comment does not specify precisely what that minimum core is.

The concept of minimum core obligation was developed by the committee to describe the minimum expected of a state in order to comply with its obligation under the Covenant. It is the floor beneath which the conduct of the state must not drop if there is to be compliance with the obligation. Each right has a "minimum essential level" that must be satisfied by the states parties. The committee developed this concept based on "extensive experience gained by [it] ... over a period of more than a decade of examining States parties' reports." The general comment is based on reports furnished by the reporting states and the general comment is therefore largely descriptive of how the states have complied with their obligations under the Covenant. The committee has also used the general comment "as a means of developing a common understanding of the norms by establishing a prescriptive definition."[31] Minimum core obligation is determined generally by having regard to the needs of the most vulnerable group that is entitled to the protection of the right in question. It is in this context that the concept of minimum core obligation must be understood in international law.

---

31. Id at 91.

It is not possible to determine the minimum threshold for the progressive realisation of the right of access to adequate housing without first identifying the needs and opportunities for the enjoyment of such a right. These will vary according to factors such as income, unemployment, availability of land and poverty. The differences between city and rural communities will also determine the needs and opportunities for the enjoyment of this right. Variations ultimately depend on the economic and social history and circumstances of a country. All this illustrates the complexity of the task of determining a minimum core obligation for the progressive realisation of the right of access to adequate housing without having the requisite information on the needs and the opportunities for the enjoyment of this right. The committee developed the concept of minimum core over many years of examining reports by reporting states. This Court does not have comparable information.

The determination of a minimum core in the context of "the right to have access to adequate housing" presents difficult questions. This is so because the needs in the context of access to adequate housing are diverse: there are those who need land; others need both land and houses; yet others need financial assistance. There are difficult questions relating to the definition of minimum core in the context of a right to have access to adequate housing, in particular whether the minimum core obligation should be defined generally or with regard to specific groups of people. As will appear from the discussion below, the real question in terms of our Constitution is whether the measures taken by the state to realise the right afforded by section 26 are reasonable. There may be cases where it may be possible and appropriate to have regard to the content of a minimum core obligation to determine whether the measures taken by the state are reasonable. However, even if it were appropriate to do so, it could not be done unless sufficient information is placed before a court to enable it to determine the minimum core in any given context. In this case, we do not have sufficient information to determine what would comprise the minimum core obligation in the context of our Constitution. It is not in any event necessary to decide whether it is appropriate for a court to determine in the first instance the minimum core content of a right.

iii) Analysis of section 26

[Section 26 provides:]

(1) Everyone has the right to have access to adequate housing.

(2) The state must take reasonable legislative and other measures, within its available resources, to achieve the progressive realisation of this right.

(3) No one may be evicted from their home, or have their home demolished, without an order of court made after considering all the relevant circumstances. No legislation may permit arbitrary evictions.

Subsections (1) and (2) are related and must be read together. Subsection (1) aims at delineating the scope of the right. It is a right of everyone including children. Although the subsection does not expressly say so, there is, at the very least, a negative obligation placed upon the state and all other entities and persons to desist from preventing or impairing the right of access to adequate housing. The negative right is further spelt out in subsection (3) which prohibits arbitrary evictions. Access to housing could also be promoted if steps are taken to make the rural areas of our country more viable so as to limit the inexorable migration of people from rural to urban areas in search of jobs.

The right delineated in section 26(1) is a right of "access to adequate housing" as distinct from the right to adequate housing encapsulated in the Covenant. This difference is significant. It recognises that housing entails more than bricks and mortar. It requires available land, appropriate services such as the provision of water and the removal of sewage and the financing of all of these, including the building of the house itself. For a person to have access to adequate housing all of these conditions need to be met: there must be land, there must be services, there must be a dwelling. Access to land for the purpose of housing is therefore included in the right of access to adequate housing in section 26. A right of access to adequate housing also suggests that it is not only the state who is responsible for the provision of houses, but that other agents within our society, including individuals themselves, must be enabled by legislative and other measures to provide housing. The state must create the conditions for access to adequate housing for people at all economic levels of our society. State policy dealing with housing must therefore take account of different economic levels in our society.

In this regard, there is a difference between the position of those who can afford to pay for housing, even if it is only basic though adequate housing, and those who cannot. For those who can afford to pay for adequate housing, the state's primary obligation lies in unlocking the system, providing access to housing stock and a legislative framework to facilitate self-built houses through planning laws and access to finance. Issues of development and social welfare are raised in respect of those who cannot afford to provide themselves with housing. State policy needs to address both these groups. The poor are particularly vulnerable and their needs require special attention. It is in this context that the relationship between sections 26 and 27 and the other socio-economic rights is most apparent. If under section 27 the state has in place programmes to provide adequate social assistance to those who are otherwise unable to support themselves and their dependants, that would be relevant to the state's obligations in respect of other socio-economic rights.

The state's obligation to provide access to adequate housing depends on context, and may differ from province to province, from city to city, from rural to urban areas and from person to person. Some may need access to land and no more; some may need access to land and building materials; some may need access to finance; some may need access to services such as water, sewage, electricity and roads. What might be appropriate in a rural area where people live together in communities engaging in subsistence farming may not be appropriate in an urban area where people are looking for employment and a place to live.

Subsection (2) speaks to the positive obligation imposed upon the state. It requires the state to devise a comprehensive and workable plan to meet its obligations in terms of the subsection. However subsection (2) also makes it clear that the obligation imposed upon the state is not an absolute or unqualified one. The extent of the state's obligation is defined by three key elements that are considered separately: (a) the obligation to "take reasonable legislative and other measures"; (b) "to achieve the progressive realisation" of the right; and (c) "within available resources."

Reasonable legislative and other measures

What constitutes reasonable legislative and other measures must be determined in the light of the fact that the Constitution creates different spheres of government: national government, provincial government and local government. The last of these may, as it does in this case, comprise two tiers. The Constitution allocates powers and functions amongst these different spheres emphasising their obligation to co-operate with one another in carrying out their constitutional tasks. In the case of housing, it is a function shared by both national and provincial government. Local governments have an important obligation to ensure that services are provided in a sustainable manner to the communities they govern. A reasonable programme therefore must clearly allocate responsibilities and tasks to the different spheres of government and ensure that the appropriate financial and human resources are available.

Thus, a co-ordinated state housing programme must be a comprehensive one determined by all three spheres of government in consultation with each other as contemplated by Chapter 3 of the Constitution. It may also require framework legislation at national level, a matter we need not consider further in this case as there is national framework legislation in place. Each sphere of government must accept responsibility for the implementation of particular parts of the programme but the national sphere of government must assume responsibility for ensuring that laws, policies, programmes and strategies are adequate to meet the state's section 26 obligations. In particular, the national framework, if there is one, must be designed so that these obligations can be met. It should be emphasised that national government bears an important responsibility in relation to the allocation of national revenue to the provinces and local government on an equitable basis. Furthermore, national and provincial government must ensure that executive obligations imposed by the housing legislation are met.

The measures must establish a coherent public housing programme directed towards the progressive realisation of the right of access to adequate housing within the state's available means. The programme must be capable of facilitating the realisation of the right. The precise contours and content of the measures to be adopted are primarily a matter for the legislature and the executive. They must, however, ensure that the measures they adopt are reasonable. In any challenge based on section 26 in which it is argued that the state has failed to meet the positive obligations imposed upon it by section 26(2), the question will be whether the legislative and other measures taken by the state are reasonable. A court considering reasonableness will not enquire whether other more desirable or favourable measures could have been adopted, or whether public money could have been better spent. The question would be whether the measures that have been adopted are reasonable. It is necessary to recognise that a wide range of possible measures could be adopted by the state to meet its obligations. Many of these would meet the requirement of reasonableness. Once it is shown that the measures do so, this requirement is met.

The state is required to take reasonable legislative *and* other measures. Legislative measures by themselves are not likely to constitute constitutional compliance. Mere legislation is not enough. The state is obliged to act to achieve the intended result, and the legislative measures will invariably have to be supported by appropriate, well-directed policies and programmes implemented by the executive. These policies and programmes must be reasonable both in their conception and their implementation. The formulation of a programme is only the first stage in meeting the state's obligations. The programme must also be reasonably implemented. An otherwise reasonable programme that is not implemented reasonably will not constitute compliance with the state's obligations.

In determining whether a set of measures is reasonable, it will be necessary to consider housing problems in their social, economic and historical context and to consider the capacity of institutions responsible for implementing the programme. The programme must be balanced and flexible and make appropriate provision for attention to housing crises and to short, medium and long term needs. A programme that excludes a significant segment of society cannot be said to be reasonable. Conditions do not remain static and therefore the programme will require continuous review.

Reasonableness must also be understood in the context of the Bill of Rights as a whole. The right of access to adequate housing is entrenched because we value human beings and want to ensure that they are afforded their basic human needs. A society must seek to ensure that the basic necessities of life are provided to all if it is to be a society based on human dignity, freedom and equality. To be reasonable, measures cannot leave out of account the degree and extent of the denial of the right they endeavour to realise. Those whose needs are the most urgent and whose ability to enjoy all rights therefore is most in peril, must not be ignored by the measures aimed at achieving realisation of the right. It may not be sufficient to meet the test of reasonableness to show that the measures are capable of achieving a statistical advance in the realisation of the right. Furthermore, the Constitution requires that everyone must be treated with care and concern. If the measures, though statistically successful, fail to respond to the needs of those most desperate, they may not pass the test.

Progressive realisation of the right

The extent and content of the obligation consist in what must be achieved, that is, "the progressive realisation of this right." It links subsections (1) and (2) by making it quite clear that the right referred to is the right of access to adequate housing. The term "progressive realisation" shows that it was contemplated that the right could not be realised immediately. But the goal of the Constitution is that the basic needs of all in our society be effectively met and the requirement of progressive realisation means that the state must take steps to achieve this goal. It means that accessibility should be progressively facilitated: legal, administrative, operational and financial hurdles should be examined and, where possible, lowered over time. Housing must be made more accessible not only to a larger number of people but to a wider range of people as time progresses. The phrase is taken from international law and Article 2.1 of the Covenant in particular. The committee has helpfully analysed this requirement in the context of housing as follows:

> Nevertheless, the fact that realization over time, or in other words progressively, is foreseen under the Covenant should not be misinterpreted as depriving the obligation of all meaningful content. It is on the one hand a necessary flexibility device, reflecting the realities of the real world and the difficulties involved for any country in ensuring full realization of economic, social and cultural rights. On the other hand, the phrase must be read in the light of the overall objective, indeed the raison d'être, of the Covenant which is to establish clear obligations for States parties in respect of the full realization of the rights in question. It thus imposes an obligation to move as expeditiously and effectively as possible towards that goal. Moreover, any deliberately retrogressive measures in that regard would require the most careful consideration and would need to be fully justified by reference to the totality of the rights provided for in the Covenant and in the context of the full use of the maximum available resources.

Although the committee's analysis is intended to explain the scope of states parties' obligations under the Covenant, it is also helpful in plumbing the meaning of "progressive realisation" in the context of our Constitution. The meaning ascribed to the phrase is in harmony with the context in which the phrase is used in our Constitution and there is no reason not to accept that it bears the same meaning in the Constitution as in the document from which it was so clearly derived.

Within available resources

The third defining aspect of the obligation to take the requisite measures is that the obligation does not require the state to do more than its available resources permit. This means that both the content of the obligation in relation to the rate at which it is achieved as well as the reasonableness of the measures employed to achieve the result are governed by the availability of resources. Section 26 does not expect more of the state than is achievable within its available resources. As Chaskalson P said in Soobramoney:

> What is apparent from these provisions is that the obligations imposed on the State by §§ 26 and 27 in regard to access to housing, health care, food, water, and social security are dependent upon the resources available for such purposes, and that the corresponding rights themselves are limited by reason of the lack of resources. Given this lack of resources and the significant demands on them that have already been referred to, an unqualified obligation to meet these needs would not presently be capable of being fulfilled.

There is a balance between goal and means. The measures must be calculated to attain the goal expeditiously and effectively but the availability of resources is an important factor in determining what is reasonable.

F. Description and evaluation of the state housing programme

In support of their contention that they had complied with the obligation imposed upon them by section 26, the appellants placed evidence before this Court of the legislative and other measures they had adopted. There is in place both national and provincial legislation concerned with housing. It was explained that in 1994 the state inherited fragmented housing arrangements which involved thirteen statutory housing funds, seven ministries and housing departments, more than twenty subsidy systems and more than sixty national and regional parastatals operating on a racial basis. These have been rationalised. The national Housing Act provides a framework which establishes the responsibilities and functions of each sphere of government with regard to housing. The responsibility for implementation is generally given to the provinces. Provinces in turn have assigned certain implementation functions to local government structures in many cases. All spheres of government are intimately involved in housing delivery and the budget allocated by national government appears to be substantial. There is a single housing policy and a subsidy system that targets low-income earners regardless of race. The White Paper on Housing aims to stabilise the housing environment, establish institutional arrangements, protect consumers, rationalise institutional capacity within a sustainable long-term framework, facilitate the speedy release and servicing of land and co-ordinate and integrate the public sector investment in housing. In addition, various schemes are in place involving public/private partnerships aimed at ensuring that housing provision is effectively financed.* * *

It emerges from the general principles read together with the functions of national, provincial and local government that the concept of housing development as defined is central to the Act. Housing development, as defined, seeks to provide citizens and permanent residents with access to permanent residential structures with secure tenure ensuring internal and external privacy and to provide adequate protection against the elements. What is more, it endeavours to ensure convenient access to economic opportunities and to health, educational and social amenities. All the policy documents before the Court are postulated on the need for housing development as defined. This is the central thrust of the housing development policy.

The definition of housing development as well as the general principles that are set out do not contemplate the provision of housing that falls short of the definition of housing development in the Act. In other words there is no express provision to facilitate access to temporary relief for people who have no access to land, no roof over their heads, for people who are living in intolerable conditions and for people who are in crisis because of natural disasters such as floods and fires, or because their homes are under threat of demolition. These are people in desperate need. Their immediate need can be met by relief short of housing which fulfils the requisite standards of durability, habitability and stability encompassed by the definition of housing development in the Act.

What has been done in execution of this programme is a major achievement. Large sums of money have been spent and a significant number of houses has been built. Considerable thought, energy, resources and expertise have been and continue to be devoted to the process of effective housing delivery. It is a programme that is aimed at achieving the progressive realisation of the right of access to adequate housing.

A question that nevertheless must be answered is whether the measures adopted are reasonable within the meaning of section 26 of the Constitution. Allocation of responsibilities and functions has been coherently and comprehensively addressed. The programme is not haphazard but represents a systematic response to a pressing social need. It takes account of the housing shortage in South Africa by seeking to build a large number of homes for those in need of better housing. The programme applies throughout South Africa and although there have been difficulties of implementation in some areas, the evidence suggests that the state is actively seeking to combat these difficulties.

Legislative measures have been taken at both the national and provincial levels. As we have seen, at the national level the Housing Act sets out the general principles applicable to housing development, defines the functions of the three spheres of government and addresses the financing of housing development. It thus provides a legislative framework within which the delivery of houses is to take place nationally. At the provincial level there is the Western Cape Housing Development Act, 1999. This statute also sets out the general principles applicable to housing development; the role of the provincial government; the role of local government; and other matters relating to housing development. Thus, like the Housing Act, this statute provides a legislative framework within which housing development at provincial level will take place. All of the measures described form part of the nationwide housing programme.

This Court must decide whether the nationwide housing programme is sufficiently flexible to respond to those in desperate need in our society and to cater appropriately for immediate and short-term requirements. This must be done in the context of the scope of the housing problem that must be addressed. This case is concerned with the situation in the Cape Metro and the municipality and the circumstances that prevailed there are therefore presented.

The housing shortage in the Cape Metro is acute. About 206,000 housing units are required and up to 25,000 housing opportunities are required in Oostenberg itself. Shack counts in the Cape Metro in general and in the area of the municipality in particular reveal an inordinate problem. 28,300 shacks were counted in the Cape

Metro in January 1993. This number had grown to 59,854 in 1996 and to 72,140 by 1998. Shacks in this area increased by 111 percent during the period 1993 to 1996 and by 21 percent from then until 1998. There were 2,121 shacks in the area of the municipality in 1993, 5,701 (an increase of 168 percent) in 1996 and 7,546 (an increase of 32 percent) in 1998. These are the results of a study commissioned by the Cape Metro.

The study concludes that the municipality "is the most critical local authority in terms of informal settlement shack growth at this point in time", this despite the fact that, according to an affidavit by a representative of the municipality, 10,577 houses had been completed by 1997. The scope of the problem is perhaps most sharply illustrated by this: about 22,000 houses are built in the Western Cape each year while demand grows at a rate of 20,000 family units per year. The backlog is therefore likely to be reduced, resources permitting and, on the basis of the figures in this study, only by 2,000 houses a year.

The housing situation is desperate. The problem is compounded by rampant unemployment and poverty. [A] quarter of the households in Wallacedene had no income at all, and more than two-thirds earned less than R500-00 per month during 1997. [M]any of the families living in Wallacedene are living in intolerable conditions. In some cases, their shacks are permanently flooded during the winter rains, others are severely overcrowded and some are perilously close to busy roads. There is no suggestion that Wallacedene is unusual in this respect. It is these conditions which ultimately forced the respondents to leave their homes there.

The Cape Metro has realised that this desperate situation requires government action that is different in nature from that encompassed by the housing development policy described earlier in this judgment. It drafted a programme (the Cape Metro land programme) in June 1999, some months after the respondents had been evicted. It wrote:

> From the above, it is seen that there is a complete mismatch between demand and supply in the housing sector, resulting in a crisis in housing delivery.

> However, the existing housing situation cannot just be accepted, as there are many families living in crisis conditions, or alternatively, there are situations in the [Cape Metro] where local authorities need to undertake legal proceedings (evictions) in order to administer and implement housing projects. A new housing programme needed [sic] to cater for the crisis housing conditions in the [Cape Metro]. The proposed programme is called an 'Accelerated Managed Land Settlement Programme'.

Later in the document, the programme is briefly described as follows:

> The Accelerated Managed Land Settlement Programme (AMSLP) can therefore be described as the rapid release of land for families in crisis, with the progressive provision of services.

> This programme should benefit those families in situations of crisis. The programme does not offer any benefits to queue jumpers, as it is the Metropolitan Local Council who determines when the progressive upgrading of services will be taken.

> The Accelerated Managed Land Settlement Programme (AMSLP) includes the identification and purchase of land, planning, identification of the beneficiaries, township approval, pegging of the erven, construction of basic services, resettlement and the transfer of land to the beneficiaries.

We were informed by counsel during the hearing that although this programme was not in force at the time these proceedings were commenced, it has now been adopted and is being implemented.

The Cape Metro land programme was formulated by the Cape Metro specifically "to assist the metropolitan local councils to manage the settlement of families in crisis." Important features of this programme are its recognition of (i) the absence of provision for people living in crisis conditions; (ii) the unacceptability of having families living in crisis conditions; (iii) the consequent risk of land invasions; and (iv) the gap between the supply and demand of housing resulting in a delivery crisis. Crucially, the programme acknowledges that its beneficiaries are families who are to be evicted, those who are in a crisis situation in an existing area such as in a flood-line, families located on strategic land and families from backyard shacks or on the waiting list who are in crisis situations. Its primary objective is the rapid release of land for these families in crisis, with services to be upgraded progressively.

In devising its programme the Cape Metro said the following:

> Local government, by virtue of the powers and functions granted to it by national and provincial legislation and policy, needs to initiate, facilitate and develop housing projects. Part of this role is also the identification of vacant land for housing. There are currently a few programmes that are available to finance housing projects, for example, the project-linked subsidy, institutional subsidy and CMIP. None of these programmes deal directly with crisis situations in the housing field. The Accelerated Managed Land Settlement Programme (AMLSP) can therefore be described as the rapid release of land for families in crisis, with the progressive provision of services.

Section 26 requires that the legislative and other measures adopted by the state are reasonable. To determine whether the nationwide housing programme as applied in the Cape Metro is reasonable within the meaning the section, one must consider whether the absence of a component catering for those in desperate need is reasonable in the circumstances. It is common cause that, except for the Cape Metro land programme, there is no provision in the nationwide housing programme as applied within the Cape Metro for people in desperate need.

Counsel for the appellants supported the nationwide housing programme and resisted the notion that provision of relief for people in desperate need was appropriate in it. Counsel also submitted that section 26 did not require the provision of this relief. Indeed, the contention was that provision for people in desperate need would detract significantly from integrated housing development as defined in the Act. The housing development policy as set out in the Act is in itself laudable. It has medium and long term objectives that cannot be criticised. But the question is whether a housing programme that leaves out of account the immediate amelioration of the circumstances of those in crisis can meet the test of reasonableness established by the section.

The absence of this component may have been acceptable if the nationwide housing programme would result in affordable houses for most people within a reasonably short time. However the scale of the problem is such that this simply cannot happen. Each individual housing project could be expected to take years and the provision of houses for all in the area of the municipality and in the Cape Metro is likely to take a long time indeed. The desperate will be consigned to their fate for the foreseeable future unless some temporary measures exist as an integral part of the nationwide housing programme. Housing authorities are understandably unable to say when housing will become available to these desperate people. The result is that people in desperate need are left without any form of assistance with no end in sight. Not only are the immediate crises not met. The consequent pressure on existing settlements inevitably results in land invasions by the desperate thereby frustrating the attainment of the medium and long term objectives of the nationwide housing programme. That is one of the main reasons why the Cape Metro land programme was adopted.

The national government bears the overall responsibility for ensuring that the state complies with the obligations imposed upon it by section 26. The nationwide housing programme falls short of obligations imposed upon national government to the extent that it fails to recognise that the state must provide for relief for those in desperate need. They are not to be ignored in the interests of an overall programme focussed on medium and long-term objectives. It is essential that a reasonable part of the national housing budget be devoted to this, but the precise allocation is for national government to decide in the first instance.

This case is concerned with the Cape Metro and the municipality. The former has realised that this need has not been fulfilled and has put in place its land programme in an effort to fulfil it. This programme, on the face of it, meets the obligation which the state has towards people in the position of the respondents in the Cape Metro. Indeed, the amicus accepted that this programme "would cater precisely for the needs of people such as the respondents, and, in an appropriate and sustainable manner." However, as with legislative measures, the existence of the programme is a starting point only. What remains is the implementation of the programme by taking all reasonable steps that are necessary to initiate and sustain it. And it must be implemented with due regard to the urgency of the situations it is intended to address.

Effective implementation requires at least adequate budgetary support by national government. This, in turn, requires recognition of the obligation to meet immediate needs in the nationwide housing programme. Recognition of such needs in the nationwide housing programme requires it to plan, budget and monitor the fulfilment of immediate needs and the management of crises. This must ensure that a significant number of desperate people in need are afforded relief, though not all of them need receive it immediately. Such planning too will require proper co-operation between the different spheres of government.

In conclusion it has been established in this case that as of the date of the launch of this application, the state was not meeting the obligation imposed upon it by section 26(2) of the Constitution in the area of the Cape Metro. In particular, the programmes adopted by the state fell short of the requirements of section 26(2) in that no provision was made for relief to the categories of people in desperate need identified earlier. I come later to the order that should flow from this conclusion.

G. Section 28(1)(c) and the right to shelter

The judgment of the High Court amounts to this: (a) section 28(1)(c) obliges the state to provide rudimentary shelter to children and their parents on demand if parents are unable to shelter their children; (b) this obligation exists independently of and in addition to the obligation to take reasonable legislative and other measures in terms of section 26; and (c) the state is bound to provide this rudimentary shelter irrespective of the availability of resources. On this reasoning, parents with their children have two distinct rights: the right of access to adequate housing in terms of section 26 as well as a right to claim shelter on demand in terms of section 28(1)(c).

This reasoning produces an anomalous result. People who have children have a direct and enforceable right to housing under section 28(1)(c), while others who have none or whose children are adult are not entitled to housing under that section, no matter how old, disabled or otherwise deserving they may be. The carefully constructed constitutional scheme for progressive realisation of socio-economic rights would make little sense if it could be trumped in every case by the rights of children to get shelter from the state on demand. Moreover, there is an obvious danger. Children could become stepping stones to housing for their parents instead of being valued for who they are.

The respondents and the amici in supporting the judgment of the High Court draw a distinction between housing on the one hand and shelter on the other. They contend that shelter is an attenuated form of housing and that the state is obliged to provide shelter to all children on demand. The respondents and the amici emphasise that the right of children to shelter is unqualified and that the "reasonable measures" qualification embodied in sections 25(5) 26, 27 and 29 are markedly absent in relation to section 28(1)(c). The appellants disagree and criticise the respondents' definition of shelter on the basis that it conceives shelter in terms that limit it to a material object. They contend that shelter is more than just that, but define it as an institution constructed by the state in which children are housed away from their parents.

I cannot accept that the Constitution draws any real distinction between housing on the one hand and shelter on the other, and that shelter is a rudimentary form of housing. Housing and shelter are related concepts and one of the aims of housing is to provide physical shelter. But shelter is not a commodity separate from housing. There is no doubt that all shelter represents protection from the elements and possibly even from danger. There are a range of ways in which shelter may be constituted: shelter may be ineffective or rudimentary at the one extreme and very effective and even ideal at the other. The concept of shelter in section 28(1)(c) is not qualified by any requirement that it should be "basic" shelter. It follows that the Constitution does not limit the concept of shelter to basic shelter alone. The concept of shelter in section 28(1)(c) embraces shelter in all its manifestations. However, it does not follow that the Constitution obliges the state to provide shelter at the most effective or the most rudimentary level to children in the company of their parents.

The obligation created by section 28(1)(c) can properly be ascertained only in the context of the rights and, in particular, the obligations created by sections 25(5), 26 and 27 of the Constitution. Each of these sections expressly obliges the state to take reasonable legislative and other measures, within its available resources, to achieve the rights with which they are concerned.[49] Section 28(1)(c) creates the right of children to basic nutrition, shelter, basic health care services and social services. There is an evident overlap between the rights created by sections 26 and 27 and those conferred on children by section 28. Apart from this overlap, the section 26 and 27 rights are conferred on everyone including children while section 28, on its face, accords rights to children alone. This overlap is not consistent with the notion that section 28(1)(c) creates separate and independent rights for children and their parents.

The extent of the state obligation must also be interpreted in the light of the international obligations binding upon South Africa. The United Nations Convention on the

---

49. Section 25(5) mandates the state to foster conditions which enables citizens to gain land on an equitable basis; section 26(2) is concerned with the right to access to adequate housing; section 27(2) with the right to access to health care services, sufficient food and water and social security including appropriate social assistance if people are unable to support themselves and their dependants.

Rights of the Child, ratified by South Africa in 1995, seeks to impose obligations upon state parties to ensure that the rights of children in their countries are properly protected. Section 28 is one of the mechanisms to meet these obligations. It requires the state to take steps to ensure that children's rights are observed. In the first instance, the state does so by ensuring that there are legal obligations to compel parents to fulfil their responsibilities in relation to their children. Hence, legislation and the common law impose obligations upon parents to care for their children. The state reinforces the observance of these obligations by the use of civil and criminal law as well as social welfare programmes.

Section 28(1)(c) must be read in this context. Subsections 28(1)(b) and (c) provide:

Every child has the right—

(b) to family care or parental care, or to appropriate alternative care when removed from the family environment;

(c) to basic nutrition, shelter, basic health care services and social services.

They must be read together. They ensure that children are properly cared for by their parents or families, and that they receive appropriate alternative care in the absence of parental or family care. The section encapsulates the conception of the scope of care that children should receive in our society. Subsection (1)(b) defines those responsible for giving care while subsection (1)(c) lists various aspects of the care entitlement.

It follows from subsection 1(b) that the Constitution contemplates that a child has the right to parental or family care in the first place, and the right to alternative appropriate care only where that is lacking. Through legislation and the common law, the obligation to provide shelter in subsection (1)(c) is imposed primarily on the parents or family and only alternatively on the state. The state thus incurs the obligation to provide shelter to those children, for example, who are removed from their families. It follows that section 28(1)(c) does not create any primary state obligation to provide shelter on demand to parents and their children if children are being cared for by their parents or families.

This does not mean, however, that the state incurs no obligation in relation to children who are being cared for by their parents or families. In the first place, the state must provide the legal and administrative infrastructure necessary to ensure that children are accorded the protection contemplated by section 28. This obligation would normally be fulfilled by passing laws and creating enforcement mechanisms for the maintenance of children, their protection from maltreatment, abuse, neglect or degradation, and the prevention of other forms of abuse of children mentioned in section 28. In addition, the state is required to fulfil its obligations to provide families with access to land in terms of section 25, access to adequate housing in terms of section 26 as well as access to health care, food, water and social security in terms of section 27. It follows from this judgment that sections 25 and 27 require the state to provide access on a programmatic and coordinated basis, subject to available resources. One of the ways in which the state would meet its section 27 obligations would be through a social welfare programme providing maintenance grants and other material assistance to families in need in defined circumstances.

It was not contended that the children who are respondents in this case should be provided with shelter apart from their parents. Those of the respondents in this case who are children are being cared for by their parents; they are not in the care of the state, in any alternative care, or abandoned. In the circumstances of this case, therefore, there was no obligation upon the state to provide shelter to those of the respondents who were children and, through them, their parents in terms of section 28(1)(c). The High Court therefore erred in making the order it did on the basis of this section.

H. Evaluation of the conduct of the appellants towards the respondents

The final section of this judgment is concerned with whether the respondents are entitled to some relief in the form of temporary housing because of their special circumstances and because of the appellants' conduct towards them.... At first blush, the respondents' position was so acute and untenable when the High Court heard the case that simple humanity called for some form of immediate and urgent relief. They had left Wallacedene because of their intolerable circumstances, had been evicted in a way that left a great deal to be desired and, as a result, lived in desperate sub-human conditions on the Wallacedene soccer field or in the Wallacedene community hall. But we must also remember that the respondents are not alone in their desperation; hundreds of thousands (possibly millions) of South Africans live in appalling conditions throughout our country.

Although the conditions in which the respondents lived in Wallacedene were admittedly intolerable and although it is difficult to level any criticism against them for leaving the Wallacedene shack settlement, it is a painful reality that their circumstances were no worse than those of thousands of other people, including young children, who remained at Wallacedene. It cannot be said, on the evidence before us, that the respondents moved out of the Wallacedene settlement and occupied the land earmarked for low-cost housing development as a deliberate strategy to gain preference in the allocation of housing resources over thousands of other people who remained in intolerable conditions and who were also in urgent need of housing relief. It must be borne in mind however, that the effect of any order that constitutes a special dispensation for the respondents on account of their extraordinary circumstances is to accord that preference.

All levels of government must ensure that the housing programme is reasonably and appropriately implemented in the light of all the provisions in the Constitution. All implementation mechanisms, and all state action in relation to housing falls to be assessed against the requirements of section 26 of the Constitution. Every step at every level of government must be consistent with the constitutional obligation to take reasonable measures to provide adequate housing.

But section 26 is not the only provision relevant to a decision as to whether state action at any particular level of government is reasonable and consistent with the Constitution. The proposition that rights are interrelated and are all equally important is not merely a theoretical postulate. The concept has immense human and practical significance in a society founded on human dignity, equality and freedom. It is fundamental to an evaluation of the reasonableness of state action that account be taken of the inherent dignity of human beings. The Constitution will be worth infinitely less than its paper if the reasonableness of state action concerned with housing is determined without regard to the fundamental constitutional value of human dignity. Section 26, read in the context of the Bill of Rights as a whole, must mean that the respondents have a right to reasonable action by the state in all circumstances and with particular regard to human dignity. In short, I emphasise that human beings are required to be treated as human beings. This is the backdrop against which the conduct of the respondents towards the appellants must be seen.

The national legislature recognises this. In the course of stating the general principles binding on all levels of government, the Housing Act provides that in the administration of any matter relating to housing development, all levels of government must respect, protect, promote and fulfil the rights in Chapter 2 of the Constitution. In addition, section 2(1)(b) obliges all levels of government to consult meaningfully with individuals and communities affected by housing development. Moreover, section 9(1)(e) obliges munic-ipalities to promote the resolution of conflict arising in the housing development process.

Consideration is now given to whether the state action (or inaction) in relation to the respondents met the required constitutional standard. It is a central feature of this judgment that the housing shortage in the area of the Cape Metro in general and Oost-enberg in particular had reached crisis proportions. Wallacedene was obviously burst-ing and it was probable that people in desperation were going to find it difficult to resist the temptation to move out of the shack settlement onto unoccupied land in an effort to improve their position. This is what the respondents apparently did.

Whether the conduct of Mrs Grootboom and the other respondents constituted a land invasion was disputed on the papers. There was no suggestion however that the re-spondents' circumstances before their move to New Rust was anything but desperate. There is nothing in the papers to indicate any plan by the municipality to deal with the occupation of vacant land if it occurred. If there had been such a plan the appellants might well have acted differently.

The respondents began to move onto the New Rust Land during September 1998 and the number of people on this land continued to grow relentlessly. I would have ex-pected officials of the municipality responsible for housing to engage with these people as soon as they became aware of the occupation. I would also have thought that some effort would have been made by the municipality to resolve the difficulty on a case-by-case basis after an investigation of their circumstances before the matter got out of hand. The municipality did nothing and the settlement grew by leaps and bounds.

There is, however, no dispute that the municipality funded the eviction of the re-spondents.... The state had an obligation to ensure, at the very least, that the eviction was humanely executed. However, the eviction was reminiscent of the past and inconsis-tent with the values of the Constitution. The respondents were evicted a day early and to make matters worse, their possessions and building materials were not merely removed, but destroyed and burnt. I have already said that the provisions of section 26(1) of the Constitution burdens the state with at least a negative obligation in relation to housing. The manner in which the eviction was carried out resulted in a breach of this obligation.

In these circumstances, the municipality's response to the letter of the respondents' attorney left much to be desired....

In all these circumstances, the state may well have been in breach of its constitutional obligations. It may also be that the conduct of the municipality was inconsistent with the provisions of the Prevention of Illegal Eviction from and Unlawful Occupation of Land Act. In addition, the municipality may have failed to meet the obligations im-posed by the provisions of sections 2(1)(b), 2(1)(h)(i) and 9(1)(e) of the Housing Act. However no argument was addressed to this Court on these matters and we are not in a position to consider them further.

At the hearing in this Court, counsel for the national and Western Cape government, tendered a statement indicating that the respondents had, on that very day, been offered some alternative accommodation, not in fulfilment of any accepted constitutional obligation, but in the interests of humanity and pragmatism. Counsel for the respon-dents accepted the offer on their behalf. We were subsequently furnished with a copy of the arrangement which read as follows:

   1.   The Department of Planning, Local Government and Housing (Western Cape
        Province) undertakes in conjunction with the Oostenberg Municipality to pro-

vide temporary accommodation to the respondents on the Wallacedene Sportsfield until they can be housed in terms of the housing programmes available to the local authority, and in particular the Accelerated Land Managed Settlement Programme.

2. The 'temporary accommodation' comprises: a marked off site; provision for temporary structures intended to be waterproof; basic sanitation, water and refuse services.

3. The implementation of such measures is to be discussed with the Wallacedene community and the respondents.

Although, as indicated earlier, the special position of the respondents was aired during argument, the relief claimed by them was always grounded only in sections 26 and 28 of the Constitution and not on the breach of any statute (such as the Prevention of Illegal Evictions Act, or the Housing Act), the common law or any other provision of the Constitution. Accordingly, it is inappropriate for this Court to order any relief on grounds other than sections 26 or 28 of the Constitution.

This judgment must not be understood as approving any practice of land invasion for the purpose of coercing a state structure into providing housing on a preferential basis to those who participate in any exercise of this kind. Land invasion is inimical to the systematic provision of adequate housing on a planned basis. It may well be that the decision of a state structure, faced with the difficulty of repeated land invasions, not to provide housing in response to those invasions, would be reasonable. Reasonableness must be determined on the facts of each case.

I. Summary and conclusion

This case shows the desperation of hundreds of thousands of people living in deplorable conditions throughout the country. The Constitution obliges the state to act positively to ameliorate these conditions. The obligation is to provide access to housing, health-care, sufficient food and water, and social security to those unable to support themselves and their dependants. The state must also foster conditions to enable citizens to gain access to land on an equitable basis. Those in need have a corresponding right to demand that this be done.

I am conscious that it is an extremely difficult task for the state to meet these obligations in the conditions that prevail in our country. This is recognised by the Constitution which expressly provides that the state is not obliged to go beyond available resources or to realise these rights immediately. I stress however, that despite all these qualifications, these are rights, and the Constitution obliges the state to give effect to them. This is an obligation that courts can, and in appropriate circumstances, must enforce.

Neither section 26 nor section 28 entitles the respondents to claim shelter or housing immediately upon demand. The High Court order ought therefore not to have been made. However, section 26 does oblige the state to devise and implement a coherent, co-ordinated programme designed to meet its section 26 obligations. The programme that has been adopted and was in force in the Cape Metro at the time that this application was brought, fell short of the obligations imposed upon the state by section 26(2) in that it failed to provide for any form of relief to those desperately in need of access to housing.

In the light of the conclusions I have reached, it is necessary and appropriate to make a declaratory order. The order requires the state to act to meet the obligation imposed upon it by section 26(2) of the Constitution. This includes the obligation to devise, fund, implement and supervise measures to provide relief to those in desperate need.

The Human Rights Commission is an amicus in this case. Section 184 (1) (c) of the Constitution places a duty on the Commission to "monitor and assess the observance of human rights in the Republic." Subsections (2) (a) and (b) give the Commission the power:

(a) to investigate and to report on the observance of human rights;

(b) to take steps to secure appropriate redress where human right have been violated.

Counsel for the Commission indicated during argument that the Commission had the duty and was prepared to monitor and report on the compliance by the state of its section 26 obligations. In the circumstances, the Commission will monitor and, if necessary, report in terms of these powers on the efforts made by the state to comply with its section 26 obligations in accordance with this judgment.

There will be no order as to costs.

J. The Order

The following order is made:

1. The appeal is allowed in part.

2. The order of the Cape of Good Hope High Court is set aside and the following is substituted for it:

It is declared that:

(a) Section 26(2) of the Constitution requires the state to devise and implement within its available resources a comprehensive and coordinated programme progressively to realise the right of access to adequate housing.

(b) The programme must include reasonable measures such as, but not necessarily limited to, those contemplated in the Accelerated Managed Land Settlement Programme, to provide relief for people who have no access to land, no roof over their heads, and who are living in intolerable conditions or crisis situations.

(c) As at the date of the launch of this application, the state housing programme in the area of the Cape Metropolitan Council fell short of compliance with the requirements in paragraph (b), in that it failed to make reasonable provision within its available resources for people in the Cape Metropolitan area with no access to land, no roof over their heads, and who were living in intolerable conditions or crisis situations....

Occupiers of 51 Olivia Road, Berea Township, and 197 Main Street, Johannesburg, Applicants v. City of Johannesburg, et al.

2008 (5) BCLR 475 (CC) (Constitutional Court of South Africa)

Before: Langa CJ, Moseneke DCJ, Madala J, Mpati AJ, Ngcobo J, Nkabinde J, Sachs J, Skweyiya J and Van der Westhuizen J, who concur in the judgment of Yacoob J.

Yacoob J:

Introduction

More than 400 occupiers of two buildings in the inner city of Johannesburg (the occupiers) applied for leave to appeal against a decision of the Supreme Court of Appeal.

They challenged the correctness of the judgment and order of that Court authorising their eviction at the instance of the City of Johannesburg (the City) based on the finding that the buildings they occupied were unsafe and unhealthy. The City was ordered to provide those of the occupiers who were "desperately in need of housing assistance with relocation to a temporary settlement area".

The appeal to the Supreme Court of Appeal was directed by the City against a judgment and order in the Johannesburg High Court (the High Court). The High Court had before it applications by the City for the ejectment of the occupiers as well as counter-applications by the latter aimed at securing alternative accommodation or housing as a pre-condition to their eviction. The judge in the High Court declared that the City's housing programme fell short of what was required, ordered the City to produce a programme to cater for those people in desperate need, and interdicted the eviction of the occupiers on certain terms.

The broad questions initially raised in the application for leave to appeal were whether the order for the eviction of the occupiers ought to have been granted and whether the City's housing programme complied with the obligations imposed upon it by section 26(3) of the Constitution. I stress that the question in both courts was not limited to whether the City had complied with its housing obligations to the occupiers. They raised, in the public interest, the broader question whether the City had made reasonable provision for housing for those thousands of people who were said to be living in desperate conditions in the inner city....

Two days after the application for leave to appeal was heard, this Court issued an interim order aimed at ensuring that the City and the occupiers engaged with each other meaningfully on certain issues....

[Subsequently] we were informed that an agreement of settlement had been entered into between the City and the occupiers.... To determine the issues that remain for decision we must first define the issues raised by the application for leave to appeal. This judgment will next set out the reasons for issuing the engagement order as well as the terms of the agreement entered into consequent upon engagement. I will then investigate the effect of the agreement on those issues. The issues that remain to be decided are those not disposed of in that part of the judgment concerned with the reasons for engagement. Further the remaining issues will call for consideration only if they raise constitutional issues and if it is in the interests of justice for us to decide them.

Issues raised by this application

The first broad issue raised by the application is whether the Supreme Court of Appeal was right when it granted an order for the ejectment of all the occupiers. This broad issue encapsulates five questions. None of these was determined in the High Court. They arise out of the defences of the occupiers to the ejectment application.[11] The first of these was that section 12 of the Act is inconsistent with the Constitution because it provides for arbitrary evictions and evictions without a court order. Second, the occupiers attacked the constitutional validity of the decision by the City to evict them as being unfair because it had been taken without giving them a hearing. The next point taken was that the administrative decision to evict them was not reasonable in all the circumstances because in particular the City did not take into account that the oc-

---

11. The High Court did not deem it necessary to decide these questions because it held that the occupiers could not be evicted until and unless alternative accommodation was found for them.

cupiers would be homeless after the eviction. Fourthly, it was contended that section 26(3) of the Constitution precluded their eviction. The final argument made was that the standards set by the Prevention of Illegal Eviction from and Unlawful Occupation of Land Act (PIE) were applicable to these evictions. The Supreme Court of Appeal dismissed all these objections and, as already mentioned, granted the eviction orders on the basis that temporary accommodation should be provided to those occupiers who fulfil certain requirements.

The housing issues raised in the counter-applications are whether the City's housing programme then in operation catered reasonably for the occupiers and whether that programme also catered reasonably for the many thousands of people who lived in desperate conditions within the inner city. The essential question to be asked is whether the High Court was right in making the orders it did. The Supreme Court of Appeal disagreed with the High Court in this regard and made a limited order for temporary accommodation.

Reasons for the engagement order

The need for meaningful engagement between the City and the occupiers was not directly raised by the parties before this Court. It was however in some sense foreshadowed by their contention that the City was obliged to give the occupiers a hearing before taking the decision to evict on the basis that the decision was an administrative one.[14] The City contended that the occupiers had indeed been given a hearing because they had had an opportunity to file affidavits in the High Court in opposition to the ejectment application.

In Grootboom[15] this Court said, on the relationship between reasonable state action and the need to treat human beings with the appropriate respect and care for their dignity to which they have a right as members of humanity—

> All levels of government must ensure that the housing program is reasonably and appropriately implemented in the light of all the provisions in the Constitution. All implementation mechanisms and all State action in relation to housing falls to be assessed against the requirements of §26 of the Constitution. Every step at every level of government must be consistent with the constitutional obligation to take reasonable measures to provide adequate housing.

> But §26 is not the only provision relevant to a decision as to whether State action at any particular level of government is reasonable and consistent with the Constitution. The proposition that rights are interrelated and are all equally important is not merely a theoretical postulate. The concept has immense human and practical significance in a society founded on human dignity, equality and freedom. It is fundamental to an evaluation of the reasonableness of State action that account be taken of the inherent dignity of human beings. The Constitution will be worth infinitely less than its paper if the reasonableness of State action concerned with housing is determined without regard to the fundamental constitutional value of human dignity. Section 26, read in the context of the Bill of Rights as a whole, must mean that the respondents have a right to reasonable action by the State in all circumstances and with particular

---

14. The decision would therefore be subject to section 3(2)(b)(ii) of the Promotion of Administrative Justice Act 3 of 2000 (PAJA) as well as jurisprudence on administrative decisions.

15. Government of the Republic of South Africa and Others v. Grootboom and Others 2001(1) SA 46 (CC); 2000 (11) BCLR 1169 (CC).

regard to human dignity. In short, I emphasise that human beings are required to be treated as human beings. This is the backdrop against which the conduct of the [State] must be seen.

The Court went on to say more specifically about engagement and its importance—

The respondents began to move onto the New Rust land during September 1998 and the number of people on this land continued to grow relentlessly. I would have expected officials of the municipality responsible for housing to engage with these people as soon as they became aware of the occupation. I would have also thought that some effort would have been made by the municipality to resolve the difficulty on a case-by-case basis after an investigation of their circumstances before the matter got out of hand. The municipality did nothing and the settlement grew by leaps and bounds.

In Port Elizabeth Municipality[18] this Court said—

… the procedural and substantive aspects of justice and equity cannot always be separated. The managerial role of the courts may need to find expression in innovative ways. Thus, one potentially dignified and effective mode of achieving sustainable reconciliations of the different interests involved is to encourage and require the parties to engage with each other in a proactive and honest endeavour to find mutually acceptable solutions. Wherever possible, respectful face-to-face engagement or mediation through a third party should replace arm's-length combat by intransigent opponents.

It became evident during argument that the City had made no effort at all to engage with the occupiers at any time before proceedings for their eviction were brought. Yet the City must have been aware of the possibility, even the probability, that people would become homeless as a direct result of their eviction at its instance. In these circumstances those involved in the management of the municipality ought at the very least to have engaged meaningfully with the occupiers both individually and collectively.

Engagement is a two-way process in which the City and those about to become homeless would talk to each other meaningfully in order to achieve certain objectives. There is no closed list of the objectives of engagement. Some of the objectives of engagement in the context of a city wishing to evict people who might be rendered homeless consequent upon the eviction would be to determine—

(a) what the consequences of the eviction might be;

(b) whether the city could help in alleviating those dire consequences;

(c) whether it was possible to render the buildings concerned relatively safe and conducive to health for an interim period;

(d) whether the city had any obligations to the occupiers in the prevailing circumstances; and

(e) when and how the city could or would fulfil these obligations.

Engagement has the potential to contribute towards the resolution of disputes and to increased understanding and sympathetic care if both sides are willing to participate in the process. People about to be evicted may be so vulnerable that they may not be able to understand the importance of engagement and may refuse to take part in the process.

---

18. Port Elizabeth Municipality v. Various Occupiers 2005 (1) SA 217 (CC); 2004 (12) BCLR 1268 (CC).

If this happens, a municipality cannot walk away without more. It must make reasonable efforts to engage and it is only if these reasonable efforts fail that a municipality may proceed without appropriate engagement. It is precisely to ensure that a city is able to engage meaningfully with poor, vulnerable or illiterate people that the engagement process should preferably be managed by careful and sensitive people on its side.

The City has constitutional obligations towards the occupants of Johannesburg. It must provide services to communities in a sustainable manner, promote social and economic development, and encourage the involvement of communities and community organisations in matters of local government. It also has the obligation to fulfil the objectives mentioned in the preamble to the Constitution to "[i]mprove the quality of life of all citizens and free the potential of each person". Most importantly it must respect, protect, promote and fulfil the rights in the Bill of Rights. The most important of these rights for present purposes is the right to human dignity and the right to life. In the light of these constitutional provisions a municipality that ejects people from their homes without first meaningfully engaging with them acts in a manner that is broadly at odds with the spirit and purpose of the constitutional obligations set out in this paragraph taken together.

But the duty of the City to engage people who may be rendered homeless after an ejectment to be secured by it is also squarely grounded in section 26(2) of the Constitution.[26] It was said in Grootboom that "[e]very step at every level of government must be consistent with the constitutional obligation to take reasonable measures to provide adequate housing." Reasonable conduct of a municipality pursuant to section 26(2) includes the reasonableness of every step taken in the provision of adequate housing. Every homeless person is in need of housing and this means that every step taken in relation to a potentially homeless person must also be reasonable if it is to comply with section 26(2).

And, what is more, section 26(2) mandates that the response of any municipality to potentially homeless people with whom it engages must also be reasonable. It may in some circumstances be reasonable to make permanent housing available and, in others, to provide no housing at all. The possibilities between these extremes are almost endless. It must not be forgotten that the City cannot be expected to make provision for housing beyond the extent to which available resources allow. As long as the response of the municipality in the engagement process is reasonable, that response complies with section 26(2). The Constitution therefore obliges every municipality to engage meaningfully with people who would become homeless because it evicts them. It also follows that, where a municipality is the applicant in eviction proceedings that could result in homelessness, a circumstance that a court must take into account to comply with section 26(3) of the Constitution is whether there has been meaningful engagement.

It has been suggested that there are around 67 000 people living in the inner city of Johannesburg in unsafe and unhealthy buildings in relation to whom ejectment orders will have to be issued and that it would be impractical to expect meaningful engagement in every case. I cannot agree. It is common cause that the implementation of the City's Regeneration Strategy is an important reason that founded the decision to evict. That strategy was adopted in 2003. If structures had been put in place with competent

---

26. Section 26(2) provides—
   The state must take reasonable legislative and other measures, within its available resources, to achieve the progressive realisation of [the right of access to adequate housing].

sensitive council workers skilled in engagement, the process could have begun when the strategy was adopted. It must then have been apparent that the eviction of a large number of people was inevitable. Indeed the larger the number of people potentially to be affected by eviction, the greater the need for structured, consistent and careful engagement. Ad hoc engagement may be appropriate in a small municipality where an eviction or two might occur each year, but is entirely inappropriate in the circumstances prevalent in the City.

It must be understood that the process of engagement will work only if both sides act reasonably and in good faith. The people who might be rendered homeless as a result of an order of eviction must, in their turn, not content themselves with an intransigent attitude or nullify the engagement process by making non-negotiable, unreasonable demands. People in need of housing are not, and must not be regarded as a disempowered mass. They must be encouraged to be pro-active and not purely defensive. Civil society organisations that support the peoples' claims should preferably facilitate the engagement process in every possible way.

Finally it must be mentioned that secrecy is counter-productive to the process of engagement. The constitutional value of openness is inimical to secrecy. Moreover, as I have already pointed out, it is the duty of a court to take into account whether, before an order of eviction that would lead to homelessness is granted at the instance of a municipality, there has been meaningful engagement or, at least, that the municipality has made reasonable efforts towards meaningful engagement. In any eviction proceedings at the instance of a municipality therefore, the provision of a complete and accurate account of the process of engagement including at least the reasonable efforts of the municipality within that process would ordinarily be essential. The absence of any engagement or the unreasonable response of a municipality in the engagement process would ordinarily be a weighty consideration against the grant of an ejectment order.

This Court made the interim order because it was not appropriate to grant any eviction order against the occupiers, in the circumstances of this case, unless there had at least been some effort at meaningful engagement. It was common cause during argument that there had been none. The ejectment of a resident by a municipality in circumstances where the resident would possibly become homeless should ordinarily take place only after meaningful engagement. Whether there had been meaningful engagement between a city and the resident about to be rendered homeless is a circumstance to be considered by a court in terms of section 26(3).

It follows that the Supreme Court of Appeal should not have granted the order of ejectment in the circumstances of this case, in the absence of meaningful engagement.

The engagement agreement

The post-engagement agreement concluded between the City and the occupiers records at its inception that it "contemplates" the resolution of two aspects of their dispute: the interim measures to be taken by the City to improve the condition of the properties as well as "[t]he City's application for the eviction of the occupiers". It is not necessary to go into these two aspects of the agreement in much detail.

The agreement makes explicit and meticulous provision for measures aimed at rendering both properties "safer and more habitable" in the interim. It is not necessary to set out each measure. They include the installation of chemical toilets, the cleaning and sanitation of the buildings, the delivery of refuse bags, the closing of a certain lift shaft and the installation of fire extinguishers. The work aimed at rendering the building more habitable was to be completed within 21 working days of the signature of the agreement. The agreement was signed on 29 October 2007.

The eviction application of the City was resolved on a somewhat different basis. The agreement obliged the City to provide all occupiers with alternative accommodation in certain identified buildings. It defined with reasonable precision the nature and standard of the accommodation to be provided and determined the way in which the rent in respect of this accommodation will be calculated. The agreement obliged all occupiers to move into alternative accommodation by yesterday[30] and stipulated that this alternative accommodation is provided "pending the provision of suitable permanent housing solutions" being developed by the City "in consultation" with the occupiers concerned.

Approval of the agreement

I have already pointed out that work on the improvement of buildings now occupied was to begin 21 days after the signature of the agreement. However the rest of the agreement was to take effect only on the date on which it was approved or endorsed by this Court. On 5 November 2007 this Court made the following order —

1. The Agreement entered into between the City of Johannesburg and those Occupiers who have signed the Agreement dated 29 October 2007 is endorsed.

2. Residual issues arising from the parties' reports will be considered in the judgment to be delivered in this matter in due course.

No reasons were given for the endorsement order. I state them briefly. This judgment holds that the City is required to respond reasonably to the process of engagement. The agreement would call for endorsement by this Court if it does indeed represent a reasonable response to the engagement process. There was no doubt that the agreement represented a reasonable response to the engagement process. The City must be commended for the fact that its position became more humane as the case proceeded through the different courts, and for its ultimate reasonable response to the engagement order.

This is the first time this Court has approved an agreement between the parties before it in circumstances where the parties required approval before important aspects of it came into operation. This Court deemed it appropriate to consider and evaluate the terms of the agreement for the purpose of deciding whether to approve it because —

(a) the City and the occupiers engaged with each other in the process of complying with the order of this Court;

(b) the parties reported to this Court also in compliance with our order;

(c) considerable expenditure on the part of the City was obviously required in the implementation of the agreement; and

(d) the City and the occupiers would have been in an invidious position if this Court had later held that the agreement was not a reasonable response to engagement.

It will not always be appropriate for a court to approve all agreements entered into consequent upon engagement. It is always for the municipality to ensure that its response to the process of engagement is reasonable. The deciding factor in this case in

---

30. 18 February 2008.

my view was that engagement was ordered by this Court, and the parties had been asked to report back on the process while proceedings were pending before it. Courts would ordinarily consider agreements entered into consequent upon engagement ordered by them in the course of litigation. It must be emphasised that the process of engagement should take place before litigation commences unless it is not possible or reasonable to do so because of urgency or some other compelling reason.

Effect of development

There are issues in relation to which there is either a dispute or, at the very least, the absence of complete agreement whether they should be considered by this Court. Apart from costs, the contention of the occupiers in relation to the disputes that remain is set out as follows—

11.1.　The relief claimed by the applicants in respect of the City's failure to formulate and implement a housing plan for the applicants and the class of persons on behalf of whom the current litigation was initiated;

11.2.　The practice to be adopted by the City in dealing with persons occupying so-called "bad" buildings in future;

11.3.　The constitutionality of Section 12(4)(b) of the National Building Regulations and Building Standards Act 103 of 1977 ("the NBRA");

11.4　The applicants' review of the City's decisions to issue the notices in terms of Section 12(4)(b) of the NBRA in respect of the 51 Olivia Road and 197 Main Street properties, assuming that the NBRA is valid;

11.5.　The applicability of the Prevention of Illegal Eviction from, and Unlawful Occupation of, Land Act 19 of 1998;

11.6.　The reach and applicability of Sections 26(1), 26(2) and 26(3) of the Constitution....

We must now determine whether any of these issues should be decided.

Relief concerning the housing plan

The occupiers contend that this Court must adjudicate their contention that the City has failed to formulate and implement a housing plan for them and the class of person they say they represent. Since the agreement has disposed of the issue of temporary accommodation, the occupiers evidently require adjudication of the housing plan in relation to whether it facilitates permanent housing solutions for them and for the thousands of other people who might later be evicted from unsafe and unhealthy buildings. The agreement acknowledges that a permanent housing solution has not yet been found and records that—

> The nature and location of any permanent housing options to be made available to the occupiers will be developed by the City in consultation with the occupiers concerned, having regard to applicable national, provincial and municipal housing policies and implementation plans.

The occupiers contend in their reporting affidavit that negotiations concerning "permanent housing solutions have been marred by the absence of any concrete plan to provide housing for the inner city poor" in general or for the occupiers in particular. The City attaches to its post-engagement settlement affidavit a housing plan and requires this Court to consider this plan in the context of the challenges and complexities inherent in the process of housing provision.[32] The occupiers in a supplementary affidavit contend that we should, if we are minded to consider the plan, give them a 30-day opportunity to deal with the plan and to provide the City with a similar opportunity to address their response before we do so.

It is not necessary for this Court to consider the question of "permanent housing solutions" for the occupiers. The City has agreed that these solutions will be developed in consultation with them. The complaint by the occupiers that negotiations have been marred by unclear and inconcrete housing plans is not in my view a sufficient reason for this Court to consider this question at this stage. There is every reason to believe that negotiations will continue in good faith. The situation now is very different from that which confronted the occupiers in the High Court. The City has shown a willingness to engage. As a result, the desperate situation of the occupiers has been alleviated by the reasonable response of the City to the engagement process. There is no reason to think that future engagement will not be meaningful and will not lead to a reasonable result. In any event this Court should not be the court of first and last instance on whether the City has acted reasonably in the process. Nor should it be the only determinant of whether the plan is reasonable in the sense of being sufficiently concrete and clear. It is the duty of both parties to continue with the process of negotiation and for the occupiers or the City to approach the High Court if this course becomes necessary.

Much the same reasoning applies to the plea of the occupiers that we consider the plight of thousands of other poor people in the inner city and evaluate the housing plan in relation to them. The housing plan before the High Court differs from the one that we are required to consider in this case. This Court should not be the court of first and last instance in deciding whether it complies with the Constitution and the law. We must bear in mind that the engagement between the occupiers and the City has resulted in an agreement that represents a reasonable response by the City. There is no reason to believe that the City will not in the future engage meaningfully with other occupants whose evictions become either necessary or desirable. The City has undertaken to negotiate permanent housing solutions for the occupiers in consultation with them. It is not unreasonable to expect that the City will, in the ordinary course, adopt a similar approach in respect of other people who are affected in the future. In the circumstances, it would be premature to examine the plan and evaluate it in a generalised way. A process of this kind comes close to an abstract evaluation which is undesirable at the best of times. A case can always be brought in the High Court in relation to particular occupiers with specific allegations as to the respects in which the housing obligations imposed by the Constitution have not been complied with. This is preferable to dealing with a generalised claim in relation to anticipated future occurrences. At the same time the High Court order has been overtaken by events and cannot be allowed to stand.

It must be apparent by now that this Court did not afford any opportunity for further response to the housing plan because, though the evaluation of these plans did raise a constitutional issue, it was not in the interests of justice to follow that course and to consider and evaluate the plan.

---

32. There is a debate about whether the plight of thousands of other poor residents of the inter city apart from occupiers has been properly raised.

* * *

Other issues that need not be decided

Enough has been said in this judgment about what the occupiers call the practice to be adopted by the City in dealing with people who occupy unsafe and unhealthy buildings in the future. I can also see no need for a further general discussion on "the reach and applicability of Sections 26(1), 26(2) and 26(3)". This judgment should say no more about these issues.

There is equally no need for this judgment to be concerned with the question whether PIE applies in the present case or to expand on the relationship between section 26 and PIE. The question may never arise if the City engages meaningfully with those people who would become homeless if evicted by it.

The section 12 issues

This leaves two matters mentioned by the occupiers. Both concern section 12 of the Act. The one is a claim for a review of the City's decision to issue the section 12(4)(b) notices. The other concerns the constitutionality of section 12(4)(b). I do not think the review remains relevant because the ejectment proceedings have been effectively settled. However it is in my view in the interests of justice to investigate the narrower question of the considerations relevant to the issuing of the section 12(4)(b) notice. The same applies to the question of the constitutionality of section 12(6). The section 12 procedure is likely to be applied by municipalities in the future and it is appropriate that some guidance be given to them. The importance of the issues to be considered will become apparent when they are discussed.

* * *

Sections 12(4), 12(5) and 12(6) provide—

(4) If the local authority in question deems it necessary for the safety of any person, it may by notice in writing, served by post or delivered—

   (a) order the owner of any building to remove, within the period specified in such notice, all persons occupying or working or being for any other purpose in such building therefrom, and to take care that any person not authorised by such local authority does not enter such building;

   (b) order any person occupying or working or being for any other purpose in any building, to vacate such building immediately or within a period specified in such notice.

(5) No person shall occupy or use or permit the occupation or use of any building in respect of which a notice was served or delivered in terms of this section or steps were taken by the local authority in question in terms of subsection (1), unless such local authority has granted permission in writing that such building may again be occupied or used.

(6) Any person who contravenes or fails to comply with any provision of this section or any notice issued thereunder, shall be guilty of an offence and, in the case of a contravention of the provisions of subsection (5), liable on conviction to a fine not exceeding R100 for each day on which he so contravened.

Relevant considerations

One of the grounds upon which the lawfulness of the City's decision to issue the section 12(4)(b) notices was challenged was that the City had failed to take relevant considerations into account. The particular contention and the way in which it was disposed of appear in one paragraph of the judgment of the Supreme Court of Appeal in the following terms—

> The second ground, namely that the city failed to take relevant considerations into account, was based on the assertion that the city failed to consider the availability of suitable alternative accommodation or land for the respondents. The submission presupposes that the right to act under § 12(4)(b) and the right to access to adequate housing are reciprocal and that the former is dependent or conditional on the latter. There is in my view no merit in the submission.

The Supreme Court of Appeal is undoubtedly right in the conclusion that the right to act under section 12(4)(b) and the right to access adequate housing are not reciprocal and that the former is neither dependent nor conditional on the latter. However the difficulty is the inescapable inference from the passage just quoted that it is neither appropriate nor necessary for a decision-maker to consider at all the availability of suitable alternative accommodation or land when making a section 12(4)(b) decision. Any suggestion that the availability of alternative accommodation need not be considered carries the implication that whether a person or family is rendered homeless after an eviction consequent upon a section 12(4)(b) decision is irrelevant to the decision itself. The reasoning postulates the false premise that there is no relationship between section 12(4)(b) of the Act and section 26(2) even if the person is rendered homeless by the decision.

It is common cause that the City in making the decision to evict the people concerned took no account whatsoever of the fact that the people concerned would be rendered homeless. This is regrettable. Municipal officials do not act appropriately if they take insulated decisions in respect of different duties that they are obliged to perform. In this case the City had a duty to ensure safe and healthy buildings on the one hand and to take reasonable measures within its available resources to make the right of access to adequate housing more accessible as time progresses on the other. It cannot be that the City is entitled to make decisions on each of these two aspects separately, one department making a decision on whether someone should be evicted and some other department in the bureaucratic maze determining whether housing should be provided. The housing provision and the health and safety provision must be read together. There is a single City. That City must take a holistic decision in relation to eviction after appropriate engagement taking into account the possible homelessness of the people concerned and the capacity of the City to do something about it.

The Supreme Court of Appeal did not wholly embrace the inter-relationship between section 12(4)(b) of the Act and section 26(2) of the Constitution. It said that the appeal before it concerned—

> ... in the main the right of a local authority to order occupiers by notice to vacate a building because it is necessary for their safety or the safety of others and its right, if they fail to comply, to apply for an order of court for their eviction.

The Court saw the case as "only peripherally about the constitutional duty of organs of state towards those who are evicted from their homes and are in a desperate condition." This characterisation is unfortunate.

The Supreme Court of Appeal was incorrect in its conclusion that the failure of the City to consider the availability of suitable alternative accommodation or land for the occupiers in the process of making a section 12(4)(b) decision was unobjectionable. The relationship between the eviction of people by the City pursuant to section 12(4)(b) and the possibility of their being rendered homeless consequent upon that eviction cannot be gainsaid. It follows that the City must take into account the possibility of the homelessness of any resident consequent upon a section 12(4)(b) eviction in the process of making the decision as to whether or not to proceed with the eviction.

The constitutional validity of section 12(6) of the Act

Sections 12(4), 12(5) and 12(6) were attacked before the Supreme Court of Appeal on numerous grounds.

There is … one finding that does occasion sufficient constitutional concern to render it in the interests of justice for it to be considered. It is the conclusion of the Supreme Court of Appeal that there is nothing objectionable about a legislative provision that permits "the issuing of an administrative order to vacate and, in the event of non-compliance, for a criminal sanction." It would have been noticed that the criminal sanction is imposed by section 12(6). Section 12(4)(b) authorises the municipality concerned by notice to "order any person occupying … any building" to "vacate" it "immediately" or within a specified period. In terms of section 12(5) no person may occupy the building after the notice has been issued without the permission of the municipality. It is in this context that section 12(6) provides that any person who continues to occupy despite the "order" is liable on conviction to a maximum fine of R100 for each day of unlawful occupation.

Section 26(3), like all provisions of the Bill of Rights, deserves a generous construction. The section prohibits eviction of people from their home absent a court order that must be made after taking into account all the relevant circumstances. It means in effect that no person may be compelled to leave their home unless there exists an appropriate court order. The provisions of section 26(3) would be virtually nugatory and would amount to little protection if people who were in occupation of their homes could be constitutionally compelled to leave by the exertion of the pressure of a criminal sanction without a court order. It follows that any provision that compels people to leave their homes on pain of criminal sanction in the absence of a court order is contrary to the provisions of section 26(3) of the Constitution. Section 12(6) provides for this criminal compulsion and is not consistent with the Constitution. Continued occupation of the property should not be a criminal offence absent a court order for eviction.

It is neither just nor equitable to set the provisions of section 12(6) of the Act aside. It is appropriate to encourage people to leave unsafe or unhealthy buildings in compliance with the court order for their eviction. A criminal sanction does have this effect. It provides an additional incentive for occupiers to leave unhealthy and unsafe buildings and reduces the need for a forced eviction at the instance of the State. A reading-in order that provides for a criminal sanction only after a court order for eviction has already been made would in my view be appropriate to save the section. As has already been pointed out in this judgment, a court must take into account all relevant circumstances before making an order for eviction. Any eviction order would also afford the occupier a reasonable time within which to vacate the property.

This is not a case in which there are a myriad ways in which the Legislature could cure the section. The order should be to the effect that section 12(6) of the National Building Regulations and Building Standards Act 103 of 1977 must be read as if the following proviso has been added: "This subsection applies only to people who, after service upon them of an order of court for their eviction, continue to occupy the property concerned."

Retrospectivity

It will not be just and equitable for this order to be retrospective. The read-in proviso should not apply to cases in which people have already been convicted of a contravention of section 12(6) of the Act, the period provided for the lodging of an application for leave to appeal has expired and no notice of appeal has been lodged.

Helen Hershkoff, *Transforming Legal Theory in the Light of Practice: The Judicial Application of Social and Economic Rights to Private Orderings,* in COURTING SOCIAL JUSTICE: JUDICIAL ENFORCEMENT OF SOCIAL AND ECONOMIC RIGHTS IN THE DEVELOPING WORLD
294-99 (Varun Gauri & Daniel M. Brinks, eds., Cambridge U. Press 2008).

Aligning Property Rights with Constitutional Goals

The classical model of constitutional enforcement remits property rights to the private sphere; when invaded—through takings or, occasionally, by other regulatory acts—the property holder is entitled to compensation from the state. As Joseph William Singer explains,

> The classical view of property concentrates on protecting those who have property.... The classical view focuses on individual owners and the actions they must take to acquire property rights, which will then be defended by the state. It assumes that the distribution of property is a consequence of the voluntary actions of individuals rather than a decision by the state. Property law does nothing more than protect property rights acquired by individual action. Distributional questions, in this conception, are foreign to property as a system.[139]

By contrast, critical theory places the distributional aspects of property law front and center, emphasizing the role of property rules in shaping social relations and perpetuating or destabilizing hierarchy.[140] The case studies suggest that in some situations, social and economic rights afford courts interpretive space within which to reconfigure property rights in the light of public aspirations. This is not to say that private property becomes collective or state-owned;[141] rather, in some situations, the inclusion of social and economic rights in a national constitution persuades a court to reconfigure the boundaries of the property right to reflect the significance of interests that in other contexts might be given less weight or not included at all in the balance.

---

139. [Joseph William] Singer 1996. No right to exclude: Public accommodations and private property. *Nw. U. L. Rev.* 90: 1283, 1466–1467.

140. *Id.* at 1474 ("Property law helps to structure and shape the contours of social relationships. Choices of property rules ineluctably entail choices about the quality and character of human relationships").

141. Cf. Liam Murphy & Thomas Nagel 2002. *The myth of ownership: Taxes and justice.* Oxford: Oxford University Press, pp. 175–176 (referring to the "conventionality of property," but emphasizing the fact that the "state does not own its citizens, nor do they own each other collectively. But individual citizens don't own anything except through laws that are enacted and enforced by the state").

Whether property rights could defeat the South African government's provision of emergency shelter to the indigent came to the forefront in the *Kyalami Ridge* case decided by the Constitutional Court.[142] In this case, petitioners challenged the state's authority to create temporary settlements on public land for indigent people made homeless through flooding caused by heavy rains. Budgetary appropriations had been made to deal with the emergency, and the government chose to site a transit camp on a prison farm using land that the government owned. Nearby residents filed suit to enjoin the siting decision. They argued that the government could not site the camp on the farm because it lacked specific legislative authorization to take such action. They also argued that the siting decision violated requirements of administrative legality because the government had failed to secure consents from ministerial functionaries, had failed to meet environmental standards, and had failed to comply with town planning ordinances. Claimants further challenged the government's decision on the ground that "the choice of the prison farm as the site of the transit camp ... will affect the character of the neighbourhood and reduce the value of their properties," and that the transit camp "would constitute a nuisance." It bears emphasis that the claimants at no point disputed the constitutional right of the flood victims to be afforded access to temporary shelter.

The Court found that the government's use of its own property was not unreasonable for the intended purpose, and, further, that existing laws neither "excluded nor limited the government's common law power to make its land available to flood victims pursuant to its constitutional duty to provide them with access to housing." In addition, even if claimants were prejudiced because of a reduction in the value of their property or a change in the "character of their neighborhood," they pointed to no "rights or legitimate expectations" that were "affected or threatened," as required to secure relief under the principle of procedural fairness. The Court left open the question whether prospective rights (as, for example, asserted by an applicant for a license) would satisfy the requirement, assuming "that procedural fairness may be required for administrative decisions affecting a material interest short of an enforceable or prospective right." Looking, then, at the competing interests of the adjacent property owners and the homeless flood victims, the Court insisted that one factor not be privileged over the other, but rather that a balance be struck, depending on "the nature of the decision, the 'rights' affected by it, the circumstances in which it is made, and the consequence[s] resulting from it":

> The fact that property values may be affected by low cost housing development on neighbouring land is a factor that is relevant to the housing policies of the government and to the way in which government discharges its duty to provide everyone with access to housing. But it is only a factor and cannot in the circumstances of the present case stand in the way of the constitutional obligation that government has to address the needs of homeless people, and its decision to use its own property for that purpose.

The Court left open whether other legal restraints might be interpreted to limit the government's conduct, emphasizing that the state "cannot ... on the basis of its rights as owner of the land and a constitutional obligation to provide access to housing, claim the power to develop its land contrary to legislation that is binding on it."[143]

---

142. Minister of Public Works and Others v. Kyalami Ridge Environmental Association and Others, 2001 (7) BCLR 652 (CC) (South Africa), available at http://www.saflii.org/za/cases/ZACC/2001/19.rtf (accessed May 20, 2008).

143. Excerpts from the court's opinions appear in *id.* at ¶¶ 94, 24, 96, 48, 92, 101, 108, and 115.

Conversely, whether the burden of the state's housing efforts can be imposed on any single property owner came to issue in the *Modderkip Boerdery* litigation,[144]which raised, but elided, the question of the horizontal application of Section 25 of the South Africa Constitution ("No one may be deprived of property except in terms of law of general application, and no law may permit arbitrary deprivation of property"[145]). Over time, the Modderklip farm became the site of informal settlements by residents from an adjacent and overcrowded township in Benoni. In May 2000, four hundred settlers came to live on the farm and resided in fifty dwellings. After discussion with the Benoni City Council, Modderklip tried to evict the settlers, but the head of the local prison requested that the prosecutions not go forward "as the prison would be hard-pressed to find space to accommodate convicted unlawful occupiers should they be sentenced to prison terms." Modderklip continued to try to resolve the matter short of eviction, going so far as offering to sell the occupied portions of the farm to the township. In the meantime, informal settlements continued to develop. By October, eighteen thousand people, in four thousand dwellings, had come to occupy Modderklip's farm; at the time of decision, the number had mounted to forty thousand, collectively organized into the Gabon Informal Settlement. Unable to evict the settlers, Modderklip filed suit in the Pretoria High Court claiming that the continued occupation of the farm constituted an unconstitutional arbitrary taking of property. In their response, the police "contended that the problem was not a police matter but one of land reform," and asked the court to consider where the settlers would live if they were evicted from the farm. The court ruled largely in favor of Modderklip, finding:

> [T]he state had breached its [constitutional] obligations ... to take reasonable steps within its available resources to realise the right of the occupiers to have accesses [sic] to adequate housing and land ... [and that] this failure by the state effectively amounted to the unlawful expropriation of Modderklip's property and also infringed Modderklip's rights to equality ... by requiring it to bear the burden of providing accommodation to the occupiers, a function that should have been undertaken by the state.

The Supreme Court of Appeal generally agreed with the lower court, declaring that Modderklip was entitled to damages for the occupation of the land, but that the settlers "are entitled to occupy the land until alternative land has been made available to them by the State or the provincial or local authority." The appeals court further found that Modderklip's rights to fair treatment under Section 25 of the Constitution had been violated by the settler[s'] occupation of the land.

The Supreme Court declined to address whether Section 25 "has horizontal application and if so, under what circumstances." But it found that "it was unreasonable of the state to stand by and do nothing in circumstances where it was impossible for Modderklip to evict the occupiers because of the sheer magnitude of the invasion and the particular circumstances of the occupiers." In crafting relief, the Court balanced Modderklip's interest in using the farm with the occupants' interest in safe and stable dwellings. The occupants were recognized to "have formed themselves into a settled

---

144. President of the Republic of South Africa and Another v. Modderklip Boerdery (Pty) Ltd. 2005 (CCT 20/04) [2005] ZACC 5; 2005 (5) SA 3 (CC) (13 May 2005) (South Africa), available at http://www.saflii.org/za/cases/ZAAC/toc-P.html (accessed May 20, 2008).

145. Quoted in *id.*

community and built homes" and to "have no other option but to remain on Modderk-lip's property." The Court, thus, held that the occupants' "investment into their own community on Modderklip's farm must be weighed against the financial waste that their eviction would represent," consistent with the overall goal of achieving "the consti-tutional vision of a caring society based on good neighbourliness and shared con-cern."[146]

The Supreme Court declined to order eviction of the occupants, pointing to their constitutional right to access to affordable shelter, or to order expropriation of the Modderklip farm, citing separation of powers concerns, despite the owner's willingness to make the sale. Instead, the Court ordered the state to compensate Modderklip for the occupants' use of the farm, even though the government had not authorized the residents to settle there. Rather than approaching the question as one of direct or indi-rect application of constitutional rights to private actors, the Court instead looked at the specific relations at issue and balanced highly contextual factors in the light of the constitutional commitment both to provide judicial access and to secure access to housing.

RECONCEPTUALIZING CONSTITUTION ENFORCEMENT IN THE LIGHT OF JUDICIAL PRACTICE

The case studies tell a story of constitutional enforcement that plainly does not map on to the classical approach. Courts in the countries surveyed do not adhere, or at least do not consistently adhere, to a binary distinction between the public and the private. Instead, constitutional norms radiate into the world of common law doctrine and re-shape private rules in specific contexts reflecting constitutional aspirations. But these judicial practices likewise do not cleanly trace the alternative horizontal models set out in the academic literature. Courts seem reluctant to decide whether constitutional rights are violated by non-state actors and, conversely, whether non-state actors owe constitutional duties to other private individuals. It is not only that courts avoid what Craig Scott has called the "stark either/or division of the applicability of rights into the categories of 'horizontal' versus 'vertical.'"[147] More than that, courts appear to avoid even the language of rights and duties when analyzing the application of constitutional provisions to non-state actors. Yet, the constitutional provisions clearly are influencing their interpretive practice.

Consider the *Modderklip* litigation. Here, the South Africa [c]ourt did not character-ize the private farm owner as owing a duty to provide access to shelter to the settlers oc-cupying the land; neither did the [c]ourt deem the settlers responsible for a "taking" of the Modderklip farm when they used it to construct an alternative community. The duty—to provide shelter or to compensate for the use of land—at all times remained with the government. But the court also recognized that Modderklip could not simply evict the settlers and leave them to the hazards of homelessness. The [c]ourt looked to social and economic norms as reflecting a constitutional vision of solidarity that altered the relation of the property owner to the settlers. The Court did not use the language of rights and duties to describe this influence. Instead, the constitutional provisions af-forded the [c]ourt interpretive authority to modify powers typically associated with

---

146. Excerpts from the court's opinion appear in *id.* ¶¶ 5, 14, 15, 21, 26, 48, 54, and 55.
147. Craig Scott 1999. Reaching beyond (without abandoning) the category of "economic, social and cultural rights." *Hum. Rts. Q.* 21: 633, 646.

common law entitlements—in this situation, the common law power of a property owner to exclude uninvited guests.[148]

One way to conceptualize the court's approach is to see it as a shift from the language of rights and duties to that of power and liability in discrete relations.[149]

In the classical conception, common law powers can be used in the holder's discretion to maximize self-utility; the egoistic exercise of power is assumed to conduce toward the general welfare. The presence of social welfare norms in a constitution alters this background assumption. From a constitutive theory of law, the powers assigned to individuals must now be interpreted and applied within the orbit of constitutional commitment and not simply within that of self-regarding concern. In some situations, the individual's private power—to extend medical services, to produce pharmaceuticals, to ensure workplace safety—will be channeled so that it is exercised beneficially for claimants who otherwise would be adversely affected in their social position. In this sense, the constitutional norm exercises a radiating effect on a legal relation and in some settings the court must recalibrate the balance of interests guiding the private entity's exercise of power.[150]

The South Africa [c]ourt, thus, made clear that Modderklip's power to control access to the farm could not be exercised in a way that would unduly burden the occupants' background right to housing, notwithstanding the fact that the farm owner does not owe a duty of shelter to the settlers. By constraining the exercise of the common law power, the court effectively altered the occupants' legal relation in the sense that they now possessed shelter. But, rather than prescribing rights directly owed from one individual to another, the court instead reshaped a power relationship in a specific context in the light of different facts and circumstances. By declining to set down a hard and fast rule for future claimants, the court's approach may introduce unpredictablility into its decision making. However, it also has the benefit of avoiding ossification, a significant attribute when dealing with social welfare norms and other complex areas that raise broad policy questions. The court's approach may be likened to forms of provisional review used by American courts, both state and federal, in structural reform litigation involving social welfare claims.[151]

---

148. Joseph William Singer explains:

If "property is a set of social relations among human beings," the legal definition of those relationships confers—or withholds—power over others. The grant of a property right to one person leaves others vulnerable to the will of the owner. Conversely, the refusal to grant a property right leaves the claimant vulnerable to the will of others, who may with impunity infringe on the interests which have been denied protection.

Singer, Sovereignty and property, p. 41.

149. According to Peter Jaffey, the formal distinction is as follows:

Y has a duty to X, which means Y is required to act or refrain from acting in a certain way (for the benefit of X), and X has a correlative right to the performance of the duty.... In a power-liability relation, by acting in the way prescribed for the exercise of the power, X can alter Y's legal relations. X's power is correlated with a liability on the part of Y to the alteration of Y's legal relations.

Peter Jaffey 2004. Hohfeld's power-liability/right-duty distinction in the law of restitution. *Can. J. L. & Juris* 17: 295. See also Walter Wheeler Cook 1919. Hohfeld's contributions to the science of law. *Yale L. J.* 28: 721, 725 (explaining that in "Hohfeld's terminology any human being who can by his acts produce changes in legal relations has a legal *power* or powers" [emphasis in original]).

150. Alexy, *A theory of constitutional rights*, p. 352.

151. See Hershkoff, Positive rights and state constitutions, [112 Harv. L. Rev. 1132, 1158 (1999)] (developing the argument that state courts in the U.S. approach state constitutional decision making with an eye toward "provisional solutions"); Michael C. Dorf & Charles F. Sabel 1998. A constitution of democratic experimentalism. *Colum. L. Rev.* 98: 267.

A Dream Denied:
The Criminalization of Homelessness in U.S. Cities

A Report by the National Coalition for the Homeless and the National Law Center on Homelessness and Poverty (Jan. 2006), pp. 18–19

Criminalization Measures Violate Human Rights Norms

While laws and practices that criminalize homelessness may violate domestic constitutional law, these measures also may violate international human rights law.

I. Using International Human Rights Law in the U.S.

The United States has signed international human rights agreements, many of which prohibit actions that target homeless people living in public spaces. Although the U.S. had signed and/or ratified several human rights treaties that would prohibit actions that criminalize homelessness, those treaties are not directly enforceable in U.S. courts (i.e., "self-executing"). However, once a country has signed an international treaty, it is obligated not to pass laws that would "defeat the object and purpose of [the] treaty."[16] Even if a treaty is not directly enforceable in domestic courts, international human rights treaties can be used persuasively to support legal arguments based on domestic law. For example, if the domestic law is ambiguous on a certain topic, courts can turn to international law for guidance.[17]

II. Provisions in International Law to Support Combating Criminalization

The U.S. Supreme Court has not ruled explicitly to protect the right to intrastate travel. However, the right to movement has been established in international human rights documents, and has been considered customary international law by both scholars and domestic courts. The International Covenant on Civil and Political Rights (ICCPR), a treaty signed and ratified by the U.S. (though not self-executing), contains provisions that protect the right to movement. The Human Rights Committee ("HRC"), which oversees the ICCPR, states that the right to movement and the freedom to choose your own residence are important rights that should only be breached by the least intrusive means necessary to keep public order.[18] Many laws that target homeless people living in public spaces interfere with their right to freedom of movement, by either keeping them out of certain areas in a city or forcing them to move to other spaces involuntarily.

In addition, the majority of international human rights agreements have non-discrimination clauses. The ICCPR protects "equal protection of the law" and prohibits discrimination based on a variety of statuses. The United States participated in the 1996 Second United Nations Conference on Human Settlements and is signatory to the Habitat Agenda, which states that no one should be "penalized for their status."[19] Laws that

---

16. The Vienna Convention on the Law of Treaties, May 23, 1969, art. 18(a), 1155 U.N.T.S. 331.

17. For more information about the status of the human right to housing in the U.S. see NLCHP, Homeless in the United States and the Human Right to Housing (2004); Maria Foscarinis et al., The Human Right to Housing, Making the Case in U.S. Advocacy, 38 Clearinghouse Review 97 (2004); Maria Foscarinis, Homelessness and Human Rights: Towards an Integrated Strategy, 19 St. Louis U. Public Law Review 317 (2000).

18. Human Rights Committee, General Comment 27, Freedom of movement (Art. 12), U.N. Doc. CCPR/C/21/Rev.1/Add.9 (1999).

19. The United Nations Conference on Human Settlements, Istanbul, June 3–4, 1996 ¶61(b), U.N. Doc. A/CONF.165/14 (1996), U.N. Doc. A/CONF.165/14. This comment is made in the context of forced evictions.

criminalize panhandling or performing life-sustaining activities in public, such as sleeping and sitting, target homeless people based on their economic and housing status. Other laws that are more neutral, such as loitering or public intoxication laws, are frequently applied in a discriminatory manner against homeless persons.*

Forced evictions have long been contrary to international human rights agreements, and the United Nations repeatedly has emphasized the importance of a person's security of tenure in his or her land and home in raising his or her standard of living. In addressing the issue of forced evictions, the Habitat Agenda explicitly prohibits punishment of homeless persons based on their status. Though the Habitat Agenda is non-binding, the U.S. publicly committed to stand behind its principles by signing the document. However, many cities across the country conduct "sweeps" that remove people from outdoor encampments without notice or relocation to other housing. These city actions are a form of forced evictions, contrary to international human rights principles.

The United States has continued to shield itself from direct enforcement of international human rights treaties, yet it continues to be a consenting party when they are drafted. Many of the rights found in these treaties are not explicitly dealt with in United States law, making the treaties useful to support domestic legal arguments. Because the criminalization of homelessness violates many rights protected by international law, advocates can use such law as a framework within which to fight criminalization.

Maria Foscarinis, Brad Paul, Bruce Porter, and Andrew Scherer, *The Human Right to Housing: Making the Case in U.S. Advocacy*
38 Clearinghouse Rev. J. of Pov.L. and Policy 97, 98–114 (2004)

* * *

The Right to Housing in International Human Rights Law

In his foreword to a recent book on national perspectives on housing rights, Nelson Mandela reflected on the phenomenon of the "globalization of human rights" and the central place of the right to housing in the modern human rights movement:

> The international world has gradually come to realise the critical importance of social and economic rights in building true democracies, which meet the basic needs of all people. The realisation of these needs is both an essential element of a genuine democracy, as well as essential for the maintenance of democracy.
>
> This is nowhere more evident than in the right to housing. Everyone needs a place where they can live with security, with dignity, and with effective protection against the elements. Everyone needs a place which is a home.[5]

This link between a secure home and the basic values of dignity, security, and democratic citizenship that lie at the heart of the international human rights movement has

---

* Editor's Note: See Jeremy Waldron, Homelessness and the Issue of Freedom, in Jeremy Waldron, Liberal Rights: Collected Papers 1981–1991 (Cambridge U. Press 1993) at 309.

5. Nelson Mandela, *Foreword*, in National Perspectives on Housing Rights xvii (Scott Leckie ed., 2003).

ensured a prominent place for the right to housing in international human rights law. The Universal Declaration of Human Rights, developed under the leadership of Eleanor Roosevelt and adopted by the U.N. General Assembly in 1948, states: "Everyone has the right to a standard of living adequate for the health and wellbeing of himself [or herself] and of his [her] family, including food, clothing, housing and medical care and necessary social services...."[6]

In 1951 the U.N. General Assembly drafted two covenants, or treaties, to develop further and to implement the Universal Declaration; these are the International Covenant on Economic Social and Cultural Rights and the International Covenant on Civil and Political Rights.[7] While the treaties are separate, both recognize their interdependence, which has been repeatedly affirmed in resolutions of the General Assembly and other international bodies.[8]

The right to housing is defined most clearly in Article 11(1) of the International Covenant on Economic, Social, and Cultural Rights and in the guidance of the committee that oversees the covenant's implementation. The right is defined to consist of seven elements: security of tenure, affordability, adequacy, accessibility, proximity to services, availability of infrastructure, and cultural adequacy. Because implementing the right fully may require allocation of resources, the obligation that the covenant imposes on states is to apply the "maximum of available resources" toward "progressive realization" of the right over time. However, the additional obligation to ensure that people can exercise the right without discrimination is effective immediately....

The U.S. Position on the Right to Housing in International Law

On the international and domestic fronts, the U.S. government has shown considerable determination to resist the growing recognition of the right to housing and other social and economic rights. At the U.N.-sponsored Istanbul Conference on Human Settlements (Habitat II), which focused on the right to housing, the United States initially contended that the conference should refuse to recognize any human right to housing. Only after significant pressure from other countries and nongovernmental organizations did the United States agree to a final declaration affirming the right.[19] The United States has not ratified most of the major treaties protecting economic and social rights. While Pres. Jimmy Carter signed the International Covenant on Economic, Social and Cultural Rights in 1977, the covenant has never been referred to the Senate for ratification. Similarly the Convention on the Elimination of All Forms of Discrimination Against Women, which guarantees the equal enjoyment of social and economic rights, was signed in 1980 but never ratified; the Convention on the Rights of the Child, which guarantees the right to housing for children, was signed by Pres. Bill Clinton in 1995

---

6. Universal Declaration of Human Rights, G.A. Res. 217(III) U.N. GAOR, 3d Sess., Supp. No. 13, at 71, U.N. Doc. A/810 (1948) (art. 25).

7. International Covenant on Economic, Social and Cultural Rights, G.A. Res. 2200A (XXI), 21 U.N. GAOR, Supp. No. 16, at 49, U.N. Doc. A/6316 (1966), 993 U.N.T.S. 3, entered into force Jan. 3, 1976 [hereinafter ICESCR]; International Covenant on Civil and Political Rights, G.A. Res. 2200A (XXI), 21 U.N. GAOR Supp. No. 16, at 52, U.N. Doc. A/6316 (1966), 999 U.N.T.S. 171, entered into force March 23, 1976 [hereinafter ICCPR].

8. Vienna Declaration and Program of Action, World Conference on Human Rights, Vienna, June 14–25, 1993, U.N. Doc. A/CONF.157/24 (pt. I) at 20 (1993).

19. Philip Alston, *The U.S. and the Right to Housing: A Funny Thing Happened on the Way to the Forum*, 1 European Human Rights Law Review 120–33 (1996); Habitat II Brings Victories, Opportunities, JUST TIMES (National Law Center on Homelessness and Poverty), Aug. 1996.

but never ratified.[20] Nevertheless, as a signatory to these treaties, the United States is obliged under international law to "refrain from acts which would defeat the object and purpose of [the] treaty ... until it shall have made its intention clear not to become a party....."[21]

Further, the United States has signed and ratified both the Convention on the Elimination of All Forms of Racial Discrimination, which includes a guarantee of equal enjoyment of the right to housing, and the International Covenant for Civil and Political Rights.[22] Although the latter does not include an explicit right to adequate housing, its preamble recognizes that "the ideal of free human beings enjoying civil and political freedom and freedom from fear and want can only be achieved if conditions are created whereby everyone may enjoy his [or her] civil and political rights, as well as his [or her] economic, social and cultural rights." In its first statement of understanding following ratification of the International Covenant for Civil and Political Rights, the United States also accepted the covenant's principle of nondiscrimination, which includes distinctions based on "property, birth and other status, subject to the understanding that distinctions on any of the grounds are permitted "when such distinctions are, at minimum, rationally related to a legitimate government objective."[23] And while the United States declared rights under the covenant to be nonself-executing, so as to avoid direct judicial enforcement of its provisions, it has accepted that "American courts are not prevented from seeking guidance from the Covenant in interpreting American law."[24] The U.N. Human Rights Committee, which oversees compliance with the treaty, finds in the context of its review of Canada that the right to life imposes direct obligations on governments to take "positive measures to address homelessness" and that the effects of cuts to social programs on women, racial minorities, people with disabilities, and children must be considered in light of the right to equality and nondiscrimination.[25] In 1995[,] in its first review of the U.S. compliance, the committee expressed its concern about the contradiction between the extent of poverty in the United States and the guarantee of equality. The concern suggested a substantive understanding of the right to equality and nondiscrimination that would view failures to address disproportionate levels of poverty and homelessness among particular groups in the United States as a potential treaty violation:

> The Committee notes with concern that information provided in the core document reveals that disproportionate numbers of Native Americans, African Americans, Hispanics and single parent families headed by women live below the poverty line and that one in four children under six [lives] in poverty. It is

20. Convention on the Elimination of All Forms of Discrimination against Women, G.A. Res. 34/180, 34 U.N. GAOR Supp. (No. 46) at 193, U.N. Doc. A/34/46, entered into force Sept. 3, 1981, arts. 14(2), 16(h); Convention on the Rights of the Child, G.A. Res. 44/25, annex, 44 U.N. GAOR Supp. (No. 49) at 167, U.N. Doc. A/44/49 (1989), entered into force Sept. 2 1990 (art. 27).

21. Vienna Convention on the Law of Treaties, art. 18, 1155, U.N.T.S. 331, entered into force Jan. 27, 1980.

22. International Convention on the Elimination of All Forms of Racial Discrimination, G.A. Res. 2106 (XX), Annex, 20 U.N. GAOR, Supp. No. 14, at 47, U.N. Doc. A/6014 (1966), 660 U.N.T.S. 195, entered into force Jan. 4, 1969 (art. 5(e)(iii)); ICCPR, *supra* note 7.

23. 23U.S. Reservations, Declarations, and Understandings, International Covenant on Civil and Political Rights, 138 Cong. Rec. S4781-01 (daily ed., April 2, 1992) (Understandings ¶ 1).

24. Concluding Observations of the Human Rights Committee: United States of America. 03/10/95. CCPR/C/79/Add.50; A/50/40, ¶¶ 275–76, Oct. 3, 1995.

25. United Nations Human Rights Committee, *Concluding Observations on Canada*, CCPR/C/79/Add. 105 (1999) (April 7, 1999) ¶¶ 12, 20. The ICCPR states: "Every human being has the inherent right to life. This right shall be protected by law. No one shall be arbitrarily deprived of his life" (art. 6, sec. 1).

concerned that poverty and lack of access to education adversely affect persons belonging to these groups in their ability to enjoy rights under the Covenant on the basis of equality.[26] * * *

A Right to Housing in the United States: Litigation and Law Reform Strategies

Under the Constitution treaties are binding law with the same status as federal statutes once ratified through the signature of the President and the advice and consent of two-thirds of the Senate.[62] However, unless ratification includes the clear intent that the treaty be directly enforceable by the courts—(i.e., "self-executing"), and unless Congress passes implementing legislation, the treaty is not judicially enforceable.[63] The Senate typically ratifies human rights treaties with "reservations" that they are not "self-executing," and the courts uphold this limitation. However, even though not directly enforceable under these circumstances, treaties are legally relevant and even determinative in certain cases. The U.S. Supreme Court holds that domestic law—federal, state, and local—must be interpreted whenever possible not to conflict with ratified treaties, whether self-executing or not, or with "customary international law."[64] The latter, another source of international law, is the general and consistent practice of nations; it is not only widespread but also based on the belief that that the practice is required. Customary international law requires no implementing legislation; it is U.S. law and has the status of federal common law.[65] Thus a federal statute overrides conflicting customary international law, but customary international law controls absent federal law on point or where that law is ambiguous. Customary international law overrides conflicting state law. The practices of other nations can also be relevant even if they do not support a claim of customary international law. Courts, including the U.S. Supreme Court, cite and rely on such practices without analyzing whether they rise to the level of customary international law. For example, in a 1997 decision concerning the constitutionality of a state law banning assisted suicide, the Court cited the practices of other countries (in particular, "Western democrac[ies]").[66] Recently individual justices also spoke of the relevance of international law and practice to U.S. law.[67]

U.S. Courts and Human Rights Law

Both federal and state courts apply international human rights law, as well as international practices, in deciding domestic cases.[68] Courts use international human rights

---

26. *Concluding Observations of the Human Rights Committee: United States of America.* 03/10/95. CCPR/C/79/Add.50; A/50/40 ¶ 291, Oct. 3, 1995.

62. U.S. CONST. art. VI, § 2; art. II, § 2.

63. Self-executing treaties are enforceable and override earlier conflicting federal statutes, according to the "last-in-time rule" (*U.S. v. Bell*, 248 F. Supp. 992 (E.D.N.Y. 1918)). They override all state statutes (*Sei Fujii v. California*, 242 P.2d 617, 621 (1952)).

64. *Murray v. Schooner Charming Betsy*, 6 U.S. (2 Cranch) 64 (1804).

65. *Banco Nacional de Cuba v. Sabbatino*, 376 U.S. 398 (1964); *The Paquete Habana*, 175 U.S. 677 (1900).

66. *Washington v. Glucksberg*, 521 U.S. 702, 710 (1997).

67. Justice Stephen Breyer, The Supreme Court and The New International Law, The American Society of International Law, 97th annual Meeting, Washington, D.C. (Apr. 4, 2003); Justice Ruth Bader Ginsburg, Remarks for the American Constitution Society, Looking Beyond Our Borders: The Value of a Comparative Perspective in Constitutional Adjudication (Aug. 2, 2003); Justice Sandra Day O'Connor, Keynote Address, American Society of International Law, Proceedings of the Ninety-Sixth Annual Meeting of the American Society of International Law (March 16, 2002). [Editor's Note: See also Roper v. Simmons, 543 U.S. 551, 560, 575–78 (2005).]

68. For a summary of some such cases, see National Law Center on Homelessness and Poverty, Human Rights Fact Sheet: U.S. Federal and State Case Law Asserting Economic and Social Rights as Human Rights, available at www.nlchp.org. See also Maria Foscarinis, Homelessness and Human

law as an interpretive guide, to give content to general concepts such as standards of need and due process, and in further support of analyses under domestic law.

For example, in *In Re White*, the California Court of Appeal cited the Universal Declaration of Human Rights in support of its conclusion that both the U.S. and California Constitutions protected the right to intrastate and intramunicipal travel, a matter upon which the U.S. Supreme Court had not ruled, as well as the right to interstate travel, which a Supreme Court ruling had protected.[69] At issue in *White* was a challenge to a condition of probation imposed for prostitution; the condition barred the probationer from entering or simply being in certain defined areas of the city.

Courts also apply the directive to interpret domestic law to be consistent with international law by looking to human rights law as a source of content in cases where domestic legal standards are ambiguous or vague. For example, in *Boehm v. Superior Court*, indigent plaintiffs sought to prevent the reduction of general assistance benefits for indigent persons.[70] A state statute provided that "[e]very county ... shall relieve and support all incompetent, poor, indigent persons" and required each county to adopt standards of aid and care. While the statute gave counties discretion to determine the type and amount of benefits, the court held that benefit levels must be sufficient for survival. In making that determination, the court required the county to consider the need for food, housing, transportation, clothing and medical care and cited the Universal Declaration of Human Rights (the declaration refers specifically to these elements).

A similar example of the use of international law is *Lareau v. Manson*, in which a federal district court considered whether alleged overcrowding and other prison conditions violated the due process clause of the U.S. Constitution.[71] As part of its analysis, the court looked to the United Nations Standard Minimum Rules for the Treatment of Prisoners, a nonbinding document. The court reasoned that these standards constituted an authoritative international statement of basic norms of human dignity and thus could help define the "'canons of decency and fairness which express the norms of justice' embodied in the Due Process Clause" and the "evolving standards of decency" relevant to evaluating Eighth Amendment challenges.

Further, the court noted that the standard minimum rules might have acquired the force of customary international law and thus constituted binding legal authority. The court also cited the International Covenant on Civil and Political Rights, which had not then been ratified by the United States. Nevertheless, the court considered it to have been so widely adopted that it constituted customary international law. This is particularly significant because the analysis supports the use in litigation of the International

---

Rights: Towards an Integrated Strategy, 19 Saint Louis U. Public Law Review 317 (2000), for a discussion of litigation and other strategies; Noah Leavitt, International Human Rights Violations Here in the U.S.: A U.N. Visit to Chicago's Cabrini-Green Housing Project, available at http://writ.news.findlaw.com/commentary/ 20040506_leavitt.html; and Laurene Heybach & Patricia Nix-Hodes, *Is Housing a Human Right?*, Homeward Bound (Chicago Coalition for the Homeless 2003).

69. *In Re White*, 168 Cal. Rptr. 562, 567 (Ct. App. 1979).

70. *Boehm v. Superior Court*, 178 Cal. App. 3d 494 (1986).

71. Lareau v. Manson, 507 F. Supp. 1177 (D.C. Conn. 1980), aff'd in relevant part, modified and remanded in part, 651 F.2d 96 (2d Cir. 1981)

Covenant on Economic, Social and Cultural Rights, the treaty that contains the most detailed protection of the right to housing (and other economic rights) but has not yet been ratified by the United States.[72]

The Human Right to Housing in the United States: Litigation Strategies

As noted, the most significant treaty protecting the right to housing is the International Covenant on Economic, Social and Cultural Rights. As a signatory, the United States is obliged under the Vienna Convention to "refrain from acts which would defeat the object and purpose of a treaty."[73] Thus the United States is bound not to take "retrogressive" actions with respect to the rights that the treaty protects. Further, as noted above, jurisprudence emanating from the Human Rights Committee under the International Covenant on Civil and Political Rights recognizes obligations under the right to life in Article 6, as well as under guarantees of nondiscrimination, to take positive measures to address poverty and homelessness. While the latter treaty is not self-executing, it can be used as an interpretive guide in cases where domestic law is absent or ambiguous; it may also be considered customary law and thus binding with the status of federal common law. A number of its provisions could be used in these ways. For example, the International Covenant on Civil and Political Rights protects the "right to liberty of movement and the freedom to choose [one's] residence," both of which are relevant to challenges to laws criminalizing homelessness.[74] However, while the U.S. Supreme Court has ruled that the Constitution protects the right to interstate travel, it has not ruled on the constitutional status (if any) of the intrastate right to travel. Some circuits protect that right while others do not; arguably U.S. law is ambiguous on this point, and the covenant could be cited to support recognition of the right. The covenant protects "equal protection of the law" and prohibits discrimination "on any ground such as race, color, sex, language, religion, political or other opinion, national or social origin, *property*, birth or *other status*."[75] This is also relevant to challenges to laws criminalizing homelessness and their unequal enforcement; such laws are often facially neutral but discriminatorily applied to homeless people based on their status—which could be considered either a property status or an "other" status of homelessness.[76] The Universal Declaration of Human Rights defines basic minimum economic standards as human rights.[77] While it is not a treaty, and thus not binding by its terms, numerous scholars argue that the declaration is binding because it has acquired the status of customary in-

---

72. Some commentators and advocates argue that state courts have a special duty to apply international human rights laws relating to economic and social rights when interpreting state constitutions and statutes. See, e.g., brief of amici curiae Center for Economic and Social Rights, International Women's Human Rights Law Clinic, and Center for Constitutional Rights (filed with the New Jersey Supreme Court) in support of plaintiff-appellants in *Sojourner A. v. New Jersey Department of Social Services*, available at www.cesr.org/PROGRAMS/us%20program/sojourner2.pdf.

73. Vienna Convention on the Law of Treaties, art. 18, 1155, U.N.T.S. 331, entered into force Jan. 27, 1980.

74. ICCPR, Dec. 16, 1966, art. 12, 99 U.N.T.S. 171.

75. *Id.*, art. 26. (emphasis added).

76. To argue, however, that the ICCPR creates protected class status on these bases, as that term is understood in U.S. constitutional law, would be much more difficult. Indeed, in ratifying the ICCPR, the United States specifically noted its understanding that distinctions were permissible if rationally related to a legitimate government purpose and that distinctions with a disparate impact on protected class members were permitted.

77. Universal Declaration of Human Rights, Dec. 10, 1948.

ternational law.[78] Citations by numerous U.S. courts lend support to that view.[79] This is particularly relevant to statutes that establish a general standard of need and to state constitutions that contain general statements about meeting needs.[80]

---

78. Scott Leckie, International Institute for Environment and Development, From Housing Needs to Housing Rights: An Analysis of the Right to Adequate Housing Under International Human Rights Law 10 (1992).

79. See, e.g. *Boehm*, 178 Cal. App. 3d at 494

80. See *National Law Center on Homelessness and Poverty*, [Homelessness in the United States and the Human Right to Housing iii–6 (2004)].

IV

Housing Rights in the United States

A. Tenants' Rights

1. Security of Tenure

Edwards v. Habib

397 F.2d 687 (D.C. Cir. 1968),
cert. denied, 393 U.S. 1016 (1969)

Mr. Brian Michael Olmstead, Des Moines, Iowa, with whom Mrs. Florence Wagman Roisman, Washington, D.C., was on the brief, for appellant.

Mr. Herman Miller, Washington, D.C., for appellee.

Messrs. Charles T. Duncan, Corporation Counsel for the District of Columbia, Hubert B. Pair, Principal Asst. Corporation Counsel, and Richard W. Barton and David P. Sutton, Asst. Corporation Counsel, filed a brief on behalf of the District of Columbia as amicus curiae, urging reversal.

Mr. Reuben B. Robertson, III, Washington, D.C., filed a brief on behalf of the National Capital Area Civil Liberties Defense and Education Fund as amicus curiae, urging reversal.

Danaher, Wright and McGowan, Circuit Judges. McGowan, Circuit Judge (concurring except as to Parts I and II). Danaher, Circuit Judge (dissenting).

J. Skelly Wright, Circuit Judge.

In March 1965 the appellant, Mrs. Yvonne Edwards, rented housing property from the appellee, Nathan Habib, on a month-to-month basis. Shortly thereafter she complained to the Department of Licenses and Inspections of sanitary code violations which her landlord had failed to remedy. In the course of the ensuing inspection, more than 40 such violations were discovered which the Department ordered the landlord to correct. Habib then gave Mrs. Edwards a 30-day statutory notice[1] to vacate and ob-

---

1. 45 D.C. Code § 902 (1967), Notices to quit—Month to month:

   A tenancy from month to month, or from quarter to quarter, may be terminated by a thirty days' notice in writing from the landlord to the tenant to quit, or by such a notice from the tenant to the landlord of his intention to quit, said notice to expire, in either case, on the day of the month from which such tenancy commenced to run.

tained a default judgment for possession of the premises.[2] Mrs. Edwards promptly moved to reopen this judgment, alleging excusable neglect for the default and also alleging as a defense that the notice to quit was given in retaliation for her complaints to the housing authorities. Judge Greene, sitting on motions in the Court of General Sessions, set aside the default judgment and, in a very thoughtful opinion, concluded that a retaliatory motive, if proved, would constitute a defense to the action for possession. At the trial itself, however, a different judge apparently deemed evidence of retaliatory motive irrelevant and directed a verdict for the landlord.

Mrs. Edwards then appealed to this court for a stay pending her appeal to the District of Columbia Court of Appeals, and we granted the stay, provided only that Mrs. Edwards continue to pay her rent. She then appealed to the DCCA, which affirmed the judgment of the trial court. In reaching its decision the DCCA relied on a series of its earlier decisions holding that a private landlord was not required, under the District of Columbia Code, to give a reason for evicting a month-to-month tenant and was free to do so for any reason or for no reason at all. The court acknowledged that the landlord's right to terminate a tenancy is not absolute, but felt that any limitation on his prerogative had to be based on specific statutes or very special circumstances.[5] Here, the court concluded, the tenant's right to report violations of law and to petition for redress of grievances was not protected by specific legislation and that any change in the relative rights of tenants and landlords should be undertaken by the legislature, not the courts. We granted appellant leave to appeal that decision to this court.[*] We hold that the promulgation of the housing code by the District of Columbia Commissioners at the direction of Congress impliedly effected just such a change in the relative rights of landlords and tenants and that proof of a retaliatory motive does constitute a defense to an action of eviction. Accordingly, we reverse the decision of the DCCA with directions that it remand to the Court of General Sessions for a new trial where Mrs. Edwards will be permitted to try to prove to a jury that her landlord who seeks to evict her harbors a retaliatory intent.

I.

Appellant has launched a constitutional challenge to the judicial implementation of 45 D.C. Code §902 and 910 in aid of a landlord who is evicting because his tenant has

---

2. 45 D.C.Code §910 (1967), Ejectment or summary proceedings:
   Whenever a lease for any definite term shall expire, or any tenancy shall be terminated by notice as aforesaid, and the tenant shall fail or refuse to surrender possession of the leased premises, the landlord may bring an action of ejectment to recover possession in the United States District Court for the District of Columbia; or the landlord may bring an action to recover possession before the District of Columbia Court of General Sessions, as provided in sections 11-701 to 11-749.

5. The DCCA acknowledged three distinct lines of cases "wherein a landlord's right to terminate a tenancy has been limited." First, where a governmental body is the landlord, it is subject to the requirements of due process and cannot act arbitrarily towards its tenants. Second, where there is emergency rent control legislation restricting the contractual rights of landlords. And third, where eviction was in retaliation for the tenant's registering to vote or actually voting. The DCCA distinguished the voting cases as involving "specific ... legislation" enacted to protect the right intimidated by eviction. The court also acknowledged, without evaluative comment, that some courts have allowed a tenant to show as a defense that his eviction was sought solely because of his race. Racially restrictive covenants are unenforceable in the District in part because their enforcement might be contrary to "the public policy of the United States." Hurd v. Hodge, 334 U.S. 24, 34 (1948).

* Editor's Note: At that time, the federal court of appeals had such discretionary jurisdiction over cases in the local courts. This ended with the District of Columbia Court Reform Act of 1970, P.L. 91-358, but this case was governed by the prior law.

reported housing code violations on the premises. We do not, however, reach the question whether it is unconstitutional for the court to apply the statute in such circumstances because we think Congress never intended that it be so applied. Nevertheless, because constitutional considerations inform the statutory construction on which our decision rests, we do discuss them briefly.[6]

Appellant argues first that to evict her because she has reported violations of the law to the housing authorities would abridge her First Amendment rights to report violations of law and to petition the government for redress of grievances. But while it is clear beyond peradventure that the making of such complaints is at the core of protected First Amendment speech,[7] and that punishment, in the form of eviction, if imposed by the state would unconstitutionally abridge First Amendment rights, it is equally clear that these rights are rights against government, not private parties. Consequently, before appellant can prevail on this theory she must show that the government is in some relevant sense responsible for inhibiting her right to petition for redress of grievances; she must show, in other words, the requisite "state action."[8] Appellant seeks to overcome this obstacle by arguing that the use of courts to effect her eviction sufficiently implicates the state as to bring into play constitutional constraints. She relies on an unreported decision of the United States District Court for the Southern District of New York, where the court invoked just such a theory to support the issuance of a preliminary injunction restraining an alleged retaliatory rent increase.

There can now be no doubt that the application by the judiciary of the state's common law, even in a lawsuit between private parties, may constitute state action which must conform to the constitutional strictures which constrain the government. New York Times Co. v. Sullivan, 376 U.S. 254 (1964). This may be so even where the court is simply enforcing a privately negotiated contract. Shelley v. Kraemer, 334 U.S. 1 (1948). But the nature and extent of the judicial involvement required to bring into play these constitutional constraints is unclear. The central case is, of course, Shelley v. Kraemer, where the Court ruled that judicial enforcement of private agreements containing restrictive covenants against selling to Negroes violated the Fourteenth Amendment's command that "no State shall ... deny to any person within its jurisdiction the equal protection of the laws." But the contours of Shelley remain undefined and it is uncertain just how far its reasoning extends.[9] Judge Greene declined to rest his opinion on Shelley for fear that if, for constitutional purposes, every private

---

6. The lurking constitutional issues are relevant to our construction of the statutes in two ways. First, where two interpretations are plausible, we should opt for the one that avoids the constitutional questions. And second, in discerning the intent of Congress we must assume that it too sought to avoid constitutional doubt and to protect the constitutional interests which are at stake. "We need not, however, decide the issue before us in terms of constitutional compulsion, for our first duty is to construe this statute. In doing so we should not assume that Congress chose to disregard a constitutional danger zone...."

7. The First Amendment gives express recognition to the right of the people "to petition the Government for a redress of grievances." U.S.Const., Amend. 1.

8. The concept of "state action" generally comes into play where there is an alleged denial of the Fourteenth Amendment's equal protection guarantee. State action is also required under the Fifteenth Amendment. The doctrine was born in the Civil Rights Cases, 109 U.S. 3 (1883). The "state action" concept is also relevant where First Amendment freedoms are at stake.

9. Shelley has been called "constitutional law's Finnegan's Wake." Kurland, Foreword: "Equal in Origin and Equal in Title to the Legislative and Executive Branches of the Government," 78 Harv. L. Rev. 143, 148 (1964). And many commentators have sought the skeleton key that adequately explains it.

right were transformed into governmental action by the mere fact of court enforcement of it, the distinction between private and governmental action would be obliterated. He accepted the reasoning of Mr. Justice Black, who joined in the Shelley
opinion but has since maintained that its doctrine applies only where, as in Shelley
itself, the court is called upon to upset a transaction between a willing buyer and a
willing seller.[10] Others, however, have urged different interpretations of Shelley, ones
which would extend its principle beyond its facts but would still leave certain private
rights, even when judicially enforced, immune from the Constitution's restraints on
government.

Some commentators have suggested that private action is subject to constitutional
scrutiny only when the state has encouraged or sanctioned it.[11] Others have gone further
and suggested that at least where racial discrimination is involved the state denies the
equal protection of the law when it does not act affirmatively to assure equal protection
by legislating against privately initiated, as well as governmental, discrimination. But
these commentators are careful to point out that Shelley should not be read to hold that
a state cannot enforce any discrimination which it could not itself make.[13] There is, on
this view, unconstitutional action by inaction except in those situations where the Constitution itself demands inaction; that is, in those situations where the state could not
legislate equality because to do so would impinge on the individual discriminator's
countervailing rights of liberty, property and privacy. The state, through its police or
courts, could aid an individual in his quest to keep Negroes from a dinner party in his
home even though it could not keep Negroes from a courthouse cafeteria or even from
a privately owned hotel solely on account of their race. Consequently this theory might
dull, but it would not obliterate, the distinction between private and state action.

Were this analysis of state action by inaction under the equal protection clause un-
qualifiedly applied where the question was governmental action under the First Amendment, there is no doubt that Mrs. Edwards' eviction could not be sustained. Not only
would the government have failed to protect her against private reprisals for the exercise
of her First Amendment rights (and clearly it could constitutionally protect her if it
chose to do so),[16] but it would, through its court, actually be aiding the individual who

---

10. Bell v. State of Maryland, 378 U.S. 226 (1964) (dissenting opinion of Mr. Justice Black). But
see dissenting opinion of Mr. Justice Douglas in Black v. Cutter Laboratories, 351 U.S. 292 (1956),
in which Mr. Justice Black joined. Professor Pollak, who thinks Shelley was rightly decided, would
apparently limit it in much the same way. "The line sought to be drawn is that beyond which the
state assists a private person in seeing to it that others behave in a fashion which the state could not
itself have ordained. The principle underlying the distinction is this: the fourteenth amendment
permits each his personal prejudices and guarantees him free speech and press and worship, together with a degree of free economic enterprise, as instruments with which to persuade others to
adopt his prejudices; but access to state aid to induce others to conform is barred." Pollak, Racial
Discrimination and Judicial Integrity: A Reply to Professor Wechsler, 108 U. Pa L. Rev. 1, 13 (1959).

11. And the state is responsible for the acts of its officials even where the acts are unauthorized
or forbidden by law. It may also be responsible where it permits private bodies to perform an essentially governmental function, or where it owns and leases property to a private body, or where a
common carrier's operations are authorized by the state, or where because of private discrimination
those discriminated against are denied equal access to governmental benefits.

13. The state court, for instance, could constitutionally probate a will leaving the deceased's
property to the Catholic Church, even though the state could not constitutionally make a comparable disposition of its own funds.

16. Even in its heyday, the state action doctrine did not preclude federal legislation protecting
from private interference the exercise of the right to report violations of law. In re Quarles and Butler, 158 U.S. 532 (1895). Unquestionably such legislation governing merely the District of Columbia
would be valid.

seeks to intimidate the exercise of those rights.[17] It may be, however, that what is state action under Fourteenth Amendment is not always state action under the First. To begin with, the Reconstruction amendments were enacted with a particular purpose in mind: to eradicate forever the vestiges of slavery and the black codes. In addition, the language of the First Amendment, "Congress shall make no law...," is not as amenable as the Fourteenth Amendment is to the construction that there is state action by inaction or by judicial action which merely gives legal effect to privately made decisions. Indeed those who have expounded this theory of state action have been careful to limit their case to the area of racial discrimination.

But this does not end the matter. In New York Times Co. v. Sullivan, supra, the state of Alabama neither forced nor even encouraged Police Commissioner Sullivan to sue the New York Times. It simply provided courts in which such a suit could be brought, and its common law provided the doctrine upon which the dispute would be settled. There was no suggestion in the Supreme Court's opinion that the doctrine was not fairly and honestly applied by the state court. Yet the Court, hardly pausing even to consider the question of state action,[20] held that a libel judgment against the Times, on the facts of that case, unconstitutionally abridged the Times' First Amendment rights as incorporated in the Fourteenth Amendment's due process clause. The fact that Congress and the state legislature had "made no law" was apparently irrelevant to this determination.[21]

A state court judgment, then, even by adjudicating private lawsuits, may unconstitutionally abridge the right of free speech as well as the right to equal protection of the laws. Of course, the federal court review in Times was technically under the due process clause of the Fourteenth Amendment as it incorporates the First, while here the challenge is made under the First Amendment itself. But there is no reason to think that review under the First Amendment is more limited.[22] In any case, review under the Fifth

---

17. Given the current state of the law in the District, it is questionable that a landlord could ever evict a resisting tenant without the aid of the courts. And in view of our stay, judicial action to effect an eviction in this case would be indispensable. To some commentators the question of "state action" turns on whether judicial action was essential to the deprivation of the alleged right.

20. "We may dispose at the outset of two grounds asserted to insulate the judgment of the Alabama courts from constitutional scrutiny. The first is the proposition relied on by the State Supreme Court—that "The Fourteenth Amendment is directed against State action and not private action." That proposition has no application to this case. Although this is a civil lawsuit between private parties, the Alabama courts have applied a state rule of law which petitioners claim to impose invalid restrictions on their constitutional freedoms of speech and press. It matters not that that law has been applied in a civil action and that it is common law only, though supplemented by statute. The test is not the form in which state power has been applied but, whatever the form, whether such power has in fact been exercised."

21. It was enough that a common law rule was applied to mediate conflicting claims of right between private parties. Though highly relevant to the Court's decision on the merits, the fact that the plaintiff was a state official was not a factor in the Court's determination that there was reviewable state action.

22. It is of course true that the First Amendment explicitly proscribes only congressional action. But at least as incorporated into the Fourteenth, it invalidates any "state action" which abridges the freedoms it protects. Action by a state legislature is not required. See New York Times Co. v. Sullivan, 376 U.S. 254 (1964). There is no more reason to require congressional action where the challenge is made under the First Amendment itself. As Mr. Justice Black put it: "The First and Fourteenth Amendments, I think, take away from government, state and federal, all power to restrict freedom of speech, press, and assembly...." Cox v. State of Louisiana, 379 U.S. 536, 578. Compare Hurd v. Hodge, "It is not consistent with the public policy of the United States to permit federal courts in the Nation's capital to exercise general equitable powers to compel action denied the state courts where such state action has been held to be violative of the guaranty of the equal protection of the laws." Of course there are acts of Congress, 45 D.C. §§ 902 and 910, 16 D.C. § 1501, at play in

Amendment's due process clause would not be. Bolling v. Sharpe, 347 U.S. 497 (1954). And it may be that the more flexible concept of due process is preferable where the question is one involving First Amendment rights and the government, though perhaps sufficiently implicated in the abridgement to bring into play constitutional constraints, is not directly responsible for it. It may be instructive to borrow again from other state action theorists whose analyses, though concerned primarily with racial discrimination, are somewhat less rigid and therefore may transfer more comfortably from the area of racial discrimination under the Fourteenth Amendment into the context of First Amendment rights.

It has been suggested that there is state action, not only when an individual asserts a claim of right against a state, but also when he asserts a claim of right against the claims of right of other persons and the state resolves the conflict according to its policy of what is reasonable under the circumstances, i.e., according to its law. Once this "state action" is established, the question then becomes simply "whether the particular state action in the particular circumstances, determining legal relations between private persons, is constitutional when tested against the various federal constitutional restrictions on state action."

The question in the instant case would then be whether a court can consistently with the Constitution prefer the interests of an absentee landlord[25] in evicting a tenant solely because she has reported violations of the housing code to those of a tenant in improving her housing by resort to her rights to petition the government and to report violations of laws designed for her protection. On this theory, if it would be unreasonable to prefer the landlord's interest, it would also be unconstitutional.[26] Mr. Justice Black, who is not prone to weigh interests where First Amendment rights are involved, seems to have taken just this approach in writing for the Court in Marsh v. State of Alabama, 326 U.S. 501 (1946), which, like the instant case, involved state-aided privately-initiated abridgement of First Amendment freedoms.[28] The question before the Court in Marsh was "whether a State, consistently with the First and Fourteenth Amendments, can impose criminal punishment on a person who undertakes to distribute religious literature

---

the instant case. But to say that these statutes, as applied here, might be unconstitutional would be an accurate but artificial way of putting the issue. In general, the statutes simply provide the landlord with a judicial mechanism for achieving what he could traditionally accomplish by self-help. They say nothing about what if any defenses are available to the tenant. Consequently a more informative way of framing the question would be: Is it unconstitutional for the court not to permit a defense under them that eviction is sought in retaliation for the exercise of First Amendment rights? Indeed, rights of federal citizenship.

25. The fact that Mrs. Edwards is not in any sense a boarder in Mr. Habib's home would, on this theory, be relevant in assessing his interest in associating with whom he pleases.

26. If Congress had made an unambiguous judgment that in the context of the instant case the landlord's interests were to be preferred to the tenant's, this court would owe that judgment great deference, more than the Supreme Court would owe comparable judgments of state legislatures. If, however, the statute was unclear, we would owe no deference to the DCCA's interpretation of it, while the Supreme Court would defer to a comparable construction by a state court of a state statute.

28. Mr. Justice Black will also apparently resort to a balancing approach where he perceives "speech plus" as he did in Cox v. State of Louisiana: "This Court does, and I agree that it should, 'weigh the circumstances' in order to protect, not to destroy, freedom of speech, press, and religion." If there is ever such a thing as "speech pure," we have it in the instant case. For Mrs. Edwards' speech itself does not interfere in any way with the legitimate property interests of her landlord or anyone else. The question on this theory would simply be whether it is unreasonable for the government not to limit property rights by forbidding retaliatory evictions in order to protect the tenant's right to report housing code violations.

on the premises of a company-owned town contrary to the wishes of the town's management." In answering it, Mr. Justice Black felt compelled to "balance the Constitutional rights of owners of property against those of the people to enjoy freedom of press and religion" and in doing so remained mindful "of the fact that the latter occupy a preferred position." He concluded that the state acted unconstitutionally in preferring the property rights of the town's owners to those of the defendant and the town's residents[29] through the application of its criminal trespass statute to Mr. Marsh. "Insofar as the State has attempted to impose criminal punishment on appellant for undertaking to distribute religious literature in a company town, its action cannot stand."

Again it should be remembered that in Times the state did not initiate the action, nor did it encourage the private parties involved to do so. And in Marsh there could have been no prosecution without a private complaint. In both cases the state simply provided courts and laws to settle essentially private disputes.[30] Where its settlement impinged on First Amendment freedoms, a balancing process was utilized on review to determine whether it did so unconstitutionally.[31] But we need not undertake such a weighing of interests here or even decide if such a process is appropriate, for we find, as indicated in Part III, that Congress, by directing the enactment of the housing code, impliedly directed the court to prefer the interests of the tenant who seeks to avail himself of the code's protection.

II.

Appellant argues that, even if Shelley and the concept of "state action" are interpreted narrowly, and if the judicial implementation of the D.C. Code to effect a retaliatory eviction does not violate her First Amendment rights, her eviction would be unconstitutional nonetheless because the right to petition the government and to report violations of law is constitutionally protected against private as well as governmental interference. There is strong support for this position. In Crandall v. State of Nevada, 73 U.S. (6 Wall.) 35 (1868), decided before the Fourteenth Amendment was enacted, the Court struck down Nevada's one-dollar tax on anyone leaving the state in part because the Court felt that such a tax might infringe the individual's right to travel to Washington to participate in, and seek redress from, the government. And in United States v. Cruikshank, 92 U.S. (2 Otto) 542 (1876), in dictum and in In re Quarles and Butler, 158 U.S. 532 (1895), as holding, the Court was even more explicit in recognizing the right to petition the government for redress of grievances and the right to inform the government of violations of law as rights of federal citizenship

---

29. Just as the interests of the company town's residents were considered by the Court in Marsh, so here the interests of other tenants who would be deterred from seeking to improve their housing by reporting code violations to the authorities would have to be considered in deciding whether Mrs. Edwards' eviction would be reasonable.

30. See also American Federation of Labor v. Swing, 312 U.S. 321 (1941), where the Supreme Court struck down an Illinois statute which gave employers the right to secure an injunction against picketing of their shops when there was no existing dispute between the employer and his employees. Nothing in the statute required or encouraged the employer to utilize the injunctive mechanism at his disposal. If he wished to permit such picketing he was free to do so. Consequently any decision to impair the alleged First and Fourteenth Amendment rights of the pickets was solely that of a private party, not that of the state. Swing was cited and relied upon in Shelley v. Kraemer, 334 U.S. 1 (1948).

31. The balance where First and Fourteenth Amendment rights are involved may be different. The individual's interest in being free to choose his associates on the basis of what they do or say may be entitled to more weight than such choices made on the basis of what they are, i.e., on the basis of race.

arising from our constitutional system as a whole, not just from the First Amendment or from any other particular constitutional clause or provision. In Quarles the Supreme Court affirmed the conviction under the Civil Rights Act of a private citizen for conspiring to "injure, oppress, threaten, or intimidate (another) in the free exercise ... of (a) right ... secured to him by the Constitution or laws of the United States, or because of his having so exercised the same." The defendant and his accomplices had threatened and beaten one Worley for informing federal officers that the defendant was violating the federal liquor law. The defendant argued that Worley had no right to inform that was protectable against private interference. But the Court rejected this argument, stating that:

> The power (to protect certain rights from private interference) arises out of the circumstance that the function in which the party is engaged, or the right which he is about to exercise, is dependent on the laws of the United States....
> It is the duty of that government to see that he may exercise this right freely, and to protect him from violence while so doing, or on account of so doing. This duty does not arise solely from the interest of the party concerned, but from the necessity of the government itself. The necessary conclusion is ... that this right is secured to the citizen by the Constitution of the United States.

This right, appellant, argues, is accordingly protected against private as well as governmental interference.[34] It is on the basis of this theory that Judge Greene found that proof of a retaliatory purpose constituted a valid defense.

But though this argument from Quarles is persuasive, it is not conclusive, for at issue in Quarles was the applicability and constitutionality of the Civil Rights Act to punish private interferences with the right to right to report violations of law, not the question, first, whether such interferences were themselves unconstitutional in the absence of remedial legislation, and second, if unconstitutional, what legal consequences attached to them. The DCCA rejected the argument for just this reason, saying that Quarles was a case where "Congress enacted special legislation to secure certain rights." Presumably the legislation referred to is the Civil Rights Act, and the DCCA apparently felt that current civil rights statutes would not apply to this case. But the enforcement section of the Civil Rights Act provided remedies for the deprivation of rights secured by the Constitution or laws of the United States. It did not create new rights. And the Supreme Court held in Quarles that the right to report violations of law was a constitutional right protectable by federal legislation against private interference, not that it was itself a right created by the Civil Rights Act. It is this constitutional right that Mrs. Edwards is setting up as a defense to the landlord's action of eviction. It is not necessarily relevant, therefore, that because of the peculiar requirements of the civil rights statutes they may not

---

34. Federal law can protect such rights (at least the right to vote) from privately exercised economic intimidation as well as from more violent forms of coercion. The current civil rights statutes do just that. See United States v. Beaty[, 288 F.2d 653 (6th 1961)]. Even "conduct that might be perfectly legal, if not colored by the bad intent of interfering with the right to [register and] vote" may become "illegal upon proof of such illegal intent." United States v. Bruce[, 353 F.2d 474 (5th 1965)], where the intimidation took the form of a conspiracy by landlords to invoke the state trespass laws to keep one Brown, a Negro insurance collector, from reaching many of his policyholders who were tenants on their land. Brown had been active in urging his friends and neighbors to vote and the court felt that the allegations of the complaint, which had been dismissed below, made a showing from which it could be inferred that the landlords' ban of Brown was in reprisal for his participation in the voter registration drive.

provide her with additional affirmative civil or criminal remedies for violation of the same right.[37]

III.

But we need not decide whether judicial recognition of this constitutional defense is constitutionally compelled. We need not, in other words, decide whether 45 D.C. Code § 910 could validly compel the court to assist the plaintiff in penalizing the defendant for exercising her constitutional right to inform the government of violations of the law; for we are confident that Congress did not intend it to entail such a result.

45 D.C. Code § 910, in pertinent part, provides:

> Whenever ... any tenancy shall be terminated by notice as aforesaid, and the tenant shall fail or refuse to surrender possession of the leased premises, ... the landlord may bring an action to recover possession before the District of Columbia Court of General Sessions.

And 16 D.C. Code § 1502, in pertinent part, provides:

> When a person detains possession of real property ... after his right to possession has ceased, the District of Columbia Court of General Sessions ... may issue a summons to the party complained of to appear and show cause why judgment should not be given against him for restitution of possession.

These provisions are simply procedural. They neither say nor imply anything about whether evidence of retaliation or other improper motive should be unavailable as a defense to a possessory action brought under them. It is true that in making his affirmative case for possession the landlord need only show that his tenant has been given the 30-day statutory notice, and he need not assign any reason for evicting a tenant who does not occupy the premises under a lease. But while the landlord may evict for any legal reason or for no reason at all, he is not, we hold, free to evict in retaliation for his tenant's report of housing code violations to the authorities.[38]

As a matter of statutory construction and for reasons of public policy,[39] such an eviction cannot be permitted.

---

37. As with Shelley, there are, conceivably, problems in containing the Quarles doctrine. Could, for instance, a landlord invite all his tenants to dinner except those who had complained of housing code violations? Again the landlord's countervailing constitutional rights of privacy and association may be the cutting edge. Or perhaps such petty slights do not rise to the level of intimidation, coercion, interference or punishment. Finally, as Judge Greene pointed out, appellant is simply setting up her constitutional right as defense, and is not seeking affirmative relief based on it.

38. In L'Orange v. Medical Protective Co., 6 Cir., 394 F.2d 57 (1968), the Sixth Circuit held that a malpractice insurer could not cancel the policy of an Ohio dentist simply because the insured testified in a malpractice suit against a colleague insured by the same company. Presumably the policy could have been cancelled for any lawful reason or for no reason at all, but it could not be cancelled for the purpose of intimidating a witness in contravention of Ohio's public policy. *See also* Petermann v. International Brotherhood of Teamsters, etc., Local 369, 174 Cal.App.2d 184, 344 P.2d 25 (1959), which held that a union could not fire one of its employees even though there was no fixed term of employment if the reason for the dismissal of the employee was his refusal to give false testimony before a legislative investigating committee. Such a dismissal, it was held, contravened California's policy against perjury.

39. Compare Hurd v. Hodge: "But even in the absence of the statute, there are other considerations which would indicate that enforcement of restrictive covenants in these cases is judicial action contrary to the public policy of the United States, and as such should be corrected by this Court in the exercise of its supervisory powers over the courts of the District of Columbia. The power of the federal courts to enforce the terms of private agreements is at all times exercised subject to the re-

The housing and sanitary codes,[40] especially in light of Congress' explicit direction for their enactment, indicate a strong and pervasive congressional concern to secure for the city's slum dwellers decent, or at least safe and sanitary, places to live.[41] Effective implementation and enforcement of the codes obviously depend in part on private initiative in the reporting of violations. Though there is no official procedure for the filing of such complaints, the bureaucratic structure of the Department of Licenses and Inspections establishes such a procedure, and for fiscal year 1966 nearly a third of the cases handled by the Department arose from private complaints.[43] To permit retaliatory evictions, then, would clearly frustrate the effectiveness of the housing code as a means of upgrading the quality of housing in Washington.

As judges, "we cannot shut our eyes to matters of public notoriety and general cognizance. When we take our seats on the bench we are not struck with blindness, and forbidden to know as judges what we see as men." Ho Ah Kow v. Nunan, 12 Fed.Cas. 252(1879). In trying to effect the will of Congress and as a court of equity we have the responsibility to consider the social context in which our decisions will have operational effect. In light of the appalling condition and shortage of housing in Washington,[45] the

---

strictions and limitations of the public policy of the United States as manifested in the Constitution, treaties, federal statutes, and applicable legal precedents."

40. The District Commissioners have promulgated extensive housing regulations which require landlords to keep their premises in "clean, safe and sanitary condition." Housing Regulations of the District of Columbia, §§ 2101, 2304 (1956). The purpose of the Regulations is:

The Commissioners of the District of Columbia hereby find and declare that there exist residential buildings and areas within said District which are slums or are otherwise blighted, and that there are, in addition, other such buildings and areas within said District which are deteriorating and are in danger of becoming slums or otherwise blighted unless action in taken to prevent their further deterioration and decline.

The Commissioners further find and declare that such unfortunate conditions are due, among other circumstances, to certain conditions affecting such residential buildings and such areas, among them being the following: dilapidation, inadequate maintenance, overcrowding, inadequate toilet facilities, inadequate bathing or washing facilities, inadequate heating, insufficient protection against fire hazards, inadequate lighting and ventilation, and other insanitary or unsafe conditions.

The Commissioners further find and declare that the aforesaid conditions, where they exist, and other conditions which contribute to or cause the deterioration of residential buildings and areas, are deleterious to the health, safety, welfare and morals of the community and its inhabitants.

41. The Commissioners of the District of Columbia are authorized and directed to make and enforce such building regulations for the said District as they may deem advisable.

Such rules and regulations made as above provided shall have the same force and effect within the District of Columbia as if enacted by Congress. 1 D.C.Code § 288 (1967).

43. Of 47,701 cases handled, almost 15,000 were initiated by private complaint. And the need for increased private and group participation in code enforcement has been widely recognized. Gribetz and Grad, Housing Code Enforcement: Sanctions and Remedies, 66 Colum.L.Rev. 1254 (1966); Note, Enforcement of Municipal Housing Codes, 78 Harv.L.Rev. 801, 843–860 (1965). See also Sax and Hiestant, Slumlordism as a Tort, 65 Mich.L.Rev. 869 (1967).

45. See Report of the National Capital Planning Commission, Problems of Housing People in Washington, D.C.:

Poor families are responding to Washington's housing shortage by doubling and overcrowding; by living in structurally substandard or other hazardous housing; by sharing or doing without hot water, heat, light, or kitchen or bathroom facilities; by farming out their children wherever they can; by denying their children exist to landlords and public officials; by paying rents which are high compared to incomes so they must sacrifice other living necessities; and by living without dignity or privacy. Each one of these features has been measured separately or has been observed in Washington's poverty areas.

expense of moving, the inequality of bargaining power between tenant and landlord, and the social and economic importance of assuring at least minimum standards in housing conditions,[47] we do not hesitate to declare that retaliatory eviction cannot be tolerated. There can be no doubt that the slum dweller, even though this home be marred by housing code violations, will pause long before he complains of them if he fears eviction as a consequence. Hence an eviction under the circumstances of this case would not only punish appellant for making a complaint which she had a constitutional right to make, a result which we would not impute to the will of Congress simply on the basis of an essentially procedural enactment, but also would stand as a warning to others that they dare not be so bold, a result which, from the authorization of the housing code, we think Congress affirmatively sought to avoid.

The notion that the effectiveness of remedial legislation will be inhibited if those reporting violations of it can legally be intimidated is so fundamental that a presumption against the legality of such intimidation can be inferred as inherent in the legislation even if it is not expressed in the statute itself. Such an inference was recently drawn by the Supreme Court from the federal labor statutes to strike down under the supremacy clause a Florida statute denying unemployment insurance to workers discharged in retaliation for filing complaints of federally defined unfair labor practices. While we are not confronted with a possible conflict between federal policy and state law, we do have the task of reconciling and harmonizing two federal statutes so as to best effectuate the purposes of each.[50] The proper balance can only be struck by interpreting 45 D.C. Code §§ 902 and 910 as inapplicable where the court's aid is invoked to effect an eviction in retaliation for reporting housing code violations.[51]

This is not, of course, to say that even if the tenant can prove a retaliatory purpose she is entitled to remain in possession in perpetuity. If this illegal purpose is dissipated, the landlord can, in the absence of legislation[52] or a binding contract, evict his tenants

---

47. "Miserable and disreputable housing conditions may do more than spread disease and crime and immorality. They may also suffocate the spirit by reducing the people who live there to the status of cattle. They may indeed make living an almost insufferable burden. They may also be an ugly sore, a blight on the community which robs it of charm, which makes it a place from which men turn. The misery of housing may despoil a community as an open sewer may ruin a river." Berman v. Parker, 348 U.S. 26 (1954). The need to maintain basic, minimal standards of housing, to prevent the spread of disease and of that pervasive break-down in the fiber of a people which is produced by slums and the absence of the barest essentials of civilized living, has mounted to a major concern of American government. According to the Report of the Planning Commission, "more than 100,000 children are growing up in Washington now under one or more housing conditions which create psychological, social, and medical impairments, and make satisfactory home life difficult or a practical impossibility."

50. When Congress enacted 45 D.C.C. §§ 902 and 910, it did not have in mind their possible use in effectuating retaliatory evictions. Indeed, when they were enacted there was no housing code at all. And in all probability Congress did not attend to the problem of retaliatory evictions when it directed the enactment of the housing code. Our task is to determine what Congress would have done, in light of the purpose and language of the statute, had it confronted the question now before the court. And where there is a possible conflict, the more recent enactment, the housing code, should be given full effect while leaving an area of effective operation for the earlier statute. This task, we think, our resolution of the issue accomplishes.

51. In a recent important decision the DCCA has held that as a matter of public policy a landlord who has rented housing space knowing that it contained housing code violations could not collect back rent from his ex-tenant. Brown v. Southall Realty Co., D.C.App., 237 A.2d 834 (1968).

52. There have been several bills introduced in Congress which deal expressly with the problem of retaliatory evictions. Hearings were held in the Senate on three bills but none was reported out of committee. H.R. 257, 90th Cong., 1st Sess. (1967), is now before the House Committee on the Dis-

or raise their rents for economic or other legitimate reasons, or even for no reason at all.[53] The question of permissible or impermissible purpose is one of fact for the court or jury, and while such a determination is not easy, it is not significantly different from problems with which the courts must deal in a host of other contexts, such as when they must decide whether the employer who discharges a worker has committed an unfair labor practice because he has done so on account of the employee's union activities. As Judge Greene said, "There is no reason why similar factual judgments cannot be made by courts and juries in the context of economic retaliation (against tenants by landlords) for providing information to the government."

Reversed and remanded.

McGowan, Circuit Judge (concurring except as to Parts I and II).

The considerations bearing upon statutory construction, so impressively marshalled by Judge Wright in Part III of his opinion, have made it unnecessary for me to pursue in any degree the constitutional speculations contained in Parts I and II; and it is for this reason that I do not join in them. The issue of statutory construction presented in this case has never seemed to me to be a difficult one, nor to require for its resolution the spur of avoidance of constitutional questions. A Congress which authorizes housing code promulgation and enforcement clearly cannot be taken to have excluded retaliatory eviction of the kind here alleged as a defense under a routine statutory eviction mechanism also provided by Congress.

Danaher, Circuit Judge (dissenting).

Basically at issue between my colleagues and me is a question as to the extent to which the power of the court may here be exercised where by their edict the landlord's right to his property is being denied. They concede as they must that in making his affirmative case for possession the landlord need only show that his tenant has been given the 30-day statutory notice, and he need not assign any reason for evicting a tenant who does not occupy the premises under a lease.

That fundamental rule of our law of property must give way, it now develops. My colleagues so rule despite the absence of a statutory prescription of discernible standards as to what may constitute "violations," or of provision for compensating[2] the landlord for the deprivation of his property. They say that the court will not "frustrate the effectiveness of the housing code as a means of upgrading the quality of housing in Washington." Since they recognize that there is an "appalling condition and shortage of housing in Washington,"[3] they say the court must take account of the "social and eco-

---

trict of Columbia. Its companion bill, S. 1910, 90th Cong., 1st Sess. (1967), has been introduced in the Senate. The bill would forbid an eviction, except for specified reasons, during the nine months following the filing of a complaint.

53. Of course, because of his prior taint the landlord may not be able to disprove an illicit motive unless he can show a legitimate affirmative reason for eviction.

2. Berman v. Parker, 348 U.S. 26 (1954) held for the first time that the government here might condemn one's property and turn it over to another private "person"—but not without due process, not without compensation.

3. It is common knowledge that following Berman v. Parker, the housing structures in one entire quadrant of the City of Washington were razed, driving thousands of tenants to seek whatever "appalling" accommodations they could find. In place of the destroyed housing, beautiful apartment buildings have been built, to be sure, with "co-ops" in some costing up to $100,000 per apartment, with rentals in others priced far beyond the capacity to pay of thousands of those who had been displaced. And even the affluent tenants having chosen to do so, must be presumed, at least until now, to have taken the premises in the condition in which they found them, cockroaches and all.

nomic importance of assuring at least minimum standards in housing conditions." So to meet such needs, the burden would now be met, not pursuant to a congressionally prescribed policy, with adequate provision for construction or acquisition costs, or for compensation to property owners, but by private landlords who will be saddled with what should have been a public charge.

The Washington Post on April 1, 1968 editorialized upon the need for a renewal project after "the wholesale bulldozing of slums and massive uprooting of families with them which characterized the Southwest development."

Note how my colleagues achieve that result as they rule:

But while the landlord may evict for any legal reason or for no reason at all, he is not, we hold, free to evict in retaliation for his tenant's report of housing code violations to the authorities. As a matter of statutory construction and for reasons of public policy, such an eviction cannot be permitted.

Just as do my colleagues, I deplore the effort of any landlord for a base reason to secure possession of his own property, but if his right so to recover in accordance with our law is to be denied, Congress should provide the basis. Appropriate standards as a pre-condition thus could be spelled out in legislation and just compensation thereupon be awarded if found to be due.[4]

I am not alone in my position, I dare say, as I read the Congressional Record for March 13, 1968, page H 1883. In President Johnson's message to the Congress he said:

One of the most abhorrent injustices committed by some landlords in the District is to evict — or threaten to evict — tenants who report building code violations to the Department of Licenses and Inspections.

This is intimidation, pure and simple. It is an affront to the dignity of the tenant. It often makes the man who lives in a cold and leaking tenement afraid to report those conditions.

Certainly the tenant deserves the protection of the law when he lodges a good faith complaint.

I recommend legislation to prevent retaliatory evictions by landlords in the District.

He seems to think as do I that congressional action is required. It may be doubted that the President would so have recommended legislation except upon the advice of the legal authorities upon whom he relies. Certainly he is aware of the due process protective considerations which must be accorded to a landlord, even one who might be guilty of "an affront to the dignity" of a tenant. He must know that a community burden is not to be borne alone by landlords, charged with allegedly "retaliatory"[6] evictions because of complaints of "violations," undefined and vague and lacking in standards.

---

4. As Chief Judge Hood observed, writing for a unanimous District of Columbia Court of Appeals: "If, as some believe, the law relating to landlords and tenants is outdated, it should be brought up-to-date by legislation and not by court edict." In note 10 he quoted from Collins v. Hardyman, 341 U.S. 651 (1951), "It is not for this Court to compete with Congress or attempt to replace it as the Nation's law-making body."

6. For background and as a matter of convenient reference, let it be noted that Edwards and Habib entered into a monthly tenancy agreement as of March 24, 1965. The tenant paid one month's rent in advance, and, of course, took the premises as she found them. The agreement provided that failure thereafter to pay the rental in advance would constitute a default and that the agreement was to operate as a notice to quit and that the statutory 30 days' notice to quit was expressly waived. Repeatedly thereafter the tenant was in default of payment of the rental. As of Octo-

That my colleagues ultimately upon reflection began to doubt the sufficiency of their position seems clear enough, for they observe:

> This is not, of course, of say that even if the tenant can prove a retaliatory purpose she is entitled to remain in possession in perpetuity.

"Of course" not, I say; not at all was the law as read, until now, I may add. My colleagues continue:

> If this illegal purpose is dissipated, the landlord can, in the absence of legislation or a binding contract, evict his tenants or raise their rents for economic or other legitimate reasons, or even for no reason at all.

And so, it may be seen according to the majority, we need never mind the Congress, the aid of which the President would invoke. We may disregard, even reject, our law of such long standing. We will simply leave it to a jury to say when a landlord may regain possession of his own property, although "the determination is not easy," my colleagues concede. [7]

I leave my colleagues where they have placed themselves.

Note to Edwards v. Habib

The constitutional discussion in Edwards v. Habib suggests two books that may be of interest: Anthony Lewis, MAKE NO LAW: THE SULLIVAN CASE AND THE FIRST AMENDMENT (1991) is, according to Professor Laurence Tribe, "a masterly tale of the most important First Amendment decision of our time." William Lee Miller, ARGUING ABOUT SLAVERY: THE GREAT BATTLE IN THE UNITED STATES CONGRESS (1996) tells the story of a battle to preserve the right to petition for redress of grievances.

Serreze[1] v. YWCA of Western Massachusetts, Inc.

330 Mass. App. Ct. 639, 572 N.E.2d 581 (Appeals Court of Massachusetts 1991)

Katherine Callaghan, for plaintiffs; Elaine M. Reall, for defendant.

Before Warner, C.J., and Brown and Greenberg, JJ.

---

ber 11, 1965, neither the appellant nor her counsel appeared in the Landlord-Tenant Branch of the Court of General Sessions. A later motion to reopen a default judgment was granted, a two-day trial followed, and a directed verdict for the landlord was entered. This court was asked to stay the judgment after the District of Columbia Court of Appeals refused to do so. I then dissented from this court's order for reasons set forth in Edwards v. Habib, 125 U.S.App. D.C. 49, 51 (1965), to which I now refer. In the meanwhile, time and again, further defaults occurred with resulting harassment and vexation to the landlord which this court as often overlooked. The landlord is still without possession of his property which should have been available to him for remodeling or sale, or even that the structure might be razed. Unless its condition could justify its condemnation by lawful authority, his should have been the option as to future use of the property. It is difficult for me to understand how this court can sustain so studied a deprivation as has here occurred.

7. And with the results in riot-torn Washington so painfully obvious the prospect now being opened up may seem horrendous indeed, whether the "violations" were committed by the tenants themselves or by others whose conduct created conditions with which the landlord must cope. I cannot accept the premise that Congress even remotely entertained any such "intent" as my colleagues so confidently proclaim.

1. Angela Anderson and Jane Doe. Jane Doe is unable to bring this suit in her own name because her former abuser continues to make efforts to locate her.

Greenberg, Justice:

The question posed by this case is whether three women residing in "chapter 707 project based units" operated by the Springfield YWCA are statutorily protected from self-help eviction. We conclude that they are and that the trial judge's dismissal of part of their claims was erroneous.

The plaintiffs, Mary Serreze, Angela Anderson and Jane Doe, filed suit against the YWCA of Western Massachusetts doing business as Springfield YWCA (YWCA), alleging violations of G.L. c. 186, §§ 14[2] and 15F,[3] claiming among other things, that when they were locked out of their apartments on May 12, 1989, they were unlawfully evicted without judicial process. They sought preliminary injunctive relief, which was denied, and damages.

The YWCA moved to dismiss the plaintiffs' complaint on the ground that the pleadings and supporting documents established that the plaintiffs' relationship to the YWCA was that of voluntary social service clients and not tenants. After a hearing, a judge in the Superior Court granted the YWCA's motion to dismiss and judgment entered accordingly.

1. The "Transitional Living Program." The YWCA leased units of a multi-unit apartment building located on South Street in Northampton to facilitate its "Transitional Living Program" (TLP) for battered women and their children. The TLP program, a blend of housing and social services, is unique in that it is designed not to provide residential therapy for mental health patients or "emergency" housing for the homeless, but rather comprehensive "second stage" support for selected families seeking transition to a life independent of their former abusers. The TLP program furnished each selected participant with her own apartment, subsidized through the Department of Community Affairs (DCA),[6] and social services, funded through the Department of Social Services (DSS) and provided by the YWCA. In return for the services received, the women were expected either to work or to attend school and to participate in regularly scheduled self-help counseling and vocational guidance sessions. The program was run largely by two YWCA employees, a program coordinator responsible for counseling, advocacy and general case management, and a children's coordinator responsible for monitoring the needs of those women with minor children.

2. The dispute. Toward the end of January, 1989, the controversy which spawned this litigation erupted between the YWCA and the plaintiffs. The plaintiffs Anderson and Doe, unhappy with the program coordinator's purported insensitivity to their case management, lodged a complaint with the executive director of the YWCA. A short time later, in a letter dated March 12, 1989, the three women articulated specific grievances against the program coordinator, including charges of breach of confidentiality, inaccessibility, lack of knowledge as to area resources, and an inability properly to facilitate sup-

---

2. G.L. c. 186, § 14, as amended by St.1984, c. 189, § 146, provides in pertinent part: "Any lessor or landlord who directly or indirectly interferes with the quiet enjoyment of any residential premises by the occupant, or who attempts to regain possession of such premises by force without benefit of judicial process ... [is subject to statutory remedies]."

3. G.L. c. 186, § 15F, inserted by St.1974, c. 575, § 2, provides as follows: "If a tenant is removed from the premises or excluded therefrom by the landlord or his agent except pursuant to a valid court order ... [a statutory remedy is available]."

6. Each of the program participants paid a monthly rent of twenty-five percent of her income pursuant to the regulation governing the determination of rents in State-aided public housing.

port group sessions.[7] Tensions mounted and culminated in Doe's refusal to attend the individual and group counseling sessions. Serreze joined the boycott shortly thereafter.

On March 29, 1989, the program coordinator, citing as grounds for termination their "voluntary" failure to participate in support services, issued Doe and Serreze thirty-day notices to vacate their apartments by April 30, 1989.[8] Concerned that the rift would jeopardize future funding for an otherwise valuable program, the YWCA executive director met with the plaintiffs on at least one occasion, on April 5, 1989, to discuss their complaints. At that meeting, the director agreed to investigate the plaintiffs' grievances, but informed them that if they failed to vacate their apartments as required in the notices, she would have the locks changed. She added that this decision was not appealable.

Anticipating a moratorium on the YWCA's ouster notices, the three women, through counsel, requested a fair hearing and conciliation conference through DSS. See 110 Code Mass.Regs. §§ 10.06, 10.08(2), 10.09 (1988). On May 12, 1989, during the DSS conciliation conference, and for reasons not entirely developed in the record, the YWCA representatives walked out of the meeting and changed the locks on the plaintiffs' apartment doors.

3. Plaintiffs' claims under G.L. c. 186. The plaintiffs contend that the YWCA, in barring them from their apartments without judicial process, violated G.L. c. 186, §§ 14 and 15F. The YWCA counters that plaintiffs were not tenants, but clients in a temporary treatment program, and, as such, licensees not statutorily protected under landlord-tenant law.

We recognize that the regulatory scheme underlying the transitional housing program suggests an intention to "depart from traditional concepts of the landlord-tenant relationship." Spence v. O'Brien, 15 Mass.App.Ct. 489, 496, 446 N.E.2d 1070 (1983). However, the existence of a classic "tenancy" between these parties is not dispositive, for G.L. c. 186, § 14, does not require such a relationship for statutory protections to attach. Because of the general disapproval of self-help evictions, the statute was drafted to prohibit a "lessor or landlord" from "directly or indirectly interfering with the quiet enjoyment of *any* residential premises by the *occupant*, or ... [from attempting] to regain possession of such premises by force without benefit of judicial process." Note 2, supra. As self-help eviction would constitute a breach of the covenant of quiet enjoyment under this provision, the plaintiffs, as "occupants" of "residential premises," qualify for its protections and remedies.[9]

The YWCA, like many landlords before them, insists that the financial integrity of this program or other like programs will be compromised each time a disruptive resident must be ousted through summary process. We recognize in this case the legitimate interests of the YWCA in preserving the viability of its TLP program, and we are conscious of the potential impediments involved. However, it is not a characteristic feature of sum-

---

7. Anderson and Doe also alleged in the complaint that a short time after the YWCA hired a child coordinator, on March 21, 1989, they believed they "witnessed the Coordinator physically and psychologically abusing a child belonging to one of the other residents."

8. In a parallel development, the program coordinator had sent Anderson a letter on March 8, 1989, ordering her out of her apartment due to her failure to attend regular meetings and because of a partial arrearage on her security deposit. On April 10, 1989, Anderson was notified that she had until April 19, 1989, to vacate her unit.

9. Because we hold that the plaintiffs are entitled to remedies afforded by G.L. c. 186, § 14, we need not reach the more difficult question whether they were "tenants" for the purposes of G.L. c. 186, § 15F. However, we note that remedial statutes, such as G.L. c. 186, § 15F, are to be liberally construed to effectuate the apparent legislative purpose. Any ambiguities are to be resolved toward the same end. Following these principles, in construing the term "tenant", courts have looked beyond rigid common law definitions to effectuate an appropriate remedy.

mary process law that the landlord who seeks possession is without speedy remedy.[10] The YWCA has offered nothing to establish what it is about the summary procedure under G.L. c. 239, §§ 1 et seq., which might justify treating the plaintiffs differently.

The mere fact that the TLP program is a condition of the occupancy agreement, and the services provided inherently restorative, should not preclude the application of G.L. c. 186, § 14. In implementing this program, the YWCA has provided a safe place for participants whose survival depends upon controlling their own habitat. The plaintiffs sought refuge from their former households because the provisions of the abuse prevention statute could not effectively "create[ ] a haven for [them] in which no further abuse need be feared...." Commonwealth v. Gordon, 407 Mass. 340, 347, 553 N.E.2d 915 (1990). TLP participants are capable of independent living,[11] and have been furnished with the means to secure themselves and their children. Under the agreements, they reside in an apartment and pay for the exclusive right of possession and control. To deny such program participants some form of predeprivation process may only perpetuate the cycle of temporary shelter and dislocation. Where, as here, the administrative process has stumbled, the courts, as "ultimate protectors of constitutional rights," may apply remedial statutes such as G.L. c. 186, § 14....

Cotton v. Alexian Brothers Bonaventure House

2003 WL 22110501 (N.D.Ill. 2003)

Richard M. Wheelock, Michelle J. Gilbert, Michelle S. Wetzel, Legal Assistance Foundation of Chicago, Chicago, IL, for Plaintiffs.

Susan G. Feibus, David Galbreath Larmore, Edward George Renner, Samera S. Ludwig, Ungaretti & Harris, Chicago, IL, for Defendant.

Matthew F. Kennelly, United States District Judge:

Alexian Brothers Bonaventure House is a supportive residence that provides a transitional living program for people with HIV/AIDS. It receives federal funding through the Housing Opportunities for People With AIDS Act ("HOPWA"), 42 U.S.C. § 12901 et seq. Plaintiffs Gregory Cotton and Emory Bolden are persons living with AIDS. They reside at Bonaventure House and participate in its transitional living program. During November, 2002, Bonaventure terminated plaintiffs' residency at its facility. At that time, plaintiffs sued separately in this Court, each seeking a temporary restraining order and preliminary injunction against Bonaventure. Each alleged that his residency had been terminated without notice and a hearing as required by HOPWA and sought to be reinstated in defendant's transitional living program. Plaintiffs also sought damages for the alleged HOPWA violation, intentional infliction of emotional distress, and alleged violations of the Illinois Forcible Entry and Detainer Act and the Chicago Resi-

---

10. Unlike several States in which anti-eviction statutes prohibit the removal of any residential occupant except for cause, Massachusetts continues to permit summary eviction of tenants at will. See and compare, the New Jersey Anti-Eviction Act, arising from a recognition of the severe housing shortage in that State. In Massachusetts, the burden remains on a tenant to establish a reasonable basis to stave off eviction proceedings.

11. In this way, these women are very different from those individuals housed in programs funded through the Department of Mental Health. See 760 Code Mass.Regs. § 39.01(1) (1988), which specifically excludes mental health programs and shelters from the Transitional Housing Program. The plaintiffs have manifested no behavioral disorders justifying substantive limitations on their living accommodations, nor has there been any allegation that the plaintiffs substantially interfered with the rights of other occupants.

dential Landlord and Tenant Ordinance, as well as declaratory and injunctive relief. On November 5, 2002, this Court granted Cotton's request for a temporary restraining order against Bonaventure House, ordering it to restore Cotton to full use and occupancy of his residence pending a hearing on his petition for a preliminary injunction. On November 20, 2002, we granted Bolden's request for a TRO, likewise ordering Bonaventure House to restore him to full use and occupancy of his residence. On December 9, 2002, the two cases were consolidated and the restraining orders against Bonaventure House were extended through the date of this Court's ruling on plaintiffs' motion for summary judgment. The Court is now presented with the parties' cross motions for summary judgment.

combined

Factual Background

Bonaventure House is a voluntary transitional living program for people with AIDS. It receives ten percent of its operating expenses from the United States Department of Housing and Urban Development ("HUD") through HOPWA. Residents must complete an application and interview prior to being accepted into Bonaventure House's program. Once admitted, residents may stay at Bonaventure House for up to twenty-four months. Each resident is required to contribute forty-five percent of his income to help offset operating expenses. Bonaventure House provides meals to its residents. In addition, each resident is given a private room that can be locked to exclude other residents. All residents share bathrooms, showering facilities and common living areas. Bonaventure House reserves the right to enter and inspect a resident's private room at any time.

provide mental health counseling

In addition to room and board, Bonaventure House provides on-site counseling to its residents. Specifically, it provides public benefits counseling, assistance in executing durable powers of attorney for health care and property, assistance in connecting residents with appropriate community psychological services, and collaboration with other community based service providers to provide residents with substance abuse and mental health counseling and treatment. It does not provide medical care to its residents, nor does it administer medication.

Don't tolerate violence

Bonaventure House has adopted a Resident Handbook that sets forth guidelines for its transitional living program. According to the Handbook, abusive language, violence and threat of violence are prohibited. A corrective action policy is in place to enforce these prohibitions. As part of the corrective action policy, Bonaventure Houses issues written or verbal warnings depending upon the nature of the infraction. In serious situations a resident may be asked to leave the program immediately. The Director of Programs and Services has the discretion to determine the amount of time the terminated resident has to vacate the premises.

Plaintiff Gregory Cotton is a person living with AIDS. He moved into Bonaventure House around January 24, 2001. On October 30, 2002, Marty Hansen, a social work supervisor for Bonaventure House[,] told Cotton that he was being terminated from the program, and that he needed to leave the building by 3:00 p.m. that day. Hansen claims that he told Cotton that he was being terminated for "inappropriate behavior." Two weeks earlier, according to Hansen, Cotton had threatened to "slice someone's throat" in the Bonaventure House dining room. Bonaventure House did not give Cotton written notice prior to first informing him that he had to leave the premises.

After some negotiations between Cotton and Bonaventure's administrative staff, Cotton was permitted to stay until 6:00 p.m. Around 5:30 p.m., Bonaventure gave Cotton a letter stating that he had to leave by 6:00 p.m. or Bonaventure House staff would call the police. The letter did not state any reasons why Cotton was being asked to leave. It did, however, provide Cotton with the names and phone numbers of persons to contact at two organizations that might be able to help him secure alternative housing and mental health treatment. The letter informed Cotton that he could return to Bonaventure House two days hence, on Friday, November 1, 2002 at 9:00 a.m, to receive a "detailed written explanation" why his residency was being terminated. The letter further stated that Cotton would be allowed to appeal the decision in writing and at an appeals meeting during which he could confront witnesses with the aid of counsel. Cotton was informed that he would receive a final decision on the matter in writing by November 8, 2002, and that his belongings would be secured at Bonaventure House until that time.

Cotton left Bonaventure House on October 30, 2002 as requested. On the nights of October 30 and 31, Cotton slept on the "L" train and in a Chicago city park. On November 1, Cotton met with his attorney who then contacted Bonaventure and advised that she intended to file suit in federal court to restore Cotton to possession of his residence. That same day, Bonaventure House wrote Cotton a letter detailing reasons for its decision to dismiss him from the program. The letter documented a series of examples of Cotton's behavior during his residency at Bonaventure, including behavior that Bonaventure characterized as "extreme," "negative" and "dangerous to the Bonaventure community." It stated that Cotton had been terminated because his "continuing belligerent and threatening verbal behaviors presented a threat to the Bonaventure community."

For the nights of November 1–4, Bonaventure House paid for Cotton to stay at the Diplomat Hotel, a single room occupancy building. On November 4, 2002, Bonaventure House sent Cotton a second letter, addressed to his attorney, which explained that Cotton could obtain reconsideration for participation in its program if he submitted to a psychological evaluation. On November 5, 2002, Cotton appeared before this Court arguing that Bonaventure House had terminated his residency without providing the notice and hearing required by HOPWA, and without the service of a summons and complaint as required by the Illinois Forcible Entry and Detainer Act and the Chicago Residential Landlord and Tenant Ordinance. We granted his motion for a temporary restraining order, directing Bonaventure House to restore Cotton to full use and occupancy of his residence. He continues to reside at Bonaventure House pending the outcome of the parties' motions for summary judgment.

Like Cotton, Emory Bolden is a person living with AIDS. He moved into Bonaventure House on November 5, 2002. Bonaventure asserts that on November 17, 2002, Bolden entered another resident's room uninvited and attempted to engage him in sexual contact. It asserts that the other resident, who had been sleeping, awoke startled, rebuffed Bolden's advances, and asked him to leave. According to Bonaventure, Bolden initially refused to leave the resident's room but eventually did so voluntarily.

After meeting with Bolden on the morning of November 19, 2002, Bonaventure terminated Bolden from its program, citing his alleged behavior on November 17. Bolden was told to leave the premises by 3:00 p.m. that day. He packed some of his personal property and left as requested. Bonaventure secured his remaining belongings and informed him that he could return to retrieve them later that evening. Bonaventure did not provide Bolden with a written explanation of the reasons for his termination. On November 20, 2002, Bolden filed suit against Bonaventure in this Court, along with a motion for a temporary restraining order. Like Cotton, he argued that Bonaventure had terminated his residence without complying with the procedural requirements imposed by HOPWA and by state and local landlord-tenant law. The Court granted his motion, ordering him to be restored to full use and occupancy of his residence. Bolden returned to Bonaventure House on the evening of November 20 and has continued to reside there since that time.

Discussion

Before the Court now are cross-motions for summary judgment. In their complaints, Cotton and Bolden allege that Bonaventure terminated their residencies without following the procedural guidelines imposed by HOPWA, and without pursuing formal eviction actions against them pursuant to Illinois law and the Chicago Residential Landlord-Tenant Ordinance. Plaintiffs further claim intentional infliction of emotional distress, alleging that the manner in which Bonaventure handled their terminations was outrageous. Plaintiffs have moved for summary judgment as to liability on all of their claims.

In its cross-motion for summary judgment, Bonaventure argues that its involuntary discharge policy complies with HOPWA regulations and that it satisfied the due process requirements imposed by the Act when it terminated Cotton and Bolden from its program. Bonaventure argues that the program is not governed by Illinois landlord-tenant law and that Bonaventure is not required to comply with the Detainer Act or the CRLTO when it decides to terminate a program participant's residency. It also argues that plaintiffs have failed to produce evidence that would support a claim for intentional infliction of emotional distress….

The parties here dispute some of the factual circumstances surrounding Cotton and Bolden's discharge from Bonaventure House. Fundamentally, however, the parties disagree about the legal requirements imposed on Bonaventure when it decides to discharge a participant from its program. We first address the issue of Bonaventure's due process obligations under HOPWA.

A. HOPWA

1. "Conditions of Occupancy"

Plaintiffs argue that in terminating their residencies and discharging them from its program, Bonaventure failed to comply with the due process requirements imposed by HOPWA's implementing regulations. They also argue that Bonaventure's involuntary discharge policy as stated in its Resident Handbook fails to comply with those regulations on its face. Though Bonaventure concedes that it is bound by HOPWA regulations generally, it denies that it is obligated to provide due process as prescribed by HOPWA when it terminates residents for violating "conditions of occupancy." Alternatively, it argues that its involuntary discharge policy and the specific procedures it followed in terminating Cotton and Bolden's residencies at Bonaventure House demonstrate full compliance with its obligations under the Act.

The HOPWA regulation at issue provides as follows:

(2) Violation of requirements.

    (i) Basis. Assistance to participants who reside in housing programs assisted under this part may be terminated if the participant violates program requirements or conditions of occupancy. Grantees must ensure that supportive services are provided, so that a participant's assistance is terminated only in the most severe cases.

(ii) Procedure. In terminating assistance to any program participant for violation of requirements grantees must provide a formal process that recognizes the rights of individuals receiving assistance to due process of law. This process must consist of:

(A) Serving the participant with a written notice containing a clear statement of the reasons for termination;

(B) Permitting the participant to have a review of the decision, in which the participant is given the opportunity to present written objections, and be represented by their own counsel, before a person other than the person (or subordinate of that person) who made or approved the termination decision; and

(C) Providing prompt written notification of the final decision to the participant.

Code of Federal Regulation

24 C.F.R. §574.310(e). To summarize, a participant's assistance may be terminated if he or she "violates program requirements or conditions of occupancy." A "formal process" recognizing the participant's right to due process of law is required for any termination "for violation of requirements."

Seizing on §574.310(e)(2)(ii)'s use of the term "requirements," Bonaventure equates that term with §574.310(e)(2)(i)'s authorization to terminate residents for violating "program requirements" and argues that §574.310(e)(2)(ii) does not require due process when it terminates a participant for violating a "condition of occupancy." Bonaventure argues that its involuntary discharge procedure, which does not expressly guarantee formal process, therefore complies with the regulation because a participant may be discharged under the procedure only for violating a condition of occupancy.

defendent claim

Leaving aside for a moment the sufficiency of Bonaventure's policies, the Court disagrees with its reading of the regulation. There is no basis to read the regulation's use of the two different terms—"requirements" and "program requirements"—to mean the same thing. A more reasonable reading is that the more general term—"requirements"—is intended to have a broader meaning than the more specific "program requirements." In any event, we are not convinced that the regulation draws any meaningful distinction between violations of "program requirements" and violations of "conditions of occupancy." As plaintiffs point out, neither of those terms are [sic; is] anywhere defined in HOPWA's implementing regulations. If, as Bonaventure contends, a program participant's minimum due process rights under HOPWA were meant to depend on whether the participant is terminated for violating a "program requirement" as opposed to a "condition of occupancy," it is reasonable to believe that the regulation would have offered some guidance as to the kind of rules that fall into each category. Otherwise, a HOPWA grantee like Bonaventure could avoid its due process obligations each time it discharged a participant by simply characterizing the basis for termination as a violation of a condition of occupancy rather than a program requirement. There is *known* no reason to believe that in promulgating regulations under a statute whose overall purpose included limiting terminations to "the most severe cases," see §574.310(e)(2)(i), with the intent of ensuring that "reasonable efforts be made to intervene before terminating assistance," S. Rep. No. 101-316 at 172, reprinted in 1990 U.S.C.A.A.N. 5763, 5934, HUD intended to create a regulatory scheme that would be so easily manipulable.

The plain language of the regulation provides that in terminating assistance to any program participant for violation of "requirements," HOPWA grantees must provide the participant with minimum procedural due process. 24 C.F.R. §574.310(e)(2)(ii),

We understand this to mean that whenever a supportive residence like Bonaventure discharges one of its residents for failure to comply with the rules established by its program, it must provide the participant with the minimum formal process outlined in §574.310(e)(2)(ii)(A)–(C). The question before us, therefore, is whether Bonaventure's involuntary discharge policy and the steps it took to discharge Cotton and Bolden from its program comported with its due process obligations under 24 C.F.R. §574.310(e).

2. Bonaventure's Involuntary Discharge Policy

We begin with Bonaventure's involuntary discharge policy. According to its Resident Handbook, a resident may be asked to leave Bonaventure House involuntarily for any of eight enumerated reasons, including participation in physical violence or abuse. Under this policy, Bonaventure's Director of Programs and Services has the discretion to determine the amount of time that the departing resident has to vacate the premises. In particularly serious situations, such as when a resident has threatened bodily harm to another person, Bonaventure reserves the right to ask the resident to leave immediately.

Plaintiffs argue that these features of Bonaventure's policy conflict with its due process obligations. This argument is based on plaintiffs' position that §574.310(e) does not permit post-deprivation hearings. Though the regulations are silent as to the issue of timing of a required hearing, plaintiffs assert that post-deprivation hearings are inadequate to protect the rights of Bonaventure's sick and impoverished residents, many of whom could be rendered immediately homeless by the decision to terminate their residency. Plaintiffs rely on Supreme Court decisions in the area of Fourteenth Amendment procedural due process to support its argument that pre-deprivation notice and hearing are required in terminating assistance to participants in HOPWA funded residential programs. See, e.g., Zinermon v. Burch, 494 U.S. 113 (1991); 397 U.S. 254 (1970). Because HOPWA and its implementing regulations are silent on the issue, we agree that the Supreme Court's treatment of constitutional due process is instructive.

The essence of due process is "the opportunity to be heard 'at a meaningful time and in a meaningful manner.'" Matthews v. Eldridge, 424 U.S. 319, 335 (1976) (quoting Armstrong v. Manzo, 380 U.S. 545, 552 (1965)). The Court has held that the extent to which *Fourteenth Amendment* procedural due process must be afforded to a recipient of public benefits is influenced by "the extent to which [a recipient] may be 'condemned to suffer grievous loss,' and depends upon whether the recipient's interest in avoiding that loss outweighs the governmental interest in summary adjudication." Goldberg. An individual is presumptively entitled to notice and an opportunity for a hearing prior to the permanent deprivation of a recognized interest in liberty or property. Logan v. Zimmerman, 455 U.S. 422 (1982). Post-deprivation process is typically inadequate "absent 'the necessity of quick action by the State or the impracticality of providing any predeprivation process.'" Logan, 455 U.S. at 436. These principles suggest that in determining the proper timing of the written notice and hearing guaranteed by HOPWA's implementing regulations, we should consider the extent to which HOPWA grantees require the flexibility to make quick decisions regarding their program participants, the general feasibility of providing predeprivation process, the consequences to program participants of losing their assistance, and the adequacy of a written notice and hearing after termination of a program participant's benefits.

There is no doubt, as plaintiffs contend, that the consequences to HOPWA program participants of losing their assistance are serious. Participants in supportive residential programs like Bonaventure's are impoverished, suffer from AIDS related illnesses, and lack adequate housing opportunities. A resident who loses his housing assistance may face homelessness and may experience psychological stress that exacerbates his illnesses. Program participants erroneously discharged from HOPWA facilities may suffer seriously during even short periods between the time their residencies are terminated and the time of any post-deprivation hearing. From this perspective, across-the-board post-deprivation hearings would be inadequate to protect the due process rights recognized by HOPWA's implementing regulations. Cf. Anast v. Commonwealth Apartments, 956 F.Supp. 792, 799 (N.D. Ill.1997) (Because an improper denial of benefits cannot be corrected easily at a later date, a pretermination hearing must be held before eviction from public housing projects) (citing Goldberg; Caulder v. Durham Housing Auth., 433 F.2d 998 (4th Cir.1970)).

On the other hand, those charged with administering HOPWA funded programs may on occasion have a legitimate need to be able to make quick decisions to protect the interests of all program participants. Bonaventure argues convincingly that in situations where a particular resident's behavior is alleged to pose an imminent threat to the safety of others, it has a legitimate interest in removing the dangerous resident immediately. Under such circumstances, it may be impracticable to provide the formal hearing contemplated by HOPWA's implementing regulations until after the resident has been removed from the premises. For this reason, we cannot say that Bonaventure's involuntary discharge policy, which allows for immediate discharge in emergency situations, facially conflicts with HOPWA's due process guarantees. Absent exigent circumstances, however, we are not convinced that it is either impracticable or unduly burdensome to require HOPWA program administrators to provide its residents with a formal hearing under § 574.310(e)(2)(ii)(B) before terminating their assistance.

[handwritten margin note: Defendent claim]

Written notification is a separate matter. The HOPWA regulations unambiguously require service of a written notice with a "clear statement" of the reasons for termination. The regulations do not, however, specifically state when this notice must be given. Bonaventure argues that HOPWA's silence entitles it to exercise discretion over when it must provide written notice. The Court disagrees. As we have discussed, the regulations incorporate general principles of due process. Meaningful due process typically requires pre-deprivation procedures, particularly where a recipient of public benefits stands to suffer serious consequences as a result of losing his assistance. Bonaventure has not argued that it would be difficult or impractical to provide departing residents with the written notification required by § 574.310(e)(2)(ii)(A), and the Court can conceive of no emergency (nor has Bonaventure identified any) that would prevent it from doing so. Unlike the hearing requirement, which contemplates a formal process allowing the participant to confront opposing witnesses and present written objections, providing written notification of the reasons for termination entails minimal preparation and no significant delay. HOPWA grantees are simply required to provide departing residents with "a clear statement of reasons for termination." 24 C.F.R. § 574.310(e)(2)(ii)(A). Even in cases where a resident becomes dangerous and must be removed quickly, there is no reason why a HOPWA program administrator could not produce this simple notice within a few minutes.

[handwritten margin note: P claim]

On the other hand, it does not follow that Bonaventure's involuntary discharge policy fails as a matter of law to comply with HOPWA's due process requirements. Bonaventure's failure to provide pre-termination notice may subject it to liability in individual cases, but there is no basis to declare its policy—which is silent on the timing issue—illegal.

3. Plaintiffs' Termination

The question remains whether Bonaventure complied with its due process obligations when it discharged Cotton and Bolden from its program. We address this question separately as to each plaintiff, beginning with Cotton.

Cotton argues that he was forced out of Bonaventure House without first being provided with written notice of the reasons for his termination and without an opportunity for a hearing. Bonaventure contends that it was under no obligation to provide pre-deprivation process. As we have discussed, however, due process as that term is used in HOPWA's implementing regulations requires that Bonaventure provide departing residents with prior written notice stating the reasons for termination. See generally, Mullane v. Central Hanover Bank & Trust Co., 339 U.S. 306, 314 (1950) ("an elementary and fundamental requirement of due process in any proceeding which is to be accorded finality is notice reasonably calculated, under all the circumstances, to apprise interested parties of the pendency of the action and afford them the opportunity to present their objections.... when notice is a person's due, process which is mere gesture is not due process"). Moreover, as previously discussed, unless Cotton posed an imminent threat to the residents and employees of Bonaventure House or some other emergency or exigent circumstance existed, he was entitled to a hearing prior to being put out on the street.

The parties agree that Cotton was asked to leave Bonaventure House on October 30, 2002. On that date, he received a letter from Marty Hansen, Bonaventure's social work supervisor, informing him that he was required to vacate the premises by 6:00 p.m. Though the letter stated that he could return the next morning to receive a detailed written explanation for his termination, the letter did not state the reasons for his termination. This was insufficient under HOPWA. Cotton was entitled to a written notice containing a clear statement of the reasons for his termination before he was discharged from Bonaventure House. The letter Bonaventure mailed Cotton, a letter two days after kicking him out which stated the reasons for his termination, did not satisfy Bonaventure's obligation to provide pre-termination notice of the reasons for its actions.

The October 30 letter stated no reasons, telling Cotton only that if he wanted to he could come back the next day to get a written explanation. Nor does Bonaventure offer any evidence that it so much as told Cotton the reasons for his termination beyond accusing him of "inappropriate behavior."[1] Nor has Bonaventure even attempted to excuse the giving of prior written notice of its reasons, such as by arguing that it had to act quickly and had no time to prepare the notice—a contention that in any event would be undermined by the fact that it had more than enough time to prepare a letter telling Cotton to leave.

Cotton also argues that a pre-deprivation hearing was required; Bonaventure, for its part, contends that its offer of a post-deprivation hearing was sufficient. Determination of this issue requires resolution of factual disputes, which we cannot do in deciding a motion for summary judgment or even in deciding cross-motions.

We next address Bonaventure's actions in terminating assistance to Bolden. According to Bonaventure, on the night of November 17, 2002, Bolden entered another resident's room uninvited, attempting to initiate sexual contact. After Bolden allegedly touched the other resident's face, the resident awoke, rebuffed Bolden's advances and

---

1. Bonaventure supervisor Marty Hansen's affidavit describes what he understood the "inappropriate behavior" to be but does not say that he communicated this to Cotton. Hansen Aff., ¶ 2.

asked him to leave. Bonaventure appears to have learned of this incident on November 18; Bolden says he got a note that day asking him to meet with Bonaventure supervisor Marty Hansen the next morning at 8:00 a.m. At that meeting, Hansen told Bolden that he was being terminated for "assaulting" the other resident and that he was to vacate the premises by 3:00 p.m. Though it prepared a letter that it later mailed to Bolden at his brother's residence, Bonaventure did not provide Bolden with written notice of any kind before he left. And it gave Bolden no indication that he was entitled to challenge the decision (either before or after his ouster), a notification clearly required by §574.310(e)(2)(ii)(B). For these reasons, the Court finds that Bonaventure violated Bolden's HOPWA right to pretermination written notice, a violation that Bonaventure makes no effort to excuse on the grounds that it had no time to provide proper notice (nor could it plausibly do so, given the passage of time between the incident and the November 19, 8:00 a.m. meeting with Bolden and the passage of time between that meeting and his removal from the premises).

plaintiff claim

Bolden also contends that he was entitled to a pre-termination hearing. Bonaventure contends that Bolden's behavior on November 17 indicated that he posed an imminent threat to other residents at Bonaventure House. Assuming an emergency truly existed, a pre-termination hearing was not legally required, and the 45-minute meeting that Hansen had with Bolden before terminating him may have been sufficient pre-depriva-tion "process," so long as the formal hearing required by HOPWA was later offered. The existence of an emergency, however, is genuinely disputed and cannot be determined on summary judgment.

defendent claim

There is also a serious question whether Bonaventure ever intended to provide a post-termination hearing. Bonaventure argues that it intended to do so but that Bolden beat them to the punch by seeking and obtaining a temporary restraining order. But Bonaventure provides no evidence to support this argument: the affidavits of the partic-ipants contain nary a hint of such a claim or intention, and as we have noted not even the post-termination notice that Bonaventure sent mentioned any right on Bolden's part to challenge Bonaventure's actions. On the other hand, as a practical matter, the quick intervention by Bolden's counsel and the court may have made a hearing a moot point for purposes of determining the relief to which Bolden may be entitled. None of these issues, however, can be determined by the Court on summary judgment.

def. claim

In sum, both plaintiffs have shown that their right to fair notice was violated, but both plaintiffs' summary judgment motions are otherwise denied, as is defendant's cross-motion.

B. State and Local Landlord Tenant Law (modified on reconsideration)

Plaintiffs contend that Bonaventure House is governed not only by the operational guidelines established by HOPWA and its implementing regulations, but also by prin-ciples of Illinois and Chicago landlord-tenant law. They argue that in addition to pro-viding the minimum formal process required by HOPWA, Bonaventure is required to file an action under the Illinois Forcible Entry and Detainer Act before it terminates as-sistance to program participants. They also argue that Bonaventure is required under the CRLTO to obtain a court order of possession before it orders residents to leave its facility. Bonaventure concedes that its involuntary discharge policy, as provided in its Handbook, does not incorporate any of the requirements of the Detainer Act or the CRLTO and that it discharged plaintiffs without considering those laws. It argues, however, that it does not maintain a landlord-tenant relationship with its program par-ticipants and is therefore not required to comply with rules governing leasehold

plaintiff's claim

Defenden claim

defendant claim

arrangements, Bonaventure insists that the procedures for discharging residents from supportive residential facilities like Bonaventure are provided for exclusively by HOPWA and the Illinois Supportive Residences Licensing Act, 210 ILCS 65/1 et seq., an Illinois law that complements HOPWA. For the reasons set forth in the Court's memorandum opinion and order dated September 9, 2003, the Court has determined, pursuant to 28 U.S.C. § 1367(c)(1), to decline to exercise jurisdiction over these state law claims. We therefore dismiss Counts 2 and 3 of both plaintiffs' complaints without prejudice and will not address the parties' arguments regarding the merits of the claims.* * *

Conclusion

For the reasons stated above, Bonaventure's motion for summary judgment is denied. Cotton and Bolden's motions for summary judgment are also denied; however, the Court finds pursuant to Federal Rule of Civil Procedure 56(d) that both plaintiffs have established a violation of their rights under HOPWA to written pre-termination notice. Counts 2 and 3 of both Cotton and Bolden's complaints are dismissed without prejudice pursuant to 28 U.S.C. § 1367(c)(1).

Thomas v. Cohen
453 F.3d 657 (6th Cir. 2006)

David A. Friedman, Fernandez, Friedman, Grossman, Kohn & Son, Louisville, KY, for Plaintiffs-Appellants.

Gregory S. Gowen, Paul V. Guagliardo, Jefferson County Attorney's Office, Louisville, KY, for Defendants-Appellees.

Before Ryan, Clay, and Gilman, Circuit Judges.

Ryan, Circuit Judge.

The district court granted summary judgment in favor of the defendant police officers in this 42 U.S.C. § 1983 civil rights action in which the plaintiffs allege that their constitutional rights were violated when the officers evicted them from a transitional homeless shelter. We affirm because the court properly concluded that, under Kentucky law, the plaintiffs lacked a protected property interest in the premises.

I.

On December 8, 1998, the defendants, all officers of the Louisville, Kentucky, police department, removed the plaintiffs, Natasha Thomas, Susan Gibbs, and Edwina Lewis, from Augusta House, a transitional shelter in which the women were residing. They did so at the request of the director of the shelter and without affording the plaintiffs legal process of any kind. The director had earlier asked the plaintiffs to leave the shelter for various violations of house rules, but they refused to leave.

At the time of the eviction, Augusta House was owned and operated by Mission House, Inc. The residence was the least restrictive stage of a three-stage transitional shelter program operated to help homeless women become financially independent members of mainstream society. There is no evidence in the record to support the dissent's characterization of Augusta House as low-income housing rather than a transitional homeless shelter, and the plaintiffs themselves presented no proof that Augusta House was not a shelter.

All Augusta House residents were homeless women with financial difficulties who had progressed through the first two stages of the Mission House program. Emmaus

House was the first stage of the program. Participants resided there for approximately two months until Mission House staff determined they were ready to advance to the next stage, the Annex. Emmaus House residents were subject to a curfew and rules governing a wide range of conduct, and Mission House staff provided constant supervision. The staff requested that each participant pay a $140 monthly shelter fee and assigned each participant a sleeping area and chores. In addition to providing shelter in a structured environment, Mission House offered Bible study opportunities and assisted program participants in obtaining social security benefits, food stamps, and employment.

As the women progressed through the program, Mission House gave them greater responsibility in order to ease their transition into mainstream society. The staff continued to assign each participant a sleeping area and chores, but the women were subject to fewer rules and received less supervision. When the women reached Augusta House, they were no longer subject to a curfew or live-in supervision. They were expected to have employment or income of some kind prior to moving into Augusta House, but the shelter fee arrangement remained unchanged. The women resided at Augusta house until "they g[o]t on their feet," which could take up to a couple of years, and, with the help of the Mission House staff, they found permanent housing.

Augusta House was located in a house in a residential neighborhood in order to provide the residents with the responsibility of maintaining a house before their transition into mainstream society. At the time of the eviction, each plaintiff was the sole occupant of her bedroom, and the plaintiffs shared the common living areas, bathroom, and kitchen with other occupants of the house. The residents were given keys to the house, and they were able to come and go freely, subject to the house rules. There was no lease between the plaintiffs and Mission House or Augusta House, and staff members were authorized to enter the bedrooms in Augusta House, move the residents to different bedrooms, and place two residents in a bedroom if they wished to do so.

In the fall of 1998, a dispute arose between the plaintiffs and the director of Augusta House, Laura Zinious, over the plaintiffs' alleged violation of house rules. After allegedly asking the residents to leave, as was standard practice when residents violated house rules, Zinious called the police to have the plaintiffs evicted. The responding officers evicted the plaintiffs over their protests that they were tenants who paid rent and despite their attempts to show the officers documents from their legal aid attorney expressing an opinion as to their tenancy.

The plaintiffs filed a complaint under 42 U.S.C. § 1983 alleging that the eviction violated their civil rights protected by the Fourth and Fourteenth Amendments to the United States Constitution. The officers moved for summary judgment, stipulating, for purposes of the motion, that the plaintiffs were tenants of Augusta House at the time of the eviction, but claiming the officers' actions were protected from suit based on qualified immunity. The court denied the motion, and the officers appealed.

A divided panel of this court concluded that the officers were entitled to qualified immunity with respect to the Fourth Amendment claim, but that the officers were not entitled to qualified immunity with respect to the Fourteenth Amendment claim. See Thomas v. Cohen, 304 F.3d 563, 565–66 (6th Cir.2002).

On remand, the defendants again moved for summary judgment, this time arguing that the plaintiffs' living arrangements were not governed by the Kentucky Uniform

Residential Landlord and Tenant Act (KURLTA) and that the plaintiffs, therefore, did not have a recognized property interest under Kentucky state law. The district court granted the defendants' motion and the plaintiffs now appeal.

III.

The district court found that no material facts were in dispute and that the plaintiffs did not have a protected property interest under Kentucky law because the KURLTA expressly provides that it does not apply to "[r]esidence at an institution, public or private, if incidental to detention or the provision of medical, geriatric, educational counseling, religious, or similar service." Ky.Rev.Stat. Ann. §383.535(1). The KURLTA does not define the term "institution," and we find no Kentucky authority applying the KURLTA's "institution exception." The plaintiffs argue that Augusta House is not an institution because it is located in a residential building and neighborhood, but we reject that argument, and, as we will explain, we agree with the district court that, as a matter of law, the plaintiffs' residence at Augusta House was incidental to the provision of "educational counseling, religious, or similar service[s]."

Although Kentucky courts have not interpreted the "institution exception" to the KURLTA, Kentucky's general rule of statutory interpretation is that, in the absence of ambiguity, the words in a statute are given their plain and ordinarily understood meaning, unless such an application would lead to an absurd result. As the dissent notes, courts have interpreted identical provisions of the Oregon and Washington versions of the URLTA. *See Burke v. Oxford House of Oregon Chapter V*, 196 Or.App. 726, 103 P.3d 1184 (Or.Ct.App.2004); *Sunrise Group Homes, Inc. v. Ferguson*, 55 Wash.App. 285, 777 P.2d 553 (Wash.Ct.App.1989). Using a dictionary definition, these courts explained that "incidental 'does not mean that room and board must be trivial or unimportant in comparison with the overall institutional purpose; it means that living there is *subordinate or attendant* to the institutional purpose.'" *Burke*, 103 P.3d at 1193 (quoting *Sunrise*, 777 P.2d at 555). The courts in *Burke* and *Sunrise* also rejected the dissent's argument that housing cannot be subordinate or attendant to an institution's provision of services when one of the institution's primary services is the provision of housing.

The court in *Sunrise* affirmed the trial court's finding that a group home for the developmentally disabled was an institution, explaining:

> [T]he room and board provided by the Olivia Park facility is incidental to the receipt of services the facility was created to provide. Congregate care homes provide those who are unable to "maintain a safe environment in an independent living arrangement" with supervision and "assistance with activities of daily living and/or health-related services[.]
>
> While congregate care facilities exist to keep developmentally disabled persons mainstreamed, and to that extent are an attempt at "deinstitutionalization," that is not to say they lack an institutional purpose above and beyond the provision of fundamental room and board services. The RLTA specifically excludes such institutional living arrangements from the scope of its provisions.

Sunrise, 777 P.2d at 555 (citation omitted).

Similarly, the court in *Burke* held that Oxford House, an unsupervised halfway house, is an institution under the Oregon Residential Landlord and Tenant Act. Oxford House was established to help "recovering drug and alcohol addicts make the transition to independent lives in an environment that allows them to continue their recovery process without professional supervision." The court explained:

[T]he environment of self-policing and mutual support at Oxford House combines with the zero-tolerance principles to amount to services similar to counseling; that is, Oxford House provides peer supervision, support, and counseling....

... People seeking membership at Oxford House are looking to maintain their sobriety, establish themselves financially, and govern their own lives without the "overseer" that typically accompanies residence at a halfway house. The fact of residence is subordinate or attendant to those purposes.

As in *Burke* and *Sunrise*, the provision of housing here was an integral part of the Mission House program, but it was incidental to Mission House's purpose of helping homeless women become financially independent members of mainstream society. The plaintiffs resided at Augusta House only as a result of their participation in the Mission House program. As the plaintiffs progressed through the program, Mission House provided them with various services to help them integrate themselves into mainstream society. In the early stages of the program, Mission House staff provided the plaintiffs assistance in obtaining social security benefits, food stamps, and employment, as well as a rigidly structured environment and constant supervision to help them get their lives back on track. As they progressed through the program to Augusta House, Mission House provided the plaintiffs with more responsibility and less structure in a home-like environment to help them learn how to achieve lasting financial independence upon leaving the program.

The "deinstitutionalized" home-like environment at Augusta House and its location in a residential neighborhood did not vitiate or in any way diminish the primary social services character of the Mission House program; rather they provided a relatively comfortable and "realistic setting" in which Mission House could more effectively achieve its purpose of helping homeless women in the program learn how to achieve lasting financial independence. Mission House provided housing in Augusta House *only* to facilitate the provision of this counseling-like service; it did not provide housing to the general public who would not participate in, or benefit from, its primary social service program.

We conclude that the plaintiffs' residence at Augusta House was incidental to the "educational counseling, religious, or similar service[s]" Mission House provided in fulfilling its mission of helping homeless women become financially independent members of mainstream society. Therefore, the plaintiffs' residence at Augusta House was not governed by the KURLTA.

IV.

In the alternative, we conclude that, even if the plaintiffs' residence at Augusta House did not fall under the KURLTA's "institution exception," the plaintiffs failed to qualify as tenants under the KURLTA because they have presented no evidence that they had a right to exclusive possession of Augusta House or their individual bedrooms. The district court also concluded that the plaintiffs did not qualify as "tenants" under Kentucky common law, but the plaintiffs do not address this issue on appeal and have therefore waived it. The plaintiffs argue only that they were tenants under the KURLTA.

The KURLTA defines a tenant as "a person entitled under a rental agreement to occupy a dwelling unit to the exclusion of others." Ky.Rev.Stat. Ann. § 383.545(15). "'Rental agreement' means all agreements, written or oral, and valid rules and regulations adopted under KRS 383.610 embodying the terms and conditions concerning the use and occupancy of a dwelling unit and premises," *id.* § 383.545(11), and a "dwelling unit" is "a structure or the part of a structure that is used as a home, residence, or sleeping place by one (1) person who maintains a household or by two (2) or more persons who maintain a common household," *id.* § 383.545(3).

Contrary to the plaintiffs' claim, it is not clear whether each plaintiff's "dwelling unit" was Augusta House as a whole or her individual bedroom, but we need not answer that question because the plaintiffs have presented no evidence that they were "entitled under a rental agreement" to occupy Augusta House or their individual bedrooms "to the exclusion of others." They merely argue that each plaintiff had a key to Augusta House and sole possession of her bedroom at the time of eviction. In contrast, the defendants have provided evidence that Mission House had an unrestricted right to house others in Augusta House as well as a right to assign Augusta House residents to different bedrooms and place more than one resident in a bedroom.

We agree with our dissenting colleague and with the court in *Torbeck v. Chamberlain,* 138 Or.App. 446, 910 P.2d 389, 392–93 (Or.Ct.App.1996), that the phrase "to the exclusion of others," does not require that a party be entitled to exclude *all* others, including cotenants, to be protected by the KURLTA. But the dissent, like the plaintiffs, confuses the plaintiffs' good fortune of exclusive possession with a right to exclusive possession. The fact that the plaintiffs had keys to Augusta House does not imply a right to exclusive possession when the landlord had a right to provide keys to whomever else it chose. Along similar lines, the fact that each plaintiff had her own bedroom, which, although its doors could not be locked, the other residents of Augusta House had no right to enter, provides no evidence of a right to exclusive possession.

Here, the plaintiffs have presented evidence only that they had the good fortune of exclusive possession of their bedrooms during their approximate two-month stay at Augusta House. The defendants presented evidence that Mission House could permit others to reside in Augusta House and could move the plaintiffs to different bedrooms or place other residents in their bedrooms at any time, and the plaintiffs present no evidence to dispute that. And, contrary to the dissent's assertion, the record does not reflect that the Mission House staff had only a limited right to enter Augusta House. It merely reflects that the staff did not reside there in furtherance of Mission House's goal of helping the plaintiffs become financially independent members of mainstream society. Therefore, there is no factual dispute that the plaintiffs were not entitled to possess Augusta House or their individual bedrooms "to the exclusion of others," and they failed to qualify as tenants under the KURLTA as a matter of law.

V.

We conclude that the plaintiffs lacked a protected property interest under Kentucky law because their residence at Augusta House constituted residence at an institution, which is not governed by the KURLTA, and, in the alternative, they failed to qualify as tenants under the KURLTA. We AFFIRM the district court's order granting summary judgment in favor of the defendants.

Clay, J., dissenting.

I.

BACKGROUND

Before delving into the legal arguments presented in this appeal, I find it necessary to briefly clarify the nature of the issue before this Court. The question this Court decides today is not, as the majority claims, whether residents of traditional shelters are "tenants" entitled to KURLTA's protections, but rather whether KURLTA permits landlords to deprive residents of low-income housing of statutorily mandated eviction procedures simply by labeling low-income housing a "shelter." Plaintiffs' residency at Augusta House was not transient; they lived at Augusta House for several months pursuant to a rental agreement and Defendant Zinious indicated that she anticipated Plaintiffs would reside at Augusta House for "a couple of years." Additionally, each Plaintiff paid $140 a month in exchange for his or her own room, which no other resident had the right to enter. Finally, no supervisory staff resided at Augusta House. Plaintiffs lived at Augusta House as independent adults.

This distinction is crucial to the instant appeal because residents at typical shelters clearly are not entitled to KURLTA's protections. As will be discussed later, typical shelter residents, unlike Plaintiffs, do not live at shelters pursuant to rental agreements. Defendants attempt to classify Augusta House as a shelter in order to escape compliance with Kentucky's statutory eviction procedures. The majority errs in accepting Defendants' characterization of Augusta House without analysis.

II.

DISCUSSION

Whether Plaintiffs are tenants under KURLTA presents a factual dispute that should not be resolved on summary judgment. As will be more fully explained below, Plaintiffs present sufficient evidence to allow a reasonable jury to conclude that their residency at Augusta House was not incidental to the provision of any services and thus that § 383.535(1) does not exclude Plaintiffs' living arrangement from KURLTA's coverage. Similarly, Plaintiffs present sufficient evidence to allow a reasonable jury to conclude that they were "tenants" as that term is defined by KURLTA. Therefore, the district court erred in granting summary judgment in favor of Defendants.* * *

B. Plaintiffs' Residency at Augusta House is Not Incidental to the Provision of Services

Section 383.535(1) of the Kentucky Revised Code does not exclude Plaintiffs' living arrangements from KURLTA's coverage. Section 383.535 provides that KURLTA shall not extend to "[r]esidence at an institution, public or private, if incidental to detention or the provision of medical, geriatric, educational counseling, religious, or similar services." Ky.Rev.Stat. Ann. §383.535(1). To fall within this exclusion, a residence must meet the following three criteria: (1) the residence must be at an institution; (2) the institution must provide medical, geriatric, educational counseling, religious, or similar services; and (3) the residence must be incidental to the provision of such services. See id. Although Plaintiffs' residency at Augusta House likely satisfies the first two criteria, Plaintiffs' residency is not incidental to the provision of services. Therefore, §383.535(1) does not exclude Plaintiffs from KURLTA's coverage.

Plaintiffs' residency at Augusta House was not "incidental" to any provision of services because Plaintiffs' landlord, Mission House, provided Plaintiffs with housing primarily to ensure that Plaintiffs were provided a place to live and not to further any other service provided by Mission House. As the majority opinion recognizes, no Kentucky court has interpreted the term "incidental" in the context of §383.535(1). At least two other state courts, however, have interpreted identical provisions in their own landlord tenant acts. These courts have recognized that a person's residency is "incidental" to the provision of services when it is "subordinate or attendant to the [relevant] institution['s] purpose." See Sunrise Group Homes, Inc. v. Ferguson, 55 Wash.App. 285, 777

P.2d 553, 555 (Wash.Ct.App.1989); see also Burke Oxford House of Oregon, 196 Or.App. 726, 103 P.3d 1184 (Or.Ct.App.2004) (en banc) (citing *Sunrise*). In this case, Mission House, the relevant institution, identifies its primary goal to be the provision of housing and shelter for the poor. Because one of Mission House's primary goal[s] is to provide housing, the provision of housing is not subordinate or attendant to Mission House's provision of other services. Indeed, it is entirely possible that Mission House's other services are actually attendant to the goal of providing housing.

Even if the so-called transitional living services were not incidental to the housing provided at Augusta House, it does not follow that the housing at Augusta House is incidental to these services. See Gray v. Pierce County Hous. Auth., 123 Wash.App. 744, 97 P.3d 26 (Wash.Ct.App.2004) (holding that a housing authority's provision of housing to individuals with low income, bad credit, criminal history, and/or history of past evictions was not excluded from the protections of Washington's Landlord Tenant Act simply because the housing authority conditioned the residency on life skills classes). The comment to § 1.202 of KURLTA makes clear that § 383.535(1) was intended to exempt housing that facilitates the provision of some primary service. Uniform Residential Landlord Tenant Act, Nat'l Conference of Comm'r on State Laws, available at Rental Housing Online, http://www.rhol.org/rental/KURLTA.htm (last visited March 6, 2006). This is evidenced through the comment's list of housing that is incidental to the provision of services: prisons, nursing homes, hospitals and college dormitories. *Id.* In all of these examples, housing is provided to facilitate services that the relevant institution was created to provide. Prisons provide housing to segregate prisoners from the public at large. Nursing homes and hospitals provide attendant housing so that doctors and nurses are able to continuously care for the sick, elderly, and disabled. Colleges provides dormitories so that students can attend college classes. In contrast, Mission House's provision of residency at Augusta House does not facilitate Mission House's ability to provide any of the so-called "transitional living services." According to the majority these services include, 1) help obtaining food stamps and social security, 2) assistance in finding employment, and 3) Bible study classes. First, food stamps and social security can be obtained in a matter of hours. Plaintiffs' residency at Augusta House, however, was permanent. Thus, it seems clear that Plaintiffs' residency at Augusta House was intended to continue long after Plaintiffs obtained food stamps and social security. If Plaintiffs already had food stamps and social security, their continued residency at Augusta House could not facilitate Mission House's ability to help them obtain food stamps and social security. Similarly, Plaintiffs were required to have employment *prior* to living at Augusta House. Thus again, it would seem that Plaintiffs' residency at Augusta House could not have facilitated Mission House's ability to assist Plaintiffs in obtaining employment. Finally, the Bible study classes were optional. If Plaintiffs were not required to attend these classes, their residency at Augusta House could not be for the purpose of facilitating such attendance. Therefore, it seems fairly clear that Plaintiffs' residency at Augusta House was not intended to facilitate Mission House's provision of transitional services and that Defendants are simply seeking away to avoid following KURLTA's eviction procedures.

The majority erroneously characterizes *Burke* and *Sunrise* as having rejected my position. This is simply not the case. *Burke* and *Sunrise* rejected the position that housing was not incidental to the provision of services simply because housing was a primary service. Here, however, the issue is not simply that housing is a primary service but that housing is the primary goal. Because providing housing is the primary goal, the provision of housing cannot be incidental to any other service. This distinction is important because in some cases, as in *Burke,* housing may be a primary service without being a primary goal. As the *Burke* court explained that while housing was "central" it was nonetheless "incidental" because it existed to facilitate the institution's sole purpose — assisting drug addicts with recovery. In other words, the housing was a means to an end. Here, that is not the case. Housing is not being provided to further any service or goal. In contrast to *Burke,* where the housing facilitated a peer counseling system for recovering drug addicts, or *Sunrise,* where the housing facilitated the defendants' provision of medical services, Plaintiffs' residency at Augusta House did not facilitate the provision of any services. Id. at 1192, 777 P.2d 553; Sunrise, 777 P.2d at 289. This is made clear by the majority's complete inability to point to any specific service that Mission House provided to Plaintiffs' *at the time of their residency at Augusta House,* let alone any service facilitated by the residency.

C. Plaintiffs Are "Tenants" as Defined by KURLTA

Similarly, Plaintiffs provide sufficient evidence to allow a reasonable juror to find that Plaintiffs are tenants within the meaning of KURLTA. KURLTA defines tenant as "a person entitled under a rental agreement to occupy a dwelling unit to the exclusion of others" Ky.Rev.Stat. Ann. § 383.545(15). The record demonstrates that Plaintiffs lived in Augusta House pursuant to a rental agreement, which arguably granted them the right to live in Augusta House to the exclusion of others. Therefore, a jury should be allowed to determine whether Plaintiffs are tenants within the meaning of Kurlta.

1. Rental Agreement

It is fairly obvious that Plaintiffs and Zinious entered into an oral rental agreement, which allowed Plaintiffs to occupy Augusta House. Section 383.545(11) defines rental agreement as "all agreements, written or oral, … embodying the terms and conditions concerning the use and occupancy of a dwelling unit and premises." Ky.Rev.Stat. Ann. § 383.545(11). In this case, Plaintiffs allege that they had an oral agreement with Mission House to use and occupy Augusta House. Plaintiffs support these allegations with evidence, namely, Plaintiffs' residency of Augusta House prior to the eviction and Plaintiffs payment of rent to Mission House. Moreover, Laura Zinious, the manager of Augusta House, admits that she had an oral agreement with Plaintiffs permitting them to use and occupy Augusta House. Therefore, Defendants' assertion that no rental agreement existed is unsupported both by Kentucky law and the record.

Defendants argue that a rental agreement does not exist because Mission House did not believe that it was entering into a rental agreement and Plaintiffs' "unilateral expectation" is insufficient to create a contract or agreement. This argument runs contrary to the facts. Zinious admits that she agreed to allow Plaintiffs' to use and occupy Augusta House. Moreover, whether Zinious considered the agreement to constitute a "rental agreement" misses the point. Whether the operative terms and understandings between the parties to the agreement constituted a rental agreement under the applicable law involves a legal determination. Factually, in the instant case, Zinious admitted the agreement embodied certain terms, which rendered it a rental agreement under Kentucky law.

2. Exclusion of Others

Next, Plaintiffs provide sufficient evidence to allow a reasonable juror to conclude that the rental agreement granted them the right to occupy Augusta House to the exclusion of others. No Kentucky court has defined the phrase "to the exclusion of others" in the context of KURLTA. However, the Oregon Court of Appeals has interpreted "to the exclusion of others" in an identical provision of its landlord tenant act. Torbeck v.

Chamberlain, 138 Or.App. 446, 910 P.2d 389 (Or.Ct.App.1996). The Oregon Court of Appeals held that exclusion of others means the exclusion of the public at large and not the exclusion of other tenants, or in some cases, even the landlord. Several considerations render the Oregon court's interpretation persuasive. First, KURLTA instructs courts to apply its provisions liberally to improve the quality of housing. Ky.Rev.Stat. Ann. § 383.505. Thus, "tenant" should be interpreted broadly to expand KURLTA's coverage, not to exclude living arrangements from KURLTA's protections. Second, the Oregon court's interpretation is in accord with the common law. At common law, a tenancy was defined as the right to occupy a premises to the exclusion of others, including the landlord. Nonetheless, common law courts have recognized exceptions to a tenant's ability to exclude others. For example, in Kentucky, common law courts have upheld the existence of a tenancy despite a landlord's contractual right to enter the premises for limited purposes. Third, tenant is defined as a person with right to exclude others, not necessarily the right to exclude *all* others.

In this case, Plaintiffs have offered evidence that they had the right to exclude the public from Augusta House. Plaintiffs each had keys to the house. Plaintiffs' possession of their own keys to the premises evidence[s] their ability to lock the members of the public out of Augusta House and quintessentially symbolizes their right to exclude others. Additionally, each Plaintiff occupied her own room and had the right to exclude other residents from her space. Finally, the record indicates that Zinious and Mission House staff had only limited rights to enter Augusta House, as opposed to a general occupancy right. That is, they could enter to enforce house rules but did not have a have the right to live at Augusta House. Therefore, whether the rental agreement granted Plaintiffs the right to occupy Augusta House to the exclusion of others is an issue for the jury.

In summary, Plaintiffs have offered sufficient evidence to allow a reasonable juror to find both that § 383.535(1) does not render KURLTA inapplicable to Plaintiffs' residency at Augusta House and that Plaintiffs are tenants within the meaning of KURLTA. Thus, summary judgment in Defendants' favor was not proper.

Burke v. Oxford House

341 Ore. 82, 137 P.3d 1278 (Supreme Court of Oregon 2006)

Edward Johnson, Oregon Law Center, Portland, argued the cause for petitioner on review. With him on the briefs were Mark G. Passannante, of Broer & Passannante, and Maureen Leonard.

Craig Colby, Portland, argued the cause for respondents on review. With him on the brief was Frank Wall.

Kathleen L. Wilde and James A. Wrigley, Oregon Advocacy Center, Portland, filed a brief on behalf of amici curiae Fair Housing Council of Oregon and Oregon Advocacy Center. Adam Scott Arms, McKanna, Bishop, Joffe & Sullivan, LLP, Portland, filed a brief on behalf of amici curiae Community Alliance of Tenants and JOIN.

Before Carson, Chief Justice,** and Gillette, Durham, Riggs, de Muniz,*** Balmer, and Kistler, Justices.

** Chief Justice when case was argued.
*** Chief Justice when decision was rendered.

Carson, J.

This case requires us to decide whether defendants were subject to the requirements of the Residential Landlord and Tenant Act (RLTA), ORS chapter 90. Plaintiff brought an action against defendants, Oxford House, Inc.; Oxford House of Oregon, Chapter V; and Oxford House-Ramona, because they evicted her from her residence without following the requirements of the RLTA. Defendants moved for summary judgment, claiming, among other things, that the nature of their relationship with plaintiff exempted them from the RLTA. The trial court, in denying defendants' motion for summary judgment, rejected that argument and granted plaintiff's cross-motion for summary judgment, concluding that the RLTA applied to defendants' arrangement with plaintiff. Defendants appealed, and the Court of Appeals reversed the judgment of the trial court, concluding that defendants' arrangement with plaintiff fit within two separate exemptions from the RLTA's requirements. We reverse the decision of the Court of Appeals and affirm the judgment of the trial court.

The following facts are undisputed. Defendant Oxford House, Inc., is a nonprofit corporation established "to allow recovering alcoholics and drug addicts to support each other on the road to independent living." To further that mission, Oxford House, Inc., grants charters to Oxford House chapters, and those chapters establish and maintain individual Oxford House residences. Those residences are unsupervised, and Oxford House provides no professional services to members living at its residences. The essential purpose of the Oxford House structure is to allow recovering alcoholics and drug addicts to live together in a common drug-and-alcohol-free residence. Oxford House, Inc., also provides support services to assist Oxford House chapters and individual Oxford Houses in establishing common residences for Oxford House members. Oxford House, Inc., requires, as a condition of being granted a charter and of maintaining that charter, that each Oxford House chapter, and the houses run by that chapter, comply with three rules: (1) each Oxford House must be run democratically, with most decisions made by a majority vote of members living in the house; (2) each Oxford House must be financially self-supporting; and (3) any member who relapses and begins using drugs or alcohol must be expelled from the house immediately.[1]

---

1. According to Oxford House rules, a member also can be expelled immediately, by a majority vote of house members, for engaging in disruptive behavior, stealing, or not paying rent. Conversely, the Residential Landlord and Tenant Act (RLTA) requires a landlord to give a tenant a minimum of 24 hours' notice before terminating a tenancy. Of particular interest here, former ORS 90.400(9) (1999), *renumbered as* 90.398 (2005), allows for speedy, although not immediate, termination of a tenancy for drug and alcohol free housing. That statute provides:

> If a tenant living for less than two years in drug and alcohol free housing uses, possesses or shares alcohol, illegal drugs, controlled substances or prescription drugs without a medical prescription, the landlord may deliver a written notice to the tenant terminating the tenancy for cause as provided in this subsection. The notice shall specify the acts constituting the drug or alcohol violation and shall state that the rental agreement will terminate in not less than 48 hours after delivery of the notice, at a specified date and time. The notice shall also state that the tenant can cure the drug or alcohol violation by a change in conduct or otherwise within 24 hours after delivery of the notice. If the tenant cures the violation within the 24-hour period, the rental agreement shall not terminate. If the tenant does not cure the violation within the 24-hour period, the rental agreement shall terminate as provided in the notice. If substantially the same act that constituted a prior drug or alcohol violation of which notice was given reoccurs within six months, the landlord may terminate the rental agreement upon at least 24 hours' written notice specifying the violation and the date and time of termination of the rental agreement. The tenant

Defendant Oxford House of Oregon, Chapter V (Oxford House Chapter V) is an unincorporated association of recovering alcoholics and drug addicts. Oxford House, Inc., has granted a charter to Oxford House Chapter V and has authorized Oxford House Chapter V to establish and maintain individual Oxford House residences.

Defendant Oxford House-Ramona is an individual Oxford House residence, established under the Oxford House Chapter V charter. Oxford House-Ramona provides housing for three to six recovering alcoholics or drug addicts in a single house leased in the name of Oxford House Chapter V. Oxford House members living in Oxford House-Ramona are assigned their own bedrooms but share all other living spaces in the house. Members pay a monthly membership fee, the majority of which goes toward paying the rent for the house. The monthly fee also covers shared expenses such as electricity and cable television, and part of the fee is sent to Oxford House, Inc., as a "contribution."

Plaintiff lived at Oxford House-Ramona. In February 2001, following a dispute with a fellow member, a majority of the members of Oxford House-Ramona found that plaintiff had violated a rule prohibiting disruptive behavior. Consequently, they evicted plaintiff from Oxford House-Ramona and gave her 15 minutes' notice to remove her belongings. Plaintiff was unable to remove all her belongings, and other Oxford House members moved the remaining belongings to the garage. Some of plaintiff's belongings were lost or stolen before she could retrieve them. Plaintiff sued defendants, seeking a declaratory judgment that defendants were subject to the requirements of the RLTA and seeking damages for her lost property and statutory damages[2] for what she asserted was an unlawful eviction. * * *

[T]he sole issue before this court is whether defendants were subject to the requirements of the RLTA. Fortunately, that issue is more interesting than it is difficult. For the reasons that follow, we conclude that the RLTA applied to the relationship between plaintiff and defendants.

The RLTA "applies to, regulates and determines rights, obligations and remedies under a rental agreement, wherever made, for a dwelling unit located within this state." ORS 90.115. However, ORS 90.110 lists various residential arrangements that are exempt from the RLTA's requirements. That statute provides, in part:

Unless created to avoid the application of [the RLTA], the following arrangements are not governed by [the RLTA]:

(1) Residence at an institution, public or private, if incidental to detention or the provision of medical, geriatric, educational, counseling, religious or similar service, but not including residence in off-campus nondormitory housing. * * *

(3) Occupancy by a member of a fraternal or social organization in the portion of a structure operated for the benefit of the organization.

shall not have a right to cure this subsequent violation.
Former ORS 90.400(9) (1999).

2. For example, ORS 90.375 allows a tenant to recover "up to two months' periodic rent or twice the actual damages sustained by the tenant * * *" for an unlawful eviction. Former ORS 90.425(16)(a) (1999), *renumbered as* ORS 90.425(a) (2005), allows a tenant to recover "up to twice the actual damages sustained by the tenant * * *" if the landlord fails to follow certain procedures when dealing with tenant property. Under ORS 90.245 a tenant may "recover in addition to the actual damages of the tenant an amount up to three months' periodic rent[ ]" if the landlord attempts to enforce certain, prohibited, rental agreement provisions.

Although not exempt from the requirements of the RLTA, drug-and-alcohol-free housing facilities enjoy expedited eviction procedures under certain circumstances. See former ORS 90.400(9) (1999), renumbered as ORS 90.398 (2005) (providing for termination of tenancy on 48 hours' notice if tenant uses drugs or alcohol while living in drug-and-alcohol-free housing). To qualify for those expedited eviction procedures, the drug-and-alcohol-free housing providers must meet the following requirements, among others:

(a) Each of the dwelling units on the premises is occupied or held for occupancy by at least one tenant who is a recovering alcoholic or drug addict and is participating in a program of recovery;

(b) The landlord is a nonprofit corporation * * * or a housing authority * * *;

(c) The landlord provides:

(A) A drug and alcohol free environment, covering all tenants, employees, staff, agents of the landlord and guests;

(B) An employee who monitors the tenants for compliance with the requirements of paragraph (d) of this subsection;

(C) Individual and group support for recovery; and

(D) Access to a specified program of recovery; and

(d) The rental agreement is in writing and includes the following provisions:

(A) That the tenant shall not use, possess or share alcohol, illegal drugs, controlled substances or prescription drugs without a medical prescription, either on or off the premises;

* * *

(C) That the tenant shall participate in a program of recovery, which specific program is described in the rental agreement;

* * *

(F) That the landlord has the right to terminate the tenant's tenancy in the drug and alcohol free housing for noncompliance with the requirements of this paragraph, pursuant to ORS 90.400(1) and (9) or 90.630.

ORS 90.243(1) (1999), amended by Or Laws 2003, ch 378, § 10.

The Court of Appeals held that defendants' arrangement with plaintiff fit into two of the exempt arrangements listed in ORS 90.110. We need not consider the correctness of that interpretation, however, because we conclude that the introductory phrase of ORS 90.110 precludes defendants from qualifying for any of the exemptions listed in ORS 90.110.

The record in this case includes a memorandum from Oxford House, Inc., that explains Oxford House operating procedures to "new [Oxford House] groups, landlords, rental agents[,] and local officials * * *." That memorandum is entitled "OXFORD HOUSE: The Legal and Policy Reasons Underlying Oxford House Group Leas[es]." A subsection of that memorandum, entitled "Who Signs the Lease," provides:

The signatory of the lease is the individual Oxford House; for example, Oxford House-Main Street. *The effect of this commitment by the group to the landlord is important because of the nature of Oxford House and the application of local landlord-tenant laws.*

Oxford House works because an individual resident who returns to using alcohol or drugs—in or outside of the house—must be immediately expelled from the house. *If the individual is a signatory to the lease the immediate eviction becomes difficult, if not impossible, because of local landlord-tenant rights.* In many jurisdictions it takes up to ninety days to evict a tenant even for non-payment of rent. *Since no individual is a signatory to a Oxford House lease, the relapsing individual who is being evicted has no legal rights to delay his or her departure.* There is no way to accomplish this result without the signature on the lease being in the name of the particular Oxford House group.

(Emphasis added.) Defendants followed the procedures explained in that memorandum when establishing the lease agreement here. Specifically, the lease for Oxford House-Ramona was signed in the name of Oxford House Chapter V.

The introductory phrase of ORS 90.110 states that various listed arrangements are exempt from the application of the RLTA "[u]nless created to avoid the application of [the RLTA] * * *." The term "arrangements" includes not only the type of rental arrangement but also the procedures by which the parties have structured the rental arrangement. See ORS 90.110(2) (exempting from coverage of RLTA occupancy by purchaser of a dwelling prior to closing or by seller following closing if the occupancy is "permitted under the terms of an agreement for sale of [the] dwelling * * *.") The Oxford House memorandum clearly illustrates that defendants structure their lease arrangements to avoid application of the landlord-tenant laws. They readily proclaim that that is the purpose of their group lease requirement. Therefore, defendants may not avail themselves of any of the exemptions listed in ORS 90.110, and defendants were subject to the requirements of the RLTA. Consequently, plaintiff was entitled to summary judgment because defendants did not comply with the requirements of the RLTA when evicting her.

The decision of the Court of Appeals is reversed. The judgment of the circuit court is affirmed.

AIMCO Properties, LLC v. Dziewisz

152 N.H. 587, 883 A.2d 310 (Supreme Court of New Hampshire 2005)

Gormley & Gormley, P.C., of Nashua (Arthur O. Gormley, III on the brief and orally), for the plaintiff.

Kasha Dziewisz, by brief, pro se.

New Hampshire Legal Assistance, of Manchester (Elliott Berry on the brief and orally), for The Way Home, as amicus curiae.

Dalianis, J. Broderick, C.J., and Duggan and Galway, JJ., concurred. Nadeu, J. concurred specially.

Dalianis, J.

The parties entered into a lease beginning on September 1, 2003, and ending on August 31, 2004. On July 12, 2004, the plaintiff sent the defendant a letter stating, in pertinent part:

Dear Ms. Dziewisz,

Please be advised your current apartment lease expires on August 31, 2004. You are hereby notified that Royal Crest Estates-Nashua does not intend to renew you [*sic*] lease. Therefore, you must vacate your apartment by Tuesday August 31, 2004.

After the defendant failed to vacate the apartment, the plaintiff filed suit seeking a writ of possession. The defendant [moved] to dismiss, arguing that the plaintiff failed to allege good cause for the eviction in the notice to quit. [T]he district court denied these motions and granted the plaintiff's request for a writ of possession.

The defendant argues that the plaintiff's "failure to state one of the statutory reasons for eviction or state good cause in the Letter of Non-Renewal" does not comply with the requirement of RSA 540:2, II (1997) that a landlord of restricted property have good cause for an eviction. RSA 540:3, III (1997) requires that the notice to quit state the reason for eviction. She contends that the expiration of the lease, in and of itself, does not constitute good cause.

RSA 540:2, II provides:

> The lessor or owner of restricted property may terminate any tenancy by giving to the tenant or occupant a notice in writing to quit the premises in accordance with RSA 540:3 and 5, but only for one of the following reasons:
>
> (a) Neglect or refusal to pay rent due and in arrears, upon demand.
>
> (b) Substantial damage to the premises by the tenant, members of his household, or guests.
>
> (c) Failure of the tenant to comply with a material term of the lease.
>
> (d) Behavior of the tenant or members of his family which adversely affects the health or safety of the other tenants or the landlord or his representatives, or failure of the tenant to accept suitable temporary relocation due to lead-based paint hazard abatement, as set forth in RSA 130-A:8-a, I.
>
> (e) Other good cause.
>
> (f) The dwelling unit contains a lead exposure-hazard which the owner will abate by:
>
>   (1) Methods other than interim controls or encapsulation;
>
>   (2) Any other method which can reasonably be expected to take more than 30 days to perform; or
>
>   (3) Removing the dwelling unit from the residential rental market.

RSA 540:2, II states that it applies to "any tenancy." The plain meaning of any is "every" or "all." Webster's Third New International Dictionary 97 (2d unabridged ed. 2002). Prior to the expiration of the lease, the defendant had a leasehold tenancy. On August 31, 2004, the defendant's lease expired; when the lease expired and the defendant did not vacate the apartment, she became a tenant at sufferance. Thus, at all times relevant to these proceedings, the plaintiff and defendant had a landlord-tenant relationship. Regardless of whether the defendant had the status of a leasehold tenant or the status of a tenant at sufferance, the plaintiff needed good cause to terminate the defendant's tenancy.

RSA 540:3, III requires that the "notice to quit shall state with specificity the reason for the eviction." Assuming, without deciding, that the plaintiff's letter of non-renewal constituted a notice to quit, the only reason that the plaintiff provided in its letter of non-renewal was the expiration of the lease. Thus, we must determine whether the expiration of a lease, alone, constitutes good cause for an eviction as required by RSA 540:2, II.

RSA 540:2, II does not provide that the expiration of a lease constitutes good cause. It does, however, contain a section describing "other good cause." RSA 540:2, II(e). The question we must answer is whether the expiration of a lease constitutes "other good cause."

RSA 540:2, V provides that other good cause "includes, but is not limited to, any legitimate business or economic reasons and need not be based on the action or inaction of the tenant, members of his family, or guests." Whether the expiration of a lease constitutes "other good cause" cannot be determined by merely looking to the plain language of RSA 540:2, II. The term "other good cause" is ambiguous. When [a] statute is ambiguous we consider legislative history to aid our analysis. Our goal is to apply statutes in light of the legislature's intent in enacting them, and in light of the policy sought to be advanced by the entire statutory scheme.

RSA 540:2, II was adopted in 1985 as part of House Bill 95, which was enacted to "limit[ ] the grounds for eviction of tenants from restricted property." It was described as "giv[ing] ... greater flexibility to landlords to evict tenants for any good reason and at the same time protect[ing] tenants from arbitrarily and/or ill motivated evictions." N.H.S. Jour. 157 (1985). Interpreting the term "other good cause" as including the mere expiration of a lease would run contrary to this legislative intent, as it would allow landlords to arbitrarily evict tenants whose leases have expired, thereby denying tenants the precise protection that RSA 540:2, II was designed to provide.

Nor would it advance the purpose of the statute to conclude that the mere expiration of a lease constitutes a legitimate business or economic reason. RSA 540:2, II only applies to landlords who rent restricted property: landlords who are generally in the business of renting residential property, and whose main concern is, presumably, profit. It does not apply to: property rented for nonresidential purposes, single-family houses if the owner of such a house does not own more than three single-family houses at one time, rental units in an owner-occupied building containing a total of four units or fewer, rental units in a vacation or recreational dwelling rented during the off-season for certain purposes, or single-family houses acquired by banks or other mortgagees through foreclosure. Replacing one tenant upon the expiration of a lease with another tenant who will pay the same rent and occupy the same position as the tenant being evicted does not, in and of itself, provide the landlord of restricted property with any economic or business advantage.

During the [S]enate debates in 1985, it was stated by the sponsor of the bill that:

> Under current law if a tenant does not have a lease, as i[s] the case with most low and moderate income tenants, he or she can be evicted without any reason whatsoever. All the landlord has to do is give the tenant a notice directing the tenant to leave in 30 days. Under HB 95, almost all landlords will be required to establish justifiable cause for eviction.

N.H.S. Jour. 1040 (1985). Were we to hold that a landlord may evict a tenant for good cause merely because a lease has expired we would eviscerate the protections that RSA 540:2, II was designed to afford; a landlord could easily avoid the requirements of RSA 540:2, II, by simply requiring tenants to sign renewable month-long leases, allowing the landlord to evict any tenant arbitrarily upon the expiration of any month's lease. A landlord would thus be able to evict tenants in the exact manner that RSA 540:2, II was designed to prohibit.

Were the mere expiration of a lease to constitute good cause, then tenants could be evicted arbitrarily from their homes through no fault of their own; such evictions, as the legislature undoubtedly realized, create substantial hardships for tenants. At worst, tenants may become homeless as a result. Even when another residence is procured, the tenant must bear the expenses and inconveniences of moving. Relationships with friends and neighbors may be disrupted, children may be forced into new school districts, and local services and support systems for elderly and disabled tenants may be lost. Such a result would be contrary to what the legislature intended.

Furthermore, were the mere expiration of the lease to constitute good cause for eviction, it could enable landlords to evict when the true reason for eviction is ill-motivated. RSA 540:2, II was enacted to prevent landlords from evicting tenants for ill-motivated reasons. If the mere expiration of the lease were to constitute good cause, a landlord who did not wish to continue renting to a tenant for any reason—for example, because the tenant became disabled during the course of the tenancy—could evict the tenant at the end of the lease without disclosing the true reason for eviction. This would be contrary to what the legislature intended.

Our holding does not restrict a landlord's ability to lease or rent to whomever the landlord chooses, within the limits imposed by other laws. The legislature only sought to establish *limited* protections for tenants who had *already* established a tenancy, as demonstrated by this exchange on the senate floor during the debate on whether to adopt the changes to RSA chapter 540:

> Senator Stephen: Isn't [*sic*] the owner or realtor, in the past, always had his choice of who to rent to. Would he still have that?
>
> Senator Boyer: Yes, he would have that. That is when the decision ought to be made whether they [*sic*] want a tenant or not.
>
> Senator Stephen: Does that give the tenant the right to stay on the premise [*sic*] forever?
>
> Senator Boyer: No.

N.H.S Jour. 1042–43 (1985). The time for a landlord to determine whether to rent to a tenant is not after the tenant has established a residence, but at the beginning of the landlord-tenant relationship. A landlord, of course, is not forced into a perpetual landlord-tenant relationship, and may terminate the tenancy for good cause as laid out in RSA 540:2, II.

The plaintiff set forth no good cause in its "notice to quit" for its desire to evict the defendant; we must, therefore, reverse the district court's denial of the second motion to dismiss.

Reversed.

Broderick, C.J., and Duggan and Galway, JJ., concurred; Nadeau, J., concurred specially.

Nadeau, J., concurring specially.

I concur in the judgment reversing the trial court's decision because the landlord *concedes* that the trial court *erred* when it ruled that the landlord did not have to serve a notice to quit upon the tenant, Kasha Dziewisz....

In light of the landlord's concession, I would not reach the issue of whether, consistent with RSA 540:2, II (1997), the trial court could have awarded the landlord possession of the premises based upon its notice of intent not to renew the lease. Additionally, unlike the majority, I would hold that, in this case, the landlord's notice met the requirements of RSA 540:2, II. Therefore, I concur only in the judgment

RSA 540:2, II provides, in pertinent part, that the "lessor or owner of restricted property may terminate any tenancy by giving to the tenant ... a notice in writing to quit the premises in accordance with RSA 540:3 and 5, but only for one of the following reasons." One of the reasons provided is "[o]ther good cause." RSA 540:2, II(e). Other good cause "includes, but is not limited to, any legitimate business or economic reason." RSA 540:2, V (1997).

The majority asserts that the mere expiration of the lease is not good cause. I disagree. I believe that the statutory language defining "[o]ther good cause" is broad enough to include terminating a tenancy at the expiration of the term of a written lease. The expiration of the term of a written lease, in my view, may, under appropriate circumstances, constitute a "legitimate business or economic reason" for terminating a tenancy. As we have no transcript of the trial court proceedings, I believe the majority is mistaken when it assumes that the landlord here could not prove *any* set of circumstances under which the expiration of the tenant's lease could be a "legitimate business or economic reason" for terminating her tenancy.

The majority contends that, under its interpretation of RSA 540:2, II, a landlord "is not forced into a perpetual landlord-tenant relationship." To the contrary, under the majority's interpretation, a landlord with a lease of a specified term is obliged to continue the tenancy absent some other "good cause." See Franklin Tower One, L.L.C. v. N.M., 157 N.J. 602, 725 A.2d 1104, 1110 (1999). Under the majority's interpretation, lease provisions purporting to limit the lease to a specified duration have no meaning. The effect of the majority's interpretation "is to create a perpetual tenancy, virtually a life interest, in favor of a tenant of [restricted property] covered by [the statute]." J.M.J. Properties v. Khuzam, 365 N.J.Super. 325, 839 A.2d 102, 106 (2004) (quotations omitted). I do not believe that was the intent of RSA 540:2.

Although the *amicus curiae* relies upon precedent developed in the context of federally subsidized housing, I believe that its reliance is misplaced. We are not bound by cases interpreting the good cause requirements imposed upon owners of federally subsidized rental housing when interpreting RSA 540:2. Moreover, although the tenant argues that she receives assistance from the federal Section 8 housing program, she has failed to demonstrate that she preserved this claim for review on appeal. Thus, we treat this claim as waived on appeal.

U.S. v. Rucker
535 U.S. 125 (2002)

James A. Feldman, Washington, DC, and Gary T. LaFayette, San Francisco, CA, for petitioners.*

Paul A. Renne, San Francisco, CA, for respondents.**

---

* Briefs amici curiae for Petitioners were filed by the Center for the Community Interest, the International City-County Management Association, National Association of Counties, National Governors Association, National League of Cities, U.S. Conference of Mayors, Washington Legal Foundation, and Allied Educational Foundation.

** Briefs amici curiae for Respondents were filed by Lawrence Lessig, John J. Donohue, James Gordley, Gary Blasi, June Carbone, Jo Carrillo, Mary Jane Foran, and Cathy Mosbrucker, National Network to End Domestic Violence, Coalition to Protect Public Housing, United Community Housing Coalition, Public Housing Resident Network, Community Alliance of Tenants, NOW Legal Defense and Education Fund, American Civil Liberties Union, Pennsylvania Association of Resident Councils, Resident Advisory Board to the Allegheny County Housing Authority, Erie Tenants Council, and Hazelton Alliance of Resident Councils, AARP, ENPHRONT, Island Tenants on the Rise, Massachusetts Union of Public Housing Tenants, Carmelitos Tenants Association, & Public Housing Resident Council.

Before Chief Justice Rehnquist and Justices Stevens, O'Connor, Scalia, Kennedy, Souter, Thomas, Ginsberg, and Breyer.

Rehnquist, C. J., delivered the opinion of the Court, in which all other Members joined, except Breyer, J., who took no part in the consideration or decision of the cases.***

With drug dealers "increasingly imposing a reign of terror on public and other federally assisted low-income housing tenants," Congress passed the Anti-Drug Abuse Act of 1988. §5122, 102 Stat. 4301, 42 U.S.C. §11901(3) (1994 ed.). The Act, as later amended, provides that each "public housing agency shall utilize leases which … provide that any criminal activity that threatens the health, safety, or right to peaceful enjoyment of the premises by other tenants or any drug-related criminal activity on or off such premises, engaged in by a public housing tenant, any member of the tenant's household, or any guest or other person under the tenant's control, shall be cause for termination of tenancy." Petitioners say that this statute requires lease terms that allow a local public housing authority to evict a tenant when a member of the tenant's household or a guest engages in drug-related criminal activity, regardless of whether the tenant knew, or had reason to know, of that activity. Respondents say it does not. We agree with petitioners.

Respondents are four public housing tenants of the Oakland Housing Authority (OHA). Paragraph 9(m) of respondents' leases, tracking the language of §1437d(l)(6), obligates the tenants to "assure that the tenant, any member of the household, a guest, or another person under the tenant's control, shall not engage in … any drug-related criminal activity on or near the premises." Respondents also signed an agreement stating that the tenant "understands that if I or any member of my household or guests should violate this lease provision, my tenancy may be terminated and I may be evicted."

In late 1997 and early 1998, OHA instituted eviction proceedings in state court against respondents, alleging violations of this lease provision. The complaint alleged: (1) that the respective grandsons of respondents William Lee and Barbara Hill, both of whom were listed as residents on the leases, were caught in the apartment complex parking lot smoking marijuana; (2) that the daughter of respondent Pearlie Rucker, who resides with her and is listed on the lease as a resident, was found with cocaine and a crack cocaine pipe three blocks from Rucker's apartment;[1] and (3) that on three instances within a 2-month period, respondent Herman Walker's caregiver and two others were found with cocaine in Walker's apartment. OHA had issued Walker notices of a lease violation on the first two occasions, before initiating the eviction action after the third violation.

United States Department of Housing and Urban Development (HUD) regulations administering §1437d(l)(6) require lease terms authorizing evictions in these circumstances. The HUD regulations closely track the statutory language,[2] and provide that "in

---

*** Editor's Note: Justice Breyer's brother, the Honorable Charles R. Breyer, was the U.S. District Judge who issued a preliminary injuction against some of the challenged evictions. Rucker v. Davis, 1998 U.S. Dist. LEXIS 9345.

1. In February 1998, OHA dismissed the unlawful detainer action against Rucker, after her daughter was incarcerated, and thus no longer posed a threat to other tenants.

2. The regulations require public housing authorities (PHAs) to impose a lease obligation on tenants:

To assure that the tenant, any member of the household, a guest, or another person under the tenant's control, shall not engage in:

(A) Any criminal activity that threatens the health, safety, or right to peaceful enjoyment of the PHA's public housing premises by other residents or employees of the PHA, or

(B) Any drug-related criminal activity on or near such premises.

deciding to evict for criminal activity, the [public housing authority] shall have discretion to consider all of the circumstances of the case...." 24 CFR § 966.4(l)(5)(i) (2001). The agency made clear that local public housing authorities' discretion to evict for drug-related activity includes those situations in which "[the] tenant did not know, could not foresee, or could not control behavior by other occupants of the unit." 56 Fed. Reg. 51560, 51567 (1991).

After OHA initiated the eviction proceedings in state court, respondents commenced actions against HUD, OHA, and OHA's director in United States District Court. They challenged HUD's interpretation of the statute under the Administrative Procedure Act, 5 U.S.C. § 706(2)(A), arguing that 42 U.S.C. § 1437d(l)(6) does not require lease terms authorizing the eviction of so-called "innocent" tenants, and, in the alternative, that if it does, then the statute is unconstitutional.[3] The District Court issued a preliminary injunction, enjoining OHA from "terminating the leases of tenants pursuant to paragraph 9(m) of the 'Tenant Lease' for drug-related criminal activity that does not occur within the tenant's apartment unit when the tenant did not know of and had no reason to know of, the drug-related criminal activity."

A panel of the Court of Appeals reversed, holding that § 1437d(l)(6) unambiguously permits the eviction of tenants who violate the lease provision, regardless of whether the tenant was personally aware of the drug activity, and that the statute is constitutional. An en banc panel of the Court of Appeals reversed and affirmed the District Court's grant of the preliminary injunction. That court held that HUD's interpretation permitting the eviction of so-called "innocent" tenants "is inconsistent with Congressional intent and must be rejected" under the first step of Chevron U.S.A. Inc. v. Natural Resources Defense Council, Inc., 467 U.S. 837, 842–843 (1984).

We granted certiorari, and now reverse, holding that 42 U.S.C. § 1437d(l)(6) unambiguously requires lease terms that vest local public housing authorities with the discretion to evict tenants for the drug-related activity of household members and guests whether or not the tenant knew, or should have known, about the activity.

That this is so seems evident from the plain language of the statute. It provides that "each public housing authority shall utilize leases which ... provide that ... any drug-related criminal activity on or off such premises, engaged in by a public housing tenant, any member of the tenant's household, or any guest or other person under the tenant's control, shall be cause for termination of tenancy." The en banc Court of Appeals thought the statute did not address "the level of personal knowledge or fault that is required for eviction." Yet Congress' decision not to impose any qualification in the statute, combined with its use of the term "any" to modify "drug-related criminal activity," precludes any knowledge requirement. As we have explained, "the word 'any' has an expansive meaning, that is, 'one or some indiscriminately of whatever kind.'" United States v. Gonzales, 520 U.S. 1, 5 (1997). Thus, *any* drug-related activity engaged in by the specified persons is grounds for termination, not just drug-related activity that the tenant knew, or should have known, about.

The en banc Court of Appeals also thought it possible that "under the tenant's control" modifies not just "other person," but also "member of the tenant's household" and

---

Any criminal activity in violation of the preceding sentence shall be cause for termination of tenancy, and for eviction from the unit. 24 CFR § 966.4(f)(12)(i) (2001).

3. Respondents Rucker and Walker also raised Americans with Disabilities Act claims that are not before this Court. And all of the respondents raised state-law claims against OHA that are not before this Court.

"guest." The court ultimately adopted this reading, concluding that the statute prohibits eviction where the tenant "for a lack of knowledge or other reason, could not realistically exercise control over the conduct of a household member or guest." But this interpretation runs counter to basic rules of grammar. The disjunctive "or" means that the qualification applies only to "other person." Indeed, the view that "under the tenant's control" modifies everything coming before it in the sentence would result in the nonsensical reading that the statute applies to "a public housing tenant … under the tenant's control." HUD offers a convincing explanation for the grammatical imperative that "under the tenant's control" modifies only "other person": "by 'control,' the statute means control in the sense that the tenant has permitted access to the premises." 66 Fed. Reg. 28781 (2001). Implicit in the terms "household member" or "guest" is that access to the premises has been granted by the tenant. Thus, the plain language of § 1437d(l)(6) requires leases that grant public housing authorities the discretion to terminate tenancy without regard to the tenant's knowledge of the drug-related criminal activity.

Comparing § 1437d(l)(6) to a related statutory provision reinforces the unambiguous text. The civil forfeiture statute that makes all leasehold interests subject to forfeiture when used to commit drug-related criminal activities expressly exempts tenants who had no knowledge of the activity: "[N]o property shall be forfeited under this paragraph … by reason of any act or omission established by that owner to have been committed or omitted without the knowledge or consent of the owner." 21 U.S.C. § 881(a)(7) (1994 ed.). Because this forfeiture provision was amended in the same Anti-Drug Abuse Act of 1988 that created 42 U.S.C. § 1437d(l)(6), the en banc Court of Appeals thought Congress "meant them to be read consistently" so that the knowledge requirement should be read into the eviction provision. But the two sections deal with distinctly different matters. The "innocent owner" defense for drug forfeiture cases was already in existence prior to 1988 as part of 21 U.S.C. § 881(a)(7). All that Congress did in the 1988 Act was to add leasehold interests to the property interests that might be forfeited under the drug statute. And if such a forfeiture action were to be brought against a leasehold interest, it would be subject to the pre-existing "innocent owner" defense. But 42 U.S.C. § 1437(d)(l)(6), with which we deal here, is a quite different measure. It is entirely reasonable to think that the Government, when seeking to transfer private property to itself in a forfeiture proceeding, should be subject to an "innocent owner defense," while it should not be when acting as a landlord in a public housing project. The forfeiture provision shows that Congress knew exactly how to provide an "innocent owner" defense. It did not provide one in § 1437d(l)(6).

The en banc Court of Appeals next resorted to legislative history. The Court of Appeals correctly recognized that reference to legislative history is inappropriate when the text of the statute is unambiguous. Given that the en banc Court of Appeals' finding of textual ambiguity is wrong, there is no need to consult legislative history.[4]

---

4. Even if it were appropriate to look at legislative history, it would not help respondents. The en banc Court of Appeals relied on two passages from a 1990 Senate Report on a proposed amendment to the eviction provision. But this Report was commenting on language from a Senate version of the 1990 amendment, which was never enacted. The language in the Senate version, which would have imposed a different standard of cause for eviction for drug-related crimes than the unqualified language of § 1437d(l)(6), was rejected at Conference. And, as the dissent from the en banc decision below explained, the passages may plausibly be read as a mere suggestion about how local public housing authorities should exercise the "*wide* discretion to evict tenants connected with drug-related criminal behavior" that the lease provision affords them. 237 F.3d at 1134 (Sneed, J., dissenting).

Respondents also cite language from a House Report commenting on the Civil Asset Forfeiture

Nor was the en banc Court of Appeals correct in concluding that this plain reading of the statute leads to absurd results.[5] The statute does not *require* the eviction of any tenant who violated the lease provision. Instead, it entrusts that decision to the local public housing authorities, who are in the best position to take account of, among other things, the degree to which the housing project suffers from "rampant drug-related or violent crime," "the seriousness of the offending action," and "the extent to which the leaseholder has … taken all reasonable steps to prevent or mitigate the offending action." It is not "absurd" that a local housing authority may sometimes evict a tenant who had no knowledge of the drug-related activity. Such "no-fault" eviction is a common "incident of tenant responsibility under normal landlord-tenant law and practice." 56 Fed. Reg., at 51567. Strict liability maximizes deterrence and eases enforcement difficulties.

And, of course, there is an obvious reason why Congress would have permitted local public housing authorities to conduct no-fault evictions: Regardless of knowledge, a tenant who "cannot control drug crime, or other criminal activities by a household member which threaten health or safety of other residents, is a threat to other residents and the project." 56 Fed. Reg., at 51567. With drugs leading to "murders, muggings, and other forms of violence against tenants," and to the "deterioration of the physical environment that requires substantial governmental expenditures," 42 U.S.C. § 11901(4) (1994 ed., Supp. V), it was reasonable for Congress to permit no-fault evictions in order to "provide public and other federally assisted low-income housing that is decent, safe, and free from illegal drugs."

In another effort to avoid the plain meaning of the statute, the en banc Court of Appeals invoked the canon of constitutional avoidance. But that canon "has no application in the absence of statutory ambiguity." "Any other conclusion, while purporting to be an exercise in judicial restraint, would trench upon the legislative powers vested in Congress by Art. I, § 1, of the Constitution." There are, moreover, no "serious constitutional doubts" about Congress' affording local public housing authorities the discretion to conduct no-fault evictions for drug-related crime.

The en banc Court of Appeals held that HUD's interpretation "raises serious questions under the Due Process Clause of the Fourteenth Amendment," because it permits "tenants to be deprived of their property interest without any relationship to individual wrongdoing." 237 F.3d, at 1124–1125 (citing Scales v. United States, 367 U.S. 203, 224-25 (1961); Southwestern Telegraph & Telephone Co. v. Danaher, 238 U.S. 482 (1915)). But both of these cases deal with the acts of government as sovereign. In Scales, the United States criminally charged the defendant with knowing membership in an organization that advocated the overthrow of the United States Government. In Danaher, an Arkansas statute forbade discrimination among customers of a telephone company. The

---

Reform Act of 2000. For the reasons discussed supra, legislative history concerning forfeiture provisions is not probative on the interpretation of § 1437d(1)(6).

A 1996 amendment to § 1437d(l)(6), enacted five years after HUD issued its interpretation of the statute, supports our holding. The 1996 amendment expanded the reach of § 1437d(l)(6), changing the language of the lease provision from applying to activity taking place "on or near" the public housing premises, to activity occurring "on or off" the public housing premises. See Housing Opportunity Program Extension Act of 1996, § 9(a)(2), 110 Stat. 836. But Congress, "presumed to be aware" of HUD's interpretation rejecting a knowledge requirement, made no other change to the statute.

5. For the reasons discussed above, no-fault eviction, which is specifically authorized under § 1437d(l)(6), does not violate § 1437d(l)(2), which prohibits public housing authorities from including "unreasonable terms and conditions [in their leases]." In addition, the general statutory provision in the latter section cannot trump the clear language of the more specific § 1437d(l)(6).

situation in the present cases is entirely different. The government is not attempting to criminally punish or civilly regulate respondents as members of the general populace. It is instead acting as a landlord of property that it owns, invoking a clause in a lease to which respondents have agreed and which Congress has expressly required. Scales and Danaher cast no constitutional doubt on such actions.

The Court of Appeals sought to bolster its discussion of constitutional doubt by pointing to the fact that respondents have a property interest in their leasehold interest, citing Greene v. Lindsey, 456 U.S. 444 (1982). This is undoubtedly true, and Greene held that an effort to deprive a tenant of such a right without proper notice violated the Due Process Clause of the Fourteenth Amendment. But, in the present cases, such deprivation will occur in the state court where OHA brought the unlawful detainer action against respondents. There is no indication that notice has not been given by OHA in the past, or that it will not be given in the future. Any individual factual disputes about whether the lease provision was actually violated can, of course, be resolved in these proceedings.[6]

We hold that "Congress has directly spoken to the precise question at issue." Chevron U.S.A. Inc. v. Natural Resources Defense Council, Inc., 467 U.S., at 842. Section 1437d(l)(6) requires lease terms that give local public housing authorities the discretion to terminate the lease of a tenant when a member of the household or a guest engages in drug-related activity, regardless of whether the tenant knew, or should have known, of the drug-related activity.

Accordingly, the judgment of the Court of Appeals is reversed, and the cases are remanded for further proceedings consistent with this opinion.

Dartmouth/Halifax County Regional Housing Authority v. Sparks
[1993] 101 D.L.R. (4th) 224 (N.S.C.A.)

Nova Scotia Supreme Court, Appeal Division

Vincent Calderhead, for appellant. Jamie S. Campbell, for respondent. Timothy J. LeMay, for intervener.

Jones, Hart, Hallett, Freeman, and Roscoe, JJ.A.

Hallett, J.A.

The appellant has been a public housing tenant for over 10 years. In accordance with the terms of her lease she was given one month's notice by the respondent to quit her residential premises. She is a single black mother with two children and is on social assistance. The respondent is a public housing authority. If the appellant had been a tenant of a private sector landlord she would have had the benefit of the so-called "security of tenure" provisions of the Residential Tenancies Act, R.S.N.S. 1989, c. 401, and could not have been given such short notice.

---

6. The en banc Court of Appeals cited only the due process constitutional concern. Respondents raise two others: the First Amendment and the Excessive Fines Clause. We agree with Judge O'Scannlain, writing for the panel that reversed the injunction, that the statute does not raise substantial First Amendment or Excessive Fines Clause concerns. Lyng v. Automobile Workers, 485 U.S. 360 (1988), forecloses respondents' claim that the eviction of unknowing tenants violates the First Amendment guarantee of freedom of association. And termination of tenancy "is neither a cash nor an in-kind payment imposed by and payable to the government" and therefore is "not subject to analysis as an excessive fine."

The Act gives residential tenants substantive rights in excess of those provided by the common law, particularly with respect to the landlord's right to terminate the tenancy by notice to quit. However, the Act's application to public housing tenants is severely limited by §§ 10(8)(d) and 25(2); the appellant challenges their constitutionality.

Sections 10(8) and 25 provide:

10 (8) Notwithstanding the periods of notice in subsection (1), (3) or (6), where a tenant, on the eighteenth day of May, 1984, or thereafter, has resided in the residential premises for a period of five consecutive years or more, notice to quit may not be given except where

(a) the residential premises are leased to a student by an institution of learning and the tenant ceases to be a student;

(b) the tenant was an employee of an employer who provided the tenant with residential premises during his employment and the employment has terminated;

(c) the residential premises have been made uninhabitable by fire, flood or other occurrence;

(d) the residential premises are operated or administered by or for the Government of Nova Scotia, the Government of Canada or a municipality;

(e) a judge is satisfied that the tenant is in default of any of his obligations under this Act, the regulations or the lease;

(f) a judge is satisfied that it is appropriate to make an order under Section 16 directing the landlord to be given possession at a time specified in the order, but not more than six months from the date of the order, where

(1) the landlord in good faith requires possession of the residential premises for the purpose of residence by himself or a member of his family,

(2) the landlord in good faith requires possession of the residential premises for the purpose of demolition, removal or making repairs or renovations so extensive as to require a building permit and vacant possession of the residential premises, and all necessary permits have been obtained, or

(3) the judge deems it appropriate in the circumstances.

25 (1) This Act governs all landlords and tenants to whom this Act applies in respect of residential premises.

(2) Where any provision of this Act conflicts with the provision of a lease granted to a tenant of residential premises that are administered by or for the Government of Canada or the Province or a municipality, or any agency thereof, developed and financed under the National Housing Act, 1954 (Canada) or the National Housing Act (Canada), the provisions of the lease govern.

Sections 10(1) and (6) are also relevant for a proper understanding of the relationship between landlords and residential tenants in Nova Scotia:

10 (1) Notwithstanding any agreement between the landlord and tenant respecting a period of notice, notice to quit residential premises shall be given

(a) where the residential premises are let from year to year, by the landlord or tenant at least three months before the expiration of any such year;

(b) where the residential premises are let from month to month,

(1) by the landlord, at least three months, and

(2) by the tenant, at least one month,

before the expiration of any such month;

(c) where the residential premises are let from week to week,

(1) by the landlord, at least four weeks, and

(2) by the tenant, at least one week,

before the expiration of any such week.

(6) Notwithstanding the periods of notice in subsection (1), where a year to year or a month to month tenancy exists or is deemed to exist and the rent payable for the residential premises is in arrears for thirty days, the landlord may give to the tenant notice to quit the residential premises fifteen days from the date the notice to quit is given.

Public housing tenants are treated differently than private sector residential tenants in that the terms of the lease with a housing authority can override the provisions of the Act and the public housing tenant in possession for five years or more by reason of § 10(8)(d) does not have "security of tenure". The appellant's lease provides for termination on one month's notice. A private sector tenant with five years' possession, subject to certain exceptions which are not relevant to this factual situation, can only be given a notice to quit if a judge is satisfied that the tenant is in default of any of the tenant's obligations under the Act, the regulations or the lease (§ 10(8) (e)).

The appellant sought a declaration that §§ 10(8)(d) and 25(2) of the Act contravened §15(1) of the Canadian Charter of Rights and Freedoms and were of no force and effect. The learned trial judge concluded that the sections did not infringe the appellant's § 15(1) equality right.

The respondents admitted that women, blacks and social assistance recipients form a disproportionally large percentage of tenants in public housing and on the waiting list for public housing. The case was argued before the learned trial judge on the basis that such persons were adversely impacted by the challenged sections.

In 1988 this court dealt with a challenge under § 5(1) of the Charter to the constitutionality of §§10(8)(d) and 25(2) of the Act. The court concluded that the sections did not offend §15(1): Bernard v. Dartmouth Housing Authority (1988), 53 D.L.R. (4th) 81, 50 R.P.R. 12, 88 N.S.R. (2d) 190. In writing for the court, Mr. Justice Pace stated at p. 90:

> There is no doubt there is a difference or inequality between the protection afforded a non-subsidized tenant and a subsidized tenant. However, not every difference or inequality gives rise to discrimination such as would necessitate the invocation of the protection afforded under the provisions of § 15(1) of the Charter.

In the present appeal, the trial judge found the appellant failed to establish a prima facie case of unequal treatment. He found that she was not treated in a prejudicial manner and that she freely took advantage of the benefits of subsidized housing with knowledge of the disadvantages.

In short, this court concluded that discrimination had not been proven at trial and dismissed the appeal; the challenge failed because of the lack of evidence of discrimination.

The learned trial judge's decision in the appeal we have under consideration concluded with the following:

> To summarize, Bernard is the law in Nova Scotia as it relates to distinctions created in the Residential Tenancies Act affecting tenants of public housing. Distinctions, differences or inequality do not necessarily give rise to discrimination. As in Bernard, the tenant here has not established a prima facie case of discrimination as it affects public housing tenants as a whole.

> With regard to the tenant's submission that she is suffering adverse affect discrimination by virtue of being black, a woman, and a recipient of social assistance, I find that she has not established a prima facie case thereof. I accordingly find that §§ 10(8)(d) and 25(2) of the Residential Tenancies Act do not contravene the provisions of §15(1) of the Charter. Because of this finding there is no necessity to consider S.1 of the Charter.

The principal focus of the appellant's argument both at trial and before this court is that the appellant suffers adverse effect discrimination because of the effect on her of the two sections in question.

The learned trial judge made the following findings:

> I accept the submissions by the tenant that single-parent mothers, and blacks, are less advantaged than the majority of other members of our society. It also goes without saying that social assistance recipients are also less advantaged, although some arguments could be made that there are certain advantages accruing to such recipients if they are able to obtain suitable public housing at a smaller percentage of their income than would be the case if they were a private sector tenant.

The learned trial judge in dealing with the issue of discrimination [stated]:

> The tenant in this case is treated differently because and solely arising from having applied and met the criteria for public housing. I agree with the submission by counsel for the landlord that the fact that public housing tenants are disproportionately black, females on social assistance tells us something about public housing but doesn't tell us anything about being black, about being female or upon [sic] being on social assistance. I agree that it is not a characteristic of any of those three groups to reside in public housing.

> I accept the submission that the legislature is not discriminating against black, female, social assistance recipients by treating public housing tenants differently.

The learned trial judge concluded that in order to succeed the appellant:

> ... would have to show that the legislation somehow exempted blacks, women, and recipients of social assistance from the protection of the statute by singling out a characteristic of being a black, female, social assistance recipient, and exempting from the protection of the Act those with that characteristic.

The law on § 15(1) of the Charter.

The most authoritative case in Canada with respect to the interpretation and application of § 15(1) of the Charter is Andrews v. Law Society of British Columbia, [(1983),

56 D.L.R. (4th) 1, [1989] 1 S.C.R. 48, 25 C.C.E.L. 255]. McIntyre J., in dealing with the "concept of equality," made the following statement:

> To approach the ideal of full equality before and under the law—and in human affairs an approach is all that can be expected—the main consideration must be the impact of the law on the individual or the group concerned.

In the Andrews case, Mr. Justice McIntyre put the burden of proving an infringement of § 15(1) on the complainant and described the extent of that burden when he stated:

> A complainant under § 15(1) must show not only that he or she is not receiving equal treatment before and under the law or that the law has a differential impact on him or her in the protection or benefit accorded by law but, in addition, must show that the legislative impact of the law is discriminatory.

Distinctions in treatment of different individuals and groups does not infringe on an individual's equality rights as provided by § 15(1) of the Charter unless the law is also discriminatory. In the Andrews case, Justice McIntyre directed his attention to the meaning of "discrimination." After reviewing several statements which aim to define the term "discrimination," he stated:

> I would say then that discrimination may be described as a distinction, whether intentional or not but based on grounds relating to personal characteristics of the individual or group, which has the effect of imposing burdens, obligations, or disadvantages on such individual or group not imposed upon others, or which withholds or limits access to opportunities, benefits, and advantages available to other members of society. Distinctions based on personal characteristics attributed to an individual solely on the basis of association with a group will rarely escape the charge of discrimination, while those based on an individual's merits and capacities will rarely be so classed.

In R. v. Turpin (1989), 48 C.C.C. (3d) 8, [1989] 1 S.C.R. 1296, 69 C.R. (3d) 97, the Supreme Court of Canada stated that finding that discrimination exists will, in most cases, entail a search for a disadvantage that exists apart from and independent of the particular legal distinction being challenged. The court went on to hold that victims of discrimination will often be members of a discrete and insular minority and, thus, come within the protection of § 15(1) of the Charter.

The Issues

Counsel for the appellant invites us to reconsider the decision of this court in the Bernard case; and secondly, to find that the learned trial judge was in error when he concluded that the appellant did not suffer from adverse effect discrimination by reason of the effect on her of the provisions of §§ 10(8)(d) and 25(2) of the Residential Tenancies Act.

The provisions of §§ 10 and 25(1) of the Act which give a residential tenant some protection from termination without cause do not, by reason of §§ 10(8)(d) and 25(2) apply to public housing tenants. The appellant asserts that the two sections infringe her § 15(1) Charter right of equality in that they discriminate against her and that the two sections cannot be saved by § 1 of the Charter.

The respondent's position is that the exempting provisions do not amount to a violation of § 15(1) since the distinction drawn by the legislation is between groups of tenants and does not relate to a prohibited ground of discrimination. The respondent relies on the notion that to constitute a violation of § 15(1) the impugned difference in treatment must relate to a "personal characteristic". Tenancy, it is argued, is not such a characteristic.

In addition, the respondent relies on the decision of this court in Bernard, where these sections were upheld. It is appropriate to reconsider the issues disposed of in Bernard for two reasons. First, the body of evidence put forward in this case is not the same as was before the court then. In this case, the appellant adduced a substantial body of evidence at trial relating to the composition of the group of public housing tenants and the social condition of this group as related to their housing needs. Secondly, significant direction respecting the application of § 15 has since been given by the Supreme Court of Canada in the Andrews and Turpin cases to which I have referred. In general, those cases provide direction on the type of legislative distinction which is discriminatory and which amount to a § 15 violation. In addition, the court gives direction as to the types of groups to be protected by § 15; the shelter of § 15 is not limited to persons and groups falling within the listed grounds of prohibited discrimination in § 15(1), but extends to those which can establish that their condition is analogous to the listed ones. In particular, such analogy is made out where the evidence discloses the group complaining of discrimination is historically disadvantaged.

The questions to be answered by this court can be stated as follows:

1. Do the exempting provisions of the Act infringe the appellant's § 15(1) Charter rights?

2. If the first question is answered in the affirmative, can the impugned provisions be saved by § 1; that is, do they constitute a reasonable limit prescribed by law and justified in a free and democratic society?

First Issue

Sections 10(8)(d) and 25(2) draw a distinction between public housing tenants and private sector tenants such that a benefit extended to the latter group is denied the former. That the distinction puts public housing tenants at a disadvantage is apparent. The question, then, is whether or not this disadvantage amounts to discrimination.

Section 15(1) of the Charter provides:

15(1) Every individual is equal before and under the law and has the right to the equal protection and equal benefit of the law without discrimination and, in particular, without discrimination based on race, national or ethnic origin, colour, religion, sex, age or mental or physical disability.

I find that the impugned provisions amount to discrimination on the basis of race, sex and income; it is not necessary in this case to show adverse effect discrimination as argued by the appellant. An adverse impact analysis has been applied in cases involving legislation which is neutral on its face. Sections 10(8)(d) and 25(2) are not neutral; they explicitly deny benefits to a certain group of the population (public housing tenants) while extending them to others.*

---

 * Editor's Note: See footnote 4 of the U.S. Supreme Court decision in U.S. v. Carolene Products, 304 U.S. 144, 153 n. 4 (1938), which states in part:

Nor need we enquire whether similar considerations enter into the review of statutes directed at particular religious, Pierce v. Society of Sisters, 268 U.S. 510, or national, Meyer v. Nebraska, 262 U.S. 390, or racial minorities, Nixon v. Herndon; Nixon v. Condon: whether prejudice against discrete and insular minorities may be a special condition, which tends seriously to curtail the operation of those political processes ordinarily to be

The fact that the legislation describes the group (public housing tenants) by reference to a factor which is not a listed ground in §15(1) does not avail the respondent. The respondent relied on the notion that the distinction drawn by the legislation is not discriminatory, since it is not "based on grounds relating to a personal characteristic" of the appellant. The respondent does not dispute that race, gender and income are personal characteristics, but argues that the legislation is not "based on" such characteristics. This position was accepted by the learned trial judge.

The phrase "based on grounds relating to personal characteristics" as used in the Andrews case cannot be taken to mean that the personal characteristics must be explicit on the face of the legislation, nor that the legislation must be manifestly directed at such characteristics. Such an interpretation would fly in the face of the effects-based approach to the Charter espoused by the Supreme Court of Canada.

It is clear that a determination of the constitutionality of legislation must take account of both the purpose and effects of that legislation. In R. v. Big M Drug Mart Ltd. (1985), 18 D.L.R. (4th) 321, 18 C.C.C. (3d) 385, [1985] 1 S.C.R. 293, Dickson J. stated at p. 350:

> In my view, both purpose and effect are relevant in determining constitutionality; either an unconstitutional purpose or an unconstitutional effect can invalidate legislation. All legislation is animated by an object the Legislature intends to achieve. This object is realized through the impact produced by the operation and application of the legislation. Purpose and effect respectively, in the sense of the legislation's object and its ultimate impact, are clearly linked, if not indivisible.

And at pp. 351–2:

> In short, I agree with the respondent that the legislation's purpose is the initial test of constitutional validity and its effects are to be considered when the law under review has passed or, at least, has purportedly passed the purpose test. If the legislation fails the purpose test, there is no need to consider further its effects, since it has already been demonstrated to be invalid. Thus, if a law with a valid purpose interferes by its impact, with rights or freedoms, a litigant could still argue the effects of the legislation as a means to defeat its applicability and possibly its validity.

Accepting, without deciding, that the purpose of the legislation is not to discriminate, we must still determine whether or not it has a discriminatory effect. To do so, it is necessary to examine the group affected. Such an examination must take account not merely of the manner in which the group is described in the legislation, in this case as "public housing tenants." In addition, regard must be had to the characteristics shared by the persons comprising the group.

Low income, in most cases verging on or below poverty, is undeniably a characteristic shared by all residents of public housing; the principal criteria of eligibility for public housing are to have a low income and have a need for better housing. Poverty is, in addition, a condition more frequently experienced by members of the three groups identified by the appellant. The evidence before us supports this.

Single mothers are now known to be the group in society most likely to experience poverty in the extreme. It is by virtue of being a single mother that this poverty is likely

---

relied upon to protect minorities, and which may call for a correspondingly more searching judicial inquiry. Compare McCulloch v. Maryland, 4 Wheat. 316, 428; South Carolina v. Barnwell Bros., 303 U.S. 177, 184, n. 2, and cases cited.

to affect the members of this group. This is no less a personal characteristic of such individuals than non-citizenship was in Andrews. To find otherwise would strain the interpretation of "personal characteristic" unduly.

Similarly, senior citizens that are in public housing are there because they qualify by reason of their low incomes and need for better housing. As a general proposition, persons who qualify for public housing are the economically disadvantaged and are so disadvantaged because of their age and correspondingly low incomes (seniors) or families with low incomes, a majority of whom are disadvantaged because they are single female parents on social assistance, many of whom are black. The public housing tenants group as a whole is historically disadvantaged as a result of the combined effect of several personal characteristics listed in § 15(1). As a result, they are a group analogous to those persons or groups specifically referred to by the characteristics set out in § 15(1) of the Charter being characteristics that are most commonly the subject of discrimination. In fact, the legislature recognized the group of persons who qualify for public housing as being disadvantaged; a subsidized housing scheme was created to alleviate their disadvantage.

Section 15(1) of the Charter requires all individuals to have equal benefit of the law without discrimination. Public housing tenants have been excluded from certain benefits private sector tenants have as provided to them in the Act. The effect of §§ 25(2) and 10(8)(d) of the Act has been to discriminate against public housing tenants who are a disadvantaged group analogous to the historically recognized groups enumerated in § 15(1). The provisions of §§ 10(8)(d) and 25(2) discriminate against them because as public housing tenants they do not have the benefit of the law provided to all residential tenants by §§ 10 and 25(1) of the Act. Public housing tenants are not welcome in the private sector rental market and the short notice to quit provisions that can be imposed on public housing tenants, as imposed on the appellant in this case, further disadvantage them as the evidence shows that they have great difficulty in securing rental accommodations in the private sector if evicted from public housing. The content of the law and its impact on public housing tenants is not only that they are treated differently, but the difference relates to the personal characteristics of the public housing tenant group. To come to any other conclusion is to close one's eyes to the make-up of the public housing tenancy group and the effect on them of the exempting sections. The two sections infringe public housing tenants' § 15(1) rights to the equal benefit of the law without discrimination. Accordingly, §§ 10(8) (d) and 25(2) of the Residential Tenancies Act are unconstitutional unless those provisions can be saved by § 1 of the Charter.

Issue 2 — § 1 of the Charter

As stated by La Forest J. in Tetreault-Gadoury v. Canada (Employment and Immigration Commission) (1991), 81 D.L.R. (4th) 358, [1991] 2 S.C.R. 22, 50 Admin. L.R. 1, the general approach to be taken by a court when determining whether a law constitutes a reasonable limit to a Charter right was initially described by the Supreme Court of Canada in R. v. Oakes (1986), 26 D.L.R. (4th) 200, 24 C.C.C. (3d) 321, [1986] 1 S.C.R. 103. The first question to be answered is whether the objectives of the two sections in question are of sufficient importance to warrant overriding the appellant's Charter right to equal benefit of the law. Counsel for the respondent argued that the public housing authorities need flexibility to administer the public housing scheme and therefore the authority should not be burdened with the tenant safeguards as provided in the Act.

Administrative flexibility in itself is generally regarded as insufficient reason to warrant overriding a Charter right. However, a degree of administrative flexibility is needed to effectively manage a public housing scheme. Certainly changes in tenants' eligibility for public housing should affect the duration of the tenancy. Therefore, there is legitimacy to the objective of not granting all the benefits of the Act to public housing tenants. However, neither the authority nor the Attorney-General has proven that the means chosen to achieve the objective are reasonable and demonstratively justified in a free and democratic society. In short, §§ 10(8)(d) and 25(2) are not properly tailored to achieve the legitimate objectives of the housing authorities. The two sections fail the proportionality test, as established by the Supreme Court of Canada, as they impair the public housing tenant's rights under the Act to such an extreme extent that the sections cannot be said to be a minimal or reasonable impairment so as to achieve the objectives of making sure that public housing is available for only those persons who qualify. Pursuant to § 25(2) of the Act the leases prepared by the authority, like that entered into between the authority and the appellant, can be drawn in such a way as to negate the legislated notice periods to terminate a residential tenancy. Secondly, a public housing tenant like the appellant who has been in possession for more than five years, can be given a notice to quit without a judge being satisfied that the public housing tenant was in default of any of the tenant's obligations under the Act, the regulations or the lease.

I am mindful of the fact that the courts should show considerable deference to the measures chosen by the legislature in balancing the competing social values of equality as guaranteed by § 15(1) of the Charter while at the same time providing a public housing scheme that is equitable and manageable. However, as noted by La Forest, J. in Tetreault-Gadoury, supra:

> … the deference that will be accorded to the government when legislating in these matters does not give them an unrestricted licence to disregard an individual's Charter rights. Where the government cannot show that it had a reasonable basis for concluding that it has complied with the requirement of minimal impairment in seeking to obtain its objectives, the legislation will be struck down.

Neither the authority nor the Attorney-General have satisfied me that there was a reasonable basis for denying carte blanche, so to speak, the benefits of the Act to public housing tenants. In my opinion, the broad scope of §§ 10(8) (d) and 25(2) show that the government really did not make an effort to strike a reasonable balance between the authority's need for some administrative flexibility and the rights of public housing tenants to the equal benefit of the law as guaranteed by § 15(1) of the Charter.

Most other provinces have achieved the legitimate objective of treating public housing tenants differently than private sector tenants without resort to the blunt instrument approach that is found in the Act. For example, in Ontario public housing tenants are exempted from the benefits of the residential tenancies legislation in three areas only. There is a provision relating to termination of tenancies for misrepresentation of family income. Considering the purposes of the public housing program that is reasonable and justifiable. Likewise, there is a provision for allowing for termination when a tenant has ceased to meet the qualifications to occupy public housing. That too is justifiable and reasonable. Finally, in Ontario a public housing tenant is not entitled to sublet. That too is reasonable and justifiable because the intent is to provide public housing to those persons who have been found to be in need and are therefore eligible. The objective of public housing to alleviate conditions of the poor in finding adequate housing would be frustrated if a tenant once qualified could sublet to anyone.

Counsel for the appellant has brought to our attention that there is in place in the province a different form of low-cost rent or subsidized housing entitled "Rent Supplement Programme". In that program, the tenants who have been approved for public housing and are on a waiting list are placed as tenants in privately owned apartment buildings. The tenant pays exactly the same rent as if he or she were in a public housing project with the Department of Housing paying the difference between the rent paid by the tenant and the market rent. But unlike the tenant in public housing, the tenant who is put into a private building has the benefit of being subject to the same terms and conditions as the lease used for other tenants in the building. These, of course, would give such a tenant all the rights provided in the Act. In short, there are two types of subsidized tenants; those who are accorded the benefits of the Act and those who are not. While I do not like to intrude on the role of the legislature, there is no evidence that a sufficient attempt was made to draft legislation that would achieve the legitimate objectives of the housing authorities while at the same time recognize the rights of public housing tenants to equal benefit of the law. Sections 10(8)(d) and 25(2) fail both the minimal or reasonable impairment test and cannot be justified as a reasonable limit on the appellant's right to the equal benefit of the law as guaranteed by § 15 of the Charter.

The Bernard Decision

In the Bernard case it would appear that the evidence before the trial judge respecting the alleged Charter infringement was so lacking that this court could have come to no other conclusion than to dismiss the appeal.

The Trial Judge's Decision

The learned trial judge, in the decision we have under review, considered himself bound by the Bernard decision.

Conclusion

Sections 10(8)(d) and 25(2) of the Act are inconsistent with the public housing tenant's right to equal benefit of the law without discrimination. The provisions are overly broad. The most appropriate and just remedy is to declare these provisions to be of no force or effect. The public housing authority is not without a remedy under the Act. If a public housing tenant with five years possession breaches the terms of a lease, the authority can avail itself of § 10(8)(e) of the Act and apply to a judge for permission to give a notice to quit on the basis of a tenant's default under his or her lease. If the judge is satisfied that there has been a default, a notice to quit can be given as provided for in the Act. I am satisfied that amendments to the Act can be designed that will meet the legitimate objectives of the legislature to give housing authorities the powers needed to properly administer the public housing scheme while at the same time complying with the tests enunciated by the Supreme Court of Canada in R. v. Oakes, supra, and the other cases to which I have referred, so as not to infringe the § 15 Charter rights of public housing tenants to the equal benefit of residential tenancy laws in the province.

Therefore, I would allow the appeal and declare §§ 10(8)(d) and 25(2) of the Residential Tenancies Act to be unconstitutional and to be of no force and effect. The appellant was represented by legal aid and there should not be an order for costs. Appeal allowed.

Carter v. Maryland Management Co.

377 Md. 596, 835 A.2d 158 (Court of Appeals of Maryland 2003)

]Gregory Leo Countess (Hannah E.M. Lieberman and Sarah Glorian of the Legal Aid Bureau, Inc., of Baltimore on brief) for petitioner.

W. Michael Pierson (Pierson & Pierson, Baltimore, Howard Cassin and Donna M. Raffaele of Sagal, Cassin, Filbert & Quasney, P.A. of Towson, MD on brief) for respondent.

Before Bell, C.J.,* and Eldridge, Raker, Wilner, Cathell, Harrell, and Battaglia, JJ.

Wilner, Judge:

In Brown v. Housing Opportunities Comm., 714 A.2d 197 ([Md.] 1998), we pointed out that the Real Property Article of the Maryland Code contains three separate and distinct provisions under which a landlord may recover possession of leased premises. Section 8-401 provides for the recovery of possession when the tenant fails to pay rent that is currently due and payable. Section 8-402 — often referred to as the "tenant holding over" statute — permits recovery upon a finding that the tenant's lease has expired, that notice to quit was given, and that the tenant has refused to vacate. Section 8-402.1 — referred to as the "breach of lease" statute — provides for recovery when the tenant has breached a covenant of the lease, other than the covenant to pay rent, and the court finds that the breach was substantial and warrants eviction.

The principal issue now before us is whether a landlord who is participating in the Federal Low-Income Housing Tax Credit (LIHTC) Program provided for in 26 U.S.C. §42 may use the tenant holding over statute to evict a tenant who qualifies for and is receiving low-income housing assistance under the voucher program provided for in 42 U.S.C. §1437f(o). The tenant here, petitioner Carter, contends that (1) provisions in 26 U.S.C. §42(h)(6)(B) and (E) preclude a participating landlord from terminating a lease except for good cause, (2) the effect of that Federal preclusion is to make the tenancy an indefinite one, without any fixed term, (3) the lease therefore does not expire, regardless of whether, on its face, it has an expiration date or provides for expiration, and (4) as a result, the tenant holding over statute (§8-402) is inapplicable. She thus avers that, in order to terminate her tenancy, other than for nonpayment of rent, the landlord must proceed under the breach of lease provision (§8-402.1). Petitioner adds that, even if the preclusion does not convert a fixed tenancy into an indefinite one, the landlord failed to establish good cause in this case for terminating her lease.

The landlord — respondent Maryland Management Co. — argues that (1) except in one particular circumstance not applicable here, the Federal law does *not* require "good cause" for termination, (2) even if it does, that does not convert a fixed-term tenancy into one that is indefinite or perpetual, (3) if the requisites of §8-402 are met, the landlord may therefore proceed, in accordance with State law, under the tenant holding over statute, and (4) if good cause is required by Federal law to be shown under the tenant holding over statute, respondent produced sufficient evidence in this case to establish such cause. The District Court concluded that good cause was required, that that requirement did not preclude use of the tenant holding over statute, and that the landlord

---

* Editor's Note: The Honorable Robert Bell, Chief Judge of the Maryland Court of Appeals, was the lead defendant in the sit-in case, Bell v. State of Maryland, 378 U.S. 226 (1964). See William L. Reynolds, Foreword: *The Legal History of the Great Sit-In Case of Bell v. Maryland*, 61 Md. L.Rev. 761 (2002).

had established good cause. It therefore entered a judgment of restitution. The Circuit Court for Baltimore City affirmed, and so shall we.

Background

On October 1, 1996, petitioner leased a townhouse in a project owned by respondent. By reason of its participation in the LIHTC program, respondent agreed to lease a certain percentage of the rental units in the project to persons, such as petitioner, who qualified for low-income rental assistance under 42 U.S.C., § 1437f.* The initial lease, for 1996–97, is not in the record, but an addendum to it is in evidence. The addendum, on a U.S. Department of Housing and Urban Development form for the "Section 8 Tenant-Based Assistance Rental Voucher Program," notes that the lease ran from October 1, 1996 to October 1, 1997. It states that the "term of the lease" would terminate if (1) the lease terminates, (2) the housing assistance payment contract between the public housing agency and the landlord terminates, or (3) the housing agency terminates program assistance for the tenant. The "lease" would terminate upon termination by the landlord, the tenant, or both.

Paragraph 10 of the addendum expressly limited the grounds upon which the landlord could terminate the tenancy to "serious or repeated violation of the terms and conditions of the lease; violation of Federal, State, or local law that imposes obligations on the tenant in connection with the occupancy or use of the contract unit and the premises; [certain] criminal activity [ ]; or other good cause." The term "other good cause" was defined in ¶ 10 c. as including, but not limited to, "living or housekeeping habits resulting in damage to the unit or property." Paragraph 11 required the landlord, as a condition of its terminating the lease, to give written notice to the tenant of the grounds for termination at or before the commencement of any eviction action. Whether this addendum, or one like it, accompanied subsequent leases is unclear. The record contains a lease for the term October 1, 2000 to October 1, 2001, but there is no addendum to it.

On September 4, 1998, a "Section 8 inspector" from the Baltimore City Housing Authority made an annual inspection of petitioner's home, in conformance with requirements of the program, and found seven violations. Petitioner was directed to patch and repaint a hole in the living room wall, clean a dirty kitchen floor and stove, clean stains in the bathtub, cover and repaint holes in two bedroom walls, clean walls or the floor in three bedrooms, and clean the carpet and floors throughout the unit. In June, 2000, respondent filed actions under both § 8-402 and § 8-402.1 to evict petitioner, but those cases were generally postponed pursuant to a settlement agreement.

The agreement allowed petitioner to remain in the home, but provided that, if she breached the lease prior to December 13, 2000, the landlord would provide notice of the breach and, within 30 days, the cases would be rescheduled for trial. If there was no request to reschedule by December 13, the cases would be dismissed. Although the agreement did not specifically call for a new lease, one was entered into on January 5,

---

* Editor's Note: The LIHTC statute provides that a LIHTC development may not discriminate against a person because that person has a Section 8 voucher. 26 U.S.C. § 42(h)(6)(B)(iv). If Maryland Management Co. were under any obligation to accept a certain number of voucher holders, that would be a requirement imposed by Maryland law, not by the LIHTC statute. The LIHTC statute does require that at least 20% of residents have incomes below 50% of area median gross income (26 USC § 42(g)(1)–(g)(8)); these people would be eligible for Section 8 vouchers, although they would not necessarily have such vouchers.

2001. As we shall see, the Federal regulations relating to leases with voucher program tenants changed considerably between 1996 and 2000, and the new lease reflected those changes. The term was one year, commencing October 1, 2000, at the end of which period the parties could renew on a month-to-month basis. In addition to the renewal provision, there was a paragraph captioned "Tenant Holding Over," which provided, in relevant part, that if the tenant continued to occupy the unit "after expiration of this Lease Agreement, or any renewal or extension thereof" and the landlord consented to such continued occupancy, the occupancy, unless agreed otherwise, would be on a month-to-month basis, at twice the rental payable under the lease, to continue until either party gave two months notice of termination. Included in the lease were certain rules and regulations, among which was a covenant by petitioner to "keep the Premises in a neat, clean, good and sanitary condition."

The next annual inspection occurred in September, 2000. This time, one violation was noted; petitioner was directed to replace broken glass in the living room. In June, 2001, respondent sent notice to petitioner of its intent to terminate the lease when it expired. In August, another annual inspection occurred and turned up seven violations. Petitioner was directed to repair or replace the bathroom door and a bedroom door, clean and paint a bedroom wall, replace inoperable smoke detectors, clean and paint the walls on the steps, replace missing screens, and clean or replace all rugs. The lease expired, by its terms, on September 30, 2001 and, when petitioner failed to vacate the premises at that time, respondent filed another tenant holding over action but did not specify in its complaint any cause for termination other than expiration of the lease. When that case came to trial, petitioner argued that respondent could not terminate her tenancy absent a showing of good cause—something more than just termination of the lease. The District Court agreed and, noting that the June, 2001 notice failed to specify any such good cause, dismissed the case.

On December 28, 2001, respondent sent a notice declaring that the lease would be terminated on February 28, 2002. The letter stated that the lease would not be renewed because petitioner had failed to maintain her unit in a neat, clean, sanitary, and safe condition. It referenced the violations noted in the September, 1998, and August, 2001 inspection reports and indicated a lack of any evidence that those deficiencies had been corrected. At the same time, respondent informed the Housing Authority that it was terminating the housing assistance contract that it had with respect to petitioner. When petitioner failed to vacate in accordance with the notice, respondent filed new actions under both § 8-402 and § 8-402.1. At trial, the various notices were admitted into evidence, along with testimony by the Housing Authority inspector, who confirmed the violations and stated that those directed to the landlord had been corrected but not those directed at petitioner. Petitioner acknowledged most of the conditions reported by the inspector. She said that respondent had repaired some of them and that she had tried to remedy others.

After listening to the evidence, the District Court found, from the various violations going back to 1998, that there was good cause for termination of the lease and that petitioner was a tenant holding over. Concluding that the tenant holding over statute was applicable, it entered judgment for restitution in favor of respondent under that statute and dismissed the action brought under the breach of lease statute. Petitioner appealed, arguing, as she does here, that (1) under Federal law, her lease was an indefinite one, without any fixed term, and that the tenant holding over statute was therefore inapplicable, and (2) respondent failed to establish good cause in any event. The Circuit Court found no merit to either argument and affirmed the District Court judgment.

Discussion

The Good Cause Requirement

The issues here depend entirely on the effect that the Federal statutes (and implementing Federal regulations) have on State landlord-tenant law. There is no substantial dispute that, if respondent had not subjected petitioner's townhouse to the Federal low-income housing program by qualifying for the Federal tax credit under 26 U.S.C. §42, and the issue were thus governed solely by Maryland landlord-tenant law, petitioner would, indeed, be a tenant holding over, and respondent would be entitled to use §8-402 to have her evicted. The one-year term of the last lease had expired, the lease had been converted by its terms into a month-to-month tenancy, and respondent had given the requisite 60-day notice to quit. It is critical, therefore, to understand the nature and requirements of the Federal statutes.

The statutory basis for the Federal low-income housing program is split between the tax code, 26 U.S.C. §42, and the general program for assisted housing, 42 U.S.C. §1437 et seq. Section 42 sets forth the eligibility criteria for the tax credit. The provisions in title 42 authorize the Secretary of Housing and Urban Development to enter into annual contributions contracts with public housing agencies in order to provide rental assistance payments to owners of certain dwelling units rented to approved low-income tenants.

In conformance with statutory guidelines, the Secretary is to establish the maximum monthly rent the owner is entitled to receive for the units and the amount of rent that the tenants are required to pay, the latter being set as a percentage of the tenants' family income. The difference is made up by the government assistance payments. For our purposes, the pertinent provision in title 42 is §1437f—the current emanation of what began as Title I, §8 of the National Housing Act of 1937—and, in particular, §1437f(o), the §8 voucher program.

Both sets of provisions—§42 and §1437f—are exceedingly long, complex, and convoluted, as befitting Federal programs in general and Federal tax laws in particular. Section 1437f and the regulations adopted pursuant to it have undergone many changes in just the past 20 years, and keeping up with the shifts in policy and approach is not easy. We shall begin with the tax provision, known as the Low Income Housing Tax Credit (LIHTC). It was enacted as part of the Tax Reform Act of 1986, as an effort to encourage the private development of low income housing.[1] Substantial amendments, relevant to the issue before us, were made as part of the Omnibus Budget Reconciliation Acts of 1989 and 1990.

Section 42 of title 26, coupled with §38 of that title, provides a tax credit, usable ordinarily over a ten-year period, for a "qualified low-income housing project." Section 42(g)(1) defines such a project as one for residential rental property in which minimum enumerated percentages of the residential units are both rent-restricted and occupied by persons whose income does not exceed certain amounts. In its initial (1986) version, the law, through its definition of "qualified low-income building," required the building to remain part of a "qualified low-income housing project" during a 15-year "compliance period."

---

1. See Marc Jolin, *Good Cause Eviction and the Low Income Housing Tax Credit*, 67 U. Chi. L. Rev. 521, 524 (2000). (The LIHTC program was created, in part, to make it financially feasible for private developers to build and maintain low-income housing and help fill the void left by cuts in public housing and Section 8 rental subsidy programs.)

The 1989 amendment added a new subsection (h)(6) to §42, in which was imposed the requirement of a further 15-year "extended use period." With that amendment, §42(h)(6)(A) makes clear that no credit is allowed with respect to a building unless an "extended low-income housing commitment," as defined in §42(h)(6)(B), is in effect at the end of the taxable year. Thus, to qualify for the tax credit, the commitment must remain in effect for a "compliance period" of 15 taxable years, dating from the first taxable year of the credit period, and an "extended use period," which, subject to §42(h)(6)(E), may not end earlier than 15 years after the close of the "compliance period." The effective commitment is thus, ordinarily, for 30 years.

Section 42(h)(6)(E) permits an early termination of the "extended use period" in two circumstances. If a mortgage on the building is foreclosed, the "extended use period" terminates on the date the building is acquired pursuant to the foreclosure. After the fourteenth year of the "compliance period," the owner may request the housing credit agency to find a buyer for the taxpayer's interest in the low-income portion of the building, and, if the agency is unable to present a qualified contract for the acquisition of that portion by a person who will continue to operate it as a low-income building, the "extended use period" ends on the last day of that one-year period. See §42(h)(6)(E)(i) and (I). Subsection 42(h)(6)(E)(ii) provides, however, that

> the termination of an extended use period under clause (i) shall not be construed to permit before the close of the 3-year period following such termination—
>
> (I) the eviction or the termination of tenancy (other than for good cause) of an existing tenant of any low-income unit; or
>
> (II) any increase in the gross rent with respect to such unit.

This provision, added as §42(h)(6)(E)(ii) by the 1989 amendment, clearly applies only in the event of an early termination of the "extended use period" and is intended to protect existing low-income tenants, as to both their tenancy and the rent, for a three-year period. A new owner who acquires the building by virtue of a foreclosure or the existing owner who is allowed to terminate the commitment under §42(h)(6)(E)(i)(II) may not evict or terminate the leases of low-income tenants, other than for good cause, or raise their gross rent beyond what is permitted during that three-year period.

The provision that lies at the heart of petitioner's indefinite tenancy argument is contained in §42(h)(6)(B) which, as noted, defines the term "extended low-income housing commitment"—the commitment that must be in effect in order to entitle the owner to the tax credit. A brief explanation is required. Section 42(a) establishes the amount of the tax credit as "(1) the applicable percentage of (2) the qualified basis of each qualified low-income building." Section 42(c), in turn, defines the "qualified basis" of a "qualified low-income building" as an amount equal to "the applicable fraction" of "the eligible basis" for the building. The "applicable fraction" is the smaller of the "unit fraction" or the "floor space fraction," each, itself, being a defined term. All of this relates to how the credit is to be calculated and, until the 1990 amendment to §42(h)(6)(B) added by Congress in the Omnibus Budget Reconciliation Act of 1990, would have been quite irrelevant to what is now before us.

As budget reconciliation Acts tend to be, the 1990 Act was comprehensive in nature.[2] Title XI, which carried its own name, the Revenue Reconciliation Act of 1990, dealt with a variety of revenue provisions. Subtitle G, captioned Tax Technical Corrections,

---

2. The comprehensiveness of this statute is illustrated by the fact that the amendment at issue here was enacted by §11,701 of the Act.

made a number of amendments to the Revenue Reconciliation Act of 1989, one of which effectively amended §42(h)(6)(B)(i). That subparagraph stated one of the six criteria for an "extended low-income housing commitment." The amendment added the language noted below in italics:

> For purposes of this paragraph, the term "extended low-income housing commitment" means any agreement between the taxpayer and the housing credit agency—
>
> (I) which requires that the applicable fraction (as defined in subsection (c)(1)) for the building for each taxable year in the extended use period will not be less than the applicable fraction specified in such agreement *and which prohibits the actions described in subclauses (I) and (II) of subparagraph (E)(ii).*

(Emphasis added.)

Petitioner views that 1990 amendment as giving the restrictions in §42(h)(6)(E)(ii) much broader effect and as mandating that an extended low-income housing commitment preclude, during both the compliance period and the extended use period, the eviction of a low-income tenant, other than for good cause. We believe that she is correct in her ultimate conclusion, but not just because of the 1990 statutory amendment.

In order to qualify for the tax credit under §42, a landlord must comply with statutory requirements and requirements imposed by authorized regulations of the Secretary of Housing and Urban Development during both the initial compliance period and the extended use period. Section 1437f(d) and (o) require that contracts for assistance payments entered into by a public housing agency and the owner of existing housing units must provide, among other things, that "during the term of the lease, the owner shall not terminate the tenancy except for serious or repeated violation of the terms and conditions of the lease, for violation of applicable Federal, State, or local law, or for other good cause." As we shall see, that requirement also appears in regulations of the Secretary. See 24 C.F.R. §247.3, applicable generally to subsidized projects, and §982.310, applicable to the voucher program in which petitioner participated.

The statutes relied upon by petitioner concern only the extended use period, first imposed by the 1989 amendment. As we observed, the "good cause" requirement for termination during the extended use period, as enacted in 1989, applied only in the event of early termination of that period, and was obviously intended to protect existing tenants for a minimum three-year period. The 1990 amendment broadened that requirement, however, and made it applicable throughout the entire extended use period, even if there was no early termination. That is clear both as a matter of ordinary statutory construction and from the legislative history of the 1990 provision. Respondent's view that the requirement remains applicable only to the three-year period following early termination makes no sense. The amendment would have been unnecessary for that purpose. The limited "grandfather" requirement applicable to early termination was already in the law. Placing the requirement in §42(h)(6)(B)(i), even though it had no relevance to the "applicable fraction," which was the subject of §42(h)(6)(B)(i), made it a condition of an "extended low-income housing commitment" and thus of the landlord's entitlement to the tax credit.

The legislative history of the 1990 amendment clearly supports that intent. Although the technical correction provisions of the 1990 Act were posited by the Chairman of the House Ways and Means Committee, upon introduction of the legislation, as making "technical and clerical corrections" to the 1989 law in an effort "to make the language of the law understandable and clear" (see remarks of Congressman Rostenkowski, 136 Cong. Rec. H 7138, 101st Cong. 2nd Sess. Aug. 3, 1990), the Report of the House Ways and Means Committee notes that "the bill *also* clarifies that the extended low-income housing commitment *must* prohibit the eviction or termination of tenancy (other than for good cause) of an existing tenant of a low-income unit or any increase in the gross rent inconsistent with the rent restrictions on the unit." (Emphasis added). 101 H. Rpt. 894 (Oct. 17, 1990). See also summary of the provisions of H.R. 5454 placed in the Congressional Record by Representative Rostenkowski upon introduction of the bill ("The bill clarifies that the extended low-income housing commitment must prohibit the eviction or termination of tenancy (other than for good cause) of an existing tenant of a low-income unit or any increase in the gross rent inconsistent with the rent restrictions on the unit"). 136 Cong. Rec. H 7138, supra. It is clear, therefore, that, both during the initial compliance period and during the extended use period, a landlord participating in the § 42 tax credit program may not terminate the tenancy of a low-income tenant other than for good cause. See Cimarron Village v. Washington, 659 N.W.2d 811 (Minn.App.2003); Templeton Arms v. Feins, 531 A.2d 361 ([N.J.] 1987).

Effect on Tenant Holding Over Statute

The requirement of good cause is but one prong of petitioner's argument. The other is that the requirement gives to petitioner a right or entitlement to continued occupancy and thus effectively converts a fixed-term lease into an indefinite one that continues in existence and does not expire until the end of the extended use period. This is based on the notion that, as good cause is required to terminate the tenancy, the tenancy cannot be terminated simply because the underlying lease expires. That second prong, indeed, is the linchpin of her argument that the tenant holding over statute is inapplicable because, until the expiration of the extended use period, she cannot be a tenant holding over. Consistently with our interpretation of 26 U.S.C. § 42, we agree with petitioner that her tenancy may not be terminated solely because of the expiration of her lease—that good cause is required to evict even as a tenant holding over—but we do not agree that she cannot be a tenant holding over, that the lease is one that continues indefinitely until the end of the extended use period.

At one time, the law may have supported petitioner's view of an indefinite lease. Prior to the consolidation of the certificate and voucher programs in a new § 1437f(o) in 1998, the leasing provisions governing those programs were contained in § 1437f(d)(1)(B), which provided, in relevant part, that (1) the lease between owner and tenant had to be for at least one year "and shall contain other terms and conditions specified by the Secretary," and (2) the owner could not "terminate the tenancy except for serious or repeated violation of the terms and conditions of the lease, for violation of applicable Federal, State, or local law, or for other good cause." Section 1437f(d)(1)(B)(iii) through (v) listed certain conduct that would be cause for termination.

In 1995, the Secretary adopted new regulations for the certificate and voucher programs. See 60 FR 34660 (July 3, 1995) adopting new 24 C.F.R. § 982.309. Those regulations required the lease to be for an initial term of at least one year and to provide either "for automatic renewal for successive definite terms (e.g., month-to-month or year-to-year); or ... for automatic indefinite extension of the lease term." § 982.309(b)(1) and (2). It provided that the term of the lease would terminate if the owner, the tenant, or the two together terminated the lease, but stated that, during the term of the lease, the owner could not terminate the lease except for good cause. §§ 982.309(b)(3), 982.310(a). In proposing those regulations, the Department noted that they were intended merely to "confirm and clarify" the existing principle that "the tenancy continues automatically after the end of the initial lease term" and that "there is no need or requirement for the parties to execute a new lease or lease extension" as "the automatic extension is provided for in the lease originally executed by the landlord and family." 58 FR 11292 (Feb. 24, 1993). It continued:

> The difference between an automatic indefinite extension and an extension for pre-defined definite terms is only a difference of form. For all program tenancies, the owner may only terminate the tenancy for statutory good cause grounds, whether during the course of the initial or extended term, or at the end of the initial or any extended term. In this respect, tenancies in the Section 8 tenant-based programs differ from private unassisted tenancies, where the owner may typically evict the tenant without cause at the end of the lease term. *In the tenant-based Section 8 programs, simple expiration of the lease term is not grounds for termination of tenancy.*

Under that regime, most of the few courts that considered the matter concluded that the requirement of good cause applied not only during the term of the lease but after the lease expired—that it governed as well the decision whether to renew or extend the lease. In Swann v. Gastonia Housing Authority, 502 F. Supp. 362, 365 (W.D.N.C.1980), aff'd in part, 675 F.2d 1342 (4th Cir. 1982), the District Court observed:

> The purpose of the Act would be frustrated if a landlord were allowed to participate in and take advantage of the economic security provided to landlords under the Act, and yet the tenant were stripped of any reciprocal security by being vulnerable to eviction without good cause at the expiration of the lease term. Congress could not have intended such unfairness and insecurity in an area as critical for low-income families as is basic housing.

That aspect of the decision was affirmed by the Fourth Circuit Court. See 675 F.2d at 1345.

A Federal court in California reached a similar conclusion, on a somewhat more precise basis. In Mitchell v. U.S. Dept. of Housing & Urban Develop., 569 F. Supp. 701, 707–08 (N.D. Cal. 1983), the court noted that the limitation in § 1437f(d) was on a termination of "the tenancy," not termination of "the lease." It concluded that, "if Congress had intended the good cause requirement to be applicable only to mid-lease evictions, it could have easily selected the phrase 'terminate the lease.'" Applying the good cause requirement to non-renewals following expiration, the court said, "is not onerous, but merely fair." Id. at 709. See also Templeton Arms v. Feins, supra, 531 A.2d 361; Cimarron Village v. Washington, supra, 659 N.W.2d 811; Joy v. Daniels, 479 F.2d 1236 (4th Cir.1973). We intimated as much, although the issue was not directly before us, in Carroll v. Housing Opportunities Comm'n, 306 Md. 515, 510 A.2d 540 (1986)....

The statutory and regulatory regime changed significantly in 1998, however, when Congress consolidated the certificate and voucher programs in a new § 1437f(o). In place of the lease requirements of § 1437f(d), the new programs became subject to § 1437f(o)(7) which, after requiring a one-year initial lease (unless the public housing agency approves a shorter term), provides that the lease shall (1) be "in a standard form used in the locality by the dwelling unit owner," (2) "contain terms and conditions that—(I) are consistent with State and local law; and (II) apply generally to tenants in the property who are not assisted under this section," and (3) "provide that during the term of the lease, the owner shall not terminate the tenancy except for serious or repeated violation of the terms and conditions of the lease, for violation of applicable Federal, State, or local law, or for other good cause." See P.L. 105-276, 112 Stat. 2461, 2599. Those are the current provisions.

In conformance with that statutory change, the applicable regulations were also significantly rewritten. See 64 FR 26632 (May 14, 1999). They continue to require an initial lease of one year, unless the public housing agency approves a shorter term, but gone are the provisions requiring automatic renewal. They are replaced by the new provisions in §982.308 requiring the lease to conform with standard leases in the community and with State landlord-tenant law. As the Department advised in proposing these new regulations, "the lease form must be in the standard form used in the locality by the owner" and "must contain terms that are consistent with State and local law, and that apply generally to unassisted tenants in the same property." 64 FR 26632, supra.

The pre-1998 version of §1437f, and the regulations implementing it, were far more consistent with the post-1990 structure of the tax credit provision in establishing that good cause was required to terminate the tenancy of a voucher program tenant, whether during the term of a lease or upon its expiration. Whether they would have gone further and supported the notion of an indefinite tenancy is a moot point now, as the provisions in the old law that may have supported that proposition have been deleted in favor of the requirement that voucher program leases be consistent with leases generally used in the community, leases, like the one in this case, that ordinarily carry fixed expiration dates and that permit eviction under the State tenant holding over law. The new, current, provisions clearly militate against the notion of an indefinite tenancy—a never-ending lease.

We do not believe that the new provisions were intended, or effective, to delete the requirement that decisions not to renew or extend a lease upon its expiration require good cause, however. For one thing, that would place §1437f(o) in conflict with 26 U.S.C. §42 which, as we noted, precludes both the "eviction" and the "termination of tenancy" of existing low-income tenants other than for good cause. The two sections are part of an integrated statutory scheme, and, as we have often said, "a provision contained within an integrated statutory scheme must be understood in that context and harmonized to the extent possible with other provisions of the statutory scheme." Balto. Gas & Elec. v. Public Serv. Comm'n, 501 A.2d 1307, 1313 ([Md.]1986).

Such a construction is also more consonant with the Congressional intent. Although the changes to §1437f were certainly intended to allow landlords more flexibility and to bring some aspects of the voucher program more in line with both private residential leasing practices and State landlord-tenant law, we do not believe that they were intended to subject voucher tenants to the arbitrary whims of landlords who are reaping a significant tax advantage from the program. If we were to conclude that the good cause requirement applies only to mid-term evictions and not to renewal decisions, the program would lose substantial stability, as tenants could be evicted for no reason at the end of a one-year lease or at any time thereafter on 60 days notice. That would hardly be consistent with the declared Congressional purpose of "aiding low-income families in obtaining a decent place to live and of promoting economically mixed housing." §1437f(a).

The two statutes can easily be read harmoniously, with each other and with the overall Congressional purpose. We hold that, whatever term may be stated in the lease, a voucher program tenant may not be evicted by a landlord who has qualified for a §42 tax credit and is continuing to receive rent subsidies, either during the term of the lease or at the expiration of that term, except for conduct or circumstances that qualify under the Federal law as good cause. We hold further, however, that neither §42 nor §1437f(o), as currently worded, precludes use of the State tenant holding over statute as a procedural mechanism to remove a tenant who is, indeed, holding over after the expiration of the term of his/her lease. To succeed under that statute, the landlord must comply with its terms and conditions *and* establish good cause for refusing to renew the tenancy.

Existence of Good Cause

We thus come to the final question of whether respondent established sufficient facts to constitute good cause for its decision to terminate petitioner's month-to-month lease. Under Maryland Rule 8-131(c), we review the case on both the law and the evidence but do not set aside the judgment on the evidence unless the judgment is clearly erroneous, giving due regard to the ability of the trial court to judge the credibility of the witnesses.

As we have indicated, the HUD regulations, 24 C.F.R. §982.310(d), provide a non-exclusive list of conduct or circumstances that might establish good cause for terminating a lease. Among them is "[a] family history of ... destruction of property, or of living or housekeeping habits resulting in damage to the unit or premises." In this case, the Housing Authority inspector found petitioner's residence to be plagued with various maintenance problems—foul odors, apparently from a cat, holes in several walls, apparently caused by petitioner's children, dirty floors, walls, and kitchen appliances, inoperable smoke detectors, missing or torn screens—some of which dated back to 1998, only two years after she commenced occupancy. Petitioner admitted to most of the problems, and the court found them to exist. We do not find its ruling to be clearly erroneous.

Judgment of Circuit Court affirmed, with costs.

Notes and Questions

1. The LIHTC statute, 26 U.S.C. §42 (h)(6)(D), provides:

   (h) Limitation on aggregate credit allowable with respect to projects located in a state. —* * *

      (6) Buildings eligible for credit only if minimum long-term commitment to low-income housing. —* * *

         (D) Extended use period. — For purposes of this paragraph, the term "extended use period" means the period—

            (i) beginning on the 1st day in the compliance period on which such building is part of a qualified low-income housing project, and

            (ii) ending on the later of—

         (I) the date specified by such agency in such agreement, or

         (II) the date which is 15 years after the close of the compliance period.

   Should the court in Carter have taken this into account? How would this have affected the decision?

2. Is it sound policy to require good cause for evictions? Consider these comments from a property manager:

   [T]he only successful method for maintaining low income complexes as safe, clean environments (which is what the "good" tenants deserve) is to rely upon a hardline, zero tolerance policy of proactive action with regards to the termination of residents whose households refuse to comply with community rules.

   The "no-cause" termination was an effective and fair tool for relative quick removal of bad tenants.... "[N]o-cause" termination provided a much larger benefit to tenants than landlords! With "no-cause" a terminated tenant was able to leave a rental property with a "clean" rental history, making it very easy for the tenant to qualify for acceptance at the next property he/she would be applying to. As the Tax Credit terminations must now be documented as "for-cause," the terminated tenant will now be burdened with a documented record of reason/s for terminations, and the property that terminated will be legally bound to provide a negative referral for the tenant when contacted by prospective properties for rental history verification.

3. Pertinent provisions of IRS Revenue Ruling 2004-82 are set out below. How will this affect a tenant in Ms. Carter's position?

C. Extended Low-income Housing Commitment Issue

Law

Section 42(h)(6)(A) provides that no credit will be allowed with respect to any building for the taxable year unless an extended low-income housing commitment (as defined in §42(h)(6)(B)) is in effect as of the end of the taxable year. Section 42(h)(6)(B)(i) provides that "the term "extended low-income housing commitment" means any agreement between the taxpayer and the housing credit agency which requires that the applicable fraction (as defined in §42(c)(1)) for the building for each taxable year in the extended use period will not be less than the applicable fraction specified in the agreement and *which prohibits the actions described in subclauses (I) and (II) of §42(h)(6)(E)(ii)*" (emphasis added).

Section 42(h)(6)(E)(ii) provides that the termination of an extended low-income housing commitment under §42(h)(6)(E)(i) will not be construed to permit before the close of the 3-year period following the termination (I) the eviction or termination of tenancy (other than for good cause) of an existing tenant of any low-income unit, or (II) any increase in the gross rent with respect to a low-income unit not otherwise permitted under §42. Section 42(h)(6)(D) defines the term "extended use period" as the period beginning on the first day in the compliance period on which the building is part of a qualified low-income housing project and ending on the later of (1) the date specified by the agency in the extended low-income housing commitment, or (2) the date which is 15 years after the close of the compliance period.

Section 42(h)(6)(J) provides that if, during a taxable year, there is a determination that a valid extended low-income housing commitment was not in effect as of the beginning of the year, the determination will not apply to any period before that year and §42(h)(6)(A) will be applied without regard to the determination provided that the failure is corrected within 1 year from the date of the determination.

In the Omnibus Budget Reconciliation Act of 1990, 1991-2 C.B. 481, 531 (the "1990 Act"), Congress amended §42(h)(6)(B)(i) by adding the language emphasized above, which prohibits the actions described in subclauses (I) and (II) of §42(h)(6)(E)(ii). At the time of this amendment, however, §42(h)(6)(E)(ii) was already part of §42.

The legislative history to §42 states that the extended low-income housing commitment must prohibit the eviction or termination of tenancy (other than for good cause) of an existing tenant of a low-income unit or any increase in the gross rent inconsistent with the rent restrictions on the unit. H. Rep. No. 894, 101st Cong., 2d Sess. 10, 13 (1990).

Q-5.

Must the extended low-income housing commitment prohibit the actions described in subclauses (I) and (II) of §42(h)(6)(E)(ii) only for the 3-year period described in §42(h)(6)(E)(ii)?

A-5.

No. Section 42(h)(6)(B)(i) requires that an extended low-income housing commitment include a prohibition during the extended use period against (1) the eviction or the termination of tenancy (other than for good cause) of an existing tenant of any low-income unit (no-cause eviction protection) and (2) any increase in the gross rent with respect to the unit not otherwise permitted under §42. When Congress amended §42(h)(6)(B)(i) to add the language emphasized above, §42(h)(6)(E)(ii) was already part of §42. As a result, Congress must have intended the amendment to §42(h)(6)(B)(i) to add an additional requirement beyond what was contained in §42(h)(6)(E)(ii), which already prohibited the actions described in that section for the 3 years following the termination of the extended use period. Because the requirements of §42(h)(6)(B)(i) otherwise apply for the extended use period, Congress must have intended the addition of the prohibition against the actions described in subclauses (I) and (II) of §42(h)(6)(E)(ii) to apply throughout the extended use period.

If it is determined by the end of a taxable year that a taxpayer's extended low-income housing commitment for a building does not meet the requirements for an extended low-income housing commitment under §42(h)(6)(B) (for example, it does not provide no-cause eviction protection for the tenants of low-income units throughout the extended use period), the low-income housing credit is not allowable with respect to the building for the taxable year, or any prior taxable year. However, if the failure to have a valid extended low-income housing commitment in effect is corrected within 1 year from the date of the determination, the determination will not apply to the current year of the credit period or any prior year.

Pursuant to this revenue ruling, each housing credit agency is required to review its extended low-income housing commitments for compliance with the interpretation of §42(h)(6)(B)(i) provided in this question and answer. This review must be completed by December 31, 2004. If during the review period the housing credit agency determines that an extended low-income housing commitment is not in compliance with the interpretation of §42(h)(6)(B)(i) provided in this question and answer, the 1-year period described under §42(h)(6)(J) will commence on the date of that determination.

2. Decent, Safe, and Sanitary Conditions

Altz v. Leiberson

233 N.Y. 16, 134 N.E. 703 (Court of Appeals of New York 1922)

Cardozo, J. Hiscock, Ch. J., Hogan, Pound, McLaughlin, and Crane, JJ., concur; Andrews, J., dissents.

Cardozo, J.

The plaintiff in November, 1917, was a tenant in the defendant's apartment house in the city of New York. She was injured while in her room by a falling ceiling, which the defendant, after timely notice of the danger, had omitted to repair.... The question to be determined is whether the omission was a breach of duty.

At common law there was no duty resting on the landlord of an apartment house to repair the rooms demised. His duty of repair was limited to those parts of the building which the occupants enjoyed in common. The Tenement House Law has changed the measure of his burden.

> A "tenement house" is any house or building, or portion thereof, which is either rented, leased, let or hired out, to be occupied, or is occupied, in whole or in part, as the home or residence of three families or more living independently of each other, and doing their cooking upon the premises, and includes apartment houses, flat houses and all other houses so occupied

> Every tenement house and all the parts thereof shall be kept in good repair.

The comprehensive sweep of this enactment admits of no exception. We are not at liberty to confine it to those parts of the building not included within the premises demised. The legislature has said that the duty shall extend, not only to some parts, but to all. Apter words could hardly have been chosen wherewith to exclude division of responsibility between one part and another. The command of the statute, directed, as it plainly is, against the owner has thus changed the ancient rule. Whether "owner" may mean at times a lessee of the whole building is a question not before us. No doubt, before a right of action will accrue in favor of the tenant, there must be notice, actual or constructive, of the defect to be repaired. No doubt the defect itself must be one that has relation to the maintenance of the building as a tenantable habitation. This limitation results by implication from the context of the section, which forms part of an article entitled "sanitary provisions." The meaning is that the premises shall not be suffered to fall into decay. The duty to prevent this, which, in part at least, once rested upon the tenant, is now cast upon another.

A narrower construction ignores, not only the letter of the statute, but the evil to be cured. A "tenement house," as the meaning is enlarged by the definition of the statute, may include the dwellings of the rich. In its primary and common application, it suggests the dwellings of the poor. We may be sure that the framers of this statute, when regulating tenement life, had uppermost in thought the care of those who are unable to care for themselves. The legislature must have known that unless repairs in the rooms of the poor were made by the landlord, they would not be made by any one. The duty imposed became commensurate with the need. The right to seek redress is not limited to the city or its officers. The right extends to all whom there was a purpose to protect. * * *

The judgment should be affirmed with costs.

Javins v. First National Realty Corp.
428 F.2d 1071 (D.C. Cir. 1970),
cert. denied, 400 U.S. 925 (1970)

Mr. Edmund E. Fleming, Boston, Mass., for appellants.

Mr. Herman Miller, Washington, D.C., for appellee.

Mrs. Caryl S. Terry, Washington, D.C., filed a brief on behalf of Washington Planning and Housing Association as amicus curiae urging reversal.

Mrs. Margaret F. Ewing, Mrs. Florence Wagman Roisman and Mrs. Patricia M. Wald, Washington, D.C., filed a brief on behalf of Neighborhood Legal Services Program as amicus curiae urging reversal.

Messrs. Myron Moskovitz and Peter Honigsberg filed a brief on behalf of National Housing Law Project as amicus curiae urging reversal.

Before Wright, McGowan, and Robb, Circuit Judges.

J. Skelly Wright, Circuit Judge.

These cases present the question whether housing code violations which arise during the term of a lease have any effect upon the tenant's obligation to pay rent. The Landlord and Tenant Branch of the District of Columbia Court of General Sessions ruled proof of such violations inadmissible when proffered as a defense to an eviction action for nonpayment of rent. The District of Columbia Court of Appeals upheld this ruling.

Because of the importance of the question presented, we granted appellants' petitions for leave to appeal.* We now reverse and hold that a warranty of habitability, measured by the standards set out in the Housing Regulations for the District of Columbia, is implied by operation of law into leases of urban dwelling units covered by those Regulations and that breach of this warranty gives rise to the usual remedies for breach of contract.

I.

The facts revealed by the record are simple. By separate written leases, each of the appellants rented an apartment in a three-building apartment complex in Northwest Washington known as Clifton Terrace. The landlord, First National Realty Corporation, filed separate actions in the Landlord and Tenant Branch of the Court of General Sessions on April 8, 1966, seeking possession on the ground that each of the appellants had defaulted in the payment of rent due for the month of April. The tenants, appellants here, admitted that they had not paid the landlord any rent for April. However, they alleged numerous violations of the Housing Regulations as "an equitable defense or (a) claim by way of recoupment or set-off in an amount equal to the rent claim," as provided in the rules of the Court of General Sessions. They offered to prove "that there are approximately 1500 violations of the Housing Regulations of the District of Columbia in the building at Clifton Terrace, where Defendant resides[,] some affecting the premises of this Defendant directly, others indirectly, and all tending to establish a course of conduct of violation of the Housing Regulations to the damage of Defendants...." Appellants conceded at trial, however, that this offer of proof reached only violations which had arisen since the term of the lease had commenced.** The Court of General Sessions refused appellants' offer of proof and entered judgment for the landlord. The District of Columbia Court of Appeals affirmed, rejecting the argument made by appellants that the landlord was under a contractual duty to maintain the premises in compliance with the Housing Regulations.

II.

Since, in traditional analysis, a lease was the conveyance of an interest in land, courts have usually utilized the special rules governing real property transactions to resolve

---

* Editor's Note: At that time, the federal court of appeals had such discretionary jurisdiction over cases in the local courts. This ended with the District of Columbia Court Reform Act of 1970, PL 91-358, 84 Stat. 473 (1970), but this case was governed by the prior law. 80 Cong. Ch. 646, 62 Stat. 869.

** Editor's Note: This became pertinent because the local court of appeals had decided Brown v. Southall Realty after the Clifton Terrace tenants had filed their answers in the landlord-tenant cases. See n. 43, infra.

controversies involving leases. However, as the Supreme Court has noted in another context, "the body of private property law..., more than almost any other branch of law, has been shaped by distinctions whose validity is largely historical." Courts have a duty to reappraise old doctrines in the light of the facts and values of contemporary life—particularly old common law doctrines which the courts themselves created and developed. As we have said before, "The continued vitality of the common law ... depends upon its ability to reflect contemporary community values and ethics."

The assumption of landlord-tenant law, derived from feudal property law, that a lease primarily conveyed to the tenant an interest in land may have been reasonable in a rural, agrarian society; it may continue to be reasonable in some leases involving farming or commercial land. In these cases, the value of the lease to the tenant is the land itself. But in the case of the modern apartment dweller, the value of the lease is that it gives him a place to live. The city dweller who seeks to lease an apartment on the third floor of a tenement has little interest in the land 30 or 40 feet below, or even in the bare right to possession within the four walls of his apartment. When American city dwellers, both rich and poor, seek "shelter" today, they seek a well known package of goods and services—a package which includes not merely walls and ceilings, but also adequate heat, light and ventilation, serviceable plumbing facilities, secure windows and doors, proper sanitation, and proper maintenance.

Professor Powell summarizes the present state of the law:

> ... The complexities of city life, and the proliferated problems of modern society in general, have created new problems for lessor and lessees and these have been commonly handled by specific clauses inserted in leases. This growth in the number and detail of specific lease covenants has reintroduced into the law of estates for years a predominantly contractual ingredient. In practice, the law today concerning estates for years consists chiefly of rules determining the construction and effect of lease covenants.... [10]

Ironically, however, the rules governing the construction and interpretation of "predominantly contractual" obligations in leases have too often remained rooted in old property law.

Some courts have realized that certain of the old rules of property law governing leases are inappropriate for today's transactions. In order to reach results more in accord with the legitimate expectations of the parties and the standards of the community, courts have been gradually introducing more modern precepts of contract law in interpreting leases. Proceeding piecemeal has, however, led to confusion where "decisions are frequently conflicting, not because of a healthy disagreement on social policy, but because of the lingering impact of rules whose policies are long since dead." [Kessler, The Protection of the Consumer Under Modern Sales Law, 74 Yale L.J. 262, 263 (1964)].

In our judgment the trend toward treating leases as contracts is wise and well considered. Our holding in this case reflects a belief that leases of urban dwelling units should be interpreted and construed like any other contract.[13]

---

10. 2 R. Powell, Real Property, para 221[1] at 179 (1967).

13. This approach does not deny the possible importance of the fact that land is involved in a transaction. The interpretation and construction of contracts between private parties has always required courts to be sensitive and responsive to myriad different factors. We believe contract doctrines allow courts to be properly sensitive to all relevant factors in interpreting lease obligations. We also intend no alteration of statutory or case law definitions of the term "real property" for purposes of statutes or decisions on recordation, descent, conveyancing, creditors' rights, etc. We contem-

III.

Modern contract law has recognized that the buyer of goods and services in an industrialized society must rely upon the skill and honesty of the supplier to assure that goods and services purchased are of adequate quality. In interpreting most contracts, courts have sought to protect the legitimate expectations of the buyer and have steadily widened the seller's responsibility for the quality of goods and services through implied warranties of fitness and merchantability. Thus without any special agreement a merchant will be held to warrant that his goods are fit for the ordinary purposes for which such goods are used and that they are at least of reasonably average quality. Moreover, if the supplier has been notified that goods are required for a specific purpose, he will be held to warrant that any goods sold are fit for that purpose. These implied warranties have become widely accepted and well established features of the common law, supported by the overwhelming body of case law. Today most states as well as the District of Columbia have codified and enacted these warranties into statute, as to the sale of goods, in the Uniform Commercial Code.

Implied warranties of quality have not been limited to cases involving sales. The consumer renting a chattel, paying for services, or buying a combination of goods and services must rely upon the skill and honesty of the supplier to at least the same extent as a purchaser of goods. Courts have not hesitated to find implied warranties of fitness and merchantability in such situations. In most areas product liability law has moved far beyond "mere" implied warranties running between two parties in privity with each other.

The rigid doctrines of real property law have tended to inhibit the application of implied warranties to transactions involving real estate. Now, however, courts have begun to hold sellers and developers of real property responsible for the quality of their product. For example, builders of new homes have recently been held liable to purchasers for improper construction on the ground that the builders had breached an implied warranty of fitness.[22] In other cases courts have held builders of new homes liable for breach of an implied warranty that all local building regulations had been complied with. And following the developments in other areas, very recent decisions[24] and commentary suggest the possible extension of liability to parties other than the immediate seller for improper construction of residential real estate.

Despite this trend in the sale of real estate, many courts have been unwilling to imply warranties of quality, specifically a warranty of habitability, into leases of apartments. Recent decisions have offered no convincing explanation for their refusal; rather they have relied without discussion upon the old common law rule that the lessor is not obligated to repair unless he covenants to do so in the written lease contract. However, the Supreme Courts of at least two states, in recent and well reasoned opinions, have held landlords to implied warranties of quality in housing leases. In our judgment, the old no-repair rule cannot coexist with the obligations imposed on the landlord by a typical modern housing code, and must be abandoned[28] in favor of an implied warranty of

---

plate only that contract law is to determine the rights and obligations of the parties to the lease agreement, as between themselves. The civil law has always viewed the lease as a contract, and in our judgment that perspective has proved superior to that of the common law.

22. See ... Schipper v. Levitt & Sons, Inc., [44 N.J. 70, 207 A.2 314 (1965)]....

24. Connor v. Great Western Savings and Loan Ass'n., 447, P.2d 609 (1968) (Traynor, Ch. J.). Chief Justice Traynor's excellent opinion utilizes tort doctrines to extend liability beyond the immediate seller.

28. As far as tort liability is concerned, we have previously held that the old common law rule has been changed by passage of the housing code and that the landlord has a duty to maintain reasonably safe premises.

habitability.[29] In the District of Columbia, the standards of this warranty are set out in the Housing Regulations.

IV.

A.

In our judgment the common law itself must recognize the landlord's obligation to keep his premises in a habitable condition. This conclusion is compelled by three separate considerations. First, we believe that the old rule was based on certain factual assumptions which are no longer true; on its own terms, it can no longer be justified. Second, we believe that the consumer protection cases discussed above require that the old rule be abandoned in order to bring residential landlord-tenant law into harmony with the principles on which those cases rest. Third, we think that the nature of today's urban housing market also dictates abandonment of the old rule.

The common law rule absolving the lessor of all obligation to repair originated in the early Middle Ages.[30] Such a rule was perhaps well suited to an agrarian economy; the land was more important[31] than whatever small living structure was included in the leasehold, and the tenant farmer was fully capable of making repairs himself.[32] These historical facts were the basis on which the common law constructed its rule; they also provided the necessary prerequisites for its application.[33]

Court decisions in the late 1800's began to recognize that the factual assumptions of the common law were no longer accurate in some cases. For example, the common law, since it assumed that the land was the most important part of the leasehold, required a tenant to pay rent even if any building on the land was destroyed.[34] Faced with such a rule and the ludicrous results it produced, in 1863 the New York Court of Appeals de-

---

29. Although the present cases involve written leases, we think there is no particular significance in this fact. The landlord's warranty is implied in oral and written leases for all types of tenancies.

30. The rule was "settled" by 1485. 3 W. Holdsworth, A History of English Law 122–123 (6th ed. 1934). The common law rule discussed in text originated in the even older rule prohibiting the tenant from committing waste. The writ of waste expanded as the tenant's right to possession grew stronger. Eventually, in order to protect the landowner's reversionary interest, the tenant became obligated to make repairs and liable to eviction and damages if he failed to do so.

31. The land was so central to the original common law conception of a leasehold that rent was viewed as "issuing" from the land: "The governing idea is that the land is bound to pay the rent.... We may almost go to the length of saying that the land pays it through (the tenant's) hand." 2 F. Pollock & F. Maitland, The History of English Law 131 (2nd ed. 1923).

32. Many later judicial opinions have added another justification of the old common law rule. They have invoked the timeworn cry of caveat emptor and argued that a lessee has the opportunity to inspect the premises. On the basis of his inspection, the tenant must then take the premises "as is," according to this reasoning. As an historical matter, the opportunity to inspect was not thought important when the rule was first devised.

33. Even the old common law courts responded with a different rule for a landlord-tenant relationship which did not conform to the model of the usual agrarian lease. Much more substantial obligations were placed upon the keepers of inns (the only multiple dwelling houses known to the common law). Their guests were interested solely in shelter and could not be expected to make their own repairs. "The modern apartment dweller more closely resembles the guest in an inn than he resembles an agrarian tenant, but the law has not generally recognized the similarity." J. Levi, P. Hablutzel, L. Rosenberg & J. White, Model Residential Landlord-Tenant Code 6–7 (Tent. Draft 1969).

34. Paradine v. Jane, Aleyn 26, 82 Eng.Rep. 897 (K.B. 1947); 1 American Law of Property ... § 3.103.

clined to hold that an upper story tenant was obliged to continue paying rent after his apartment building burned down. The court simply pointed out that the urban tenant had no interest in the land, only in the attached building.

Another line of cases created an exception to the no-repair rule for short term leases of furnished dwellings. The Massachusetts Supreme Judicial Court, a court not known for its willingness to depart from the common law, supported this exception, pointing out:

> ... [A] different rule should apply to one who hires a furnished room, or a furnished house, for a few days, or a few weeks or months. Its fitness for immediate use of a particular kind, as indicated by its appointments, is a far more important element entering into the contract than when there is a mere lease of real estate. One who lets for a short term a house provided with all furnishings and appointments for immediate residence may be supposed to contract in reference to a well-understood purpose of the hirer to use it as a habitation.... It would be unreasonable to hold, under such circumstances, that the landlord does not impliedly agree that what he is letting is a house suitable for occupation in its condition at the time....

These as well as other similar cases demonstrate that some courts began some time ago to question the common law's assumptions that the land was the most important feature of a leasehold and that the tenant could feasibly make any necessary repairs himself. Where those assumptions no longer reflect contemporary housing patterns, the courts have created exceptions to the general rule that landlords have no duty to keep their premises in repair.

It is overdue for courts to admit that these assumptions are no longer true with regard to all urban housing. Today's urban tenants, the vast majority of whom live in multiple dwelling houses, are interested, not in the land, but solely in "a house suitable for occupation." Furthermore, today's city dweller usually has a single, specialized skill unrelated to maintenance work; he is unable to make repairs like the "jack-of-all-trades" farmer who was the common law's model of the lessee. Further, unlike his agrarian predecessor who often remained on one piece of land for his entire life, urban tenants today are more mobile than ever before. A tenant's tenure in a specific apartment will often not be sufficient to justify efforts at repairs. In addition, the increasing complexity of today's dwellings renders them much more difficult to repair than the structures of earlier times. In a multiple dwelling repair may require access to equipment and areas in the control of the landlord. Low and middle income tenants, even if they were interested in making repairs, would be unable to obtain any financing for major repairs since they have no long-term interest in the property.

Our approach to the common law of landlord and tenant ought to be aided by principles derived from the consumer protection cases referred to above. In a lease contract, a tenant seeks to purchase from his landlord shelter for a specified period of time. The landlord sells housing as a commercial businessman and has much greater opportunity, incentive and capacity to inspect and maintain the condition of his building. Moreover, the tenant must rely upon the skill and bona fides of his landlord at least as much as a car buyer must rely upon the car manufacturer. In dealing with major problems, such as heating, plumbing, electrical or structural defects, the tenant's position corresponds precisely with "the ordinary consumer who cannot be expected to have the knowledge or capacity or even the opportunity to make adequate inspection of mechanical instrumentalities, like automobiles, and to decide for himself whether they are reasonably fit for the designed purpose." Henningsen v. Bloomfield Motors, Inc., 161 A.2d 69, 78 (1960).[42]

Since a lease contract specifies a particular period of time during which the tenant has a right to use his apartment for shelter, he may legitimately expect that the apartment will be fit for habitation for the time period for which it is rented. We point out that in the present cases there is no allegation that appellants' apartments were in poor condition or in violation of the housing code at the commencement of the leases.[43] Since the lessees continue to pay the same rent, they were entitled to expect that the landlord would continue to keep the premises in their beginning condition during the lease term. It is precisely such expectations that the law now recognizes as deserving of formal, legal protection.

Even beyond the rationale of traditional products liability law, the relationship of landlord and tenant suggests further compelling reasons for the law's protection of the tenants' legitimate expectations of quality. The inequality in bargaining power between landlord and tenant has been well documented.[44] Tenants have very little leverage to enforce demands for better housing. Various impediments to competition in the rental housing market, such as racial and class discrimination and standardized form leases, mean that landlords place tenants in a take it or leave it situation. The increasingly severe shortage of adequate housing further increases the landlord's bargaining power and escalates the need for maintaining and improving the existing stock. Finally, the findings by various studies of the social impact of bad housing has led to the realization that poor housing is detrimental to the whole society, not merely to the unlucky ones who must suffer the daily indignity of living in a slum.[48]

Thus we are led by our inspection of the relevant legal principles and precedents to the conclusion that the old common law rule imposing an obligation upon the lessee to repair during the lease term was really never intended to apply to residential urban leaseholds. Contract principles established in other areas of the law provide a more rational framework for the apportionment of landlord-tenant responsibilities; they strongly suggest that a warranty of habitability be implied into all contracts for urban dwellings.

B.

We believe, in any event, that the District's housing code requires that a warranty of habitability be implied in the leases of all housing that it covers. The housing code—formally designated the Housing Regulations of the District of Columbia—was established and authorized by the Commissioners of the District of Columbia on August 11, 1955. Since that time, the code has been updated by numerous orders of the Commissioners. The 75 pages of the Regulations provide a comprehensive regulatory scheme

---

42. Nor should the average tenant be thought capable of "inspecting" plaster, floorboards, roofing, kitchen appliances, etc. To the extent, however, that some defects are obvious, the law must take note of the present housing shortage. Tenants may have no real alternative but to accept such housing with the expectation that the landlord will make necessary repairs. Where this is so, caveat emptor must of necessity be rejected.

43. In Brown v. Southall Realty Co., 237 A.2d 834 (1968), the District of Columbia Court of Appeals held that unsafe and unsanitary conditions existing at the beginning of the tenancy and known to the landlord rendered any lease of those premises illegal and void.

44. See Edwards v. Habib, 397 F.2d 687, 701 (1968); 2 R. Powell, supra note 10, P221(1) at 183; President's Committee on Urban Housing, A Decent Home 96 (1968).

48. A. Schorr, Slums and [Social] Insecurity (1963); J. Levi, et al., supra note 33, at 7–8.

setting forth in some detail: (a) the standards which housing in the District of Columbia must meet; (b) which party, the lessor or the lessee, must meet each standard; and (c) a system of inspections, notifications and criminal penalties. The Regulations themselves are silent on the question of private remedies.

Two previous decisions of this court, however, have held that the Housing Regulations create legal rights and duties enforceable in tort by private parties. In Whetzel v. Jess Fisher Management Co., 282 F.2d 943 (1960), we followed the leading case of Altz v. Lieberson, 134 N.E. 703 (1922), in holding (1) that the housing code altered the common law rule and imposed a duty to repair upon the landlord, and (2) that a right of action accrued to a tenant injured by the landlord's breach of this duty. As Judge Cardozo wrote in Lieberson:

> We may be sure that the framers of this statute, when regulating tenement life, had uppermost in thought the care of those who are unable to care for themselves. The Legislature must have known that unless repairs in the rooms of the poor were made by the landlord, they would not be made by any one. The duty imposed became commensurate with the need. The right to seek redress is not limited to the city or its officers. The right extends to all whom there was a purpose to protect.

134 N.E. at 107. Recently in Kanelos v. Kettler, 132 U.S. App. D.C. 133, 135, 406 F.2d 951, 953 (1968), we reaffirmed our position in *Whetzel*, holding that "the Housing Regulations did impose maintenance obligation upon appellee [landlord] which he was free to ignore."

* * *

The District of Columbia Court of Appeals gave further effect to the Housing Regulations in Brown v. Southall Realty Co., 237 A.2d 834 (1968). There the landlord knew at the time the lease was signed that housing code violations existed which rendered the apartment "unsafe and unsanitary." Viewing the lease as a contract, the District of Columbia Court of Appeals held that the premises were let in violation of Sections 2304[53] and 2501 of the Regulations and that the lease, therefore, was void as an illegal contract. In the light of Brown, it is clear not only that the housing code creates privately enforceable duties as held in Whetzel, but that the basic validity of every housing contract depends upon substantial compliance with the housing code at the beginning of the lease term. The Brown court relied particularly upon Section 2501 of the Regulations which provides:

> Every premises accommodating one or more habitations shall be maintained and kept in repair so as to provide decent living accommodations for the occupants. This part of this Code contemplates more than mere basic repairs and maintenance to keep out the elements; its purpose is to include repairs and maintenance designed to make a premises or neighborhood healthy and safe.

By its terms, this section applies to maintenance and repair during the lease term. Under the Brown holding, serious failure to comply with this section before the lease term begins renders the contract void. We think it untenable to find that this section has no effect on the contract after it has been signed. To the contrary, by signing the lease

---

53. "No person shall rent or offer to rent any habitation, or the furnishings thereof, unless such habitation and its furnishings are in a clean, safe and sanitary condition, in repair, and free from rodents or vermin."

the landlord has undertaken a continuing obligation to the tenant to maintain the premises in accordance with all applicable law.

This principle of implied warranty is well established. Courts often imply relevant law into contracts to provide a remedy for any damage caused by one party's illegal conduct. In a case closely analogous to the present ones, the Illinois Supreme Court held that a builder who constructed a house in violation of the Chicago building code had breached his contract with the buyer:

> The law existing at the time and place of the making of the contract is deemed a part of the contract, as though expressly referred to or incorporated in it. The rationale for this rule is that the parties to the contract would have expressed that which the law implies "had they not supposed that it was unnecessary to speak of it because the law provided for it." Consequently, the courts, in construing the existing law as part of the express contract, are not reading into the contract provisions different from those expressed and intended by the parties, as defendants contend, but are merely construing the contract in accordance with the intent of the parties.[56]

We follow the Illinois court in holding that the housing code must be read into housing contracts—a holding also required by the purposes and the structure of the code itself.[57] The duties imposed by the Housing Regulations may not be waived or shifted by agreement if the Regulations specifically place the duty upon the lessor. Criminal penalties are provided if these duties are ignored. This regulatory structure was established by the Commissioners because, in their judgment, the grave conditions in the housing market required serious action. Yet official enforcement of the housing code has been far from uniformly effective. Innumerable studies have documented the desperate condition of rental housing in the District of Columbia and in the nation. In view of these circumstances, we think the conclusion reached by the Supreme Court of Wisconsin as to the effect of a housing code on the old common law rule cannot be avoided:

> The legislature has made a policy judgment—that it is socially (and politically) desirable to impose these duties on a property owner—which has rendered the old common law rule obsolete. To follow the old rule of no implied warranty of habitability in leases would, in our opinion, be inconsistent with the current legislative policy concerning housing standards.

We therefore hold that the Housing Regulations imply a warranty of habitability, measured by the standards which they set out, into leases of all housing that they cover.

V.

In the present cases, the landlord sued for possession for nonpayment of rent. Under contract principles,[61] however, the tenant's obligation to pay rent is dependent upon the landlord's performance of his obligations, including his warranty to maintain the premises in habitable condition. In order to determine whether any rent is owed to the

---

56. See Schiro v. W.E. Gould & Co., 165 N.E.2d 286 (1960).

57. The housing and sanitary codes, especially in light of Congress' explicit direction for their enactment, indicate a strong and pervasive congressional concern to secure for the city's slum dwellers decent, or at least safe and sanitary, places to live.

61. In extending all contract remedies for breach to the parties to a lease, we include an action for specific performance of the landlord's implied warranty of habitability.

landlord, the tenants must be given an opportunity to prove the housing code violations alleged as breach of the landlord's warranty.[62]

At trial, the finder of fact must make two findings: (1) whether the alleged violations[63] existed during the period for which past due rent is claimed, and (2) what portion, if any or all, of the tenant's obligation to pay rent was suspended by the landlord's breach. If no part of the tenant's rental obligation is found to have been suspended, then a judgment for possession may issue forthwith. On the other hand, if the jury determines that the entire rental obligation has been extinguished by the landlord's total breach, then the action for possession on the ground of nonpayment must fail.[64]

The jury may find that part of the tenant's rental obligation has been suspended but that part of the unpaid back rent is indeed owed to the landlord. In these circumstances, no judgment for possession should issue if the tenant agrees to pay the partial rent found to be due. If the tenant refuses to pay the partial amount, a judgment for possession may then be entered.

The judgment of the District of Columbia Court of Appeals is reversed and the cases are remanded for further proceedings consistent with this opinion.[67]

So ordered.

Circuit Judge Robb concurs in the result and in Parts IV-B and V of the opinion.

Note

For further information about Javins, "arguably the most influential landlord-tenant case of the twentieth century," see Richard H. Chused, Saunders (a.k.a. Javins) v. First

---

62. To be relevant, of course, the violations must affect the tenant's apartment or common areas which the tenant uses. Moreover, the contract principle that no one may benefit from his own wrong will allow the landlord to defend by proving the damage was caused by the tenant's wrongful action. However, violations resulting from inadequate repairs or materials which disintegrate under normal use would not be assignable to the tenant. Also we agree with the District of Columbia Court of Appeals that the tenant's private rights do not depend on official inspection or official finding of violation by the city government.

63. The jury should be instructed that one or two minor violations standing alone which do not affect habitability are de minimis and would not entitle the tenant to a reduction in rent.

64. As soon as the landlord made the necessary repairs rent would again become due. Our holding, of course, affects only eviction for nonpayment of rent. The landlord is free to seek eviction at the termination of the lease or on any other legal ground.

67. Appellants in the present cases offered to pay rent into the registry of the court during the present action. We think this is an excellent protective procedure. If the tenant defends against an action for possession on the basis of breach of the landlord's warranty of habitability, the trial court may require the tenant to make future rent payments into the registry of the court as they become due; such a procedure would be appropriate only while the tenant remains in possession. The escrowed money will, however, represent rent for the period between the time the landlord files suit and the time the case comes to trial. In the normal course of litigation, the only factual question at trial would be the condition of the apartment during the time the landlord alleged rent was due and not paid.

As a general rule, the escrowed money should be apportioned between the landlord and the tenant after trial on the basis of the finding of rent actually due for the period at issue in the suit. To insure fair apportionment, however, we think either party should be permitted to amend its complaint or answer at any time before trial, to allege a change in the condition of the apartment. In this event, the finder of fact should make a separate finding as to the condition of the apartment at the time at which the amendment was filed. This new finding will have no effect upon the original action; it will only affect the distribution of the escrowed rent paid after the filing of the amendment.

National Realty Corporation, 11 Geo. J. on Pov. L. & Pol'y 191, 193 (2004). An abridged version of this article is in Property Stories 121-68 (Gerald Korngold & Andrew P. Morriss, eds., Foundation Press 2004).

Timeline with Respect to Development of the Implied Warranty of Habitability

1949   Housing Act declares the national housing goal: "the realization, as soon as feasible of the goal of a decent home and a suitable living environment for every American family."[1]

The Act's redevelopment title (Title I) also requires consideration of whether "local public bodies" had "undertaken positive programs" to prevent "the spread or recurrence ... of slums and blighted areas through the adoption, improvement, and modernization of local codes and regulations relating to land use and adequate standards of health, sanitation, and safety for dwelling accommodations."[2]

When the 1949 Act was being debated, the Senate rejected an amendment that would have prohibited racial segregation in public housing, thus encouraging the continued racial segregation in federal housing programs.[3]

1954   Housing Act conditions provision of federal urban renewal funds on each locality's adoption of a "Workable Program for Community Improvement" and mentions a housing code as a possible element of a workable program.[4] The Housing and Home Finance Agency (HHFA), the predecessor of HUD, de-

---

1. Title V of the Housing Act of 1949, Pub. L. 81-171, 82 Stat. 518 as amended, 42 U.S.C. § 1451 et. seq. (October 25, 1949).

2. Title I, §101, 63 Stat. 414 (1949) as amended, 42 U.S.C. § 1450 (1949). "This provision, the ancestor of the 'workable program' requirement, implied, though it did not yet require, stringent use of local housing codes to jack up housing standards in renewal areas, if not elsewhere in the city." Lawrence M. Friedman, Government and Slum Housing: A Century of Frustration 150 (Rand McNally 1968).

3. "Republican senators John Bricker of Ohio and Harry P. Cain of Washington, implacable foes of public housing, unabashedly injected the race issue into congressional debate over the bill in an attempt to derail it. The Bricker-Cain amendment called for a flat prohibition on segregation and reflected the sponsors' calculation that its adoption would strip away vital southern support. Indeed, Democrat Allen Ellender of Louisiana, who pioneered the housing bill, vowed to vote against it should the amendment be passed. Liberal Paul Douglas candidly acknowledged it as the 'death knell' of slum clearance and redevelopment...." Senator Douglas and others voted against the Bricker-Cain amendment. "Within months, high [federal] PHA officials made clear their refusal to require nonsegregation in federally supported projects.... 'PHA felt it could not do, by its regulations ... what Congress did not see fit to do by legislation.'" Arnold R. Hirsch, *Searching for a 'Sound Negro Policy': A Racial Agenda for the Housing Acts of 1949 and 1954*, 11 Housing Policy Debate 393, 400–401 (2000).

4. Friedman, supra note 2, at 49. The statute required that a workable program "utilize appropriate private and public resources to eliminate and prevent the development or spread of slums and urban blight, to encourage needed urban rehabilitation, [and] to provide for the redevelopment of blighted, deteriorated, or slum areas." Housing Act of 1954, Pub. L. 89-171, 68 Stat. 623 as amended, 42 U.S.C. § 1451 (1967).

fines "Workable Program" to include adoption of a housing code.[5]

1962	Publication of Michael Harrington, The Other America: Poverty in the United States (Penguin 1962).
	President Kennedy directs Attorney General Robert Kennedy "to assemble a task force charged with developing a coordinated program to alleviate poverty."[6]
January 1964	President Johnson declares War on Poverty in his State of the Union address (available at http://www.lbjlib.utexas.edu/johnson/archives.hom/speeches.hom/640108.asp).
1964	Freedom Summer.
June 21, 1964	Michael Schwerner, James Chaney, and Andrew Goodman murdered in Philadelphia, Mississippi.
1964	Riots in New York, New Jersey, Chicago, and Philadelphia.
	Housing Act makes Workable Program requirement mandatory.[7]
January–March 1965	Selma to Montgomery March
February 1965	Bayard Rustin, "a frequent strategist for the movement, explained the necessity for … redirection northward:
[W[hile school integration proceeds at a snail's pace in the South, the number of Northern schools with an excessive proportion of minority youth proliferates. And behind this is the continuing growth of racial slums, spreading over our central cities and trapping Negro youth in a milieu which, whatever its legal definition, sows an unimaginable demoralization."[8]
February 19, 1965	Schipper v. Levitt decided (44 N.J. 70 (Supreme Court of New Jersey 1965)).
February 21, 1965	Malcolm X assassinated.
March 2, 1965	President Johnson asks Congress to create a commission to study housing issues.
April 1965	James Bevel, a chief lieutenant of Dr. Martin Luther King, Jr., announces in Chicago that "'the nonviolent movement … will call on Chicago to address itself on the racist attitude that is denying Negroes the right to live in adequate housing.'"[9]

---

5. Friedman, supra note 2, at 49. The statute required that a workable program "utilize appropriate private and public resources to eliminate and prevent the development or spread of, slums and urban blight, to encourage needed urban rehabilitation, [and] to provide for the redevelopment of blighted, deteriorated, or slum areas." Housing Act of 1954, 80 Cong. Ch. 649, 68 Stat. 590, 623 as amended 42 U.S.C. § 1451 (1954).

6. John Charles Boger, *Race and the American City: The Kerner Commission in Retrospect—An Introduction*, 71 N.C.L.Rev.1289, 1291 (1993).

7. Friedman, supra note 2, at 162; Housing Act of 1954, 83 Cong. Ch. 649, 68 Stat. 590, 623 as amended 42 U.S.C § 1451(c) (1967).

8. Boger, supra note 6, at 1289 n. 1, quoting Bayard Rustin, *From Protest to Politics: The Future of the Civil Rights Movement*, Commentary, Feb. 1965, at 25, 26.

9. James R. Ralph, Jr., Northern Protest: Martin Luther King, Jr., Chicago, and the Civil Rights Movement 1 (Harvard U. Press 1993).

August 11–16, 1965	Riot in the Watts area of Los Angeles, killing 34 people and causing $40 million in property damage.
August 1965	Dr. Martin Luther King, Jr. announces that he and the Southern Christian Leadership Conference will launch a nonviolent campaign in Chicago for the "teeming millions of Negroes hovered in ghettoes...."[10]
August 10, 1965	Housing Act includes mandate for study (Douglas Commission).
1965	Publication of Kenneth B. Clark, Dark Ghetto: Dilemmas of Social Power (Wesleyan U. Press 1965).
Summer 19671	Riots in 127 cities in U.S., "killing at least 77 and injuring at least 4,000 people."[11] In DC, "an episode of arson and rock throwing...."[12]
July 23, 1967	Riot in Detroit kills 43 people and destroys 1300 buildings. "[T]he disturbances were so severe that federal troops were called in—the first use of federal troops to maintain order since 1942."[13]
1968	Publication of Lawrence M. Friedman: Government and Slum Housing: A Century of Frustration (Rand McNally 1968).
March 1, 1968	Kerner Commission Report issued.
April 4, 1968	Dr. King assassinated.
April 11, 1968	Title VIII enacted.
May 17, 1968	Edwards v. Habib decided.
June 5, 1968	Robert Kennedy assassinated.
June17, 1968	Jones v. Mayer decided.
August 1, 1968	1968 Housing Act enacted.
December 1968	Douglas Commission Report issued.

3. Freedom from Discrimination

Jancik v. Department of Housing and Urban Development
44 F.3d 553 (7th Cir. 1995)

Henry T. Synek, Richard J. Synek (argued), Synek & Synek, Chicago, IL, for petitioner.

David K. Flynn, Asst. Atty. Gen., Miriam R. Eisenstein, Asst. Atty. Gen. (argued), Dept. of Justice, Civil Rights Div., Appellate Section, Roberta Achtenberg, Carole Wilson, Harry L. Carey, Eileen F. Ray, U.S. Dept. of Housing and Urban Development, Washington, DC, for Dept. of Housing & Urban Development.

---

10. Id. at 7.
11. Edward H. Rabin, *The Revolution in Residential Landlord-Tenant Law: Causes and Consequences*, 69 Cornell L.Rev. 517, 547 (1984).
12. Id.
13. Id.

Edward A. Voci, Leadership Council for Metropolitan Open Communities (argued), Chicago, IL, for Leadership Council for Metropolitan Open Communities, Marsha Allen.

Before Eschbach, Ripple, and Rovner, Circuit Judges.

Rovner, Circuit Judge.

Stanley Jancik petitions for review of a decision of the Department of Housing and Urban Development ("HUD"), which found that he discriminated in the rental of an apartment on the basis of both race and family status in violation of 42 U.S.C. § 3604(c). He also petitions for review of an order awarding attorney fees to the Leadership Council for Metropolitan Open Communities. We affirm.

I.

Stanley Jancik owns Building No. 44 in King Arthur's Court, a large housing complex in the Chicago suburb of Northlake. King Arthur's Court houses people of all ages, including children, and although all of the apartments in Jancik's building have only one bedroom, they are large enough to house more than one occupant under local codes. The claims in this case arise out of Jancik's conduct in the rental of an apartment in that building. On August 29, 1990, Jancik placed this ad in a local suburban newspaper:

> NORTHLAKE deluxe 1 BR apt, a/c, newer quiet bldg, pool, prkg, mature person preferred, credit checked. $395....

Suspecting that the request for a "mature person" might reflect a violation of the Act, the Leadership Council's Investigations Manager Glenn Brewer decided to "test" the property. In that process, "testers" bearing fictitious identities pose as potential renters in order to check for discriminatory practices. In this instance, Brewer chose to use volunteer testers Cindy Gunderson, who is white, and Marsha Allen, who is African American, for the task.

Gunderson spoke with Jancik by telephone on the evening of September 7, 1990. She subsequently related that after asking Gunderson her age and learning that she was 36, Jancik told her "that was good—he doesn't want any teenagers in there." Jancik also asked Gunderson her name and, upon hearing it, inquired "what kind of name" it was. Learning that the name was Norwegian, Jancik asked whether "that's white Norwegian or black Norwegian" and repeated the question a second time after Gunderson failed to answer. Gunderson asked Jancik whether he was inquiring as to her race and, after he responded affirmatively, told him that she was white. Gunderson then asked to view the apartment and the two arranged for her to do so the following morning.

Marsha Allen spoke with Jancik two hours later the same evening. Jancik asked Allen her occupation, income, age, marital status, race and whether she had any children or pets. Allen did not reveal her race, but in response to that question asked Jancik why he needed this information. He responded, in her words, "that he had to screen the applicants because the tenants in the building were middle-aged and he did not want anyone moving in who was loud, made a lot of noise and had children or pets." When Allen told Jancik that she did not have any children or pets he said "wonderful," and the two arranged for Allen to see the apartment the next morning. Both testers arrived the next morning at approximately 10:00, and Jancik's rental manager separately informed each that the apartment had been rented earlier that morning.

Based on the reports filed by Gunderson and Allen, the Leadership Council filed an administrative complaint with HUD ... charg[ing] that Jancik had violated section 804(c) of the FHA, 42 U.S.C. § 3604(c), which makes it unlawful:

To make, print, or publish, or cause to be made, printed, or published any notice, statement, or advertisement, with respect to the sale or rental of a
dwelling that indicates any preference, limitation, or discrimination based on
race, color, religion, sex, handicap, familial status, or national origin, or an intention to make any such preference, limitation, or discrimination.

The Leadership Council claimed that Jancik's print advertisement violated the section by indicating a preference based on family status and that his interviews with the
testers violated the section by indicating a preference based on both race and family status. After HUD's General Counsel issued a "Determination of Reasonable Cause and
Charge of Discrimination," the matter was set for hearing before Administrative Law
Judge ("ALJ") William C. Cregar, as provided by 42 U.S.C. §3612(b). With the Council
and Marsha Allen as intervenors, the ALJ conducted a two-day hearing ... and issued a
21-page Initial Decision and Order..., which found that Jancik had violated section
3604(c). The ALJ awarded damages to the Leadership Council ($21,386.14) and to Mar-
sha Allen ($2,000), assessed a civil penalty of $10,000, and enjoined Jancik from engaging in further acts of discrimination.... The Leadership Council subsequently filed a
petition requesting $23,842.50 in attorney's fees. Although Jancik did not raise any fac-
tual objections to the fee petition, which was supported by affidavits, he did request a
hearing on the fees issue. [T]he ALJ denied that request and granted the fees petition
for the full amount requested. Jancik now seeks review of both of the ALJ's orders.

II.

We will reverse the Secretary's decision only if it is "not in accordance with law,"
"without observance of procedure required by law," or "unsupported by substantial evidence." 5 U.S.C. §706(2)(A), (D) & (E). Substantial evidence is "such relevant evidence
as a reasonable mind might accept as adequate to support a conclusion." "Although we
review the entire record, we may not decide the facts anew, reweigh the evidence, or
substitute our own judgment for that of the Secretary." We accord considerable deference to the credibility determinations of the ALJ.

Section 3604(c) prohibits the making or publishing of any statement or advertisement
that "indicates" any preference or limitation based on, among other factors, race or family status. Whether a given statement or advertisement "indicates" such a preference is
therefore central to our analysis. Although we have not previously dealt with the "indicates" aspect of section 3604(c), the circuit courts that have done so have employed a relatively straightforward approach, which we also find appropriate. First, every circuit that
has considered a claim under section 3604(c) has held that an objective "ordinary reader"
standard should be applied in determining what is "indicated" by an ad. Thus, "the
statute [is] violated if an ad for housing suggests to an ordinary reader that a particular
[protected group] is preferred or dispreferred for the housing in question." Ragin v. New
York Times Co., 923 F.2d 995 (2d Cir).[4] In applying the "ordinary reader" test, courts
have not required that ads jump out at the reader with their offending message, but have
found instead that the statute is violated by "any ad that would discourage an ordinary
reader of a particular [protected group] from answering it." Ragin.

Significantly, no showing of a subjective intent to discriminate is therefore necessary
to establish a violation of the section. At the same time, however, evidence of such intent is not irrelevant. Evidence that the author or speaker intended his or her words to

---

4. Ragin further explained that "an ordinary reader is neither the most suspicious nor the most
insensitive of our citizenry."

indicate a prohibited preference obviously bears on the question of whether the words in fact do so. Thus, if such proof exists, it may provide an alternative means of establishing a violation of the section.

In view of these guidelines, the ALJ's finding that Jancik's advertisement and statements expressed a preference based on family status in violation of section 804(c) was certainly supported by substantial evidence. First, Jancik told Allen that he did not want any families with children and told Gunderson that he did not want any teenagers in the building. In our view, both of these statements quite clearly would suggest to an "ordinary" listener that Jancik had a preference or limitation based on family status. The advertisement indicating his preference for a "mature person" was similarly problematic. Not only do we view that term as suggesting an unlawful preference to an ordinary reader,[5] the term is noted in the implementing regulation as being among "those most often used in residential real estate advertising to convey either overt or tacit discriminatory preferences or limitations." 24 C.F.R. § 109.20(b)(7). Of course, as Jancik points out, use of the listed terms does not violate the Act per se, but it does "indicate a possible violation of the act and establish a need for further proceedings on the complaint, if it is apparent from the context of the usage that discrimination within the meaning of the act is likely to result." Here, the context of the usage, which included explicit verification of Jancik's preference to each of two prospective tenants who responded to the ad, makes clear that the usage was meant to convey an unlawful preference.[6]

And, although we have no doubt that the Act has been violated based solely on this objective analysis, the record was also replete with evidence of Jancik's subjective intent to discriminate against families with children. For example, Jancik admitted at the hearing that he had told prospective tenants with children that there was no school in the area, when there was in fact a high school located on adjacent property and an elementary school within one mile. Jancik also told the HUD investigator that he had previously turned away a single parent with a ten-year-old child.

Although the question of whether Jancik violated section 3604(c) by asking Gunderson and Allen about their race is somewhat more difficult, the ALJ's determination in that regard is also supported by substantial evidence. Unlike his comments regarding family status, Jancik did not expressly indicate a preference based on race, but merely asked the testers about their race. In the only case that has commented on the issue, the Second Circuit has indicated by way of dicta in Soules that questions about race standing alone are sufficient to violate the section because "there is simply no legitimate reason for considering an applicant's race." We need not decide that question here, however, because the context of the questions makes clear they did indicate an intent to discriminate on the basis of race. First, each question came in the midst of conversations in which Jancik was expressing other impermissible preferences. Hearing an inquiry about race immediately after being asked about children and told that applicants with children were undesirable, would, in our view, suggest to an ordinary listener that

---

5. Cf. [United States v.] Hunter, 459 F.2d [205,] 215 [(4th Cir. 1972), cert. denied, 409 U.S. 934 (1972)] (to the ordinary reader, the term "white home" indicates a racial preference and therefore violates section 3604(c).)

6. Jancik cites Soules [v. United States Department of Housing and Urban Development], 967 F.2d 817 (2nd Cir. 1992)] for the proposition that questions about children may sometimes be asked for legitimate reasons, such as local zoning ordinances that limit the number of permitted occupants or conditions in the neighborhood that are dangerous to children. Not only is the record here completely devoid of evidence suggesting that Jancik's questions were asked for any such permissible reasons, it makes clear that his reasons were impermissible.

the racial question was part of the same screening process. Indeed, when Allen asked Jancik the purpose of his question about her race, he admitted that he was, in her words, "screening the applicants." Jancik's unlawful purpose was similarly revealed in his conversation with Gunderson by the pointedness of his inquiry. After asking the origins of the Gunderson name and learning that it was Norwegian, he twice inquired whether Gunderson was "white Norwegian or black Norwegian" and subsequently admitted, in answer to her question, that he was inquiring as to her race. It is unlikely that if the inquiry had been merely conversational, as Jancik has contended, he would have pursued it with such determination. In addition, the fact that Jancik had never rented to an African American tenant before the Leadership Council filed its complaint in this case further bolsters the ALJ's conclusion that Jancik's question reflected an intent to exclude tenants on the basis of race.

III. Attorney's Fees

Jancik does not contest the amount of attorney's fees awarded, but argues only that the ALJ abused his discretion in denying Jancik's request for a hearing on the issue. Aside from arguing in general that the fees were excessive, however, Jancik raised no factual objections to the fees petition. The ALJ addressed each of Jancik's legal challenges to the fees petition in a thorough order disposing of the matter. Because no facts were in dispute, the ALJ's determination that an evidentiary hearing was "unnecessary" was not an abuse of discretion.

IV.

For the foregoing reasons, we find that each of the ALJ's orders is both in accordance with law and supported by substantial evidence. Jancik's petitions for review are therefore denied.

DiCenso v. Cisneros
96 F.3d 1004 (7th Cir. 1996)

James P. Baker, Springfield, IL, for Petitioner.

Thomas E. Chandler, Jessica Dunsay Silver, Department of Justice, Civil Rights Division, Appellate Section, Washington, DC, Harry L. Carey, Nelson Diaz, Department of Housing and Urban Development, Washington, DC, for Respondent.

Christina L. Brown, Respondent, Decatur, IL, pro se.

Before Bauer, Eschbach, and Flaum, Circuit Judges.

Bauer, Circuit Judge.

This case raises the question of whether one incident of harassment was sufficiently egregious to create a hostile environment sex discrimination cause of action under the Fair Housing Act. An Administrative Law Judge ("ALJ") thought it was not, but the Housing and Urban Development Secretary's Designee disagreed, and remanded the case to the ALJ for a determination of damages. On remand, the ALJ awarded Christina Brown $5,000 in compensatory damages, assessed a $5,000 civil penalty, and entered injunctive relief. The landlord who committed the harassment now seeks relief from the Secretary's Order.

Background

The events of this lawsuit arose in the context of Christina Brown's tenancy at 522 1/2 West Allen Street in Springfield, Illinois. Brown, who at the time was 18 years old, lived in one of the four apartment units with Thomas Andrews and their infant daughter Sara. Beginning in June 1990, they leased the apartment from Albert DiCenso, who owned and managed the building, did most of the cleaning and maintenance, and collected the rents.

Brown and Andrews signed a six-month lease with an option for six more months. During the first few months a family friend stayed with them, and their rent was $300 per month. When the friend moved out in September, DiCenso reduced the rent to $275 per month. At first, Brown and her co-tenants delivered the rent checks to Di-Censo's home, but eventually DiCenso started going to the apartment to collect the payments.

Sometime in mid-October or early November, DiCenso came to Brown's apartment to collect the rent. According to the ALJ's findings, the following exchange took place:

> While [Brown] stood at the door, [DiCenso] asked about the rent and simultaneously began caressing her arm and back. He said to her words to the effect that if she could not pay the rent, she could take care of it in other ways. [Brown] slammed the door in his face. [DiCenso] stood outside calling her names—a "bitch" and "whore," and then left.

On January 15, 1991, DiCenso again went to the apartment to collect the monthly rent. While there, he became involved in a confrontation with Andrews and the police were called. DiCenso informed the police that the disagreement was over Andrews' refusal to pay the rent. Brown and Andrews told DiCenso that they would be leaving the apartment within the next ten days. According to the police report, the two parties "both came to the decision of settling the matter in court."

Brown and Andrews did not move out, however, and in late January, DiCenso served them with a five-day notice to quit the premises. On January 31, Brown filed a housing discrimination complaint alleging that DiCenso had harassed her and her boyfriend, and had made sexual advances toward her.[1] DiCenso denied the allegations, and asserted that he had had problems collecting the December 1990 and January 1991 rent, and that Andrews not only refused to pay the rent, but had threatened to hurt him. DiCenso felt that the discrimination complaint was a "plot" by Brown and Andrews to avoid paying the rent that was due.[2]

The Department investigated Brown's complaint and determined that reasonable cause existed to believe that discrimination had occurred. [T]he Department issued a charge against DiCenso for violations of sections 804(b) and 818 of the Fair Housing Act.... A HUD ALJ conducted a hearing ... [and] issued a thorough decision, in which she acknowledged that any finding that the alleged acts occurred rested solely on credibility determinations. In making these determinations, the ALJ relied on the witnesses' demeanor while testifying, their ability and opportunity to observe what happened, their memory, any interest or bias they might have, the consistency of their statements, and the reasonableness of their testimony in light of all of the evidence received. On the

---

1. In addition to the aforementioned incident, Brown's complaint alleged other incidents of purported harassment as well as unauthorized entries into the apartment. However, the mid-October exchange is the only incident for which the ALJ found DiCenso responsible. The ALJ heard the evidence, and observed the demeanor and testimony of the witnesses. Moreover, the Secretary's designee accepted the ALJ's findings of fact. Accordingly, we will consider only the mid-October exchange in determining whether Brown has stated an actionable claim.

2. DiCenso also filed suit against Brown and Andrews in the Circuit Court of Sangamon County to collect the unpaid January 1991 rent. After an evidentiary hearing, the court entered judgment in favor of DiCenso in the sum of $275.00 plus court costs.

whole, the ALJ found Brown more credible than DiCenso. However, the ALJ also found that Brown's testimony established only one act of sexual harassment by DiCenso—the mid-October incident. On this set of facts, the ALJ concluded that DiCenso's conduct did not rise to the level of severity required to create a hostile housing environment. Consequently, the ALJ found that Brown had failed to establish a claim of sex discrimination and dismissed the complaint.

The Department, acting on Brown's behalf, sought review of the ALJ's order pursuant to 42 U.S.C. §3612(h). The HUD Secretary's Designee affirmed the ALJ's findings of fact, but reached a different conclusion on the issue of whether the single incident amounted to a hostile housing environment for purposes of the Fair Housing Act. Finding for Brown on the issue of liability, the Secretary's Designee vacated the ALJ's decision and remanded the case for a determination of damages. The ALJ awarded Brown $5,000 in compensatory damages, assessed a $5,000 civil penalty against DiCenso and entered injunctive relief.... DiCenso filed a petition for review in this court....

Analysis

A. Standard of Review

Before addressing whether DiCenso's conduct constitutes unlawful discrimination, we first must address the applicable standard of review. Both parties correctly acknowledge that we defer to the ALJ's findings of fact where they are supported by substantial evidence on the record as a whole. The issue, then, is whether we also should defer to the Department's legal conclusions. DiCenso understandably argues that we should review the legal conclusion de novo. *from the beginning*

Chevron [U.S.A., Inc. v. National Resources Defense Council, Inc., 467 U.S. 837 (1984)] requires us to defer to the decisions of executive agencies where the agency has a particular expertise in the conflicting policy considerations that underlie a statute, or where the agency previously has considered the matter at issue in a detailed and reasoned fashion. Neither of these situations exists here. In Meritor Savings Bank, FSB v. Vinson, 477 U.S. 57 (1986), the Supreme Court commented on the deference given to EEOC guidelines defining sexual harassment as a form of sex discrimination. Although those guidelines "constitute a body of experience and informed judgment to which courts and litigants may properly resort for guidance," they are not "controlling upon the courts by reason of their authority." In this case, by contrast, HUD has not even enacted guidelines regarding hostile housing environment sex discrimination. Rather, as the HUD Secretary's Designee acknowledged, a determination of what constitutes a hostile environment in the housing context requires the same analysis courts have undertaken in the Title VII context. Such a determination does not require deference to an administrative agency.

[T]he Department now argues that we should subject determinations of whether an incident of harassment is sufficiently egregious to constitute sex discrimination to a clearly erroneous standard.... In [other employment] cases, we held that the existence of harassment in a hostile work environment involved an application of facts to law. Therefore, the clearly erroneous standard governed. In this case, the existence of harassment is not at issue. The sole question is whether the incident of harassment that occurred is sufficient to state a cause of action under the Fair Housing Act. This is purely a question of law which we review de novo. *Brown*

B. Hostile Environment Sex Discrimination

Title VII of the Civil Rights Act of 1964 allows a cause of action for harassment that creates a hostile or offensive working environment. Meritor. Claims of hostile environment sex discrimination in the housing context have been far less frequent. The first district court to apply the hostile environment cause of action to housing discrimination did so in Shellhammer v. Lewallen, Fair Hous.-Fair Lend. Rep. (P-H) 15,742 (W.D. Ohio Nov. 22, 1983), affirmed by 1985 WL 13505 (6th Cir. July 31, 1985). Since Shellhammer, one court of appeals also has recognized sexual harassment as a basis for a Fair Housing Act discrimination claim. See Honce v. Vigil, 1 F.3d 1085 (10th Cir. 1993). Like Shellhammer and Honce, other courts that have found harassment to create an actionable form of housing discrimination also have incorporated Title VII doctrines into their analyses. See Beliveau v. Caras, 873 F. Supp. 1393 (C.D. Cal. 1995); see also Abrams v. Merlino, 694 F. Supp. 1101 (S.D.N.Y. 1988) (alleging a pattern of race and sex discrimination in the provision of real estate brokerage services).

Like the Tenth Circuit, we recognize a hostile housing environment cause of action, and begin our analysis with the more familiar Title VII standard. For sexual harassment to be actionable in the Title VII context, it must be sufficiently severe or pervasive to alter the conditions of the victim's employment and create an abusive working environment. Meritor. "Conduct that is not severe or pervasive enough to create an objectively hostile or abusive work environment—an environment that a reasonable person would find hostile or abusive—is beyond Title VII's purview." Harris v. Forklift Systems, Inc., 510 U.S. 17 (1993). Applied to the housing context, a claim is actionable "when the offensive behavior unreasonably interferes with use and enjoyment of the premises." Honce, 1 F.3d at 1090. Whether an environment is "hostile" or "abusive" can be determined only by looking at all the circumstances, and factors may include the frequency of the discriminatory conduct; its severity; whether it is physically threatening or humiliating, or a mere offensive utterance; and whether it unreasonably interferes with an employee's work performance. Harris, 510 U.S. at 23.

We repeatedly have held that isolated and innocuous incidents do not support a finding of sexual harassment. For example, in Saxton v. American Tel. & Tel. Co., 10 F.3d 526 (7th Cir. 1993), the defendant on one occasion put his hand on the plaintiff's leg and kissed her until she pushed him away. Three weeks later, the defendant lurched at the plaintiff from behind some bushes and unsuccessfully tried to grab her. While these incidents were subjectively unpleasant, the defendant's conduct was not frequent or severe enough to create a hostile environment. Similarly, in Weiss v. Coca-Cola Bottling Co. of Chicago, 990 F.2d 333 (7th Cir. 1993), the defendant asked the plaintiff for dates on repeated occasions, placed signs which read "I love you" in her work area, and twice attempted to kiss her. These incidents also were too isolated and insufficiently severe to create a hostile work environment. Common to all of these examples is an emphasis on the frequency of the offensive behavior. "Though sporadic behavior, if sufficiently abusive, may support a [discrimination] claim, success often requires repetitive misconduct." Chalmers v. Quaker Oats Co., 61 F.3d 1340 (7th Cir. 1995).

In this context, the problem with Brown's complaint is that although DiCenso may have harassed her, he did so only once. Moreover, DiCenso's conduct, while clearly unwelcome, was much less offensive than other incidents which have not violated Title VII. DiCenso's comment vaguely invited Brown to exchange sex for rent, and while DiCenso caressed Brown's arm and back, he did not touch an intimate body part, and did not threaten Brown with any physical harm. There is no question that Brown found DiCenso's remarks to be subjectively unpleasant, but this alone did not create an objectively hostile environment.

We stress in closing that our decision today should not be read as giving landlords one free chance to harass their tenants. We do not condone DiCenso's conduct, nor do we hold that a single incident of harassment never will support an actionable claim. Considering the totality of the circumstances in this case, we agree with the ALJ that DiCenso's conduct was not sufficiently egregious to create an objectively hostile housing environment. * * *

Flaum, Circuit Judge, dissenting.

The majority correctly notes that this case raises the purely legal issue of whether a particular incident of harassment was sufficiently egregious to create a hostile housing environment claim under the Fair Housing Act. The majority reviews this legal issue de novo and concludes that Albert DiCenso's conduct did not create an objectively hostile environment. Because, in my view, we must defer to HUD's reasonable interpretation of what constitutes a hostile housing environment, I respectfully dissent from the majority's decision.

It is well-established that considerable weight should be given to an agency's construction of a statutory scheme that it has been entrusted to administer. See Chevron, U.S.A., Inc. v. National Resources Defense Council, Inc., 467 U.S. 837 (1984). The Supreme Court has held that HUD's interpretation of the FHA "ordinarily commands considerable deference" since "HUD [is] the federal agency primarily assigned to implement and administer Title VIII." Gladstone, Realtors v. Village of Bellwood, 441 U.S. 91 (1979). The majority recognizes that Chevron calls for deference where an agency has expertise in reconciling conflicting policy considerations that underlie a statute, but posits that, because HUD has not enacted hostile housing environment guidelines, we need not defer to HUD's construction of the FHA. Yet an agency is free to formulate policy through individual adjudicative proceedings rather than rulemaking. NLRB v. Bell Aerospace Co., 416 U.S. 267 (1974). Thus an agency's interpretation of the statute that it administers commands deference, irrespective of whether that interpretation emerges as a result of an adjudicative proceeding or a rulemaking process. Pfaff [v. U.S. Dept. of Housing and Urban Dev.], 88 F.3d [739,] 747 [(9th Cir. 1996)]; see Edward J. DeBartolo Corp. v. Florida Gulf Coast Bldg. & Constr. Trades Council, 485 U.S. 568 (1988) (applying Chevron deference in the context of an adjudicative proceeding); Federal Election Comm'n v. Democratic Senatorial Campaign Comm., 454 U.S. 27 (1981) (finding that interpretation developed by agency during adjudication was entitled to deference). The scope of our review of this agency action is therefore clearly limited. We "may not substitute [our] own construction of a statutory provision for a reasonable interpretation made by the administrator of an agency." Chevron, 467 U.S. at 844.

In the current case, the Secretary of HUD has taken the position that DiCenso's conduct was sufficiently severe as to create a claim for hostile housing environment under the FHA. Section 804(b) of the FHA prohibits genderbased discrimination in the sale or rental of a dwelling, or in the "provision of services" in connection with such sale or rental. The Secretary, consistently with the approach adopted by the majority, believes that a hostile housing environment claim is actionable "when the offensive behavior unreasonably interferes with use and enjoyment of the premises." Honce v. Vigil, 1 F.3d 1085 (10th Cir. 1993). The Secretary concludes that DiCenso's offensive conduct was sufficiently severe to satisfy this test, despite the fact that the conduct only occurred once. DiCenso's unwelcome caressing of Brown, combined with his offer of "sex for rent" and his hurling of gender-oriented epithets after Brown's rejection of his offer, certainly provides the Secretary with ample support for this conclusion. Although the majority may very well be correct in stating that DiCenso's conduct would not be sufficient to give rise to a claim for sexual harassment under our Title VII precedent, the majority provides no basis for doubting the reasonableness of the Secretary's interpretation of the FHA. In conclusion it is my judgment that the Secretary's interpretation of the FHA is a reasonable one and is therefore entitled to deference.

Note

Chevron, U.S.A., Inc. v. National Resources Defense Council, 467 U.S. 837, 843 (1984), holds that when

> a court reviews an agency's construction of the statute which it administers, it is confronted with two questions. First, always, is the question whether Congress has directly spoken to the precise question at issue. If the intent of Congress is clear, that is the end of the matter; for the court, as well as the agency, must give effect to the unambiguously expressed intent of Congress. If, however, the court determines Congress has not directly addressed the precise question at issue, the court does not simply impose its own construction on the statute, as would be necessary in the absence of an administrative interpretation. Rather, if the statute is silent or ambiguous with respect to the specific issue, the question for the court is whether the agency's answer is based on a permissible construction of the statute.

Krueger v. Cuomo
115 F.3d 487 (7th Cir. 1997)

Gerald A. Goldman, Arthur R. Ehrlich, Jonathan C. Goldman (argued), Chicago, IL, for Petitioner.

Jessica Dunsay Silver, Department of Justice, Civil Rights Division, Appellate Section, Washington, DC, Elizabeth Crowder, U.S. Department of Housing and Urban Development, Chicago, IL, Nelson Diaz, Department of Housing and Urban Development, Washington, DC, Michelle M. Aronowitz (argued), United States Department of Justice, Washington, DC, for Respondent.

Before Flaum, Kanne, and Rovner, Circuit Judges.

Flaum, Circuit Judge:

Lyle Krueger petitions for review of a decision and order of the Secretary of the Department of Housing and Urban Development ("HUD") concluding that Krueger violated the Fair Housing Act, 42 U.S.C. § 3601 et seq., by sexually harassing one of his tenants. We affirm.

I.

In April 1992, Debbie Maze was living in Kenosha, Wisconsin with her two children, ages four and three, in her sister's two-bedroom apartment, also home to the sister's boyfriend and four children. Maze had been searching for an apartment for three months, and her section 8 housing voucher was due to expire in late May. So when she saw a "for rent" sign on an apartment owned by Lyle Krueger, she inquired within and found Krueger, who gave her a rental application and suggested they meet the next morning for breakfast.

At the breakfast meeting, it became apparent that Maze could not afford the three-bedroom, $547-a-month apartment, for her housing voucher provided only $395 for a two-bedroom apartment, to which she was expected to add a personal contribution of $52 per month. Although Krueger initially refused to rent the apartment to Maze, he soon changed his mind. He located Maze through her sister, a former tenant, and arranged for another breakfast meeting. At this second meeting, Krueger told Maze that she could pay money on the side or "fool around or something" to make up the $100 shortfall. She declined this payment scheme, but Krueger nevertheless agreed to rent her the apartment. Maze did not own a car, and Krueger gave her a ride home from their meeting. In his car, Krueger rubbed Maze's thigh and predicted, "we're going to be close." Maze asked Krueger not to touch her.

On May 11, Krueger and Maze went to the Kenosha Housing Authority to sign a rental agreement. In the elevator on the way to the office, Krueger touched Maze, rubbed her, and tried to kiss her. She told him to stop, a request he greeted with laughter. After the two had signed the lease, an undaunted Krueger once again prophesied that he and Maze "were going to be real close." Maze was so disturbed by Krueger's behavior that, later the same day, she returned alone to the Housing Authority. There, she reported Krueger's advances to a Housing Authority official, Paula Lattergrass, who urged her not to take the apartment. Maze felt that she had few alternatives other than to move into the apartment, but she did, at the suggestion of Lattergrass, file complaints against Krueger with the Urban League and HUD.

Krueger's unwelcome advances continued after Maze moved into the apartment on May 13. He made a habit (three to four times a week, Maze recalled) of arriving unannounced; he would knock on the first-floor doorway, enter before Maze could respond, and climb the internal staircase to her apartment. Once inside, he would grab and touch Maze, doing so on at least one occasion in front of her children. He suggested that she send the children to her mother's so that she and Krueger could go away together. On another occasion, he repeated his hope that they would be "real close" and asked if they were "going to do good in bed." When Maze demurred, he told Maze that he was losing money because of her and reminded her that he could have rented the apartment to someone else. Krueger also asked Maze out for drinks. Maze, who is black, told Krueger, who is white, that she did not date white men. Four or five times, she observed him parked outside her home watching her apartment. Maze began to seek ways to minimize contact with Krueger. In order to do so, she brought her rent checks to Lattergrass, who forwarded them to Krueger.

Under these circumstances, it would be inapt to speak of a deterioration in the relationship between Krueger and Maze; but from Krueger's perspective at least, matters did take a turn for the worse after he learned that Maze had filed harassment charges against him. In a series of letters written during the summer of 1992, Krueger expressed his dissatisfaction with Maze as a tenant. These letters explicitly linked the perceived decline in their relations to Maze's filing of harassment charges against Krueger ("Before you moved in you were very friendly..., you were a pleasure to be with and then you filed sexual harassment charges."), informed Maze that Krueger would be willing to break the year-long lease, and repeatedly suggested that Maze "think about moving." The letters also referred to a ten-dollar fee, imposed as a result of the Housing Authority's purported delay in forwarding Maze's rent check, and to the cost of repairs made to the apartment, both of which Krueger intended to deduct from Maze's rent payments. In October, the letters became more official in tone. On October 20, Krueger informed

Maze that, because lead had been detected in her children's blood, she would have to vacate the apartment and remove all of her belongings, including furniture, in order for him to take "corrective action." (In fact, Krueger only painted over the lead-based paint; Maze and her children were able to spend daytime hours at her mother's for the two or three days required to complete the painting.) The most recent letter in the record, dated October 22, 1992, came from Krueger's lawyer, who instructed Maze that she must either pay "unpaid rent" or vacate her apartment within five days.

As Krueger indicated in his letters, the "unpaid rent" represented the cost of repairs that he had deducted from Maze's rent payments, as well as the ten-dollar late fee. The repairs in question were the unclogging of Maze's toilet and sink and the replacement of her apartment door, which she had forced open after one of her children locked himself inside the apartment. Prior to Krueger's attempt to evict Maze, the landlord and tenant had met at the Housing Authority in an attempt to resolve the payment dispute, and Lattergrass had presented a compromise solution, under which Maze would pay for a portion of the repairs. (Based on her inspection of the apartment, Lattergrass believed that Maze was only partly responsible for the plumbing difficulties and that the broken door had needed only a new lock, not complete replacement.) Nevertheless, Krueger refused to accept any money from Maze.

Krueger continued to sexually harass Maze after she became pregnant in October 1992. In February 1993, Maze moved out of her apartment and into her mother's home, a two-bedroom unit shared by Maze's stepfather and her brother. She did not find another apartment until May 1993.

Maze's complaint against Krueger came before an administrative law judge ("ALJ") in December 1995. After hearing testimony from Krueger, Maze, her sister Barbara Maze, Lattergrass, and a HUD investigator, the ALJ ruled in favor of Maze. In his decision and order, dated June 7, 1996, the ALJ noted that, in contrast to Debbie Maze's "straightforward, consistent, and credible" testimony, which was corroborated by Lattergrass and Barbara Maze, Krueger's testimony was "riddled with inconsistencies" and, in places, "simply … not believable."[1] Significantly, the ALJ found that Krueger's conduct had caused Maze to move out of her apartment. Krueger "made Maze's tenancy untenable," in the ALJ's view; "Eventually the tenancy became so miserable that she felt compelled to move out." The ALJ also rejected Krueger's proffered explanations for his attempts to evict Maze (her hostility toward him, her failure to pay rent) and found that Krueger's actions were a direct response to her refusal to submit to his demands and to her filing of harassment charges. Because Maze's rejection of Krueger's advances resulted in an adverse consequence (i.e., being forced out of her apartment), the ALJ concluded that Krueger had engaged in quid pro quo sexual harassment. Accordingly, the ALJ held that Krueger had violated 42 U.S.C. § 3604(b), which forbids discrimination on the basis of sex "in the terms, conditions, or privileges of sale or rental of a dwelling, or in the provision of services or facilities in connection therewith.…" The ALJ also held that Krueger's continued campaign of harassment—an interference with Maze's right to quiet enjoyment of her tenancy—and his retaliation against Maze for her filing a complaint each independently violated 42 U.S.C. § 3617, which makes it "unlawful to coerce, intimidate, threaten, or interfere with any person in the exercise or enjoyment of, or on account of his having exercised or enjoyed … any right granted or protected by section … 3604 … of [Title 42]." Krueger was enjoined from committing future acts

---

1. Krueger denied virtually all of the sexual harassment attributed to him by Maze. Our account of the underlying facts relies mainly on the ALJ's findings.

of discrimination, assessed a civil penalty of $10,000, and ordered to pay Maze $622 for alternative housing costs, $2,000 to compensate for the inconvenience occasioned by her loss of the apartment, and $20,000 for Maze's emotional distress. On July 7, 1996, the ALJ's ruling became the final order of the Secretary pursuant to 42 U.S.C. § 3612(h)(1). Krueger now appeals the agency's liability determination and argues that the damages and civil penalty are excessive.

II.

Krueger's challenge to HUD's conclusion that he violated sections 3604(b) and 3617 warrants little discussion. This court has recognized that sexual harassment in the housing context can violate the Fair Housing Act, see DiCenso v. Cisneros, 96 F.3d 1004, 1008 (7th Cir. 1996), and Krueger does not argue otherwise. Moreover, although he purports to raise legal issues subject to our plenary review, the legal standards Krueger proposes do nothing to undermine the agency's analysis. Krueger's arguments ultimately rest on the assertion that he attempted to evict Maze for "legitimate business reasons" and that there was "no causal connection between Krueger's alleged sexual advances and her moving out of the apartment"—a view of the evidence directly in conflict with the ALJ's findings. From our perspective, those findings need only be supported by substantial evidence: "we may not decide the facts anew, reweigh the evidence, or substitute our own judgment for that of the Secretary." Jancik v. Department of Housing and Urban Development, 44 F.3d 553, 556 (7th Cir. 1995). "'[A]n ALJ's credibility determinations,'" we have explained, "'will be overturned ... only when extraordinary circumstances so require.'" Certainly, no such "extraordinary circumstances" are present in this case, in which Maze buttressed her convincing testimony with the testimony of a disinterested witness (Lattergrass) to whom she had promptly reported the misconduct at issue. On this record, we have no basis for upsetting the agency's findings.

III.

Krueger also argues that the civil fine assessed against him ($10,000) and the damages awarded Maze ($622 in alternative housing costs and $22,000 for emotional distress and inconvenience) were excessive.

The ALJ based his award of alternative housing costs on Maze's estimate of her moving expenses and the rent she paid for three months to her mother and for one month to her new landlord, less the amount she would have had to contribute during this period under her lease with Krueger. On appeal, Krueger complains that Maze introduced no corroborating testimony or documentation and that the money Maze furnished her mother was not rent but went to pay the cable or phone bill. We, however, agree with HUD that the relevant inquiry is not how Maze's mother chose to apply the funds Maze contributed. Rather, it is enough that Maze paid this money in consideration of her being permitted to live in her mother's apartment. Further, Krueger has cited to us no authority for the proposition that Maze was required to document her alternative housing costs with exacting specificity, and we have not uncovered any. To the contrary, we believe that the ALJ was entitled to make a reasonable estimate, based on all of the evidence before him, of Maze's alternative housing costs. Cf. Horn v. Duke Homes, 755 F.2d 599, 607 (7th Cir. 1985) ("The calculation is not precise, but unrealistic exactitude is not required in this context....") (discussing damages calculation in employment discrimination cases).

Similarly, the evidence was sufficient to support the award of damages for emotional distress. Krueger observes that the direct evidence of Maze's emotional distress was limited almost entirely to her own testimony. He argues that because the ALJ's decision focused primarily upon Krueger's behavior, rather than Maze's reaction to that behavior, the award constitutes an unrequested, and therefore improper, punitive sanction. What Krueger neglects, however, is that the ALJ was obligated to "look at both the direct evidence of emotional distress and the circumstances of the act that allegedly caused the distress." United States v. Balistrieri, 981 F.2d 916, 932 (7th Cir. 1992). "The more inherently degrading or humiliating the defendant's action is, the more reasonable it is to infer that a person would suffer humiliation or distress from that action; consequently, somewhat more conclusory evidence of emotional distress will be acceptable to support an award for emotional damages." Id. It demands little in the way of either empathy or imagination to appreciate the predicament of a woman who is harassed in full view of her children, whose home becomes not a sanctuary but the situs of her torment, and who concludes that she has no alternative but to leave a long sought-for apartment. Maze testified that Krueger made her feel "real dirty," "like a bad person," and "scared" her. She was not required, as Krueger appears to believe, to call an expert witness.

Also without merit is Krueger's appeal of the Secretary's award of $2,000 to compensate Maze for her inconvenience. In ordering this relief, the ALJ noted that Maze had to search for new housing during the winter, to live for three months in crowded conditions in her mother's apartment, and eventually to accept a smaller, less well-heated apartment. Krueger's argument to this court—that Maze could have moved during the summer, when Krueger "actually tried to evict her" and that she "did not have to move in with her mother," but "could have waited and moved into a new apartment"—contradicts itself. Worse, it ignores both the limited options available to Maze and the egregiousness of Krueger's misconduct. From all that appears, Maze dealt as well as could be expected with an intolerable situation.

Finally, we are not persuaded that the $10,000 civil fine—the maximum penalty authorized under the governing statute, see 42 U.S.C. §3612(g)(3)(A)—was excessive. In opposition to this fine, Krueger contends that "to pay this civil penalty, he would have to sell one of [his four] properties, which is too severe a penalty for [his] alleged conduct." Yet difficulty paying is not inability to pay, and a painless sanction would have little deterrent effect. In arriving at the $10,000 figure, the ALJ did consider Krueger's financial resources, as well as the seriousness of his misconduct and the need to deter him and other landlords from repeating the harassment that Maze experienced. Section 3612(g)(3) of Title 42 authorizes civil penalties "to vindicate the public interest," and the ALJ acted well within his authority in imposing the maximum fine available.

The order of the Secretary is affirmed.

4. Proposed Rules

Department of Housing and Urban Development
24 CFR Part 100
Fair Housing Act Regulations Amendments
Standards Governing Sexual Harassment Cases
65 Fed. Reg. 67666 (Mon., Nov. 13, 2000)
AGENCY: Office of the Assistant Secretary for Fair Housing and Equal Opportunity, HUD.

DATES: Comment due date: January 12, 2001.

SUPPLEMENTARY INFORMATION: The Fair Housing Act (42 U.S.C. 3600–3620) (referred to as "the Act" in this rule) prohibits discrimination on the basis of sex. Sexual harassment related to housing has been uniformly recognized by courts as a form of discrimination based on sex and a violation of the Fair Housing Act. Sexual harassment may violate sections 804(a), 804(b), 804(c), 805, 806 or 818 under the Act. As the Department's current Fair Housing regulations do not address the standards to be applied in cases of sexual harassment, courts have looked to Title VII of the Civil Rights Act of 1964 (42 U.S.C. 2000 et. seq.) (Title VII), and associated case law and regulations for guidance in Fair Housing Act cases. (See Grieger v. Sheets, 1989 WL 38707 (N.D. Ill); see also Henson v. City of Dundee, 682 F.2d 897 (11th Cir. 1982); Shellhammer v. Lewallen, 770 F.2d 167 (6th Cir. 1985); Honce v. Vigil, 1 F.3d 1085 (10th Cir. 1993); Beliveau v. Caras, 873 F. Supp. 1393 (D. Cal. 1995); Krueger v. Cuomo, 115 F.3d 487 (7th Cir. 1997).) One court has expressed concern about the Department's lack of published standards concerning sexual harassment as a violation of the Act. (See DiCenso v. Cisneros, 96 F.3d 1004, 1007 (7th Cir. 1996)).

The Department is promulgating this proposed rule to provide guidance on key aspects of evaluating sexual harassment claims. In formulating the Department's position on sexual harassment, the Department carefully reviewed case law applying the Fair Housing Act, case law governing Title VII, and the Equal Employment Opportunity Commission's (EEOC) guidelines and policy statements.

Victims of sexual harassment at home lose their traditional place of refuge. "When the harassment occurs in a woman's home, it is a complete invasion in her life. Ideally, the home is the haven from the troubles of the day, when home is not a safe place, a woman may feel distressed and often immobile." (Regina Cahan, *Home is No Haven: An Analysis of Sexual Harassment in Housing*, 1987 Wis. L. Rev. 1061, 1072 (1987).) At least two courts have recognized that sexual harassment in the home may have more severe effects than harassment in the workplace. (See Beliveau v. Caras, 873 F. Supp. 1393, 1397 (C.D. Cal. 1995); Williams v. Poretsky Management, 955 F. Supp. 490, 497 (S.D. Md. 1996).)

Sexual harassment violates the prohibitions against discrimination on the basis of sex found in sections 804(a), 804(b), 804(c), 805, or 806 of the Act. Sexual harassment can also violate section 818 of the Act, which prohibits threatening, intimidating or coercive verbal or physical conduct that occurs because of an individual's membership in a protected class. Threatening, intimidating or coercive verbal or physical conduct, which occurs between neighbors or tenants, may constitute sexual harassment and, if so, the offending neighbor or tenant will be liable under section 818 of the Act.

There are two types of actionable sexual harassment claims: "quid pro quo" claims and "hostile environment" claims. There will be cases where the conduct in question may support both quid pro quo and hostile environment claims of sexual harassment.

Proposed § 100.500(a)(1) — Quid Pro Quo

A "quid pro quo" claim exists when submission to unwelcome sexual advances and requests for sexual favors is made a term or condition of housing related to the sale or rental of dwellings, the provision of services in connection therewith, or the availability of residential real estate-related transactions. Such a claim may be established if submission to or rejection of such conduct is used as the basis for decisions affecting the provision of housing or residential real estate-related transactions and related benefits or services. Generally, an individual asserting a quid pro quo claim of sexual harassment must establish the existence of an unwelcome demand for sexual favors based on the individual's sex and that the harassment adversely affected one or more terms, conditions, or privileges of housing or a residential real estate-related transaction or associated benefits or services.

Proposed § 100.500(a)(2) — Hostile Environment

A person creates a hostile environment when that person's unwelcome conduct is sufficiently severe or pervasive that it results in the creation of an environment that a reasonable person in the aggrieved person's position would find intimidating, hostile, offensive, or otherwise significantly less desirable. Generally, an individual asserting a hostile environment sexual harassment claim generally must establish that he or she was subjected to unwelcome verbal or physical conduct; the conduct was severe or pervasive; the conduct was based upon the individual's sex; and the conduct made the environment burdensome and significantly less desirable than if the conduct had not occurred.

Reasonable person standard. Whether conduct creates a hostile environment will be evaluated from the perspective of a reasonable person in the aggrieved person's position. The perspective of a reasonable person in the aggrieved person's position is that of an ordinary person in like circumstances. The Department believes that the purpose and intent of the Act is best served by adhering to the reasonable person standard and adopts this standard for cases under the Act. This standard recognizes that men, as well as women, may be victims of sexual harassment. (Oncale v. Sundowner Offshore Services, Inc., 523 U.S. 75 (1998).) This standard also recognizes that either opposite-sex or same-sex discrimination violates the Fair Housing Act if the challenged conduct occurred because of the victim's sex. (Id.)

The reasonable person standard is the perspective from which the victim's reaction to the harasser's conduct should be analyzed to determine whether an actionable sexual harassment claim exists. Use of the reasonable person standard to determine liability should not be confused with the standard used to determine appropriate damages to aggrieved persons in housing discrimination cases. It is a well-established principle in fair housing law that perpetrators of housing discrimination must take their victims as they find them; that is, damages are measured based on the injuries actually suffered by the victim, not on the injuries that would have been suffered by a reasonable person. (Alan W. Heifetz and Thomas C. Heinz, Separating the Objective, the Subjective and the Speculative: Assessing Compensatory Damages in Fair Housing Adjudications, 26 John Marshall Law Review 3, 21 (1992).)

Proposed § 100.500(b) — Totality of the Circumstances

Whether any conduct in question constitutes sexual harassment in violation of the Act will depend on the totality of the circumstances involved in each particular situation on a case by case basis. (Harris v. Forklift Systems, Inc., 510 U.S. 17, 22 (1993).) Critical factors to examine include, but are not limited to, the context, nature, severity, scope, frequency, duration, and location of the incidents, as well as the identity, number, relative ages and relationships of the persons involved.

This proposed regulation does not impose a quantitative requirement on the incidents of harassment that will constitute sexual harassment under the Act. (Harris, 510 U.S. at 22 "[t]his is not ... a mathematically precise test.") A quantitative requirement unfairly penalizes the person who takes affirmative steps to avoid further harassment by avoiding the harasser. (Gnerre v. Massachusetts Commission Against Discrimination, 524 N.E. 2d 84, 89 (Mass. 1988)). A single incident of conduct may constitute unlawful sexual harassment.

Proposed § 100.500(c) — Unwelcome Conduct

As evidenced by case law, unwelcome verbal conduct without physical conduct may independently support a sexual harassment claim. (See e.g., Grieger, 1989 WL 38707 (N.D. Ill.).) Verbal conduct includes, but is not limited to, the use of sexual epithets. Since verbal harassment may by itself support a sexual harassment claim under the Act, it follows that proof of physical harm is not necessary to establish a sexual harassment claim.

An intentional touching of any part of the body may constitute unwelcome conduct. To establish that conduct is sexual harassment, it is not necessary that intentional physical conduct involve an intimate body part. Evidence of unwelcome conduct need not be sexual in nature to support a claim for sexual harassment. (Id.*3 (citing cases from the Eighth, Tenth, and District of Columbia Circuits).)

Proposed § 100.500(d) — Liability

(1) A person is responsible for his or her acts.

(2) A person shall be vicariously liable for sexual harassment by his or her agents. An alleged perpetrator's responsibilities, duties and functions should be carefully examined to establish whether the perpetrator was acting in an agency capacity before determining whether a principal is liable. This principle is fully consistent with the Department's position on a principal's liability for the acts of agents. (See 24 CFR 103.20 (1999), and preamble to final rule implementing the Fair Housing Act Amendments of 1988, 54 FR 3232, 3260–3261, January 23, 1989.)

The duty of a property owner not to discriminate in the leasing or sale of property is non-delegable. (Alexander v. Riga, 208 F.3d 419, 432–434 (3rd Cir. 2000); Walker v. Crigler, 976 F.2d 900, 904 (4th Cir. 1992); Marr v. Rife, 503 F.2d 735, 741 (6th Cir. 1974); City of Chicago v. Matchmaker Real Estate Sales Center, Inc., 982 F.2d 1086, 1096 (7th Cir. 1996); Coates v. Bechtel, 811 F.2d 1045, 1051 (7th Cir. 1987); Phiffer v. Proud Parrot Motor Hotel, Inc., 648 F.2d 548 (9th Cir. 1980)). The Department invites comment on whether an affirmative defense, similar to the one that was created for employers by the Supreme Court in Title VII cases (Burlington Industries, Inc. v. Ellerth, 524 U.S. 742 (1998), and Faragher v. City of Boca Raton, 524 U.S. 775 (1998)) would be appropriate in the Fair Housing context. The Department also solicits comments on methods by which it can incorporate in the regulation provisions regarding training and other methods to educate individuals as to the prohibitions against sexual harassment under the Fair Housing Act.

(3) A person shall be responsible for acts of sexual harassment by third parties, where he or she, or his or her agent, knew or should have known of the conduct and failed to take immediate and appropriate corrective action, and had a duty to do so. (Reeves v. Carrolsburg Condominium Unit Owners Association, 1997 U.S. Dist. LEXIS 21762 *23; Cf. Bradley v. Carydale Enterprises, 707 F. Supp. 217 (E.D. VA 1989).) The duty to take corrective action may be established by leases, contracts, condominium by-laws and local ordinances. (Reeves, 1997 U.S. Dist., LEXIS 21762, *23.) Examples of third parties include tenants and independent contractors.

The Department solicits comments on other mechanisms that may create a duty to take corrective action and factors the Department should consider when determining whether such a duty exists.

Proposed § 100.500(e) — Other Related Conduct

When a housing-related opportunity or benefit is granted because of an individual's submission to sexual advances or requests for sexual favors, a person may be held liable for sexual harassment by other individuals who were qualified for and had a reasonable expectation of receiving an opportunity or benefit, but were denied. (Cf., Broderick v. Ruder, 685 F. Supp., 1269 (D.D.C. 1988).) For example, the manager of a housing complex with a long waiting list offers to move applicants to the top of the waiting list in exchange for sexual favors. Other applicants, even if they were not propositioned, but lost housing opportunities because of the manager's preferential treatment of others in exchange for sexual favors are aggrieved persons under the Fair Housing Act.

Proposed § 100.500(f) — Evidence of Psychological Harm

Evidence relating to the relative mildness or severity of an aggrieved person's psychological harm is not relevant to whether a respondent has violated the Fair Housing Act's prohibition against sexual harassment. (Harris, 510 U.S. 17 (1993)) Evidence of psychological harm may be considered in determining the proper amount of any money damages to which an aggrieved person may be entitled in compensation for emotional distress suffered.

Accordingly, 24 CFR part 100 is proposed to be amended as follows:

Part 100 — Discriminatory Conduct under the Fair Housing Act

1. The authority citation for 24 CFR part 100 continues to read as follows:

    Authority: 42 U.S.C. 3535(d), 3600–3620.

    § 100.65 Discrimination in terms, conditions and privileges and in services and facilities.

2. Section 100.65 is amended by removing paragraph (b)(5).

    Subpart G — Prohibited Sexual Harassment

3. In part 100, a new subpart G that consists of new § 100.500 is added to read as follows:

    § 100.500 Prohibited sexual harassment.

    (a) Sexual harassment can violate the prohibitions against discrimination on the basis of sex found in sections 804(a), 804(b), 804(c), 805, or 806 of the Act. Sexual harassment can also violate section 818 of the Act. There are two types of actionable sexual harassment claims:

       (1) Quid pro quo. Unwelcome sexual advances, requests for sexual favors, and other verbal or physical conduct of a sexual nature constitute sexual harassment when submission to the conduct, either explicitly or implicitly, is made a term or condition relating to the sale or rental of dwellings, the provision of benefits or services in connection therewith, or the availability of residential real estate-related transactions.

       (2) Hostile environment. Unwelcome sexual advances, requests for sexual favors, and other verbal or physical conduct constitute sexual harassment when the conduct has the effect of creating an environment which a rea-

sonable person in the aggrieved person's position would consider intimidating, hostile, offensive, or otherwise significantly less desirable in connection with the sale or rental of dwellings, the provision of benefits or services in connection therewith, and the availability of residential real estate-related transactions. Proof of an adverse action is not necessary to create an actionable hostile environment claim.

(b) Totality of the circumstances. Whether any particular conduct constitutes sexual harassment will depend upon the totality of the circumstances, including the nature of the conduct and the context in which the incident(s) occurred. Critical factors to examine include, but are not limited to, the context, nature, severity, scope, frequency, duration, and location of the incidents, as well as the identity, number, relative ages and relationships of the persons involved. A single incident of conduct may constitute hostile environment sexual harassment.

(c) Unwelcome conduct. Unwelcome verbal conduct may include, but is not limited to, sexual epithets. Unwelcome physical conduct may include, but is not limited to, contact with an intimate body part.

(d) Liability.

(1) A person is responsible for his or her acts.

(2) A person is vicariously liable to a victimized individual for sexual harassment by his or her agents.

(3) With respect to liability for sexual harassment by a third party, a person is responsible for acts of sexual harassment where the person, or his or her agents, knew or should have known of the third party's conduct and did not take immediate and appropriate corrective action and had a duty to do so.

(e) Other related conduct. When a housing-related opportunity or benefit is granted because of an individual's submission to sexual advances or requests for sexual favors, a person may be held liable by other individuals who were qualified for and had a reasonable expectation of receiving the opportunity or benefit, but were denied.

(f) Evidence of psychological harm. Evidence relating to the relative mildness or severity of an aggrieved person's psychological harm from such conduct is not relevant to a determination of whether a respondent violated the Act, but such evidence will be considered in determining the proper amount of any money damages to which an aggrieved person may be entitled in compensation for emotional distress suffered.

Dated: August 21, 2000.

Eva M. Plaza,

Assistant Secretary for Fair Housing and Equal Opportunity.

Wisconsin ex rel. Sprague v. City of Madison
205 Wis.2d 110, 555 N.W.2d 409 (1996)

Before Dykman, P.J., and Gartzke and Sundby, JJ.

Sundby, J.

Ann Hacklander-Ready and Maureen Rowe appeal from a decision affirming the Madison Equal Opportunity Commission's (MEOC) Decision and Order which found that they refused to rent housing to Carol Sprague as their housemate because of her sexual orientation, in violation of §3.23(4)(a) of the Madison General Ordinances (MGO). MEOC awarded Sprague $3,000 in damages for emotional distress, and $300 for the loss of a security deposit on another apartment. We conclude that the trial court correctly found that §3.23, MGO, unambiguously applied to housemates at the time this action arose. We therefore affirm MEOC's award of damages for Sprague's loss of her security deposit. However, we reverse the award for emotional distress because we conclude that MEOC had no power to award such damages. We further affirm MEOC's award of costs and reasonable attorney's fees to Sprague. Although Sprague is not entitled to damages for emotional distress, she is the prevailing party because she established that appellants discriminated against her.

Background

At all times relevant to this action Hacklander-Ready leased a four-bedroom house. She had the owner's permission to allow others to live with her and share in the payment of rent. In the fall of 1988, Maureen Rowe began living with Hacklander-Ready and paying rent. In April 1989 they advertised for housemates to replace two women who were moving out. They chose Sprague from among numerous applicants. They knew her sexual orientation when they extended their offer to her. Sprague accepted their offer and made a rent deposit on May 4, 1989. However, the following day Hacklander-Ready informed Sprague that they were withdrawing their offer because they were not comfortable living with a person of her sexual orientation.

Sprague filed a complaint with MEOC alleging that appellants discriminated against her on the basis of sexual orientation. The administrative law judge agreed and awarded Sprague $2,000 for emotional distress, $1,000 punitive damages, and $300 for the security deposit she lost trying to secure another apartment, together with costs and reasonable attorney's fees. Appellants appealed to MEOC. On July 10, 1992, MEOC vacated the hearing examiner's Findings of Fact and Conclusions of Law and Order on the grounds that the Madison City Council intended to exempt roommate arrangements from the ordinance. MEOC did not state its reasons for this conclusion, nor did it address the legal arguments the parties raised.

Sprague petitioned the circuit court for a writ of certiorari to review MEOC's decision. She argued that the ordinance unambiguously applied to housemate arrangements. On August 19, 1993, the trial court reversed MEOC's order. The court found that the language of the ordinance was "crystal clear" and that MEOC had jurisdiction to provide Sprague with relief. The trial court retained jurisdiction and remanded the matter to MEOC. On February 10, 1994, MEOC issued a Decision and Order on Remand which affirmed, in part, the decision of the hearing examiner. MEOC reversed the hearing examiner's award of punitive damages but increased the award of damages for Sprague's emotional distress to $3,000. The total award remained $3,300. MEOC awarded Sprague costs and reasonable attorney's fees.

Applicable Ordinances

At the time of the events in issue, §3.23, MGO, provided:

(1) Declaration of Policy. The practice of providing equal opportunities in housing ... without regard to ... sexual orientation ... is a desirable goal of the City of Madison and a matter of legitimate concern to its government ... In order that the peace, freedom, safety and general welfare of all inhabitants of the City

may be protected and ensured, it is hereby declared to be the public policy of the City of Madison to foster and enforce to the fullest extent the protection by law of the rights of all its inhabitants to equal opportunity to … housing.…

(2) (b) "Housing" shall mean any building, structure, or part thereof which is used or occupied, or is intended, arranged or designed to be used or occupied, as a residence, home or place of habitation of one or more human beings, including a mobile home as defined in Section 66.058 of the Wisconsin Statutes and a trailer as defined in Section 9.23 of the Madison General Ordinances.… Such definition of "housing" is qualified by the exceptions contained in Section 3.23(4)(a).…

(4) It shall be an unfair discrimination practice and unlawful and hereby prohibited:

(a) For any person having the right of ownership or possession or the right of transfer, sale, rental or lease of any housing, or the agent of any such person, to refuse to transfer, sell, rent or lease, or otherwise to deny or withhold from any person such housing because of … sexual orientation …

(b) Nothing in this ordinance shall prevent any person from renting or leasing housing, or any part thereof, to solely male or female persons if such housing or part thereof is rented with the understanding that toilet and bath facilities must be shared with the landlord or with other tenants.

Decision

On certiorari we review the decision of the administrative agency. Our review is limited to (1) whether MEOC kept within its jurisdiction, (2) whether it acted according to the law, (3) whether its action was arbitrary, oppressive, or unreasonable and represented its will and not its judgment, and (4) whether the evidence was such that MEOC might reasonably have made the order or determination in question.

Sprague claims that § 3.23, MGO, was intended to apply to housemate arrangements.[1] The interpretation of a statute or ordinance is a question of law which we decide without deference to the trial court. Where a statute is unambiguous there is no need to go beyond the clear language of the statute.

Section 3.23(4), MGO, unambiguously prohibits any person having right of rental to refuse to rent to any person because of the person's sexual orientation. Hacklander-Ready concedes that she held the lease to the house and that she had the right to rent the property to others. Further, she and Rowe admit that the sole reason they withdrew their offer was Sprague's sexual orientation. Finally, the room that appellants sought to rent falls within the definition of housing under § 3.23(2)(b), MGO, as a part of a building intended as a place of habitation for one or more human beings.

While appellants correctly argue that a statute is ambiguous if it may be construed in different ways by reasonably well-informed persons, we fail to see any reasonable interpretation that would make § 3.23, MGO, inapplicable in this case. Appellants also correctly note that a court may resort to construction if the literal meaning of a statute produces an absurd or unreasonable result. However, applying § 3.23(4) to the rental of a room within a house with shared common areas is not unreasonable or absurd.

---

1. In September 1989, subsequent to the commencement of this action, the Madison City Council amended the Equal Opportunities Ordinance by adding § 3.23(c), MGO, which states, "Nothing in this ordinance shall affect any person's decision to share occupancy of a lodging room, apartment or dwelling unit with another person or persons."

Because we find that the ordinance clearly and unambiguously applies to the subleasing of housing by a person having the right of rental, our inquiry in this respect is at an end.

Appellants argue that to apply the ordinance to the lease of housing by a tenant to a housemate makes § 3.24(4)(a), MGO, unconstitutional in its application....

Appellants cite many cases which they argue support their constitutional challenge: NAACP v. Alabama, 357 U.S. 449 (1958): Griswold v. Connecticut, 381 U.S. 479 (1965); City of Ladue v. Gilleo, 512 U.S. 43 (1994); Payton v. New York, 445 U.S. 573 (1980); Moore v. City of East Cleveland, 431 U.S. 494 (1977); City of Wauwatosa v. King, 49 Wis.2d 398 (1971). However, those cases deal either with the right to privacy in the home or family or the right to engage in first amendment activity free of unwarranted governmental intrusion. Appellants gave up their unqualified right to such constitutional protection when they rented housing for profit. The restrictions placed by the Madison City Council on persons who rent housing for profit are not unreasonable and do not encroach upon appellant's constitutional protections. We therefore reject appellants' challenge to the constitutionality of § 3.24, MGO, as applied.

[The court held that MEOC exceeded its jurisdiction and acted contrary to law when it awarded Sprague damages for emotional distress.]

Appellants also argue that the $300 award for the lost security deposit should be vacated because it reflects MEOC's will and not its judgment. However, we find that MEOC's determination that appellants' illegal refusal to rent to Sprague was the proximate cause of the lost security deposit is reasonably supported by the evidence and is an appropriate restitutionary remedy.

Finally, appellants contend that Sprague's inquiries as to whether the household would respect her sexual orientation constituted a waiver of her rights under § 3.23, MGO. To hold that a prudent inquiry about the environment in which one will live waived the protections afforded by § 3.23, MGO, would be an unreasonable construction of the ordinance. We therefore hold that by her inquiries Sprague did not waive her rights under the ordinance.

Because we hold that in enacting § 3.23(9)(c)2.b, MGO, the Common Council did not authorize MEOC to award damages for emotional distress, we do not decide whether the award violated appellants' right to a jury trial. Further, we need not consider the broader question whether municipalities generally have the power to authorize administrative agencies to award compensatory damages.

Order affirmed in part and reversed in part.

Levin v. Yeshiva University
96 N.Y.2d 484, 754 N.E.2d 1099 (Court of Appeals of New York 2001)

James D. Esseks, for appellants.* Mark A. Jacoby, for respondents.

Judges Levine, Wesley, Rosenblatt, and Graffeo concur. Judge Smith concurs in result in an opinion. Chief Judge Kaye concurs in part and dissents in part in an opinion.

---

* Attorney General of the State of New York; Lambda Legal Defense and Education Fund, et al.; Audre Lorde Project, et al.; Association of the Bar of the City of New York; NAACP Legal Defense and Educational Fund, Inc., et al.; Gay and Lesbian Law Students Alliance et al., amici curiae.

Ciparick, J.

The New York City Human Rights Law, like the State Human Rights Law, protects certain groups from policies or practices that discriminate against them in areas such as employment, public accommodations and housing. The City's Human Rights Law goes the additional step of prohibiting policies or practices which, though neutral on their face and neutral in intent, have an unjustified disparate impact upon one or more of the covered groups. In contrast to the State law, the New York City law explicitly extends protection to persons discriminated against on the basis of sexual orientation.

Plaintiffs Sara Levin and Maggie Jones are lesbians enrolled at defendant Yeshiva University's Albert Einstein College of Medicine (AECOM) in the Bronx.[1] … The complaint alleges the following facts, which we must accept as true for present purposes: Yeshiva maintains a number of different sized apartments near AECOM for the housing of medical students. AECOM's housing policy restricts university-owned housing to medical students, their spouses and children. All apartment vacancies are filled from a waiting list on a first-come, first-served basis. Married couples, however, receive priority for studio apartments. One-bedroom apartments must be shared by a minimum of two students or a married couple. Two-bedroom apartments must be shared by a minimum of three individuals, with married couples having one or more children receiving priority.[2] To receive housing priority, married couples must provide Yeshiva's housing office with acceptable proof of marriage.

Prior to her first year of medical school, plaintiff Sara Levin requested housing for herself and her partner of five years. Pursuant to its policy, AECOM informed her that she had to produce proof of marriage in order to live with a non-student. Unable to produce proof of marriage, Levin accepted housing in an on-campus three-bedroom apartment with two other students. Levin's request for housing with her partner was again denied the following year. Eventually, Levin and her partner moved into an off-campus apartment in Brooklyn. In her first year of medical school, plaintiff Maggie Jones was also denied housing with her partner. Jones accepted a one-bedroom apartment with another AECOM student during her first year, but then also relinquished campus housing to live with her partner off-campus.

Plaintiffs commenced this action in 1998 claiming that defendants' housing policy discriminated against them based on marital status in violation of the New York State and City Human Rights Laws and that it had a disparate impact against lesbians and gay men in violation of the City Human Rights Law.… Supreme Court … dismissed the complaint.… The Appellate Division affirmed, agreeing that there was no discrimination or disparate impact on homosexuals, since defendant's policy "had the same impact on non-married heterosexual medical students as it had on non-married homosexual medical students." Because plaintiffs have pleaded allegations sufficient to raise an issue of fact as to whether defendants' housing policy has a disparate impact on the basis of sexual orientation under the New York City law, we now modify the order of the Appellate Division and remit this case to the Supreme Court for further proceedings.

---

1. All parties agree that Yeshiva's religious affiliations have no bearing on this appeal. Also, plaintiffs did not plead claims based on either the State or Federal Constitution.

2. The complaint alleges, at paragraph (9), that university-owned housing is restricted to "Yeshiva students, their spouses and children." Presumably, a single parent, regardless of sexual orientation, would be eligible to reside in university-owned housing with his or her child. The complaint is silent on this subject. However, defendants appear to concede the point in their brief.

Marital Status

Contrary to plaintiffs' assertions, AECOM's policy did not discriminate on the basis of marital status on its face. This question is settled by our prior holdings.

As we held in [earlier cases], for purposes of applying the statutory proscription, a distinction must be made between the complainant's marital status as such, and the existence of the complainant's disqualifying relationship—or absence thereof—with another person. Just as the lease provision in Hudson View did not turn on the marital status of the tenant, but instead validly limited occupancy to only those in a legal, family relationship with the tenant, AECOM's housing policy is restricted to those in legally recognized, family relationships with a student, not the student's marital status.

In our view, AECOM's housing policy—limiting cohabitational housing eligibility to students, their spouses and dependent children—is substantially indistinguishable from the policy considered in Hudson View limiting occupancy to tenants and their "immediate family." For this reason, the policy does not facially discriminate on the basis of marital status....

Sexual Orientation

Section 8-107(5)(a)(1) of the Administrative Code of the City of New York makes it an unlawful discriminatory practice to refuse housing accommodations to any person because of that person's "actual or perceived race, creed, color, national origin, gender, age, disability, *sexual orientation*, marital status, or alienage or citizenship status." (emphasis supplied). At the outset, we note that this provision applies to those who provide public or private housing accommodations, and so Yeshiva's status as a private institution does not exempt it from the enactment. While denying its violation, Yeshiva concedes that it is subject to the City Human Rights Law....

A claim of discrimination based on sexual orientation can be stated where a facially neutral policy or practice has a disparate impact on a protected group ([NYC Admin.] Code §8-107[17][a][1]–[2]). Under that section, a claim is established where a plaintiff demonstrates that a defendant's policy or practice "results in a disparate impact to the detriment of any group protected" under the City Human Rights Law (id.).[3] Our inquiry at this stage concerns whether the complaint sufficiently pleads that AECOM's housing policy has such a disparate impact on the basis of sexual orientation. How impact is measured is obviously a critical determination.

Instructive in this regard is Griggs v. Duke Power Co., 401 U.S. 424 [(1971)]. In Griggs, plaintiffs, African-American employees of the defendant utility, alleged that their employer violated [T]itle VII of the Civil Rights Act of 1964 by instituting a policy that required all applicants for certain positions to have earned a high school diploma and/or pass a standardized test. Plaintiffs argued that the policy was discriminatory not because it targeted African-Americans but because, statistically, it disqualified African-Americans at a higher rate than white candidates. The lower courts held that defendant's policy was not suspect because it was keyed solely to educational achievement, and there had been no showing of discriminatory intent.

---

3. Once that showing has been made, defendant has an opportunity to plead and prove as an affirmative defense that the policy or practice complained of "bears a significant relationship to a significant business objective." The defense is defeated, however, when plaintiff produces substantial evidence of an available alternative policy or practice with less disparate impact, and defendant fails to prove that the alternative policy or practice would not serve defendant's significant business objective as well as the complained-of policy or practice.

The United States Supreme Court reversed, holding that under the Civil Rights Act, "practices, procedures or tests neutral on their face, and even neutral in terms of intent, cannot be maintained if they operate to freeze the status quo of prior discriminatory employment practices." Looking beyond facial neutrality the Court stated "[the Civil Rights] Act proscribes not only overt discrimination but also practices that are fair in form, but discriminatory in operation." The Court concluded that the facially neutral hiring and promotional requirements operated to exclude African-Americans at a significantly higher rate than similarly situated white applicants. In such a context, a prima facie case of disparate impact is established when it is demonstrated that a test or policy "select[s] applicants for hire or promotion in a racial pattern significantly different from that of the pool of applicants" (Albemarle Paper Co. v. Moody, 422 U.S. 405, 425 [(1975)]; see also, Dothard v. Rawlinson, 433 U.S. 321, 329–330 [(1977)] [comparing ratio of men to women nationally to ratio of men to women who had qualified for positions as corrections officers]).

Twenty years after Griggs, in 1991, the City of New York enacted Human Rights Law section 8-107(17), explicitly creating a disparate impact cause of action for plaintiffs who can demonstrate "that a policy or practice of a covered entity [e.g., employer, housing provider] or a group of policies or practices of a covered entity results in a disparate impact to the detriment of any [protected] group." Unlike the State Human Rights Law, the City law both specifies a right of action for policies or practices that have a disparate impact and specifically prohibits any form of discrimination based on sexual orientation. The New York City Council also explicitly made "disparate impact" applicable to discrimination claims outside of the employment context.

Here, the Appellate Division held that, as a matter of law, AECOM's housing policy did not have a disparate impact on plaintiffs on the basis of sexual orientation. It reached that conclusion by also ruling as a matter of law that married students had to be excluded from consideration for purposes of comparison between the benefitted and excluded classes. We conclude that the court erred in dismissing the complaint on that basis.

The exclusion of married students from the necessary comparison group conflicts with controlling disparate impact methodology and analysis. Self-evidently, married students make up a significant portion of the very class of persons made eligible by AECOM's policy for the substantial economic and social benefits of cohabiting with non-students in university-owned housing. In no presently authoritative precedent, either Federal or from our Court, has a plaintiff in a disparate impact discrimination case been precluded from pointing to the composition of the class of persons rendered eligible for benefits under the challenged policy at issue. Excluding a large portion of the class benefitted by this policy from the disparate impact comparison group would render the disparate impact analysis articulated in Griggs meaningless. To illustrate, the result in Griggs would have been entirely different had the plaintiffs been prevented from analyzing the racial composition of those actually offered employment under the company's hiring policy requiring successful test completion and/or a high school diploma. As a result, just as in the Appellate Division's ruling here, the only comparison would have been between those African-American and white persons without high school diplomas or passing test scores. And, since 100% of both classes were not the recipients of favorable treatment, no disparate impact would have been established, thereby frustrating [C]ongressional policy as applied to that case.

Here, the Appellate Division declared that only unmarried AECOM students were the proper comparison group, citing Hudson View Properties v. Weiss, 59 N.Y.2d 733 [(1983)], as its basis. In so doing, the court apparently adopted one of defendants' two principal justifications for excluding consideration of married students.

According to defendants, Hudson View established the legality of their housing policy, based upon the marital relationships of students and non-students, as against *any* discrimination challenge. On the basis of that assumption, defendants conclude that "married students are not similarly situated to other students because the distinction that the housing policy draws on the basis of marital relationship is a *lawful* one." The fallacy of this premise is easily demonstrated.

Hudson View holds only that a landlord's restriction limiting occupancy to a tenant's immediate family does not violate prohibitions against facial discrimination based upon marital status. It does not, however, determine the question of whether the same policy would constitute prohibited disparate treatment or disparate impact discrimination based upon sexual orientation or, indeed, discrimination against any other statutorily protected class. Thus, if AECOM had limited cohabitational university housing to married students of a particular race and their non-student spouses, such a policy would arguably be "lawful" with respect to marital status discrimination under Hudson View, since it would be based upon the relationships and characteristics of the particular partners, not upon their marital status as such. No one would seriously contend, however, that such a policy would not constitute illegal discrimination based upon race. Likewise here, the legality of AECOM's policy with respect to a marital status discrimination claim cannot insulate it from a sexual orientation discrimination claim.

Defendants' alternative argument is likewise unavailing. They assert that, because State law limits marriage to a union between a man and a woman, marriage-based requirements, by their very terms, *facially* discriminate on the basis of sexual orientation. "It is analytically false to characterize a 'marriage-based requirement' as being a 'facially neutral policy' vis a vis sexual orientation" (Defendants' Brief, at 34). From that proposition, defendants draw the conclusion that married students must therefore be entirely excluded from the disparate impact analysis: "Because being married is not a facially neutral criterion as to appellants' claims of discrimination on the basis of sexual orientation, the courts below were correct in excluding married students from the composition of the similarly situated groups to be compared" (id.).

This reasoning is flawed in two critical respects. First, a university's housing policy could not be facially discriminatory on the basis of sexual orientation if the criterion used to determine whether housing was awarded operated to exclude both heterosexual and homosexual students while [it], at the same time, conferred housing to a distinct group, also comprised of both homosexual and heterosexual students.

That is exactly the case here. As defendants have conceded, not only students with spouses, but also students with dependent children, *regardless of sexual orientation*, are entitled to housing priorities under AECOM's policy. Conversely, not only gay and lesbian students and their partners are excluded from cohabitational housing, but also heterosexual students and their partners who, for whatever reason, are unable or unwilling to marry, as well as heterosexual and homosexual students who wish to live with relatives not qualifying as dependent children. Second, even if we were to accept defendants' proposition that AECOM's housing policy lacks facial neutrality "vis a vis sexual orientation," then AECOM would be compelled to acknowledge that its policy was facially discriminatory and, thus, in direct violation of the City's Human Rights Law on the basis of disparate treatment, without the necessity of establishing disparate impact.

Defendants' position here essentially distills to the proposition that AECOM's policy must be viewed as distinguishing between two nonsimilarly-situated groups: married students on the one hand who, by law, do not include homosexuals, and non-married students on the other. In short, AECOM's premise is that the comparison groups must be separated along the facially neutral lines drawn by its policy. The flaw in this analysis is demonstrated in the Congressional repudiation of both the result *and* the reasoning of the Supreme Court's decision in General Electric Co. v. Gilbert, 429 U.S. 125 [(1976)]; *see*, Newport News Shipbuilding and Dry Dock Co. v. EEOC, 462 U.S. 669 [(1983)].

At issue in General Electric v. Gilbert was a company employee disability plan that gave its workers benefits during periods of disability due to all nonoccupational causes except pregnancy. The majority in Gilbert held that the plaintiffs failed to establish a Civil Rights Act [T]itle VII violation for discrimination based upon gender, employing a rationale almost indistinguishable from that advanced here by defendants. That is, that the disability plan created two separate and dissimilar groups: (1) pregnant women (based on their physical condition, not gender); and (2) nonpregnant men and women, who were treated equally for benefit eligibility. The dissenters in Gilbert rejected that analysis as "simplistic and misleading." The relevant comparison, according to the dissenters, had to be the overall disability coverage afforded men as against that afforded women. Under that analytical framework, the General Electric plan—which insured employees, male and female, against all risks of disability except pregnancy, the single risk that is unique to women—was discriminatory based upon gender under the proper disparate impact analysis.

As fully explained in Newport News Shipbuilding and Drydock Co., in 1978, Congress overruled and repudiated the reasoning of Gilbert, and the legislative history expressly adopted the views of the dissenters in that case. Just as in Gilbert, the attempt here is to extract married medical students—the very group benefitted by AECOM's housing policy—from consideration in any disparate impact analysis thereby obscuring any realistic examination of the discriminatory effects of that policy.

In order to determine whether AECOM's housing policy has a disparate impact that falls along the impermissible lines of sexual orientation, there must be a comparison that includes consideration of the full composition of the class actually benefitted under the challenged policy. Because the Appellate Division's exclusion of at least a significant portion of that benefitted group constituted error as a matter of law, the cause of action alleging disparate impact discrimination based on sexual orientation as proscribed by the New York City Human Rights Law §8-107(17) was improperly dismissed on the pleadings and must be reinstated and remitted to Supreme Court for further proceedings. If, upon remittal, plaintiffs establish that AECOM's policy regarding university-owned housing with non-students disproportionately burdens lesbians and gay men, the City Administrative Code requires that defendants justify their policy as bearing a "significant relationship to a significant business objective." ...

Giebeler v. M & B Associates

343 F.3d 1143 (9th Cir. 2003)

Elizabeth Brancart, Brancart & Brancart, Pescadero, CA, for the appellant.

David R. Sylva and David S. Hoffman, Campbell, CA, for the appellee.

Before Thompson, W. Fletcher, and Berzon, Circuit Judges.

Berzon, Circuit Judge.

John Giebeler has AIDS. Because he has AIDS, he is disabled and can no longer work, although he had worked and earned an adequate living until he became ill. Once he was no longer earning a salary, his former apartment became too expensive for him. In addition, he needed assistance with daily matters because of his illness and so wanted to live closer to his mother.

Giebeler's lack of an income stream meant that he could not meet the minimum financial qualifications of the apartment complex where he sought an apartment. Giebeler's mother, however, did meet those standards, and offered to rent the apartment so that her son could live in it. The owners of the apartment complex refused to rent either to Giebeler or to his mother, citing a management company policy against cosigners.

The question in this case is whether the Fair Housing Amendments Act (FHAA), 42 U.S.C. § 3601 et seq. (1995), required the apartment owners reasonably to accommodate Giebeler's disability by assessing individually the risk of nonpayment created by his specific proposed financial arrangement, rather than inflexibly applying a rental policy that forbids cosigners. Concluding that the statute does so require, we reverse the district court's grant of summary judgment and remand the case for further proceedings.

Background

John Giebeler had worked as a psychiatric technician for approximately five years before becoming disabled by AIDS. At the time Giebeler had to leave work because of his disability, he was earning approximately $36,000 per year. Since 1996, Giebeler has supported himself through monthly disability benefits under the Social Security Disability Insurance (SSDI) program and housing assistance from the Housing Opportunities for People with AIDS program (HOPWA).

In May 1997, Giebeler sought to move from his two-bedroom apartment at the Elan at River Oaks complex (Elan) to an available one-bedroom unit at the Park Branham Apartments (Branham), a rental property owned by defendants (M & B). Giebeler wanted to move to the Branham unit because the rent, $875 per month, was less expensive than the $1,545 per month rent at Elan, and the Branham unit was closer to his mother's home. At the time Giebeler inquired about the Branham unit, he was receiving $837 from SSDI per month, $300 to $400 per month in a HOPWA subsidy, and varied amounts of financial support from his mother. He had a record of consistent and prompt payment of rent during his six years of residency at Elan, and his credit record contained no negative notations.

Branham resident manager Jan Duffus informed Giebeler that he did not qualify for tenancy at Branham because he did not meet the minimum income requirements. Duffus stated that Branham required prospective tenants to have a minimum gross monthly income equaling three times the monthly rent. For the apartment Giebeler wished to rent, the minimum required income was $2,625 per month, an amount less than Giebeler had earned before he became ill.

After he was informed of his ineligibility, Giebeler asked his mother, Anne Giebeler, to assist him in renting the apartment. Anne Giebeler went to the Branham office the next day for the purpose of renting an apartment that would be occupied by her son.

Like her son, Anne Giebeler had a credit record with no negative entries. Anne Giebeler had owned the same home for 27 years and had completely paid off her mortgage. The home was located less than a mile from Branham. Anne Giebeler's income was $3,770.26 per month.

Both John Giebeler and Anne Giebeler filled out application forms for the one-bedroom Branham apartment, indicating that John Giebeler would be the only resident. On his rental application, Giebeler listed his current gross income as $837 and his present occupation as "disabled." The Branham property manager rejected the applications on the basis that M & B considered Anne Giebeler a cosigner and has a policy against allowing co-signers on lease agreements.

Following the denial of his rental application, Giebeler contacted AIDS Legal Services for assistance. Attorney John Doherty wrote a letter to the Branham property manager on Giebeler's behalf, stating that Giebeler was disabled and that, under 42 U.S.C. §3604(f)(3)(B) of the FHAA, unlawful discrimination against disabled persons in housing includes "a refusal to make reasonable accommodations in rules, policies, practices, or services, when such accommodations may be necessary to afford such person equal opportunity to use and enjoy a dwelling." Doherty's letter requested a reasonable accommodation for Giebeler, suggesting use of a cosigner or other alternative arrangements to meet the financial requirements for tenancy.

Branham's attorney responded to Doherty's letter by confirming the rejection of Giebeler's rental application and denying that federal law required them to grant Giebeler's request for reasonable accommodation. Branham management never checked Giebeler's references or his rental or credit history nor inquired into Anne Giebeler's financial qualifications or connections to the area. Nor did the Branham management ever ask Giebeler about any additional sources of income or discuss with him any alternatives to the minimum income requirement.

In February 1998, Giebeler filed an action under the federal FHAA, the California Fair Employment and Housing Act (FEHA), the California Business and Professions Code, the California Civil Code section 54.1, and common law negligence. Giebeler's FHAA claim advanced three theories of discrimination: disparate impact, intentional discrimination, and failure to reasonably accommodate Giebeler's disability through refusal to waive the no-cosigner policy. The district court held that Giebeler had made out a prima facie case of intentional discrimination under the FHAA, violation of the California Business and Professions Code, and violation of the FEHA. The court granted summary judgment for M & B, however, on Giebeler's state law negligence claim and his FHAA disparate impact and reasonable accommodation claims. In ruling on Giebeler's reasonable accommodation claim, the district court held that "an accommodation which remedies the economic status of a disabled person is not an 'accommodation' as contemplated by the FHA." Only the grant of summary judgment for M & B on Giebeler's reasonable accommodation claim is before us on appeal.

Discussion

The FHAA provides that it is unlawful to discriminate against disabled persons[2]

_____

2. This opinion uses the terms "disability" and "disabled," except when referring to the FHAA's statutory language, which uses "handicap" and "handicapped." See Helen D. v. DiDario, 46 F.3d 325, 330 n.8 (3d Cir. 1995) ("The change in nomenclature from 'handicap' [in the Rehabilitation Act] to 'disability' [in the Americans With Disabilities Act] reflects Congress' awareness that individuals with disabilities find the term 'handicapped' objectionable.") When used, the terms "handicap" and "handicapped" have interchangeable meaning with "disability" and "disabled."

in the sale or rental, or to otherwise make unavailable or deny, a dwelling to any buyer or renter because of a handicap of—

(A) that buyer or renter,

(B) a person residing in or intending to reside in that dwelling after it is so sold, rented, or made available; or

(C) any person associated with that buyer or renter.

42 U.S.C. § 3604(f)(1).

The FHAA's definition of prohibited discrimination encompasses "a refusal to make reasonable accommodations in rules, policies, practices, or services, when such accommodations may be necessary to afford such person equal opportunity to use and enjoy a dwelling." 42 U.S.C. § 3604(f)(3)(B). Thus, the FHAA "imposes an affirmative duty upon landlords reasonably to accommodate the needs of handicapped persons," United States v. California Mobile Home Park Mgmt. Co., 29 F.3d 1413, 1416 (9th Cir. 1994) ("Mobile Home I"), not only with regard to the physical accommodations, see 42 U.S.C. § 3604(f)(3)(A) and (C), but also with regard to the administrative policies governing rentals.

To make out a claim of discrimination based on failure to reasonably accommodate, a plaintiff must demonstrate that (1) he suffers from a handicap as defined by the FHAA; (2) defendants knew or reasonably should have known of the plaintiff's handicap; (3) accommodation of the handicap "may be necessary" to afford plaintiff an equal opportunity to use and enjoy the dwelling; and (4) defendants refused to make such accommodation. United States v. California Mobile Home Park Mgmt. Co., 107 F.3d 1374, 1380 (9th Cir. 1997) ("Mobile Home II").

A. Giebeler's Disability

The defendants do not dispute that Giebeler is disabled for the purposes of the FHAA and that they knew of his disability, nor do they deny that they refused to make the accommodation Giebeler requested. The defendants contend, rather, that the accommodation Giebeler requested is not one the FHAA requires them to accord. For the purposes of our analysis of the scope of the accommodation to which Giebeler may have been entitled, however, it is important to understand precisely why Giebeler's disability entitled him to the protections of the FHAA.

The FHAA defines "handicap" as "a physical or mental impairment which substantially limits one or more of such person's major life activities." 42 U.S.C. § 3602(h)(1). Infection with HIV, the virus that causes AIDS, qualifies as a "physical or mental impairment" for the purposes of the FHAA. 24 C.F.R. § 100.201(a)(2); Bragdon v. Abbott, 524 U.S. 624, 639–642 (1998) (HIV infection is a disability under the ADA because it substantially limits major life activities). FHAA regulations further define "major life activities" to include "functions such as caring for one's self, performing manual tasks, walking, seeing, hearing, speaking, breathing, learning, and *working*." 24 C.F.R. § 100.201(b).

Giebeler's AIDS-related impairments substantially—indeed, entirely—limited his ability to work.[3] Giebeler had to leave his job as a psychiatric technician because of his

---

3. M&B does not challenge the validity of the regulations designating work as a major life activity. See, e.g., Sutton v. United Air Lines, Inc., 527 U.S. 471, 480 (1999) (assuming validity of regulation defining major life activity under ADA).

illness and can no longer work. Consequently, his income stream was limited to whatever he received in disability and HOWPA payments, supplemented by financial assistance from his mother. Because of his reduced income, Giebeler did not meet the minimum income defendants' policies require of Branham tenants. If Giebeler were still able to work in the position he held before becoming ill, he would have met Branham's financial requirements. A direct causal link therefore existed between Giebeler's impairment, his inability to work, and his inability to comply with defendants' minimum income requirement relying solely on his individual income.

Given these undisputed facts, we must determine whether relaxation of Branham's no-cosigner policy to allow Giebeler to live in an apartment rented for him by his mother constituted a reasonable accommodation required by the FHAA.

B. Accommodation under the FHAA

The central issue in dispute in this case is whether bending a landlord's usual *means* of testing a prospective tenant's likely ability to pay the rent over the course of the lease is an "accommodation" at all within the meaning of the FHAA, let alone a reasonable one. Permitting Giebeler to live in an apartment rented for him by his qualified mother would have adjusted for his inability, because of his disability, to earn his own income, while providing M & B with substantial assurance that the full rent—not a discounted amount—would be paid monthly. Branham maintains, however, that an adjustment of this kind is not the type of alteration in housing policy that Congress had in mind in enacting the FHAA. Noting that Branham's no-cosigner rule adversely affects many prospective tenants who cannot meet the financial specifications without relying on the income or assets of a relative or friend, M & B would have us hold that altering that rule to aid a disabled potential tenant does not come within the FHAA's concept of accommodation because it would (1) prefer disabled over nondisabled impecunious individuals; (2) accommodate Giebeler's poverty rather than his disability; and (3) increase M & B's financial exposure, with potential cost to the landlord should its fears that it could not collect the rent prove true. We conclude that the FHAA's accommodation requirement does reach adjustments in the means of proving financial responsibility, and that each of Branham's arguments to the contrary runs afoul of binding case law elucidating the "accommodation" concept in the FHAA and related statutes.

Before explaining our reasoning on the reach of the "accommodation" concept, we note that only "reasonable" accommodations are required by the FHAA. 42 U.S.C. § 3604(f)(3)(B). There is some tendency in the case law to truncate the "accommodation" concept so as to preclude requirements that unreasonably burden housing providers, rather than conducting the two-step analysis mandated by the statute. So it is important to bear in mind that a conclusion that a type of alteration to a policy is an "accommodation" within the meaning of the statute is only the first step in a multi-prong statutory analysis.

1. The plain language of the FHAA provides scant guidance concerning the reach of the accommodation requirement. See 42 U.S.C. § 3604(f)(3)(B); see also 42 U.S.C. §§ 3607; 3604(f)(5)(C); 42 U.S.C. § 3604(f)(9) (listing exemptions to FHAA coverage and limitations on the duty to accommodate). Similarly, the FHAA's legislative history and regulations provide us with little specific guidance as to the scope and limitations of "accommodation" under the FHAA.

The House Committee Report on the FHAA does state, however, that the interpretations of "reasonable accommodation" in Rehabilitation Act ("RA") regulations and case law should be applied to the FHAA's reasonable accommodation provision:

New subsection 804(f)(3)(B) makes it illegal to refuse to make reasonable accommodation in rules, policies, practices, or services if necessary to permit a person with handicaps equal opportunity to use and enjoy a dwelling. The concept of "reasonable accommodation" has a long history in regulations and case law dealing with discrimination on the basis of handicap. [Footnote citing, inter alia, 45 C.F.R. § 84.12.][4] A discriminatory rule, policy, practice, or service is not defensible simply because that is the manner in which such rule or practice has traditionally been constituted. This section would require that changes be made to such traditional rules or practices if necessary to permit a person with handicaps an equal opportunity to use and enjoy a dwelling. H.R. Rep. No. 100-711, at 25 (1988), reprinted in 1988 U.S.C.C.A.N. 2173, 2186.

See also id. at 28 ("In adopting this amendment, the Committee drew on case law developed under Section 504 of the Rehabilitation Act of 1973.").

Consistent with the Report's recommendation, we have applied RA regulations and case law when interpreting the FHAA's reasonable accommodation provisions. Also, since the enactment of the Americans with Disabilities Act (ADA), 42 U.S.C. 12101 et seq., we have relied on ADA cases in applying the RA, because, as a general matter, "there is no significant difference in the analysis or rights and obligations created by the two Acts." Vinson v. Thomas, 288 F.3d 1145, 1152 n.7 (9th Cir. 2002).

The concept that policies and practices must be modified in some instances to accommodate the needs of the disabled is common to all three statutory schemes. We therefore look to both RA and ADA interpretations of "accommodation" of disabled individuals as indicative of the scope of "accommodation" under the FHAA. In doing so, we interpret the FHAA's accommodation provisions with the specific goals of the FHAA in mind: "to protect the right of handicapped persons to live in the residence of their choice in the community," and "to end the unnecessary exclusion of persons with handicaps from the American mainstream." City of Edmonds [v. Oxford House], 18 F.3d [802,] 806 [(9th Cir. 1994)].*

2. The Supreme Court's most extensive discussion of the overall scope of the accommodation concept appears in a recent ADA case, U.S. Airways v. Barnett, 535 U.S. 391 (2002). Barnett guides our analysis concerning the reach of the accommodation obligation under the FHAA, in two respects: First, Barnett holds that an accommodation may indeed result in a preference for disabled individuals over otherwise similarly situated non-disabled individuals. And second, Barnett indicates that

---

4. The cited regulation is a Department of Health and Human Services—previously, the Department of Health, Education and Welfare—regulation promulgated under § 504. At the time of the Committee Report, the regulation read as here pertinent:

(a) A recipient shall make reasonable accommodation to the known physical or mental limitations of an otherwise qualified handicapped applicant or employee unless the recipient can demonstrate that the accommodation would impose an undue hardship on the operation of its program....

(c) In determining pursuant to paragraph (a) of this section whether an accommodation would impose an undue hardship on the operation of a recipient's program, factors to be considered include ...

(3) The nature and cost of the accommodation needed.

The present regulation is identical to the 1988 version except that "individual" has been substituted for "applicant or employee." The regulation pertains most directly to workplace accommodation, so some of the subsections are not relevant to the present issue.

* Editor's Note: This is the decision that the U.S. Supreme Court reviewed *sub. nom.* City of Edmonds v. Oxford House, 514 U.S. 725 (1995), *infra* p. 461.

accommodations may adjust for the practical impact of a disability, not only for the immediate manifestations of the physical or mental impairment giving rise to the disability.

In Barnett, an airline cargo handler requested, as accommodation of his back injuries, an exception to the company's seniority system so that he could transfer to a less physically demanding position. The airline refused to authorize a departure from its seniority rules, contending that because the ADA ensures *equal* treatment of persons with disabilities, any sort of preferential exception to a disability-neutral policy was outside the scope of the "reasonable accommodations" mandated by the statute.

Rejecting the airline's narrow interpretation of "reasonable accommodation," Barnett held that the ADA requires reasonable accommodations necessary to meet the disability-created needs of a disabled person, so that the disabled person may enjoy the same workplace opportunities enjoyed by non-disabled persons. Such reasonable accommodation in the service of equal opportunity may require preferential treatment of the disabled:

> [P]references will sometimes prove necessary to achieve the [Americans with Disabilities] Act's basic equal opportunity goal. The Act requires preferences in the form of "reasonable accommodations" that are needed for those with disabilities to obtain the *same* workplace opportunities that those without disabilities enjoy. By definition any special "accommodation" requires the employer to treat an employee with a disability differently, *i.e.,* preferentially. And the fact that the difference in treatment violates an employer's disability-neutral rule cannot by itself place the accommodation beyond the Act's potential reach.

> Were that not so, the "reasonable accommodation" provision could not accomplish its intended objective.... Many employers will have neutral rules governing the kinds of actions most needed to reasonably accommodate a worker with a disability.

The objection that Branham need not permit Giebeler to live in an apartment rented by his financially-qualified mother because other prospective tenants unable to meet the financial qualifications on their own also cannot rent apartments therefore runs afoul of Barnett. Just as Barnett was not disqualified from an adjustment to his seniority rank simply because other, non-disabled employees desired the position he sought but were barred from obtaining it by the seniority policy, so Giebeler was not disqualified from an adjustment in Branham's financial qualification/no cosigner standard simply because there were other prospective tenants similarly unable—albeit for reasons other than disability—to earn enough money to meet the rental company's credit standards.

Additionally, Barnett indicates, inferentially if not expressly, that a required accommodation need not address "barriers that would not be barriers *but for* the [individual's] disability." Barnett, 535 U.S. at 413 (Scalia, J., dissenting). Justice Scalia maintained vigorously in his dissent in Barnett that "the ADA eliminates workplace barriers only if a disability prevents an employee from overcoming them" and does not require adjustment of "rules and practices that bear no more heavily upon the disabled employee than upon others—even though an exemption from such a rule or practice might in a sense 'make up for' the employee's disability." Changes in seniority rules, maintained Justice Scalia, cannot be accommodations on this understanding of the accommodation concept, as "a seniority system ... burdens the disabled and non-disabled alike...," and so is not "a disability-related obstacle."

The majority in Barnett did not accept this reasoning. *Id.* at 1521 (rejecting "the position taken by … Justice Scalia to the contrary" of the opinion's holding regarding preferential treatment). Instead, the opinion held that in some circumstances—circumstances having to do with the nature of the employer's commitment to its seniority system, not with the obstacles faced by a particular disabled employee—modification of a seniority system might be a required accommodation. Barnett therefore recognized that the obligation to "accommodate" a disability can include the obligation to alter policies that can be barriers to non-disabled persons as well.

It is worth noting that Giebeler's inability to pay the rent without drawing on his mother's financial resources was *not,* in Justice Scalia's words, the result of "obstacles that have nothing to do with the disability." Although Barnett's inability to meet the seniority requirement for the position he wanted was simply the result of his tenure in his job, not of his disability, the reason Giebeler could not pay the rent from his own income was that his disability prevented him from working and earning a monthly paycheck as he used to. So, applying Justice Scalia's understanding of the accommodation concept, Giebeler's request that he be permitted to assure his prospective landlord of payment through his mother's financial resources rather than his own would qualify as an accommodation. Yet, under Barnett, even if one disregards the fact that Giebeler had formerly held a qualifying job and was forced to leave it because of his disability, the accommodation he seeks might still qualify as an accommodation under the FHAA, as long as adjusting Branham's method of judging financial responsibility would aid him in obtaining an apartment he could otherwise not inhabit because of his disability.[5]

Our cases involving FHAA challenges to generally applicable zoning policies confirm that reasonable accommodations can function to adjust for special needs that flow from the inability of disabled residents to meet otherwise applicable financial requirements. In Turning Point, Inc. v. Caldwell, 74 F.3d 941 (9th Cir. 1996), for example, we held that the City of Caldwell had unlawfully refused to accommodate disabled residents of Turning Point, a nonprofit homeless shelter, by refusing to waive annual review of the special use permit that allowed the shelter to house more than the maximum number of persons dictated by the area zoning policy.

In so holding, we observed that 75% of the shelter's residents had serious mental or physical disabilities that "prevent these persons from maintaining employment, obtaining education or securing permanent housing." The district court had found that the maximum occupancy limit "was a severe financial burden on [the shelter] that would eventually force it to close." Relying on this finding, we reasoned that annual review of the special use permit—a process that threatened to discontinue the financially necessary waiver of the maximum occupancy rule in the future—was unjustified and violated the FHAA's reasonable accommodation mandate.

Similarly, in City of Edmonds v. Washington State Bldg. Code Council, we held that a residence for recovering alcoholics and drug addicts that required six or more residents per house to be financially self-sufficient, to comply with federal requirements for

---

5. An example might be an individual who needed a ground floor apartment because of his disability, where such apartments are more expensive. If the individual was able to work but did not earn enough money to qualify for the more expensive apartment, Barnett suggests that—if the accommodation were adjudged reasonable—the landlord could be required to accommodate the disabled renter by accepting a cosigner or allowing him to live in an apartment rented by a relative. We need not decide whether Barnett so requires, however, as Giebeler's disability *is* the barrier that prevents him from meeting the financial responsibility standard in the manner Branham prescribes.

start-up loans, and to provide a supportive atmosphere for the residents, might be entitled to a variance from a single-family zoning ordinance that restricted the number of unrelated persons who could reside in a single home in a residential neighborhood. We noted that zoning regulations would not always be immune from FHAA requirements:

> Courts must ask whether a city's zoning satisfied FHAA standards, or whether a city has to alter neutral zoning policies to reasonably accommodate and integrate handicapped persons. The answers will vary depending on the facts of a given case. But these questions must be posed, or the policies the FHAA seeks to enforce will be frustrated.

Thus, in City of Edmonds we recognized that even when a neutral policy's adverse effect on disabled persons is attributable to financial limitations faced by disabled persons in securing housing, the FHAA may require an exception to the policy as a reasonable accommodation.[6]

3. There is one additional principle regarding the general nature of the concept of accommodations that is pertinent here as well: Accommodations need not be free of all possible cost to the landlord (although, again, a landlord need not incur a cost or risk of cost that is not "reasonable," a major qualification that we discuss later).

Mobile Home I establishes that financial considerations do not *automatically* disqualify a requested accommodation:

> We find the effort to distinguish accommodations that have a financial cost from other accommodations unconvincing. Besides the fact that §3604's reasonable accommodations requirement contains no exemption for financial costs to the landlord, the history of the FHAA clearly establishes that Congress anticipated that landlords would have to shoulder certain costs involved, so long as they are not unduly burdensome.

29 F.3d at 1416. Cf. Cripe v. City of San Jose, 261 F.3d 877, 880 (9th Cir. 2001) (stating that the ADA "requires every type of employer [to] find ways to bring the disabled into its ranks, even when doing so imposes some costs and burdens"); Arneson v. Sullivan, 946 F.2d 90, 92 (8th Cir. 1991) (requiring employer to expend a "reasonable amount … to provide a distraction-free environment," and, if necessary, to provide the plaintiff with a "reader" to assist him in his assigned tasks as reasonable accommodations under the Rehabilitation Act). Thus, disability-neutral administrative policies like Branham's tenant income qualifications do not escape all scrutiny under the FHAA's reasonable accommodation mandate simply because they are based on financial considerations or may involve a *risk* of some financial cost to the landlord.[7]

---

6. In similar circumstances, other circuits have also recognized that exceptions to neutral policies may be mandated by the FHAA where disabled persons' disability-linked needs for alterations to the policies are essentially financial in nature. See, e.g., Smith & Lee Assocs. v. City of Taylor, 102 F.3d 781, 795–96 (6th Cir. 1996) (holding that, where group homes were necessary to prevent the exclusion of disabled persons from residential neighborhoods but were not economically feasible without nine residents, City had to reasonably accommodate by altering the six-person occupancy limit specified by law for residentially-zoned areas); Elderhaven, Inc. v. City of Lubbock, 98 F.3d 175, 179 (5th Cir. 1996) ("[T]he economics of group living arrangements often require a critical mass of residents in order to make feasible the type of alternative living arrangements that the Fair Housing Act was designed to encourage.")

7. It is quite possible—indeed, likely—that in fact there will be *no* financial loss to the defendants. Giebeler requested only a different way of proving that the same rent will be paid for the apartment he lives in as is paid for similar apartments in the complex. He did not seek to pay less

4. Despite this solid line of Supreme Court and Ninth Circuit precedent, the district court and the defendants rely on two out-of-circuit cases that hold that however reasonable the requested accommodation, the FHAA does not require landlords or cities to accommodate needs generated by the inability of disabled individuals to generate income by working. See Salute v. Stratford Greens Garden Apartments, 136 F.3d 293 (2d Cir. 1998); Hemisphere Building Co. v. Village of Richton Park, 171 F.3d 437 (7th Cir. 1999).

Salute held that accommodations of one's personal economic situation are outside the scope of the FHAA's reasonable accommodation requirement, apparently even where the disabled individual's economic status is the direct result of her disability. * * *

We reject the reasoning of Salute and Hemisphere, despite the facial appeal of some of the slippery-slope reasoning of those opinions, for three reasons we find compelling:

First, both Salute and Hemisphere were decided before Barnett, and their reasoning cannot be reconciled with the Supreme Court's analysis in that case. Barnett, as we have explained, held that accommodation requirements (1) do sometimes require preferring disabled individuals over others who are otherwise similarly situated but are not disabled; and (2) are not limited only to lowering barriers created by the disability itself. Limiting accommodation to those "rules, policies, etc. that hurt handicapped people *by reason of their handicap,*" Hemisphere, 171 F.3d at 440, or requiring that accommodations be "framed by the nature of the particular handicap," Salute, 136 F.3d at 301, because "the FHAA does not elevate the rights of the handicapped poor over the rights of the nonhandicapped poor," id. at 302, contradicts both principles embraced by Barnett.[8]

Second, the reasoning of these two opinions captures concerns that *are* taken into account within the analysis required by Barnett and by the FHAA as we understand it. Under the FHAA, as under the RA and the ADA, only *reasonable* accommodations that do not cause undue hardship or mandate fundamental changes in a program are required. Barnett held that although adjustments in seniority rules could be accommodations within the intendment of the disability statutes, such adjustments are ordinarily not *reasonable* accommodations, and therefore are required only in unusual circumstances. Similarly, it is probable that all or most of the changes in long-established policies that Salute and Hemisphere march out as inevitably mandated by the FHAA unless the economic circumstances caused by disability are cordoned off entirely from the accommodation requirement would be deemed, on examination, unreasonable "ordinarily or in the run of cases," Barnett, 535 U.S. at 401, and therefore not required. We expect, for example, that mandating lower rents for disabled individuals would fail the kind of reasonableness inquiry conducted in Barnett. But Salute and Hemisphere held, inconsistently with Barnett, that courts should never *get* to the reasonableness inquiry where economic circumstances related to disability are at stake. Now that Barnett has been decided, that approach is foreclosed.

---

rent or to provide evidence of a lower monthly income with which to pay the rent—he only asked that the income relied upon be his mother's instead of his own.

8. In a case decided after Barnett, Oconomowoc Residential Programs Inc. v. City of Milwaukee, 300 F.3d 775, 787 (7th Cir. 2002), the Seventh Circuit appears to have taken a different view of the obligation to accommodate disability-caused economic circumstances from the one embraced in Hemisphere. In that case, the Court of Appeals reasoned that a zoning variance was necessary to provide plaintiffs with an equal opportunity to use and enjoy a dwelling, in part because "neither woman could afford to purchase a home on her own." The court also acknowledged that its ruling would grant preferential treatment of disabled over non-disabled persons: "Group living arrangements can be essential for disabled persons who cannot live without the services such arrangements provide, and not similarly essential for the non-disabled." Id.

Finally, the Second Circuit's decision in Salute and the Seventh Circuit's decision in Hemisphere are in tension with our zoning cases, already discussed, which recognize that governmental entities may be required to bend zoning and land use requirements in recognition of the need of disabled individuals for group living arrangements. Disabled individuals, true, may need group homes not only to have somewhere they can afford to live but also to have access to physical therapy, nursing care, and other medical needs. But those resources can be, and are, provided in individual houses or apartments to more prosperous individuals. The need to take advantage of economies of scale to make such resources available to the less well-off is the result of the economic circumstances of the residents.

We conclude that Giebeler's request that he be permitted to reside in an apartment rented by his financially qualified mother is a request for an accommodation that, under the FHAA, he was entitled to receive *if* the adjustment both "may be necessary to afford [him] equal opportunity to use and enjoy a dwelling" and was "reasonable" within the meaning of that statute. See 42 U.S.C. §3604(f)(3)(B). It is to those questions that we now turn.

C. Causation and Reasonableness

1. Causation

To prove that an accommodation is necessary, "plaintiffs must show that, but for the accommodation, they likely will be denied an equal opportunity to enjoy the housing of their choice." Smith & Lee, 102 F.3d at 795. Put another way, "without a causal link between defendants' policy and the plaintiff's injury, there can be no obligation on the part of defendants to make a reasonable accommodation." Mobile Home II, 107 F.3d at 1380.

Imposition of burdensome policies, including financial policies, can interfere with disabled persons' right to use and enjoyment of their dwellings, thus necessitating accommodation. See Shapiro v. Cadman Towers, 51 F.3d 328, 335–36 (2d Cir. 1995) (holding that a landlord's failure to grant a disabled tenant an exception to "first come-first served" waiting list for tenant parking substantially affected tenant's use and enjoyment of her dwelling); Samuelson v. Mid-Atlantic Realty, 947 F. Supp. 756, 761 (D. Del. 1996) (finding waiver of a landlord's required lease termination fee a necessary reasonable accommodation under the FHAA because "it is clear that generally applicable fees … can interfere with the use and enjoyment of housing by the handicapped"). While in some cases the plaintiff will not be able to show that alteration of a particular policy "may be necessary" to her use and enjoyment of the property, the causation requirement poses little hurdle in a case such as this one, where a landlord's policy entirely prevents a tenant from living in a dwelling. See [Mobile Home II, 10 F.3d] at 1382 n. 3 (holding that, in zoning cases, causation is not a hurdle in proving necessity of accommodation because "the city policies directly interfere with use and enjoyment because they prevent the housing from being built").

Here, the causal link between Branham's failure to accommodate and Giebeler's disability is obvious. Giebeler was unemployed because of his disability and therefore had insufficient income to qualify for the apartment. Once Branham refused to allow Anne Giebeler to rent an apartment for her son to live in, Giebeler could not show financial ability to pay the rent and therefore could not live in the housing complex. Allowing Anne Giebeler to rent an apartment on her son's behalf, or in some other manner accommodating his inability to prove financial responsibility in the usual way, was necessary to enable Giebeler to live in an apartment at Branham.

In addition to causation, equal opportunity is a key component of the necessity analysis; an accommodation must be possibly necessary to afford the plaintiff equal opportunity to use and enjoy a dwelling. M & B's refusal to allow Anne Giebeler to rent an apartment for her son denies him an opportunity for which he would otherwise be qualified. With Anne Giebeler as renter, Giebeler could satisfy Branham's minimum income requirement and ensure that Branham receives its monthly rent. Giebeler is similarly situated to other tenants at Branham in terms of the financial resources he can bring to a tenancy at Branham. It is his way of demonstrating and deploying these resources that is different.[9] So defendants' relaxation of their no cosigner policy "may be necessary" to afford Giebeler equal opportunity to use and enjoy a dwelling at Branham.

2. Reasonableness

(a) Burden of Proof: We have not decided previously whether the plaintiff or the defendant in an FHAA case bears the burden of showing whether a proposed accommodation is reasonable. There is, however, both RA and ADA precedent on the question.

Under the RA case law, a plaintiff requesting accommodation bears the "initial burden of producing evidence that a reasonable accommodation was possible." Vinson, 288 F.3d at 1154. Once evidence of the possibility is produced, the burden shifts to the other party to produce rebuttal evidence that the requested accommodation is not reasonable. Id.

In the ADA employment context, Barnett articulates the applicable burden of proof slightly differently: Barnett places the burden of showing the reasonableness of an accommodation on the plaintiff. Barnett stresses, however, that the plaintiff need only show that an accommodation "seems reasonable on its face, i.e., ordinarily or in the run of cases." Once the plaintiff has made this showing, the burden shifts to the defendant to demonstrate that the accommodation would cause undue hardship in the particular circumstances. If the plaintiff cannot make the initial showing that the requested accommodation is reasonable in the run of cases, he "nonetheless remains free to show that special circumstances warrant a finding that ... the requested 'accommodation' is 'reasonable' on the particular facts." Thus, under Barnett, case-specific circumstances may make it reasonable for certain defendants to make accommodations even where such accommodations are not reasonable in most cases.

As we have already observed, this court ordinarily applies RA case law in applying the reasonable accommodation provisions of the FHAA, but also generally applies RA and ADA case law interchangeably. That three-way interaction leaves us a bit up in the air at this juncture, as Barnett may have application to the RA mode of proof and therefore the mode of proof to be applied in FHAA cases. Vinson was filed four days after Barnett, and, not surprisingly, does not discuss the Barnett mode of proving the reasonableness of a proposed accommodation. There is no need in this case, though, to decide whether Vinson and Barnett state essentially the same allocation of burdens or

---

9. Unlike the ADA, the FHAA does not explicitly require that a disabled individual must be "qualified" except for his disability or able to meet the "essential" requirements of the housing he seeks to occupy. Even if similar requirements are implicit in the "reasonable accommodation" requirement, a question we do not decide, Giebeler meets them: He has been a model tenant in his other apartments; he has good credit; and relaxation of the no cosigner policy does not waive the essential financial requirement for tenancy, namely, access to sufficient financial resources to pay the monthly rent.

differ in a way likely to be outcome determinative in some instances.[10] Either description of the burden allocation leads to the same result in this case: Giebeler's requested accommodation was reasonable.

(b) Merits of the Reasonableness Analysis: Ordinarily, an accommodation is reasonable under the FHAA "when it imposes no 'fundamental alteration in the nature of the program' or 'undue financial or administrative burdens.'" Howard, 276 F.3d at 806 (quoting Southeastern Community College v. Davis, 442 U.S. 397, 410, 412 (1979)); see also PGA Tour, Inc. v. Martin, 532 U.S. 661, 689 (2001) (holding, in an ADA reasonable accommodation case, that where a rule is peripheral to the nature of defendants' activities, "it may be waived in individual cases without working a fundamental alteration").

In this case, Giebeler has met his burden of demonstrating that the particular accommodation he requests—allowing an eligible relative to rent an apartment for him—is "reasonable on its face, i.e., ordinarily or in the run of cases." He has also met his burden, as articulated in Vinson, of producing evidence showing that the accommodation was reasonable and possible.

The record reveals that, as one would expect, the purpose of M & B's minimum income requirement is to ensure that tenants have sufficient income to pay rent consistently and promptly. This interest is, of course, considerable. However, allowing a financially eligible relative to rent an apartment for a disabled individual who, except for his current financial circumstances, is qualified to be a tenant does not unreasonably threaten this interest.

The rental arrangement requested by Giebeler would not require Branham to accept less rent, would not otherwise alter the essential obligations of tenancy at Branham (such as appropriate behavior and care of the premises), and would provide a lessee with the proper financial qualifications and credit history. As the official renter of the apartment, Anne Giebeler would be primarily responsible for the rent, thereby obviating the need for M & B to first go to her son to collect rent before pursuing her for unpaid rent. Rentals by parents for children are not unusual in most rental markets. Even if M & B does not ordinarily permit such rentals at the Branham complex, asking a landlord to accept an alternative way of proving financial responsibility acceptable to many other landlords is likely to be reasonable in the run of cases.

Indeed, the FHAA recognizes that nondisabled persons may choose to rent apartments for occupancy by disabled persons and protects these arrangements: "It shall be unlawful ... to discriminate in the sale or rental, or to otherwise make unavailable or deny, a dwelling to any buyer or renter because of a handicap of ... a person residing in or intending to reside in that dwelling after it is so sold, rented, or made available." 42 U.S.C. § 3604(f)(1). Thus, the FHAA appears to protect not just disabled people who buy or rent their own residences, but also disabled people who reside in a residence rented by a non-disabled person, the arrangement Giebeler sought in this case.

Giebeler made the necessary initial showing that the requested accommodation was reasonable on the particular facts of this case. Barnett, 535 U.S. at 405 (Whether waiver of a no cosigner policy would be reasonable accommodation in the run of cases is a

---

10. In Oconomowoc, the Seventh Circuit applied Barnett's burden-shifting regime in a suit under the FHAA placing the burden on the plaintiffs to show that the accommodation they sought was reasonable on its face.

question we do not decide.) Branham, however, failed to meet its burden of demonstrating that in the particular circumstances of this case the requested accommodation would cause it to suffer undue hardship. Branham also failed to carry its burden as articulated in Vinson of rebutting the showing made by Giebeler that the requested accommodation was in fact reasonable.

There is no evidence in the record demonstrating that M & B is in any way unusual among landlords in its need to insist that the resident alone rather than a relative sign the lease and take responsibility for paying the rent. The particular parent seeking to rent for her disabled child, Anne Giebeler, presented no unusual risks either. Although, like any other such parent, she would not have lived on-site, she was both a good credit risk and easy to track down; her income, based on monthly pension checks, was a reliable and ample source of rent funds; and she had an unblemished credit record.[11] Anne Giebeler also had significant assets, including a home which she had owned and resided in for 27 years and for which she had paid off the mortgage in full. Her home is located less than a mile from the Branham complex. In short, by allowing Anne Giebeler to rent the apartment so that her disabled son could live in it, Branham would not assume any substantial financial or administrative risk or burden.

Even if one views the requested arrangement as the defendants did—i.e., as a cosignership, requiring waiver of the partnership's no-cosigner policy—the requested accommodation was still reasonable on the particular facts here. While Branham managers have identified some administrative burdens and expenses that could result from having to track down a cosigner when a tenant fails to pay rent, they have on occasion waived the minimum income requirement and allowed cosigners and other alternative arrangements. See Barnett, 535 U.S. at 405 (although modification to a seniority system is not ordinarily a reasonable accommodation, a plaintiff can demonstrate that reasonableness in particular circumstances, such as when the system "already contains exceptions such that, in the circumstances, one further exception is unlikely to matter.").[12]

We stress once more that Giebeler was in no way trying to avoid payment of the usual rent for the apartment he wanted to live in, nor was he proposing to leave M & B without a means of ascertaining that an individual with the means to pay that rent

---

11. Ann Giebeler died during the course of this litigation. The fate of the lease upon Ann Giebeler's death would presumably be the same as if she was a resident of the apartment. There is no indication in the record that the reason M & B refused to rent to Ann Giebeler so that her son could live there is that it was concerned that she was likely to die during the term of the lease.

12. Viewed either as a rental by a parent for a disabled child or as a cosigner arrangement, the requested accommodation in this case differs from the one requested in Salute in two ways that could be significant in a reasonableness analysis (although we do not, of course, decide whether the accommodation requested in Salute was or was not reasonable under the FHAA, as the question is not before us).

In Salute, the accommodation requested was waiver of an established policy against accepting vouchers under Section 8 ... as payment for the rent. Salute emphasized that Congress had recognized the considerable bureaucratic entanglement entailed by Section 8 and consequently included in Section 8 an explicit policy against compelling landlords to accept Section 8 tenants. Here, conversely, the statute appears affirmatively to protect arrangements whereby a disabled person lives in an apartment rented by another.

Additionally, unlike the tenants in Salute, Giebeler proffered a proposed lessee, Ann Giebeler, who more than met the economic qualifications required to rent at Branham and demanded no special, burdensome rights as a condition of her tenancy. In contrast, the Salute court was concerned that "participation in a federal program will or may entail financial audits, maintenance requirements, increased risk of litigation, and so on."

would be responsible for doing so. Giebeler's modest request that his financially qualified mother be allowed to rent an apartment for him to live in, affording him the opportunity to live in a suitable dwelling despite his disability, was a request for a reasonable accommodation within the intendment of the FHAA, and should have been honored....

B. Landowners' Rights

1. Nuisance

Armory Park Neighborhood Association v. Episcopal Community Services in Arizona

148 Ariz. 1, 712 P.2d 914 (Supreme Court of Arizona 1985)

Gonzales & Villarreal by Elizabeth C. Peasley, Tucson, for plaintiff/appellee.

Molloy, Jones, Donahue, Trachta & Childers, by Earl F. Daniels III, Tucson, for defendant/appellant.

In Banc. Feldman, Justice. Holohan, C.J., Gordon, V.C.J., and Hays and Cameron, JJ., concur.

Feldman, Justice.

On December 11, 1982, defendant Episcopal Community Services in Arizona (ECS) opened the St. Martin's Center (Center) in Tucson. The Center's only purpose is to provide one free meal a day to indigent persons. Plaintiff Armory Park Neighborhood Association (APNA) is a non-profit corporation organized for the purpose of "improving, maintaining and insuring the quality of the neighborhood known as Armory Park Historical Residential District." The Center is located on Arizona Avenue, the western boundary of the Armory Park district. On January 10, 1984, APNA filed a complaint seeking to enjoin ECS from operating its free food distribution program. The complaint alleged that the Center's activities constituted a public nuisance and that the Armory Park residents had sustained injuries from transient persons attracted to their neighborhood by the Center.

The superior court held a hearing on APNA's application for preliminary injunction. At the commencement of the hearing, the parties stipulated that "... there is no issue concerning any State, County, or Municipal zoning ordinance, or health provision, before the Court. And, the Court may find that defendants are in compliance with the same." The residents then testified about the changes the Center had brought to their neighborhood. Before the Center opened, the area had been primarily residential with a few small businesses. When the Center began operating in December 1982, many transients crossed the area daily on their way to and from the Center. Although the Center was only open from 5:00 to 6:00 p.m., patrons lined up well before this hour and often lingered in the neighborhood long after finishing their meal. The Center rented an adjacent fenced lot for a waiting area and organized neighborhood cleaning projects, but the trial judge apparently felt these efforts were inadequate to control the activity stemming from the Center. Transients frequently trespassed onto residents' yards, sometimes urinating, defecating, drinking and littering on the residents' property. A few broke into storage areas and unoccupied homes, and some asked residents for handouts. The number of arrests in the area increased dramatically. Many residents were frightened or annoyed by the transients and altered their lifestyles to avoid them.

Following the hearing, ECS filed a motion to dismiss the complaint based on three grounds: 1) that compliance with all applicable zoning and health laws constituted a complete defense to a claim of public nuisance; 2) that there had been no allegation or evidence of a violation of a criminal statute or ordinance, which it argues is a prerequisite to a finding of public nuisance; and 3) that APNA lacked standing to bring an action to abate a public nuisance because it had neither pled nor proved any special injury differing in kind and degree from that suffered by the public generally.

Based on the hearing testimony, the trial court granted the preliminary injunction and denied ECS' motion to dismiss. In its order, the court noted that ECS could be enjoined because its activities constituted both a public and a private nuisance. After its motion for reconsideration was denied, ECS filed a special action in the court of appeals, and shortly thereafter filed a notice of appeal from the order granting the injunction. The court of appeals consolidated the proceedings and stayed enforcement of the trial court's order pending a final decision.

A divided court of appeals reversed the trial court's order. In the view of the majority, a criminal violation was a prerequisite to a finding of public nuisance; because plaintiff had alleged no criminal violation, the injunction was improperly granted. The majority also concluded that the trial court abused its discretion by finding both a public and a private nuisance when the plaintiff had not alleged a private nuisance. Finally, the court held that compliance with zoning provisions was a complete defense. The court vacated the order for preliminary injunction and remanded the matter to the trial court with directions to grant ECS' motion to dismiss. We granted review in this case because of the importance of the following questions:

1) When does a voluntary association have standing to bring an action for public nuisance on behalf of its members?

2) May a lawful business be enjoined for acts committed off its premises by clients who are not under its control or direction?

3) Is it necessary to plead and prove a zoning or criminal violation by the defendant, or may a lawful activity be enjoined because the manner in which it is conducted is unreasonable and therefore constitutes a public nuisance?

The Concept of "Nuisance"

Now considered a tort, a public nuisance action originated in criminal law. Early scholars defined public nuisance as "an act or omission 'which obstructs or causes inconvenience or damage to the public in the exercise of rights common to all her Majesty's subjects.'" Prosser, W. and W.P. Keeton, Handbook on the Law of Torts, § 90, at 643 (5th ed. 1984), quoting Stephen, General View of the Criminal Law in England 105 (1890). The sole remedy was criminal prosecution. Prosser, supra, § 86, at 618.

Historically, the remedy for a private nuisance was an action "upon the case," as it was an injury consequential to the act done and found its roots in civil law. Pearce, E. and D. Meston, Handbook on the Law Relating to Nuisances 2 (1926). A private nuisance is strictly limited to an interference with a person's interest in the enjoyment of real property. The Restatement defines a private nuisance as "a nontrespassory invasion of another's interest in the private use and enjoyment of land." Restatement (Second) of

Torts § 821D. A public nuisance, to the contrary, is not limited to an interference with the use and enjoyment of the plaintiff's land. It encompasses any unreasonable interference with a right common to the general public. Restatement, supra, § 821B. Accord, Prosser, supra, § 86, at 618.

We have previously distinguished public and private nuisances. In City of Phoenix v. Johnson, 75 P.2d 30 (1938), we noted that a nuisance is public when it affects rights of "citizens as a part of the public, while a private nuisance is one which affects a single individual or a definite number of persons in the enjoyment of some private right which is not common to the public." A public nuisance must also affect a considerable number of people. See also Spur Industries v. Del Webb Development Co. The legislature has adopted a similar requirement for its criminal code, defining a public nuisance as an interference "with the comfortable enjoyment of life or property by an entire community or neighborhood, or by a considerable number of persons...." A.R.S. § 13-2917.

The defendant contends that the trial court erred in finding both public and private nuisances when the plaintiff had not asserted a private nuisance claim. The defendant has read the trial court's minute entry too strictly. While we acknowledge that public and private nuisances implicate different interests, we recognize also that the same facts may support claims of both public and private nuisance. As Dean Prosser explained:

> When a public nuisance substantially interferes with the use or enjoyment of the plaintiff's rights in land, it never has been disputed that there is a particular kind of damage, for which the private action will lie. Not only is every plot of land traditionally unique in the eyes of the law, but in the ordinary case the class of landowners in the vicinity of the alleged nuisance will necessarily be a limited one, with an interest obviously different from that of the general public. The interference itself is of course a private nuisance; but is none the less particular damage from a public one, and the action can be maintained upon either basis, or upon both. [Prosser, *Private Action for Public Nuisance*, 52 Va.L.Rev. 997, 1018 (1966).]

Thus, a nuisance may be simultaneously public and private when a considerable number of people suffer an interference with their use and enjoyment of land. See Spur Industries. The torts are not mutually exclusive. Some of plaintiff's members in this case have suffered an injury to the use and enjoyment of their land. Any reference to both a public and a private nuisance by the trial court was, we believe, merely a recognition of this well-accepted rule and not error. However, both because plaintiff did not seek relief under the theory of private nuisance and because that theory might raise standing issues not addressed by the parties, we believe plaintiff's claim must stand or fall on the public nuisance theory alone.

Standing to Bring the Action

1. Do the residents have standing?

Defendant argues that the Association has no standing to sue and that, therefore, the action should be dismissed. The trial court disagreed and defendant claims it erred in so doing. Two standing questions are before us. The first pertains to the right of a private person, as distinguished from a public official, to bring a suit to enjoin the maintenance of a public nuisance. The original rule at common law was that a citizen had no standing to sue for abatement or suppression of a public nuisance since such inconvenient or troublesome offences [sic], as annoy the whole community in general, and not merely some particular persons; and therefore are indictable only, and not actionable; as it would be unreasonable to multiply suits, by giving every man a separate right of action, by what damnifies him in common only with the rest of his fellow subjects.

IV Blackstone Commentaries 167 (1966). It was later held that a private individual might have a tort action to recover personal damages arising from the invasion of the public right. Y.B. 27 Hen. VIII, Mich, pl. 10, cited in Restatement, supra, § 821C comment a. However, the individual bringing the action was required to show that his damage was different in kind or quality from that suffered by the public in common. Prosser, supra, § 90, at 646; Harper & James, The Law of Torts § 1.23, at 64–5 (1956).

The rationale behind this limitation was two-fold. First, it was meant to relieve defendants and the courts of the multiple actions that might follow if every member of the public were allowed to sue for a common wrong. Second, it was believed that a harm which affected all members of the public equally should be handled by public officials. Restatement, supra, § 821C comment a. Considerable disagreement remains over the type of injury which the plaintiff must suffer in order to have standing to bring an action to enjoin a public nuisance. However, we have intimated in the past that an injury to plaintiff's interest in land is sufficient to distinguish plaintiff's injuries from those experienced by the general public and to give the plaintiff-landowner standing to bring the action. This seems also to be the general rule accepted in the United States. See Prosser, supra, § 90, at 651; Restatement, supra, § 821C comment d.

We hold, therefore, that because the acts allegedly committed by the patrons of the neighborhood center affected the residents' use and enjoyment of their real property, a damage special in nature and different in kind from that experienced by the residents of the city in general, the residents of the neighborhood could bring an action to recover damages for or enjoin the maintenance of a public nuisance.

2. May the Association bring the action on behalf of its members?

We have not previously decided whether an association or other organization has standing to assert the claims of its members in a representational capacity. The federal courts, confined by the "case or controversy" requirements of article III, § 2, cl. 1 of the United States Constitution, have enunciated a three-part test. The United States Supreme Court has held that an association has standing to sue on behalf of its members when (a) its members would have standing to sue in their own right; (b) the interests which the association seeks to protect are relevant to the organization's purpose; and (c) neither the claim asserted nor the relief requested requires the participation of individual members. Warth v. Seldin, 422 U.S. 490 (1975); Hunt v. Washington State Apple Advertising Commission, 432 U.S. 333 (1977).

We have previously determined that the question of standing in Arizona is not a constitutional mandate since we have no counterpart to the "case or controversy" requirement of the federal constitution. In addressing the question of standing, therefore, we are confronted only with questions of prudential or judicial restraint. We impose that restraint to insure that our courts do not issue mere advisory opinions, that the case is not moot and that the issues will be fully developed by true adversaries. Our court of appeals has explained that these considerations require at a minimum that each party possess an interest in the outcome. Thus, the question of standing in Arizona cases such as this need not be determined by rigid adherence to the three-prong test of Warth, although those factors may be considered. The issue in Arizona is whether, given all the circumstances in the case, the association has a legitimate interest in an actual controversy involving its members and whether judicial economy and administration will be promoted by allowing representational appearance. As indicated earlier, individual residents whose land was affected by the actions of defendant's patrons would have had standing to bring an action in their own name. Testimony was offered indicating that the purpose of APNA was to promote and preserve the use and enjoyment of the neighborhood by its residents. We believe this purpose is sufficiently relevant to the issues presented in this action so that APNA will adequately and fairly represent the interests of those of its members who would have had standing in their individual capacities. Further, APNA seeks an injunction rather than damages for separate property owners. Principles of judicial economy are advanced by allowing the issues to be settled in a single action rather than in a multitude of individual actions because the relief sought is universal to all of its members and requires no individual quantification by the court. We hold, therefore, that APNA has standing to bring the action as the representative of its members.

Defendant's Derivative Responsibility

Defendant claims that its business should not be held responsible for acts committed by its patrons off the premises of the Center. It argues that since it has no control over the patrons when they are not on the Center's premises, it cannot be enjoined because of their acts. We do not believe this position is supported either by precedent or theory.

In Shamhart v. Morrison Cafeteria Co., 32 So.2d 727 (1947), the defendant operated a well-frequented cafeteria. Each day customers waiting to enter the business would line up on the sidewalk, blocking the entrances to the neighboring establishments. The dissenting justices argued that the defendant had not actually caused the lines to form and that the duty to prevent the harm to the plaintiffs should be left to the police through regulation of the public streets. The majority of the court rejected this argument, and remanded the case for a determination of the damages. See, also, Reid v. Brodsky, 156 A.2d 334 (1959) (operation of a bar enjoined because its patrons were often noisy and intoxicated; they frequently used the neighboring properties for toilet purposes and sexual misconduct); Barrett v. Lopez, 262 P.2d 981 (1953) (operation of a dance hall enjoined, the court finding that "mere possibility of relief from another source [police] does not relieve the courts of their responsibilities"); Wade v. Fuller, 365 P.2d 802 (1961) (operation of drive-in cafe enjoined where patrons created disturbances to nearby residents); McQuade v. Tucson Tiller Apartments, 543 P.2d 150 (1975) (music concerts at mall designed to attract customers enjoined because of increased crowds and noise in residential area).

Under general tort law, liability for nuisance may be imposed upon one who sets in motion the forces which eventually cause the tortious act; liability will arise for a public nuisance when "one person's acts set in motion a force or chain of events resulting in the invasion." Restatement, supra, §824 comment b. We hold, therefore, that defendant's activity may be enjoined upon the showing of a causal connection between that activity and harm to another.

The testimony at the hearing establishes that it was the Center's act of offering free meals which "set in motion" the forces resulting in the injuries to the Armory Park residents. Several residents testified that they saw many of the same transients passing through the neighborhood and going in and out of the Center. We find the testimony sufficient to support the trial judge's finding of a causal link between the acts of ECS and the injuries suffered by the Armory Park residents. The court of appeals thus erred by holding that there was no evidence from which the trial court could have concluded that ECS had engaged in conduct which would render it causally responsible for the interferences. The question is not whether defendant directly caused each improper act, but whether defendant's business operation frequently attracted patrons whose conduct violated the rights of residents to peacefully use and enjoy their property.

Reasonableness of the Interferences

Since the rules of a civilized society require us to tolerate our neighbors, the law requires our neighbors to keep their activities within the limits of what is tolerable by a reasonable person. However, what is reasonably tolerable must be tolerated; not all interferences with public rights are public nuisances. As Dean Prosser explains, "[t]he law does not concern itself with trifles, or seek to remedy all of the petty annoyances and disturbances of everyday life in a civilized community even from conduct committed with knowledge that annoyance and inconvenience will result." Prosser, supra, §88, at 626. Thus, to constitute a nuisance, the complained-of interference must be substantial, intentional and unreasonable under the circumstances. Restatement, supra, §826 comment c and §821F. Our courts have generally used a balancing test in deciding the reasonableness of an interference. The trial court should look at the utility and reasonableness of the conduct and balance these factors against the extent of harm inflicted and the nature of the affected neighborhood. We noted in the early case of Mac-Donald v. Perry:

> What might amount to a serious nuisance in one locality by reason of the density of the population, or character of the neighborhood affected, may in another place and under different surroundings be deemed proper and unobjectionable. What amount of annoyance or inconvenience caused by others in the lawful use of their property will constitute a nuisance depends upon varying circumstances and cannot be precisely defined.

See, also, Spur Industries.

The trial judge did not ignore the balancing test and was well aware of the social utility of defendant's operation. His words are illuminating:

> It is distressing to this Court that an activity such as defendants [sic] should be restrained. Providing for the poor and the homeless is certainly a worthwhile, praisworthy [sic] activity. It is particularly distressing to this Court because it [defendant] has no control over those who are attracted to the kitchen while they are either coming or leaving the premises. However, the right to the comfortable enjoyment of one's property is something that another's activities should not affect, the harm being suffered by the Armory Park Neighborhood and the residents therein is irreparable and substantial, for which they have no adequate legal remedy.

We believe that a determination made by weighing and balancing conflicting interests or principles is truly one which lies within the discretion of the trial judge. We defer to that discretion here. The evidence of the multiple trespasses upon and defacement of the residents' property supports the trial court's conclusion that the interference caused by defendant's operation was unreasonable despite its charitable cause.

The common law has long recognized that the usefulness of a particular activity may outweigh the inconveniences, discomforts and changes it causes some persons to suffer. We, too, acknowledge the social value of the Center. Its charitable purpose, that of feeding the hungry, is entitled to greater deference than pursuits of lesser intrinsic value. It appears from the record that ECS purposes in operating the Center were entirely admirable. However, even admirable ventures may cause unreasonable interferences. We do not believe that the law allows the costs of a charitable enterprise to be visited in their entirety upon the residents of a single neighborhood. The problems of dealing with the unemployed, the homeless and the mentally ill are also matters of community or governmental responsibility.

Zoning

ECS argues that its compliance with City of Tucson zoning regulations is a conclusive determination of reasonableness. We agree that compliance with zoning provisions has some bearing in nuisance cases. We would hesitate to find a public nuisance, if, for example, the legislature enacted comprehensive and specific laws concerning the manner in which a particular activity was to be carried out. Accord Restatement, supra, § 821B comment f. We decline, however, to find that ECS' compliance with the applicable zoning provisions precludes a court from enjoining its activities. The equitable power of the judiciary exists independent of statute. Although zoning and criminal provisions are binding with respect to the type of activity, they do not limit the power of a court acting in equity to enjoin an unreasonable, albeit permitted, activity as a public nuisance.

The determination of the type of business to be permitted in a particular neighborhood, therefore, may be left to administrative agencies or legislative bodies. However, the judgment concerning the manner in which that business is carried out is within the province of the judiciary. Restatement, supra, § 821B comment f. See also J. Joyce, Treatise on the Law Governing Nuisances § 73, at 115 (1906). Zoning provisions may permit one's neighbor to operate a business. This does not give him license to use one's yard, nor permit his customers to do so. * * *

Criminal Violation

Occasionally we have indicated that conduct which violates a specific criminal statute is an element of public nuisance for civil tort claims. These cases did not face the issue whether a tort claim for public nuisance exists independent of statute. ECS argued that there is no criminal violation and that a tort claim for nuisance must be based on such a violation. The trial court did find that the consequences of ECS' activities fit within A.R.S. § 13-2917, which defines a criminal nuisance as an interference with the "comfortable enjoyment of life or property." We need not reach this issue nor need we rule on the constitutionality of the statute. We do not find it fatal that the plaintiff failed to allege a statutory violation. The statute in question adds little to APNA's claim. It does not proscribe specific conduct nor define what conduct constitutes a public nuisance, but only declares, in effect, that a public nuisance is a crime. We are squarely faced, therefore, with the issue of whether a public nuisance may be found in the absence of a statute making specific conduct a crime.

In MacDonald v. Perry, we indicated that the inquiry in a nuisance claim is not whether the activity allegedly constituting the nuisance is lawful but whether it is reasonable under the circumstances. The Restatement states that a criminal violation is only one factor among others to be used in determining reasonableness. That section reads:

(1) A public nuisance is an unreasonable interference with a right common to the general public.

(2) Circumstances that may sustain a holding that an interference with a public right is unreasonable include the following:

    (a) Whether the conduct involves a significant interference with the public health, the public safety, the public peace, the public comfort or the public convenience, *or*

    (b) whether the conduct is proscribed by a statute, ordinance or administrative regulation, *or*

    (c) whether the conduct is of a continuing nature or has produced a permanent or long-lasting effect, and, as the actor knows or has reason to know, has a significant effect upon the public right.

Restatement, supra, § 821B. Comment d to that section explains:

> It has been stated with some frequency that a public nuisance is always a criminal offense. This statement is susceptible of two interpretations. The first is that in order to be treated as a public nuisance, conduct must have been already proscribed by the state as criminal. This is too restrictive.... [T]here is clear recognition that a defendant need not be subject to criminal responsibility.

Our earlier decisions indicate that a business which is lawful may nevertheless be a public nuisance. For example, in Spur Industries, we enjoined the defendant's lawful business. We explained that "Spur is required to move not because of any wrongdoing on the part of Spur, but because of a proper and legitimate regard of the courts for the rights and interests of the public." This rule is widely accepted. Joyce, supra, § 99 at 146; Harper and James, § 1.30 at 90.

We hold, therefore, that conduct which unreasonably and significantly interferes with the public health, safety, peace, comfort or convenience is a public nuisance within the concept of tort law, even if that conduct is not specifically prohibited by the criminal law.* * *

CONCLUSION

The trial court's order granting the preliminary injunction is affirmed. By affirming the trial court's preliminary orders, we do not require that he close the center permanently. It is of course, within the equitable discretion of the trial court to fashion a less severe remedy, if possible. The opinion of the court of appeals is vacated. The case is remanded for further proceedings.

City of Gary, Indiana v. Smith & Wesson Corp.

801 N.E.2d 1222 (Supreme Court of Indiana 2003)

Attorneys for Appellant: James B. Meyer, Lukas I. Cohen, W. Anthony Walker, Gary, Indiana. Dennis A. Henigan, Brian J. Siebel, Daniel R. Vice, Washington, DC.

Attorneys for Appellees: James P. Dorr, Sarah L. Olson, Chicago, Illinois. Terence M. Austgen, Elizabeth M. Bezak, Munster, Indiana. Kenneth D. Reed, John P. Reed, Hammond, Indiana. John E. Hughes, Merrillville, Indiana. Stephen E. Scheele, Highland, Indiana, Ihor A. Woloshanski, Merrillville, Indiana.

Boehm, Justice. Shepard, C.J., and Dickson, Sullivan, and Rucker, JJ., concur.

Boehm, Justice.

The City of Gary sued for injunctive relief and money damages for the harm it alleges is caused by the unlawful marketing and distribution of handguns. The City alleges claims for public nuisance and negligence against manufacturers, wholesalers, and distributors of these products. We hold that the City's complaint states a claim against certain sales practices of all defendants. We also hold that the City's negligent design claim states a claim against the manufacturer-defendants.

Factual and Procedural Background

In September 1999, the City filed this action in state court against a number of participants at various stages in the manufacture and distribution of handguns. After an amended complaint disposed of some defendants, the remaining named defendants are eleven manufacturers, one wholesaler, and five retailers. The City has also named multiple John Doe defendants in all three categories.

The complaint alleges that manufacturers of handguns typically sell to "distributors" who resell at wholesale to "dealers" who in turn sell at retail to the general public. Some categories of persons are prohibited by law from purchasing guns, and all dealer-defendants are alleged to have knowingly sold to illegal buyers through intermediaries in "straw purchases." Specifically, three dealers, Cash America, Ameri-Pawn, and Blythe's Sporting Goods, are alleged to have engaged in straw purchases that were the subject of a "sting" operation conducted by the Gary police department against suspected violators of the gun distribution laws. The police employed a variety of techniques in these operations. In general, an undercover officer first told a dealer's salesperson that he could not lawfully purchase a gun, for example, because he had no license or had been convicted of a felony, and a second undercover officer then made a purchase with the clerk's knowledge that the gun would be given to the first. Some other practices of dealers are also alleged to generate illegal purchases. These include failure by some dealers to obtain the required information for background checks required by federal law, sales of a number of guns to the same person, and intentional "diversion" of guns by some dealers to illegal purchasers.

The City alleges that the manufacturers know of these illegal retail sales of handguns, and know that a small percentage of dealers, including the dealer-defendants here, account for a large portion of illegally obtained handguns. The City alleges the manufacturers and distributors have the ability to change the distribution system to prevent these unlawful sales but have intentionally failed to do so.

The City alleges that these and other practices generate substantial additional cost to the public in general and the City in particular. Possession of unlawfully purchased guns is claimed to contribute to crime that requires expenditure of public resources in addition to the obvious harm to the victims. The complaint alleges that seventy murders with handguns took place in Gary in 1997, and another fifty-four in 1998. From 1997 through 2000, 2,136 handguns used in crimes were recovered. Of these, 764 were sold through dealers who are defendants in this suit. The City also asserts that harm is suffered by the City at the time of the sale of an illegal handgun because these unlawful sales generate additional requirements to investigate and prosecute the violations of law.

In addition to challenging the distribution practice of the defendants, the City also alleges negligent design of the handguns by the manufacturers that contributes to these injuries. Finally, the City alleges that the manufacturers engage in deceptive advertising of their product by asserting that a gun in the home offers additional safety for the occupants when in fact the contrary is the case.

Count I of the complaint alleges that these facts support a claim for public nuisance. Count II asserts a claim for negligence in distribution of guns and Count III presents a claim for their negligent design. The trial court granted a motion by all defendants to dismiss both counts for failure to state a claim. The Court of Appeals affirmed the dismissal of the negligence count as to all defendants. Dismissal of the claim for public nuisance was affirmed as to the manufacturers and distributors, but the Court of Appeals concluded that the complaint stated a claim for public nuisance as to the dealers to the extent it alleged that they engaged in "straw purchases."

I. Public Nuisance

The City asserts that public nuisance is an independent cause of action and that any business unreasonably and unnecessarily operating in a dangerous manner can constitute a nuisance. It contends that its allegations against the defendants meet that standard.

A. Public Nuisance as an Unreasonable Interference with a Public Right

The essence of the City's claim is that handgun manufacturers, distributors, and dealers conduct their business in a manner that unreasonably interferes with public rights in the City of Gary, and therefore have created a public nuisance. In addressing this contention all parties to the lawsuit look to the Restatement (Second) of Torts section 821(B), which defines a public nuisance as "an unreasonable interference with a right common to the general public." Indiana nuisance law is grounded in a statute enacted in 1881, and now appearing at Indiana Code section 32-30-6-6. It reads:

Whatever is:

(1) injurious to health;

(2) indecent;

(3) offensive to the senses; or

(4) an obstruction to the free use of property;

so as essentially to interfere with the comfortable enjoyment of life or property, is a nuisance, and the subject of an action.

The Indiana statute, unlike the Restatement and most common law formulations of public nuisance, makes no explicit mention of the "reasonableness" of the conduct that is alleged to constitute a nuisance. However, the language of the statute is very broad, and if read literally would create a cause of action for many activities not actionable as nuisances at common law and not generally viewed as improper even though they produce, at least to some extent, one or more of the effects listed in the statute. In recognition of this practical reality, over the intervening 122 years, Indiana courts have consistently referred to the common law reasonableness standard in applying the Indiana nuisance statute. Indeed, in 1881, the year of the statute's enactment, this Court referred to the need to avoid "unnecessary" inconvenience or annoyance to others. Owen v. Phillips, 73 Ind. 284 (1881), was a private nuisance case by adjoining property owners seeking to have a mill declared a nuisance. This Court pointed out the need to balance the usefulness of the activity against the harm to others in evaluating a claim of nuisance:

We approve, in its fullest extent, the doctrine, that in some localities a business will be considered a nuisance, while it would not be so in others. But wherever the mill or factory may be located, whatever its surroundings, property owners of the vicinity have a right to require that it shall be properly managed, conducted with ordinary care and proper regard for the rights of others, and in such a way as that no unnecessary inconvenience or annoyance shall be caused them.

Id. at 295–96.

More recently, in addressing a nuisance claim based on an alleged hazardous use of real property, this Court adopted a more modern formulation of essentially the same concept. A public nuisance was described as an activity "reasonably and naturally calculated to injure the general public:"

> Not every dangerous agency is a nuisance, and we believe it can be said generally that an instrumentality maintained upon private premises may only be said to be a nuisance upon the ground that it is calculated to produce personal injuries when it is of such character, and so maintained, that it is reasonably and naturally calculated to injure the general public or strangers who may come upon the premises.

Town of Kirklin v. Everman, 688, 28 N.E.2d 73, 75 (1940). In addition, several Indiana Court of Appeals decisions, including that of the Court of Appeals in this case, have adopted the Restatement's formulation of a nuisance as an "unreasonable" interference with common or public rights.

Despite the statute's absolutist approach, all parties to this lawsuit have couched their arguments in terms of the reasonableness of the defendant's conduct. Given this consistent interpretation of a statute long on the books, we reaffirm that a nuisance claim is, as the Restatement says, predicated on unreasonable interference with a public right. "Reasonableness" in evaluating a nuisance claim appears to have been used by Indiana courts in two related but facially different senses. Defining a nuisance as conduct "reasonably calculated to injure" seems to focus on the predictability of resulting injury. "Reasonable" conduct, on the other hand, focuses on the activity claimed to constitute a nuisance. The formulation of the Restatement seems consistent with the first view, by looking to the resulting injury to the public as the test of "unreasonable" interference. Comment (e) to the Restatement section 821(B) defines an unreasonable interference: "the defendant is held liable for a public nuisance if his interference with the public right was intentional or was unintentional and otherwise actionable under the principles controlling liability for negligent or reckless conduct or for abnormally dangerous activities.... If the interference with the public right is intentional, it must also be unreasonable." Restatement (Second) of Torts § 821(B) cmt. e.

We think this boils down to the same question for the trier of fact framed by Owen over a century ago: a nuisance is an activity that generates injury or inconvenience to others that is both sufficiently grave and sufficiently foreseeable that it renders it unreasonable to proceed at least without compensation to those that are harmed. Whether it is unreasonable turns on whether the activity, even if lawful, can be expected to impose such costs or inconvenience on others that those costs should be borne by the generator of the activity, or the activity must be stopped or modified. W. Page Keeton, Prosser and Keeton on The Law of Torts § 88 at 629–30 (5th ed. 1984). And of course the same activity may constitute a nuisance in some contexts, but be acceptable in others where its adverse effects are not sufficient to require a remedy.

B. The City's Public Nuisance Claim

The City alleges that the manufacturers, distributors, and dealers knowingly participate in a distribution system that unnecessarily and sometimes even intentionally provides guns to criminals, juveniles, and others who may not lawfully purchase them. Specifically, the City asserts that "defendants affirmatively rely upon the reasonably foreseeable laxness of dealers, and employees, and the ingenuity of criminals to ensure that thousands of handguns find their way into their expected place in the illegal secondary market."

The defendants first contend that the lawful distribution of their products cannot constitute a public nuisance. The manufacturers point out, correctly, that "in every one of over 1,000 Indiana state court and 50 federal public nuisance decisions" courts have recognized public nuisance claims only in two circumstances. Either a statute is violated, or the nuisance stems from use of real property. A variation on this argument is the contention advanced by one retailer that an independent tort must be pleaded to support a public nuisance claim. From this the defendants infer that it is a requirement of a public nuisance action that the claim be based on either misuse of real property or unlawful conduct in the form of either a violation of a statute or an independent tort. The use of real property is not at issue here as to the manufacturers and distributors. The only question, at least as to those defendants, is whether a statutory violation or an underlying tort is required in order to assert a public nuisance claim. The defendants contend that there is no underlying tort here, and also argue that their conduct is legislatively authorized and therefore cannot be a public nuisance. The defendants further contend that even if a public nuisance action could survive, they do not have sufficient control over the handguns at the time of the injury to be liable for harm from their misuse. Similarly, the manufacturers and distributors disclaim control over any unlawful sales and therefore deny liability for any harm generated by the sale of a weapon.

Courts are divided on the same or very similar issues under the laws of several other states. For the reason explained below, we conclude that a public nuisance has been alleged under Indiana law and the City is a proper party to assert that claim.

1. Unlawful Activity or Use of Land as a Prerequisite for Nuisance

We are not persuaded that a public nuisance necessarily involves either an unlawful activity or the use of land. Defendants cite no Indiana case that establishes this requirement, but point out that all Indiana cases to date have fallen into one of these two categories. We think that is due to the happenstance of how the particular public nuisance actions arose and not to any principle of law. The Court of Appeals reached a similar conclusion in rejecting the contention that a party must be the owner or controller of property to be held liable for a nuisance: "although most nuisance cases refer to the controversy as being between two landowners, it is because this is the norm, not because the law requires either party to be a landowner." Gray v. Westinghouse Elec. Corp., 624 N.E.2d 49, 53 (Ind. Ct. App. 1993) (citations omitted). The court went on to point out that the nuisance statute:

> uses the broad term "whatever" to define the possible sources of a nuisance and it does not contain any reference to property ownership by the party creating the nuisance. This indicates the focus of the legislature was on protecting an individual's right to enjoy property from infringement by any source. We hold that the party which causes a nuisance can be held liable, regardless of whether the party owns or possesses the property on which the nuisance originates.

Id. at 53. The same reasoning applies to the claim that use of real estate or conduct of an unlawful activity is a prerequisite of a public nuisance. The fact that public nuisance has never been applied to situations other than those involving real property or an unlawful activity does not mean it cannot arise in other contexts.

The Restatement also supports the view that neither real estate nor unlawful conduct is a requirement of a public nuisance claim. It is explicit that "unlike a private nuisance, a public nuisance does not necessarily involve interference with use and enjoyment of land." Restatement (Second) of Torts § 821(B), cmt. h (1977). The requirement that a public nuisance arise from unlawful conduct is found in subsection (b) of Restatement (Second) section 821B(2). But subsection (b) is only one of three "circumstances" that may give rise to a public nuisance. Restatement (Second) section 821(B), reads in full:

(1) A public nuisance is an unreasonable interference with a right common to the general public.

(2) Circumstances that may sustain a holding that an interference with a public right is unreasonable include the following:

(a) Whether the conduct involves a significant interference with the public health, the public safety, the public peace, the public comfort or the public convenience, or

(b) whether the conduct is proscribed by a statute, ordinance or administrative regulation, or

(c) whether the conduct is of a continuing nature or has produced a permanent or long-lasting effect, and, as the actor knows or has reason to know, has a significant effect upon the public right.

Subsection (a) acknowledges that a nuisance may arise from a "significant interference" with public health, safety or convenience. Subsection (c) recognizes that a predictable "significant effect upon the public right" may constitute a nuisance. The three subsections are plainly alternative means of imposing an "unreasonable interference," and the limitations of subsection (b) do not apply to either subsection (a) or (c).

In sum, neither the language of the Indiana statute nor the standard case law formulation of public nuisance places those limits on the doctrine. Indeed, courts in this state and elsewhere have typically rejected any such requirement. Accordingly, we hold that there is no requirement that the activity involve an unlawful activity or use of land. If an activity meets the requirements of an unreasonable interference with a public right, it may constitute a public nuisance.

A. Other jurisdictions have reached similar conclusions in the context of handgun cases.

We also conclude that a public nuisance may exist without an underlying independent tort, although some elements of the two may be indistinguishable in practical terms, as the allegations of this complaint demonstrate. Here the complaint does allege negligence and resulting predicable injury. But a nuisance claim may be predicated on a lawful activity conducted in such a manner that it imposes costs on others.[9] This is the case whether the actor intends the adverse consequences or merely is charged with

---

9. Nuisances may arise from a lawful activity. Our Court of Appeals has held that "while the keeping of hogs, being a lawful enterprise, cannot be characterized as an absolute nuisance or a nuisance, per se, such an activity can become a nuisance per accidens by reason of the manner in which the hogs are kept, the locality or both." Yeager & Sullivan, Inc. v. O'Neill, 324 N.E.2d 846, 852 (1975) (citations omitted).

knowledge of the reasonably predictable harm to others. In either case, the law of public nuisance is best viewed as shifting the resulting cost from the general public to the party who creates it. If the marketplace values the product sufficiently to accept that cost, the manufacturer can price it into the product. If the manufacturers and users of the offending activity conclude that the activity is not worthwhile after absorbing these costs, that is their choice. In either case, there is no injustice in requiring the activity to tailor itself to accept the costs imposed on others or cease generating them. Finally, as City of Chicago noted "[o]ne is subject to liability for a nuisance caused by an activity, not only when he carries on the activity but also when he participates to a substantial extent in carrying it on." City of Chic., 785 N.E.2d at 29.

2. Compliance with Regulatory Statutes as a Defense

The Court of Appeals held that legislative authorization of the defendants' activities served as an affirmative defense to any public nuisance claim and insulated the defendants from liability for a harmful activity. We disagree. Presumably the legislative authorization to which the Court of Appeals referred is found either in Indiana Code sections 35-47-2.5-1 through 15, dealing with the sale of handguns, or Article I, section 32 of the Indiana Constitution, which gives Indiana citizens the right to bear arms in defense of themselves and others. But, as established in Part A, an activity can be lawful and still be conducted in an unreasonable manner so as to constitute a nuisance. The Indiana statutes detail the procedure to be used by a dealer in every handgun transaction involving background checks and furnishing information on gun purchasers to the state police. Intentional failure to observe a statutory standard is presumptively unreasonable. Indeed, the doctrine has been specifically applied to unlawful gun sales. Over a decade ago the Court of Appeals held that sales in violation of gun registration laws are negligence per se for which the seller may be civilly liable. Some of the activity alleged in the complaint presumably violates those regulatory statutes, either directly in the case of the dealers or as knowing accomplices in the case of the other defendants.

More generally, gun regulatory laws leave room for the defendants to be in compliance with those regulations while still acting unreasonably and creating a public nuisance. As the court in AcuSport recently pointed out, "the fact that conduct is otherwise lawful is no defense where ... the actions or failures to act of multiple defendants creating in the aggregate a public nuisance can justify liability...." NAACP v. AcuSport, Inc., 271 F. Supp. 2d 435, 482 (E.D. N.Y. 2003). The essence of a nuisance claim is the foreseeable harm unreasonably created by the defendants' conduct. In any event, the City alleges that the defendants, though subject to regulatory schemes, either directly or as accomplices, are not in compliance with applicable laws. The City has alleged that (1) dealers engage in illegal sales, and (2) the distributors and manufacturers know of their practice and have it within their power to curtail them but do not do so for profit reasons. More specifically, the City claims that manufacturers are on notice of the concentration of illegal handgun sales in a small percentage of dealers, and the ability to control distribution through these dealers, but continue to facilitate unlawful sales by failing to curtail supply. The City also alleges substantial and ongoing human and financial harm from these unlawful sales. These allegations state a claim.

D. Damages Under the Nuisance Claim

In addition to its claim for injunctive relief, the City also seeks damages as a party uniquely injured by the nuisance. In particular, the City points to public costs for the "care and treatment of … gunshot injuries" and economic injuries in the form of increased spending on law enforcement, emergency rescue services, security at public buildings, pensions, benefits, and jail costs. The City also asserts that the widespread presence of guns in illegal hands results in lower tax revenues and lower property values. In addition to costs imposed by use of lawfully distributed guns, the City claims harm at the time of an unlawful sale in the form of increased costs in tracking down illegal handguns. Indiana Code section 32-30-6-8 explicitly allows monetary damages to be recovered by any successful plaintiff in a nuisance action. This includes the City as well as private parties. To the extent the City can establish its claim for damages as an injured party it has a claim for money damages just as any other injured party.

The City does not claim damage to its property from use of illegally sold guns. Rather, it seeks compensation for various forms of responses to gun use or illegal sales. Some courts have concluded that the difficulty of proof of damages bars a nuisance claim altogether. We believe these holdings are inapplicable here for the simple reason that Indiana statutes explicitly provide for a municipality to bring an action to enjoin or abate a nuisance. Thus, even if money damages are ultimately found to be barred by doctrines of remoteness, proximate cause, or the like, injunctive relief is available.

We respectfully disagree with those jurisdictions that have dismissed a complaint on the ground that money damages are too remote from the activity of some defendants to be recoverable. Related contentions are that administration of such a claim is judicially unmanageable, and that municipal costs are not recoverable. Although the City is authorized to sue for "money damages," we conclude that the limitations on types of damages recoverable under a negligence theory are equally applicable to a nuisance claim. Legislative authorization to sue for money damages carries with it the common law limitations on damages. As explained in Part II.(B), the City's claims for damages raise a number of issues and the discussion of damages in Part II.(B) applies equally to the damages the City claims under its nuisance count. These issues do not warrant dismissal of the complaint, however. It is sufficient here to observe that the complaint alleges the City has incurred damages from the nuisance. This is a conventional tort pleading subject to no requirement of specificity. What form the City's proof will take is currently not before us and we cannot say as a matter of law it cannot establish some items of damage if liability is proven. As set forth in Part II, we agree that there may be major, perhaps insurmountable, obstacles to establishing some or all of the damage items the City cites. But that is not a basis to dismiss the complaint before discovery has refined these issues and the precise nature of the City's case is known.

2. Servitudes

Hill v. Community of Damien of Molokai

121 N.M. 353, 911 P.2d 861 (Supreme Court of New Mexico 1996)

Protection and Advocacy System, Nancy Koenigsberg, Albuquerque, for Appellant.

William J. Darling & Associates, P.A., William J. Darling, Margaret P. Armijo, Albuquerque, Sylvain Segal, Albuquerque, for Appellees.*

---

* Michael B. Browde, Albuquerque, Singer, Smith & Williams, Nan E. Burke, Albuquerque, for Amici Curiae ACLU, et al.

Stanley F. Frost, Justice; Joseph F. Baca, Chief Justice, Richard E. Ransom, Gene E. Franchini, and Pamela B. Minzer, Justices, concur.

Frost, Justice.

Defendant-Appellant Community of Damien of Molokai (Community) appeals from the district court's ruling in favor of Plaintiffs-Appellees, enjoining the further use of the property at 716 Rio Arriba, S.E., Albuquerque, as a group home for individuals with AIDS. Plaintiffs-Appellees argue that the group home violates a restrictive covenant. The Community contends that the group home is a permitted use under the covenant and, alternatively, that enforcing the restrictive covenant against the group home would violate the Federal Fair Housing Act, 42 U.S.C. §§ 3601–3631 (1988) [hereinafter FHA]. We ... reverse.

I. Facts

The Community is a private, nonprofit corporation which provides homes to people with AIDS as well as other terminal illnesses. In December 1992 the Community leased the residence at 716 Rio Arriba, S.E., Albuquerque, located in a planned subdivision called Four Hills Village, for use as a group home for four individuals with AIDS. The four residents who subsequently moved into the Community's group home were unrelated, and each required some degree of in-home nursing care.

Plaintiffs-Appellees, William Hill, III, Derek Head, Charlene Leamons, and Bernard Dueto (hereinafter Neighbors) live in Four Hills Village on the same dead-end street as the group home. Shortly after the group home opened, the Neighbors noticed an increase in traffic on Rio Arriba street, going to and from the group home. The Neighbors believed that the Community's use of its house as a group home for people with AIDS violated one of the restrictive covenants applicable to all the homes in the sixteenth installment of Four Hills Village. Installment sixteen encompasses the Community's group home and the Neighbors' houses. The applicable covenant provides in relevant part:

> No lot shall ever be used for any purpose other than *single family residence purposes*. No dwelling house located thereon shall ever be used for other than *single family residence purposes*, nor shall any outbuildings or structure located thereon be used in a manner other than incidental to such *family residence purposes*. The erection or maintenance or use of any building, or the use of any lot for other purposes, including, but not restricted to such examples as stores, shops, flats, duplex houses, apartment houses, rooming houses, tourist courts, schools, churches, hospitals, and filling stations is hereby expressly prohibited.

After hearing evidence at two separate hearings, the trial court held that the restrictive covenant prevented the use of the Community's house as a group home for people with AIDS and issued a permanent injunction against the Community. * * *

II. Four Hills Restrictive Covenants

The first issue before us is the applicability of the Four Hills restrictive covenant to the Community's group home....

A. Operating a Group Home Constitutes a Residential Use

In reaching its conclusion that the group home violated the residential use restriction, the trial court made two specific findings regarding the nature of the current use of the home. The court found that the …"Community uses of the residence are much closer to the uses commonly associated with health care facilities, apartment houses, and rooming houses than uses which are commonly associated with single family residences."

It is undisputed that the group home is designed to provide the four individuals who live in the house with a traditional family structure, setting, and atmosphere, and that the individuals who reside there use the home much as would any family with a disabled family member. The four residents share communal meals. They provide support for each other socially, emotionally, and financially. They also receive spiritual guidance together from religious leaders who visit them on Tuesday evenings.

To provide for their health care needs, the residents contract with a private nursing service for health-care workers. These health-care workers do not reside at the home, and they are not affiliated with the Community in any way. The number of hours of service provided by the health-care workers is determined by a case-management group assigned by the state pursuant to a state program. The in-home health services that the residents receive from the health-care workers are precisely the same services to which any disabled individual would be entitled regardless of whether he or she lived in a group home or alone in a private residence.

The Community's role in the group home is to provide oversight and administrative assistance. It organizes the health-care workers' schedules to ensure that a nurse is present twenty-four hours per day, and it provides oversight to ensure that the workers are doing their jobs properly. It also receives donations of food and furniture on behalf of the residents. A Community worker remains at the house during the afternoon and evening but does not reside at the home. The Community, in turn, collects rent from the residents based on the amount of social security income the residents receive, and it enforces a policy of no drinking or drug use in the home.

The Community's activities in providing the group home for the residents do not render the home a nonresidential operation such as a hospice or boarding house. As the South Carolina Supreme Court noted when faced with a similar situation involving a group home for mentally impaired individuals:

> This Court finds persuasive the reasoning of other jurisdictions which have held that the incident necessities of operating a group home such as maintaining records, filing accounting reports, managing, supervising, and providing care for individuals in exchange for monetary compensation are collateral to the prime purpose and function of a family housekeeping unit. Hence, these activities do not, in and of themselves, change the character of a residence from private to commercial.

Rhodes v. Palmetto Pathway Homes, Inc., 400 S.E.2d 484, 485–86 (S.C. 1991). In Jackson v. Williams, 714 P.2d 1017, 1022 (Okla. 1985), the Oklahoma Supreme Court similarly concluded:

> The essential purpose of the group home is to create a normal family atmosphere dissimilar from that found in traditional institutional care for the mentally handicapped. The operation of a group home is thus distinguishable from a use that is commercial—i.e., a boarding house that provides food and lodging only—or is institutional in character.

We agree with the conclusions reached by the South Carolina Supreme Court and other jurisdictions that the purpose of the group home is to provide the residents with a traditional family structure and atmosphere.

B. Residents of a Group Home Meet Single Family Requirement

The Neighbors also argue on appeal that the four, unrelated residents of the group home do not constitute a "single family" as required by the restrictive covenant. The Neighbors contend that the restrictive covenant should be interpreted such that the term "family" encompasses only individuals related by blood or by law. We disagree.

The word "family" is not defined in the restrictive covenant and nothing in the covenant suggests that it was the intent of the framers to limit the term to a discrete family unit comprised only of individuals related by blood or by law. Accordingly, the use of the term "family" in the covenant is ambiguous. As we noted above, we must resolve any ambiguity in the restrictive covenant in favor of the free enjoyment of the property. This rule of construction therefore militates in favor of a conclusion that the term "family" encompasses a broader group than just related individuals and against restricting the use of the property solely to a traditional nuclear family.

In addition, there are several other factors that lead us to define the term "family" as including unrelated individuals. First, the Albuquerque municipal zoning ordinance provides a definition of family that is at odds with the restrictive definition suggested by the Neighbors. The Albuquerque zoning ordinance includes within the definition of the term "family," "any group of not more than five [unrelated] persons living together in a dwelling."

The Neighbors argue that the zoning code definition is irrelevant to the scope of the covenant. They point to Singleterry v. City of Albuquerque, 632 P.2d 345, 347 ([N.M.] 1981), in which this Court stated, "It is well established that zoning ordinances cannot relieve private property from valid restrictive covenants if the ordinances are less restrictive." However, we agree with the Colorado Court of Appeals which noted, "While [the zoning] statute has no direct applicability to private covenants, it is some indication of the type of groups that might logically, as a matter of public policy, be included within the concept of a single family." Turner v. United Cerebral Palsy Ass'n, 772 P.2d 628, 630 (Colo. Ct. App. 1988) (construing term "family" in covenant to include unrelated group home residents), cert. denied, (Apr. 24, 1989); see also Gregory, 495 A.2d at 1002 n. 3 (referring to zoning ordinances when construing the term "family," as used in covenant). In the present case, we are not using the zoning ordinances to relieve the Community of its obligations under the restrictive covenant. We are instead looking to the definition of family within the zoning ordinance as persuasive evidence for a proper interpretation of the ambiguous term in the covenant. The Albuquerque zoning ordinance would include the residents of the group home within its definition of family.

Second, there is a strong public policy in favor of including small group homes within the definition of the term "family." The federal government has expressed a clear policy in favor of removing barriers preventing individuals with physical and mental disabilities from living in group homes in residential settings and against restrictive definitions of "families" that serve to exclude congregate living arrangements for the disabled. The FHA squarely sets out this important public policy. As the court in United States v. Scott, 788 F. Supp. 1555, 1561 n. 5 (D. Kan. 1992), stated, "The legislative history of the amended Fair Housing Act reflects the national policy of deinstitutionalizing disabled individuals and integrating them into the mainstream of society." The Scott court further noted that the Act "is intended to prohibit special restrictive covenants or other terms or conditions, or denials of service because of an individual's handicap and which ... exclude, for example, congregate living arrangements for persons with handicaps." Id.... This policy is applicable to the present case because the FHA's protections for handicapped people extend to individuals with AIDS. See Support Ministries for Persons with AIDS, Inc. v. Village of Waterford, 808 F. Supp. 120, 129 (N.D.N.Y.1992). The Developmental Disabilities Assistance and Bill of Rights Act, 42 U.S.C. §6000 (1988 & Supp. II 1990), and the Rehabilitation Act of 1973, 29 U.S.C. §701 (1988 & Supp. IV 1992), also identify a national policy favoring persons with disabilities living independently in normal communities and opposing barriers to this goal. See Scott, 788 F. Supp. at 1561 n. 5.

In New Mexico, the Developmental Disabilities Act, NMSA 1978, §28-16A-2 (Cum. Supp. 1995), expresses a clear state policy in favor of integrating disabled individuals into communities.* * *

Accordingly, we reject the Neighbors' claim that the term "family" in the restrictive covenants should be read to include only individuals related by blood or by law. We agree with the court in Open Door Alcoholism Program, Inc. v. Board of Adjustment, 200 N.J. Super. 191, 491 A.2d 17, 21 (N.J. Super. Ct. App. Div. 1985), which noted, "The controlling factor in considering whether a group of unrelated individuals living together as a single housekeeping unit constitutes a family ... is whether the residents bear the generic character of a relatively permanent functioning family unit.["] As we already discussed above, the individuals living in the Community's group home do operate as a family unit. Much of the activities of the residents are communal in nature. More importantly, the residents provide moral support and guidance for each other and together create an environment that assists them in living with the disease that has afflicted them. We find that the Community's group home "exhibits [the] kind of stability, permanency and functional lifestyle which is equivalent to that of the traditional family unit." *491 A.2d at 22.* We therefore conclude that the Community's use of the property as a grouop home does not violate the Four Hills restrictive covenant.

C. Findings Regarding Increased Traffic

The Neighbors strenuously argue that the covenant should be interpreted to exclude the group home because the group home's operation has an adverse impact on the neighborhood. In support of this claim, the Neighbors point to the trial court's findings that "the amount of vehicular traffic generated by [the] Community's use of the house ... greatly exceeds what is expected in an average residential area" and that, as a result, "the character of [the] residential neighborhood relative to traffic and to parked vehicles has been significantly altered to the detriment of this residential neighborhood and is [sic] residents." The Neighbors contend that these facts are uncontradicted and point out that this Court is bound by the factual findings of the trial court unless the findings are not supported by substantial evidence.

However, the Neighbors fail to appreciate that the amount of traffic generated by the group home simply is not relevant to determining whether the use of the house as a group home violated the covenant in this case. A review of all the provisions in the covenant reveals that the restrictive covenants for the Four Hills Village, sixteenth installment, are not directed at controlling either traffic or on-street parking. The various covenants merely regulate the structural appearance and use of the homes. For example, the covenants regulate building architecture, views, frontage, setback, visible fences and walls, signs and billboards, trash and weeds, trailers and campers parked in yards, maintaining livestock, and of course nonresidential uses of homes. However, not one of the fifteen provisions and numerous paragraphs of the covenants attempts to control the number of automobiles that a resident may accommodate on or off the property nor the amount of traffic a resident may generate.

The Neighbors do not contend that the amount of traffic and parking generated by the Community's home violates any covenant in and of itself, nor could they. The Neighbors do suggest, however, that the volume of traffic demonstrates that the group home is not functionally equivalent to a traditional single-family residence, as required by the covenants. However, the question whether the group home is equivalent to a traditional family residence must be evaluated in relation to the requirements of the covenants, which in this case are directed to maintaining the structural appearance of the house and restricting nonresidential uses. Cf. Turner, 772 P.2d at 630 (looking to other provisions of covenant to define nature of "family" restriction). There is no evidence that the volume of traffic generated by the group home interferes with the structural appearance of the house in violation of the covenants. Nor does the amount of traffic or parked vehicles alter the residential nature of the group home or modify the familial relationship of the residents. * * *

We conclude that the Community is entitled to continue operating its group home for individuals with AIDS both under the Four Hills restrictive covenants and under the Fair Housing Act. Accordingly, for the reasons discussed above, the trial court's ruling is reversed and the injunction is vacated. The trial court's dismissal of the counterclaim is affirmed.

[The discussion of the Fair Housing Act is omitted.]

Simovits v. The Chanticleer Condominium Association
933 F.Supp. 1394 (N.D. IL 1996)

For Stephen S. Simovits, Jr., Kathleen Simovits, and Hope Fair Housing Center, an Illinois Not-for-Profit Corporation, plaintiffs: Jeffrey Lynn Taren, Kinoy, Taren, Geraghty & Potter, Chicago, IL.

For The Chanticleer Condominium Association, defendant: Reese J. Peck, Rathje, Woodward, Dyer & Burt, Wheaton, IL.

Arlander Keys, United States Magistrate Judge.

Statement of Facts

The Simovits[es] owned a condominium in the Chanticleer Condominium Complex ("Chanticleer"), an eighty-four unit housing facility located in Hinsdale, Illinois. Since 1985, the Association has had a restrictive covenant ("the Covenant") in its Declaration of Condominium Ownership, stating that "no minor children under the age of eighteen (18) years may reside in any unit purchased after the effective date of this amendment," without the prior written approval of the Board of Managers. Residents of Chanticleer who violate the Covenant are subject to injunctive relief and a $10,000 fine. This provision is construed as barring an owner from selling a unit to anyone with children under the age of eighteen.

A large number of Chanticleer's residents are fifty-five years of age or older. However, there is no requirement that residents must be fifty-five years old or older. According to the president of the Association, Jim Londos, Chanticleer is intended for people who are "any age over 18." In fact, the last two sales of Chanticleer units have been to people under the age of fifty-five.

The Simovits[es] purchased their Chanticleer condominium in June of 1993, for $130,000. Prior to the closing, they appeared before the Association's screening committee. The purpose of this meeting was to explain the Association's rules and regulations, including the Covenant. Mr. Simovits informed the board that he believed the Covenant to be illegal.[2] Nonetheless, the Simovits[es] signed a statement acknowledging the rules and agreeing to abide by them.[3]

Shortly after moving into Chanticleer, Mr. Simovits ran for a position on the Association's board. During his campaign, he published a newsletter to introduce himself to the residents of Chanticleer. In that newsletter, Mr. Simovits stated that "I like Chanticleer as an adult community and would like to keep it that way." He testified that these comments were politically motivated: "by that time, I knew that many of the residents were elderly and they liked the place as it was. I needed some votes." Mr. Simovits lost the election.

While living at Chanticleer, the Simovits[es] made several improvements to their condominium. They remodeled the kitchen with new cabinets and remodeled the bathroom with amenities, such as a Jacuzzi. The Simovits[es] installed a new furnace and central air-conditioning. They also converted the attic into a third bedroom, with air-conditioning. The Simovits[es] expended almost $20,000 in materials on these improvements.

The Simovits[es] put their Chanticleer condominium on the market in May of 1995, for $187,500.[4] A prospective buyer, represented by real estate agent Karen Jones, expressed an interest in the condominium. However, the Simovits[es] decided not to enter into negotiations with that individual because she had a minor child and they did not wish to cause any problems. After several weeks passed without any interested buyers, the Simovits[es] were forced to lower their asking price. They lowered it to $179,500 in July and again, in August, to $169,900. In early November, another prospective buyer, represented by realtor Bonita Swartz, expressed an interest in the Simovits[es]' condominium. According to Ms. Swartz's testimony, the prospect was interested in making an offer on the condominium. At that time, the condominium was on the market for $169,900. The potential buyer had three children, all under the age of eighteen.

When Mr. Simovits informed Mr. Londos that he had a potential buyer with minor children, Mr. Londos replied that the Covenant prohibited such a sale. Mr. Londos also told Ms. Swartz about the Covenant. Ms. Swartz testified that, after she told the prospective buyer about the rule, the prospect was no longer interested in making an offer.

On the same day he informed Mr. Simovits that he could not sell to this prospective buyer, Mr. Londos contacted the Association's lawyer, who called the Simovits[es] on November 8, 1995, warning them that the Covenant prohibited a sale to a person with minor children. On November 14, 1995, Mr. Londos received a letter from the Association's lawyer regarding the Simovits[es] and the questionable legality of the Covenant. The letter warned Mr. Londos that discriminating against families with children is illegal. The letter stated that the statutory exemptions to the FHA are "strictly construed" and that "unless Chanticleer can produce hard evidence that the community meets these narrowly construed exemptions, the financial liability to Chanticleer could be substantial." Mr. Londos shared the contents of this letter with the Association's board members on

---

2. Although Mr. Simovits is primarily employed as a mechanical engineer, he is also a licensed real estate agent.

3. Mr. Simovits testified that his lawyer informed him that, despite his belief regarding the illegality of the Covenant, he had to sign this statement in order to finalize the closing on the condominium.

4. Mr. Simovits testified that he "was planning to come down possibly about $10,000 or so" from this initial asking price.

the day he received it. Despite the warnings in the letter, the Association decided to continue to prevent the Simovits[es] from selling to a buyer with minor children.

Immediately after contacting the Association's lawyer in early November, Mr. Londos began to compile a list of all the Chanticleer residents' ages in order to determine the percentage of residents who were fifty-five years of age or older. This was the first time the Association had conducted a survey of this nature. In compiling the survey, Mr. Londos speculated as to the residents' ages. He testified that he "had a pretty good idea ... in [his] head who was of what age." He did not take any steps to verify these presumptions. Consequently, the list contained inaccuracies.

In preparation for the hearing herein, Mr. Londos conducted another similar survey. In this May 21, 1996 survey, conducted two days prior to the hearing, Mr. Londos used signed affidavits to verify the residents' ages. However, he did not obtain affidavits from all of Chanticleer's residents. He resorted to guessing the ages of those residents who did not submit an affidavit.[7]

On April 15, 1996, the Simovits[es] entered into a contract to sell their condominium to Brian Weigus and Ramona Caracheo, a couple without children, for $145,000. However, the buyers were young, and thus wanted the Covenant waived. The Association agreed to waive it, and the deal closed on April 30, 1996.

The Simovits[es] allege that, as a result of the Covenant, they lost numerous opportunities to sell their condominium at a higher price.... They enlisted HOPE Fair Housing Center ("HOPE"), a not-for-profit agency dedicated to promoting equal opportunity housing, to challenge the legality of the Covenant.

The Simovits[es] brought suit for the economic damages that they suffered as a result of the Covenant. They allege that the Covenant diminished the value of their condominium by $30,000. Real estate appraiser Robert A. Napoli testified on behalf of Plaintiffs, and appraisers Brent Baldwin and Anthony Uzemack testified on behalf of Defendant. All agreed that the Simovits[es]' condominium was worth $145,000 with the Covenant. However, the appraisers disagreed as to the condominium's value without the Covenant. To determine the effect of the Covenant on the value of the condominium, Mr. Napoli looked at recent sales prices of five condominiums, similar in size and location to the Simovits[es],' that were not subject to a restrictive covenant. He opined that the Simovits[es]' condominium, without the Covenant, was worth $175,000. Mr. Uzemack, looking at three of the same properties as Mr. Napoli,[8] opined that the Covenant had no "measurable" effect on the value of the Simovits[es]' condominium—that it was worth $145,000, with or without the Covenant.[9]

In addition to diminishing the value of their condominium, the Simovits[es] allege that the Covenant caused them to incur additional mortgage obligations. Because the

---

7. Mr. Londos' testimony regarding how he determined the ages of those residents who did not submit an affidavit illustrates the speculative nature of these surveys. When asked how he knew one resident was over the age of fifty-five, Mr. Londos stated that "I have seen her at the meetings. She is definitely over 55."

8. Mr. Uzemack generally agreed with Mr. Napoli that the properties at 5715 Sutton Place and 498 Old Surrey were comparable to the Simovits[es]' condominium. Those properties had recently sold for $157,000 and $140,000, respectively. Mr. Uzemack testified further that the $157,000 sale price of the Sutton Place property was consistent with the sale prices of comparable Chanticleer units based on his analysis of sales activity in that subdivision.

9. The Association's other appraiser, Brent Baldwin, agreed with Mr. Uzemack that the value of the Simovits[es]' condominium, with or without the Covenant, was $145,000.

Covenant delayed the sale of their condominium, the Simovits[es] allege that they paid an extra $3,560.15 in mortgage payments. They testified that making these additional mortgage payments caused them financial strain.

Moreover, the Simovits[es] allege that they were emotionally injured as a result of the enforcement of the Covenant. Mr. Simovits testified to a special sensitivity to discrimination due to events in his past.[11] Mrs. Simovits testified that her husband suffered from chest and stomach pains, as well as sleeplessness, as a result of their inability to sell the condominium.[12] Mrs. Simovits testified that she suffered from extreme anxiety, headaches, and abdominal distress due to their inability to sell. Mr. and Mrs. Simovits seek $10,000 each in emotional injury damages.

HOPE also alleges economic injuries as a result of the Covenant. HOPE is suing for the time and money it devoted to helping the Simovits[es]. HOPE alleges that it diverted its time and resources away from housing counseling in order to help the Simovits[es] pursue this action against the Association. According to Bernard Kliena, HOPE's executive director, HOPE spent $2,806 in out-of-pocket expenses and $4,424 in staff time on the Simovits[es]' case. Additionally, HOPE asks for $35,000 in monitoring and compliance expenses.

The Simovits[es] and HOPE both seek punitive damages in the amount of $10,000 from the Association. In addition, the Simovits[es] and HOPE seek a 5 year injunction against the Association, requiring them to permit residency at Chanticleer regardless of family status.

Discussion

The following issues are before the Court: (1) whether the Simovits[es] and/or HOPE have standing to sue under the FHA; (2) whether the Association is liable under the FHA for discrimination based on familial status; (3) whether the Association's defenses to liability are viable; and (4) if the Court finds the Association liable and its defenses untenable, what remedies are available to the Simovits[es] and HOPE.* * *

II. Liability

The question of the Association's liability under the FHA for discrimination based on familial status turns on whether or not Chanticleer meets the exemption for "housing for older persons" in § 3607(b)(2) of the FHA. One category of "housing for older persons" is "housing intended and operated for occupancy by persons 55 years and older."

42 U.S.C. § 3607(b)(2)(C).*

Prior to December 28, 1995, the FHA required the following to meet the "55 years and older" exemption: (1) the facility has significant facilities and services specifically

---

11. Mr. Simovits testified that he "grew up under Nazi occupied Hungary" and that he was "an anti-Communist in Budapest."

12. Mr. Simovits did not mention any of these problems during his testimony.

* Editor's Note. Sections 3607(b)(1) and (2) provide:

(b)(1) Nothing in this title limits the applicability of any reasonable local, State, or Federal restrictions regarding the maximum number of occupants permitted to occupy a dwelling. Nor does any provision in this title regarding familial status apply with respect to housing for older persons.

(2) As used in this section, "housing for older persons" means housing—

(A) provided under any State or Federal program that the Secretary determines is specifically designed and operated to assist elderly persons (as defined in the

designed to meet the physical and social needs of older persons; (2) at least eighty percent of the units are occupied by one person age fifty-five or over; and (3) the complex publishes and adheres to policies which demonstrate an intent to provide housing for persons age fifty-five and older.

However, on December 28, 1995, Congress eliminated this "significant facilities and services" requirement. See Housing for Older Persons Act of 1995. Under the Housing for Older Persons Act of 1995, the following are the requirements to qualify as "age 55 years and older" housing: (1) at least eighty percent of the occupied units are occupied by at least one person who is fifty-five years of age or older; (2) the housing facility publishes and adheres to policies and procedures that demonstrate the intent to provide housing for persons age fifty-five or older; and (3) the housing facility complies with HUD rules and regulations for verification of occupancy.[15] 42 U.S.C. § 3607(b)(2)(C)(i)–(iii). The statute requires that the defendant meet all of the above requirements to qualify for the exemption. In addition, the defendant has the burden of proving that it meets the above requirements.

A. Eighty Percent Test

The Association has failed to provide reliable evidence that, since 1985,[16] eighty percent of the occupied dwellings at Chanticleer have had at least one person fifty-five years of age or older in residence. The Association relies on the results of the two surveys conducted by Mr. Londos to qualify for the exemption. Such reliance, however, is misplaced. Most significant, in the first survey, is the absence of corroborating source documentation. Mr. Londos merely estimated the ages of the Chanticleer residents, neglecting to verify them by using affidavits or other signed statements. A survey compiled

---

State or Federal program); or

(B) intended for, and solely occupied by, persons 62 years of age or older; or

(C) intended and operated for occupancy by persons 55 years of age or older, and—

   (i)   at least 80 percent of the occupied units are occupied by at least one person who is 55 years of age or older;

   (ii) the housing facility or community publishes and adheres to policies and procedures that demonstrate the intent required under this subparagraph; and

   (iii) the housing facility or community complies with rules issued by the Secretary for verification of occupancy, which shall—

        (I) provide for verification by reliable surveys and affidavits; and

        (II) include examples of the types of policies and procedures relevant to a determination of compliance with the requirement of clause (ii). Such surveys and affidavits shall be admissible in administrative and judicial proceedings for the purposes of such verification.

(3) Housing shall not fail to meet the requirements for housing for older persons by reason of:

(A) persons residing in such housing as of the date of enactment of this Act who do not meet the age requirements of subsections (2)(B) or (C): Provided, That new occupants of such housing meet the age requirements of subsections (2)(B) or (C); or (B) unoccupied units: Provided, That such units are reserved for occupancy by persons who meet the age requirements of subsections (2)(B) or (C).

15. The amended statute applies to the case at bar because the Association continued its discriminatory conduct of enforcing the Covenant subsequent to the passage of the new law. Thus, there is no issue of retroactivity in this case.

16. The Association's alleged discrimination began in 1985, when the Covenant was added to the Declaration of Condominium Ownership.

in such an unscientific manner does not provide reliable evidence that eighty percent of the occupied dwellings had at least one person age fifty-five or older in residence. Moreover, the circumstances surrounding the taking of this survey—upon the advice of counsel in response to Mr. Simovits' threat to file a lawsuit—makes it clear that, even if the eighty percent requirement were met, it was merely fortuitous and is not indicative of any intent to provide housing for persons age fifty-five or older.

As to the second survey, the corroborating source documentation is incomplete. Mr. Londos did not obtain affidavits from every resident at Chanticleer, and he speculated as to the ages of those residents from whom he did not obtain an affidavit. Consequently, the survey's results are totally unreliable.[17] Accordingly, the Court finds that the Association has failed to meet the eighty percent test.

B. Policies and Procedures Test

The Association freely admits that it does not publish and adhere to policies and procedures that demonstrate an intent to provide housing for persons aged fifty-five years or older.[18] 42 U.S.C. § 3607(b)(2)(C)(ii). Thus, the Association has, in fact, conceded its liability under the FHA, since qualification for the exemption requires that all three of its requirements be met. HUD provides a list of six nonexclusive factors for determining whether a facility is in compliance with this test. These factors are: (1) the housing facility's written rules and regulations; (2) the manner which the housing is described to prospective residents; (3) the nature of advertising; (4) age verification procedures; (5) lease provisions; and (6) the actual practices of the management in enforcing the relevant rules and regulations.[19] 24 C.F.R. § 100.316(b)(1)–(6) (1995).

The Association argues, unpersuasively, that these six factors are no longer applicable, in determining whether on not the policies and procedures prong is met, because HUD eliminated § 100.316 on April 25, 1996. The Federal Register, on which the Association's argument is based, states that "the provisions describing the 'significant facilities and services' requirement for '55 or over' housing in §§ 100.306, 100.307, 100.310, and 100.316 were deleted to conform to the new requirements of '55 or over' housing established by the Housing for Older Persons Act." Regulatory Reinvention; Streamlining of HUD's Regulations Implementing the Fair Housing Act, 61 Fed. Reg. 18,248 (1996). Clearly, only the provisions relating to the "significant facilities and services requirement" were deleted. The provisions in § 100.316 relating to the policies and procedures requirement remain intact.[20]

---

17. Assuming, arguendo, that the Court did rely on Mr. Londos' uncorroborated survey, the survey fails to support the Association's assertions that exactly eighty percent of Chanticleer's dwellings are occupied by at least one person fifty-five years of age or older. Mr. Londos erred by including the Simovits[es] in this second survey, even though they sold their condominium almost a month before the survey was completed. If the buyers of the Simovits[es]' condominium, Mr. Weigus and Ms. Caracheo, are included in the survey, instead of the Simovits[es], the percentage of residents at Chanticleer who are fifty-five years or older falls below eighty.

18. The Association argues that it is in "effective compliance" with this prong of the statute because Chanticleer has a "longstanding reputation" in the community as a facility for older persons. However, the "exemptions from the Fair Housing Act are to be construed narrowly, in recognition of the important goal of preventing housing discrimination." See Massaro[v. Mainlands Section 1 & 2 Civic Ass'n, Inc.], 3 F.3d [1472,] 1475 [(Fla. 1993)]. The Association's argument for "effective compliance" directly conflicts with this principle of narrow construction.

19. Obviously, not all factors are applicable in every case. See Massaro, 3 F.3d at 1477–1478. Further, other factors, not included in this list, may be relevant.

20. Section 100.316(b) states that "the following factors, *among others*, are relevant in determining whether the owner or manager of a housing facility has complied with the requirements of

The finding that these six factors are still applicable under the amended statute is consistent with the legislative history of the Housing For Older Persons Act of 1995. 42 U.S.C. § 3607(b)(2)(C) (1995). According to the Senate Report, "the purpose of the [December 28, 1995 amendment] was to eliminate the burden of the significant facilities and services requirement." S. Rep. No. 172, 104th Cong., 3d. Sess. 4 (1995). Congress deleted this requirement because "nobody, including the Government, can figure out what the phrase 'significant facilities and services' means." However, nothing in the legislative history suggests that Congress intended the policies and procedures prong to change. In fact, the statutory language describing the test in the amended statute is exactly the same as it was in the old statute. Thus, because the policies and procedures prong remains entirely unchanged, so do the criteria for analyzing it. In the case at bar, neither the Association's written rules and regulations, nor its age verification procedures, demonstrate an intent to provide housing for persons age fifty-five and older.

1. Written Rules and Regulations

The Association's written rules and regulations fail to demonstrate an intent to provide housing to persons fifty-five years of age or older. To demonstrate this intent, the Association's rules and regulations must explicitly restrict residency to persons fifty-five years or older. See Massaro, 3 F.3d at 1479 (holding that, where a facility's only written rule was a restriction against children, the facility failed to show that it was intended for older persons). There has never been a rule at Chanticleer specifically requiring residents to be fifty-five years of age or older. Indeed, the Association has done nothing to actively pursue prospective residents age fifty-five or over, and all of its sales in 1995 and 1996 were to individuals under the age of fifty-five. Rather, the only rule relating to age is the one prohibiting residency by children under eighteen. Therefore, the Association's "no children" policy does not adequately demonstrate an intent to provide housing to persons fifty-five years of age and older.

2. Age Verification Procedures

Insofar as the Association has belatedly implemented age verification procedures, the Record does not demonstrate that those procedures are consistent with an intent to maintain the fifty-five year and older exemption. In order to establish the requisite intent, the Association's age verification procedures must be reliable. Massaro, 3 F.3d at 1478 (emphasizing that survey is unreliable if not supported by corroborating documentation, such as driver's licenses or birth certificates, that verifies the residents' ages); HUD v. TEMS, 2 Fair Housing-Fair Lending (P-H) ¶ 25,028, 25,308 (HUD ALJ 1992) (holding that survey containing several misstatements of the residents' ages is not reliable). For the reasons previously discussed, neither of Mr. Londos' surveys is reliable.

In addition, age verification procedures must be performed on a consistent basis. The Association, however, has not consistently verified the ages of the Chanticleer residents. The timing of the events in early November strongly suggests that Mr. Londos only began compiling his surveys once he was warned, by the Association's lawyer, of a potential legal conflict with the Simovits[es]. See Massaro, 3 F.3d at 1478 (minimizing a survey's import in establishing the intent to provide housing for older persons because

---

§ 100.316." 24 C.F.R. § 100.316(b) (emphasis added). If this section was deleted in its entirety, as the Association suggests, then no factors at all would be relevant in analyzing a facility's policies and procedures. Clearly, the Association's interpretation of this April 25, 1996 amendment is not what was intended by HUD.

it was compiled subsequent to the alleged discriminatory actions). Moreover, the Record contains no evidence that the Association ever performed any age verification surveys of the residents prior to those completed by Mr. Londos. The age verification procedures used by the Association, therefore, fall short of demonstrating an intent to provide housing for persons age fifty-five and older.

C. Compliance with HUD Rules

The Association has not complied with the HUD rules for verification of occupancy. The statute requires that the HUD rules: (1) provide for verification by reliable surveys and affidavits; and (2) include examples of the types of policies and procedures relevant to a determination of intent to provide housing for persons fifty-five years and older. These requirements for the HUD rules duplicate the requirements under the eighty percent test and the policies and procedures test. As previously discussed, the Association does not meet either of these two prongs. Thus, the Association fails this third statutory prong as well.

In sum, the Court finds that the Association does not qualify for the exemption in § 3607(b)(2)(C) of the FHA. The Association failed all three requirements of the "fifty-five and older" exemption. Therefore, the Association is liable for familial status discrimination that occurred as a result of the Covenant.

III. Defenses

The [court rejected] the argument that the Simovits[es] should be barred from enforcing their rights under the FHA by the equitable defenses of estoppel, laches, unclean hands and waiver. * * *

IV. Remedies

The FHA provides that, where a defendant has engaged in a discriminatory housing practice, "the court may award to the plaintiff actual and punitive damage ... and as the court deems appropriate ... any permanent or temporary injunction." 42 U.S.C. § 3613(c)(1). The Simovits[es] and HOPE have asked for: (1) an award of damages as compensation for economic losses; (2) an award of punitive damages; and (3) injunctive relief to ensure that the Association will not engage in unlawful housing practices in the future. Additionally, the Simovits[es] have asked for an award of damages as compensation for emotional distress.

A. Economic Damages

The FHA provides that relief may include the actual damages suffered by the plaintiff. 42 U.S.C. § 3613(c)(1). In this case, the Simovits[es] seek $30,000 in damages as compensation for the reduction in the value of their condominium due to the Covenant. The parties agreed that the condominium's value, subject to the Covenant, was $145,000. However, they disagreed as to the condominium's value without the Covenant. Without the Covenant, the Simovits[es] valued the condominium at $175,000. The Association asserts that the Covenant had no effect, and that the condominium was worth $145,000, with or without the Covenant. It sold for $145,000.

While all three experts are professional real estate appraisers, and all valued the Simovits[es]' condominium the same, with the Covenant, their differences of opinion as to whether and to what extent the Covenant has an impact on the value of the property is inexplicable and irreconcilable and can be attributable only to their alignments with the respective parties. The Defendants' experts' opinion that the Covenant has no impact on the value of the units simply defies logic. On the other hand, Plaintiffs' expert's opinion that the Covenant decreases the value of the property by $30,000 appears excessive. The Court discredits Defendant's experts in this regard and credits Plaintiff's expert only to the extent that the Covenant had *some* adverse impact on the value of the property. The Court, then, is left with the necessity of determining a non-arbitrary figure regarding the diminution in value of the property as a result of the Covenant.

[T]he Court finds that the Simovits[es]' condominium, without the Covenant, would have sold for at least $500 more, or $157,500. Therefore, the Simovits[es] are entitled to the difference between the amount at which they sold their property, $145,000, and what they reasonably could have realized but for the Covenant, $157,500. Accordingly, they are awarded $12,500 in damages as compensation for the reduction in value of their condominium.

The Simovits[es] also seek recovery for unnecessary mortgage payments made on their Chanticleer condominium. The Covenant created a delay in selling the condominium (by deterring prospective buyers), causing the Simovits[es] to incur $3,560.15 in additional mortgage obligations. This Court finds that, but for the Covenant, the Simovits[es] would not have incurred these costs. Thus, the Simovits[es] are entitled to the $3,560.15 they paid in unnecessary mortgage payments.

HOPE seeks recovery of $7,230 in economic losses stemming from the time and resources it devoted to helping the Simovits[es]. The Court awards these damages. The Court, however, declines to award the $35,000 in monitoring and compliance costs sought by HOPE. The goals of monitoring the Association can be achieved through more equitable means, as set forth in the Court's Order below.

B. Emotional Distress Damages

Mr. and Mrs. Simovits seek $10,000 each in emotional injury damages. In order for the Simovits[es] to recover for emotional injuries, a causal connection must exist between their alleged injuries and the Association's discriminatory conduct. Nekolny v. Painter, 653 F.2d 1164, 1172 (7th Cir. 1981), cert. denied, 455 U.S. 1021 (1982) (rejecting award for emotional injury damages because mere conclusory statement that plaintiff was "very depressed" failed to establish causal connection between plaintiff's injuries and defendant's discriminatory conduct); but see Douglas v. Metro Rental Serv., Inc., 827 F.2d 252, 257 (7th Cir. 1987) (affirming award of $2,500 for emotional distress where the plaintiffs were denied access to an apartment because of their race).

In this case, neither Mr. nor Mrs. Simovits' testimony indicates a causal link between their alleged emotional distress and enforcement of the Covenant. The Court finds that the Association's enforcement of the Covenant did not cause Mr. Simovits any compensable indignity or emotional harm, especially in light of his "feigned" approval of it. Hence, the Simovits[es] suffered, at most, only indirect effects of the "no children" policy; they were not denied housing on the basis of their familial status. The Simovits[es] have cited no authority to support compensation for these indirect emotional injuries. Even if compensation for this indirect emotional distress were available, Mr. Simovits did not provide any testimony of specific injuries he suffered as a result of the Covenant. His only testimony regarding his emotional distress was that he had "very deep rooted emotions about discrimination." Clearly, Mr. Simovits' vagueness precludes the Court from finding that enforcement of the Covenant caused him any compensable emotional injury.

Mrs. Simovits, like her husband, was not the direct victim of the Association's discrimination. Therefore, the Court is unable to find a causal connection between her alleged injuries and enforcement of the Covenant. In fact, Mrs. Simovits did not even allege that her emotional distress was caused by the indignity of discrimination against families with children. Rather, she testified that the inability to sell their condominium caused her emotional distress. Moreover, although Mrs. Simovits testified to suffering anxiety and headaches, there is no indication that these injuries were atypical of the normal stresses associated with the sale of one's home. Therefore, the Record does not support an award for emotional damages for either Mr. or Mrs. Simovits.

C. Punitive Damages

The Simovits[es] and HOPE seek $10,000 each (for a total of $20,000) in punitive damages from the Association. Under §3613(c)(1) of the FHA, the court may award punitive damages to a prevailing party in a housing discrimination case. Generally, punitive damages are awarded in cases where the defendant shows a reckless or callous disregard for the plaintiff's rights. The Record in this case contains overwhelming evidence of the Association's reckless disregard for the Simovits[es]' and HOPE's rights. Most significant is the Association's failure to heed the warnings of its lawyer. The November 14, 1995 letter stated that the statutory exemptions to the FHA are "strictly construed" and that "housing discrimination based upon familial status is against federal and state law." Further, it warned the Association of the substantial monetary sanctions it could face in the event it were found in violation. Despite these warnings, the Association persisted in enforcing the Covenant against the Simovits[es], and prevented them from selling to buyers with children under the age of eighteen. The Minutes of the Association's November 14, 1995 Board of Managers' meeting show that this was a calculated gamble. Moreover, the Association republished its resident directory containing the rules and regulations, including the Covenant, to all residents in March, 1996. This callous and reckless disregard for the Simovits[es]' rights entitles them to punitive damages.

Likewise, the Association showed a reckless disregard for HOPE's rights. The Association's continued publication and enforcement of the Covenant, despite warnings of the Covenant's illegality, directly conflicted with HOPE's mission of providing equal housing opportunities to the people of DuPage County. This reckless disregard for HOPE's rights entitles them to punitive damages.

There is no formula for determining the amount of punitive damages; however, the size of the award should be sufficient to "'punish [the defendant] for his outrageous conduct and to deter him and others like him from similar conduct in the future.'" Smith, 461 U.S. at 54 (quoting Restatement 2d of Torts, §908(1) (1979)). At the end of 1995, the Association had a cash balance of $44,000. A punitive award of $20,000, approximately one-half of its cash reserves, certainly serves the goals of punishment and deterrence. Moreover, a $20,000 punitive award is not excessive; the Seventh Circuit has affirmed even larger punitive awards in past housing discrimination cases.[26] Thus, a $10,000 award to the Simovits[es] and another $10,000 award to HOPE constitute reasonable punitive awards.

D. Injunctive Relief

Section 3613(c)(1) also authorizes the Court to order injunctive relief. Equitable remedies serve the purpose of "eliminating the effects of past discrimination and pre-

---

26. In Phillips v. Hunter Trails Comm. Ass'n, 685 F.2d 184, 191 (7th Cir. 1982), the Seventh Circuit affirmed a punitive award of $100,000 to a married couple.

venting future discrimination." The testimony herein shows that the Association has no intention of discontinuing the enforcement of the Covenant unless enjoined and that an injunction is necessary to redress its "long-standing reputation ... within the community as a community for older persons." The Court is unaware of the pervasiveness of this reputation; however, it is certain that, since the enactment of the Covenant in 1985, families with children have been wrongfully denied the opportunity to live at Chanticleer. Although this type of harm can not be cured by monetary awards alone, the Court has adequate flexibility in fashioning equitable relief to remedy the effects of the Association's discrimination. The remedial plan set forth in the Order below is both reasonable and necessary to redress the Association's discrimination....

Order

It is Hereby Ordered That:

1. By the close of business on September 6, 1996, the Association shall pay the Simovits[es] $26,060.15 in damages. The $26,060.15 consists of:

    a. $12,500 for the reduction in value of the Simovits[es]' condominium;

    b. $3,560.15 for the additional mortgage payments made on the Chanticleer condominium; and

    c. $10,000 in punitive damages.

2. By the close of business on September 6, 1996, the Association shall pay HOPE $17,230 in damages. The $17,230 consists of:

    a. $7,230 for HOPE's out-of-pocket expenses and staff time spent on the Simovits[es]' case; and

    b. $10,000 in punitive damages.

3. From August 1, 1996 through August 1, 1999, the Association is hereby enjoined from attempting to qualify for any of the "housing for older persons" exemptions provided for in §3607(b)(2) of the FHA.

4. The Association shall, no later than August 15, 1996, remove from its by-laws, rules, regulations and/or Declaration of Condominium Ownership any policies that discriminate against families with children. Written notification of such action shall be sent to all owners and tenants of units at Chanticleer and to HOPE.

5. By the close of business on the first Friday of January, beginning January 3, 1997, and continuing through January 7, 2000, the Association shall submit annual reports to HOPE containing the following information:

    a. A copy of every person's application for the Association's approval to purchase at Chanticleer during the prior year, and a statement indicating the person's name and familial status, whether that person was rejected or accepted, the date on which the person was notified of acceptance or rejection, and, if rejected, the reason for such rejection; and

    b. Current occupancy statistics of Chanticleer, indicating the ages of all residents occupying each of the units at Chanticleer.

6. By the close of business on August 26, 1996, the Association shall send written notice, to all real estate brokerage firms listed in the Hinsdale Yellow Pages, consisting of a statement explaining that the Association's discriminatory policies are no

longer in effect and that families with children are welcome to reside at Chanticleer. A copy of each letter shall also be sent to HOPE.

Lobato v. Taylor
Supreme Court of Colorado
En Banc.
71 P.3d 938 (2002)

Eley, Goldstein and Dodge, LLC, Jeffrey A. Goldstein, Otten, Johnson, Robinson, Neff & Ragonetti, PC, William F. Schoeberlein, Robert Maes, David Martinez, Walters & Joyce, PC, Julia T. Waggener, Kelly, Haglund, Garnsey & Kahn LLC, Norman D. Haglund, Don Hiller & Galleher, PC, Watson Galleher, Elisabeth Arenales, Denver, CO, Attorneys for Petitioners.

Wolf & Slatkin, PC, Albert B. Wolf, Raymond P. Micklewright, Jonathan L. Madison, Denver, CO, Attorneys for Respondent.

Richard Garcia, Denver, CO, Peter Reich, Costa Mesa, CA, Attorneys for Amici Curiae Bi-National Human Rights Commission, International Indian Treaty Council, National Chicano Human Rights Council, Comision De Derechos Humanos De Seminario Permanente De Estudios Chicanos Y De Fronteras.

Federico Cheever, Gorsuch Kirgis, LLP, Loretta P. Martinez, Denver, CO, Attorneys for Amicus Curiae Colorado Hispanic Bar Association.

David J. Stephenson, Jr., Denver, CO, Attorney for Amicus Curiae Rocky Mountain Human Rights Law Group.

Before: Chief Justice Mullarkey and Justices Hobbs, Martinez, Bender, Rice, Coats, and Eid.

Kourlis, J., dissented and filed opinion in which Rice, J., joined.

Martinez, J., dissented in part and filed opinion.

Chief Justice Mullarkey delivered the Opinion of the Court.

The history of this property rights controversy began before Colorado's statehood, at a time when southern Colorado was part of Mexico; at a time when all of the parties' lands were part of the one million acre Sangre de Cristo grant, an 1844 Mexican land grant. Here, we determine access rights of the owners of farmlands in Costilla County to a mountainous parcel of land now known as the Taylor Ranch. As successors in title to the original settlers in the region, the landowners exercised rights to enter and use the Taylor Ranch property for over one hundred years until Jack Taylor fenced the land in 1960 and forcibly excluded them. These rights, they assert, derive from Mexican law, prescription, and an express or implied grant, and were impermissibly denied when the mountain land was fenced.

We are reviewing this case for the second time in this protracted twenty-one year litigation. In the first phase of this litigation, the trial court dismissed the plaintiffs' claims, holding that a federal decision in the 1960s on the same issue barred their suit. We reversed and remanded, holding that the notice given in the federal case did not comport with due process. The subject matter of the current appeal is the landowners' substantive claims of rights. The trial court and the court of appeals held that the landowners failed to prove rights on any of their three theories.

We find that evidence of traditional settlement practices, repeated references to settlement rights in documents associated with the Sangre de Cristo grant, the one hun-

dred year history of the landowners' use of the Taylor Ranch, and other evidence of necessity, reliance, and intention support a finding of implied rights in this case. While we
reject the landowners' claims for hunting, fishing, and recreation rights, we find that
the landowners have rights of access for grazing, firewood, and timber through a prescriptive easement, an easement by estoppel, and an easement from prior use. Furthermore, we retain jurisdiction in order to examine the trial court's due process determination.

I. Facts and Prior Proceedings

In 1844, the governor of New Mexico granted two Mexican nationals a one million-
acre land grant, located mainly in present-day southern Colorado (Sangre de Cristo
grant), for the purpose of settlement. The original grantees died during the war between the United States and Mexico. The land was not settled in earnest until after the
cessation of the war, and Charles (Carlos) Beaubien then owned the grant.

In 1848, the United States and Mexico entered into the Treaty of Guadalupe Hidalgo,
ending the war between the two countries. Pursuant to the treaty, Mexico ceded land to
the United States, including all of California, Nevada, and Utah; most of New Mexico
and Arizona; and a portion of Colorado. The United States agreed to honor the existing
property rights in the ceded territory. Relevant to the Sangre de Cristo grant, Congress
asked the Surveyor General of the Territory of New Mexico to determine what property
rights existed at the time of the treaty. On the Surveyor General's recommendation,
Congress confirmed Carlos Beaubien's claim to the Sangre de Cristo grant in the 1860
Act of Confirmation.

In the early 1850s, Beaubien successfully recruited farm families to settle the Colorado portion of the Sangre de Cristo grant. He leased a portion of his land to the
United States government to be used to establish Fort Massachusetts and recruited farm-
ers to settle other areas. The settlement system he employed was common to Spain and
Mexico: strips of arable land called vara strips were allotted to families for farming, and
areas not open for cultivation were available for common use. These common areas were
used for grazing and recreation and as a source for timber, firewood, fish, and game.

In 1863, Beaubien gave established settlers deeds to their vara strips. That same year,
Beaubien executed and recorded a Spanish language document that purports to grant
rights of access to common lands to settlers on the Sangre de Cristo grant (Beaubien
Document). In relevant part, this document guarantees that "all the inhabitants will
have enjoyment of benefits of pastures, water, firewood and timber, always taking care
that one does not injure another."

A year later, Beaubien died. Pursuant to a prior oral agreement, his heirs sold his interest in the Sangre de Cristo grant to William Gilpin, who was Colorado's first territorial governor. The sales agreement (Gilpin agreement) stated that Gilpin agreed to provide vara strip deeds to settlers who had not yet received them. The agreement further
stated that Gilpin took the land on condition that certain "settlement rights before then
conceded ... to the residents of the settlements ... shall be confirmed by said William
Gilpin as made by him."

In 1960, Jack Taylor, a North Carolina lumberman, purchased roughly 77,000 acres
of the Sangre de Cristo grant (mountain tract) from a successor in interest to William
Gilpin. Taylor's deed indicated that he took the land subject to "claims of the local people by prescription or otherwise to right to pasture, wood, and lumber and so-called
settlement rights in, to, and upon said land."

Despite the language in Taylor's deed, he denied the local landowners access to his land and began to fence the property. Taylor then filed a Torrens title action in the United States District Court for the District of Colorado to perfect his title (Torrens action).[1] The district court found that the local landowners did not have any rights to the mountain tract; the Tenth Circuit Court of Appeals affirmed. Sanchez v. Taylor, 377 F.2d 733 (10th Cir.1967).

In 1973, Taylor purchased an adjoining, roughly 2,500 acre parcel that was also part of the Sangre de Cristo grant (Salazar estate). Taylor's predecessor in title to the Salazar estate had also filed a Torrens title action in 1960 which determined that local landowners had no rights in the estate. Together, the mountain tract and the Salazar estate are known as the Taylor Ranch.

The current case began in 1981. In that year a number of local landowners filed suit in Costilla County District Court. The landowners asserted that they had settlement rights to the Taylor Ranch and that Taylor had impermissibly denied those rights.[2] The court held that the doctrine of res judicata barred the suit because the Salazar Torrens action and the Sanchez decision regarding Taylor's Torrens action were binding upon the plaintiffs.

The court of appeals affirmed. This court granted certiorari and reversed and remanded, questioning the constitutional adequacy of the publication notice in the Torrens action. Rael v. Taylor, 876 P.2d 1210, 1228 (Colo.1994). We directed the trial court to determine which of the plaintiffs received adequate notice in the Torrens action and to hold a trial on the merits for those who did not have proper notice.

On remand, the trial court granted Taylor's motion for summary judgment on the Mexican law claim. The court then bifurcated the proceedings: it determined the due process and class action certification issues before holding a trial on the merits. During the due process phase, the court dismissed most of the plaintiffs. The court determined that seven of the plaintiffs could pursue their claims regarding the mountain tract and that three of the plaintiffs could proceed with their claims regarding the Salazar estate. Without further hearing, the court denied class certification. The court then held a trial on the merits.

After the trial, the court made a finding of fact that the landowners or their predecessors in title had "grazed cattle and sheep, harvested timber, gathered firewood, fished, hunted and recreated on the land of the defendant from the 1800s to the date the land was acquired by the defendant, in 1960." The trial court further found that the community referred to Taylor Ranch as "open range," and that prior to 1960, the landowners "were never denied access to the land." The court also stated that it did "not dispute" that the settlers could not have survived without use of the mountain area of the grant.

Despite theses findings, the court determined that the landowners had not proved prescriptive rights because their use was not adverse. The court further held that the

---

1. The Colorado Torrens Title Registration Act allowed land owners to file an action that would essentially quiet title to their land. Because Taylor was a North Carolina resident he invoked diversity jurisdiction.

2. Jack Taylor died during the pendency of this litigation. His son, Zachary Taylor, stepped in as the executor of his father's estate. At some point, the Taylor estate sold the Taylor Ranch to another party. This party bought the land subject to the landowners' claims and subject to this litigation. For the sake of simplicity, Jack Taylor and his successors in title are referred to as "Taylor" in this opinion.

Beaubien Document was not an effective express grant of rights because it did not identify the parties to the rights or the locations where the rights should be exercised. Regarding an implied grant by Beaubien, the court concluded that Colorado law did not
recognize the implied rights the landowners claimed. The landowners appealed both
the due process determination and the rulings on their claim of rights.

The court of appeals affirmed. The court agreed with the trial court's conclusions regarding all three of the landowners' theories. Regarding an express grant of rights, the
court of appeals engaged in a technical application of the 1863 property laws of the Colorado Territory. The court concluded that the document included neither the "christian
and surnames" of the grantees nor an accurate description of the property to be burdened. Furthermore, the court of appeals noted that that because the document does
not use the words, "and heirs and assigns" it does not indicate that Beaubien intended
any rights to run with the land. Because the court rejected all of the landowners' substantive claims, the court did not reach the question of whether the trial court erred in
its due process decision.

We granted certiorari.

II. Analysis

The landowners claim rights to graze livestock, gather firewood and timber, hunt,
fish, and recreate. Before discussing the sources of the settlement rights, we characterize
the claimed rights in order to determine the rules of law that govern them.

A. The Rights at Issue

The parties agree that the rights at issue are most appropriately characterized as profits à prendre. A profit à prendre—in modern parlance, a profit—"is an easement that
confers the right to enter and remove timber, minerals, oil, gas, game, or other substances from land in the possession of another." Restatement (Third) of Property: Servitudes § 1.2(2) (1998) [hereinafter Restatement]. Thus, a profit is a type of easement.

This court has described an easement as "a right conferred by grant, prescription or
necessity authorizing one to do or maintain something on the land of another which,
although a benefit to the land of the former, may be a burden on the land of the latter."
Lazy Dog Ranch v. Telluray Ranch Corp., 965 P.2d 1229, 1234 (Colo.1998).

An easement can be in gross or appurtenant. An easement in gross does not belong
to an individual by virtue of her ownership of land, but rather is a personal right to use
another's property. An easement appurtenant, on the other hand, runs with the land. It
is meant to benefit the property, or an owner by virtue of her property ownership. An
easement is presumed to be appurtenant, rather than in gross. Restatement, supra,
§ 4.5(2).

In this case, the landowners allege that the settlement rights were to be used in connection with their land. They argue that the firewood was used to heat their homes, the
timber to frame their adobe houses, and the grazing necessary to the viability of their
farms. The landowners also assert that the settlement rights were granted to their predecessors in title by virtue of their interest in their vara strips and were in fact a necessary incentive for settlement in the area.

We conclude that the rights the landowners are claiming are best characterized as
easements appurtenant to the land. We reach this conclusion from the evidence that
under Mexican custom access to common land was given to surrounding landowners,

the evidence that this access was used to benefit the use of the land, and the presumption in favor of appurtenant easements.

Having established the nature of the rights at issue, we now turn to the sources of these rights.

B. Sources of the Rights

The landowners argue that their settlement rights stem from three sources: Mexican law, prescription, and an express or implied grant from Beaubien.

Regarding the Mexican law claim, the landowners claim that community rights to common lands not only are recognized by Mexican law, but also are integral to the settlement of an area. The landowners further point out that in the Treaty of Guadalupe Hidalgo, the United States government agreed that the land rights of the residents of the ceded territories would be "inviolably respected." Under the landowners' theory, the treaty dictates that the court apply Mexican law to the Taylor Ranch and accordingly recognize the settlement rights.

The landowners further argue that use rights can be found via prescription. For this claim, they point to their regular use of the Taylor Ranch land for over one hundred years until the area was fenced in 1960.

Lastly, the landowners assert that their use rights were obtained by either an express or implied grant from Carlos Beaubien. For this claim, the landowners rely primarily on the Beaubien Document.

The trial court dismissed the Mexican law claim on motion for summary judgment, and after a trial on the merits, rejected the two remaining claims. The court of appeals affirmed. The court of appeals held that the Mexican law claim failed because whatever rights may have existed at the time of the Treaty of Guadalupe Hidalgo were subsequently extinguished by Congress's 1860 Act of Confirmation. The court further held that the landowners could not claim prescriptive rights because their use of the Taylor Ranch was not adverse. Lastly, the court held that the Beaubien Document fails as an express grant of rights and that Colorado does not recognize implied easements in the form of profits.

We agree that the landowners cannot claim rights under Mexican law. Their predecessors in title did not settle on the Sangre de Cristo grant until after the land was ceded to the United States and thus their use rights developed under United States law. Mexican land use and property law are highly relevant in this case in ascertaining the intentions of the parties involved. However, because the settlement of the grant occurred after the land was ceded to the United States, we conclude that Mexican law cannot be a source of the landowners' claims.

We disagree, however, with the court of appeals' resolution of the landowners' other claims. While the Beaubien Document cannot support an express grant of rights, when coupled with the Gilpin agreement and other evidence, it supports a finding of a prescriptive easement, an easement by estoppel, and an easement from prior use.

1. The Beaubien Document

As evidence of a grant of rights from Carlos Beaubien, the landowners rely primarily on the Beaubien Document. The document was written by Beaubien in 1863, one year before his death.

One English translation of the document reads, in part:

Plaza of San Luis de la Culebra, May 11, 1863.

> It has been decided that the lands of the Rito Seco remain uncultivated for the benefit of the community members (gente) of the plazas of San Luis, San Pablo and Los Ballejos and for the other inhabitants of these plazas for pasturing cattle by the payment of a fee per head, etc. and that the water of the said Rito remains partitioned among the inhabitants of the same plaza of San Luis and those from the other side of the vega who hold lands almost adjacent to it as their own lands, that are not irrigated with the waters of the Rio Culebra. The vega, after the measurement of three acres from it in front of the chapel, to which they have been donated, will remain for the benefit of the inhabitants of this plaza and those of the Culebra as far as above the plaza of Los Ballejos.... Those below the road as far as the narrows will have the right to enjoy the same benefit.... *[No one may] place any obstacle or obstruction to anyone in the enjoyment of his legitimate rights....* Likewise, each one should take scrupulous care in the use of water without causing damage with it to his neighbors nor to anyone. According to the corresponding rule, *all the inhabitants will have enjoyment of benefits of pastures, water, firewood and timber, always taking care that one does not injure another.*

(Emphases added.)

The landowners assert that this document evidences an express grant of settlement rights on the Taylor Ranch land. The trial court concluded that the Beaubien Document did not vest any rights in the Taylor Ranch. The court noted that although the document lists rights of pasture, water, firewood, and timber, the only locations specified for access are the Rito Seco and the vega, two areas that the parties agree are not part of the Taylor Ranch. The trial court did admit extrinsic evidence to determine whether there was a "latent ambiguity" in the document. However, because the court ultimately found that the document was unambiguous, it ruled that extrinsic evidence could not be considered in interpreting the document.

The court of appeals affirmed. The appeals court agreed that the Beaubien Document was ultimately unambiguous and that the trial court properly treated the extrinsic evidence of Beaubien's intent. The court then applied 1863 Colorado property law and concluded that the Beaubien Document did not meet the formal requirements for conveying rights to the landowners' predecessors in title. Moreover, the court held that profits must be expressly granted and thus rejected any claim of implied rights.

We agree that the Beaubien Document does not meet the formal requirements for an express grant of rights. However, we find that the document, when taken together with the other unique facts of this case, establishes a prescriptive easement, an easement by estoppel, and an easement from prior use.

Extrinsic evidence is relevant in interpreting the Beaubien Document. In Lazy Dog [Ranch v. Telluray Ranch Corp., 965 P.2d 1229 (Colo. 1998)], we articulated when a court could examine extrinsic evidence in order to ascertain the nature of an easement. In that case, we expressly followed the Restatement and concluded that "[o]ur paramount concern in construing a deed is to ascertain the intentions of the parties." We also recognized that "circumstances surrounding the grant may be relevant to interpreting the language of the grant." Id. at 1236; see also Restatement, supra, § 4.1(1) (noting that an easement "should be interpreted to give effect to the intention of the parties ascertained from the language used in the instrument, or the circumstances surrounding creation of the servitude, and to carry out the purpose for which it was created"). Moreover, the question of whether or not the document is ambiguous "may be answered by reference to extrinsic evidence." Lazy Dog, 965 P.2d at 1235.

Here, we look to extrinsic evidence to construe the Beaubien Document for two reasons. First, as Lazy Dog tells us, extrinsic evidence may reveal ambiguities. Second, the document is ambiguous on its face with respect to where the landowners could exercise their rights.

Lazy Dog tells us that extrinsic evidence may reveal ambiguities in modern documents; that principle can be only more true with respect to the Beaubien Document. We are attempting to construe a 150 year-old document written in Spanish by a French Canadian who obtained a conditional grant to an enormous land area under Mexican law and perfected it under American law. Beaubien wrote this document when he was near the end of his adventurous life in an apparent attempt to memorialize commitments he had made to induce families to move hundreds of miles to make homes in the wilderness. It would be the height of arrogance and nothing but a legal fiction for us to claim that we can interpret this document without putting it in its historical context.

For the most part, the document is reasonably specific in identifying places where rights are to be exercised. That is not true with respect to the rights asserted by the landowners. The key language reads: "According to the corresponding rule, all the inhabitants will have enjoyment of benefits of pastures, water, firewood and timber, always taking care that one does not injure another."

Thus, given the specificity of other parts of the document, the lack of specificity in this sentence creates an ambiguity. We cannot determine from the face of the document what lands were burdened by the rights Beaubien conveyed to the first settlers.

Following Lazy Dog, we look to the extrinsic evidence in this case. Amici assert that the contrast between the specificity of the majority of the Beaubien Document and the casual reference to the settlement rights at the end of the document can best be explained by the events surrounding the execution of the document. Beaubien penned the document at a time when settlement was moving to the northern area of the grant, which lies northwest of the Taylor Ranch area. At that time, he wrote the Beaubien Document to establish common rights to the area in and around San Luis and at the same time memorialize settlement rights that had already been in existence in the more southern areas of the grant, where Taylor Ranch is located.

We agree with the amici. From the trial court findings, expert testimony, the documents associated with the grant, and a review of the settlement system under which Beaubien and the settlers were operating, we draw two conclusions. First, we conclude that the location for the settlement rights referenced in the Beaubien Document is the mountainous area of the grant on which Taylor Ranch is located. Second, we conclude that Beaubien meant to grant permanent access rights that run with the land.

We first discuss the location for the rights. The evidence in this case establishes that the reference to pasture, water, firewood, and timber in the Beaubien Document refers to access on the mountain area of the grant of which Taylor Ranch is a part.

First, the trial court found that the landowners or their predecessors in title accessed the Taylor Ranch land for over one hundred years to exercise the rights outlined in the Beaubien Document. This strongly suggests that the parties understood that the Taylor Ranch land was the location of their access rights.

Second, experts testified that the resources listed in the document were only available in the Taylor Ranch area of the grant. Expert testimony established that summer grazing, wood, and timber were only available in the mountain area of the grant. This is perhaps the most significant evidence that points to the Taylor Ranch as the location of the rights.

Third, the landowners' access rights are expressly mentioned in Taylor's deed. The deed subjects his property interest not only to "rights of way of record," but also to "all rights of way heretofore located and now maintained and used on, through, over, and across the same." It further subjects the conveyance to "claims of the local people by pre-scription or otherwise to rights to *pasturage, wood, and lumber and so-called settlement rights* in, to, and upon said land." (Emphasis added.) This resolves any doubt that the access rights were meant to burden Taylor's land.

There is also ample evidence that the document was meant to create permanent rights that run with the land. Both the settlement system under which Beaubien and the settlers were operating and the Gilpin agreement are strong evidence of this.

Access to common areas was an integral feature of the settlement system under which the settlers and Beaubien were operating. Under Spanish and Mexican law, the govern-ment awarded community and private grants for the purpose of settling the frontier. See Malcolm Ebright, Land Grants and Lawsuits in Northern New Mexico 23 (1994).

The Mexican grants were issued under specific procedures. The governor would refer a petition to the local *alcalde* (mayor) for his recommendations on whether the grant should be made. Availability of pasture, water, and firewood on common lands was among the primary considerations:

> The primary considerations were whether the land was being used or claimed by others, the sufficiency of the petitioner's qualifications, and in the case of a community grant, *the availability of resources like pasture, water, and firewood.*

Id. (emphasis added). Large private grants were made during the Mexican period. If the recommendation from the *alcalde* was favorable, the governor would make the private grant to an individual. The individual's ownership, however, was conditional upon suc-cessful settlement of the grant.

Agriculture and stock raising were the primary means of subsistence for the settlers on the grants. Id. at 25. The settlers supplemented their irrigated plots by use of commonly accessible community or private grant lands for gathering firewood and grazing livestock:

> The pattern of land tenure and use was the foundation for these tightly knit communities. Produce from their small irrigated plots *supplemented by the use of common lands for gathering firewood and for grazing a few head of livestock* furnished the bare necessities for the village families, a lifestyle to which they were accustomed.

Ira G. Clark, Water in New Mexico, A History of Its Management and Use 34 (1987) (emphasis added).

Under colonial and Mexican law, the difference between a community grant[7] and a private grant was that the common lands of the community could not be sold; the grantee of a private grant could sell the lands. See Ebright, supra, at 25.

---

7. Because the lands of a community grant could not be sold and were held in common in per-petuity, settlers could use them for hunting, fishing, gathering herbs, and rock quarrying, among other uses, without any question or conflict with subsequent landowners or the need of courts to define the intended uses. Some private grants operated like community grants; others did not. See Ebright, supra, at 25. Two examples of community grants in the Sangre de Cristo grant are the San

Expert reports submitted in this case reveal that Beaubien and the original settlers operated under this traditional system. Common areas were not only a typical feature but a necessary incentive for settlement.

As discussed above, because the Sangre de Cristo grant was part of the United States at the time permanent settlement began, this Mexican settlement tradition is not the source of the landowners' rights. However, because the settlers and Beaubien were so familiar with the settlement system, it is highly relevant in ascertaining the parties' intentions and expectations.

The express language in the Gilpin agreement, recorded one year after the Beaubien Document, further supports the conclusion that the rights referenced in the Beaubien Document were meant to burden the land. Gilpin was Beaubien's immediate successor as owner of the grant land. The Gilpin agreement contains an express condition confirming the settlers' rights:

> [Gilpin agrees to the] express condition that the settlement rights before then conceded by said Charles Beaubien to residents of Costilla, Culebra & Trinchera, within said Tract included, shall be confirmed by the said William Gilpin as confirmed by him.

This deed also recites that the settlers paid consideration to Beaubien for those rights and that Gilpin succeeds to the settlers' obligations to Beaubien, including payments due on promissory notes held by Beaubien and his agents. The Gilpin agreement is in Taylor's chain of title and Taylor's own deed expressly refers to the landowners' settlement rights.

Thus, we conclude both that rights were granted and exercised from the time of settlement and that the Beaubien Document memorialized them. Moreover, we conclude that the location for the rights is the mountain portion of the grant of which Taylor Ranch is a part, and that the benefit and burden of these rights were meant to run with the land.

We do not take issue with the court of appeals' application of 1863 Colorado property law to the Beaubien Document. It is not surprising that Carlos Beaubien failed to comply with the nuances and technical requirements of the conveyance of real property rights. Beaubien's failure to comply with the territorial property law, however, is not the end of the inquiry. The territorial supreme court made it clear that rights to access and use the property of another landowner could be found in the law of implied easements. Yunker v. Nichols, 1 Colo. 551 (1872). The law of implied easements recognizes that rights may be implied even though they were not properly expressly conveyed. This well-established area of property law is concerned with honoring the intentions of the parties to land transactions and avoiding injustice.

2. Implied Grant of Settlement Rights

The evidence in this case overwhelmingly supports the conclusion that the landowners have implied rights in the Taylor Ranch. We first review the law of implied servitudes. Second, we discuss how traditional settlement practices, repeated

---

Luis vega and chapel referenced in the Beaubien Document. The chapel and the vega continue to exist in the town of San Luis and they are used for the originally intended purposes as a church and as a common pasture. Although a portion of the Beaubien Document establishes these two community grants, the general references to settlement rights were meant to memorialize access and use rights. This is clear from the Gilpin agreement.

references to settlement rights in documents associated with the Sangre de Cristo grant, the hundred year history of the landowners' use of the Taylor Ranch, and other evidence of necessity, reliance, and intention support a finding of implied rights in this case.

a. Implied Servitudes

An easement is created if the owner of the servient estate either enters into a contract or makes a conveyance intended to create a servitude that complies with the Statute of Frauds or an exception to the Statute of Frauds. Restatement, supra, §2.1.

> Servitudes that are not created by contract or conveyance include servitudes created by dedication, prescription, and estoppel. Those which are not created by express contract or conveyance are the implied servitudes, which may be based on prior use, map or boundary descriptions, necessity, or other circumstances surrounding the conveyance of other interests in land, which give rise to the inference that the parties intended to create a servitude.

Id. §2.8 cmt. b; see also Wright v. Horse Creek Ranches, 697 P.2d 384, 387-88 (Colo.1985) (noting that an easement may be established by "necessity; by preexisting use; by express or implied grant; or by prescription"); Wagner v. Fairlamb, 151 Colo. 481, 484, 379 P.2d 165, 167 (1963) (noting that implied easements are "not expressed by the parties in writing, but ... arise [ ] out of the existence of certain facts implied from the transaction").

Easements can be implied in a number of situations. Easements created by prescription, Restatement, supra, §2.17; easements by estoppel, id. §2.10; and easements implied from prior use, id. §2.12, are the most relevant to this case. We discuss each of these in turn, discussing both Colorado case law and the Restatement, which is consistent with our precedent.

An easement by prescription is established when the prescriptive use is: 1) open or notorious, 2) continued without effective interruption for the prescriptive period, and 3) the use was either a) adverse or b) pursuant to an attempted, but ineffective grant.

A court can imply an easement created by estoppel when 1) the owner of the servient estate "permitted another to use that land under circumstances in which it was reasonable to foresee that the user would substantially change position believing that the permission would not be revoked," 2) the user substantially changed position in reasonable reliance on that belief, and 3) injustice can be avoided only by establishment of a servitude. Id. §2.10. Whether reliance is justified depends upon the nature of the transaction, including the sophistication of the parties. Id. §2.9 cmt. e. The Restatement does not have a requirement of deception; neither does Colorado. An easement by estoppel is an equitable remedy. It recognizes that when a landowner induces another to change position in reliance upon his promise, he is estopped from then denying the existence of the rights simply because they did not meet the formal conveyance rules. The rule "is founded on the policy of preventing injustice."

Colorado law has repeatedly recognized this equitable right. For example, in Graybill [v. Corlett, 60 Colo. 551 (Colo. 1916)], we examined a landowner's right to maintain a water ditch across the land of his neighbor. The owner of the servient estate had granted the owner of the dominant estate the right to establish a ditch across his land. This was an oral promise; the parties did not comply with conveyance and recording formalities. In reliance on the parol agreement, the owner of the dominant estate used the ditch as the irrigation source for his land and cleaned, repaired, and made improvements to the ditch. On these facts, we noted that, "[i]t is too well settled to require discussion that under the circumstances above stated a licensee holds under an irrevocable license, and his right is as valid as if acquired by grant." Id. at 553, 154 P. at 731; see also Hoehne Ditch Co. [v. John Flood Ditch Co.], 68 Colo. 531, 191 P. 108 [(Colo. 2002)] (applying the "well settled" rule that "although an oral contract relating to realty is within the statute [of frauds], where a consideration has passed, and it has been fully performed by both parties and possession taken in pursuance thereof, the bar of the statute is removed and equity will enforce the right thus acquired").

An easement implied from prior use is created when 1) the servient and dominant estates were once under common ownership, 2) the rights alleged were exercised prior to the severance of the estate, 3) the use was not merely temporary, 4) the continuation of this use was reasonably necessary to the enjoyment of the parcel, and 5) a contrary intention is neither expressed nor implied. Restatement, supra §2.12. The rationale for this servitude is as follows:

> The rule stated in this section is not based solely on the presumed actual intent of the parties. It furthers the policy of protecting reasonable expectations, as well as actual intent, of parties to land transactions.

Restatement, supra, §2.12 cmt. a.

Colorado has long applied this implied easement. This court has found an easement from prior use in Lee. In Lee, the owner of one parcel of land claimed a right of way across his neighbor's land to access his property. The servient and dominant estates had once been under common ownership and this right of way was used before the severance of title. Seven years after the severance of title, the defendant bought the servient estate and attempted to block the right of way, claiming a lack of an enforceable agreement. This court found that an easement from prior use had been established. Lee [v. School Dist. No. R-1 in Jefferson County], 164 Colo. [326], 333, 435 P.2d [232], 236 [(Colo. 1967)].

Similarly, the court of appeals found an easement from prior use in Proper. There, the plaintiff landowner used his neighbor's land to access his property. This use had begun when the two plots were under common ownership. Although the neighbor allowed this use, there was no formal agreement. The neighbor sought to rescind his permission after twenty-five years of the easement's use, and to construct a fence. Proper [v. Granger], 827 P.2d [591], 592 [(Colo. App. 1992)]. The court found that under these facts, an easement from prior use had been established.

Having outlined the law of implied easements, we now turn to the facts of this case.

b. Application to the Landowners' Claims

Despite the long history of implied easements in Colorado, the court of appeals in this case rejected the landowners' claims of an implied easement. The court did so because it believed that, although easements in the form of access rights could be implied, easements in the form of profits could not. In reaching this conclusion, the court misapplied a 1964 decision of this court, Dawson v. Fling, 155 Colo. 599, 396 P.2d 599 (1964).

In Dawson, the Flings claimed easement rights to a lake owned by a corporation. The document establishing the rights was a deed which read, in part, that the lake could be used "for boating and swimming purposes, for the use of said grantees by themselves, their heirs and assigns, their servants, agents, friends, guests, and whomever they may select." Although the deed specified boating and swimming rights, the Flings petitioned the court to find that they had the right to fish as well. This court concluded that the language of the conveyance clearly limited the rights to boating and swimming and thus declined to imply fishing rights as well.

In dicta, this court asserted that "[a] right to profits à prendre must be expressly granted." However, from the circumstances of the case it is clear that this court declined to find implied rights because the deed of conveyance expressly limited the rights: "A court cannot rewrite a contract and thereby change its terms when it is plain, clear and unambiguous." Id. at 604-05, 396 P.2d at 602. In Dawson, then, a crucial element of an implied easement was missing because a contrary intention was expressly stated in the deed. For that reason, we declined to imply additional profits in Dawson.

Although this court has not addressed implied profits for over thirty-five years, there is a modern trend to apply the same rules to easements of access and to profits. Figliuzzi v. Carcajou Shooting Club, 184 Wis.2d 572, 516 N.W.2d 410, 415 (1994) (applying a statutory rule of easements to profits in part because the court was persuaded by the Restatement of Property § 450 Special Note (1944), which states that it treats "easements" and "profits" the same because "in no case was there a rule applicable to one of these interests which was not also applicable to the other").

The Restatement explains that, although some profits such as mineral and water rights have specific rules, generally as between easements in the form of access rights and easements in the form of profits, "there are no doctrinal differences between them." Restatement, supra, § 1.2 reporter's note.[10] "Generally, the rules governing creation, interpretation, transfer, and termination of easements and profits are the same in American law." Id. § 1.2 cmt. e.

Easements and profits are treated equally because the same public policy and practical considerations that underlie implied rights of access also underlie implied profits. A recognition that parties do not always comply with strict rules of express conveyance, a desire to effectuate the intent of the parties, and the aim of fairness apply equally to easements and profits.

Colorado law is replete with precedent that reflects a strong policy to be true to parties' intentions and recognizes that Colorado's unique history and geography further necessitate judicial recognition of implied rights in land. See, e.g., Roaring Fork Club v. St. Jude's Co., 36 P.3d 1229, 1231 (Colo.2001) (noting that "our lawmakers [have] recognized that our arid climate require[s] the creation of a right to appropriate and convey water across the land of another"); Lazy Dog Ranch, 965 P.2d at 1235 (in determining the scope of an easement, noting that the "paramount concern" is to ascertain the intentions of the parties and that when a deed is silent as to a particular right, the court shall look at the circumstances surrounding the transaction); Thompson [v. Whinnery], 895 P.2d [537], 540 [(Colo. 1995)] (in implying an easement, noting that "sound public policy dictates that land should not be rendered unfit for occupancy and that there is a presumption, therefore, that whenever a party conveys property he conveys whatever is necessary for the beneficial use of that property"); Yunker [v. Nichols], 1 Colo. [551], 554 [1872 WL 149 (Colo. Terr. 1872)] (noting that certain water rights are necessary for enjoying land and that the law will "imply a grant of such easement where it is especially necessary to the enjoyment of the dominant estate," and that such rights come not out of the literal terms of the contract, but rather out of "pre-existing and

---

10. The first Restatement of Property, concluding that the same rules apply to easements of access as to profits, dropped the term "profit." However, because the word "profit" is useful as a descriptive term, it survives. Restatement, supra, § 1.2 cmt. e.

higher authority of laws of nature, of nations, or of the community to which the parties belong").

Thus, the aim of honoring parties' intentions and avoiding injustice that the Restatement expresses has long been the goal of Colorado law. Specifically, Colorado has a strong history of implying servitudes based on equitable concerns. As the Restatement concludes, it is arbitrary and inconsistent to apply these principles to easements of access but not to profits.[11] Such a limitation would be directly contrary to our legacy of implied easements.

Having concluded that the trial court and court of appeals in this case incorrectly held that Colorado law does not recognize implied easements in the form of profits, we now apply the law of implied easements to the landowners' claims.

Our review of the record leads us to conclude that there is ample evidence to imply certain rights in the landowners to access and use the Taylor Ranch. The prior unity of title of the landowners' and Taylor's land; the necessity of the rights; the significant reliance upon the promise of these rights; the fact that the rights were exercised for over one hundred years; and [the] fact that these rights were memorialized in the Beaubien Document, the Gilpin agreement, and every deed of conveyance in Taylor's chain of title, satisfy every element of the Restatement test and the implied easements we recognized in the cases discussed above.

i. Prescriptive Easement

Because Taylor's deed indicates that Taylor's ownership of the land is subject to the landowners' prescriptive rights, we begin with an application of the law of prescriptive easements. The court of appeals in this case concluded that the landowners failed to prove a prescriptive easement claim because their use was not adverse. The court erred in this respect.

Although adversity is a necessary requisite for adverse possession claims it is not required for a prescriptive easement. Courts often find prescriptive easements even when the owner of the servient estate allows the use. Significantly, the Restatement articulates that a prescriptive use is either:

(1) a use that is adverse to the owner of the land or the interest in land against which the servitude is claimed, or

(2) a use that is made pursuant to the terms of an intended but imperfectly created servitude, or the enjoyment of the benefit of an intended but imperfectly created servitude.

Restatement, supra, § 2.16.

Although an easement by prescription without adversity has been codified only in the recent restatement, "it has always been present in American servitudes law." Id. § 2.16 cmt. a. Because many jurisdictions technically required adversity for a prescriptive easement, decisions in those states often used "convoluted explanations" to explain how a permitted use was actually hostile and met the adversity requirement. Id. Some

---

11. Notably, one of the goals of the Restatement is to "present [ ] a comprehensive modern treatment of the law of servitudes that substantially simplifies and clarifies one of the most complex and archaic bodies of 20th century American law.... It is designed to allow both traditional and innovative land-development practices using servitudes without imposing artificial constraints as to form or arbitrary limitations as to substance." Restatement, supra, Introduction at 3.

courts acknowledged an exception to the adversity rule in certain circumstances. Other jurisdictions, such as Colorado, simply glossed over the adversity requirement without comment.

It has long been established, then, that the element of adversity is not required in all circumstances. It is not required when other evidence makes clear that the parties intend an easement, but fail "because they do not fully articulate their intent or reduce their agreement to writing, or because they fail to comply with some other formal requirement imposed in the jurisdiction." Restatement, supra, §2.16, cmt. a. Thus, the court of appeals in the current case erred when it required a finding of adversity in all circumstances.

Having established that adversity is not required when a grant has been imperfectly attempted, we turn to the facts of the current case. The trial court's findings of fact and our interpretation of the Beaubien Document fit every element of a prescriptive easement.

First, the use must be open and notorious. There is no doubt that the landowners' use was well known to Taylor and his predecessors in title. The trial court noted that Taylor's predecessors in title not only knew of the landowners' access, but they even went so far as to direct the location of grazing. Most significantly, Taylor and his predecessors in title had express notice of the landowners' claims of right from the language of their deeds. The use was open and notorious.

Second, the use must continue without effective interruption for the prescriptive period. In Colorado, the statutory period is eighteen years. Here, the trial court explicitly found that the landowners and their predecessors in title "grazed cattle and sheep, harvested timber, gathered firewood, fished, hunted and recreated on the land of the defendant from the 1800s to the date the land was acquired by the defendant, in 1960." The trial court also found that this access was never denied. This more than satisfies the statutory time period.

Third, the access must either be adverse or pursuant to an intended, but imperfectly executed, grant. Here, the access was permissive, rather than adverse. However, there is ample evidence of an intended grant of these rights. The Beaubien Document, although imperfect as an express grant, evidences Beaubien's intent to grant rights to the landowners' predecessors in title (see supra). Moreover, the express language in the deeds of conveyance for the Taylor Ranch, from Gilpin ultimately to Taylor, indicate[s] an intention that the rights burden the land.

Thus, the landowners have established a prescriptive claim.[12]

ii. Easement by Estoppel

The landowners have also established every element of an easement by estoppel. First, Taylor's predecessors in title "permitted [the settlers] to use [the] land under circum-

---

12. The trial court in the current case heard evidence and ruled on the prescription claim as a matter of judicial economy. However, the court also ruled that the landowners could not bring a prescription claim because Taylor did not have adequate notice. Our review of the record does not support this determination. Although the landowners did not formally file for leave to add a prescription claim until 1992, all of their factual allegations from the birth of this case clearly implicate prescriptive rights—particularly their claim that they and their predecessors in title continuously accessed the Taylor Ranch for over one hundred years. Significantly, the deed of conveyance explicitly informed Taylor that he purchased the land subject to the "claims of the local people by *prescription* or otherwise." (Emphasis added.) Taylor had adequate notice of this claim.

stances in which it was reasonable to foresee that the [settlers] would substantially change position believing that the permission would not be revoked." Restatement, supra, § 2.10. The settlers' reliance was reasonable because rights were expected, intended, and necessary. It was expected because of the Mexican settlement system discussed above. Also discussed above, this settlement system, combined with the actual practices and the deeds associated with the Taylor Ranch, show that rights were intended.

The rights were also necessary. The plaintiffs' expert, Dr. Marianne Stoller, testified that access to wood was necessary to heat homes, access to timber was necessary to build homes, and access to grazing was necessary for maintaining livestock.[13] Moreover, Beaubien included each of these resources in a lease to the United States for the first military post in Colorado. See LeRoy R. Hafen & Ann W. Hafen, Colorado: A Story of the State and its People 130 (1947). The trial court found that during the 1850s Beaubien executed a lease to the United States government for the maintenance of Fort Massachusetts on grant land. In this lease Beaubien granted the army the right to "pasture, cut grass, timber and collect firewood" on Beaubien's land. We can safely assume that the United States was more sophisticated in its dealings with Beaubien than were the landowners' predecessors in title and that it insisted on putting Beaubien's promises into writing.[14] Under these circumstances, it is reasonable to foresee that that a settler would substantially change position believing that the permission would not be revoked.

The second element, that the user substantially change position in reasonable reliance on the belief, is easily found. The landowners' predecessors in title settled Beaubien's grant for him. They moved onto the land and established permanent farms.

The third element, the avoidance of injustice, is also undeniably present. The original Sangre de Cristo grant was given on the condition that it be settled. Indeed, under Mexican law, the grant would have been revoked if settlement did not succeed. The settlers, then, fulfilled the condition of the grant that made Beaubien fee owner of one million acres of land.

Beaubien attracted settlers to the area by convincing them that he would provide them with the rights they needed for survival. Beaubien knew that families would rely on his promises and leave their homes to travel hundreds of miles on foot or horseback to establish new homes.

A condition of the conveyance of Beaubien's land, from Gilpin down to Taylor, was that the owner honor these rights. Although these promised rights were exercised for over one hundred years, although these rights were necessary to the settlers' very existence, and although Taylor had ample notice of these rights, Taylor fenced his land over forty years ago. It is an understatement to say that this is an injustice.

The landowners have established each element of an easement by estoppel.

---

13. Dr. Stoller, at one point in her testimony, also mentioned that the settlers fished, hunted, and recreated on the land. She did not, however, indicate that such practices were necessary. Significantly, in her written report, which the landowners submitted to the trial court, Dr. Stoller lists the landowners' rights as use rights to "pasture, firewood, timber, and water."

14. The landowners' expert, Dr. Stoller, agreed that the rights included in Beaubien's lease to the government were significant: "he gave [the United States Army] use rights for pasture, cutting grass, firewood and timber to the adjacent lands.... Thus he was following the same practice in the 1863 document for his settlers, and for the same reasons—the need for these resources for human survival."

iii. Easement From Prior Use

Lastly, every element of an easement from prior use has been shown. First, both Taylor's and the landowners' lands were originally under the common ownership of Beaubien who owned the entire Sangre de Cristo grant before settlement.

Second, the rights were exercised prior to the severance of the estate. As discussed above, many of the rights the landowners claim were needed and expected for life in the San Luis Valley. This necessity existed from the first days of settlement—indicating that these rights were exercised prior to severance of title.

The third and fourth prongs—that the use was not merely temporary and is reasonably necessary to the enjoyment of the land—are also easily established. The trial court's findings of fact establish that the rights were exercised from the time of settlement until Taylor came on the scene. Moreover, as discussed above, the rights were reasonably necessary.

Lastly, no contrary intention is expressed or implied; thus, the fifth element is present. Custom, expectation, practice, and language in the documents and deeds surrounding the Taylor ranch property indicate not only that a contrary intention did not exist, but that the parties affirmatively intended for these rights to exist.

All five elements of an easement from prior use have been established.

C. Extent of the Rights

Having found that the landowners have implied profits in the Taylor Ranch, we now must address the scope of those rights. We imply the rights memorialized in the Beaubien Document. We do so for four reasons.

First, the document is the strongest evidence we have of the parties' intentions and expectations. Second, the rights in the document were likely the most necessary. Third, the Fort Massachusetts lease lists these same rights. Fourth, the document is the only evidence we have of an attempted express grant. This is particularly important for the prescriptive easement claim. See Restatement, supra, § 2.16 cmt. a.[15]

Accordingly, we hold that the landowners have implied rights in Taylor's land for the access detailed in the Beaubien Document—pasture, firewood, and timber. These easements should be limited to reasonable use—the grazing access is limited to a reasonable number of livestock given the size of the vara strips; the firewood limited to that needed for each residence; and the timber limited to that needed to construct and maintain residence and farm buildings located on the vara strips.

III. Remaining Issues

As a matter of judicial economy, and as a matter of fairness, given the forty-one year denial of access to the Taylor Ranch and this twenty-one year litigation, we decline to

---

15. The landowners acknowledge that the Beaubien Document does not reference rights for hunting, fishing, and recreation and thus that there is no evidence of an express or implied grant of these rights from Carlos Beaubien. However the landowners claim that these rights exist via a prescriptive easement. We disagree. As discussed above, in order to find a prescriptive easement in the absence of adversity, there must be evidence of an attempted express grant. In this case, the Beaubien Document is the only evidence of an attempted express grant to the landowners. Because it makes no reference to hunting, fishing, or recreation, there can be no prescriptive easement for those rights.

remand this case to the court of appeals for a determination of [a remaining] issue. Rather, we will revisit the due process issue after full briefing, in a separate opinion.

IV. Conclusion

In sum, we imply access rights in the landowners to the Taylor Ranch for reasonable grazing, firewood, and timber. We reject the landowner's claims for hunting, fishing, and recreation. Before we remand to the trial court for a permanent order of access, additional briefing is necessary in order to determine which landowners received adequate notice in the Taylor and Salazar Torrens actions. The clerk of this court will set a briefing schedule for the parties.

3. Eminent Domain

Berman v. Parker
348 U.S. 26 (1954)

James C. Toomey and Joseph H. Schneider argued the cause for appellants. With them on the brief was Albert Ginsberg.

Solicitor General Sobeloff argued the cause for appellees. Assistant Attorney General Morton, Oscar H. Davis, Roger P. Marquis, George F. Riseling, and William S. Cheatham were with him on a brief for the District of Columbia Redevelopment Land Agency and the National Capital Planning Commission, appellees.

Vernon E. West, Chester H. Gray, Milton D. Korman, Harry L. Walker, and J. Hampton Baumgartner, Jr. filed a brief for Renah F. Camalier and Louis W. Prentiss, Commissioners of the District of Columbia, appellees.

Before Chief Justice Warren and Justices Black, Reed, Frankfurter, Douglas, Burton, Clark, Minton, and Harlan.

Mr. Justice Douglas delivered the opinion of the Court.

This is an appeal from the judgment of a three-judge District Court which dismissed a complaint seeking to enjoin the condemnation of appellants' property under the District of Columbia Redevelopment Act of 1945. The challenge was to the constitutionality of the Act, particularly as applied to the taking of appellants' property. The District Court sustained the constitutionality of the Act.

By § 2 of the Act, Congress made a "legislative determination" that "owing to technological and sociological changes, obsolete lay-out, and other factors, conditions existing in the District of Columbia with respect to substandard housing and blighted areas, including the use of buildings in alleys as dwellings for human habitation, are injurious to the public health, safety, morals, and welfare, and it is hereby declared to be the policy of the United States to protect and promote the welfare of the inhabitants of the seat of the Government by eliminating all such injurious conditions by employing all means necessary and appropriate for the purpose."[1]

---

1. The Act does not define either "slums" or "blighted areas." Section 3(r), however, states: "Substandard housing conditions" means the conditions obtaining in connection with the existence of any dwelling, or dwellings, or housing accommodations for human beings, which because of lack of sanitary facilities, ventilation, or light, or because of dilapidation, overcrowding, faulty interior arrangement, or any combination of these factors, is in

Section 2 goes on to declare that acquisition of property is necessary to eliminate these housing conditions.

Congress further finds in § 2 that these ends cannot be attained "by the ordinary operations of private enterprise alone without public participation"; that "the sound replanning and redevelopment of an obsolescent or obsolescing portion" of the District "cannot be accomplished unless it be done in the light of comprehensive and coordinated planning of the whole of the territory of the District of Columbia and its environs"; and that "the acquisition and the assembly of real property and the leasing or sale thereof for redevelopment pursuant to a project area redevelopment plan ... is hereby declared to be a public use."

Section 4 creates the District of Columbia Redevelopment Land Agency (hereinafter called the Agency), composed of five members, which is granted power by § 5(a) to acquire and assemble, by eminent domain and otherwise, real property for "the redevelopment of blighted territory in the District of Columbia and the prevention, reduction, or elimination of blighting factors or causes of blight."

Section 6(a) of the Act directs the National Capital Planning Commission (hereinafter called the Planning Commission) to make and develop "a comprehensive or general plan" of the District, including "a land-use plan" which designates land for use for "housing, business, industry, recreation, education, public buildings, public reservations, and other general categories of public and private uses of the land." Section 6(b) authorizes the Planning Commission to adopt redevelopment plans for specific project areas. These plans are subject to the approval of the District Commissioners after a public hearing; and they prescribe the various public and private land uses for the respective areas, the "standards of population density and building intensity," and "the amount or character or class of any low-rent housing."

Once the Planning Commission adopts a plan and that plan is approved by the Commissioners, the Planning Commission certifies it to the Agency. At that point, the Agency is authorized to acquire and assemble the real property in the area.

After the real estate has been assembled, the Agency is authorized to transfer to public agencies the land to be devoted to such public purposes as streets, utilities, recreational facilities, and schools, and to lease or sell the remainder as an entirety or in parts to a redevelopment company, individual, or partnership. The leases or sales must provide that the lessees or purchasers will carry out the redevelopment plan and that "no use shall be made of any land or real property included in the lease or sale nor any building or structure erected thereon" which does not conform to the plan. Preference is to be given to private enterprise over public agencies in executing the redevelopment plan.

The first project undertaken under the Act relates to Project Area B in Southwest Washington, D.C. In 1950 the Planning Commission prepared and published a comprehensive plan for the District. Surveys revealed that in Area B, 64.3% of the dwellings were beyond repair, 18.4% needed major repairs, only 17.3% were satisfactory; 57.8% of the dwellings had outside toilets, 60.3% had no baths, 29.3% lacked electricity, 82.2% had no wash basins or laundry tubs, 83.8% lacked central heating. In the judgment of the District's Director of Health it was necessary to redevelop Area B in the interests of public health. The population of Area B amounted to 5,012 persons, of whom 97.5% were Negroes.

---

the opinion of the Commissioners detrimental to the safety, health, morals, or welfare of the inhabitants of the District of Columbia.

The plan for Area B specifies the boundaries and allocates the use of the land for various purposes. It makes detailed provisions for types of dwelling units and provides that at least one-third of them are to be low-rent housing with a maximum rental of $17 per room per month.

After a public hearing, the Commissioners approved the plan and the Planning Commission certified it to the Agency for execution. The Agency undertook the preliminary steps for redevelopment of the area when this suit was brought.

Appellants own property in Area B at 712 Fourth Street, S.W. It is not used as a dwelling or place of habitation. A department store is located on it. Appellants object to the appropriation of this property for the purposes of the project. They claim that their property may not to taken constitutionally for this project. It is commercial, not residential property; it is not slum housing; it will be put into the project under the management of a private, not a public, agency and redeveloped for private, not public, use. That is the argument; and the contention is that appellants' private property is being taken contrary to two mandates of the Fifth Amendment—(1) "No person shall ... be deprived of ... property, without due process of law"; (2) "nor shall private property be taken for public use, without just compensation." To take for the purpose of ridding the area of slums is one thing; it is quite another, the argument goes, to take a man's property merely to develop a better balanced, more attractive community. The District Court, while agreeing in general with that argument, saved the Act by construing it to mean that the Agency could condemn property only for the reasonable necessities of slum clearance and prevention, its concept of "slum" being the existence of conditions "injurious to the public health, safety, morals and welfare."

The power of Congress over the District of Columbia includes all the legislative powers which a state may exercise over its affairs. We deal, in other words, with what traditionally has been known as the police power. An attempt to define its reach or trace its outer limits is fruitless, for each case must turn on its own facts. The definition is essentially the product of legislative determinations addressed to the purposes of government, purposes neither abstractly nor historically capable of complete definition. Subject to specific constitutional limitations, when the legislature has spoken, the public interest has been declared in terms well-nigh conclusive. In such cases the legislature, not the judiciary, is the main guardian of the public needs to be served by social legislation, whether it be Congress legislating concerning the District of Columbia or the States legislating concerning local affairs. This principle admits of no exception merely because the power of eminent domain is involved. The role of the judiciary in determining whether that power is being exercised for a public purpose is an extremely narrow one.

Public safety, public health, morality, peace and quiet, law and order—these are some of the more conspicuous examples of the traditional application of the police power to municipal affairs. Yet they merely illustrate the scope of the power and do not delimit it. Miserable and disreputable housing conditions may do more than spread disease and crime and immorality. They may also suffocate the spirit by reducing the people who live there to the status of cattle. They may indeed make living an almost insufferable burden. They may also be an ugly sore, a blight on the community which robs it of charm, which makes it a place from which men turn. The misery of housing may despoil a community as an open sewer may ruin a river.

We do not sit to determine whether a particular housing project is or is not desirable. The concept of the public welfare is broad and inclusive. The values it represents are spiritual as well as physical, aesthetic as well as monetary. It is within the power of the legislature to determine that the community should be beautiful as well as healthy, spacious as well as clean, well-balanced as well as carefully patrolled. In the present case, the Congress and its authorized agencies have made determinations that take into account a wide variety of values. It is not for us to reappraise them. If those who govern the District of Columbia decide that the Nation's Capital should be beautiful as well as sanitary, there is nothing in the Fifth Amendment that stands in the way.

Once the object is within the authority of Congress, the right to realize it through the exercise of eminent domain is clear. For the power of eminent domain is merely the means to the end. Once the object is within the authority of Congress, the means by which it will be attained is also for Congress to determine. Here one of the means chosen is the use of private enterprise for redevelopment of the area. Appellants argue that this makes the project a taking from one businessman for the benefit of another businessman. But the means of executing the project are for Congress and Congress alone to determine, once the public purpose has been established. The public end may be as well or better served through an agency of private enterprise than through a department of government—or so the Congress might conclude. We cannot say that public ownership is the sole method of promoting the public purposes of community redevelopment projects. What we have said also disposes of any contention concerning the fact that certain property owners in the area may be permitted to repurchase their properties for redevelopment in harmony with the overall plan. That, too, is a legitimate means which Congress and its agencies may adopt, if they choose.

In the present case, Congress and its authorized agencies attack the problem of the blighted parts of the community on an area rather than on a structure-by-structure basis. That, too, is opposed by appellants. They maintain that since their building does not imperil health or safety nor contribute to the making of a slum or a blighted area, it cannot be swept into a redevelopment plan by the mere dictum of the Planning Commission or the Commissioners. The particular uses to be made of the land in the project were determined with regard to the needs of the particular community. The experts concluded that if the community were to be healthy, if it were not to revert again to a blighted or slum area, as though possessed of a congenital disease, the area must be planned as a whole. It was not enough, they believed, to remove existing buildings that were insanitary or unsightly. It was important to redesign the whole area so as to eliminate the conditions that cause slums—the overcrowding of dwellings, the lack of parks, the lack of adequate streets and alleys, the absence of recreational areas, the lack of light and air, the presence of outmoded street patterns. It was believed that the piecemeal approach, the removal of individual structures that were offensive, would be only a palliative. The entire area needed redesigning so that a balanced, integrated plan could be developed for the region, including not only new homes but also schools, churches, parks, streets, and shopping centers. In this way it was hoped that the cycle of decay of the area could be controlled and the birth of future slums prevented. Such diversification in future use is plainly relevant to the maintenance of the desired housing standards and therefore within congressional power.

The District Court below suggested that, if such a broad scope were intended for the statute, the standards contained in the Act would not be sufficiently definite to sustain the delegation of authority. We do not agree. We think the standards prescribed were adequate for executing the plan to eliminate not only slums as narrowly defined by the District Court but also the blighted areas that tend to produce slums. Property may of course be taken for this redevelopment which, standing by itself, is innocuous and unoffending. But we have said enough to indicate that it is the need of the area as a whole which Congress and its agencies are evaluating. If owner after owner were permitted to resist these redevelopment programs on the ground that his particular property was not being used against the public interest, integrated plans for redevelopment would suffer greatly. The argument pressed on us is, indeed, a plea to substitute the landowner's standard of the public need for the standard prescribed by Congress. But as we have already stated, community redevelopment programs need not, by force of the Constitution, be on a piecemeal basis — lot by lot, building by building.

It is not for the courts to oversee the choice of the boundary line nor to sit in review on the size of a particular project area. Once the question of the public purpose has been decided, the amount and character of land to be taken for the project and the need for a particular tract to complete the integrated plan rests in the discretion of the legislative branch.

The District Court indicated grave doubts concerning the Agency's right to take full title to the land as distinguished from the objectionable buildings located on it. We do not share those doubts. If the Agency considers it necessary in carrying out the redevelopment project to take full title to the real property involved, it may do so. It is not for the courts to determine whether it is necessary for successful consummation of the project that unsafe, unsightly, or insanitary buildings alone be taken or whether title to the land be included, any more than it is the function of the courts to sort and choose among the various parcels selected for condemnation.

The rights of these property owners are satisfied when they receive that just compensation which the Fifth Amendment exacts as the price of the taking.

The judgment of the District Court, as modified by this opinion, is affirmed.

County of Wayne v. Hathcock

471 Mich. 445, 684 N.W.2d 765 (Supreme Court of Michigan 2004)

Zausmer, Kaufman, August & Caldwell, P.C. (by Mark J. Zausmer and Mischa M. Gibbons), Farmington Hills, MI, for the plaintiff.

Ackerman & Ackerman, P.C. (by Alan T. Ackerman and Darius W. Dynkowski), Troy, MI, Plunkett & Cooney, P.C. (by Mary Massaron Ross), Detroit, MI, and Allan Falk, P.C. (by Allan S. Falk), Okemos, MI, for the defendants.

Martin N. Fealk, Taylor, MI, for defendants Speck.*

---

* Kupelian Ormond & Magy, P.C. (by Stephon B. Bagne), Southfield, for amici curiae the International Council of Shopping Centers, Inc.
Secrest, Wardle, Lynch, Hampton, Truex and Morley (by Gerald A. Fisher and Thomas R. Schultz), Farmington Hills, for amici curiae the Public Corporation Law Section of the State Bar of Michigan.
Miller, Canfield, Paddock and Stone, P.L.C. (by Thomas C. Phillips, Clifford T. Flood, Jaclyn Shoshana Levine, and Thomas C. Phillips), Lansing, for amici curiae the Michigan Municipal League.
Dykema Gossett P.L.L.C. (by Richard D. McLellan and Julie A. Karkosak), Lansing, for amici curiae the Michigan Economic Development Corporation.
Monghan, LoPrete, McDonald, Yakima, Grenke & McCarthy (by Thomas J. McCarthy), Bloomfield Hills, for amici curiae the city of Dearborn.
Steinhardt Pesick & Cohen, P.C. (by H. Adam Cohen and Jason C. Long), for amici curiae the Adell Children's Funded Trusts.
Lewis & Munday, P.C. (by David Baker Lewis, Brian J. Kott, Susan D. Hoffman, and Darice E. Weber), Detroit, for amici curiae the Economic Development Corporation of the City of Detroit,

Before Justices Robert P. Young Jr., Maura D. Corrigan, Clifford W. Taylor, Stephen J. Markman, Elizabeth A. Weaver, Michael F. Cavanagh, and Marilyn J. Kelly.

Young, J.

We are presented again with a clash of two bedrock principles of our legal tradition: the sacrosanct right of individuals to dominion over their private property, on the one hand and, on the other, the state's authority to condemn private property for the commonweal. In this case, Wayne County would use the power of eminent domain to condemn defendants' real properties for the construction of a 1,300-acre business and technology park. This proposed commercial center is intended to reinvigorate the struggling economy of southeastern Michigan by attracting businesses, particularly those involved in developing new technologies, to the area.

Defendants argue that this exercise of the power of eminent domain is neither authorized by statute nor permitted under article 10 of the 1963 Michigan Constitution, which requires that any condemnation of private property advance a "public use." Both the Wayne Circuit Court and the Court of Appeals rejected these arguments—compelled, in no small measure, by this Court's opinion in Poletown Neighborhood Council v. Detroit....

We conclude that, although these condemnations are authorized by MCL 213.23, they do not pass constitutional muster under art. 10, §2 of our 1963 constitution. Section 2 permits the exercise of the power of eminent domain only for a "public use." In this case, Wayne County intends to transfer the condemned properties to private parties in a manner wholly inconsistent with the common understanding of "public use" at the time our Constitution was ratified. Therefore, we reverse the judgment of the Court of Appeals and remand the case to the Wayne Circuit Court for entry of summary disposition in defendants' favor. * * *

B. Art 10, §2

Art. 10, §2 of Michigan's 1963 Constitution provides that "private property shall not be taken for public use without just compensation therefor being first made or secured in a manner prescribed by law." Plaintiffs contend that the proposed condemnations are not "for public use," and therefore are not within constitutional bounds. Accordingly, our analysis must now focus on the "public use" requirement of Art. 10, §2.

---

the City of Detroit Downtown Development Authority, and the Michigan Downtown and Financing Association.

Williams Acosta, P.L.L.C. (by Avery K. Williams), Detroit, for amici curiae the city of Detroit.

Michael A. Cox, Attorney General, Thomas L. Casey, Solicitor General, and S. Peter Manning, Assistant Attorney General, Lansing, for amici curiae the Environment, Natural Resources, and Agriculture Division.

Ronald Reosti, Detroit, Ralph Nader, Washington, D.C., and Alan Hirsch, Williamstown, MA, for amici curiae the citizens of Michigan.

John F. Rohe, Petoskey, MI, and Georgetown Environmental Law & Policy Institute (by Robert G. Dreher), Washington, D.C., for amici curiae the National Congress for Community Economic Development.

Marc K. Shaye, Franklin, MI, James S. Burling, and Timothy Sandefur, Sacramento, CA, for amici curiae the Pacific Legal Foundation.

Kary L. Moss and Michael J. Steinberg, Detroit, for amici curiae the American Civil Liberties Union Fund of Michigan.

Law Office of Parker and Parker (by John Ceci), Howell, MI, and Institute for Justice (by Dana Berliner, William H. Mellor, Washington, D.C., and Ilya Somin, Assistant Professor of Law), Arlington, VA, for amici curiae the Institute for Justice and Mackinac Center for Public Policy.

1. "Public Use" as a Legal Term of Art

This case does not require that this Court cobble together a single, comprehensive definition of "public use" from our pre-1963 precedent and other relevant sources. The question presented here is a fairly discrete one: are the condemnation of defendants' properties and the subsequent transfer of those properties to private entities pursuant to the Pinnacle Project consistent with the common understanding of "public use" at ratification? For the reasons stated below, we answer that question in the negative.

2. "Public Use" and Private Ownership

When our Constitution was ratified in 1963, it was well-established in this Court's eminent domain jurisprudence that the constitutional "public use" requirement was not an absolute bar against the transfer of condemned property to private entities. It was equally clear, however, that the constitutional "public use" requirement worked to prohibit the state from transferring condemned property to private entities for a *private* use. Thus, this Court's eminent domain jurisprudence—at least that portion concerning the reasons for which the state may condemn private property—has focused largely on the area between these poles.

Justice Ryan's Poletown dissent accurately describes the factors that distinguish takings in the former category from those in the latter according to our pre-1963 eminent domain jurisprudence. Accordingly, we conclude that the transfer of condemned property is a "public use" when it possesses one of the three characteristics in our pre-1963 case law identified by Justice Ryan.

First, condemnations in which private land was constitutionally transferred by the condemning authority to a private entity involved "public necessity of the extreme sort otherwise impracticable." The "necessity" that Justice Ryan identified in our pre-1963 case law is a specific kind of need:

> [T]he exercise of eminent domain for private corporations has been limited to those enterprises generating public benefits whose very *existence* depends on the use of land that can be assembled only by the coordination central government alone is capable of achieving.

Justice Ryan listed "highways, railroads, canals, and other instrumentalities of commerce" as examples of this brand of necessity. A corporation constructing a railroad, for example, must lay track so that it forms a more or less straight path from point A to point B. If a property owner between points A and B holds out—say, for example, by refusing to sell his land for any amount less than fifty times its appraised value—the construction of the railroad is halted unless and until the railroad accedes to the property owner's demands. And if owners of adjoining properties receive word of the original property owner's windfall, they too will refuse to sell.

The likelihood that property owners will engage in this tactic makes the acquisition of property for railroads, gas lines, highways, and other such "instrumentalities of commerce" a logistical and practical nightmare. Accordingly, this Court has held that the exercise of eminent domain in such cases—in which collective action is needed to acquire land for vital instrumentalities of commerce—is consistent with the constitutional "public use" requirement.

Second, this Court has found that the transfer of condemned property to a private entity is consistent with the constitution's "public use" requirement when the private entity remains accountable to the public in its use of that property. * * *

Finally, condemned land may be transferred to a private entity when the selection of the land to be condemned is itself based on public concern. In Justice Ryan's words, the property must be selected on the basis of "facts of independent public significance," meaning that the underlying purposes for resorting to condemnation, rather than the subsequent use of condemned land, must satisfy the Constitution's public use requirement.

The primary example of a condemnation in this vein is found in In re Slum Clearance, a 1951 decision from this Court. In that case, we considered the constitutionality of Detroit's condemnation of blighted housing and its subsequent resale of those properties to private persons. The city's *controlling purpose* in condemning the properties was to remove unfit housing and thereby advance public health and safety; subsequent resale of the land cleared of blight was "incidental" to this goal. We concluded, therefore, that the condemnation was indeed a "public use," despite the fact that the condemned properties would inevitably be put to private use. In re Slum Clearance turned on the fact that the act of condemnation *itself*, rather than the use to which the condemned land eventually would be put, was a public use. Thus, as Justice Ryan observed, the condemnation was a "public use" because the land was selected on the basis of "facts of independent public significance" — namely, the need to remedy urban blight for the sake of public health and safety.

The foregoing indicates that the transfer of condemned property to a private entity, seen through the eyes of an individual sophisticated in the law at the time of ratification of our 1963 Constitution, would be appropriate in one of three contexts: (1) where "public necessity of the extreme sort" requires collective action; (2) where the property remains subject to public oversight after transfer to a private entity; and (3) where the property is selected because of "facts of independent public significance," rather than the interests of the private entity to which the property is eventually transferred.

3. Poletown, the Pinnacle Project, and Public Use

The exercise of eminent domain at issue here — the condemnation of defendants' properties for the Pinnacle Project and the subsequent transfer of those properties to private entities — implicates none of the saving elements noted by our pre-1963 eminent domain jurisprudence.

The Pinnacle Project's business and technology park is certainly not an enterprise "whose very *existence* depends on the use of land that can be assembled only by the coordination central government alone is capable of achieving." To the contrary, the landscape of our country is flecked with shopping centers, office parks, clusters of hotels, and centers of entertainment and commerce. We do not believe, and plaintiff does not contend, that these constellations required the exercise of eminent domain or any other form of collective public action for their formation.

Second, the Pinnacle Project is not subject to public oversight to ensure that the property continues to be used for the commonwealth after being sold to private entities. Rather, plaintiff intends for the private entities purchasing defendants' properties to pursue their own financial welfare with the single-mindedness expected of any profit-making enterprise. The public benefit arising from the Pinnacle Project is an epiphenomenon of the eventual property owners' collective attempts at profit maximization. No formal mechanisms exist to ensure that the businesses that would occupy what are now defendants' properties will continue to contribute to the health of the local economy.

Finally, there is nothing about the *act* of condemning defendants' properties that serves the public good in this case. The only public benefits cited by plaintiff arise after the lands are acquired by the government and put to private use. Thus, the present case is quite unlike Slum Clearance because there are no facts of independent public significance (such as the need to promote health and safety) that might justify the condemnation of defendants' lands.

We can only conclude, therefore, that no one sophisticated in the law at the 1963 Constitution's ratification would have understood "public use" to permit the condemnation of defendants' properties for the construction of a business and technology park owned by private entities. Therefore, the condemnations proposed in this case are unconstitutional under art. 10, § 2.

Indeed, the only support for plaintiff's position in our eminent domain jurisprudence is the majority opinion in Poletown. In that opinion per curiam, a majority of this Court concluded that our Constitution permitted the Detroit Economic Development Corporation to condemn private residential properties in order to convey those properties to a private corporation for the construction of an assembly plant.

As an initial matter, the opinion contains an odd but telling internal inconsistency. The majority first acknowledges that the property owners in that case "urge[d the Court] to distinguish between the terms 'use' and 'purpose,' asserting they are not synonymous and have been distinguished in the law of eminent domain." This argument, of course, was central to plaintiffs' case, because the Constitution allows the exercise of eminent domain only for a "public *use*." The Court then asserted that the plaintiffs *conceded* that the Constitution allowed condemnation for a "public use" *or* a "public purpose," despite the fact that such a concession would have dramatically undermined plaintiffs' argument:

> There is no dispute about the law. All agree that condemnation for a public use or purpose is permitted.... The heart of this dispute is whether the proposed condemnation is for the primary benefit of the public or the private user.

The majority therefore contended that plaintiffs waived a distinction they had "urged" upon the Court. And in so doing, the majority was able to avoid the difficult question whether the condemnation of private property for another private entity was a "public use" as that phrase is used in our Constitution.[78]

This inconsistency aside, the majority opinion in Poletown is most notable for its radical and unabashed departure from the entirety of this Court's pre-1963 eminent domain jurisprudence. The opinion departs from the "common understanding" of "public use" at the time of ratification in two fundamental ways.

First, the majority concluded that its power to review the proposed condemnations is limited because

> the determination of what constitutes a public purpose is primarily a legislative function, subject to review by the courts when abused, and the determination of the legislative body of that matter should not be reversed except in instances where such determination is palpable and manifestly arbitrary and incorrect.

The majority derived this principle from a *plurality* opinion of this Court and supported the application of the principle with a citation of an opinion of the United States

---

78. Moreover, as Justice Ryan noted, the majority also conflated the broad construction of "public purpose" in our taxation jurisprudence with the more limited construction of "public purpose" in the eminent domain context.

Supreme Court concerning judicial review of congressional acts under the Fifth Amendment of the federal constitution.[81] Neither case, of course, is binding on this Court in construing the takings clause of our state Constitution, and neither is persuasive authority for the use to which they were put by the Poletown majority.

It is not surprising, however, that the majority would turn to nonbinding precedent for the proposition that the Court's hands were effectively tied by the Legislature. As Justice Ryan's dissent noted:

> In point of fact, this Court has *never* employed the minimal standard of review in an eminent domain case which is adopted by the [Poletown] majority.... Notwithstanding explicit legislative findings, this Court has always made an *independent* determination of what constitutes a public use for which the power of eminent domain may be utilized.

Our eminent domain jurisprudence since Michigan's entry into the union amply supports Justice Ryan's assertion. Questions of public *purpose* aside, whether the proposed condemnations were consistent with the Constitution's "public use" requirement was a constitutional question squarely within the Court's authority. The Court's reliance on Gregory Marina and Berman for the contrary position was, as Justice Ryan observed, "disingenuous."

Second, the Poletown majority concluded, for the first time in the history of our eminent domain jurisprudence, that a generalized economic benefit was sufficient under art. 10, § 2 to justify the transfer of condemned property to a private entity. Before Poletown, we had never held that a private entity's pursuit of profit was a "public use" for constitutional takings purposes simply because one entity's profit maximization contributed to the health of the general economy. * * *

Because Poletown's conception of a public use — that of "alleviating unemployment and revitalizing the economic base of the community" — has no support in the Court's eminent domain jurisprudence before the Constitution's ratification, its interpretation of "public use" in art. 10, § 2 cannot reflect the common understanding of that phrase among those sophisticated in the law at ratification. Consequently, the Poletown analysis provides no legitimate support for the condemnations proposed in this case and, for the reasons stated above, is overruled. * * *

We conclude that the condemnations proposed in this case do not pass constitutional muster because they do not advance a public use as required by Const. 1963, art. 10, § 2. Accordingly, this case is remanded to the Wayne Circuit Court for entry of summary disposition in defendants' favor. * * *

Kelo v. City of New London, Connecticut

545 U.S. 469 (2005)

Institute for Justice, William H. Mellor, Scott G. Bullock, Counsel of Record, Dana Berliner, Steven Simpson, Washington, DC, Sawyer Law Firm, LLC, Scott W. Sawyer, New London, CT, Counsel for Petitioners.

Wesley W. Horton, Counsel of Record, Daniel J. Krisch, Horton, Shields & Knox, P.C., Hartford, CT, Thomas J. Londregan, Jeffrey T. Londregan, Conway & Londregan, P.C.,

---

81. Berman v. Parker, 348 U.S. 26 (1954). Justice Ryan noted in his Poletown dissent that the majority's reliance on this case "[was] particularly disingenuous." Poletown [Neighborhood Council v. City of Detroit, 304 N.W.2d 455], 668 [(1981)].

New London, CT, Edward B. O'Connell, David P. Condon, Waller, Smith & Palmer, P.C., New London, CT, Counsel for the Respondents.

Stevens, J., delivered the opinion of the Court, in which Kennedy, Souter, Ginsburg, and Breyer, JJ., joined. Kennedy, J., filed a concurring opinion. O'Connor, J., filed a dissenting opinion, in which Rehnquist, C. J., and Scalia and Thomas, JJ., joined. Thomas, J., filed a dissenting opinion.

Justice Stevens delivered the opinion of the Court.

In 2000, the city of New London approved a development plan that, in the words of the Supreme Court of Connecticut, was "projected to create in excess of 1,000 jobs, to increase tax and other revenues, and to revitalize an economically distressed city, including its downtown and waterfront areas." In assembling the land needed for this project, the city's development agent has purchased property from willing sellers and proposes to use the power of eminent domain to acquire the remainder of the property from unwilling owners in exchange for just compensation. The question presented is whether the city's proposed disposition of this property qualifies as a "public use" within the meaning of the Takings Clause of the Fifth Amendment to the Constitution.[1]

I.

The city of New London (hereinafter City) sits at the junction of the Thames River and the Long Island Sound in southeastern Connecticut. Decades of economic decline led a state agency in 1990 to designate the City a "distressed municipality." In 1996, the Federal Government closed the Naval Undersea Warfare Center, which had been located in the Fort Trumbull area of the City and had employed over 1,500 people. In 1998, the City's unemployment rate was nearly double that of the State, and its population of just under 24,000 residents was at its lowest since 1920.

These conditions prompted state and local officials to target New London, and particularly its Fort Trumbull area, for economic revitalization. To this end, respondent New London Development Corporation (NLDC), a private nonprofit entity established some years earlier to assist the City in planning economic development, was reactivated. In January 1998, the State authorized a $5.35 million bond issue to support the NLDC's planning activities and a $10 million bond issue toward the creation of a Fort Trumbull State Park. In February, the pharmaceutical company Pfizer Inc. announced that it would build a $300 million research facility on a site immediately adjacent to Fort Trumbull; local planners hoped that Pfizer would draw new business to the area, thereby serving as a catalyst to the area's rejuvenation. After receiving initial approval from the city council, the NLDC continued its planning activities and held a series of neighborhood meetings to educate the public about the process. In May, the city council authorized the NLDC to formally submit its plans to the relevant state agencies for review. Upon obtaining state-level approval, the NLDC finalized an integrated development plan focused on 90 acres of the Fort Trumbull area.

The Fort Trumbull area is situated on a peninsula that juts into the Thames River. The area comprises approximately 115 privately owned properties, as well as the 32 acres of land formerly occupied by the naval facility (Trumbull State Park now occupies

---

1. "[N]or shall private property be taken for public use, without just compensation." U.S. Const., Amdt. 5. That Clause is made applicable to the States by the Fourteenth Amendment. See Chicago, B. & Q.R. Co. v. Chicago, 166 U.S. 226 (1897).

18 of those 32 acres). The development plan encompasses seven parcels. Parcel 1 is designated for a waterfront conference hotel at the center of a "small urban village" that will include restaurants and shopping. This parcel will also have marinas for both recreational and commercial uses. A pedestrian "riverwalk" will originate here and continue down the coast, connecting the waterfront areas of the development. Parcel 2 will be the site of approximately 80 new residences organized into an urban neighborhood and linked by public walkway to the remainder of the development, including the state park. This parcel also includes space reserved for a new U.S. Coast Guard Museum. Parcel 3, which is located immediately north of the Pfizer facility, will contain at least 90,000 square feet of research and development office space. Parcel 4A is a 2.4-acre site that will be used either to support the adjacent state park, by providing parking or retail services for visitors, or to support the nearby marina. Parcel 4B will include a renovated marina, as well as the final stretch of the riverwalk. Parcels 5, 6, and 7 will provide land for office and retail space, parking, and water-dependent commercial uses.

The NLDC intended the development plan to capitalize on the arrival of the Pfizer facility and the new commerce it was expected to attract. In addition to creating jobs, generating tax revenue, and helping to "build momentum for the revitalization of downtown New London," the plan was also designed to make the City more attractive and to create leisure and recreational opportunities on the waterfront and in the park.

The city council approved the plan in January 2000, and designated the NLDC as its development agent in charge of implementation. The city council also authorized the NLDC to purchase property or to acquire property by exercising eminent domain in the City's name. The NLDC successfully negotiated the purchase of most of the real estate in the 90-acre area, but its negotiations with petitioners failed. As a consequence, in November 2000, the NLDC initiated the condemnation proceedings that gave rise to this case.

II.

Petitioner Susette Kelo has lived in the Fort Trumbull area since 1997. She has made extensive improvements to her house, which she prizes for its water view. Petitioner Wilhelmina Dery was born in her Fort Trumbull house in 1918 and has lived there her entire life. Her husband Charles (also a petitioner) has lived in the house since they married some 60 years ago. In all, the nine petitioners own 15 properties in Fort Trumbull—4 in parcel 3 of the development plan and 11 in parcel 4A. Ten of the parcels are occupied by the owner or a family member; the other five are held as investment properties. There is no allegation that any of these properties is blighted or otherwise in poor condition; rather, they were condemned only because they happen to be located in the development area.

In December 2000, petitioners brought this action in the New London Superior Court. They claimed, among other things, that the taking of their properties would violate the "public use" restriction in the Fifth Amendment. After a 7-day bench trial, the Superior Court granted a permanent restraining order prohibiting the taking of the properties located in parcel 4A (park or marina support). It, however, denied petitioners relief as to the properties located in parcel 3 (office space).[4]

---

4. While this litigation was pending before the Superior Court, the NLDC announced that it would lease some of the parcels to private developers in exchange for their agreement to develop the land according to the terms of the development plan. Specifically, the NLDC was negotiating a 99-year ground lease with Corcoran Jennison, a developer selected from a group of applicants. The negotiations contemplated a nominal rent of $1 per year, but no agreement had yet been signed.

After the Superior Court ruled, both sides took appeals to the Supreme Court of Connecticut. That court held, over a dissent, that all of the City's proposed takings were valid. It began by upholding the lower court's determination that the takings were authorized by chapter 132, the State's municipal development statute. That statute expresses a legislative determination that the taking of land, even developed land, as part of an economic development project is a "public use" and in the "public interest." Next, relying on cases such as Hawaii Housing Authority v. Midkiff, 467 U.S. 229 (1984), and Berman v. Parker, 348 U.S. 26 (1954), the court held that such economic development qualified as a valid public use under both the Federal and State Constitutions.

Finally, adhering to its precedents, the court went on to determine, first, whether the takings of the particular properties at issue were "reasonably necessary" to achieving the City's intended public use, and, second, whether the takings were for "reasonably foreseeable needs." The court upheld the trial court's factual findings as to parcel 3, but reversed the trial court as to parcel 4A, agreeing with the City that the intended use of this land was sufficiently definite and had been given "reasonable attention" during the planning process.

The three dissenting justices would have imposed a "heightened" standard of judicial review for takings justified by economic development. Although they agreed that the plan was intended to serve a valid public use, they would have found all the takings unconstitutional because the City had failed to adduce "clear and convincing evidence" that the economic benefits of the plan would in fact come to pass.

We granted certiorari to determine whether a city's decision to take property for the purpose of economic development satisfies the "public use" requirement of the Fifth Amendment.

III.

Two polar propositions are perfectly clear. On the one hand, it has long been accepted that the sovereign may not take the property of A for the sole purpose of transferring it to another private party B, even though A is paid just compensation. On the other hand, it is equally clear that a State may transfer property from one private party to another if future "use by the public" is the purpose of the taking; the condemnation of land for a railroad with common-carrier duties is a familiar example. Neither of these propositions, however, determines the disposition of this case.

As for the first proposition, the City would no doubt be forbidden from taking petitioners' land for the purpose of conferring a private benefit on a particular private party. Nor would the City be allowed to take property under the mere pretext of a public purpose, when its actual purpose was to bestow a private benefit. The takings before us, however, would be executed pursuant to a "carefully considered" development plan. The trial judge and all the members of the Supreme Court of Connecticut agreed that there was no evidence of an illegitimate purpose in this case.[6] Therefore, as was true of

---

6. See 268 Conn., at 159, 843 A.2d, at 595 (Zarella, J., concurring in part and dissenting in part) ("The record clearly demonstrates that the development plan was not intended to serve the interests of Pfizer, Inc., or any other private entity, but rather, to revitalize the local economy by creating temporary and permanent jobs, generating a significant increase in tax revenue, encouraging spin-off economic activities and maximizing public access to the waterfront"). And while the City intends to transfer certain of the parcels to a private developer in a long-term lease—which developer, in turn, is expected to lease the office space and so forth to other private tenants—the identities of those private parties were not known when the plan was adopted. It is, of course, difficult to accuse the government of having taken A's property to benefit the private interests of B when the identity of B was unknown.

the statute challenged in Midkiff, the City's development plan was not adopted "to benefit a particular class of identifiable individuals."

On the other hand, this is not a case in which the City is planning to open the condemned land—at least not in its entirety—to use by the general public. Nor will the private lessees of the land in any sense be required to operate like common carriers, making their services available to all comers. But although such a projected use would be sufficient to satisfy the public use requirement, this "Court long ago rejected any literal requirement that condemned property be put into use for the general public." Indeed, while many state courts in the mid-19th century endorsed "use by the public" as the proper definition of public use, that narrow view steadily eroded over time. Not only was the "use by the public" test difficult to administer (e.g., what proportion of the public need have access to the property? at what price?), but it proved to be impractical given the diverse and always evolving needs of society. Accordingly, when this Court began applying the Fifth Amendment to the States at the close of the 19th century, it embraced the broader and more natural interpretation of public use as "public purpose." Thus, in a case upholding a mining company's use of an aerial bucket line to transport ore over property it did not own, Justice Holmes' opinion for the Court stressed "the inadequacy of use by the general public as a universal test." Strickley v. Highland Boy Gold Mining Co., 200 U.S. 527, 531 (1906).[9] We have repeatedly and consistently rejected that narrow test ever since.

The disposition of this case therefore turns on the question whether the City's development plan serves a "public purpose." Without exception, our cases have defined that concept broadly, reflecting our longstanding policy of deference to legislative judgments in this field.

In Berman v. Parker (1954), this Court upheld a redevelopment plan targeting a blighted area of Washington, D. C., in which most of the housing for the area's 5,000 inhabitants was beyond repair. Under the plan, the area would be condemned and part of it utilized for the construction of streets, schools, and other public facilities. The remainder of the land would be leased or sold to private parties for the purpose of redevelopment, including the construction of low-cost housing.

The owner of a department store located in the area challenged the condemnation, pointing out that his store was not itself blighted and arguing that the creation of a "better balanced, more attractive community" was not a valid public use. Writing for a unanimous Court, Justice Douglas refused to evaluate this claim in isolation, deferring instead to the legislative and agency judgment that the area "must be planned as a whole" for the plan to be successful. The Court explained that "community redevelopment programs need not, by force of the Constitution, be on a piecemeal basis—lot by lot, building by building." The public use underlying the taking was unequivocally affirmed:

> We do not sit to determine whether a particular housing project is or is not desirable. The concept of the public welfare is broad and inclusive.... The values it represents are spiritual as well as physical, aesthetic as well as monetary. It is within the power of the legislature to determine that the community should be beautiful as well as healthy, spacious as well as clean, well-balanced as well as carefully patrolled. In the present case, the Congress and its authorized agencies

---

9. See also Clark v. Nash, 198 U.S. 361 (1905) (upholding a statute that authorized the owner of arid land to widen a ditch on his neighbor's property so as to permit a nearby stream to irrigate his land).

have made determinations that take into account a wide variety of values. It is not for us to reappraise them. If those who govern the District of Columbia decide that the Nation's Capital should be beautiful as well as sanitary, there is nothing in the Fifth Amendment that stands in the way."

In Hawaii Housing Authority v. Midkiff (1984), the Court considered a Hawaii statute whereby fee title was taken from lessors and transferred to lessees (for just compensation) in order to reduce the concentration of land ownership. We unanimously upheld the statute and rejected the Ninth Circuit's view that it was "a naked attempt on the part of the state of Hawaii to take the property of A and transfer it to B solely for B's private use and benefit." Reaffirming Berman's deferential approach to legislative judgments in this field, we concluded that the State's purpose of eliminating the "social and economic evils of a land oligopoly" qualified as a valid public use. Our opinion also rejected the contention that the mere fact that the State immediately transferred the properties to private individuals upon condemnation somehow diminished the public character of the taking. "[I]t is only the taking's purpose, and not its mechanics," we explained, that matters in determining public use.

In that same Term we decided another public use case that arose in a purely economic context. In Ruckelshaus v. Monsanto Co., 467 U.S. 986 (1984), the Court dealt with provisions of the Federal Insecticide, Fungicide, and Rodenticide Act under which the Environmental Protection Agency could consider the data (including trade secrets) submitted by a prior pesticide applicant in evaluating a subsequent application, so long as the second applicant paid just compensation for the data. We acknowledged that the "most direct beneficiaries" of these provisions were the subsequent applicants, but we nevertheless upheld the statute under Berman and Midkiff. We found sufficient Congress' belief that sparing applicants the cost of time-consuming research eliminated a significant barrier to entry in the pesticide market and thereby enhanced competition.

Viewed as a whole, our jurisprudence has recognized that the needs of society have varied between different parts of the Nation, just as they have evolved over time in response to changed circumstances. Our earliest cases in particular embodied a strong theme of federalism, emphasizing the "great respect" that we owe to state legislatures and state courts in discerning local public needs. See Hairston v. Danville & Western R. Co., 208 U.S. 598, 606–607 (1908) (noting that these needs were likely to vary depending on a State's "resources, the capacity of the soil, the relative importance of industries to the general public welfare, and the long-established methods and habits of the people"). For more than a century, our public use jurisprudence has wisely eschewed rigid formulas and intrusive scrutiny in favor of affording legislatures broad latitude in determining what public needs justify the use of the takings power.

IV.

Those who govern the City were not confronted with the need to remove blight in the Fort Trumbull area, but their determination that the area was sufficiently distressed to justify a program of economic rejuvenation is entitled to our deference. The City has carefully formulated an economic development plan that it believes will provide appreciable benefits to the community, including—but by no means limited to—new jobs and increased tax revenue. As with other exercises in urban planning and development,[12] the City is endeavoring to coordinate a variety of commercial, residential, and

---

12. Cf. Village of Euclid v. Ambler Realty Co., 272 U.S. 365 (1926).

recreational uses of land, with the hope that they will form a whole greater than the sum of its parts. To effectuate this plan, the City has invoked a state statute that specifically authorizes the use of eminent domain to promote economic development. Given the comprehensive character of the plan, the thorough deliberation that preceded its adoption, and the limited scope of our review, it is appropriate for us, as it was in Berman, to resolve the challenges of the individual owners, not on a piecemeal basis, but rather in light of the entire plan. Because that plan unquestionably serves a public purpose, the takings challenged here satisfy the public use requirement of the Fifth Amendment.

To avoid this result, petitioners urge us to adopt a new bright-line rule that economic development does not qualify as a public use. Putting aside the unpersuasive suggestion that the City's plan will provide only purely economic benefits, neither precedent nor logic supports petitioners' proposal. Promoting economic development is a traditional and long accepted function of government. There is, moreover, no principled way of distinguishing economic development from the other public purposes that we have recognized. In our cases upholding takings that facilitated agriculture and mining, for example, we emphasized the importance of those industries to the welfare of the States in question, we endorsed the purpose of transforming a blighted area into a "well-balanced" community through redevelopment,[13] in Midkiff, we upheld the interest in breaking up a land oligopoly that "created artificial deterrents to the normal functioning of the State's residential land market," and in Monsanto we accepted Congress' purpose of eliminating a "significant barrier to entry in the pesticide market." It would be incongruous to hold that the City's interest in the economic benefits to be derived from the development of the Fort Trumbull area has less of a public character than any of those other interests. Clearly, there is no basis for exempting economic development from our traditionally broad understanding of public purpose.

Petitioners contend that using eminent domain for economic development impermissibly blurs the boundary between public and private takings. Again, our cases foreclose this objection. Quite simply, the government's pursuit of a public purpose will often benefit individual private parties. For example, in Midkiff, the forced transfer of property conferred a direct and significant benefit on those lessees who were previously unable to purchase their homes. In Monsanto, we recognized that the "most direct beneficiaries" of the data-sharing provisions were the subsequent pesticide applicants, but benefiting them in this way was necessary to promoting competition in the pesticide market.[14] The owner of the department store in Berman objected to "taking from one businessman for the benefit of another businessman," referring to the fact that under the redevelopment plan land

---

13. It is a misreading of Berman to suggest that the only public use upheld in that case was the initial removal of blight. The public use described in Berman extended beyond that to encompass the purpose of *developing* that area to create conditions that would prevent a reversion to blight in the future.... Had the public use in Berman been defined more narrowly, it would have been difficult to justify the taking of the plaintiff's nonblighted department store.

14. Any number of cases illustrate that the achievement of a public good often coincides with the immediate benefiting of private parties. See, e.g., National Railroad Passenger Corporation v. Boston & Maine Corp., 503 U.S. 407 (1992) (public purpose of "facilitating Amtrak's rail service" served by taking rail track from one private company and transferring it to another private company); Brown v. Legal Foundation of Wash., 538 U.S. 216 (2003) (provision of legal services to the poor is a valid public purpose). It is worth noting that in Hawaii Housing Authority v. Midkiff (1984), Monsanto, and Boston & Maine Corp., the property in question retained the same use even after the change of ownership.

would be leased or sold to private developers for redevelopment.[15] Our rejection of that contention has particular relevance to the instant case: "The public end may be as well or better served through an agency of private enterprise than through a department of government—or so the Congress might conclude. We cannot say that public ownership is the sole method of promoting the public purposes of community redevelopment projects."[16]

It is further argued that without a bright-line rule nothing would stop a city from transferring citizen A's property to citizen B for the sole reason that citizen B will put the property to a more productive use and thus pay more taxes. Such a one-to-one transfer of property, executed outside the confines of an integrated development plan, is not presented in this case. While such an unusual exercise of government power would certainly raise a suspicion that a private purpose was afoot, the hypothetical cases posited by petitioners can be confronted if and when they arise.[18] They do not warrant the crafting of an artificial restriction on the concept of public use.[19]

Alternatively, petitioners maintain that for takings of this kind we should require a "reasonable certainty" that the expected public benefits will actually accrue. Such a rule, however, would represent an even greater departure from our precedent. "When the legislature's purpose is legitimate and its means are not irrational, our cases make clear that empirical debates over the wisdom of takings—no less than debates over the wisdom of other kinds of socioeconomic legislation—are not to be carried out in the federal courts." Midkiff. The disadvantages of a heightened form of review are especially pronounced in this type of case. Orderly implementation of a comprehensive redevelopment plan obviously requires that the legal rights of all interested parties be established before new construction can be commenced. A constitutional rule that required postponement of the judicial approval of every condemnation until the likelihood of

---

15. Notably, as in the instant case, the private developers in Berman were required by contract to use the property to carry out the redevelopment plan.

16. Nor do our cases support Justice O'Connor's novel theory that the government may only take property and transfer it to private parties when the initial taking eliminates some "harmful property use." There was nothing "harmful" about the nonblighted department store at issue in Berman; nothing "harmful" about the lands at issue in the mining and agriculture cases; and certainly nothing "harmful" about the trade secrets owned by the pesticide manufacturers in Monsanto. In each case, the public purpose we upheld depended on a private party's *future* use of the concededly nonharmful property that was taken. By focusing on a property's future use, as opposed to its past use, our cases are faithful to the text of the Takings Clause. See U.S. Const., Amdt. 5. ("[N]or shall private property be taken for public use, without just compensation"). Justice O'Connor's intimation that a "public purpose" may not be achieved by the action of private parties confuses the *purpose* of a taking with its *mechanics,* a mistake we warned of in Midkiff. See also Berman ("The public end may be as well or better served through an agency of private enterprise than through a department of government").

18. Cf. Panhandle Oil Co. v. Mississippi ex rel. Knox, 277 U.S. 218(1928) (Holmes, J., dissenting) ("The power to tax is not the power to destroy while this Court sits").

19. A parade of horribles is especially unpersuasive in this context, since the Takings Clause largely "operates as a conditional limitation, permitting the government to do what it wants so long as it pays the charge." Eastern Enterprises v. Apfel, 524 U.S. 498, 545 (1998) (Kennedy, J., concurring in judgment and dissenting in part). Speaking of the takings power, Justice Iredell observed that "[i]t is not sufficient to urge, that the power may be abused, for, such is the nature of all power—such is the tendency of every human institution: and, it might as fairly be said, that the power of taxation, which is only circumscribed by the discretion of the Body, in which it is vested, ought not to be granted, because the Legislature, disregarding its true objects, might, for visionary and useless projects, impose a tax to the amount of nineteen shillings in the pound. We must be content to limit power where we can, and where we cannot, consistently with its use, we must be content to repose a salutary confidence." Calder [v. Bull, 3 U.S. 386, 400 (1798)] (opinion concurring in result).

success of the plan had been assured would unquestionably impose a significant impediment to the successful consummation of many such plans.

Just as we decline to second-guess the City's considered judgments about the efficacy
of its development plan, we also decline to second-guess the City's determinations as to
what lands it needs to acquire in order to effectuate the project. "It is not for the courts
to oversee the choice of the boundary line nor to sit in review on the size of a particular
project area. Once the question of the public purpose has been decided, the amount
and character of land to be taken for the project and the need for a particular tract to
complete the integrated plan rests in the discretion of the legislative branch." Berman.

In affirming the City's authority to take petitioners' properties, we do not minimize
the hardship that condemnations may entail, notwithstanding the payment of just compensation. We emphasize that nothing in our opinion precludes any State from placing
further restrictions on its exercise of the takings power. Indeed, many States already impose "public use" requirements that are stricter than the federal baseline. Some of these
requirements have been established as a matter of state constitutional law,[22] while others
are expressed in state eminent domain statutes that carefully limit the grounds upon
which takings may be exercised.[23] As the submissions of the parties and their *amici*
make clear, the necessity and wisdom of using eminent domain to promote economic
development are certainly matters of legitimate public debate.[24] This Court's authority,
however, extends only to determining whether the City's proposed condemnations are
for a "public use" within the meaning of the Fifth Amendment to the Federal Constitution. Because over a century of our case law interpreting that provision dictates an affirmative answer to that question, we may not grant petitioners the relief that they seek.

The judgment of the Supreme Court of Connecticut is affirmed. * * *

**Justice O'Connor, with whom The Chief Justice, Justice Scalia, and Justice Thomas
join, dissenting.**

Over two centuries ago, just after the Bill of Rights was ratified, Justice Chase wrote:

> An ACT of the Legislature (for I cannot call it a law) contrary to the great first
> principles of the social compact, cannot be considered a rightful exercise of
> legislative authority.... A few instances will suffice to explain what I mean....
> [A] law that takes property from A. and gives it to B: It is against all reason and
> justice, for a people to entrust a Legislature with SUCH powers; and, therefore,
> it cannot be presumed that they have done it. Calder v. Bull, 3 Dall. 386, 388
> (1798) (emphasis deleted).

Today the Court abandons this long-held, basic limitation on government power.
Under the banner of economic development, all private property is now vulnerable to

---

22. See, e.g., County of Wayne v. Hathcock, 471 Mich. 445 (2004).

23. Under California law, for instance, a city may only take land for economic development purposes in blighted areas.

24. For example, some argue that the need for eminent domain has been greatly exaggerated because private developers can use numerous techniques, including secret negotiations or precommit-
ment strategies, to overcome holdout problems and assemble lands for genuinely profitable projects.
See Brief for Jane Jacobs as *Amicus Curiae* 13–15; see also Brief for John Norquist as *Amicus Curiae*.
Others argue to the contrary, urging that the need for eminent domain is especially great with regard to older, small cities like New London, where centuries of development have created an extreme overdivision of land and thus a real market impediment to land assembly. See Brief for Connecticut Conference for Municipalities et al. as *Amici Curiae* 13, 21; see also Brief for National
League of Cities et al. as *Amici Curiae*.

being taken and transferred to another private owner, so long as it might be up-graded—i.e., given to an owner who will use it in a way that the legislature deems more beneficial to the public—in the process. To reason, as the Court does, that the incidental public benefits resulting from the subsequent ordinary use of private property render economic development takings "for public use" is to wash out any distinction between private and public use of property—and thereby effectively to delete the words "for public use" from the Takings Clause of the Fifth Amendment. Accordingly I respectfully dissent.

I.

Petitioners are nine resident or investment owners of 15 homes in the Fort Trumbull neighborhood of New London, Connecticut. Petitioner Wilhelmina Dery, for example, lives in a house on Walbach Street that has been in her family for over 100 years. She was born in the house in 1918; her husband, petitioner Charles Dery, moved into the house when they married in 1946. Their son lives next door with his family in the house he received as a wedding gift, and joins his parents in this suit. Two petitioners keep rental properties in the neighborhood.

In February 1998, Pfizer Inc., the pharmaceuticals manufacturer, announced that it would build a global research facility near the Fort Trumbull neighborhood. Two months later, New London's city council gave initial approval for the New London Development Corporation (NLDC) to prepare the development plan at issue here. The NLDC is a private, nonprofit corporation whose mission is to assist the city council in economic development planning. It is not elected by popular vote, and its directors and employees are privately appointed. Consistent with its mandate, the NLDC generated an ambitious plan for redeveloping 90 acres of Fort Trumbull in order to "complement the facility that Pfizer was planning to build, create jobs, increase tax and other revenues, encourage public access to and use of the city's waterfront, and eventually 'build momentum' for the revitalization of the rest of the city."

Petitioners own properties in two of the plan's seven parcels—Parcel 3 and Parcel 4A. Under the plan, Parcel 3 is slated for the construction of research and office space as a market develops for such space. It will also retain the existing Italian Dramatic Club (a private cultural organization) though the homes of three plaintiffs in that parcel are to be demolished. Parcel 4A is slated, mysteriously, for "'park support.'" At oral argument, counsel for respondents conceded the vagueness of this proposed use, and offered that the parcel might eventually be used for parking.

To save their homes, petitioners sued New London and the NLDC, to whom New London has delegated eminent domain power. Petitioners maintain that the Fifth Amendment prohibits the NLDC from condemning their properties for the sake of an economic development plan. Petitioners are not hold-outs; they do not seek increased compensation, and none is opposed to new development in the area. Theirs is an objection in principle: They claim that the NLDC's proposed use for their confiscated property is not a "public" one for purposes of the Fifth Amendment. While the government may take their homes to build a road or a railroad or to eliminate a property use that harms the public, say petitioners, it cannot take their property for the private use of other owners simply because the new owners may make more productive use of the property.

II.

The Fifth Amendment to the Constitution, made applicable to the States by the Fourteenth Amendment, provides that "private property [shall not] be taken for public use, without just compensation." When interpreting the Constitution, we begin with the unremarkable presumption that every word in the document has independent meaning, "that no word was unnecessarily used, or needlessly added." Wright v. United States, 302 U.S. 583 (1938). In keeping with that presumption, we have read the Fifth Amendment's language to impose two distinct conditions on the exercise of eminent domain: "the taking must be for a 'public use' and 'just compensation' must be paid to the owner." Brown v. Legal Foundation of Wash., 538 U.S. 216, 231–232 (2003).

These two limitations serve to protect "the security of Property," which Alexander Hamilton described to the Philadelphia Convention as one of the "great obj[ects] of Gov[ernment]." 1 Records of the Federal Convention of 1787, p. 302 (M. Farrand ed.1934). Together they ensure stable property ownership by providing safeguards against excessive, unpredictable, or unfair use of the government's eminent domain power—particularly against those owners who, for whatever reasons, may be unable to protect themselves in the political process against the majority's will.

While the Takings Clause presupposes that government can take private property without the owner's consent, the just compensation requirement spreads the cost of condemnations and thus "prevents the public from loading upon one individual more than his just share of the burdens of government." Monongahela Nav. Co. v. United States, 148 U.S. 312, 325 (1893). The public use requirement, in turn, imposes a more basic limitation, circumscribing the very scope of the eminent domain power: Government may compel an individual to forfeit her property for the *public's* use, but not for the benefit of another private person. This requirement promotes fairness as well as security.

Where is the line between "public" and "private" property use? We give considerable deference to legislatures' determinations about what governmental activities will advantage the public. But were the political branches the sole arbiters of the public-private distinction, the Public Use Clause would amount to little more than hortatory fluff. An external, judicial check on how the public use requirement is interpreted, however limited, is necessary if this constraint on government power is to retain any meaning.

Our cases have generally identified three categories of takings that comply with the public use requirement, though it is in the nature of things that the boundaries between these categories are not always firm. Two are relatively straightforward and uncontroversial. First, the sovereign may transfer private property to public ownership—such as for a road, a hospital, or a military base. Second, the sovereign may transfer private property to private parties, often common carriers, who make the property available for the public's use—such as with a railroad, a public utility, or a stadium. But "public ownership" and "use-by-the-public" are sometimes too constricting and impractical ways to define the scope of the Public Use Clause. Thus we have allowed that, in certain circumstances and to meet certain exigencies, takings that serve a public purpose also satisfy the Constitution even if the property is destined for subsequent private use. See, e.g., Berman v. Parker (1954); Hawaii Housing Authority v. Midkiff (1984).

This case returns us for the first time in over 20 years to the hard question of when a purportedly "public purpose" taking meets the public use requirement. It presents an issue of first impression: Are economic development takings constitutional? I would hold that they are not. We are guided by two precedents about the taking of real property by eminent domain. In Berman, we upheld takings within a blighted neigh-

borhood of Washington, D.C. The neighborhood had so deteriorated that, for example, 64.3% of its dwellings were beyond repair. It had become burdened with "overcrowding of dwellings," "lack of adequate streets and alleys," and "lack of light and air."
Congress had determined that the neighborhood had become "injurious to the public
health, safety, morals, and welfare" and that it was necessary to "eliminat[e] all such
injurious conditions by employing all means necessary and appropriate for the purpose," including eminent domain. Mr. Berman's department store was not itself
blighted. Having approved of Congress' decision to eliminate the harm to the public
emanating from the blighted neighborhood, however, we did not second-guess its decision to treat the neighborhood as a whole rather than lot-by-lot. See also Midkiff,
467 U.S., at 244 ("it is only the taking's purpose, and not its mechanics, that must pass
scrutiny").

In Midkiff, we upheld a land condemnation scheme in Hawaii whereby title in real
property was taken from lessors and transferred to lessees. At that time, the State and
Federal Governments owned nearly 49% of the State's land, and another 47% was in the
hands of only 72 private landowners. Concentration of land ownership was so dramatic
that on the State's most urbanized island, Oahu, 22 landowners owned 72.5% of the fee
simple titles. The Hawaii Legislature had concluded that the oligopoly in land ownership was "skewing the State's residential fee simple market, inflating land prices, and in-
juring the public tranquility and welfare," and therefore enacted a condemnation
scheme for redistributing title.

In those decisions, we emphasized the importance of deferring to legislative judgments about public purpose. Because courts are ill-equipped to evaluate the efficacy of
proposed legislative initiatives, we rejected as unworkable the idea of courts' "'deciding
on what is and is not a governmental function and … invalidating legislation on the
basis of their view on that question at the moment of decision, a practice which has
proved impracticable in other fields.'" Id., at 240–241 (quoting United States ex rel.
TVA v. Welch, 327 U.S. 546, 552 (1946)); see Berman, supra, at 32 ("[T]he legislature,
not the judiciary, is the main guardian of the public needs to be served by social legislation"). Likewise, we recognized our inability to evaluate whether, in a given case, eminent domain is a necessary means by which to pursue the legislature's ends. Midkiff,
supra, at 242; Berman, supra, at 103.

Yet for all the emphasis on deference, Berman and Midkiff hewed to a bedrock principle without which our public use jurisprudence would collapse: "A purely private taking could not withstand the scrutiny of the public use requirement; it would serve no
legitimate purpose of government and would thus be void." Midkiff, 467 U.S., at 245,
id., at 241 ("[T]he Court's cases have repeatedly stated that 'one person's property may
not be taken for the benefit of another private person without a justifying public purpose, even though compensation be paid.'" To protect that principle, those decisions reserved "a role for courts to play in reviewing a legislature's judgment of what constitutes
a public use … [though] the Court in Berman made clear that it is 'an extremely narrow' one." Midkiff, supra, at 240 (quoting Berman, supra, at 32).

The Court's holdings in Berman and Midkiff were true to the principle underlying
the Public Use Clause. In both those cases, the extraordinary, precondemnation use of
the targeted property inflicted affirmative harm on society—in Berman through blight
resulting from extreme poverty and in Midkiff through oligopoly resulting from extreme wealth. And in both cases, the relevant legislative body had found that eliminating the existing property use was necessary to remedy the harm. Thus a public purpose
was realized when the harmful use was eliminated. Because each taking *directly* achieved

a public benefit, it did not matter that the property was turned over to private use. Here, in contrast, New London does not claim that Susette Kelo's and Wilhelmina Dery's well-maintained homes are the source of any social harm. Indeed, it could not so claim without adopting the absurd argument that any single-family home that might be razed to make way for an apartment building, or any church that might be replaced with a retail store, or any small business that might be more lucrative if it were instead part of a national franchise, is inherently harmful to society and thus within the government's power to condemn.

In moving away from our decisions sanctioning the condemnation of harmful property use, the Court today significantly expands the meaning of public use. It holds that the sovereign may take private property currently put to ordinary private use, and give it over for new, ordinary private use, so long as the new use is predicted to generate some secondary benefit for the public—such as increased tax revenue, more jobs, maybe even aesthetic pleasure. But nearly any lawful use of real private property can be said to generate some incidental benefit to the public. Thus, if predicted (or even guaranteed) positive side-effects are enough to render transfer from one private party to another constitutional, then the words "for public use" do not realistically exclude *any* takings, and thus do not exert any constraint on the eminent domain power.

There is a sense in which this troubling result follows from errant language in Berman and Midkiff. In discussing whether takings within a blighted neighborhood were for a public use, Berman began by observing: "We deal, in other words, with what traditionally has been known as the police power." From there it declared that "[o]nce the object is within the authority of Congress, the right to realize it through the exercise of eminent domain is clear." Following up, we said in Midkiff that "[t]he 'public use' requirement is coterminous with the scope of a sovereign's police powers." This language was unnecessary to the specific holdings of those decisions. Berman and Midkiff simply did not put such language to the constitutional test, because the takings in those cases were within the police power but also for "public use" for the reasons I have described. The case before us now demonstrates why, when deciding if a taking's purpose is constitutional, the police power and "public use" cannot always be equated. The Court protests that it does not sanction the bare transfer from A to B for B's benefit. It suggests two limitations on what can be taken after today's decision. First, it maintains a role for courts in ferreting out takings whose sole purpose is to bestow a benefit on the private transferee—without detailing how courts are to conduct that complicated inquiry. For his part, Justice Kennedy suggests that courts may divine illicit purpose by a careful review of the record and the process by which a legislature arrived at the decision to take—without specifying what courts should look for in a case with different facts, how they will know if they have found it, and what to do if they do not. (Concurring opinion). Whatever the details of Justice Kennedy's as-yet-undisclosed test, it is difficult to envision anyone but the "stupid staff[er]" failing it. See Lucas v. South Carolina Coastal Council, 505 U.S. 1003, 1025-1026, n. 12 (1992). The trouble with economic development takings is that private benefit and incidental public benefit are, by definition, merged and mutually reinforcing. In this case, for example, any boon for Pfizer or the plan's developer is difficult to disaggregate from the promised public gains in taxes and jobs.

Even if there were a practical way to isolate the motives behind a given taking, the gesture toward a purpose test is theoretically flawed. If it is true that incidental public benefits from new private use are enough to ensure the "public purpose" in a taking, why should it matter, as far as the Fifth Amendment is concerned, what inspired the taking in the first place? How much the government does or does not desire to benefit a favored private party has no bearing on whether an economic development taking will or will not generate secondary benefit for the public. And whatever the reason for a given condemnation, the effect is the same from the constitutional perspective—private property is forcibly relinquished to new private ownership.

A second proposed limitation is implicit in the Court's opinion. The logic of today's decision is that eminent domain may only be used to upgrade—not downgrade—property. At best this makes the Public Use Clause redundant with the Due Process Clause, which already prohibits irrational government action. See Lingle, 544 U.S. [528], 125 S.Ct. 2074. The Court rightfully admits, however, that the judiciary cannot get bogged down in predictive judgments about whether the public will actually be better off after a property transfer. In any event, this constraint has no realistic import. For who among us can say she already makes the most productive or attractive possible use of her property? The specter of condemnation hangs over all property. Nothing is to prevent the State from replacing any Motel 6 with a Ritz-Carlton, any home with a shopping mall, or any farm with a factory. Cf. Bugryn v. Bristol, 63 Conn.App. 98, 774 A.2d 1042 (2001) (taking the homes and farm of four owners in their 70's and 80's and giving it to an "industrial park"); 99 Cents Only Stores v. Lancaster Redevelopment Agency, 237 F.Supp.2d 1123 (C.D.Cal.2001) (attempted taking of 99 Cents store to replace with a Costco); Poletown Neighborhood Council v. Detroit, 410 Mich. 616, 304 N.W.2d 455 (1981) (taking a working-class, immigrant community in Detroit and giving it to a General Motors assembly plant), overruled by County of Wayne v. Hathcock, 471 Mich. 445, 684 N.W.2d 765 (2004); Brief for the Becket Fund for Religious Liberty as *Amicus Curiae* 4–11 (describing takings of religious institutions' properties); Institute for Justice, D. Berliner, Public Power, Private Gain: A Five-Year, State-by-State Report Examining the Abuse of Eminent Domain (2003) (collecting accounts of economic development takings).

The Court also puts special emphasis on facts peculiar to this case: The NLDC's plan is the product of a relatively careful deliberative process; it proposes to use eminent domain for a multipart, integrated plan rather than for isolated property transfer; it promises an array of incidental benefits (even aesthetic ones), not just increased tax revenue; it comes on the heels of a legislative determination that New London is a depressed municipality. See, e.g., ante, at 16 ("[A] one-to-one transfer of property, executed outside the confines of an integrated development plan, is not presented in this case"). Justice Kennedy, too, takes great comfort in these facts. Ante, at 4 (concurring opinion). But none has legal significance to blunt the force of today's holding. If legislative prognostications about the secondary public benefits of a new use can legitimate a taking, there is nothing in the Court's rule or in Justice Kennedy's gloss on that rule to prohibit property transfers generated with less care, that are less comprehensive, that happen to result from less elaborate process, whose only projected advantage is the incidence of higher taxes, or that hope to transform an already prosperous city into an even more prosperous one.

Finally, in a coda, the Court suggests that property owners should turn to the States, who may or may not choose to impose appropriate limits on economic development takings. This is an abdication of our responsibility. States play many important functions in our system of dual sovereignty, but compensating for our refusal to enforce properly the Federal Constitution (and a provision meant to curtail state action, no less) is not among them. * * *

It was possible after Berman and Midkiff to imagine unconstitutional transfers from A to B. Those decisions endorsed government intervention when private property use had veered to such an extreme that the public was suffering as a consequence. Today nearly all real property is susceptible to condemnation on the Court's theory. In the prescient words of a dissenter from the infamous decision in Poletown, "[n]ow that we have authorized local legislative bodies to decide that a different commercial or industrial use of property will produce greater public benefits than its present use, no homeowner's, merchant's or manufacturer's property, however productive or valuable to its owner, is immune from condemnation for the benefit of other private interests that will put it to a 'higher' use." 410 Mich., at 644–645, 304 N.W.2d, at 464 (opinion of Fitzgerald, J.). This is why economic development takings "seriously jeopardiz[e] the security of all private property ownership." Id., at 645, 304 N.W.2d, at 465 (Ryan, J., dissenting).

Any property may now be taken for the benefit of another private party, but the fallout from this decision will not be random. The beneficiaries are likely to be those citizens with disproportionate influence and power in the political process, including large corporations and development firms. As for the victims, the government now has license to transfer property from those with fewer resources to those with more. The Founders cannot have intended this perverse result. "[T]hat alone is a *just* government," wrote James Madison, "which *impartially* secures to every man, whatever is his *own*." For the National Gazette, Property, (Mar. 29, 1792), reprinted in 14 Papers of James Madison 266 (R. Rutland et al. eds.1983).

I would hold that the takings in both Parcel 3 and Parcel 4A are unconstitutional, reverse the judgment of the Supreme Court of Connecticut, and remand for further proceedings.

Norwood v. Horney

853 N.E.2d 1115 (Supreme Court of Ohio 2006), 2006 OH 3799

Wood & Lamping, L.L.P., and Robert P. Malloy; and Institute for Justice, Dana Berliner, Scott G. Bullock, William H. Mellor, Robert W. Gall, and David Roland, for appellants.*

---

* Coolidge, Wall, Womsley & Lombard Co., L.P.A., and John C. Chambers, urging affirmance in case Nos. 2005-1210 and 2005-1211 on behalf of amici curiae First Suburbs Consortium of Northeast Ohio, Central Ohio First Suburbs Consortium, First Suburbs Consortium of Southwest Ohio, and First Tier Suburbs Consortium.

Lindner & Weaver, L.L.P., and Daniel F. Lindner, urging affirmance in case Nos. 2005-1210 and 2005-1211 on behalf of amici curiae American Planning Association and Ohio Planning Conference.

Baker & Hostetler, L.L.P., John H. Burtch, David C. Levine, and Marcella L. Lape, urging reversal in case Nos. 2005-1210 and 2005-1211 on behalf of amicus curiae Ohio Association of Realtors.

Michael R. Gareau & Associates, L.P.A., and David M. Gareau, urging reversal in case Nos. 2005-1210 and 2005-1211 on behalf of amici curiae Pacific Legal Foundation and the Claremont Institute.

Jones Day, Mark Herrmann, and Mary Beth Young; and Derek L. Gaubatz, Anthony R. Picarello Jr., and Jared N. Leland, urging reversal in case Nos. 2005-1210 and 2005-1211 on behalf of amicus curiae Becket Fund for Religious Liberty.

Barbara J. Morley and Donald Gallick, urging reversal in case Nos. 2005-1210 and 2005-1211 on behalf of amicus curiae the Reason Foundation.

Gibson Dunn & Crutcher, L.L.P., Jeffrey A. Wadsworth, and Rachel Zwolinski, urging reversal in case Nos. 2005-1210 and 2005-1211 on behalf of amicus curiae Individual Ohio Home and Business Owners.

Hughes & Luce, L.L.P., and Matthew R. Miller, urging reversal in case Nos. 2005-1210 and 2005-1211 on behalf of amicus curiae Property & Environment Research Center.

Jones Day, Douglas M. Mansfield, and Chad A. Readler, urging reversal in case Nos. 2005-1210 and 2005-1211 on behalf of amici curiae Ohio Farm Bureau Federation and Hamilton County Farm Bureau.

Manley Burke, L.P.A., Timothy M. Burke, Gary E. Powell, and Daniel J. McCarthy; and Rick G. Gibson, City of Norwood Law Director, and Theodore E. Kiser, Assistant Law Director, for appellee city of Norwood.

Dinsmore & Shohl, L.L.P., Mark A. Vander Laan, Bryan E. Pacheco, Lawrence R. Elleman, and Richard B. Tranter, for appellee Rookwood Partners, Ltd.

Moyer, C.J., Resnick, Pfeifer, Lundberg Stratton, O'Donnell and Lanzinger, JJ., concur.

James A. Brogan, J., of the Second Appellate District, sitting for Resnick, J.

O'Connor, J.

In [these] case[s], we decide the constitutionality of a municipality's taking of an individual's property by eminent domain and transferring the property to a private entity for redevelopment. In doing so, we must balance two competing interests of great import in American democracy: the individual's rights in the possession and security of property, and the sovereign's power to take private property for the benefit of the community.

In case Nos. 2005-0227 and 2005-0228, we determine the constitutionality of the provision in R.C. 163.19 prohibiting a court from enjoining the taking and using of property appropriated by the government and transferred to a private party for redevelopment, after the compensation for the property has been deposited with the court but prior to appellate review of the taking.

Our consideration does not take place in a vacuum. We recognize that eminent domain engenders great debate. Its use, though necessary, is fraught with great economic, social, and legal implications for the individual and the community. See, generally, Keasha Broussard, *Social Consequences of Eminent Domain: Urban Revitalization Against the Backdrop of the Takings Clause* (2000), 24 Law & Psychology Rev. 99.

Appropriation cases often represent more than a battle over a plot of cold sod in a farmland pasture or the plat of municipal land on which a building sits. For the individual property owner, the appropriation is not simply the seizure of a house. It is the taking of a home—the place where ancestors toiled, where families were raised, where memories were made. Fittingly, appropriations are scrutinized by the people and debated in their institutions.

In reviewing an appropriation similar to that at issue here, a sharply divided United States Supreme Court recently upheld the taking over a federal Fifth Amendment challenge mounted by individual property owners. Kelo v. New London (2005). Although it determined that the federal constitution did not prohibit the takings, the court acknowledged that property owners might find redress in the states' courts and legislatures, which remain free to restrict such takings pursuant to state laws and constitutions.

Browning & Meyer Co., L.P.A., and William J. Browning; and O'Melveny & Myers, L.L.P., Brian P. Brooks, and Garrett W. Wotkyns, urging reversal in case Nos. 2005-1210 and 2005-1211 on behalf of amici curiae Ohio Conference of the National Association for the Advancement of Colored Persons and National Institute for Urban Entrepreneurship.

Porter Wright Morris & Arthur, L.L.P., David C. Tryon, Jeffrey J. Weber, and Patrick T. Lewis, urging reversal in case Nos. 2005-1210 and 2005-1211 on behalf of amici curiae National Federation of Independent Business Legal Foundation and American Association of Small Property Owners.

William G. Batchelder; and Kirkland & Ellis, L.L.P., Douglas G. Smith, Larry J. Obhof, and Andrew P. Bautista, urging reversal in case Nos. 2005-1210 and 2005-1211 on behalf of amici curiae Ashbrook Center for Public Affairs and William G. Batchelder.

Ely M.T. Ryder urging affirmance in case Nos. 2005-1210 and 2005-1211 on behalf of amici curiae Donna Laake, William Pierani, and Paul Triance.

In response to that invitation in Kelo, Ohio's General Assembly unanimously enacted 2005 Am.Sub.S.B. No. 167. The legislature expressly noted in the Act its belief that as a result of Kelo, "the interpretation and use of the state's eminent domain law could be expanded to allow the taking of private property that is not within a blighted area, ultimately resulting in ownership of that property being vested in another private person in violation of Sections 1 and 19 of Article I, Ohio Constitution." Section 4(A), 2005 Am.Sub.S.B. No. 167. The Act created a task force to study the use and application of eminent domain in Ohio, and imposed "a moratorium on any takings of this nature by any public body until further legislative remedies may be considered."[2]

We now turn to the cases pending before us, which raise social and legal issues similar to those in Kelo.

The appellants' property was appropriated by the city of Norwood after the city determined that the appellants' neighborhood was a "deteriorating area," as that term is defined in the provisions governing appropriations in the Codified Ordinances of the City of Norwood ("Norwood Code"). Although, as we shall discuss below, we have held that a city may take a slum, blighted, or deteriorated property for redevelopment, State ex rel. Bruestle v. Rich (1953), 159 Ohio St. 13, 50 O.O. 6, 110 N.E.2d 778, and suggested that the taking is proper even when the city transfers the appropriated property to a private party for redevelopment, AAAA Ents., Inc. v. River Place Community Urban Redevelopment Corp. (1990), 50 Ohio St.3d 157, 553 N.E.2d 597, we have never been asked whether a city may appropriate property that the city determines is in an area that may deteriorate in the future.

We hold that although economic factors may be considered in determining whether private property may be appropriated, the fact that the appropriation would provide an economic benefit to the government and community, standing alone, does not satisfy the public-use requirement of Section 19, Article I of the Ohio Constitution.

We also hold that the void-for-vagueness doctrine applies to statutes that regulate the use of eminent-domain powers. Courts shall apply heightened scrutiny when reviewing statutes that regulate the use of eminent-domain powers. Applying that standard, we find that Norwood's use of "deteriorating area" as a standard for appropriation is void for vagueness. We further hold that the use of the term "deteriorating area" as a standard for a taking is unconstitutional because the term inherently incorporates speculation as to the future condition of the property to be appropriated rather than the condition of the property at the time of the taking.

Finally, we hold that the provision in R.C. 163.19 that prohibits a court from enjoining the taking and using of property appropriated by the government after the compensation for the property has been deposited with the court but prior to appellate review of the taking violates the separation-of-powers doctrine and is therefore unconstitutional. We further hold that the unconstitutional portion of R.C. 163.19 can be severed from the rest of the statute, and, accordingly, the remainder of the statute remains in effect.

I. Relevant Background

A. Norwood and its Denizens

The city of Norwood is a modern urban environment. Surrounded by the city of Cincinnati, Norwood was once home to several manufacturing plants and businesses

---

2. The moratorium expires on December 31, 2006.

that provided a substantial tax base for the municipality. Despite that industrial component, Norwood was, and for many remains, a desirable place to live. Norwood's neighborhoods were comprised of traditional single family houses and duplexes that provided homes to generations of families and many individuals.[3]

Over the past 40 years, however, Norwood underwent many changes. Like many
municipalities in Ohio, Norwood's industrial base eroded, taking with it tax dollars
vital to the city. Municipal jobs and many services were eliminated, and the city is millions of dollars in debt. Though the financial outlook of Norwood has been altered
greatly over the years, perhaps the most significant change for our purposes here is its
physical nature of the city itself.

In the 1960s, property was appropriated from the appellants' neighborhood and
used in the construction of a major highway — Interstate 71 — through Cincinnati. In
the neighborhoods affected, numerous homes were razed and front yards diminished in
order to make way for the access roads and ramps to the highway. The streets became
busier, creating safety problems for residents who had to back onto busy roadways from
their driveways. Residential roads that once ran between major thoroughfares were dis-
sected by the new highway, creating dead-end streets.

Over time, businesses arose in places where houses once stood. The neighborhood
became less residential and more commercial. Other changes in the neighborhood's
character followed. Traffic increased dramatically due to motorists seeking the highway and businesses in the area. Noise increased and light pollution became more
prevalent.

The parties vehemently disagree as to the extent to which these changes adversely affected the physical functionality, aesthetic appeal, and quality of living in the neighborhood. There is no disagreement, however, that the property held commercial value and
that proposed plan for development would raise money for the city.

A private, limited-liability company, Rookwood Partners, Ltd. ("Rookwood"), entered discussions with Norwood about redeveloping the appellants' neighborhood. The
preliminary plans for the development call for the construction of more than 200 apartments or condominiums and over 500,000 square feet of office and retail space (all of
which would be owned by Rookwood), as well as two large public-parking facilities
(which would be owned by Norwood) with spaces for more than 2,000 vehicles. The
city expects the redeveloped area to result in nearly $2,000,000 in annual revenue for
Norwood.

Norwood, operating with a deficit, was unable to fix the problems or redevelop the
appellants' neighborhood on its own, and thus city council was interested in the project.
Discussions between Norwood and Rookwood culminated in a redevelopment contract
in which Rookwood agreed to reimburse the city for the expenses of the project, including the costs arising from any need to use eminent domain to appropriate the property
necessary for the project.

Rookwood preferred that Norwood acquire the property needed for the project through
eminent domain, but Norwood resisted. It encouraged Rookwood to purchase the property through voluntary sales of homes and businesses, without the city's intervention.

---

3. Appellants Carl and Joy Gamble lived in the neighborhood for over 35 years before the appropriation. They raised their children there and planned to live the rest of their lives there. Appellants
Joseph P. Horney and his wife, Carol Gooch, once lived in the neighborhood and though now residing elsewhere, owned and operated rental properties in the neighborhood before the appropriation.

Rookwood was largely successful; it secured acquisition agreements from a substantial majority of the owners of the property necessary to complete the project. The appellants, however, refused to sell.

Because the appellants refused to sell their property, Rookwood asked Norwood to appropriate the appellants' properties and transfer them to Rookwood. Rookwood, in turn, agreed to raze the existing structures (including the appellants' homes), reconfigure the streets, and redevelop the area.

B. The Takings

Pursuant to the Norwood Code, an urban-renewal study must be completed before the city can institute eminent-domain proceedings. Norwood used funds provided by Rookwood to retain a consulting firm, Kinzelman Kline Grossman ("KKG"), to prepare an urban-renewal study of the appellants' neighborhood. The study concluded that the construction of I-71 and ensuing conversion of residential and industrial properties to commercial use had led to significant, negative changes in Norwood. Despite acknowledging that many homes were in fair to good condition, KKG concluded that the neighborhood was a "deteriorating area" as that term is defined in the Norwood Code.[5] KKG further determined that the neighborhood would continue to deteriorate and that there would be "continuing piecemeal conversion" of residences to businesses that could be detrimental to the area.

After public hearings and town meetings were held and the local planning commission recommended approval of the redevelopment plan, Norwood City Council passed a series of ordinances adopting the plan and authorizing the mayor to enter the redevelopment agreement with Rookwood and to appropriate the appellants' property. The city then filed complaints against the appellants to appropriate their properties.

At trial, Norwood relied on the testimony of KKG employees to support its conclusion that the appellants' neighborhood was deteriorating. KKG employees testified that the neighborhood was not a slum, blighted, or deteriorated area as that term is defined in the Norwood Code. The trial court found that the critical evidence presented by Norwood conflicted as to the conclusions to be drawn about the neighborhood. In her findings of fact, the trial judge noted that although one KKG witness opined that the

---

5. Norwood Code 163.02(b) defines a "[s]lum, blighted or deteriorated area" as "an area * * * in which there are a majority of structures or other improvements, which, by reason of dilapidation, deterioration, age or obsolescence, inadequate provision for ventilation, light, air, sanitation, or open spaces, high density of population and overcrowding, unsafe and unsanitary conditions or the existence of conditions which endanger life or property by fire or other hazards and causes, or any combination of such factors, and an area with overcrowding or improper location of structures on the land, excessive dwelling unit density, detrimental land uses or conditions, unsafe, congested, poorly designated streets or inadequate public facilities or utilities, all of which substantially impairs the sound growth and planning of the community, is conducive to ill health, transmission of disease, infant mortality, juvenile delinquency and crime, and is detrimental to the public health, safety, morals and general welfare."

Norwood Code 163.02(c) defines a "deteriorating area" as "an area, whether predominantly built up or open, which is not a slum, blighted or deteriorated area but which, because of incompatible land uses, nonconforming uses, lack of adequate parking facilities, faulty street arrangement, obsolete platting, inadequate community and public utilities, diversity of ownership, tax delinquency, increased density of population without commensurate increases in new residential buildings and community facilities, high turnover in residential or commercial occupancy, lack of maintenance and repair of buildings, or any combination thereof, is detrimental to the public health, safety, morals and general welfare, and which will deteriorate, or is in danger of deteriorating, into a blighted area."

neighborhood was blighted and in a deteriorating condition, he also admitted that the area was not a deteriorated area as that term is defined by the Norwood Code. The trial judge also found that another KKG witness testified that the neighborhood was neither a slum nor blighted or deteriorated and was not on its way to becoming blighted, that he could not conclude that the neighborhood was conducive to ill health, transmission of disease, or juvenile delinquency and crime, or that it was detrimental to public health, safety, morals or general welfare. At best, he testified that he believed that the neighborhood was deteriorating as a single-family-residence neighborhood and that the quality of life of the neighborhood's residents was decreasing. The trial judge similarly found that Norwood's planning director testified only that the neighborhood "probably would" deteriorate or was in danger of deteriorating into a blighted area.

After a hearing that lasted several days, the trial court rendered findings of fact and conclusions of law regarding whether the taking was lawful. The court found that KKG's study of the neighborhood contained numerous flaws and errors. Although the court did not enumerate all of the flaws and errors, it specifically noted that KKG had counted several negative factors twice, erroneously included factors that should not have been considered, and improperly conflated the criteria necessary to establish a slum, blighted, or deteriorated area with the mutually exclusive criteria for establishing a deteriorating area. The court found that, despite its errors, KKG's study was not devoid of reliability and validity and that it complied with the Norwood Code. In rejecting the appellants' contention that Norwood had not used sound reasoning in determining that their neighborhood was deteriorating, the court determined that certain conditions in the neighborhood were established beyond dispute, including those related to the increase in traffic, diversity of ownership, the safety issues related to dead-end streets and driveways off busy roads, and incompatible land uses. The court then determined the conclusions to be drawn from those conditions.

Significantly, the court found that Norwood had abused its discretion insofar as it had found that the neighborhood was a "slum, blighted or deteriorated area." That conclusion was based on the paucity of evidence supporting the necessary finding that a "majority of structures" in the neighborhood were conducive to ill health and crime, detrimental to the public's welfare, or otherwise satisfied the criteria of a slum, blighted, or deteriorated area. The court concluded, however, that there was no showing that Norwood had abused its discretion in finding that the neighborhood was a "deteriorating area."

The latter conclusion seems to have been driven by the deferential standard that the trial court believed it was required to use in evaluating Norwood's conclusion:

> The issue is whether [Norwood] abused its discretion in finding that the area was in danger of deteriorating into a blighted area. The Court does not need to conclude that it would reach the same judgment as Norwood, but only that there was a sound reasoning process and that Council did not abuse its discretion. The Court finds that this is a more difficult issue [than the issue of whether the neighborhood was a slum, blighted, or deteriorated area]. On the one hand, it is undisputed that all the buildings in the area are in good to fair condition, generally well maintained with no tax delinquencies, none were "dilapidated," and none were "obsolete." The KKG principal responsible for the [Urban-Renewal] Plan concluded that the area was not in danger of deteriorating into a blighted area. He did testify that the area was deteriorating as a single family neighborhood; however, this is not the test. The area must be in

danger of deteriorating into a blighted area. On the other hand, it is undisputed that there are safety issues and traffic concerns causing unsafe conditions (especially with dead-end streets with little or no turnaround for emergency vehicles), a predominance of inadequate street layout, faulty lot layout, and diversity of ownership, which in combination are in the City Council's judgment causing the area to be deteriorating. There was evidence that the conditions could lead to impairment of sound growth, an economic liability and a menace to the public welfare. The Planning Director for the City testified that the area was in danger of deteriorating into a blighted area. The other KKG witness also testified that the area was in danger of deteriorating into a blighted area.

Judicial deference to City Council's decisions is required because in our system of government, legislatures are better able to assess what public purpose should be advanced by the exercise of eminent domain. (Emphasis added and footnote deleted.)

Having found that the taking was justified because of the deteriorating condition of the neighborhood, the trial court returned the causes (which had been consolidated) to their originally assigned judges to hold trials on the issue of compensation. After the juries rendered their verdicts on the value of appellants' properties, Norwood deposited with the court the full amount awarded in each valuation action. Norwood obtained the titles to the properties and transferred them to Rookwood, which began demolishing the houses in the neighborhood.

The trial court refused to enjoin Rookwood from using or damaging the property pending appeal, and a divided court of appeals denied a stay of the trial court's judgment, finding that R.C. 163.19 prohibited such relief. Upon appeal of those rulings, we accepted the causes and issued orders preventing the appellees from destroying or otherwise altering the properties pending our review of the taking.

With this background in mind, we turn to the law relevant to these cases.

Constitutional Considerations

"Wherever there is sovereignty, whether in the old world, where it is held in trust for the people by things called kings, or in this country where the people wear it upon their own shoulders, two great and fundamental rights exist: the right of eminent domain in all the people, and the right of private property in each. These great rights exist over and above, and independent of all human conventions, written and unwritten." Proprietors of the Spring Grove Cemetery v. Cincinnati, Hamilton & Dayton RR. Co. (Super.1849), 1 Ohio Dec. Reprint 316, reversed on other grounds (Ohio 1850), 1 Ohio Dec. Reprints 343.

A. Individual Property Rights

The rights related to property, i.e., to acquire, use, enjoy, and dispose of property, Buchanan v. Warley (1917), 245 U.S. 60, 74, are among the most revered in our law and traditions. Indeed, property rights are integral aspects of our theory of democracy and notions of liberty. See, e.g., Robert Meltz, Dwight H. Merriam, and Richard M. Frank, The Takings Issue: Constitutional Limits on Land Use Control and Environmental Regulation (1999) 10; Bernard H. Siegan, Property and Freedom: The Constitution, the Courts, and Land-Use Regulation (1997) 14-18; *The Private Use of Public Power: The Private University and the Power of Eminent Domain* (1974), 27 Vand.L.Rev. 681, 683, and fn. 1.

Believed to be derived fundamentally from a higher authority and natural law, property rights were so sacred that they could not be entrusted lightly to "the uncertain virtue of those who govern." Parham v. Justices of Decatur Cty. Inferior Court (Ga.1851), 9 Ga. 341, 348. As such, property rights were believed to supersede constitutional principles. "To be * * * protected and * * * secure in the possession of [one's] property is a right inalienable, a right which a written constitution may recognize or declare, but which existed independently of and before such recognition, and which no government can destroy." Henry v. Dubuque Pacific RR. Co. (1860), 10 Iowa 540, 543. As Chief Justice Bartley eloquently described more than 150 years ago:

> The right of private property is an *original* and *fundamental* right, existing anterior to the formation of the government itself; the civil rights, privileges and immunities authorized by law, are *derivative*—mere *incidents* to the political institutions of the country, conferred with a view to the public welfare, and therefore *trusts* of civil power, to be exercised for the public benefit. * * * Government is the necessary burden imposed on man as the only means of securing the protection of his rights. And this protection—the primary and only legitimate purpose of civil government, is accomplished by protecting man in his rights of personal security, personal liberty, and private property. The right of private property being, therefore, an *original right,* which it was one of the primary and most sacred objects of government to secure and protect, is widely and essentially distinguished in its nature, from those exclusive political rights and special privileges * * * which are created by law and conferred upon a few * * *. The fundamental principles set forth in the bill of rights in our constitution, declaring the inviolability of private property, were evidently designed to protect the right of private property as one of the primary and original objects of civil society * * *. (Emphasis sic.) Bank of Toledo, 1 Ohio St. at 632.

In light of these Lockean notions of property rights, see, e.g., Richard A. Epstein, Takings: Private Property and the Power of Eminent Domain (1985) 10–18, it is not surprising that the founders of our state expressly incorporated individual property rights into the Ohio Constitution in terms that reinforced the sacrosanct nature of the individual's "inalienable" property rights, Section 1, Article I,[6] which are to be held forever "inviolate." Section 19, Article I. See, also, Section 5, Article XIII; Sections 4, 10, and 11, Article XVIII (requiring compensation for municipal appropriations of private property for public rights of way, utilities, and improvements).

Ohio has always considered the right of property to be a fundamental right. There can be no doubt that the bundle of venerable rights associated with property is strongly protected in the Ohio Constitution and must be trod upon lightly, no matter how great the weight of other forces.

B. The State's Power of Eminent Domain

Like the individual's right to property, the state's great power to seize private property predates modern constitutional principles. Understood as "the offspring of political necessity," Kohl v. United States (1875), 91 U.S. 367, 371, eminent domain is, like the taxation and police powers, "an inseparable incident of sovereignty." See, also, Cooper v. Williams (1831), 4 Ohio 253, 286 ("by virtue of its transcendent sovereignty (*dominium eminens*), [the state has] a power to appropriate private property for public

---

6. "All men * * * have certain inalienable rights, among which are those of * * * acquiring, possessing, and protecting property."

uses, for the purpose of promoting the general welfare. This power is inherent in every government"). At the time the Constitution was adopted, eminent domain was so familiar that "[i]ts existence * * * in the grantee of that power [was] not to be questioned." Kohl, 91 U.S. at 372. The founders recognized the necessity of the takings power and expressly incorporated it into the Fifth Amendment to the United States Constitution. But though its existence is undeniable and its powers are sweepingly broad, the power is not unlimited.

There is an inherent tension between the individual's right to possess and preserve property and the state's competing interests in taking it for the communal good. Mindful of that friction and the potential for misuse of the eminent-domain power, James Madison's proposed draft of the Takings Clause included two equitable limitations on its use that were eventually incorporated into the Fifth Amendment:[7] the "public use" requirement and the "just compensation" rule. Charles E. Cohen, *Eminent Domain after Kelo v. City of New London: An Argument for Banning Economic Development Takings* (2006), 29 Harv.J.L. & Pub. Policy 491, 532; William B. Stoebuck, *A General Theory of Eminent Domain* (1972), 47 Wash.L.Rev. 553, 595. The amendment confirms the sovereign's authority to take, but conditions the exercise of that authority upon satisfaction of two conjunctive standards: that the taking is for a "public use" and that "just compensation" for the taking is given to the property owner. Kelo, 545 U.S. 469, 125 S.Ct. at 2672, ; Brown v. Legal Found. of Washington (2003), 538 U.S. 216, 231–232.

Similarly, almost every state constitution eventually included provisions related to eminent-domain powers. Both the Northwest Ordinance and the Ohio Constitution[8] recognized the state's right to take property from an individual, but conditioned the right to take on the equitable considerations of just compensation and public use. Section 19, Article I requires that the taking be necessary for the common welfare and, to "insure that principle of natural justice," that the persons deprived of their property will be compensated for "every injury resulting from this act," "every infringement on their [property] rights," and "every injurious interference with the control of their property."

The binary constitutional inquiry in an eminent-domain case is whether both the compensation requirement and the public-use tests were satisfied. The issue of compensation is not presented in these appeals, but the latter, more difficult question of "public use" is.

It is axiomatic that the federal and Ohio constitutions forbid the state from taking private property for the sole benefit of a private individual, even when just compensation for the taking is provided. A sine qua non of eminent domain in Ohio is the understanding that the sovereign may use its appropriation powers only upon necessity for the common good. Buckingham v. Smith (1840), 10 Ohio 288, 297 (eminent domain "is founded on the superior claims of a whole community over an individual citizen; but then in those cases only where private property is wanted for *public use,* or demanded by the *public welfare*" [emphasis sic]). As we explained in Cooper, the exercise of sovereignty in eminent-domain cases is predicated on the notion that such a taking

---

7. "No person shall be * * * deprived of life, liberty, or property, without due process of law; nor shall private property be taken for public use, without just compensation."

8. "Private property shall ever be held inviolate, but subservient to the public welfare. When taken in time of war or other public exigency, imperatively requiring its immediate seizure, or for the purpose of making or repairing roads, * * * a compensation shall be made to the owner, in money, and in all other cases, where private property shall be taken for public use, a compensation therefor shall first be made in money, or first secured by a deposit of money, and such compensation shall be assessed by a jury * * * ." Section 19, Article I, Ohio Constitution.

can be permitted only "for the use and benefit of the people," which is "distinct from government interest, profit, or concern." "It is only this great and common benefit to all the people alike that creates a necessity authorizing and justifying the seizure * * *. It is the people's prerogative, exists in the social compact, and is founded in the maxim, '*salus populi suprema est lex.*'"

Despite such commanding language, however, the concept of public use has been malleable and elusive. As eminent-domain doctrine developed over the years, understanding of the term "public use" often varied greatly, leaving case law in "'doctrinal and conceptual disarray'" and causing uncertainty for attorneys and jurists. Given its fluid nature, it is necessary to consider the evolution of the public-use determinations that dominate the instant cases.

In America's nascent period, there was an abundance of unclaimed land, limited government activity, and little controversy over the use of eminent domain to develop land and natural resources. When takings occurred, they were rarely believed to be unwarranted. Typically, the appropriation was of obvious necessity and had clear, palpable benefits to the public, as in cases in which the property was taken for roadways and navigable canals, government buildings, or other uses related to the protection and defense of the people. In this early period, "public use" was often equated to "public benefit."

The early legal authority for the rare challenge to such takings was also circumscribed. Before the Civil War and the adoption of the Fourteenth Amendment, the federal courts held the Fifth Amendment inapplicable to the states. See, e.g., Barron v. Mayor & Baltimore City Council (1833), 32 U.S. (7 Pet.) 243, 250–251, 8 L.Ed. 672 (refusing to impose the Fifth Amendment's limitations on eminent domain on the states). Thus, the federal courts did not restrain the states' exercise of eminent-domain powers to take private property.[10]

Although the takings were occasionally challenged in state courts, only in rare instances did the courts interfere. Generally, the state courts upheld the authority for the taking.

As America shifted from an agrarian society to an industrialized and increasingly urban one, the economy grew. Social policy and legal philosophy fed more probing inquiries into the nature, scope, and application of all of the sovereign powers, including eminent domain. The takings doctrine was used widely to support the creation of the nation's physical infrastructure and those enterprises necessary for continued expansion and development, such as utilities, railroads, and mines. Though these takings often involved a fairly significant benefit to individuals and individual corporations, many legislatures and courts affirmed their use under the principle that they afforded some larger, general benefit to the public. Wendell E. Pritchett, *The "Public Menace" of Blight: Urban Renewal and the Private Uses of Eminent Domain* (2003), 21 Yale L. & Policy Rev. 1, 9–10; *The Private Use of Public Power*, 27 Vand. L.Rev. at 702.

By the mid-19th century, there was some movement within the state courts to limit broad interpretations of public benefit and to more strongly guard individual property rights. This retrenchment from former broad readings often required creative evasion of precedent, recasting the takings as an exercise of the police power not related to eminent domain.

---

10. The federal government did not assert authority to take state lands in its own name until the Antebellum period, and the federal courts were not called on to address federal appropriations of state lands until the closing of the Reconstruction Era. See Kohl [v. U.S., 91 U.S. 367, 373 (1875)].

By the end of the 19th century, the federal courts had established that the Due Process Clause of the Fourteenth Amendment endowed them with authority to review state takings, but they employed broad constructions of "public use" in doing so, particularly when the taking expanded the economy or provided vital resources, as with mining operations or irrigation systems necessary for settlement and development of the western regions. See, e.g., Strickley v. Highland Boy Gold Mining Co. (1906), 200 U.S. 527 (affirming use of eminent domain to permit a private mining company to run lines for transporting ore over private property); Clark v. Nash (1905), 198 U.S. 361 (affirming use of eminent domain to grant a right of way over private land for the enlargement of an irrigation ditch for the benefit of another private individual).

The broader concept of public use set forth in these cases eventually dominated and became entrenched in early 20th century eminent-domain jurisprudence. In this view, the fact that an "incidental benefit" flowed to a private actor was not a critical aspect of the analysis (even if that benefit was significant) provided that there was a clear public benefit in the taking. The expansive reading of public use, however, must be understood properly.

Central to the broad construction of public use was the courts' understanding that any workable definition of public use in an industrial age had to be "capable of meeting new conditions and improvements, and the ever-increasing needs of society." Significantly, the more liberal framing of public use was not a retreat from the fundamental understanding that a taking was not warranted for private benefit alone. As Justice Peckham explained in Clark:

> [W]e do not desire to be understood by this decision as approving of the broad proposition that private property may be taken in all cases where the taking may promote the public interest and tend to develop the natural resources of the state. We simply say that in this particular case, and upon the facts stated in the findings of the court, and having reference to the conditions already stated, we are of the opinion the use is a public one, although the taking of the right of way is for the purpose simply of thereby obtaining the water for an individual, where it is absolutely necessary to enable him to make any use whatever of his land, and which will be valuable and fertile only if water can be obtained. Other landowners adjoining the [beneficiary of the taking], if any there are, might share in the use of the water by themselves taking the same proceedings to obtain it, and we do not think it necessary, in order to hold the use to be a public one, that all should join in the same proceeding, or that a company should be formed to obtain the water." 198 U.S. at 369–370, 25 S.Ct. 676, 49 L.Ed. 1085.

Thus, rather than forging a new notion of public use, Clark is more properly seen as an extension of the court's decision in Fallbrook Irrigation Dist. v. Bradley (1896), 164 U.S. 112, which found sufficient public use in a taking that granted a private corporation land to create reservoirs and ditches to supply landowners with water.

The doctrinal evolution of eminent domain thus reflects judicial understandings that the public-use test required flexibility and consideration of diverse local conditions rather that rigid, uniform application. See, also, Clark, 198 U.S. at 370 (describing differences in the rights of riparian owners in the eastern and western regions of the country). This acceptance of the need for an elastic standard in considering public use became widely ingrained and was fully adopted by this court by midcentury. See, e.g., State ex rel. Gordon v. Rhodes (1951), 156 Ohio St. 81, 91–92, 45 O.O. 93, 100 N.E.2d

225, quoting 37 American Jurisprudence (1941) 734, Municipal Corporations, Section 120 ("'A public use changes with changing conditions of society, new appliances in the sciences, and other changes brought about by an increase in population and by new modes of transportation and communication. The courts as a rule have attempted no judicial definition of a public as distinguished from a private purpose, but have left each case to be determined by its own peculiar circumstances. Generally, a public purpose has for its objective the promotion of the public health, safety, morals, general welfare, security, prosperity, and contentment of all the inhabitants or residents within the municipal corporation, the sovereign powers of which are used to promote such public purpose. * * * The modern trend of decision is to expand and liberally construe the term "public use" in considering state and municipal activities'"); State v. Buckley (1968), 16 Ohio St.2d 128, 132, 45 O.O.2d 469, 243 N.E.2d 66 ("concepts of police power change with the times").

While broad conceptualizations of public use evolved during the first decades of the 20th century, civic and government leaders became increasingly concerned with living conditions in urban areas and the array of social problems caused by the lack of adequate and safe affordable housing in cities. The federal government eventually enacted sweeping legislation in an attempt to ameliorate some of those concerns. See, generally, ... Sayre v. United States (N.D.Ohio 1967), 18 Ohio Misc. 23, 282 F.Supp. 175, 187–188 (describing federal urban-renewal funding statutes); State ex rel. Allerton Parking Corp. v. Cleveland (1965), 4 Ohio App.2d 57, 67–68, 33 O.O.2d 91, 211 N.E.2d 203 (noting the adoption of urban-renewal programs by cities across the nation). These modern urban-renewal and redevelopment efforts fostered the convergence of the public-health police power and eminent domain.

In this paradigm, the concept of public use was altered. Rather than furthering a public benefit by appropriating property to *create* something needed in a place where it did not exist before, the appropriations power was used to *destroy* a threat to the public's general welfare and well-being: slums and blighted or deteriorated property. As set forth in a seminal case on such actions:

"The public evils, social and economic, of [unwholesome] conditions [in the slums], are unquestioned and unquestionable. Slum areas are the breeding places of disease which take toll not only from denizens, but, by spread, from the inhabitants of the entire city and state. Juvenile delinquency, crime, and immorality are there born, find protection, and flourish. Enormous economic loss results directly from the necessary expenditure of public funds to maintain health and hospital services for afflicted slum dwellers and to war against crime and immorality. * * * Time and again * * * the use by the Legislature of the power of taxation and of the police power in dealing with the evils of the slums, has been upheld by the courts. Now, in continuation of a battle, which if not entirely lost, is far from won, the Legislature has resorted to the last of the trinity of sovereign powers by giving to a city agency the power of eminent domain." New York City Hous. Auth. v. Muller (1936), 270 N.Y. 333, 339, 1 N.E.2d 153.

Historic notions equating physical, moral, and social illnesses with slums and blighted areas were reinforced. The term "blight" itself, borrowed from science and connoting an organism that promotes disease, became synonymous with urban decay, and courts were soon invoking the language of disease. See, e.g., Berman v. Parker (1954), 348 U.S. 26, 34 ("The experts concluded that if the community were to be healthy, if it were not to revert again to a blighted or slum area, as though possessed of a congenital disease, the area must be planned as a whole"); State ex rel. Ryan v. Gahanna City Council (1984), 9 Ohio St.3d 126, 131, 9 OBR 377, 459 N.E.2d 208 (Locher, J., concurring) (equating "urban blight" to "malignant cancer"); Pritchett, 21 Yale L. & Policy Rev. at 3 (noting the "disease" rhetoric adopted by renewal advocates); Lawrence M. Friedman, Government and Slum Housing: A Century of Frustration (1968) 169 (noting references to blight as "a disease of urban life" and as a "kind of cancer"). Urban renewal, through the force of eminent domain, became the treatment for saving the body politic from the spread of blight,[11] see Pritchett, 21 Yale L. & Policy Rev. at 4, and there was little doubt that a taking of blighted property for purposes of redevelopment was within the broad and inclusive concept of public use. See Berman, 348 U.S. at 33. . . . Almost all courts, including this one, have consistently upheld takings that seized slums and blighted or deteriorated private property for redevelopment, even when the property was then transferred to a private entity, and continue to do so. These rulings properly employed an elastic public-use analysis to promote eminent domain as an answer to clear and present public health concerns, permitting razing and "slum clearance."

But to some they also signaled an almost unbridled expansion of the notion of public use, which led commentators to suggest that the public-use requirement was dead or dying. Although the death knell has not officially sounded, the modern understanding of public use has permitted somewhat novel findings. See, e.g., Hawaii Hous. Auth. v. Midkiff (1984), 467 U.S. 229, 241–244 (finding sufficient public benefit in the abolition of a land oligopoly to warrant taking private property by eminent domain). In some jurisdictions, a belief has taken hold that general economic development is a public use. See, e.g., Poletown Neighborhood Council v. Detroit (1981), 410 Mich. 616, 304 N.W.2d 455, overruled by Wayne Cty. v. Hathcock (2004), 471 Mich. 445, 684 N.W.2d 765; Thomas W. Merrill, The Economics of Public Use (1986), 72 Cornell L.Rev. 61. Kelo confirmed this view for purposes of federal constitutional analysis, despite the fact that many legal commentators have expressed alarm at the potential abuse of the eminent-domain power in such circumstances.

Inherent in many decisions affirming pronouncements that economic development alone is sufficient to satisfy the public-use clause is an artificial judicial deference to the state's determination that there was sufficient public use. Similarly, in the cases before us, the trial and appellate courts below seem to have been mistaken regarding the scope of review to be employed.

The trial court properly found an abuse of discretion in Norwood's finding that the area targeted for redevelopment was slum, blighted, or deteriorated. But notwithstanding what seems to have been a significant question about whether the taking of the neighborhood could be based on its designation as a "deteriorating area," the trial court appears to have felt constrained by its interpretation of prior cases, stating that judicial review of appropriations is limited and must be deferential to the municipality. In reviewing that decision, the appellate court repeatedly framed its inquiries as whether Norwood abused its discretion by finding that the area was blighted or in danger of deteriorating into a blighted area—inquiries that it answered negatively after applying broad deference and liberal interpretation to Norwood's conclusions.

---

11. And zoning regulations—the preventive medicine to ward off blight—have been upheld as valid exercises of the police powers over due-process challenges. Euclid v. Ambler Realty Co. (1926), 272 U.S. 365, 386–387.

The trial and appellate courts correctly stated that, absent a showing of abuse of discretion, deference was due to the city's determination that the area was blighted and deteriorated. (And although deference is certainly due to such findings, it is not absolute deference—as evidenced by the trial judge's correct conclusion that there was an abuse of discretion in the city's determination in these cases.) But for reasons that we more fully set forth later in our analysis, the courts' conclusion that eliminating a "deteriorating area" satisfied the public-use requirement was an erroneous one. We believe that that error occurred, at least in part, because of a misunderstanding of the scope of review to be given in such inquiries.

The use of "deteriorating area" as a standard for a taking has never been adopted by this court, but the trial court apparently believed that deference must be given to a city's conclusion that a taking is proper. In affirming the trial court's judgment, the appellate court engaged in a limited independent analysis, noting that "[w]here the exercise of eminent domain is rationally related to a conceivable public purpose, the United States Supreme Court has never held a compensated taking to be prohibited by the public-use clause."[C]iting Hawaii Hous. Auth. v. Midkiff, 467 U.S. 229.

In addressing the meaning of the public-use clause in Ohio's Constitution, we are not bound to follow the United States Supreme Court's determinations of the scope of the public-use clause in the federal constitution, Hathcock, 471 Mich. at 479–480, 684 N.W.2d 765, and we decline to hold that the Takings Clause in Ohio's Constitution has the sweeping breadth that the Supreme Court attributed to the United States Constitution's Takings Clause in Midkiff, which presented a novel use of eminent-domain law. Moreover, the court in Midkiff noted that "there is, of course, a role for the courts to play in reviewing a legislature's judgment of what constitutes a public use." See 467 U.S. at 240, 104 S.Ct. 2321, 81 L.Ed.2d 186.

Although there is merit in the notion that deference must be paid to a government's determination that there is sufficient evidence to support a taking in a case in which the taking is for a use that has previously been determined to be a public use, see Kelo, 545 U.S. at __, 125 S.Ct. at 2669 (Kennedy, J., concurring) (comparing the deference to rational-basis review in an equal-protection challenge but not foreclosing the possibility that heightened scrutiny might be applied properly in some cases), that deferential review is not satisfied by superficial scrutiny. Id. ("A court applying rational-basis review under the Public Use Clause should strike down a taking that, by a clear showing, is intended to favor a particular private party, with only incidental or pretextual public benefits * * * "). "Even under * * * a deferential standard * * * public use is not established as a matter of law whenever the legislative body acts." We agree that the public-use requirement cannot be reduced to mere "hortatory fluff." Kelo, 545 U.S. at __, 125 S.Ct. at 2673, (O'Connor, J., dissenting). To the contrary, it remains an essential and critical aspect in the analysis of any proposed taking.

Despite the relative reluctance of courts to intervene in determinations that a sufficient public benefit supported the taking, the separation-of-powers doctrine "would be unduly restricted" if the state could invoke the police power to virtually immunize all takings from judicial review. See United States ex rel. Tennessee Valley Auth. v. Welch (1946), 327 U.S. 546, 556–557 (Reed, J., concurring). See, also, id. at 557, 327 U.S. 546, 66 S.Ct. 715, 90 L.Ed. 843 (Frankfurter, J., concurring) (the fact that a court has never struck down a legislative determination of public use as unconstitutional "does not mean that the power to review is wanting"). Though narrow in scope, judicial review is not meaningless in an eminent-domain case. To the contrary, "defining the parameters of the power of eminent domain is a judicial function," and we remain free to define the proper limits of the doctrine. Merrill v. Manchester (1985), 127 N.H. 234, 236, 499 A.2d 216 ("Whether a particular use is a public use is a question of law to be resolved by the courts").

As the Supreme Court of Illinois has observed, "The Constitution and the essential liberties we are sworn to protect control. * * * While we do not question the legislature's discretion in allowing for the exercise of eminent domain power, 'the government does not have unlimited power to redefine property rights.' Loretto v. Teleprompter Manhattan CATV Corp., 458 U.S. 419, 439 (1982). The power of eminent domain is to be exercised with restraint, not abandon." Though the Ohio Constitution may bestow the sovereign with a magnificent power to take private property against the will of the individual who owns it, it also confers an "inviolable" right of property on the people. When the state elects to take private property without the owner's consent, simple justice requires that the state proceed with due concern for the venerable rights it is preempting.

There can be no doubt that our role—though limited—is a critical one that requires vigilance in reviewing state actions for the necessary restraint, including review to ensure that the state takes no more than that necessary to promote the public use, and that the state proceeds fairly and effectuates takings without bad faith, pretext, discrimination, or improper purpose. In the proper exercise of our duty to ensure that property rights are protected, we have held that the state may not take to secure a financial gain by resale of, or taxation on, appropriated land. Thus, our precedent does not demand rote deference to legislative findings in eminent-domain proceedings, but rather, it preserves the courts' traditional role as guardian of constitutional rights and limits. Accordingly, "questions of public *purpose* aside, whether * * * proposed condemnations [are] consistent with the Constitution's 'public use' requirement [is] a constitutional question squarely within the Court's authority." (Emphasis sic.) Hathcock, 471 Mich. at 480, 684 N.W.2d 765. See, also, Cincinnati v. Vester (1930), 281 U.S. 439, 446, 50 S.Ct. 360, 74 L.Ed. 950 ("It is well established that, in considering the application of the Fourteenth Amendment to cases of expropriation of private property, the question what is a public use is a judicial one. In deciding such a question, the Court has appropriate regard to the diversity of local conditions and considers with great respect legislative declarations and in particular the judgments of state courts as to the uses considered to be public in light of local exigencies. But the question remains a judicial one which this Court must decide in performing its duty of enforcing the provisions of the Federal Constitution"); Kelo, 545 U.S. 469, 125 S.Ct. at 2684, 162 L.Ed.2d 439 (Thomas, J., dissenting) (advocating that no deference should be given to "a legislature's judgment concerning the quintessentially legal question of whether government owns, or the public has the right to use, the taken property").

The scrutiny by the courts in appropriation cases is limited in scope, but it clearly remains a critical constitutional component. The sovereign's right to take property may be conferred through the legislature to municipalities, which enjoy broad discretion in determining whether a proposed taking serves the public. But it is for the courts to ensure that the legislature's exercise of power is not beyond the scope of its authority, and that the power is not abused by irregular or oppressive use, or use in bad faith. And when the authority is delegated to another, the courts must ensure that the grant of authority is construed strictly and that any doubt over the propriety of the taking is resolved in favor of the property owner. In reviewing an appropriation, we thus act with deference to legislative pronouncements, but we are independent of them. See Hathcock, quoting Justice Ryan's dissenting opinion in Poletown Neighborhood Council v. Detroit ("'In point of fact, this Court has never employed the minimal standard of review in an eminent domain case which is adopted by the majority [in Poletown] * * *.

Notwithstanding explicit legislative findings, this Court has always made an independent determination of what constitutes a public use for which the power of eminent domain may be utilized'"). See, also, Merrill v. Manchester, 127 N.H. at 237–239, 499 A.2d 216 (holding that in light of declared legislative policy of preserving open lands, plaintiffs' open lands could not be taken for construction of an industrial park, because an industrial park did not provide a direct public benefit); In re Petition of Seattle (1981), 96 Wash.2d 616, 627–629, 638 P.2d 549 (without giving deference to legislature's determination, court concluded that primary purpose of planned redevelopment was to promote retail and therefore the contemplated use was "a predominantly private, rather than public, use," and court noted that "[a] beneficial use is not necessarily a public use"); Owensboro v. McCormick (Ky.1979), 581 S.W.2d 3, 7–8 (invalidating a statute to the extent that it granted the city or other governmental unit "unconditional right to condemn private property which [was] to be conveyed by the local industrial development authority for private development for industrial or commercial purposes"); Karesh v. Charleston City Council (1978), 271 S.C. 339, 343, 247 S.E.2d 342 (holding that a city could not condemn land and lease it to developer for parking garage and convention center, because there was no assurance that the new use would provide more than a "negligible advantage to the general public"); Baycol, Inc. v. Fort Lauderdale Downtown Dev. Auth. (Fla.1975), 315 So.2d 451, 456–458 (holding that the economic benefit that would come from an appropriation of land for a parking garage and a shopping mall did not satisfy the public-use requirement despite potential economic benefits and holding that any public benefit from construction of the garage was "incidental" and insufficient to justify the use of eminent domain); Little Rock v. Raines (1967), 241 Ark. 1071, 1083–1084, 411 S.W.2d 486 (holding that a proposed taking for an industrial park did not satisfy the public-use clause); Opinion of the Justices (1957), 152 Me. 440, 447, 131 A.2d 904 (advisory opinion concluding that a proposed statute that would authorize the city to use eminent domain for the development of an industrial park was unconstitutional).

A court's independence is critical, particularly when the authority for the taking is delegated to another or the contemplated public use is dependent on a private entity. In such cases, the courts must ensure that the grant of authority is construed strictly and that any doubt over the propriety of the taking is resolved in favor of the property owner.

Similarly, when the state takes an individual's private property for transfer to another individual or to a private entity rather than for use by the state itself, the judicial review of the taking is paramount. A primordial purpose of the public-use clause is to prevent the legislature from permitting the state to take private property from one individual simply to give it to another. Such a law would be a flagrant abuse of legislative power, see Calder v. Bull (1798), 3 U.S. (3 Dall.) 386, 388, 1 L.Ed. 648, and to give deference to it would be a wholesale abdication of judicial review. See Kelo, 545 U.S. at __, 125 S.Ct. at 2676–2677, 162 L.Ed.2d 439 (O'Connor, J., dissenting).

As Justice O'Connor correctly discerned in her analysis of the taking in Kelo, when the state takes an individual's property and gives it to another based solely on the economic gain afforded by the transfer, the "private benefit and [the] incidental public benefit are, by definition, merged and mutually reinforcing." We agree that due to the mutuality of public and private interests in such cases, a danger exists that the state's decision to take may be influenced by the financial gains that would flow to it or to the private entity because of the taking—a danger that is not apparent when the state or its designee determines whether the appropriation is warranted by communal need and public benefit. See Kelo [v. City of New London, Connecticut, 545 U.S. 469, 503

(2005)] 268 Conn. at 129–130, 843 A.2d 500 (Zarella, J., concurring in part and dissenting in part) ("Because public agencies must work hand in glove with private developers to achieve plan objectives, the taking agency may employ the power to favor purely private interests). The trial court in the present case recognized this problem when it stated in its memorandum of decision that 'powerful business groups or companies [may] exercise their influence to gain their ends with * * * little corresponding benefit to the public.' The majority makes a similar observation. See part IIA of the majority opinion (recognizing 'potential for abuse of the eminent domain power')"). In such circumstances, both common sense and the law command independent judicial review of the taking. "[T]he mere recitation of a benign * * * purpose is not an automatic shield which protects against any inquiry into the actual purposes underlying a statutory scheme." See Weinberger v. Wiesenfeld (1975), 420 U.S. 636.

Given the individual's fundamental property rights in Ohio, the courts' role in reviewing eminent-domain appropriations, though limited, is important in all cases. Judicial review is even more imperative in cases in which the taking involves an ensuing transfer of the property to a private entity, where a novel theory of public use is asserted, and in cases in which there is a showing of discrimination, bad faith, impermissible financial gain, or other improper purpose. With our proper role as arbiters of the scope of eminent domain clarified, we turn to the public use at issue in these cases.

Although we have permitted economic concerns to be considered in addition to other factors, such as slum clearance,[12] when determining whether the public-use requirement is sufficient, we have never found economic benefits alone to be a sufficient public use for a valid taking. We decline to do so now.

Rather, we find that the analysis by the Supreme Court of Michigan in Hathcock, and those presented by the dissenting judges of the Supreme Court of Connecticut and the dissenting justices of the United States Supreme Court in Kelo are better models for interpreting Section 19, Article I of Ohio's Constitution. In Hathcock, the court overruled its prior holding in Poletown Neighborhood Council v. Detroit, a case which the court characterized as a "radical and unabashed departure" from eminent-domain jurisprudence. Poletown had found a generalized economic benefit in the transfer of private property to a private entity sufficient to satisfy the public-use requirement. In overturning Poletown, the court in Hathcock correctly observed:

> Every business, every productive unit in society, * * * contribute[s] in some way to the commonwealth. To justify the exercise of eminent domain solely on the basis of the fact that the use of that property by a private entity seeking its own profit might contribute to the economy's health is to render impotent our constitutional limitations on the government's power of eminent domain. Poletown's 'economic benefit' rationale would validate practically *any* exercise

---

12. Any suggestion that our past decisions finding a public use in urban redevelopment support the notion that appropriations for purely economic purposes must also be permitted is incorrect. In past cases, we found that the removal of blight alone conferred a sufficient public benefit to warrant the taking because the discrete act of removing blight served to remove an extant health threat to the public. Although Justice Stevens suggested that the ensuing redevelopment of the blighted property at issue in Berman was a critical complement to the razing of the blighted property, we disagree that the secondary step of remediation is necessarily critical in all cases. A public benefit may inure from redevelopment, but such a benefit might also be conferred by the preservation of open land to secure recreational, ecological, and aesthetic value in a community. See, e.g., Merrill, 127 N.H. at 237–238, 499 A.2d 216.

of the power of eminent domain on behalf of a private entity. After all, if one's ownership of private property is forever subject to the government's determination that another private party would put one's land to better use, then the ownership of real property is perpetually threatened by the expansion plans of any large discount retailer, 'megastore,' or the like. Indeed, it is for precisely this reason that this Court has approved the transfer of condemned property to private entities only when certain other conditions * * * are present.

Our understanding of the individual's fundamental rights in property, as guaranteed by the Ohio Constitution and our consistent holdings throughout the past two centuries that a genuine public use must be present before the state invokes its right to take, is better reflected by Hathcock 's holdings that economic development by itself is not a sufficient public use to satisfy a taking. Although economic benefit can be considered as a factor among others in determining whether there is a sufficient public use and benefit in a taking, it cannot serve as the sole basis for finding such benefit.

Eminent domain is a power of last resort for the good of the public; it "is not simply a vehicle for cash-strapped municipalities to finance community improvements." See, also, Hudson Hayes Luce, The Meaning of Blight: A Survey of Statutory and Case Law (2000), 35 Real Prop. Probate & Trust J. 389, 401 (noting only a small minority of states' eminent-domain statutes permit the consideration of economic use in determining whether property is blighted).

We hold that an economic or financial benefit alone is insufficient to satisfy the public-use requirement of Section 19, Article I. In light of that holding, any taking based solely on financial gain is void as a matter of law and the courts owe no deference to a legislative finding that the proposed taking will provide financial benefit to a community.

C. The Void-for-Vagueness Doctrine

Due process demands that the state provide meaningful standards in its laws. A law must give fair notice to the citizenry of the conduct proscribed and the penalty to be affixed if that law is breached. Implicitly, the law must also convey an understandable standard capable of enforcement in the courts, for judicial review is a necessary constitutional counterpoise to the broad legislative prerogative to promulgate codes of conduct.

When a statute is challenged under the due-process doctrine prohibiting vagueness, the court must determine whether the enactment (1) provides sufficient notice of its proscriptions to facilitate compliance by persons of ordinary intelligence and (2) is specific enough to prevent official arbitrariness or discrimination in its enforcement. The determination of whether a statute is impermissibly imprecise, indefinite, or incomprehensible must be made in light of the facts presented in the given case and the nature of the enactment challenged.

In undertaking that inquiry into the statute or ordinance at issue, the courts are to apply varying levels of scrutiny. "The difference between the various levels of scrutiny for vagueness has never been definitively spelled out, as in equal protection jurisprudence." Though the degree of review is not described with specificity, regulations that are directed to economic matters and impose only civil penalties are subject to a "less strict vagueness test," but if the enactment "threatens to inhibit the exercise of constitutionally protected rights," a more stringent vagueness test is to be applied.

In either rubric, however, a statute is not void simply because it could be worded more precisely or with additional certainty. The critical question in all cases is whether the law affords a reasonable individual of ordinary intelligence fair notice and sufficient definition and guidance to enable him to conform his conduct to the law; those that do not are void for vagueness.

The vagueness doctrine is usually applied in criminal law and First Amendment claims, but neither the rationale underlying the doctrine nor the case law interpreting it suggests that it should not be applied in any case in which the statute challenged substantially affects other fundamental constitutional rights. And, of course, the Due Process Clause of the Fourteenth Amendment demands that fair notice be given to a property owner in an appropriation action. See, e.g., Walker v. Hutchinson (1956), 352 U.S. 112, 115–117 (notice by publication held inadequate in appropriation case). See, also, Lambert v. California (1957), 355 U.S. 225, 229, 78 S.Ct. 240 ("Notice is required before property interests are disturbed, before assessments are made, before penalties are assessed").

Given that eminent domain necessarily entails the state's intrusion onto the individual's right to garner, possess, and preserve property and that sufficient notice is the critical core of the void-for-vagueness doctrine, the doctrine has utility in eminent-domain cases. We hold that when a court reviews an eminent-domain statute or regulation under the void-for-vagueness doctrine, the court shall utilize the heightened standard of review employed for a statute or regulation that implicates a First Amendment or other fundamental constitutional right. See Hoffman Estates, [v. Flipside, Hoffman Estates, Inc., 455 U.S. 489, 498–499 (1982)].

With the controlling constitutional law established, we turn now to its particular applications in the instant cases.

Application of the Law to the Facts

A. Norwood Code's Use of "Deteriorating Area" as a Standard for a Taking

This court has affirmed cases in which a taking of property was upheld upon a showing that the property was a slum, or blighted, or, in effect, deteriorated. But this is the first time that we have reviewed a judgment that condoned the taking of property upon a finding that the property is in an area that is deteriorating. We refuse to affirm it.

The takings in the instant cases were based solely on a finding that the neighborhood was a deteriorating area. But what notice does the term "deteriorating area" give to an individual property owner?

As defined by the Norwood Code, a "deteriorating area" is not the same as a "slum, blighted or deteriorated area," the standard typically employed for a taking. And here, of course, there was no evidence to support a taking under that standard. To the contrary, the buildings in the neighborhood were generally in good condition and the owners were not property-tax delinquent. There is no suggestion that the area was vermin-infested, was subject to high crime rates or outbreaks of disease, or otherwise posed an impermissible risk to the larger community.

The Norwood Code sets forth a fairly comprehensive array of conditions that purport to describe a "deteriorating area," including those found by the trial judge in this case: incompatible land uses, nonconforming uses, lack of adequate parking facilities, faulty street arrangement, obsolete platting, diversity of ownership. In addition, the trial court identified the following factors as supporting the determination that the neighborhood was deteriorating: increased traffic, dead-end streets that impede public safety vehicles, numerous curb cuts and driveways, and small front yards. But all of those factors exist in virtually every urban American neighborhood.[13] Because the Norwood Code's definition of a deteriorating area describes almost any city, it is suspect. See Beach-Courchesne, 80 Cal.App.4th at 407, 95 Cal.Rptr.2d 265 ("If the showing made in [this] case were sufficient to rise to the level of blight, it is the rare locality in California that is not afflicted with that condition"); Birmingham v. Tutwiler Drug Co. (Ala.1985), 475 So.2d 458, 466 (the area alleged to be blighted "was typical of much of downtown Birmingham").

Similarly, some of the factors upon which the court relied, such as diversity of ownership, could apply to many neighborhoods. And although the term commonly appears in eminent-domain cases and regulations, it is susceptible of many meanings and to manipulation.

Here, the term appears in the Norwood Code but is not defined. The trial court held that the term could mean either "several owners of a single property or several owners of different properties" but that the latter definition applied in the instant cases. Other courts seem to have attributed the former meaning to the term. See Beach-Courchesne, 80 Cal.App.4th at 405, 95 Cal.Rptr.2d 265 ("The mere fact of multiple ownership does not establish blight. Otherwise a condominium development would by definition be blighted"). The ambiguity of the term portends impermissible vagueness because it does not afford fair warning to property owners and permits arbitrary or discriminatory enforcement.

Moreover, diversity of ownership is a factor of questionable weight. As seems to have been the case here, diversity of ownership is typically considered to be a negative factor for a neighborhood because it purportedly impedes development. Yet Rookwood was able to secure virtually every property owner's assent to sale without any apparent difficulty. Thus, though diversity of ownership may be a factor to consider in determining whether an area is deteriorated, it is not a compelling one.

In the cases before us, we cannot say that the appellants had fair notice of what conditions constitute a deteriorating area, even in light of the evidence adduced against them at trial. The evidence is a morass of conflicting opinions on the condition of the neighborhood. Though the Norwood Code's definition of "deteriorating area" provides a litany of conditions, it offers so little guidance in application that it is almost barren of any practical meaning.

In essence, "deteriorating area" is a standardless standard. Rather than affording fair notice to the property owner, the Norwood Code merely recites a host of subjective factors that invite ad hoc and selective enforcement—a danger made more real by the malleable nature of the public-benefit requirement. We must be vigilant in ensuring that so great a power as eminent domain, which historically has been used in areas in which the most marginalized groups lived, is not abused.

As important, the standard for "deteriorating area" defined in the Norwood Code is satisfied not just upon a finding that a neighborhood *is* deteriorating or *will* deteriorate, but is also satisfied by a finding that it "*is in danger of* deteriorating into a blighted area." The statutory definition, therefore, incorporates not only the existing condition of a

---

13. The conditions found by the trial court here are endemic to urban neighborhoods, including some of the most exclusive in America, e.g., Beacon Hill in Boston, Greenwich Village and Tribeca in lower Manhattan, and Nob Hill in San Francisco.

neighborhood, but also extends to what that neighborhood might become. But what it *might* become may be no more likely than what *might not* become. Such a speculative standard is inappropriate in the context of eminent domain, even under the modern, broad interpretation of "public use."

A municipality has no authority to appropriate private property for only a contemplated or speculative use in the future. As we said in O'Neil :

> Public use cannot be determined as of the time of completion of a proposed development, but must be defined in terms of present commitments which in the ordinary course of affairs will be fulfilled.

> "'* * * If the public use is contingent and prospective and the private use or benefit is actual and present, the public use would be incidental to the private use, and in such a case the power of eminent domain clearly could not lawfully be exercised.' Kessler v. City of Indianapolis (1927), 199 Ind. 420, 430, 157 N.E. 547, 550, 3 AL.R. 1." O'Neil, 3 Ohio St.2d at 58, 32 O.O.2d 42, 209 N.E.2d 393.

A fundamental determination that must be made before permitting the appropriation of a slum, blighted, or deteriorated property for redevelopment is that the property, because of its existing state of disrepair or dangerousness, poses a threat to the public's health, safety, or general welfare. Although we adhere to a broad construction of "public use," we hold that government does not have the authority to appropriate private property based on mere belief, supposition or speculation that the property may pose such a threat in the future. To hold otherwise would permit the derogation of a cherished and venerable individual right based on nothing more than "a plank of hypothesis flung across an abyss of uncertainty." Edith Wharton, The Descent of Man, 35 Scribner's Magazine (Mar.1904) 313, 321, reprinted in 1 The Selected Short Stories of Edith Wharton (1991) 49, 62. To permit a taking of private property based solely on a finding that the property is deteriorating or in danger of deteriorating would grant an impermissible, unfettered power to the government to appropriate.

We therefore hold that the use of "deteriorating area" as a standard for determining whether private property is subject to appropriation is void for vagueness and offends due-process rights because it fails to afford a property owner fair notice and invites subjective interpretation. Further, we hold that the term "deteriorating area" cannot be used as a standard for a taking, because it inherently incorporates speculation as to the future condition of the property into the decision on whether a taking is proper rather than focusing that inquiry on the property's condition at the time of the proposed taking.

Because Norwood may not justify its taking of appellants' property on either the basis that the neighborhood was deteriorating or on the basis that the redeveloped area would bring economic value to the city, there is no showing that the taking was for public use. Our conclusion is not altered by the amount of compensation offered to the property owners in this case, even if it was in excess of the fair market value of their property. Though the questions of just compensation and public use are both critical in an eminent-domain analysis, they must be assessed and satisfied independently. Here, there is not an adequate showing that the takings were for a public use. Accordingly, we reverse the judgment of the court of appeals that affirmed the trial court's holding that the appropriation of the appellants' property was permitted.

[The discussion of the constitutionality of R.C. 163.19 has been omitted.]

4. Zoning

City of Edmonds v. Oxford House, Inc.
514 U.S. 725 (1995)

W. Scott Snyder argued the cause and filed briefs for petitioner.*

William F. Sheehan argued the cause for private respondents. With him on the brief were Elizabeth M. Brown, David E. Jones, John P. Relman, Robert I. Heller, and Steven R. Shapiro.

Deputy Solicitor General Bender argued the cause for respondent United States. With him on the brief were Solicitor General Days, Assistant Attorney General Patrick, Cornelia T. L. Pillard, Jessica Dunsay Silver, and Gregory B. Friel.**

Before Chief Justice Rehnquist and Justices Stevens, O'Connor, Scalia, Kennedy, Souter, Thomas, Ginsberg, and Breyer.

Ginsberg, J. delivered the opinion of the Court, in which Rehnquist, C.J., and Stevens, O'Connor, Souter, and Breyer, J.J., joined. Thomas, J., filed a dissenting opinion, in which Scalia and Kennedy, J.J. joined.

Justice Ginsberg delivered the opinion of the Court.

I.

In the summer of 1990, Oxford House opened a group home in the City of Edmonds, Washington for 10 to 12 adults recovering from alcoholism and drug addiction. The group home, called Oxford House-Edmonds, is located in a neighborhood zoned for single-family residences. Upon learning that Oxford House had leased and was operating a home in Edmonds, the City issued criminal citations to the owner and a resident of the house. The citations charged violation of the zoning code rule that defines who may live in single-family dwelling units. The occupants of such units must compose a "family," and family, under the City's defining rule, "means an individual or

---

* Briefs of amici curiae urging reversal were filed for the City of Lubbock by Jean E. Shotts, Jr.; for the City of Mountlake Terrace by Gregory G. Schrag; for the Township of Upper St. Clair by Robert N. Hackett; and for the International City/County Management Association et al. by Richard Ruda, Lee Fennell, and Michael J. Wahoske.

Briefs of amici curiae were filed for the City of Fultondale by Palmer W. Norris and Fred Blanton, Jr.; and for the Pacific Legal Foundation by Ronald A. Zumbrun and Anthony T. Caso.

** Briefs of amici curiae urging affirmance were filed for the Commonwealth of Massachusetts et al. by Scott Harshbarger, Attorney General of Massachusetts, and Stanley J. Eichner, Donna L. Palermino, and Leo T. Sorokin, Assistant Attorneys General, and by the Attorneys General for their respective jurisdictions as follows: Grant Woods of Arizona, Winston Bryant of Arkansas, Alan G. Lance of Idaho, Thomas J. Miller of Iowa, Richard P. Ieyoub of Louisiana, Frankie Sue Del Papa of Nevada, Tom Udall of New Mexico, Charles W. Burson of Tennessee, Dan Morales of Texas, Jan Graham of Utah, Rosalie Simmonds Ballantine of the Virgin Islands, and Darrell V. McGraw, Jr., of West Virginia; for the American Association on Mental Retardation et al. by Lois G. Williams, Jerrold J. Ganzfried, Gregg A. Hand, Leonard S. Rubenstein, and Ira A. Burnim; for the American Association of Retired Persons by Steven S. Zaleznick, Michael Schuster, Bruce B. Vignery, and Deborah M. Zuckerman; for the American Planning Association by Brian W. Blaesser and Daniel M. Lauber; for the American Society of Addiction Medicine et al. by Paul M. Smith, Seth P. Stein, Robert L. Schonfeld, Richard Taranto, and Carolyn I. Polowy; for the American Train Dispatchers Division of Brotherhood of Locomotive Engineers et al. by Lawrence M. Mann; and for the National Fair Housing Alliance by Timothy C. Hester, Robert A. Long, Jr., and Christina T. Uhlrich.

two or more persons related by genetics, adoption, or marriage, or a group of five or fewer persons who are not related by genetics, adoption, or marriage." Oxford House-Edmonds houses more than five unrelated persons, and therefore does not conform to the code.

Oxford House asserted reliance on the Fair Housing Act which declares it unlawful "to discriminate in the sale or rental, or to otherwise make unavailable or deny, a dwelling to any buyer or renter because of a handicap ... of that buyer or a renter." The parties have stipulated that the residents of Oxford House-Edmonds "are recovering alcoholics and drug addicts and are handicapped persons within the meaning" of the Act.

Discrimination covered by the FHA includes "a refusal to make reasonable accommodations in rules, policies, practices, or services, when such accommodations may be necessary to afford [handicapped] person[s] equal opportunity to use and enjoy a dwelling."§3604(f)(3)(B). Oxford House asked Edmonds to make a "reasonable accommodation" by allowing it to remain in the single-family dwelling it had leased. Group homes for recovering substance abusers, Oxford urged, need 8 to 12 residents to be financially and therapeutically viable. Edmonds declined to permit Oxford House to stay in a single-family residential zone, but passed an ordinance listing group homes as permitted uses in multifamily and general commercial zones.

Edmonds sued Oxford House ... seeking a declaration that the FHA does not constrain the City's zoning code family definition rule. Oxford House counterclaimed..., charging the City with failure to make a "reasonable accommodation".... The United States filed a separate action on the same FHA "reasonable accommodation" ground, and the two cases were consolidated....

[T]he District Court held that ECDC §21.30.010, defining "family," is exempt from the FHA under §3607(b)(1) as a "reasonable ... restriction regarding the maximum number of occupants permitted to occupy a dwelling." The Ninth Circuit reversed.... The Ninth Circuit's decision conflicts with an Eleventh Circuit decision....

II.

The sole question before the Court is whether Edmonds' family composition rule qualifies as a "restriction regarding the maximum number of occupants permitted to occupy a dwelling" within the meaning of the FHA's absolute exemption. 42 U.S.C. §3607(b)(1).[4] In answering this question, we are mindful of the Act's stated policy "to provide, within constitutional limitations, for fair housing throughout the United States." §3601. We also note precedent recognizing the FHA's "broad and inclusive" compass, and therefore according a "generous construction" to the Act's complaint-filing provision. Trafficante v. Metropolitan Life Ins. Co. 409 U.S. 205 (1972). Accordingly, we regard this case as an instance in which an exception to "a general statement of policy" is sensibly read "narrowly in order to preserve the primary operation of the [policy]." Commissioner v. Clark, 489 U.S. 726 (1989).

A.

Congress enacted §3607(b)(1) against the backdrop of an evident distinction between municipal land use restrictions and maximum occupancy restrictions.

---

4. Like the District Court and the Ninth Circuit, we do not decide whether Edmonds' zoning code provision defining "family," as the City would apply it against Oxford House, violates the FHA's prohibitions against discrimination set out in 42 U.S.C. §§3604(f)(1)(A) and (f)(3)(B).

Land use restrictions designate "districts in which only compatible uses are allowed and incompatible uses are excluded." These restrictions typically categorize uses as single-family residential, multiple-family residential, commercial, or industrial.

Land use restrictions aim to prevent problems caused by the "pig in the parlor instead of the barnyard." Village of Euclid v. Ambler Realty Co. 272 U.S. 365 (1926). In particular, reserving land for single-family residences preserves the character of neighborhoods, securing "zones where family values, youth values, and the blessings of quiet seclusion and clean air make the area a sanctuary for people." Village of Belle Terre v. Boraas, 416 U.S. 1 (1974); see also Moore v. East Cleveland, 431 U.S. 494 (1977) (Burger, C. J., dissenting) (purpose of East Cleveland's single-family zoning ordinance "is the traditional one of preserving certain areas as family residential communities"). To limit land use to single-family residences, a municipality must define the term "family"; thus, family composition rules are an essential component of single-family residential use restrictions.

Maximum occupancy restrictions, in contradistinction, cap the number of occupants per dwelling, typically in relation to available floor space or the number and type of rooms. See, e.g., Uniform Housing Code § 503(b) (1988); BOCA National Property Maintenance Code §§ PM-405.3, PM-405.5 (1993); Standard Housing Code §§ 306.1, 306.2 (1991); APHA-CDC Recommended Minimum Housing Standards § 9.02, p. 37 (1986). These restrictions ordinarily apply uniformly to *all* residents of *all* dwelling units. Their purpose is to protect health and safety by preventing dwelling overcrowding.

We recognized this distinction between maximum occupancy restrictions and land use restrictions in Moore v. City of East Cleveland. In Moore, the Court held unconstitutional the constricted definition of "family" contained in East Cleveland's housing ordinance. East Cleveland's ordinance "selected certain categories of relatives who may live together and declared that others may not;" in particular, East Cleveland's definition of "family" made "a crime of a grandmother's choice to live with her grandson." In response to East Cleveland's argument that its aim was to prevent overcrowded dwellings, streets, and schools, we observed that the municipality's restrictive definition of family served the asserted, and undeniably legitimate, goals "marginally, at best." Another East Cleveland ordinance, we noted, "specifically addressed ... the problem of overcrowding"; that ordinance tied "the maximum permissible occupancy of a dwelling to the habitable floor area." Justice Stewart, in dissent, also distinguished restrictions designed to "preserve the character of a residential area," from prescription of "a minimum habitable floor area per person," the interest of community health and safety.

Section 3607(b)(1)'s language — "restrictions regarding the maximum number of occupants permitted to occupy a dwelling" — surely encompasses maximum occupancy restrictions.[8] But the formulation does not fit family composition rules typically tied to land use restrictions. In sum, rules that cap the total number of occupants in order to prevent overcrowding of a dwelling "plainly and unmistakably" fall within

---

8. The plain import of the statutory language is reinforced by the House Committee Report, which observes: "A number of jurisdictions limit the number of occupants per unit based on a minimum number of square feet in the unit or the sleeping areas of the unit. Reasonable limitations by governments would be allowed to continue, as long as they were applied to all occupants, and did not operate to discriminate on the basis of race, color, religion, sex, national origin, handicap or familial status." H. R. Rep. No. 100-711, p. 31 (1988).

§ 3607(b)(1)'s absolute exemption from the FHA's governance; rules designed to preserve the family character of a neighborhood, fastening on the composition of households rather than on the total number of occupants living quarters can contain, do not.[9]

B.

Turning specifically to the City's Community Development Code, we note that the provisions Edmonds invoked against Oxford House are classic examples of a use restriction and complementing family composition rule. These provisions do not cap the number of people who may live in a dwelling. In plain terms, they direct that dwellings be used only to house families. Captioned "USES," ECDC § 16.20.010 provides that the sole "Permitted Primary Use" in a single-family residential zone is "single-family dwelling units." Edmonds itself recognizes that this provision simply "defines those uses permitted in a single family residential zone."

A separate provision caps the number of occupants a dwelling may house, based on floor area:

> Floor Area. Every dwelling unit shall have at least one room which shall have not less than 120 square feet of floor area. Other habitable rooms, except kitchens, shall have an area of not less than 70 square feet. Where more than two persons occupy a room used for sleeping purposes, the required floor area shall be increased at the rate of 50 square feet for each occupant in excess of two. ECDC § 19.10.000 (adopting Uniform Housing Code § 503(b) (1988)).

This space and occupancy standard is a prototypical maximum occupancy restriction.

Edmonds nevertheless argues that its family composition rule, ECDC § 21.30.010, falls within § 3607(b)(1), the FHA exemption for maximum occupancy restrictions, because the rule caps at five the number of unrelated persons allowed to occupy a single-family dwelling. But Edmonds' family composition rule surely does not answer the question: "What is the maximum number of occupants permitted to occupy a house?" So long as they are related "by genetics, adoption, or marriage," any number of people can live in a house. Ten siblings, their parents and grandparents, for example, could dwell in a house in Edmonds' single-family residential zone without offending Edmonds' family composition rule.

Family living, not living space per occupant, is what ECDC § 21.30.010 describes. Defining family primarily by biological and legal relationships, the provision also accommodates another group association: five or fewer unrelated people are allowed to live together as though they were family. This accommodation is the peg on which Edmonds rests its plea for § 3607(b)(1) exemption. Had the City defined a family solely by biological and legal links, § 3607(b)(1) would not have been the ground on which Edmonds staked its case. It is curious reasoning indeed that converts a family values pre-

---

9. Tellingly, Congress added the § 3607(b)(1) exemption for maximum occupancy restrictions at the same time it enlarged the FHA to include a ban on discrimination based on "familial status." The provision making it illegal to discriminate in housing against families with children under the age of 18 prompted fears that landlords would be forced to allow large families to crowd into small housing units. Section 3607(b)(1) makes it plain that, pursuant to local prescriptions on maximum occupancy, landlords legitimately may refuse to stuff large families into small quarters. Congress further assured in § 3607(b)(1) that retirement communities would be exempt from the proscription of discrimination against families with minor children. In the sentence immediately following the maximum occupancy provision, § 3607(b)(1) states: "Nor does any provision in this subchapter regarding familial status apply with respect to housing for older persons."

server into a maximum occupancy restriction once a town adds to a related persons prescription "and also two unrelated persons."[11]

Edmonds additionally contends that subjecting single-family zoning to FHA scrutiny will "overturn Euclidian zoning" and "destroy the effectiveness and purpose of single-family zoning." This contention both ignores the limited scope of the issue before us and exaggerates the force of the FHA's antidiscrimination provisions. We address only whether Edmonds' family composition rule qualifies for § 3607(b)(1) exemption. Moreover, the FHA antidiscrimination provisions, when applicable, require only "reasonable" accommodations to afford persons with handicaps "equal opportunity to use and enjoy" housing.

The parties have presented, and we have decided, only a threshold question: Edmonds' zoning code provision describing who may compose a "family" is not a maximum occupancy restriction exempt from the FHA under § 3607(b)(1). It remains for the lower courts to decide whether Edmonds' actions against Oxford House violate the FHA's prohibitions against discrimination set out in §§ 3604(f)(1)(A) and (f)(3)(B)....

Justice Thomas, with whom Justice Scalia and Justice Kennedy join, dissenting. * * *

I.

To my mind, the rule that "no house ... shall have more than five occupants" (a "five-occupant limit") readily qualifies as a "restriction regarding the maximum number of occupants permitted to occupy a dwelling." In plain fashion, it "restrict[s]"—to five—"the maximum number of occupants permitted to occupy a dwelling." To be sure, as the majority observes, the restriction imposed by petitioner's zoning code is not an absolute one, because it does not apply to related persons. But § 3607(b)(1) does not set forth a narrow exemption only for "absolute" or "unqualified" restrictions regarding the maximum number of occupants. Instead, it sweeps broadly to exempt *any* restrictions *regarding* such maximum number. It is difficult to imagine what broader terms Congress could have used to signify the categories or kinds of relevant governmental restrictions that are exempt from the FHA. * * *

The majority does not ask whether petitioner's zoning code imposes any restrictions regarding the maximum number of occupants permitted to occupy a dwelling. Instead, observing that pursuant to ECDC § 21.30.010, "any number of people can live in a house," so long as they are "related 'by genetics, adoption, or marriage,'" the majority concludes that § 21.30.010 does not qualify for § 3607(b)(1)'s exemption because it "surely does not answer the question: 'What is the maximum number of occupants permitted to occupy a house?'" The majority's question, however, does not accord with the text of the statute. To take advantage of the exemption, a local, state, or federal law need not impose a restriction *establishing* an *absolute* maximum number of occupants; under § 3607(b)(1), it is necessary only that such law impose a restriction "regarding" the maximum number of occupants. Surely, a restriction can "regard"—or "concern," "re-

---

11. This curious reasoning drives the dissent. If Edmonds allowed only related persons (whatever their number) to dwell in a house in a single-family zone, then the dissent, it appears, would agree that the § 3607(b)(1) exemption is unavailable. But so long as the City introduces a specific number—*any* number (two will do)—the City can insulate its single-family zone *entirely* from FHA coverage. The exception-takes-the-rule reading the dissent advances is hardly the "generous construction" warranted for antidiscrimination prescriptions. See Trafficante v. Metropolitan Life Ins. Co.

late to," or "bear on"—the maximum number of occupants without establishing an absolute maximum number in all cases.[2]

I would apply §3607(b)(1) as it is written. Because petitioner's zoning code imposes a qualified "restriction regarding the maximum number of occupants permitted to occupy a dwelling," and because the statute exempts from the FHA "any" such restrictions, I would reverse the Ninth Circuit's holding that the exemption does not apply in this case.

II.

The majority's failure to ask the right question about petitioner's zoning code results from a more fundamental error in focusing on "maximum occupancy restrictions" and "family composition rules." These two terms—and the two categories of zoning rules they describe—are simply irrelevant to this case.

A.

As an initial matter, I do not agree with the majority's interpretive premise that "this case [is] an instance in which an exception to 'a general statement of policy' is sensibly read 'narrowly in order to preserve the primary operation of the [policy].'" ....

[T]he majority's interpretive premise clashes with our decision in Gregory v. Ashcroft, 501 U.S. 452 (1991), in which we held that state judges are not protected by the Age Discrimination in Employment Act of 1967 (ADEA)....

Behind our refusal in Gregory to give a narrow construction to the ADEA's exemption for "appointee[s] on the policymaking level" was our holding that the power of Congress to "legislate in areas traditionally regulated by the States" is "an extraordinary power in a federalist system," and "a power that we must assume Congress does not exercise lightly." Thus, we require that "'Congress should make its intention "clear and manifest" if it intends to pre-empt the historic powers of the States.'" It is obvious that land use—the subject of petitioner's zoning code—is an area traditionally regulated by the States rather than by Congress, and that land use regulation is one of the historic powers of the States. As we have stated, "zoning laws and their provisions ... are peculiarly within the province of state and local legislative authorities." Warth v. Seldin[, 422 U.S. 490 (1975)]; Village of Belle Terre v. Boraas (Marshall, J., dissenting) ("I am in full agreement with the majority that zoning ... may indeed be the most essential function performed by local government"). Accordingly, even if it might be sensible in other contexts to construe exemptions narrowly, that principle has no application in this case.

B.

I turn now to the substance of the majority's analysis, the focus of which is "maximum occupancy restrictions" and "family composition rules." The first of these two terms has

---

2. It is ironic that the majority cites Uniform Housing Code §503(b) (1988), which has been incorporated into petitioner's zoning code as a "prototypical maximum occupancy restriction" that would qualify for §§3607(b)(1)'s exemption. Because §503(b), as the majority describes it, "caps the number of occupants a dwelling may house, *based on floor area*," it actually caps the *density* of occupants, not their *number*. By itself, therefore, §503(b) "surely does not answer the question: 'What is the maximum number of occupants permitted to occupy a house?'" That is, even under §503(b), there is no single absolute maximum number of occupants that applies to every house in Edmonds. Thus, the answer to the majority's question is the same with respect to both §503(b) and ECDC §21.30.010: "It depends." With respect to the former, it depends on the size of the house's bedrooms; with respect to the latter, it depends on whether the house's occupants are related.

the sole function of serving as a label for a category of zoning rules simply invented by the majority: rules that "cap the number of occupants per dwelling, typically in relation to available floor space or the number and type of rooms," that "ordinarily apply uniformly to *all* residents of *all* dwelling units," and that have the "purpose ... to protect health and safety by preventing dwelling overcrowding." The majority's term does bear a familial resemblance to the statutory term "restrictions regarding the maximum number of occupants permitted to occupy a dwelling," but it should be readily apparent that the category of zoning rules the majority labels "maximum occupancy restrictions" does not exhaust the category of restrictions exempted from the FHA by § 3607(b)(1). The plain words of the statute do not refer to "available floor space or the number and type of rooms"; they embrace no requirement that the exempted restrictions "apply uniformly to *all* residents of *all* dwelling units"; and they give no indication that such restrictions must have the "purpose ... to protect health and safety by preventing dwelling overcrowding." * * *

In sum, it does not matter that ECDC § 21.030.010 describes "family living, not living space per occupant" because it is immaterial under § 3607(b)(1) whether § 21.030.010 constitutes a "family composition rule" but not a "maximum occupancy restriction." The sole relevant question is whether petitioner's zoning code imposes "any ... restrictions regarding the maximum number of occupants permitted to occupy a dwelling." Because I believe it does, I respectfully dissent.

Southern Burlington County N.A.A.C.P. v. Township of Mount Laurel
92 N.J. 158, 456 A.2d 390 (1983)

John E. Harrington, submitted briefs on behalf of appellant (Hartman, Schlesinger, Schlosser & Faxon, attorneys).

Thomas R. Farino, Jr., submitted briefs on behalf of respondent Township Committee of the Township of Monroe.*

J. William Barba and Glenn S. Pantel, argued the cause for amici curiae Assemblyman James J. Barry, Jr., Senator James S. Cafiero, Senator Lee B. Laskin, Senator S. Thomas Gagliano, Senator Walter E. Foran, Senator Wayne Dumont, Jr., Senator Donald T. DiFrancesco, Senator John H. Dorsey, Senator James P. Vreeland, Jr., Senator Garrett W. Hagedorn, Senator John H. Ewing, Assemblyman James R. Hurley, Assemblyman John A. Rocco, Assemblyman Thomas J. Shusted, Assemblyman H. James Saxton, As-

---

* Henry D. Blinder, Deputy Attorney General, submitted briefs on behalf of amicus curiae Department of Community Affairs, John J. Degnan, Attorney General of New Jersey, attorney; Stephen Skillman, Assistant Attorney General, of counsel; Henry D. Blinder, Dennis R. Casale and Daniel P. Reynolds, Deputy Attorneys General, on the briefs).

Alphonse A. Stanzione, Jr., submitted a brief on behalf of amici curiae The Manufactured Housing Association in New Jersey and Manufactured Housing Institute, Inc. (A-35/36) (Stanzione & Stanzione, attorneys; Edward F. Canfield and Robert E. Heggestad, members of the District of Columbia bar, of counsel).

Thomas Norman submitted a brief on behalf of amicus curiae American Planning Association, New Jersey Chapter.

Martin F. Murphy submitted a brief on behalf of amicus curiae Township of West Milford (Johnson, Johnson & Murphy, attorneys).

Samuel W. Lambert, III submitted a brief on behalf of amicus curiae Environmental Defense Fund, Inc.(Smith, Cook, Lambert & Miller, attorneys; James T. B. Tripp, a member of the New York bar, of counsel).

semblyman Clifford W. Snedeker, Assemblyman William F. Dowd, Assemblyman Anthony M. Villane, Jr., Assemblyman John O. Bennett, Assemblywoman Marie S. Muhler, Assemblyman Robert E. Littell, Assemblyman Walter J. Kavanaugh, Assemblyman Elliott F. Smith, Assemblyman Robert D. Franks, Assemblyman William J. Maguire, Assemblyman Arthur R. Albohn, Assemblywoman Barbara A. Curran, Assemblyman Dean A. Gallo, Assemblywoman Jane Burgio, Assemblyman Frederic Remington, Assemblyman Carl A. Orechio, Assemblyman Anthony Imperiale, Assemblyman Emil Olszowy, Assemblyman Louis F. Kosco, Assemblyman John B. Paolella, Assemblyman Gerald Cardinale, Assemblyman John W. Markert, Assemblyman Walter M. D. Kern, Jr., Assemblyman Karl Weidel and Assemblyman Charles L. Hardwick (Shanley & Fisher, attorneys; J. William Barba, Glenn S. Pantel and Richard A. Levao, on the briefs).

Arnold K. Mytelka, argued the cause for amicus curiae City of Newark (Clapp & Eisenberg, attorneys; Philip S. Elberg, of counsel).

Marilyn J. Morheuser, and Martin E. Sloane, a member of the District of Columbia bar, argued the cause for appellants (Marilyn J. Morheuser, attorney; Martin E. Sloane and Roger C. Rosenthal, a member of the District of Columbia bar, of counsel).

Philip Lindeman, II, argued the cause for appellants and cross-respondents (Hellring, Lindeman, Goldstein & Siegal, attorneys).

Robert Benbrook, argued the cause for appellant (A-8) (Morrow & Benbrook, attorneys; Robert Benbrook and James W. Tubbs, on the briefs).

Richard F. Bellman, a member of the New York bar, argued the cause for appellants (Courter, Kobert & Pease, attorneys; Joel Kobert, on the briefs).

Michael J. Herbert, argued the cause for appellant (Sterns, Herbert & Weinroth, attorneys; Michael J. Herbert and Joel H. Sterns, of counsel and on the briefs).

Carl S. Bisgaier, Director, Division of Public Interest Advocacy, and Kenneth E. Meiser, Deputy Director, Division of Public Interest Advocacy, argued the cause for appellants and amicus curiae Department of the Public Advocate, and Kenneth E. Meiser submitted a brief on behalf of respondents (Stanley C. Van Ness, Public Advocate, attorney; Peter J. O'Connor, of counsel; Carl S. Bisgaier, Kenneth E. Meiser, Linds R. Hurd and Linda R. Pancotto and Stephen Eisdorfer, Assistant Deputy Public Advocates, on the briefs).

S. David Brandt, argued the cause for intervenor and cross-respondent and submitted a brief on behalf of intervenor-respondent (Brandt, Haughey, Penberthy, Lewis & Hyland, attorneys; S. David Brandt and Gerald E. Haughey, on the briefs).

John E. Patton and John W. Trimble argued the cause for respondent and cross-appellant (A-35/36) (Trimble & Master, attorneys).

William C. Moran, Jr., argued the cause for respondent Township Committee of the Township of Cranbury (Huff & Moran, attorneys).

Bertram E. Busch argued the cause for respondent Township Committee of the Township of East Brunswick (Busch & Busch, attorneys).

Daniel S. Bernstein argued the cause for respondent Township Committee of the Township of Piscataway (Sachar, Bernstein, Rothberg, Sikora & Mongello, attorneys; Daniel S. Bernstein and Marilyn R. Frankenthaler, on the briefs).

Joseph L. Stonaker argued the cause for respondent Township Committee of the Township of Plainsboro (A-4) (Stonaker & Stonaker, attorneys; Joseph L. Stonaker and Janice B. Stonaker, on the briefs).

Barry C. Brechman argued the cause for respondent Township Committee of the Township of South Brunswick.

Sanford E. Chernin argued the cause for respondent Mayor and Council of the Borough of South Plainfield (Chernin & Freeman, attorneys).

Alfred L. Ferguson argued the cause for respondents and cross-appellants (McCarter & English, attorneys).

Richard G. O'Brien argued the cause for respondents (Bowers, Rinehart, Murphy & O'Brien, attorneys; Richard G. O'Brien and Steven B. Lieberman, on the briefs).

Brian T. Campion argued the cause for respondent (A-18) (Breslin & Breslin, attorneys).

Roger M. Cain argued the cause for respondents Township of Clinton, etc. and Township Council of the Township of Clinton (Felter, Cain & Shurts, attorneys; Roger M. Cain and William A. Shurts, on the briefs).

Francis P. Sutton, argued the cause for respondent Planning Board of the Township of Clinton.

Chief Justice Wilentz and Justices Sullivan, Pashman, Clifford, Schreiber, Handler, and Pollock.

Wilentz, C.J.

This is the return, eight years later, of Southern Burlington County N.A.A.C.P. v. Township of Mount Laurel, 67 N.J. 151, 336 A.2d 713 (1975) (Mount Laurel I). We set forth in that case, for the first time, the doctrine requiring that municipalities' land use regulations provide a realistic opportunity for low and moderate income housing. The doctrine has become famous. The Mount Laurel case itself threatens to become infamous. After all this time, ten years after the trial court's initial order invalidating its zoning ordinance, Mount Laurel remains afflicted with a blatantly exclusionary ordinance. Papered over with studies, rationalized by hired experts, the ordinance at its core is true to nothing but Mount Laurel's determination to exclude the poor. Mount Laurel is not alone; we believe that there is widespread non-compliance with the constitutional mandate of our original opinion in this case.

To the best of our ability, we shall not allow it to continue. This Court is more firmly committed to the original Mount Laurel doctrine than ever, and we are determined, within appropriate judicial bounds, to make it work. The obligation is to provide a realistic opportunity for housing, not litigation. We have learned from experience, however, that unless a strong judicial hand is used, Mount Laurel will not result in housing, but in paper, process, witnesses, trials and appeals. We intend by this decision to strengthen it, clarify it, and make it easier for public officials, including judges, to apply it.

This case is accompanied by five others, heard together and decided in this opinion. All involve questions arising from the Mount Laurel doctrine. They demonstrate the need to put some steel into that doctrine. The deficiencies in its application range from uncertainty and inconsistency at the trial level to inflexible review criteria at the appellate level. The waste of judicial energy involved at every level is substantial and is matched only by the often needless expenditure of talent on the part of lawyers and experts. The length and complexity of trials is often outrageous, and the expense of litigation is so high that a real question develops whether the municipality can afford to defend or the plaintiffs can afford to sue.

There is another side to the story. We believe, both through the representations of counsel and from our own research and experience, that the doctrine has done some good, indeed, perhaps substantial good. We have tried to make the doctrine clearer for we believe that most municipal officials will in good faith strive to fulfill their constitutional duty. There are a number of municipalities around the State that have responded to our decisions by amending their zoning ordinances to provide realistic opportunities for the construction of low and moderate income housing. Further, many other municipalities have at least recognized their obligation to provide such opportunities in their ordinances and master plans. Finally, state and county government agencies have responded by preparing regional housing plans that help both the courts and municipalities themselves carry out the Mount Laurel mandate. Still, we are far from where we had hoped to be and nowhere near where we should be with regard to the administration of the doctrine in our courts.

These six cases not only afford the opportunity for, but demonstrate the necessity of reexamining the Mount Laurel doctrine. We do so here. The doctrine is right but its administration has been ineffective.

A brief statement of the cases may be helpful at this point. Mount Laurel II results from the remand by this Court of the original Mount Laurel case. The municipality rezoned, purportedly pursuant to our instructions, a plenary trial was held, and the trial court found that the rezoning constituted a bona fide attempt by Mount Laurel to provide a realistic opportunity for the construction of its fair share of the regional lower income housing need. Reading our cases at that time (1978) as requiring no more, the trial court dismissed the complaint of the N.A.A.C.P. and other plaintiffs but granted relief in the form of a builder's remedy, to a developer-intervenor who had attacked the total prohibition against mobile homes. Plaintiffs' appeal of the trial court's ruling sustaining the ordinance in all other respects was directly certified by this Court, as ultimately was defendant's appeal from the grant of a builder's remedy allowing construction of mobile homes. We reverse and remand to determine Mount Laurel's fair share of the regional need and for further proceedings to revise its ordinance; we affirm the grant of the builder's remedy. * * *

I.

Background

A. History of the Mount Laurel Doctrine

In Mount Laurel I, this Court held that a zoning ordinance that contravened the general welfare was unconstitutional. We pointed out that a developing municipality violated that constitutional mandate by excluding housing for lower income people; that it would satisfy that constitutional obligation by affirmatively affording a realistic opportunity for the construction of its fair share of the present and prospective regional need for low and moderate income housing. [ ] This is the core of the Mount Laurel doctrine. Although the Court set forth important guidelines for implementing the doctrine, their application to particular cases was complex, and the resolution of many questions left uncertain. Was it a "developing" municipality? What was the "region," and how was it to be determined? How was the "fair share" to be calculated within that region? Precisely what must that municipality do to "affirmatively afford" an opportunity for the construction of lower income housing? Other questions were similarly troublesome. When should a court order the granting of a building permit (i.e., a builder's remedy) to a plaintiff-developer who has successfully challenged a zoning ordinance on Mount Laurel grounds? How should courts deal with the complicated procedural aspects of Mount Laurel litigation, such as the appointment of experts and masters, the joinder of defendant municipalities, and the problem of interlocutory appeals? These have been the principal questions that New Jersey courts have faced in attempting to implement the Mount Laurel mandate, and the principal questions dealt with in this opinion. * * *

B. Constitutional Basis for Mount Laurel and the Judicial Role

The constitutional basis for the Mount Laurel doctrine remains the same. The constitutional power to zone, delegated to the municipalities subject to legislation, is but one portion of the police power and, as such, must be exercised for the general welfare. When the exercise of that power by a municipality affects something as fundamental as housing, the general welfare includes more than the welfare of that municipality and its citizens: it also includes the general welfare—in this case the housing needs—of those residing outside of the municipality but within the region that contributes to the housing demand within the municipality. Municipal land use regulations that conflict with the general welfare thus defined abuse the police power and are unconstitutional. In particular, those regulations that do not provide the requisite opportunity for a fair share of the region's need for low and moderate income housing conflict with the general welfare and violate the state constitutional requirements of substantive due process and equal protection. * * *

Subject to the clear obligation to preserve open space and prime agricultural land, a builder in New Jersey who finds it economically feasible to provide decent housing for lower income groups will no longer find it governmentally impossible. Builders may not be able to build just where they want—our parks, farms, and conservation areas are not a land bank for housing speculators. But if sound planning of an area allows the rich and middle class to live there, it must also realistically and practically allow the poor. And if the area will accommodate factories, it must also find space for workers. The specific location of such housing will of course continue to depend on sound municipal land use planning.

While Mount Laurel I discussed the need for "an appropriate variety and choice of housing," the specific constitutional obligation addressed there, as well as in our opinion here, is that relating to low and moderate income housing. All that we say here concerns that category alone; the doctrine as we interpret it has no present applicability to other kinds of housing. It is obvious that eight years after Mount Laurel I the need for satisfaction of this doctrine is greater than ever. Upper and middle income groups may search with increasing difficulty for housing within their means; for low and moderate income people, there is nothing to search for.

No one has challenged the Mount Laurel doctrine on these appeals. Nevertheless, a brief reminder of the judicial role in this sensitive area is appropriate, since powerful reasons suggest, and we agree, that the matter is better left to the Legislature. We act first and foremost because the Constitution of our State requires protection of the interests involved and because the Legislature has not protected them. We recognize the social and economic controversy (and its political consequences) that has resulted in relatively little legislative action in this field. We understand the enormous difficulty of achieving a political consensus that might lead to significant legislation enforcing the constitutional mandate better than we can, legislation that might completely remove this Court from those controversies. But enforcement of constitutional rights cannot await a supporting political consensus. So while we have always preferred legislative to judicial action in this field, we shall continue—until the Legislature acts—to do our best to uphold the constitutional obligation that underlies the Mount Laurel doctrine. That is our duty. We may not build houses, but we do enforce the Constitution.

C. Summary of Rulings

Our rulings today have several purposes. First, we intend to encourage voluntary compliance with the constitutional obligation by defining it more clearly. We believe that the use of the State Development Guide Plan and the confinement of all Mount Laurel litigation to a small group of judges, selected by the Chief Justice with the approval of the Court, will tend to serve that purpose. Second, we hope to simplify litigation in this area. While we are not overly optimistic, we think that the remedial use of the SDGP may achieve that purpose, given the significance accorded it in this opinion. Third, the decisions are intended to increase substantially the effectiveness of the judicial remedy. In most cases, upon determination that the municipality has not fulfilled its constitutional obligation, the trial court will retain jurisdiction, order an immediate revision of the ordinance (including, if necessary, supervision of the revision through a court appointed master), and require the use of effective affirmative planning and zoning devices. The long delays of interminable appellate review will be discouraged, if not completely ended, and the opportunity for low and moderate income housing found in the new ordinance will be as realistic as judicial remedies can make it. We hope to achieve all of these purposes while preserving the fundamental legitimate control of municipalities over their own zoning and, indeed, their destiny. * * *

II.

Resolution of the Issues

A. Defining the Mount Laurel Obligation

The Constitution of the State of New Jersey does not require bad planning. It does not require suburban spread.... There is nothing in our Constitution that says that we cannot satisfy our constitutional obligation to provide lower income housing and, at the same time, plan the future of the state intelligently.

Sound planning requires that municipalities containing "growth areas" have a Mount Laurel obligation and that, together, all of those municipalities affirmatively provide a realistic opportunity for the construction of sufficient lower income housing to meet the needs of New Jersey's lower income population. * * *

As noted before, all municipalities' land use regulations will be required to provide a realistic opportunity for the construction of their fair share of the region's present lower income housing need generated by present dilapidated or overcrowded lower income units, including their own. Municipalities located in "growth areas" may, of course, have an obligation to meet the present need of the region that goes far beyond that generated in the municipality itself; there may be some municipalities, however, in growth areas where the portion of the region's present need generated by that municipality far exceeds the municipality's fair share. The portion of the region's present need that must be addressed by municipalities in growth areas will depend, then, on conventional fair share analysis, some municipality's fair share being more than the present need generated within the municipality and in some cases less. In non-growth areas, however (limited growth, conservation, and agricultural), no municipality will have to provide for more than the present need generated within the municipality, for to require more than that would be to induce growth in that municipality in conflict with the SDGP. * * *

C. Calculating Fair Share

The most troublesome issue in Mount Laurel litigation is the determination of fair share. It takes the most time, produces the greatest variety of opinions, and engenders doubt as to the meaning and wisdom of Mount Laurel. Determination of fair share has required resolution of three separate issues: identifying the relevant region, determining its present and prospective housing needs, and allocating those needs to the municipality or municipalities involved. Each of these issues produces a morass of facts, statistics, projections, theories and opinions sufficient to discourage even the staunchest supporters of Mount Laurel. The problem is capable of monopolizing counsel's time for years, overwhelming trial courts and inundating reviewing courts with a record on review of superhuman dimensions.

We have had enough experience with Mount Laurel litigation to warrant procedural modifications designed, over a period of time, to simplify these determinations. The procedural modification provided in this opinion (confining all Mount Laurel litigation to a limited number of judges) is well within conventional judicial techniques. * * *

As for fair share, we offer some suggestions. Formulas that accord substantial weight to employment opportunities in the municipality, especially new employment accompanied by substantial ratables, shall be favored; formulas that have the effect of tying prospective lower income housing needs to the present proportion of lower income residents to the total population of a municipality shall be disfavored; formulas that have the effect of unreasonably diminishing the share because of a municipality's successful exclusion of lower income housing in the past shall be disfavored.

In determining fair share, the court should decide the proportion between low and moderate income housing unless there are substantial reasons not to do so. The provisions and devices needed to produce moderate income housing may fall short of those needed for lower. Since there are two fairly distinct lower income housing needs, an effort must be made to meet both. * * *

D. Meeting the Mount Laurel Obligation

1. Removing Excessive Restrictions and Exactions

In order to meet their Mount Laurel obligations, municipalities, at the very least, must remove all municipally created barriers to the construction of their fair share of lower income housing. Thus, to the extent necessary to meet their prospective fair share and provide for their indigenous poor (and, in some cases, a portion of the region's poor), municipalities must remove zoning and subdivision restrictions and exactions that are not necessary to protect health and safety. * * *

2. Using Affirmative Measures

Despite the emphasis in Mount Laurel I on the affirmative nature of the fair share obligation, the obligation has been sometimes construed as requiring in effect no more than a theoretical, rather than realistic, opportunity. As noted later, the alleged realistic opportunity for lower income housing in Mount Laurel II is provided through three zones owned entirely by three individuals. There is absolutely no assurance that there is anything realistic in this "opportunity": the individuals may, for many different reasons, simply not desire to build lower income housing. They may not want to build any housing at all, they may want to use the land for industry, for business, or just leave it vacant. It was never intended in Mount Laurel I that this awesome constitutional obligation, designed to give the poor a fair chance for housing, be satisfied by meaningless amendments to zoning or other ordinances. "Affirmative," in the Mount Laurel rule, suggests that the municipality is going to do something, and "realistic opportunity" suggests that what it is going to do will make it realistically possible for lower income housing to be built. Satisfaction of the Mount Laurel doctrine cannot depend on the inclination of developers to help the poor. It has to depend on affirmative inducements to make the opportunity real. * * *

There are two basic types of affirmative measures that a municipality can use to make the opportunity for lower income housing realistic: (1) encouraging or requiring the use of available state or federal housing subsidies, and (2) providing incentives for or requiring private developers to set aside a portion of their developments for lower income housing. Which, if either, of these devices will be necessary in any particular municipality to assure compliance with the constitutional mandate will be initially up to the municipality itself. Where necessary, the trial court overseeing compliance may require their use. We note again that least-cost housing will not ordinarily satisfy a municipality's fair share obligation to provide low and moderate income housing unless and until it has attempted the inclusionary devices outlined below or otherwise has proven the futility of the attempt.

E. Judicial Remedies

If a trial court determines that a municipality has not met its Mount Laurel obligation, it shall order the municipality to revise its zoning ordinance within a set time period to comply with the constitutional mandate; if the municipality fails adequately to revise its ordinance within that time, the court shall implement the remedies for noncompliance outlined below; and if plaintiff is a developer, the court shall determine whether a builder's remedy should be granted.

1. Builder's Remedy

Builder's [sic] remedies have been one of many controversial aspects of the Mount Laurel doctrine. Plaintiffs, particularly plaintiff-developers, maintain that these remedies are (i) essential to maintain a significant level of Mount Laurel litigation, and the only effective method to date of enforcing compliance; (ii) required by principles of fairness to compensate developers who have invested substantial time and resources in pursuing such litigation; and (iii) the most likely means of ensuring that lower income housing is actually built. Defendant municipalities contend that even if a plaintiff-developer obtains a judgment that a particular municipality has not complied with Mount Laurel, that municipality, and not the developer, should be allowed to determine how and where its fair share obligation will be met.

In [Oakwood at Madison, Inc. v. Township of] Madison, this Court, while granting a builder's remedy to the plaintiff appeared to discourage such remedies in the future by stating that "such relief will ordinarily be rare." Experience since Madison, however, has demonstrated to us that builder's remedies must be made more readily available to achieve compliance with Mount Laurel. We hold that where a developer succeeds in Mount Laurel litigation and proposes a project providing a substantial amount of lower income housing, a builder's remedy should be granted unless the municipality establishes that because of environmental or other substantial planning concerns, the plaintiff's proposed project is clearly contrary to sound land use planning. We emphasize that the builder's remedy should not be denied solely because the municipality prefers some other location for lower income housing, even if it is in fact a better site. Nor is it essential that considerable funds be invested or that the litigation be intensive.

Other problems concerning builder's remedies require discussion. Care must be taken to make certain that Mount Laurel is not used as an unintended bargaining chip in a builder's negotiations with the municipality, and that the courts not be used as the enforcer for the builder's threat to bring Mount Laurel litigation if municipal approvals for projects containing no lower income housing are not forthcoming. Proof of such threats shall be sufficient to defeat Mount Laurel litigation by that developer. * * *

It would be useful to remind ourselves that the doctrine does not arise from some theoretical analysis of our Constitution, but rather from underlying concepts of fundamental fairness in the exercise of governmental power. The basis for the constitutional obligation is simple: the State controls the use of land, all of the land. In exercising that control it cannot favor rich over poor. It cannot legislatively set aside dilapidated housing in urban ghettos for the poor and decent housing elsewhere for everyone else. The government that controls this land represents everyone. While the State may not have the ability to eliminate poverty, it cannot use that condition as the basis for imposing further disadvantages. And the same applies to the municipality, to which this control over the land has been constitutionally delegated.

Huntington Branch, N.A.A.C.P. v. Town of Huntington
844 F.2d 926 (2d Cir. 1988)
aff'd in part, 488 U.S. 15 (1988) (*per curiam*)

Richard F. Bellman, Steel, Bellman and Levine, P.C., New York, (Lewis M. Steel, Miriam F. Clark, New York, Grover G. Hankins, General Counsel, National Association for the Advancement of Colored People, Baltimore, Maryland, on the brief), for Plaintiffs-Appellants.

Richard C. Cahn, Cahn, Wishod, Wishod, and Lamb, Melville, New York (Scott M. Carson, on the brief), for Defendants-Appellees.

Before Kaufman, Oakes, and Newman, Circuit Judges.

Kaufman, Circuit Judge.

Twenty years ago, widespread racial segregation threatened to rip civil society asunder. In response, Congress adopted broad remedial provisions to promote integration. One such statute, Title VIII of the Civil Rights Act of 1968, was enacted "to provide, within constitutional limitations, for fair housing throughout the United States." 42 U.S.C. § 3601. Today, we are called upon to decide whether an overwhelmingly white suburb's zoning regulation, which restricts private multi-family housing projects to a largely minority "urban renewal area," and the Town Board's refusal to amend that ordinance to allow construction of subsidized housing in a white neighborhood violate the Fair Housing Act.

[Plaintiffs-Appellants are] the Huntington Branch of the National Association for the Advancement of Colored People (NAACP), Housing Help, Inc. (HHI), and two black, low-income residents of Huntington. HHI sought to construct an integrated, multi-family subsidized apartment complex in Greenlawn/East Northport, a virtually all-white neighborhood. The Town's zoning ordinance, however, prohibited private construction of multi-family housing outside a small urban renewal zone in the Huntington Station neighborhood, which is 52% minority. [Plaintiffs] petitioned the Town to revise its code to accommodate the project. When the Town refused, [they sued]. * * *

[T]he district court refused to invalidate the zoning restriction. The district judge, however, incorrectly employed an intent-based standard for the disparate impact claim asserted here both in analyzing the showing of effect and in scrutinizing the validity of the Town's reasons for rejection. Accordingly, we reverse and, finding a Title VIII violation, grant appellants' request for site-specific relief.

Huntington is a town of approximately 200,000 people located in the northwest corner of Suffolk County, New York. In 1980, 95% of its residents were white. Blacks comprised only 3.35% of the Town's population and were concentrated in areas known as Huntington Station and South Greenlawn. Specifically, 43% of the total black population lived in four census tracts in Huntington Station and 27% in two census tracts in the South Greenlawn area. Outside these two neighborhoods, the Town's population was overwhelmingly white. Of the 48 census tracts in the Town in 1980, 30 contained black populations of less than 1%.

The district court found that the Town has a shortage of affordable rental housing for low and moderate-income households. The Town's Housing Assistance Plan (HAP), which is adopted by the Town Board and filed with HUD as part of Huntington's application for federal community development funds, reveals that the impact of this shortage is three times greater on blacks than on the overall population. Under the 1982-1985 HAP, for example, 7% of all Huntington families required subsidized housing, while 24% of black families needed such housing.

In addition, a disproportionately large percentage of families in existing subsidized projects are minority. In Gateway Gardens, a public housing project built in 1967, 38 of 40 units were occupied by blacks and Hispanics in 1984. Seventy-four percent of those on the project's waiting list were minority. In Whitman Village, a 260-unit HUD subsidized development built in 1971, 56% of the families were minority in 1984. Lincoln Manor, which was built in 1980, is a 30-unit HUD Section 8 project. Thirty percent of the households and 45% of those on the waiting list were minority in 1984. In January 1984, 68% of families holding Section 8 certificates and 61% of those on the waiting list were minority.

Although a disproportionate number of minorities need low-cost housing, the Town has attempted to limit minority occupancy in subsidized housing projects. The Director of Huntington's Community Development agency and the Executive Director of the Huntington Housing Authority repeatedly told whites opposing the Lincoln Manor project that they would impose a racial quota on occupancy. [A 5% minority quota was set.] HUD advised the Huntington Housing Authority that it would not permit a racial quota at Lincoln Manor. The Town similarly attempted to impose racial quotas on occupancy at a proposed 150-unit subsidized housing project. When HUD's Area Director wrote that "limitations on minority occupancy of housing on the Huntington Station site are not justifiable and will not be permitted," the Town Board unanimously passed a resolution withdrawing its support for the project because they could not "ensure a particular ethnic mix."

Under the Town's zoning ordinance, multi-family housing is permitted only in an "R-3M Apartment District." ... On its face, this provision limits private construction of multi-family housing to the Town's urban renewal area, where 52% of the residents are minority.[4] It does permit the Huntington Housing Authority (HHA) to build multi-family housing townwide. But HHA's only project, Gateway Gardens, is in the urban renewal zone. The private housing projects are also in or nearby the urban renewal area. Whitman Village is adjacent to Gateway Gardens in census blocks that are over 40% minority. Lincoln Manor, only a few blocks from the projects in the urban renewal area, is also in a racially impacted census block.

The Town's zoning ordinance also includes a special category for multi-family housing for senior citizens called "R-RM Retirement Community District." Only one such development—Paumanack Village—has been built in Huntington. It is the only multi-family housing for low income people which is situated in an overwhelmingly white neighborhood. The development itself is largely white, having a black occupancy of 3%.

Only one vacant parcel of land in Huntington currently is zoned R-3M and thus would be eligible for the appellants' proposed development: the MIA site. The Town in 1980 requested pre-approval for 150 units of Section 8 housing on this site.[5]

In response to the great need for subsidized housing in the Town, HHI decided to sponsor an integrated housing project for low-income families. HHI determined that the project could foster racial integration only if it were located in a white neighborhood outside the Huntington Station and South Greenlawn areas. This decision eliminated consideration of the MIA site, the only vacant R-3M property located in the urban renewal area.

In its effort to create racially integrated, low-cost housing, HHI actively sought the assistance of Town officials. In response to [an official's] suggestion, HHI commissioned a study to assess whether [rehabilitation of a vacant school were feasible; the conclusion was negative.]. Throughout 1979, [the official] assured HHI that existing zoning should not impede their efforts because the Town Board would amend the zoning ordinance if it supported the organization's project.

After a lengthy search, HHI determined that a 14.8 acre parcel located at the corner of Elwood and Pulaski Roads in the Town was well suited for a 162-unit housing project. This flat, largely cleared and well-drained property was near public transportation, shopping and other services, and immediately adjacent to schools.

Ninety-eight percent of the population within a one-mile radius of the site is white. HHI set a goal of 25% minority occupants. The district court found that "a significant percentage of the tenants [at Matinecock Court] would have belonged to minority groups."

[The official] assured [HHI] that the property's R-40 designation (single family homes on one-acre lots) should not be an obstacle because the Town Board, if it supported the project, would simply amend the zoning ordinance.

HHI obtained its option to purchase the Elwood-Pulaski parcel [and asked] the Town Board to rezone the property. In August 1980, HHI and National Housing Partnership, an owner-manager of federally subsidized housing, filed a joint application with HUD for Section 8 funding for the project.

---

4. The Town claims a broadened interpretation of the R-3M provision. That [interpretation is in a letter] dated August 22, 1978 ... [which states that] "so long as the subject premises is within a community development area" it can be rezoned as R-3M property. The Town claims it informed HHI of this interpretation. The letter, however, was not made public until 1984 in the midst of this litigation.

5. Although pre-approval was granted, the project was delayed by community opposition and by an attempt to reserve 30 units for the elderly and to set a limit on black participation of 10%....

At the time HHI applied for the Section 8 funding, Huntington had a Housing Assistance Plan, which had been approved by HUD. Pursuant to the provisions of the Housing and Community Development Act of 1974, when a town has such a plan, HUD must refer a Section 8 application to the Town for comment. The Town Supervisor set forth seven reasons why Huntington opposed the project.

The Town's professional staff in the Planning, Legal and Community Development Departments have reviewed the proposal and have submitted the following comments:

1. The HUD-approved Housing Assistance Plan (both the three-year goal submitted with the Community Development Block Grant 1979–80 application and the annual goal submitted with the 1980–1981 Community Development Block Grant) contains no "new construction" units as a program goal.

2. The plan for development cannot be carried out within the existing single family R-40 (1 acre) zoning.

3. The development is located at the intersection of two heavily trafficked streets.

4. The site plan presents a poor parking plan in terms of location with respect to the units, substandard in size and the lack of streets results in very poor fire protection access.

5. The development is located adjacent to both the Long Island Railroad as well as a LILCO substation. This is in addition to the heavy traffic conditions.

6. The site plan shows recreation and/or play areas very inadequate for the number and type of dwelling units being proposed.

7. The three and four-bedroom units are quite undersized; have poor layout; bedrooms are much too small; living space is unrealistic; no storage; one full and two half-baths for a family of 6 to 8 is not realistic.

When the proposal became public, substantial community opposition developed. A group called the Concerned Citizens Association was formed, and a petition containing 4,100 signatures against the proposal was submitted to the Town Board. A protest meeting in November drew about 2,000 persons. Supervisor Butterfield was the principal speaker and assured the audience of his opposition to the project. Matinecock Court came before the Town Board at a meeting on January 6, 1981. The Board rejected the proposed zoning change and adopted [a] resolution [that concluded]:

that although favoring housing for the senior citizens and others, in appropriate areas, that the location referred to herein is not an appropriate location due to lack of transportation, traffic hazard and disruption of the existing residential patterns in the Elwood area and requests that (HUD) reject the application. * * *

[T]he [district] court adopted the four-prong disparate impact test set out in Metropolitan Housing Development. v. Village of Arlington Heights [558 F.2d 1283, 1290 (7th Cir. 1977)] (Arlington Heights II):

(1) how strong is the plaintiff's showing of discriminatory effect; (2) is there some evidence of discriminatory intent, though not enough to satisfy the constitutional standard of Washington v. Davis; (3) what is the defendant's interest in taking the action complained of; and (4) does the plaintiff seek to compel the defendant to affirmatively provide housing for members of minority groups or merely to restrain the defendant from interfering with individual property owners who wish to provide such housing.

On the first prong, the court found that the showing of discriminatory effect was "not particularly strong." Although the judge held that a shortage of rental housing existed, that a disproportionately large percentage of the households using subsidized rental units are minority, and, accordingly, that a "significant percentage" of Matinecock Court tenants would be minority, he compared the larger absolute number of white poor (22,160) with minority poor (3,671) and concluded that the beneficiaries "might not come disproportionately from minority groups." On the second factor, Judge Glasser found no proof of segregative intent, deeming this a plus in the Town's favor. In so holding, he determined that appellants had failed to prove that the Town was motivated by segregative intent when it confined subsidized housing to the urban renewal area. The third prong of Arlington Heights II, he concluded, was satisfied by "legitimate, nondiscriminatory reasons for [the Town's] conduct." He deemed the fourth factor to cut in favor of appellants because they were not asking the Town to provide housing. Nevertheless, because the first three factors weighed in favor of appellees, he held that the appellants had failed to demonstrate a prima facie case.

[Finally], the court applied the test set forth in McDonnell Douglas Corp. v. Green, 411 U.S. 792 (1973), as a final determination on the merits for Title VII disparate treatment cases. According to this formula, if plaintiffs establish a prima facie case of disparate treatment, the "burden shifts to the defendant to articulate some legitimate, nondiscriminatory reason for the employee's rejection." If defendants meet this burden, plaintiffs must show that the legitimate justifications offered were pretextual and not the employer's true reasons. Applying this test, the court below found that, even if appellants had demonstrated a prima facie showing of discriminatory effect, the Town's justifications for rejecting the project were legitimate and non-discriminatory reasons which "have not been exposed as pretextual."

[We] start by pointing out that this case requires what has been called "disparate impact" or "disparate effects" analysis, not "disparate treatment" analysis. A disparate impact analysis examines a facially-neutral policy or practice, such as a hiring test or zoning law, for its differential impact or effect on a particular group. Disparate treatment analysis, on the other hand, involves differential treatment of similarly situated persons or groups. The line is not always a bright one, but does adequately delineate two very different kinds of discrimination claims.

Here, appellees would collapse the distinction between disparate impact and disparate treatment by characterizing this as a "mixed" impact and treatment case. Thus, they argue, "treatment" analysis should be applied to the Town's refusal to rezone the Matinecock Court site, while "impact" analysis should be applied to the zoning ordinance's restriction of multi-family housing to the urban renewal area. Under appellees' methodology, however, every disparate impact case would include a disparate treatment component. This cannot be the case. There is always some discrete event (refusal to rezone property, refusal to hire someone because he did not graduate from high school) which touches off litigation challenging a neutral rule or policy.

The prima facie standard for Title VIII disparate impact cases involving public defendants is a question of first impression in this circuit. In Boyd v. Lefrak Org. [509 F.2d 1110 (2d Cir. 1975)], a divided panel, considering a Title VIII case against a private defendant, doubted the relevance of the methodology used in Title VII litigation. Since then, however, we have pointedly accepted the relevance of Title VII cases to Title VIII cases. See United States v. Starrett City Assoc., 840 F.2d 1096 (2d Cir. 1988) (cert. denied 448 U.S. 946). Thus, even if the views expressed in Lefrak still apply in a Title VIII case against a private defendant, a matter of considerable uncertainty, the disparate impact approach of Title VII cases is fully applicable to this Title VIII case brought against a public defendant.

Under disparate impact analysis, as other circuits have recognized, a prima facie case is established by showing that the challenged practice of the defendant "actually or predictably results in racial discrimination; in other words that it has a discriminatory effect." The plaintiff need not show that the decision complained of was made with discriminatory intent. In determining whether discriminatory effect is sufficient, we look to congressional purpose, as gleaned from the legislative history of Title VIII, related Title VII jurisprudence, and practical concerns. Although none of these considerations is alone determinative, taken together they strongly suggest that discriminatory impact alone violates Title VIII.

The Act's stated purpose to end discrimination requires a discriminatory effect standard; an intent requirement would strip the statute of all impact on de facto segregation. Congress appears not to have resolved this precise question. Nonetheless, the legislative history provides some indication that an intent standard was not contemplated. The Rizzo court [the Third Circuit] attached significance to the Senate's rejection of an amendment that would have required "proof of discriminatory intent to succeed in establishing a Title VIII claim." The amendment, however, was far less sweeping than Rizzo suggests because it applied only to a single-family owner-occupied house. Nevertheless, its rejection does underscore congressional willingness to broaden Title VIII to encompass segregation resulting from the application of facially neutral rules, even in the absence of discriminatory intent.

More persuasive is the parallel between Title VII and Title VIII. The two statutes are part of a coordinated scheme of federal civil rights laws enacted to end discrimination; the Supreme Court has held that both statutes must be construed expansively to implement that goal. Courts and commentators have observed that the two statutes require similar proof to establish a violation. Thus, just as the Supreme Court held that Title VII is violated by a showing of discriminatory effect, we hold that a Title VIII violation can be established without proof of discriminatory intent.

Practical concerns also militate against inclusion of intent in any disparate impact analysis. First, as this court noted in Robinson, "clever men may easily conceal their motivations." This is especially persuasive in disparate impact cases where a facially neutral rule is being challenged. Often, such rules bear no relation to discrimination upon passage, but develop into powerful discriminatory mechanisms when applied. Second, inclusion of intent undermines the trial judge's inquiry into the impact of an action. The lower court's insistence on probing the "pretextual" nature of appellees' justifications vividly demonstrates the extent to which an intent-based standard can infect an analysis and draw it away from its proper focus. Accordingly, we will not require proof of discriminatory intent to establish a prima facie disparate impact case under Title VIII.

Confusion concerning the content of a prima facie disparate impact case under Title VIII has been engendered by the tendency of some courts to consider factors normally advanced as part of a defendant's justification for its challenged action in assessing whether the plaintiff has established a prima facie case. That appears to have occurred in this case when Judge Glasser analyzed the factors set forth in Arlington Heights II in the course of concluding that a prima facie case was not established. Though, as will shortly appear, we are not persuaded to adopt precisely the formulation of the Arlington Heights II factors, we agree with the Third Circuit that factors such as those mentioned in Arlington Heights II are to be considered in a final determination on the merits rather than as a requirement for a prima facie case. Nothing in Arlington Heights II indicates the court saw its test as anything but a final determination on the merits. Furthermore, treating the four factors as steps necessary to make out a prima facie case places too onerous a burden on appellants. The legislative history of the Fair Housing Act, although sparse, argues persuasively against so daunting a prima facie standard.

As Senator Mondale, the bill's author, said, the proposed law was designed to replace the ghettos "by truly integrated and balanced living patterns." In Trafficante, the Supreme Court held that Title VIII should be broadly interpreted to fulfill this congressional mandate. Moreover, both the majority and the thoughtful dissent in Starrett City, agree: Congress intended that broad application of the anti-discrimination provisions would ultimately result in residential integration. Employing the test in Arlington Heights II as a prima facie hurdle would cripple Title VIII.

Once a prima facie case of adverse impact is presented, as occurred here, the inquiry turns to the standard to be applied in determining whether the defendant can nonetheless avoid liability under Title VIII. The Third Circuit in Rizzo and the Seventh Circuit in Arlington Heights II have both made useful contributions to this inquiry. Both circuits essentially recognize that in the end there must be a weighing of the adverse impact against the defendant's justification. As phrased by the Third Circuit, the defendant must prove that its actions furthered, in theory and in practice, a legitimate, bona fide governmental interest and that no alternative would serve that interest with less discriminatory effect. We agree with that formulation. Furthermore, according to the Third Circuit, "Title VIII criteria [would] emerge, then, on a case-by-case basis." The Seventh Circuit adds two other factors that can affect the ultimate determination on the merits. One factor is whether there is any evidence of discriminatory intent on the part of the defendant. Though we have ruled that such intent is not a requirement of the plaintiff's prima facie case, there can be little doubt that if evidence of such intent is presented, that evidence would weigh heavily on the plaintiff's side of the ultimate balance. The other factor is whether the plaintiff is suing to compel a governmental defendant to build housing or only to require a governmental defendant to eliminate some obstacle to housing that the plaintiff itself will build. In the latter circumstance, a defendant would normally have to establish a somewhat more substantial justification for its adverse action than would be required if the defendant were defending its decision not to build.

In this case, we are obliged to refine the standard for assessing a Title VIII defendant's justification somewhat beyond what was said in either Rizzo or Arlington Heights II. In Rizzo, two of the defendants offered no justification for the adverse decision, and the municipal defendant offered only the entirely unacceptable apprehension of violence. The Third Circuit therefore did not have anything of substance to weigh on the defendants' side. In Arlington Heights II, the consideration of the defendant's justification scarcely moved past inquiring whether the municipal defendant was acting within the scope of zoning authority granted by state law.

In considering the defendant's justification, we start with the framework of Title VII analysis. When an employer's facially neutral rule is shown to have a racially disproportionate effect on job applicants, that rule must be shown to be substantially related to job performance. In a zoning case, the facially neutral rule is the provision of the zoning ordinance that bars the applicant and, in doing so, exerts a racially disproportionate effect on minorities. The difficulty, however, is that in Title VIII cases there is no single objective like job performance to which the legitimacy of the facially neutral rule may be related. A town's preference to maintain a particular zoning category for particular sections of the community is normally based on a variety of circumstances. The complexity of the considerations, however, does not relieve a court of the obligation to assess whatever justifications the town advances and weigh them carefully against the degree of adverse effect the plaintiff has shown. Though a town's interests in zoning requirements are substantial, they cannot, consistently with Title VIII, automatically outweigh significant disparate effects.

The discriminatory effect of a rule arises in two contexts: adverse impact on a particular minority group and harm to the community generally by the perpetuation of segregation. In analyzing Huntington's restrictive zoning, however, the lower court concentrated on the harm to blacks as a group, and failed to consider the segregative effect of maintaining a zoning ordinance that restricts private multi-family housing to an area with a high minority concentration. Yet, recognizing this second form of effect advances the principal purpose of Title VIII to promote "open, integrated residential housing patterns."

Seventy percent of Huntington's black population reside in Huntington Station and South Greenlawn. Matinecock Court, with its goal of 25% minorities, would begin desegregating a neighborhood which is currently 98% white. Indeed, the district court found that a "significant percentage of the tenants" at Matinecock Court would belong to minority groups. The court, however, failed to take the logical next step and find that the refusal to permit projects outside the urban renewal area with its high concentration of minorities reinforced racial segregation in housing.[8] This was erroneous. Similarly, the district court found that the Town has a shortage of rental housing affordable for low and moderate-income households, that a "disproportionately" large percentage of the households using subsidized rental units are minority citizens, and that a disproportionately large number of minorities are on the waiting lists for subsidized housing and existing Section 8 certificates. But it failed to recognize that Huntington's zoning ordinance, which restricts private construction of multi-family housing to the largely minority urban renewal area, impedes integration by restricting low-income housing needed by minorities to an area already 52% minority.[9] We thus find that Huntington's refusal to amend the restrictive zoning ordinance to permit privately-built multi-family housing outside the urban renewal area significantly perpetuated segregation in the Town.

On the question of harm to blacks as a group, the district court emphasized that 22,160 whites and 3,671 minorities had incomes below 200% of the poverty line, a cutoff close to the Huntington Housing Authority's qualification standards. Thus, the district court focussed on the greater absolute number of poor whites compared with indigent minorities in Huntington. The district court, however, did not analyze the disproportionate burden on minorities as required by Griggs v. Duke Power Co. [401 U.S. 424] (1971). By relying on absolute numbers rather than on proportional statistics, the district court significantly underestimated the disproportionate impact of the Town's policy.

The parties have stipulated that 28% of minorities in Huntington and 11% of whites have incomes below 200% of the poverty line. What they dispute is the meaning of

---

8. There would likely also be a desegregative effect on Huntington Township as a whole in comparison to the region, given the tight housing market throughout the area. Appellees assert that there is no statistical disparity between the Town and its surrounding region, the Nassau-Suffolk Standard Metropolitan Statistical Area. We need not reach this question, however, because we find sufficient desegregative impact within Huntington itself from the project.

9. The lower court opinion's sole reference to the zoning ordinance's perpetuation of segregation is contained in its discussion of the Town's discriminatory intent. Judge Glasser failed to consider the impact of the zoning ordinance on the perpetuation of segregation.

these statistics. Judge Glasser found no discriminatory effect because a majority of the victims are white. We disagree for reasons analogous to those the Supreme Court enumerated in Griggs. The disparity is of a magnitude similar to that in Griggs, where the Court found discriminatory an employer's policy of hiring only high school graduates because 12% of black males in North Carolina had high school diplomas while 34% of white males were high school graduates. But the plaintiffs presented even stronger evidence reflecting the disparate impact of preventing the project from proceeding. Under the Huntington HAP for 1982–1985, 7% of all Huntington families needed subsidized housing, while 24% of the black families needed such housing. In addition, minorities constitute a far greater percentage of those currently occupying subsidized rental projects compared to their percentage in the Town's population. Similarly, a disproportionately high percentage (60%) of families holding Section 8 certificates are minorities, and an equally disproportionate percentage (61%) of those on the waiting list for such certificates are minorities. Therefore, we conclude that the failure to rezone the Matinecock Court site had a substantial adverse impact on minorities.

In sum, we find that the disproportionate harm to blacks and the segregative impact on the entire community resulting from the refusal to rezone create a strong prima facie showing of discriminatory effect—far more than the Rizzo test would require. Thus, we must consider the Town's asserted justifications.

Once a plaintiff has made a prima facie showing of discriminatory effect, a defendant must present bona fide and legitimate justifications for its action with no less discriminatory alternatives available. Following McDonnell Douglas, a disparate treatment case, Judge Glasser held that if appellees articulated a legitimate, nondiscriminatory reason for their conduct, appellants must show that the reason is a "pretext." He went on to list the seven reasons in Butterfield's October 14, 1980, letter and found them "legitimate, nondiscriminatory" reasons which "have not been exposed as pretextual." The McDonnell Douglas test, however, is an intent-based standard for disparate treatment cases inapposite to the disparate impact claim asserted here. No circuit, in an impact case, has required plaintiffs to prove that defendants' justifications were pretextual. In Black Jack, [U.S. v. City of Black Jack, Missouri, 508 F.2d 1179, 1185 (8th Cir. 1974)] for example, the court required defendants to show that their conduct was necessary to promote a "compelling governmental interest." The Third Circuit in Rizzo rejected this standard for its own test of legitimate and bona fide concerns.

The Rizzo approach has two components: (1) whether the reasons are bona fide and legitimate; and (2) whether any less discriminatory alternative can serve those ends. For analytical ease, the second prong should be considered first. Concerns can usually be divided between "plan-specific" justifications and those which are "site-specific." "Plan-specific" problems can be resolved by the less discriminatory alternative of requiring reasonable design modifications. "Site-specific" justifications, however, would usually survive this prong of the test. Those remaining reasons are then scrutinized to determine if they are legitimate and bona fide. By that, we do not intend to devise a search for pretext. Rather, the inquiry is whether the proffered justification is of substantial concern such that it would justify a reasonable official in making this determination. Of course, a concern may be non-frivolous, but may not be sufficient because it is not reflected in the record.

Appellants challenge both the ordinance which restricts privately-built multi-family housing to the urban renewal area and the Town Board's decision to refuse to rezone the site. All the parties and the district court judge, however, focussed on the latter issue. Indeed, appellees below simply relied on the existence of the Housing Assistance

Plan and the zoning ordinance and failed to present any substantial evidence indicating a significant interest in limiting private developers to the urban renewal area. On appeal, appellees now contend that the ordinance is designed to encourage private developers to build in the deteriorated area of Huntington Station. Although we believe that the Town's failure to raise this argument below precludes its consideration here, we briefly address this contention. The Town asserts that limiting multi-family development to the urban renewal area will encourage restoration of the neighborhood because, otherwise, developers will choose to build in the outlying areas and will bypass the zone. The Town's goal, however, can be achieved by less discriminatory means, by encouraging development in the urban renewal area with tax incentives or abatements. The Town may assert that this is less effective, but it may actually be more so.

Developers are not wed to building in Huntington; they are filling a perceived economic void. Developments inside the urban renewal area and outside it are not fungible. Rather, developers prevented from building outside the urban renewal area will more likely build in another town, not the urban renewal area. Huntington incorrectly assumes that developers limit their area of interest by political subdivision. In fact, the decision where to build is much more complex. Hence, if the Town wishes to encourage growth in the urban renewal area, it should do so directly through incentives which would have a less discriminatory impact on the Town.

We turn next to the Town's reasons rejecting the Elwood-Pulaski site. The 1980 letter written by Town Supervisor Butterfield detailed seven justifications for the Town's refusal to rezone: (1) inconsistency with the Town's Housing Assistance Plan; (2) inconsistency with zoning; (3) traffic considerations; (4) parking and fire protection problems; (5) proximity to the railroad and Long Island Lighting Company substation; (6) inadequate recreation and play areas; and (7) undersized and unrealistic units. As the judge below noted, the first two beg the question because appellants are challenging the Town's zoning ordinance. More significantly, as we have already indicated, the Town simply relied on the existence of the Housing Assistance Plan and the zoning ordinance and failed to present any substantial evidence indicating why precluding plaintiff from building a multi-family housing project outside the urban renewal area would impair significant interests sought to be advanced by the HAP and the ordinance. The fourth, sixth and seventh problems are "plan-specific" issues which could presumably have been solved with reasonable design modifications at the time appellants applied for rezoning of the parcel. The fifth concern also is largely plan-specific because proper landscaping could shield the project from the railroad and substation.

Thus, only the traffic issue and health hazard from the substation are site-specific. At trial, however, none of Huntington's officials supported these objections. Butterfield was primarily concerned that the Matinecock Court project would "torpedo" the Town's plan to develop [another] site ... in the urban renewal area in Huntington Station.... Moreover, Huntington's only expert, planner David Portman, set forth entirely different problems than were contained in Butterfield's letters. Specifically, he noted sewage concerns, lack of conformity with the low density of the surrounding neighborhood, and inaccessibility of the site to public transportation Once during his testimony, he did mention "the relationship [of the site] to the power station.".... Never, however, did he raise any concern about a health hazard from the proximity to the substation. Indeed, appellees do not broach this issue in their brief to this court. Accordingly, we find the reasons asserted are entirely insubstantial.

The sewage problem was first raised at trial by appellees' expert Portman. Appellees now advance it as an additional concern. The district court, however, chose not to consider it. We agree. Post hoc rationalizations by administrative agencies should be af-forded "little deference" by the courts, Securities Indus. Ass'n. v. Board of Governors, 468 U.S. 137 (1984), and therefore cannot be a bona fide reason for the Town's action. Moreover, the sewage concern could hardly have been significant if municipal officials only thought of it after the litigation began. If it did not impress itself on the Town Board at the time of rejection, it was obviously not a legitimate problem. In sum, the only factor in the Town's favor was that it was acting within the scope of its zoning au-thority, and thus we conclude that the Town's justifications were weak and inadequate.

In balancing the showing of discriminatory effect against the import of the Town's justifications, we note our agreement with the Seventh Circuit that the balance should be more readily struck in favor of the plaintiff when it is seeking only to enjoin a mu-nicipal defendant from interfering with its own plans rather than attempting to compel the defendant itself to build housing. As the Arlington Heights II court explained, "courts are far more willing to prohibit even nonintentional action by the state which interferes with an individual's plan to use his own land to provide integrated housing." Bearing in mind that the plaintiffs in this case seek only the freedom to build their own project, we conclude that the strong showing of discriminatory effect resulting from the Town's adherence to its R-3M zoning category and its refusal to rezone the Matinecock Court site far outweigh the Town's weak justifications. Accordingly, to recapitulate, we find that the Town violated Title VIII by refusing to amend the zoning ordinance to per-mit private developers to build multi-family dwellings outside the urban renewal area. We also find that the Town violated Title VIII by refusing to rezone the Matinecock Court site.

Appellees argue that we should deny site-specific relief because there are 64 "commu-nity development" sites available for low-cost multi-family housing in Huntington.... [To the contrary], there is only one site, not 64 sites, zoned and available for private low-cost multi-family housing. However, even as to the one site—the MIA site in Huntington Station—by the time of trial, HUD had determined it was in an area with a high concentration of minorities and therefore an inappropriate location for a feder-ally subsidized housing development.

Ordinarily, HHI would not be automatically entitled to construct its project at its preferred site. The Town might well have legitimate reasons for preferring some al-ternative site to the one preferred by HHI. On the other hand, the Town would not be permitted to select a site that suits the Town's preference if that site imposed undue hardships on the applicant, such as distance from public transportation or other services. Thus, we would ordinarily remand this case to the district court to af-ford the appellees an opportunity to identify an alternative site, outside the urban re-newal area, that would be appropriate for HHI's project and eligible for the same fi-nancial arrangements and assistance available at the Matinecock Court site. If the Town identified such a site, it would then have the burden of persuading the district court that there were substantial reasons for using its preferred site and that those reasons did not impose undue hardships on the appellants. If the district court was not persuaded on balance of the benefits of an alternative site, it would then enter an appropriate judgment to enable HHI to proceed with its project at the Matinecock Court site.

This case, however, is not ordinary. First, we recognize the protracted nature of this litigation, which has spanned over seven years. Further delay might well prove fatal to this private developer's plans. Second, other than its decision in December 1987 to build 50 units of low-income housing in the Melville section, the Town has demonstrated little good faith in assisting the development of low-income housing. After the Town began receiving federal community development funds, HUD found it necessary to pressure the Town continually to include commitments for construction of subsidized family housing in the Town's HAPs. Because of the Town's lack of progress in constructing such housing, HUD imposed special conditions on the Town's community development grants for the 1978 fiscal allocation. Thereafter, HUD continued to express its dissatisfaction with the Town's performance. This history, while it does not rise to a showing of discriminatory intent, clearly demonstrates a pattern of stalling efforts to build low-income housing.

Third, the other 63 parcels outside the urban renewal area are not presently zoned for multi-family housing and, indeed, the zoning ordinance presently forbids rezoning of these properties. Thus, this situation differs from Arlington Heights II, where 60 tracts currently zoned for multi-family housing were available and, accordingly, the Seventh Circuit remanded the case to the district court to determine if one of those sites were suitable.... We therefore refuse to remand this case to the district court to determine the suitability of the 63 sites outside the urban renewal area. Rather, we find that site-specific relief is appropriate in this case.

Accordingly, we direct the district court to include in its judgment provision ordering the Town to rezone the 14.8 acre Matinecock Court site located at the corner of Elwood and Pulaski Roads in Huntington Township to R-3M status. The judgment should also order the Town to strike from its R-3M zoning ordinance that portion which limits private multi-family housing projects to the urban renewal area.

In the U.S. Supreme Court

Justice White, Justice Marshall, and Justice Stevens would note probable jurisdiction and set the case for oral argument.

Per Curiam. * * *

Following a bench trial, the District Court rejected appellees' Title VIII claims. The Court of Appeals for the Second Circuit reversed as to both claims. 844 F. 2d 926 (1988). The Court of Appeals held that, in order to establish a prima facie case, a Title VIII plaintiff need only demonstrate that the action or rule challenged has a discriminatory impact. As to the failure to amend the zoning ordinance (which is all that concerns us here), the court found discriminatory impact because a disproportionately high percentage of households that use and that would be eligible for subsidized rental units are minorities, and because the ordinance restricts private construction of low-income housing to the largely minority urban renewal area, which "significantly perpetuated segregation in the Town." The court declared that in order to rebut this prima facie case, appellants had to put forth "bona fide and legitimate" reasons for their action and had to demonstrate that no "less discriminatory alternative can serve those ends." The court found appellants' rationale for refusal to amend the ordinance—that the restriction of multifamily projects to the urban renewal area would encourage developers to invest in a deteriorated and needy section of town—clearly inadequate. In the court's view, that restriction was more likely to cause developers to invest in towns other than Huntington than to invest in Huntington's depressed urban renewal area, and tax incentives would have been a more efficacious and less discriminatory means to the desired end.

After concluding that appellants had violated Title VIII, the Court of Appeals directed Huntington to strike from § 198-20 the restriction of private multifamily housing projects to the urban renewal area and ordered the town to rezone the project site to R-3M.

Huntington seeks review pursuant to 28 U.S.C. § 1254(2) on the basis that, in striking the zoning limitation from the Town Code, the Court of Appeals invalidated "a State statute … as repugnant to" Title VIII, a "la[w] of the United States." Viewing the case as involving two separate claims, as presented by the parties and analyzed by the courts below, we note jurisdiction, but limit our review to that portion of the case implicating our mandatory jurisdiction. Thus, we expressly decline to review the judgment of the Court of Appeals insofar as it relates to the refusal to rezone the project site.

Since appellants conceded the applicability of the disparate-impact test for evaluating the zoning ordinance under Title VIII, we do not reach the question whether that test is the appropriate one. Without endorsing the precise analysis of the Court of Appeals, we are satisfied on this record that disparate impact was shown, and that the sole justification proffered to rebut the prima facie case was inadequate. The other points presented to challenge the court's holding with regard to the ordinance do not present substantial federal questions. Accordingly, the judgment of the Court of Appeals is

Affirmed.

Larkin v. State of Michigan Department of Social Services

89 F.3d 285 (6th Cir. 1996)

For Geraldine Larkin, Plaintiff-Appellee: Gregory J. Bator, argued, briefed, Bator & Zartarian, Birmingham, MI.

For Michigan Protection and Advocacy Service, Intervenor: Stewart R. Hakola, briefed, Michigan Protection & Advocacy Service, Marquette, MI. Gayle C. Rosen, argued, briefed, Michigan Protection and Advocacy Service, Livonia, MI. Beth Pepper, briefed, Stein & Schonfeld, Baltimore, MD.

For Michigan Department of Social Services, Defendant-Appellant: Stephen H. Garrard, Asst. Attorney Gen., argued, briefed, Department of Attorney General, Social Services Division, Lansing, MI.[+]

Suhrheinrich and Siler, Circuit Judges; Aldrich, District Judge.[*]

Aldrich, District Judge.

I.

Geraldine Larkin sought a license to operate an adult foster care (AFC) facility which would provide care for up to four handicapped adults in Westland, Michigan. The

---

[+]. For Ypsilanti Township, Amicus Curiae: William D. Winters, Angela B. King, briefed, McLain & Winters, Ypsilanti, MI. For National Association of Protection and Advocacy Systems, Amicus Curiae: Roy W. Froemming, Wisconsin Coalition for Advocacy, Madison, WI. For Arc of Michigan, Amicus Curiae: Kathy L. Peterson, briefed, Ypsilanti, MI. For Autism Society of Michigan, United Cerebral Palsy of Michigan, Association for Community Advocacy, Disability Network, American Disabled for Assistant Programs Today (ADAPT) of Michigan, Amicus Curiae: Kathy L. Peterson, Ypsilanti, MI. For Michigan Townships Association, Amicus Curiae: Kenneth C. Sparks, Bauckham, Reed, Lang, Schaefer & Travis, Kalamazoo, MI. For United States of America, Amicus Curiae: Rebecca K. Troth, argued, briefed, U.S. Dept. of Justice, Civil Rights Division, Appellate Section, Washington, DC.

[*] The Honorable Ann Aldrich, United States District Judge for the Northern District of Ohio, sitting by designation.

Michigan Adult Foster Care Licensing Act (MAFCLA) ... prevents the issuance of a temporary license if the proposed AFC facility would "substantially contribute to an excessive concentration" of community residential facilities within a municipality. Moreover, it requires compliance with section 3b of the state's zoning enabling act [which] provides in part:

> At least 45 days before licensing a residential facility [which provides resident services or care for six or fewer persons under 24-hour supervision], the state licensing agency shall notify the council ... or the designated agency of the city or village where the proposed facility is to be located to review the number of existing or proposed similar state licensed residential facilities whose property lines are within a 1,500-foot radius of the property lines of the proposed facility. The council of a city or village or an agency of the city or village to which the authority is delegated, when a proposed facility is to be located within the city or village, shall give appropriate notification ... to those residents whose property lines are within a 1,500-foot radius of the property lines of the proposed facility. A state licensing agency shall not license a proposed residential facility if another state licensed residential facility exists within the 1,500-foot radius of the proposed location, unless permitted by local zoning ordinances or if the issuance of the license would substantially contribute to an excessive concentration of state licensed residential facilities within the city or village.

MAFCLA also requires notice to the municipality in which the proposed AFC facility will be located.

Michigan Department of Social Services (MDSS) notified Westland of Larkin's application. Westland determined that there was an existing AFC facility within 1,500 feet of the proposed facility and so notified MDSS. It also notified MDSS that it was not waiving the spacing requirement, so that MDSS could not issue a license to Larkin. When MDSS informed Larkin of Westland's action, Larkin withdrew her application.

Larkin filed suit alleging that Michigan's statutory scheme violates the Fair Housing Act (FHA) [and] the equal protection clause of the fourteenth amendment.

[T]he district court ruled that the 1500-foot spacing requirement and the notice requirements were preempted by the FHAA (Fair Housing Amendments Act) because they were in conflict with it [and] that these statutes violated the equal protection clause.

III.

[T]he Fair Housing Act of 1968, as amended by the Fair Housing Amendments Act of 1988, makes it unlawful to:

> discriminate in the sale or rental, *or to otherwise make unavailable or deny*, a dwelling to any buyer or renter because of a handicap of—

> (B) a person residing in or intending to reside in that dwelling after it is so sold, rented, or made available.

42 U.S.C. § 3604(f)(1) (emphasis added). It is well-settled that the FHAA applies to the regulation of group homes. Moreover, Congress explicitly intended for the FHAA to apply to zoning ordinances and other laws which would restrict the placement of group homes. See H. Rep. No. 711, 100th Cong., 2d Sess. 24 (1988).

A. Preemption

The plaintiffs argue, and the district court found, that the MAFCLA provisions at issue discriminate in violation of the FHAA, and are therefore preempted by it. Congress may preempt state law in one of three ways. First, Congress may explicitly preempt state laws. Second, it may preempt by "occupying the field." Finally, federal law preempts state law when they actually conflict, i.e., it is not possible to comply with both the state and the federal laws. In this case, the FHAA expressly provides that any state law "that purports to require or permit any action that would be a discriminatory housing practice under this subchapter shall to that extent be invalid." 42 U.S.C. § 3615. Thus, the FHAA expressly preempts those state laws with which it conflicts, and the first and third types of preemption merge in this case.

B. Discrimination

This brings us to the crux of the case: whether the statutes at issue discriminate against the disabled in violation of the FHAA. The district court held that two different aspects of MAFCLA violate the FHAA: (1) the 1500-foot spacing requirement and (2) the notice requirements.[3]

Most courts applying the FHA have analogized it to Title VII of the Civil Rights Act of 1964 which prohibits discrimination in employment. They have concluded that a plaintiff may establish a violation under the FHA by showing either: (1) that the defendants were motivated by an intent to discriminate against the handicapped ("discriminatory intent" or "disparate treatment"); or (2) that the defendant's otherwise neutral action has an unnecessarily discriminatory effect ("disparate impact"). Some courts have identified a third type of case where a challenged practice discriminates against the handicapped on its face. However, facially discriminatory actions are just a type of intentional discrimination or disparate treatment, and should be treated as such. This is also the approach taken by the Supreme Court in employment discrimination cases.

Here, the challenged portions of MAFCLA are facially discriminatory. The spacing requirement prohibits MDSS from licensing any new AFC facility if it is within 1500 feet of an existing AFC facility. The notice requirements require MDSS to notify the municipality of the proposed facility, and the local authorities to then notify all residents within 1500 feet of the proposed facility. By their very terms, these statutes apply only to AFC facilities which will house the disabled, and not to other living arrangements. As we have previously noted, statutes that single out for regulation group homes for the handicapped are facially discriminatory. Accordingly, this is a case of intentional discrimination or disparate treatment, rather than disparate impact.

MDSS argues that the statutes at issue cannot have a discriminatory intent because they are motivated by a benign desire to help the disabled. This is incorrect as a matter of law. The Supreme Court has held in the employment context that "the absence of a malevolent motive does not convert a facially discriminatory policy into a neutral policy with a discriminatory effect." Following Johnson Controls [International Union, United Auto. Aerospace & Agricultural Implement Workers v. Johnson Controls, Inc., 499 U.S. 187 (1991)] all of the courts which have considered this issue under the FHAA have con-

---

3. As noted above, although the district court mentioned the prohibition against an excessive concentration of AFC facilities, it did not hold that it violated the FHAA or the equal protection clause, and it did not enjoin the enforcement of M.C.L. § 400.716(1). MDSS does not raise this as error on appeal, and the plaintiffs did not file a cross-appeal. Therefore, the prohibition against excessive concentration is not before us.

cluded the defendant's benign motive does not prevent the statute from being discriminatory on its face. MDSS relies on Familystyle of St. Paul, Inc. v. City of St. Paul, 728 F. Supp. 1396 (D. Minn.1990), aff'd, 923 F.2d 91 (8th Cir.1991), for the proposition that proof of a discriminatory motive is required for a finding of discriminatory intent. However, both decisions in Familystyle preceded the Supreme Court's opinion in Johnson Controls. Thus, they have been implicitly overruled by Johnson Controls in this regard.

Because the statutes at issue are facially discriminatory, the burden shifts to the defendant to justify the challenged statutes. However, it is not clear how much of a burden shifts. MDSS urges us to follow the Eighth Circuit and rule that discriminatory statutes are subject to a rational basis scrutiny, i.e., they will be upheld if they are rationally related to a legitimate government objective. Plaintiffs urge us to reject the rational basis test and adopt the standard announced by the Tenth Circuit, which requires the defendant to show that the discriminatory statutes either (1) are justified by individualized safety concerns; or (2) really benefit, rather than discriminate against, the handicapped, and are not based on unsupported stereotypes.

Although we have never explicitly decided the issue, we have held that in order for special safety restrictions on homes for the handicapped to pass muster under the FHAA, the safety requirements must be tailored to the particular needs of the disabled who will reside in the house. We rejected the ordinances at issue in an earlier case because they required nearly every safety requirement that one might think of as desirable to protect persons handicapped by any disability—mental or physical; and all the requirements applied to all housing for developmentally disabled persons, regardless of the type of mental condition that causes their disabilities or of the ways in which the disabilities manifest themselves.

Therefore, in order for facially discriminatory statutes to survive a challenge under the FHAA, the defendant must demonstrate that they are "warranted by the unique and specific needs and abilities of those handicapped persons" to whom the regulations apply.

MDSS has not met that burden. MDSS claims that the 1500-foot spacing requirement integrates the disabled into the community and prevents "clustering" and "ghettoization." In addition, it argues that the spacing requirement also serves the goal of de-institutionalization by preventing a cluster of AFC facilities from recreating an institutional environment in the community.

As an initial matter, integration is not a sufficient justification for maintaining permanent quotas under the FHA or the FHAA, especially where, as here, the burden of the quota falls on the disadvantaged minority. See United States v. Starrett City Associates, 840 F.2d 1096 (2nd Cir. 1988), cert. denied, 488 U.S. 946 (1988). The FHAA protects the right of individuals to live in the residence of their choice in the community. If the state were allowed to impose quotas on the number of minorities who could move into a neighborhood in the name of integration, this right would be vitiated.

MDSS argues that the state is not imposing a quota because it is not limiting the number of disabled who can live in a neighborhood, it is merely limiting the number of AFC facilities within that neighborhood. However, as we have previously noted, disabled individuals who wish to live in a community often have no choice but to live in an AFC facility. Alternatively, if the disabled truly have the right to live anywhere they choose, then the limitations on AFC facilities do not prevent clustering and ghettoization in any meaningful way. Thus, MDSS's own argument suggests that integration is not the true reason for the spacing requirements.

Moreover, MDSS has not shown how the special needs of the disabled warrant intervention to ensure that they are integrated. MDSS has produced no evidence that AFC facilities will cluster absent the spacing statute. In fact, this statute was not enforced from 1990 to 1993, and MDSS has offered no evidence that AFC facilities tended to cluster during that period.

Instead, MDSS simply assumes that the disabled must be integrated, and does not recognize that the disabled may choose to live near other disabled individuals. The result might be different if some municipalities were forcing the disabled to segregate, or cluster, in a few small areas. However, Michigan already prohibits such behavior:

> In order to implement the policy of this state that persons in need of community residential care shall not be excluded by zoning from the benefits of a normal residential surroundings, a state licensed residential facility providing supervision or care, or both, to 6 or less persons shall be considered a residential use of property for purposes of zoning and a permitted use in all residential zones, including those zoned for single family dwellings, *and shall not be subject to a special use or conditional use permit or procedure different from those required for other dwellings of similar density in the same zone.*

M.C.L. § 125.583b(2) (emphasis added). The only clustering or segregation that will occur, then, is as the result of the free choice of the disabled. In other words, the state's policy of forced integration is not protecting the disabled from any forced segregation; rather, the state is forcing them to integrate based on the paternalistic idea that it knows best where the disabled should choose to live.

In contrast, deinstitutionalization is a legitimate goal for the state to pursue. However, MDSS does not explain how a rule prohibiting two AFC facilities from being within 1500 feet of each other fosters deinstitutionalization in any real way. Two AFC facilities 500 feet apart would violate the statute without remotely threatening to recreate an institutional setting in the community. In fact, the spacing requirement may actually inhibit the goal of deinstitutionalization by limiting the number of AFC facilities which can be operated within any given community.

MDSS relies again on Familystyle, where both the district court and the Eighth Circuit found that the goal of deinstitutionalization justified facially discriminatory spacing requirements. However, Familystyle is distinguishable from the present case. In Familystyle, the plaintiff already housed 119 disabled individuals within a few city blocks. The courts were concerned that the plaintiffs were simply recreating an institutionalized setting in the community, rather than deinstitutionalizing the disabled.

Here, however, Larkin seeks only to house four disabled individuals in a home which happens to be less than 1500 feet from another AFC facility. The proposed AFC facility, and many more like it that are prohibited by the spacing requirement, do not threaten Michigan's professed goal of deinstitutionalization. Because it sweeps in the vast majority of AFC facilities which do not seek to recreate an institutional setting, the spacing requirement is too broad, and is not tailored to the specific needs of the handicapped.[4]

In summary, MDSS's justifications do not pass muster under the standard announced in Marbrunak. Therefore, the 1500-foot spacing requirement violates the FHAA and is preempted by it.

---

4. We express no opinion on whether a more narrowly tailored law prohibiting such a concentration would pass muster under the FHAA.

MDSS also has failed to provide an adequate justification for the notice requirements. MDSS merely offers the same justifications for the notice requirements as it offers for the spacing requirements, i.e., integration and deinstitutionalization. Notifying the municipality or the neighbors of the proposed AFC facility seems to have little relationship to the advancement of these goals. In fact, such notice would more likely have quite the opposite effect, as it would facilitate the organized opposition to the home, and animosity towards its residents. Furthermore, MDSS has offered no evidence that the needs of the handicapped would warrant such notice. We find that the notice requirements violate the FHAA and are preempted by it.

By this holding, we in no way mean to intimate that the FHA, as amended by the FHAA, prohibits reasonable regulation and licensing procedures for AFC facilities. As was stated in Marbrunak [v. City of Stow, Ohio, 974 F.2d 43, 47 (6th Cir. 1992)], "the FHAA does not prohibit the city from imposing *any* special safety standards for the protection of developmentally disabled persons." Rather, it merely prohibits those which are not "demonstrated to be warranted by the unique and specific needs and abilities of those handicapped persons."

IV.

Because the statutes at issue are preempted by the FHAA, we need not reach the equal protection claims.

5. Inequality

Melvin Oliver and Thomas Shapiro, BLACK WEALTH/WHITE WEALTH: A NEW PERSPECTIVE ON RACIAL INEQUALITY
(Routledge 1995), pp. 1–10, 15–18

Introduction

Each year two highly publicized news reports capture the attention and imagination of Americans. One lists the year's highest income earners. Predictably, they include glamorous and highly publicized entertainment, sport, and business personalities. For the past decade that list has included many African Americans: musical artists such as Michael Jackson, entertainers such as Bill Cosby and Oprah Winfrey, and sports figures such as Michael Jordan and Magic Johnson. During the recent past as many as half of the "top ten" in this highly exclusive rank have been African Americans.

Another highly publicized list, by contrast, documents the nation's wealthiest Americans. The famous *Forbes* magazine profile of the nation's wealthiest 400 focus not on income but on wealth. This list includes those people whose assets—or command over monetary resources—place them at the top of the American economic hierarchy. Even though this group is often ten times larger than the top earners list, it contains few if any African Americans. An examination of these two lists creates two very different perceptions of the well-being of America's black community on the eve of the twenty-first century. The large number of blacks on the top income list generates an optimistic view of how black Americans have progressed economically in American society. The near absence of blacks in the *Forbes* listing, by contract, presents a much more pessimistic outlook on blacks' economic progress.

This book develops a perspective on racial inequality that is based on the analysis of private wealth. Just as a change in focus from income to wealth in the discussion above provides a different perspective on racial inequality, our analysis reveals deep patterns of racial imbalance not visible when viewed only through the lens of income. This analysis provides a new perspective on racial inequality by exploring how material assets are created, expanded, and preserved.

The basis of our analysis is the analytical distinction between wealth and other traditional measures of economic status, of how people are "making it" in America (for example, income, occupation, and education). Wealth is a particularly important indicator of individual and family access to life chances. Income refers to a flow of money over time, like a rate per hour, week, or year; wealth is a stock of assets owned at a particular time. Wealth is what people own, while income is what people receive for work, retirement, or social welfare. Wealth signifies the command over financial resources that a family has accumulated over its lifetime along with those resources that have been inherited across generations. Such resources, when combined with income, can create the opportunity to secure the "good life" in whatever form is needed—education, business, training, justice, health, comfort, and so on. Wealth is a special form of money not used to purchase milk and shoes and other life necessities. More often it is used to create opportunities, secure a desired stature and standard of living, or pass class status along to one's children. In this sense the command over resources that wealth entails is more encompassing than is income or education, and closer in meaning and theoretical significance to our traditional notions of economic well-being and access to life chances.

More important, wealth taps not only contemporary resources but material assets that have historic origins. Private wealth thus captures inequality that is the product of the past, often passed down from generation to generation. Given this attribute, in attempting to understand the economic status of blacks, a focus on wealth helps us avoid the either-or view of a march toward progress or a trail of despair. Conceptualizing racial inequality through wealth revolutionizes our conception of its nature and magnitude, and of whether it is declining or increasing. While most recent analyses have concluded that contemporary class-based factors are most important in understanding the sources of continuing racial inequality, our focus on wealth sheds light on both the historical and the contemporary impacts not only of class but of race.

The empirical heart of our analysis resides in an examination of differentials in black and white wealth holdings. This focus paints a vastly different empirical picture of social inequality than commonly emerges from analyses based on traditional inequality indicators. The burden of our claim is to demonstrate not simply the taken-for-granted assumption that wealth reveals "more" inequality—income multiplied x time is not the correct equation. More importantly we show that wealth uncovers a qualitatively different pattern of inequality on crucial fronts. Thus the goal of this work is to provide an analysis of racial differences in wealth holding that reveals dynamics of racial inequality otherwise concealed by income, occupational attainment, or education. It is our argument that wealth reveals a particular network of social relations and a set of social circumstances that convey a unique constellation of meanings pertinent to race in America. This perspective significantly adds to our understanding of public policy issues related to racial inequality; at the same time it aids us in developing better policies for the future. In stating our case, we do not discount the important information that the traditional indicators provide, but we argue that by adding to the latter an analysis of wealth a more thorough, comprehensive and powerful explanation of social inequality can be elaborated.

Our argument supporting the importance of wealth in understanding contemporary racial inequality develops and unfolds in three parts. Chapters 1 and 2 introduce the importance of wealth to racial inequality, Chapters 3 through 5 present a detailed analysis of wealth holding in America with an emphasis on how class and race have structured racial inequality. The final two chapters identify the main sources of enormous racial wealth disparity and proposes preliminary means of addressing that disparity. Through the development of a "sociology of wealth and racial inequality" we situate the study of wealth among contemporary concerns with race, class, and social inequality.

Economists argue that racial differences in wealth are a consequence of disparate class and human capital credentials (age, education, experience, skills), propensities to save, and consumption patterns. A sociology of wealth seeks to properly situate the social context in which wealth generation occurs. Thus the sociology of wealth accounts for racial differences in wealth holding by demonstrating the unique and diverse social circumstances that blacks and whites face. One result is that blacks and whites also face different structures of investment opportunity, which have been affected historically and contemporaneously by both race and class. We develop three concepts to provide a sociologically grounded approach to understanding racial differentials in wealth accumulation. These concepts highlight the ways in which this opportunity structure has disadvantaged blacks and helped contribute to massive wealth inequalities between the races.

Our first concept, "racialization of state policy," refers to how state policy has impaired the ability of many black Americans to accumulate wealth—and discouraged them from doing so—from the beginning of slavery throughout American history. From the first codified decision to enslave African Americans to the local ordinances that barred blacks from certain occupations to the welfare state policies of today that discourage wealth accumulation, the state has erected major barriers to black economic self-sufficiency. In particular, state policy has structured the context within which it has been possible to acquire land, build community, and generate wealth. Historically, policies and actions of the United States government have promoted homesteading, land acquisition, home ownership, retirement, pensions, education, and asset accumulation for some sectors of the population and not for others. Poor people— blacks in particular—generally have been excluded from participation in these state-sponsored opportunities. In this way, the distinctive relationship between whites and blacks have been woven into the fabric of state actions. The modern welfare state has racialized citizenship, social organization, and economic status while consigning blacks to a relentlessly impoverished and subordinate position within it.

Our second focus, on the "economic detour," helps us understand the relatively low level of entrepreneurship among and the small scale of the businesses owned by black Americans. While blacks have historically sought out opportunities for self-employment, they have traditionally faced an environment, especially from the postbellum period to the middle of the twentieth century, in which they were restricted by law from participation in business in the open market. Explicit state and local policies restricted the rights of blacks as free economic agents. These policies had a devastating impact on the ability of blacks to build and maintain successful enterprises. While blacks were limited to a restricted African American market to which others (for example, whites and other ethnics) also had easy access, they were unable to tap the more lucrative and expansive mainstream white markets. Blacks thus had fewer opportunities to develop successful businesses. When businesses were developed that competed in size and scope with white businesses, intimidation and ultimately, in some cases, violence were used to curtail their expansion or get rid of them altogether. The lack of important assets and indigenous community development has thus played a crucial role in limiting the wealth-accumulating ability of African Americans.

The third concept we develop is synthetic in nature. The notion embodied in the "sedimentation of racial inequality" is that in central ways the cummulative effects of the past have seemingly cemented blacks to the bottom of society's economic hierarchy. A history of low wages, poor schooling, and segregation affected not one or two generations of blacks but practically all African Americans well into the middle of the twentieth century. Our argument is that the best indicator of the sedimentation of racial inequality is wealth. Wealth is one indicator of material disparity that captures the historical legacy of low wages, personal and organizational discrimination, and institutionalized racism. The low levels of wealth accumulation evidenced by current generations of black Americans best represent the economic status of blacks in the American social structure.

To argue that blacks form the sediment of the American stratificational order is to recognize the extent to which they began at the bottom of the hierarchy during slavery, and the cumulative and reinforcing effects of Jim Crow and de facto segregation through the mid-twentieth century. Generation after generation of blacks remained anchored to the lowest economic status in American society. The effect of this inherited poverty and economic scarcity for the accumulation of wealth has been to "sediment" inequality into the social structure. The sedimentation of inequality occurred because the investment opportunity that blacks faced worked against their quest for material self-sufficiency. In contrast, whites in general, but well-off whites in particular, were able to amass assets and use their secure financial status to pass their wealth from generation to generation. What is often not acknowledged is that the same social system that fosters the accumulation of private wealth for many whites denies it to blacks, thus forging an intimate connection between white wealth accumulation and black poverty. Just as blacks have had "cumulative disadvantages," many whites have had "cumulative advantages." Since wealth builds over a lifetime and is then passed along to kin, it is, from our perspective, an essential indicator of black economic well-being. By focusing on wealth we discover how blacks' socioeconomic status results from a socially layered accumulation of disadvantages passed on from generation to generation. In this sense we uncover a racial wealth tax.

Our empirical analysis enables us to raise and answer several key questions about wealth: How has wealth been distributed in American society over the twentieth century? What changes in the distribution of wealth occurred during the 1980s? And finally, what are the implications of these changes for black-white inequality?

During the eighties the rich got much richer, and the poor and middle classes fell further behind. Why? We will show how the Reagan tax cuts provided greater discretionary income for middle- and upper-class taxpayers. One asset whose value grew dramatically during the eighties was real estate, an asset that is central to the wealth portfolio of the average American. Home ownership makes up the largest part of wealth held by the middle class, whereas the upper class more commonly hold a greater degree of their wealth in financial assets. Owning a house is the hallmark of the American Dream, but it is becoming harder and harder for average Americans to afford their own home and fewer are able to do so.

In part because of the dramatic rise in home values, the wealthiest generation of elderly people in America's history is in the process of passing along its wealth. Between 1987 and 2011 the baby boom generation stands to inherit approximately $7 trillion. Of course, all will not benefit equally, if at all. One-third of the worth of all estates will be divided by the richest 1 percent, each legatee receiving an average inheritance of $6 million. Much of this wealth will be in the form of property, which, as the philosopher Robert Nozick is quoted as saying in a 1990 *New York Times* piece, "sticks out as a special kind of unearned benefit that produces unequal opportunities." Kevin, a seventy-five-year-old retired homemaker interviewed for this study, captures the dilemma of unearned inheritance:

> You heard that saying about the guy with the rich father? The kid goes through life thinking that he hit a triple. But really he was born on third base. He didn't hit no triple at all, but he'll go around telling everyone he banged the fucking ball and it was a triple. He was born there!

Inherited wealth is a very special kind of money imbued with the shadows of race. Racial difference in inheritance is a key feature of our story. For the most part, blacks will not partake in divvying up the baby boom bounty. America's racist legacy is shutting them out. The grandparents and parents of blacks under the age of forty toiled under segregation, where education and access to decent jobs and wages were severely restricted. Racialized state policy and the economic detour constrained their ability to enter the post-World War II housing market. Segregation created an extreme situation in which earlier generations were unable to build up much, if any, wealth. We will see how the average black family headed by a person over the age of sixty-five has no net financial assets to pass down to its children. Until the late 1960s there were few older African Americans with the ability to save much at all, much less invest. And no savings and no inheritance meant no wealth.

The most consistent and strongest common theme to emerge in interviews conducted with white and black families was that family assets expand choices, horizons, and opportunities for children while lack of assets limit opportunities. Because parents want to give their children whatever advantages they can, we wondered about the ability of the average American household to expend assets on their children. We found that the lack of private assets intrudes on the dreams that many Americans have for their children. Extreme resource deficiency characterizes several groups. It may surprise some to learn that 62 percent of households headed by single parents are without savings or other financial assets, or that two of every five households without a high school degree lack a financial nest egg. Nearly one-third of all households—and about 61 percent of all black households—are without financial resources. These statistics lead to our focus on the most resource-deficient households in our study—African Americans.

We argue that, materially, whites and blacks constitute two nations. One of the analytic centerpieces of this work tells a tale of two middle classes, one white and one black. Most significant, the claim made by blacks to middle-class status depends on income and not assets. In contrast, a wealth pillar supports the white middle class in its drive for middle-class opportunities and a middle-class standard of living. Middle-class blacks, for example, earn seventy cents for every dollar earned by middle-class whites but they possess only fifteen cents for every dollar of wealth held by middle-class whites. For the most part, the economic foundation of the black middle class lacks one of the pillars that provide stability and security to middle-class whites—assets. The black middle class positions is precarious and fragile with insubstantial wealth resources. This analysis means it is entirely premature to celebrate the rise of the black middle class. The glass is both half empty and half full, because the wealth data reveal the paradoxical situation in which blacks' wealth has grown while at the same time falling further and further behind that of whites.

The social distribution of wealth discloses a fresh and formidable dimension of racial inequality. Blacks' achievement at any given level not only requires that greater effort be expended on fewer opportunities but also bestows substantially diminished rewards. Examining blacks and whites who share similar socioeconomic characteristics brings to light persistent and vast wealth discrepancies. Take education as one prime example: the most equality we found was among the college educated, but even here at the pinnacle of achievement whites controlled four times as much wealth as blacks with the same degrees. This predicament manifests a disturbing break in the link between achievement and results that is essential for democracy and social equality.

The central question of this study is, Why do the wealth portfolios of blacks and whites vary so drastically? The answer is not simply that blacks have inferior remunerable human capital endowments—substandard education, jobs, and skills, for example—or do not display the characteristics most associated with higher income and wealth. We are able to demonstrate that even when blacks and whites display similar characteristics—for example, are on a par educationally and occupationally—a potent difference of $43,143 in home equity and financial assets still remains. Likewise, giving the average black household the same attributes as the average white household leaves a $25,794 racial gap in financial assets alone.

The extent of discrimination in institutions and social policy provides a persuasive index of bias that undergirds the drastic difference between blacks and whites. We show that skewed access to mortgage and housing markets result in enormous racial wealth disparity. Banks turn down qualified blacks much more often for home loans than they do similarly qualified whites. Blacks who do qualify, moreover, pay higher interest rates on home mortgages than whites. Residential segregation persists into the 1990s, and we found that the great rise in housing values is color-coded. Why should the mean value of the average white home appreciate at a dramatically higher rate than the average black home? Home ownership is without question the single most important means of accumulating assets. The lower values of black homes adversely affect the ability of blacks to utilize their residences as collateral for obtaining personal, business, or educational loans. We estimate that institutional biases in the residential arena have cost the current generation of blacks about $82 billion. Passing inequality along from one generation to the next casts another racially stratified shadow on the making of American inequality. Institutional discrimination in housing and lending markets extends into the future the effects of historical discrimination within other institutions.

Placing these findings in the larger context of public policy discussions about racial and social justice adds new dimensions to these discussions. A focus on wealth changes our thinking about racial inequality. The more one learns about wealth differences, the more mistaken current policies appear. To take these findings seriously, as we do, means not shirking the responsibility of seeking alternative policy ideas with which to address issues of inequality. We might even need to think about social justice in new ways. In some key respects our analysis of disparities in wealth between blacks and whites forms an agenda for the future, the key principle of which is to link opportunity structures to policies promoting asset formation that begin to close the racial wealth gap.

Closing the racial gap means that we have to target policies at two levels. First, we need policies that directly address the situation of African Americans. Such policies are necessary to speak to the historically generated disadvantages and the current racially based policies that have limited the ability of blacks, as a group, to accumulate wealth resources.

Second, we need policies that directly promote asset opportunities for those on the bottom of the social structure, both black and white, who are locked out of the wealth accumulation process. More generally, our analysis clearly suggests the need for massive re-distributional policies in order to reforge the links between achievement, reward, social equality, and democracy. These policies must take aim at the gross inequality generated by those at the very top of the wealth distribution. Policies of this type are the most difficult ones on which to gain consensus but the most important in creating a more just society.

This book's underlying goal is to establish a way to view racial inequality that will serve as a guide in securing racial equality in the twenty-first century. Racial equality is not an absolute or idealized state of affairs, because it cannot be perfectly attained. Yet the fact that it can never be perfectly attained in the real world is a wholly insufficient excuse for dismissing it as utopian or impossible. What is important are the bearings by which a nation chooses to orient its character. We can choose to let racial inequality fes-ter and risk heightened conflict and violence. Americans can also make a different choice, a commitment to equality and to closing the gap as much as possible. We must reexamine the values, preferences, interests, and ideals that define us. Fundamental change must be addressed before we can begin to affirmatively answer Rodney King's poignant plea: "Can we all just get along?" This book was written to help us understand how far we need to go and what we need to do to get there.* * *

The Suburbanization of America
The Making of the Ghetto

> Because of racial discrimination, blacks were unable to enter the housing mar-ket on the same terms as other groups before them. Thus, the most striking feature of black life was not slum conditions, but the barriers that middle-class blacks encountered trying to escape the ghetto.
>
> —Kenneth T. Jackson, *Crabgrass Frontier*

> A government offering such bounty to builders and lenders could have re-quired compliance with nondiscriminatory policy.... Instead, FHA adopted a racial policty that could well have been culled from the Nuremberg laws. From its inception FHA set itself up as the protector of the all-white neighborhood. It sent its agents into the field to keep Negroes and other minorities from buy-ing houses in white neighborhoods.
>
> —Charles Abrams, *Forbidden Neighbors*

The suburbanization of America was principally financed and encouraged by actions of the federal government, which supported suburban growth from the 1930s through the 1960s by way of taxation, transportation, and housing policy. Taxation policy, for ex-ample, provided greater tax savings for businesses relocating to the suburbs than to those who stayed and made capital improvements to plants in central city locations. As a con-sequence, employment opportunities steadily rose in the suburban rings of the nation's major metropolitan areas. In addition, transportation policy encouraged freeway con-struction and subsidized cheap fuel and mass-produced automobiles. These factors made living on the outer edges of cities both affordable and relatively convenient. How-ever, the most important government policies encouraging and subsidizing suburbaniza-tion focused on housing. In particular, the incentives that government programs gave for the acquisition of single-family detached housing spurred both the development and fi-nancing of the tract home, which became the hallmark of suburban living. While these governmental policies collectively enabled over thirty-five million families between 1933 and 1978 to participate in homeowner equity accumulation, they also had the adverse ef-fect of constraining black Americans' residential opportunities to central-city ghettos of major U.S. metropolitan communities and denying them access to one of the most successful generators of wealth in American history—the suburban tract home.

This story begins with the government's initial entry into home financing. Faced with mounting foreclosures, President Roosevelt urged passage of a bill that authorized the Home Owners Loan Corporation (HOLC). According to Kenneth Jackson's *Crabgrass Frontier*, the HOLC "refinanced tens of thousands of mortgages in danger of default or foreclosure." Of more importance to this story, however, it also introduced standardized appraisals of the fitness of particular properties and communities for both individual and group loans. In creating "a formal and uniform system of appraisal, reduced to writing, structured in defined procedures, and implemented by individuals only after intensive training, government appraisals institutionalized in an rational and bureaucratic framework a racially discriminatory practice that all but eliminated black access to the suburbs and to government mortgage money." Charged with the task of determining the "useful or productive life of housing" they considered to finance, government agents methodically included in their procedures the evaluation of the racial composition or potential racial composition of the community. Communities that were changing racially or were already black were deemed undesirable and placed in the lowest category. The categories, assigned various colors on a map ranging from green for the most desirable, which included new, all-white housing that was always in demand, to red, which included already racially mixed or all-black, old, and undesirable areas, subsequently were used by Federal Housing Authority (FHA) loan officers who made loans on the basis of these designations.

Established in 1934, the FHA aimed to bolster the economy and increase employment by aiding the ailing construction industry. The FHA ushered in the modern mortgage system that enabled people to buy homes on small down payments and at reasonable interest rates, with lengthy repayment periods and full loan amortization. The FHA's success was remarkable: housing starts jumped from 332,000 in 1936 to 619,000 in 1941. The incentive for home ownership increased to the point where it became, in some cases, cheaper to buy a home than to rent one. As one former resident of New York City who moved to suburban New Jersey pointed out, "We had been paying $50 per month rent, and here we come up and live for $29.00 a month." This included taxes, principal, insurance, and interest.

This growth in access to housing was confined, however, for the most part to suburban areas. The administrative dictates outlined in the original act, while containing no antiurban bias, functioned in practice to the neglect of central cities. Three reasons can be cited: first, a bias toward the financing of single-family detached homes over multifamily projects favored open areas outside of the central city that had yet to be developed over congested central-city areas; second, a bias toward new purchases over repair of existing homes prompted people to move out of the city rather than upgrade or improve their existing residences; and third, the continued use of the "unbiased professional estimate" that made older homes and communities in which blacks or undesirables were located less likely to receive approval for loans encouraged purchases in communites where race was not an issue.

While the FHA used as its model the HOLC's appraisal system, it provided more precise guidance to its appraisers in its *Underwriting Manual*. The most basic sentiment underlying the FHA's concern was its fear that the property values would decline if rigid black and white segregation was not maintained. The *Underwriting Manual* openly stated that "if a neighborhood is to retain stability, it is necessary that properties shall continue to be occupied by the same social and racial classes" and further recommended that "subdivision regulations and suitable restrictive covenants" are the best way to ensure such neighborhood stability. The FHA's recommended use of restrictive covenants continued until 1949, when, responding to the Supreme Court's outlawing of such covenants in 1948 (*Shell[e]y v. Kraemer*), it announced that "as of February 15, 1950, it would not insure mortgages on real estate subject to covenants."

Even after this date, however, the FHA's discriminatory practices continued to have an impact on the continuing suburbanization of the white population and the deepening ghettoization of the black population. While exact figures regarding the FHA's discrimination against blacks are not available, data by county show a clear pattern of "redlining" in central-city counties and abundant loan activity in suburban counties.

The FHA's actions have had a lasting impact on the wealth portfolios of black Americans. Locked out of the greatest mass-based opportunity for wealth accumulation in American history, African Americans who desired and were able to afford home ownership found themselves consigned to central-city communities where their investments were affected by the "self-fulfilling prophecies" of the FHA appraisers: cut off from sources of new investment their homes and communities deteriorated and lost value in comparison to those homes and communities that FHA appraisers deemed desirable. One infamous housing development of the period—Levittown—provides a classic illustration of the way blacks missed out on this asset-accumulating opportunity. Levittown was built on a mass scale, and housing there was eminently affordable, thanks to the FHA's and VA's accessible financing, yet as late as 1960 "not a single one of the Long Island Levittown's 82,000 residents was black."

Spencer Overton, Racial Disparities and the Political Function of Property
49 U.C.L.A. L. Rev. 1553, 1553–1574 (2002)

Introduction

[D]isparities arising from past discriminatory policies not only limit substantive rights to control economic resources and to enjoy educational and employment opportunities, but also limit political rights to participate in the democratic process.

An examination of the current privately funded campaign finance system illustrates how the distribution of private property creates racial disparities in the political sphere. In Buckley v. Valeo, [424 U.S. 1 (1976)] the U.S. Supreme Court, concluding that money is necessary for effective political speech, curtailed the extent to which legislatures may restrict campaign contributions and spending on political activity. Discriminatory laws that have shaped the existing distribution of resources,[3] however,

---

3. For example, typical white households control an income stream that is about 156 percent of that controlled by African American and Latino households. See U.S. Bureau of the Census, Money Income in the United States: 1995, at viii (1996) (showing that in 1995, the median household income was $35,766 for whites, $22,860 for Latinos, and $22,391 for African Americans). White households also possess a median net worth that is over eight times greater than that of African American households and over twelve times greater than that of Latino households. See Chuck Collins et al., Shifting Fortunes: The Perils of the Growing American Wealth Gap 57 (1999) (finding that in 1995, the median household net worth for whites was $61,000, for African Americans was $7400, and for Hispanics was $5000, and that the financial wealth (net worth minus equity in

also restrict individual political expression and association. Studies reveal that although people of color comprise approximately 30 percent of the nation's population, they represent only about 1 percent of those who make significant political contributions to federal campaigns. In a political system that deems money to be necessary for effective speech, the allocation of economic resources shapes the distribution of political power no less than the location of the boundary lines that define legislative districts....

[T]his Article illuminates the political function of property rights and asserts that past discriminatory laws that impact the present distribution of economic resources also affect the ability of people of color to exercise political liberties. The impairment of political rights may be among the most troubling effects of discriminatory policies that have shaped the distribution of property, as political rights allow individuals to secure and to preserve other substantive rights and opportunities. Political rights also give individuals a sense of full citizenship within a community and serve as a "vehicle for self-development and identification, and a means for creating alliances."

This Article complements rather than subverts race theorists' efforts to emphasize socioeconomic disparities, for a recognition of how property rights function in the political arena may lead to more comprehensive discussion about the racial misallocation of economic resources. Theorists can more clearly articulate the consequences of past discriminatory policies and tailor remedies to address these consequences. Indeed, discussions about political process may allow for meaningful exchange and progress when discussions about substantive entitlements have stalled, as many who tolerate economic disparities along racial lines may be less comfortable with political disparities. Finally, an acknowledgment of the political function of property pierces the veil between wealthy private actors and facially race-neutral state actions that effectively perpetuate, and often exacerbate, racial disparities.

Part I of this Article reviews the literature of theorists who connect past discrimination to existing economic and social disparities. Part II examines the link between the exercise of property rights and effective political participation that served as the foundation of the Court's decision in Buckley v. Valeo. Part III explains that liberties are suppressed not only by government restrictions on the use and conveyance of resources in politics, but also by allocation rules that determine how decisionmaking authority over particular resources is ordered and distributed. Past discriminatory allocation rules hinder the extent to which many people of color are able to contribute money to political campaigns and to spend money on political expression. These rules also limit the extent to which people of color exercise political liberties in other contexts. For example, discriminatory allocation rules influence the ownership of media outlets, access to high-quality voting technology, and a host of other legal relationships that provide select populations a greater opportunity to exercise political liberties.

I. Race Theory and Property

Race theorists assert that formal equality in civil and political rights is insufficient to alter racial hierarchy.[13] "Economic and social rights," the argument goes, should be

---

owner-occupied housing) for the typical white household was $18,100, for African Americans was $200, and for Hispanics was zero).

13. See Kimberlé W. Crenshaw, *Race, Reform, and Retrenchment: Transformation and Legitimation in Antidiscrimination Law*, 101 Harv. L. Rev. 1331, 1378, 1384 (1988). Crenshaw observes:

Yet the attainment of formal equality is not the end of the story. Racial hierarchy cannot be cured by the move to facial race-neutrality in the laws that structure the economic, po-

viewed "as part of the tapestry of rights that are fundamental, in addition to civil and political rights."[14] The theorists claim that racial history and context should play a significant role in legal analysis generally. Legal decisionmakers create and interpret laws, the race theorists argue, based on the false assumption that the settled distribution of property is "a legitimate and natural baseline,"[16] and thereby mask the effects of past discriminatory policies that benefited whites.[17]

For example, laws and policies that allowed confiscation of land from Native Americans[18] and Mexican Americans,[19] promoted enslavement of African Americans, and prohibited immigration from non-European countries triggered racial disparities in the

---

litical, and social lives of Black people....

... The removal of formal barriers, although symbolically significant to all and materially significant to some, will do little to alter the hierarchical relationship between Blacks and whites until the way in which white race consciousness perpetuates norms that legitimate Black subordination is revealed.... [U]ntil the distinct racial nature of class ideology is itself revealed and debunked, nothing can be done about the underlying structural problems that account for the disparities.

Id.

14. Berta Esperanza Hernandez-Truyol & Shelbi D. Day, *Wealth, Inequality and Human Rights: A Formula for Reform*, 34 Ind. L. Rev. 1213, 1233 (2001); see also Derrick A. Bell, Property Rights in Whiteness—Their Legal Legacy, Their Economic Costs, in Critical Race Theory: The Cutting Edge 71, 77 (Richard Delgado ed., 2d ed. 2000) ("[T]he rhetoric of freedom so freely voiced in this country is no substitute for the economic justice that has been so long denied."); Derrick A. Bell, *Racism: A Prophecy for the Year 2000*, 42 Rutgers L. Rev. 93, 106 (1989) [hereinafter Bell, Prophecy] ("The ultimate challenge for all progressives, black and white, is to broaden the Constitution's protections to include economic rights. Recognition of entitlement to basic needs—jobs, housing, food, health care, education and security—as essential property rights of all individuals is the fundamental issue."). The economic rights versus political rights debate has been foundational in race literature. See Booker T. Washington, Opening of the Cotton States' Exposition in Atlanta, Ga., September, 1895, in Selected Speeches of Booker T. Washington 32–36 (E. Davidson Washington ed., 1932) (urging blacks to aim for economic prosperity and to forego demands for civil rights and suffrage); W.E.B. DuBois, The Souls of Black Folk 36–51 (Penguin Books 1989) (1903) (criticizing Washington's advocacy of "submission and silence as to civil and political rights"); Robert E. Suggs, *Bringing Small Business Development to Urban Neighborhoods*, 30 Harv. C.R.-C.L. L. Rev. 487, 487 n.1 (1995) (observing that although Booker T. Washington "established the National Negro Business League in 1900 for the purpose of promoting commercial achievement that would pave the way to economic independence.... [t]he leadership that won the civil rights victories of the 1960s ... descended from DuBois"); see also Crenshaw, supra note 13, at 1384.

16. Cheryl I. Harris, *Whiteness as Property*, 106 Harv. L. Rev. 1707, 1714 (1993) ("After legalized segregation was overturned, whiteness as property evolved into a more modern form through the law's ratification of the settled expectations of relative white privilege as a legitimate and natural baseline.").

17. Although this Article focuses on past state-sponsored discrimination, which most commentators acknowledge and condemn, many race theorists also focus on present discrimination sponsored by the state and discrimination practiced by private actors. See, e.g., John O. Calmore, *Race/ism Lost and Found: The Fair Housing Act at Thirty*, 52 U. Miami L. Rev. 1067, 1070 (1998) (asserting that contemporary racism frustrates "the ability of fair housing to render a more inclusive and open society").

18. See Joseph W. Singer, *The Continuing Conquest: American Indian Nations, Property Law, and Gunsmoke*, 1 Reconstruction 97, 102 (1991) ("[P]roperty and sovereignty in the United States have a racial basis. The land was taken by force by white people from peoples of color thought by the conquerors to be racially inferior.").

19. See Frank D. Bean & Marta Tienda, The Hispanic Population of the United States 17–22 (1987) (discussing the oppression of Mexican American landowners by Anglo settlers after the Mexican-American War); Charles F. Marden et al., Minorities in American Society 135, 142, 152, 259–91 (1992) (discussing Mexican American immigration and dominance by Anglo settlers); Martin N. Marger, Race and Ethnic Relations 285–90 (2000) (noting that Mexicans' property was taken "through official and unofficial force and fraud").

control of resources. Policies that mandated segregation in education, employment, housing, and business exacerbated these disparities. Even after courts invalidated facially discriminatory laws, such structural phenomena as intergenerational transfers of wealth and depressed housing values in minority neighborhoods carried forward racial disparities in the control of resources.

Current legal doctrines protect expectations over distributions of resources that have been shaped by past discrimination, and thus reinforce and "reproduce subordination in the present."[25] Such subordination manifests itself in the form of racial disparities in wealth, income, education, unemployment, mortality rates, incarceration rates, and other socioeconomic indicators.[26]

Consequently, theorists argue, race-conscious policies such as affirmative action depart from the false neutrality of the status quo and are not unfairly discriminatory. Theorists also use historical discrimination to justify reparations and other legal changes that would improve the socioeconomic condition of people of color.

In setting forth these important socioeconomic insights, race theorists have necessarily moved beyond an exclusive focus upon civil and political inequalities. But in making this move, they need not — indeed, must not — abandon the language of political rights altogether. The political function of property, as discussed below, reveals that economic liberties and political liberties are closely interrelated.

II. The Political Function of Property

While the concept of property serves a variety of functions related to general welfare, productivity, and development, property also serves a political function.[31] In Buckley v.

---

25. Harris, supra note 16, at 1714 ("Through this entangled relationship between race and property, historical forms of domination have evolved to reproduce subordination in the present."); cf. Crenshaw, supra note 13, at 1351–52 ("Law ... embodies and reinforces ideological assumptions about human relations that people accept as natural or even immutable.... Yet by accepting the view of the world implicit in the law, people are also bound by its conceptual limitations. Thus conflict and antagonism are contained: the legitimacy of the entire order is never seriously questioned.").

26. See [Randall] Robinson, [The Debt: What America Owes to Blacks (2000)], at 59–80 (focusing on harms of past discrimination, including high infant mortality, low income, high unemployment, substandard education, and high morbidity); [John O.] Calmore, [*Spacial Equality and the Kerner Commission Report: A Back-to-the-Future Essay*, 71 N.C. L. Rev. 1487 (1993)], at 1489 ("Spatial inequality's harms are reflected in persistent segregative disadvantage in education, employment, security, and residence."); see also Richard F. America, Paying the Social Debt: What White America Owes Black America 19 (1993) (discussing various models for calculating the debt of past discrimination and estimating that the figure may be between five and ten trillion dollars); Anthony E. Cook, *King and the Beloved Community: A Communitarian Defense of Black Reparations*, 68 Geo. Wash. L. Rev. 959, 1011 (2000) ("In the case of African-Americans, some economists have calculated the debt for the unpaid wages of slavery plus accumulated interest to be over four trillion dollars.").

31. Cf. Gregory S. Alexander, Commodity & Propriety: Competing Visions of Property in American Legal Thought, 1776–1970, 2 (1997) (asserting that the proprietarian conception of property is committed to the idea that "the core purpose of property is ... to fulfill some prior normative vision of how society and the polity that governs it should be structured"); C. Edwin Baker, *Property and its Relation to Constitutionally Protected Liberty*, 134 U. Pa. L. Rev. 741, 744 (1986) ("People rely on, consume, or transform resources in many of their self-expressive, developmental, productive, and survival activities."); Frank I. Michelman, *Mr. Justice Brennan: A Property Teacher's Appreciation*, 15 Harv. C.R.-C.L. L. Rev. 296, 299–304 (1980) (asserting that property is "an essential component of individual competence in social and political life" and necessary for "self-determination and self-expression"); Frank I. Michelman, *Process and Property in Constitutional Theory*, 30 Clev. St. L. Rev. 577, 578 (1982) (asserting that "the constitutional right to property is well under-

Valeo, for example, the Supreme Court accorded heightened protection to an owner's right to use and convey resources to engage in political expression and association.[32]

As legal commentators have long recognized, property is not a set of "things." It is a cultural and legal creation that, like a "bundle of sticks," encompasses various entitlements to control resources. These entitlements often include the privilege to use resources, the right to prevent others from using the resources without consent, and the power to transfer resources. Classical liberal theorists conceptualize property as embodying an owner's absolute ability to control a particular resource to the exclusion of the rights of others. Modern theorists, however, recognize that an owner's entitlements are not always absolute. Various federal, state, and local legal directives that arise from constitutions, statutes, regulations, and judicial opinions qualify the extent to which society will respect an individual's right to use, convey, or otherwise control a particular resource for a particular function.[37]

In Buckley, the Supreme Court extended to individuals expansive rights to use, control, and convey financial resources to communicate political messages.[38] Buckley in-

standable as one of the preconditions of a fair democratic system for the determination of the principles of social ordering through public decision").

32. 424 U.S. 1, 58–59 (1976). One might argue that Buckley v. Valeo, 424 U.S. 1 (1976), focuses on expression, rather than property. Ownership of property, however, is the operative factor in determining whether courts will protect an actor's use of property for political purposes. A nonowner does not receive judicial protection from the enforcement of legal restrictions that prevent the nonowner from using another's property to promote the nonowner's views. See Lloyd Corp. v. Tanner, 407 U.S. 551, 567–68 (1972) ("Although ... the courts properly have shown a special solicitude for the guarantees of the First Amendment, this Court has never held that a trespasser or an uninvited guest may exercise general rights of free speech on property privately owned."). But see N.J. Coalition Against War in the Middle East v. J.M.B. Realty Corp., 650 A.2d 757, 760–62 (N.J. 1994) (finding a right of access for uninvited speakers to distribute leaflets at privately owned malls under the New Jersey constitution, reasoning that the leafleters' expressive rights outweigh any interference with the mall owners' property rights, and finding that such access is necessary for speakers without resources to spend on mass communication).

37. See Jeremy Bentham, The Theory of Legislation 111–13 (C.K. Ogden ed., Richard Hildreth trans., 1931) ("Property and law are born together, and die together. Before laws were made there was no property; take away laws, and property ceases."); Baker, supra note 31, at 744 ("Property rules determine when the community will recognize a person's assertion of a right to use a particular resource for these purposes."); Margaret Jane Radin, The Liberal Conception of Property: Cross Currents in the Jurisprudence of Takings, 88 Colum. L. Rev. 1667, 1678 (1988) ("[E]very regulation of any portion of an owner's 'bundle of sticks,' is a taking of the whole of that particular portion considered separately. Price regulations 'take' that particular servitude curtailing free alienability, building restrictions 'take' a particular negative easement curtailing control over development, and so on.").

Just as property commentators have described the rights associated with property as arising from legal directives, democracy scholars have noted that democracy does not consist simply of individual citizens exercising political liberties in a neutral, pre-political world; rather, democracy is also shaped by institutional and legal structures that determine the boundaries of possible political outcomes. See Samuel Issacharoff, Pamela S. Karlan & Richard H. Pildes, The Law of Democracy: Legal Structure of the Political Process 1–2 (2d ed. 2001) (stating that "[t]he kind of democratic politics we have is always and inevitably itself a product of institutional forms and legal structures" which "limit and define the decisions available through democratic politics itself"). A racial analysis reveals that laws governing property and laws governing democracy are not mutually exclusive, but overlap to shape both the meaning of property and the meaning of democracy. The rules and doctrines that govern democracy, such as the Court's invalidation of expenditure limits in Buckley, shape the contours of property rights. At the same time, the rules and doctrines that govern property, such as past discriminatory allocation rules, shape the contours of democracy.

38. See Buckley, 424 U.S. at 14–23. See also Daniel A. Farber, Afterword: Property and Free Speech, 93 Nw. U. L. Rev. 1239, 1239 (1999) ("Property, as first-year law students learn, is like a

volved a challenge to expenditure and contribution limitations contained in the Federal Election Campaign Act Amendments of 1974 (the 1974 Act). Invoking the First Amendment, the Court invalidated an array of expenditure limitations, including provisions that limited the amounts that could be spent by a campaign, by a candidate from her personal funds, and by a noncandidate on behalf of a candidate. In contrast, the Court upheld contribution limits, including a provision that prohibited individuals from contributing more than one thousand dollars to a candidate for federal office.

The Court deemed individuals to have an absolute right to exercise proprietary liberties[42] in spending resources to produce political communication. In explaining its holding, the Court emphasized the essential function of property in exercising expressive and political liberties, stating that

> virtually every means of communicating ideas in today's mass society requires the expenditure of money. The distribution of the humblest handbill or leaflet entails printing, paper, and circulation costs. Speeches and rallies generally necessitate hiring a hall and publicizing the event. The electorate's increasing dependence on television, radio, and other mass media for news and information has made these expensive modes of communication indispensable instruments of effective political speech.[44]

The Court reasoned that spending money is so closely connected to effective political communication that expenditure limits restrict the use "of virtually every means of communicating information." Therefore, the Court concluded, any restriction on expenditures impermissibly restricts political communication.

Although the Court did not extend to individuals such extensive rights to contribute financial resources to campaigns, the Court prohibited excessive legislative restrictions on the exercise of these liberties. The Court upheld the one-thousand-dollar contribution limit, reasoning that contributions are not as closely related to expression as expenditures[46] and that the contribution limits are needed to prevent corruption and the ap-

---

'bundle of sticks,' composed of various powers, rights, and immunities. Among those sticks is the capacity to use property for communicative purposes—either directly, as when we post a sign on our front lawn, or indirectly, as when we use money to pay for a newspaper ad."). In the first 150 years of the existence of the United States, property served other political functions. Property was seen as the basis for liberty, and thus property rights were less prone to political reallocation. Further, many jurisdictions conditioned the franchise on property ownership because of the assumption that property holders could best exercise independent judgment. See Dirk Hoerder, Crowd Action in Revolutionary Massachusetts, 1765–1780, at 371 (1977) (observing that at the time of the American Revolution, "[p]roperty was the basis for liberty"). According to contemporary ideology, it made men independent from the influence of others"); Daniel R. Ortiz, *The Democratic Paradox of Campaign Finance Reform*, 50 Stan. L. Rev. 893, 906 (1998) ("Originally ... property qualifications were thought to promote a vital goal: ensuring that voters had a stake in political matters and exercised independent political judgment.").

42. See Buckley, 424 U.S. at 45. Economic liberties, or freedom in "choices and modes of productive activity and investment," are sometimes distinguished from proprietary liberties, or freedom in "retention, use, and disposition of lawfully obtained holdings of wealth." Frank I. Michelman, *Liberties, Fair Values, and Constitutional Method*, 59 U. Chi. L. Rev. 91, 95 (1992). This Article, however, uses these terms interchangeably.

44. Buckley, 424 U.S. at 19. The Court suggested that money is needed for political communication just as gas is needed to drive a car. See id. at 18 n.18 ("Being free to engage in unlimited political expression subject to a ceiling on expenditures is like being free to drive an automobile as far and as often as one desires on a single tank of gasoline.").

46. See [Buckley, 424 U.S. at 21–23]. The Court attributed its tolerance of contribution ceilings to the unique characteristics of contributions:

A limitation on the amount of money a person may give to a candidate or campaign orga-

pearance of corruption. Despite this holding, the Court noted that contribution restrictions must not be too extensive because of "the important role of contributions in financing political campaigns." The Court observed that effective campaigning relies on broadcast and newspaper advertisements, mass mailings, and polling operations, all of which are often made possible by contributions. With regard to associational interests, contributions enable "like-minded persons to pool their resources in furtherance of common political goals." Because contributions allow candidates and political committees to amass resources necessary for political dialogue, the Court determined that contribution limits must be sufficiently high so as not to interfere with the ability of candidates to engage in effective advocacy.

The Court extended enhanced protection to the exercise of property rights to make expenditures and contributions because of the unique values associated with political expression and association. According to the Court, these property rights are necessary to promote the "'the widest possible dissemination of information from diverse and antagonistic sources.[']" The Court stated that such an exercise of property rights promotes the "'interchange of ideas for the bringing about of political and social changes desired by the people.[']" The exercise of such rights ensures that "the people ... individually as citizens and candidates and collectively as associations and political committees ... retain control over the quantity and range of debate on public issues in a political campaign."

III. Discriminatory Allocation Rules Limit the Exercise of Political Liberties

In drawing an explicit connection between the use of wealth and political liberty, the Court in Buckley made apparent a crucial argument that advances the critical race project. Following the reasoning of Buckley, past discriminatory laws inevitably impair the ability of people of color to exercise rights over economic resources to participate in the political process.

In addition to rules that restrict or protect one's control over her property, allocation rules "structure people's opportunities and incentives to obtain and use resources." Allocation rules are not pre-political. Instead, they are shaped by culture, history, and politics,[56] and essentially determine how decisionmaking authority over particular resources is organized and distributed.[57] Consequently, allocation rules are related to individual exercises of substantive liberty in that they establish "the frame-

---

nization thus involves little direct restraint on his political communication, for it permits the symbolic expression of support evidenced by a contribution but does not in any way infringe the contributor's freedom to discuss candidates and issues. While contributions may result in political expression if spent by a candidate or an association to present views to the voters, the transformation of contributions into political debate involves speech by someone other than the contributor....

....

... In sum, although the Act's contribution and expenditure limitations both implicate fundamental First Amendment interests, its expenditure ceilings impose significantly more severe restrictions on protected freedoms of political expression and association than do its limitations on financial contributions.

56. See [Baker, supra note 31] at 743 ("Culture, history, and politics (broadly defined) necessarily determine both the content of the specific property rules accepted in a given society and the resulting property allocations. I will here assume what I think should be obvious: that the notion of a complete set of timeless, natural, or proper property rules is absurd.").

57. See id. at 779–80 ("'[A]llocation rules' determine who is entitled to make and carry out any particular decision. They embody the criteria that identify the possessor of a property right, that is, the possessor of decision-making authority....").

work within which liberty exists."[58] People who have benefited from allocation rules are able to exercise liberties related to property for political purposes; those who have not benefited are unable to do so. Thus, allocation rules are inextricably tied to the value of liberty associated with property, and determine the value of one person's liberties relative to those of another.[59] Allocation rules are no less important to the value of liberty than rules that directly restrict or expand the formal exercise of property rights.[60]

The Court has recognized that biased allocation rules can unfairly disadvantage particular actors in their exercise of political liberties. In contrast to the First Amendment absolutism of Buckley, the Court tolerated expenditure limitations in Austin v. Michigan Chamber of Commerce.[61] In Austin, the Court upheld a Michigan statute that prohibited corporations from using money from their general treasuries to make contributions or expenditures on behalf of candidates. To the Court, special allocation rules, such as "limited liability, perpetual life, and favorable treatment of the accumulation and distribution of assets," gave corporations "legal advantages" in amassing wealth. The Court stated that aggregations of wealth that are "accumulated with the help of the corporate form" can "influence unfairly the outcome of elections." The Court concluded that "the unique state-conferred corporate structure that facilitate[d] the amassing of large treasuries warrants the limit on independent expenditures." Some commentators view Austin as an anomaly. Nonetheless, the case recognizes that allocation rules determine the value of expressive and proprietary liberties and may warrant legislative intervention that reallocates the value of these liberties.

In addition to laws that give special benefits to corporations, allocation rules include past racially discriminatory laws that have shaped the distribution of property, along with laws and practices that have carried racial disparities forward. Because of discriminatory allocation rules, many whites are more able and more likely to exercise liberties related to property for political purposes, while many people of color are less able and less likely to do so.[69]

---

58. Id. at 780 ("Because the existence of these types of rules or practices is inevitable, they should not be seen as necessarily inconsistent with all meaningful conceptions of liberty. Rather, they are better seen as establishing the framework within which liberty exists.").

59. See Michelman, supra note 42, at 99. One commentator describes the connection between distribution and the value of liberty as follows:

> In a capitalist order, one person's proprietary value (or power) is obviously relative to other people's. A constitutional system of proprietary liberty is, therefore, incomplete without attending to the configurations of the values of various people's proprietary liberties. The question of distribution is endemic in the very idea of a constitutional scheme of proprietary liberty. Thus, it can by no means be said of laws aimed at nothing but property distributions that they are ipso facto antithetical to that idea.

Id.

60. Cf. John Rawls, A Theory of Justice 178–79 (rev. ed. 1999) (explaining that liberties have value only when individuals possess sufficient resources to take advantage of them, and concluding that any theory of political justice must be accompanied by a theory of just economic distribution).

61. 494 U.S. 652 (1990).

69. Research suggests that the failure of minorities to make political contributions is attributable more to a lack of resources than a lack of desire to donate money:

> When it comes to time, minority activists are not less active than their white counterparts.... The situation is different with respect to money. Among contributors, whites—who are, as we saw, slightly more likely than African Americans and considerably more likely than Latinos to make campaign donations—give substantially more than African Americans or Latinos do when they contribute.

Henry E. Brady et al., Race, Ethnicity, and Political Participation, in Classifying by Race 354,

Studies confirm this insight. Large contributions play a crucial role in funding American politics, but a disproportionately small number of such contributions come from people of color. Even though people of color comprise approximately 30 percent of the nation's population, they represent only about 1 percent of those who make reportable contributions to federal candidates. Residents in the average American zip code make federal contributions at three times the rate of residents in zip codes populated predominantly by people of color. The 41.3 million inhabitants of America's 2492 predominantly nonwhite zip codes collectively gave less money than the 680,000 inhabitants of the 26 zip codes with the highest rates of giving.[74] Even elected officials who represent districts that are populated predominantly by people of color tend to receive most of their campaign money from white contributors.[75] Thus, the nature of political debate in minority communities "is largely dependent on the behavior of whites."

Although limitations on the size of contributions and expenditures may restrict the liberty of some individuals, discriminatory allocation rules restrict the political liberties of many people of color in contravention of the reasoning of Buckley. Because money plays a crucial role in political communication, the rules disadvantage many people of color in "virtually every means of communicating ideas." People of color have less access to "indispensable instruments of effective political speech" such as television, radio, and other mass media outlets. People of color control fewer resources and are thus less able to pool resources with like-minded persons in furtherance of common political goals. Discriminatory allocation rules also hinder fundraising and effective advocacy by those candidates that people of color support.[79] Such rules prevent "'the widest possible dissemination of information from diverse and antagonistic sources[']" as well as an "'interchange of ideas[']" that will bring about "'political and social changes desired[']" by

361–62 (Paul E. Peterson, ed. 1995); see Henry E. Brady et al., *Beyond SES: A Resource Model of Political Participation*, 89 Am. Pol. Sci. Rev. 271, 283 (1995) ("[T]he major determinant of giving money is having money. Years of education also matter, but neither free time nor civic skills affect monetary contributions."). Minority participation is much higher in other forms of political activity that are not so closely related to control over economic resources. For example, even though minorities give only about 1 percent of political contributions, they cast 23 percent of the votes in the 2000 general presidential election. See Marjorie Connelly, Who Voted: A Portrait of American Politics, 1976–2000, N.Y. Times, Nov. 12, 2000, § 4 (Week in Review) at 4; see also Sidney Verba et. al., *Voice and Equality: Civil Voluntarism in American Politics* 233 (1995) ("When it comes to activity within a campaign, African Americans are more likely to say that they have worked in a campaign but less likely to say that they have given money.").

74. See [Public Campaign, The Color of Money: Campaign Contributions and Race,] 37 (1998). For general information on Public Campaign and an abbreviated version of the study, see http://www.publicampaign.org. Racial disparities in political spending have not been studied as extensively as racial disparities in individual contributions. The lack of spending limits, however, suggests it is very possible that racial disparities in political spending are even greater.

75. See Robert Singh, The Congressional Black Caucus: Racial Politics in the U.S. Congress 125–26 (1998) ("The funding of black campaigns remains substantially the province of political actors external to black communities.... Without exception, over every congressional election cycle, CBC members raise more funds from PACs alone than their challengers raise from all sources combined."); Robert C. Smith, *Financing Black Politics: A Study of Congressional Elections*, 17 Rev. of Black Pol. Econ. 5, 24 (1988) (observing that "congressional elections in the black community tend to be financed largely by white dominated PACs and disproportionately by large (probably white) individual contributors").

79. Cf. John Theilmann & Al Wilhite, Discrimination and Congressional Campaign Contributions 78 (1991) ("After controlling for attributes such as candidate strength, opposition strength, party affiliation, and the incumbency advantage, black candidates received substantially lower levels of funds than did nonblack candidates.... [T]he differential appears to be racially motivated.").

many people of color. The rules thus hinder the individual autonomy, self-expression, and self-determination of people of color.[82]

This Article focuses on campaign finance to illustrate how past discriminatory allocation rules infringe on the present value of both the economic liberties and the political liberties of people of color, but these harms are much broader. Even outside of the campaign finance context, discriminatory allocation rules infringe upon the ability of people of color to exercise political liberties.[83]

First, past discrimination impairs the extent to which people of color spend money to exercise other, related political liberties. For example, on the whole, whites are better positioned to pool their resources and to hire a lobbyist or to purchase airtime to promote their personal opinions on affirmative action, criminal sentencing, and other general political issues. Such spending on lobbying and "issue advertisements" may significantly impact legislative outcomes. Further, wealthier whites disproportionately own and control major newspapers and television news operations, and thus people of color exercise minimal control over endorsements, editorials, and news reports that discuss candidates and ballot initiatives.[84] Similarly, people of color own and control few book publishing companies, recording companies, movie studios, and other major entities that produce expression. Through a barrage of images related to language, conduct,

---

82. While Buckley allows for a more comprehensive understanding of the harms caused by discriminatory laws that have deprived many people of color of resources, the opinion is troubling in the absence of some sort of redistribution that offsets past discriminatory allocation rules. Another way to view this problem, at least in the campaign finance context, involves a focus on not merely the discriminatory allocation rules themselves, but on the decision in Buckley to defer to a distribution of resources shaped by discriminatory allocation rules as a baseline for political participation. The Buckley Court constitutionalizes a right to exercise control over resources for political expression that is dependent on discriminatory allocation rules that we would today consider unconstitutional. Without some form of redistribution of liberties, Buckley effectively advances the political ideologies of those who have profited from the discriminatory misallocation of property. Indeed, Buckley's additional protection of settled expectations is in itself an allocation rule. The decision multiplies the rights associated with property ownership and expands disparities between those who have benefited from past discriminatory allocation rules and those who have not. Along similar lines, if property is an aspect of social relations between people that focuses on "rights" rather than "things," recognition of the political function of property contributes to a better understanding of how these rights shape social relations in the context of a democracy. See generally [Spencer] Overton, [*But Some Are More Equal: Race, Exclusion, and Campaign Finance*, 80 Tex L. Rev. 987 (2002)].

83. Past state-sponsored discrimination also impairs the ability of people of color to use resources to exercise a variety of other liberties, such as those related to counsel, privacy, and religion. Just as past discrimination shapes disparities in campaign contributions and expenditures, it may also contribute to racial disparities in criminal convictions, out-of-wedlock pregnancies, and other social circumstances.

84. See Metro Broad., Inc. v. FCC, 497 U.S. 547, 553–54 (1990) ("[I]n 1986, [minorities] owned just 2.1 percent of the more than 11,000 radio and television stations in the United States.... [T]hese statistics fail to reflect the fact that, as late entrants who often have been able to obtain only the less valuable stations, many minority broadcasters serve geographically limited markets with relatively small audiences."); Leonard M. Baynes, *Life After Adarand: What Happened to the Metro Broadcasting Diversity Rationale for Affirmative Action in Telecommunications Ownership?*, 33 Mich J.L. Reform 87, 88 (1999) (reporting that in 1998 only 2.9 percent of broadcast properties were owned by minority-owned businesses); Felicity Barringer, Editors Debate Realism vs. Retreat in Newsroom Diversity, N.Y. Times, Apr. 6, 1998, at D1 (reporting that only "11.4 percent of the nation's 54,700 newspaper reporters, photographers and editors are black, Asian, Hispanic or [N]ative American"); Newspaper Ass'n of Am., Facts About Newspapers 2001, at 29 (2001) (reporting that a 1998 survey of U.S. daily newspapers found that "[m]inorities represent 7.7% of news executives") available at http://www.naa.org/info/facts01/29_ minwomen/index.html (last visited May 14, 2002).

and values, these entities enjoy significant influence not simply over election results and government policy, but also over the meaning of racial identity (as understood by people of color as well as by whites).[86] Due to a lack of ownership and other legal relationships that allow for control of resources used for expression, people of color are hindered in their ability to counter oppressive images in the marketplace of ideas. Further, people of color are less able to demand alternative programming because they do not form a high-end target audience for advertisers.[87]

Second, past discriminatory allocation rules effectively interfere with the opportunity of many people of color to cast a vote. Certain technologies, such as optical scanning machines that more accurately record votes and Internet voting programs that allow individuals to vote from home, may appear to open the process and allow for enhanced participation. Just as individuals who have benefited from discriminatory allocation rules are better equipped to pay poll taxes, own property, and pass literacy tests, however, they also may have greater access to optical scanning machines and Internet voting. Thus, such technologies may skew the distribution of political liberties. To the extent that incarceration rates correspond with poverty, felon disenfranchisement laws disproportionately impact those disadvantaged by discriminatory allocation rules.[92] One could also assert that discriminatory allocation rules affect the racial distribution of educational opportunities, subsistence, health care, and shelter, all of which individuals need to influence political debate and to cast an informed vote.

Conclusion

While past racially discriminatory laws impact the distribution of substantive property rights, they also establish the framework within which individuals exercise political rights. As Buckley shows, resources are needed to engage in effective political communication and to participate in the democratic process. Because the value of political liberties depends on the existing distribution of economic resources, discriminatory allocation rules hinder the ability of people of color to forge political identities, to develop alliances with others, and

---

86. Some race theorists have rejected the near-absolute judicial protection of hate speech and other racially demeaning messages, arguing that the power of racist cultural messages should be curtailed in light of context, history, and politics. See, e.g., Mari J. Matsuda et al., Words that Wound: Critical Race Theory, Assaultive Speech, and the First Amendment (1993); Richard Delgado, *Toward a Legal Realist View of the First Amendment*, 113 Harv. L. Rev. 778, 779 (2000) (reviewing Steven H. Shiffrin, Dissent, Injustice, and the Meaning of America (1999)) ("Under the influence of radical feminism and Critical Race Theory, this last remnant of 1890s mechanical jurisprudence is beginning to give way to a view of speech that is flexible, policy-sensitive, and mindful of communication theory, politics, and setting."); Richard Delgado, *First Amendment Formalism Is Giving Way to First Amendment Legal Realism*, 29 Harv. C.R.-C.L. L. Rev. 169 (1994); Charles R. Lawrence III, *If He Hollers Let Him Go: Regulating Racist Speech on Campus*, 1990 Duke L.J. 431 (1990). The problem arises, however, not simply from the images themselves, but also from the inability of people of color to counter derogatory images with more constructive images, which arises in large part from racial disparities in wealth.

87. Cf. Kurt A. Wimmer, *The Future of Minority Advocacy Before the FCC: Using Marketplace Rhetoric To Urge Policy Change*, 41 Fed. Comm. L.J. 133, 141–42 (1989) ("All viewers are not valued equally by advertisers.... [A] large audience may be desirable, prompting programmers to tailor programming to ... majority interests.... [A] small, high-income demographic may be desirable, prompting programmers to tailor programming to the young, white audience.... Under either scenario, minority audiences are disenfranchised.").

92. See Issacharoff, Karlan, & Pildes, supra note 37, at 43 ("Nationally, 13 percent of black men cannot vote because of criminal records; in Alabama and Florida, nearly one in three black men are permanently disenfranchised. No other democracy appears to disenfranchise as many people due to criminal records.").

to secure and preserve substantive rights and opportunities. Those who are not adversely impacted by these rules are better able to exercise their political liberties and to secure legislative pronouncements that effectively perpetuate, and often exacerbate, racial disparities.

Concerns about political liberties need not distract from race theorists' concerns about economic opportunity, but can fortify claims to economic entitlement. A consideration of how property functions in the political arena allows for a more comprehensive understanding of the harms of discriminatory allocation rules, and enhances the claims of race theorists. If the use of resources for politics is so important that it justifies judicial protection from excessive legislative restrictions, it follows that discriminatory allocations that interfere with the ability of people of color to use resources for politics deserve closer examination.

6. Foreclosure

Associates Home Equity Group, Inc. v. Troup
343 N.J.Super. 254, 778 A.2d 529 (2001)

Madeline L. Houston, argued the cause for appellants (Houston & Totaro, attorneys; Ms. Houston and Melissa J. Totaro, on the brief).

Anthony J. Laura, Newark, argued the cause for respondent Associates Home Equity Services, Inc. f/k/a Ford Consumer Finance Company (Reed, Smith, attorneys; Mr. Laura and Greg A. Dadika, on the brief).

Kathleen Cavanaugh, Parsippany, argued the cause for respondents East Coast Mortgage Corp and Jeffrey Ahrens (Greiner, Gallagher & Cavanaugh, attorneys; Ms. Cavanaugh, on the brief).

Kenneth Zimmerman of the D.C. Bar, admitted pro hac vice, Washington, DC, argued the cause for New Jersey Institute for Social Justice, Inc. and amicus curiae for appellants Beatrice Troup and Curtis Troup (Gibbons, Del Deo, Dolan, Griffinger & Vecchione, attorneys; Lawrence S. Lustberg and Risa E. Kaufman, Newark, on the brief).

Before Judges Havey, Cuff and Lisa.

Havey, P.J.A.D.

This is a foreclosure action. Defendants Beatrice and Curtis Troup, African-Americans, obtained a mortgage loan from third-party defendant East Coast Mortgage Corp. (ECM) to pay for repairs on their Newark home made by third-party defendants Gary Wishnia, General Builders Supply, Inc. and Property Redevelopment Center, Inc. (collectively Wishnia). The mortgage and note were assigned by ECM to Associates Home Equity Services, Inc. (Associates). When the Troups defaulted, Associates instituted this foreclosure proceeding. The Troups filed a counterclaim against Associates and a third-party complaint against Wishnia and ECM, claiming violations of the Consumer Fraud Act (CFA), N.J.S.A. 56:8-1 to -106, the Law Against Discrimination (LAD), N.J.S.A. 10:5-1 to -49, the Fair Housing Act (FHA), 42 U.S.C.A. §§ 3601 to 3631, the Civil Rights Act (CRA), 42 U.S.C.A. § 1981, and the Truth-In-Lending Act (TILA), 15 U.S.C.A. § 1635. The trial court granted summary judgment dismissing all of the Troups' claims against Associates and ECM, and entered a judgment of foreclosure in favor of Associates. The court found that the terms of ECM's construction loan were not unconscionable and that the Troups' affirmative claims under the applicable state and federal laws were barred by the governing statute of limitations. We granted the Troups' motion for leave to appeal.

We affirm in part and reverse in part. We conclude that it was premature to dismiss the Troups' claim that Associates engaged in predatory lending activities. The Troups are entitled to discovery on this claim. Further, although the Troups' affirmative claims against Associates under the governing statutes are time-barred, they may be considered in support of the affirmative defense of equitable recoupment. We further conclude that genuine issues of material fact exist respecting whether the "Holder Rule," 16 C.F.R. § 433, applies in this case, subjecting ECM to liability for the wrongdoings of Wishnia, the home repair contractor. Fact issues also exist as to whether defendants engaged in unconscionable business practices under the CFA.

Considering the evidentiary material in a light most favorable to the Troups, these are the facts. Beatrice Troup, a seventy-four year old African American, has lived at 62 Vanderpool Street in Newark for approximately forty years. Following a telephone solicitation by Gary Wishnia, an agent for General Builders Supply, Inc., Beatrice and her son Curtis executed a contract for exterior home repairs with General on September 1, 1995. The contract price was $38,500, payable "$479.75 for 240 months." Beatrice claims that Wishnia told her "not to worry, he would get me financing." An amended contract was executed on November 16, 1995, for additional interior home repairs, increasing the contract price to $49,990. The agreement provided that "[payments] are to be made beginning January 1, 1996 payable to Property Redevelopment Center, Inc. until permanent financing is obtained."

Some time before September 14, 1995, Jeffrey Ahrens, ECM's representative, prepared the Troups' loan application. A credit search was conducted. According to Beatrice, the Troups had no personal dealings with ECM. She and her son Curtis dealt directly with Wishnia who arranged a limousine to transport the Troups to ECM's office to close the loan. Also, Wishnia did the "leg work" in processing the loan and obtained all income documentation required by ECM.

The Troups' loan application, dated September 14, 1995, but not signed by them until the closing date of April 27, 1996, provided for a $46,500 loan at an annual interest rate of 11.65 percent, adjustable after six months. The Truth-In-Lending disclosure form signed by the Troups at closing stated that the loan was a "balloon" type, payable in fifteen years, with the last payment being $41,603.58. The Troups were also charged four points, or four percent of the total loan amount. At the closing, Beatrice was required to execute a deed conveying the property to herself and her son.

At some point after April 27, 1996, ECM assigned the mortgage and note to Associates. On May 11, 1998, Associates filed a foreclosure complaint alleging that the Troups had failed to make the required payments under the mortgage and note. The Troups filed an answer, counterclaim and third-party complaint consisting of fifteen counts against the Wishnia defendants, ECM and Associates. Pertinent here are the counts charging Wishnia with "unconscionably poor" workmanship, and that Wishnia had conspired with ECM to place the mortgage financing with ECM and "to reap profits by subjecting the Troups to unconscionable, illegal and fraudulent home repair and financing transactions." The Troups charged Associates and third-party defendants with unconscionable and deceptive conduct in violation of the CFA. They further allege that ECM violated the TILA by failing to provide them with a "clear and conspicuous notice" of the expiration date of their right to rescind, failing to make proper disclosures, and materially understating the finance charges. Finally, the Troups asserted that Associates "participated in, authorized and/or ratified and/or had constructive knowledge of" the deceptive unconscionable acts of ECM and engaged in predatory lending practices in violation of the FHA, the CRA, and the LAD.

In dismissing all of the Troups' claims against ECM and Associates, and entering a judgment of foreclosure in Associates' favor, the trial court found that the terms of the mortgage loan given to the Troups were not "unconscionable when looked at in its entirety," given the fact that, although a 6.6 percent rate was available to "prime borrowers," the Troups "did not appear to be AAA rating." The claims against ECM based on Wishnia's deceptive and unconscionable conduct and workmanship were dismissed because, according to the court, ECM could not be held accountable for Wishnia's conduct. The court also determined that all of the Troups' claims against ECM and Associates were barred by the governing statutes of limitations under the LAD, the FHA and the CFA. Finally, the court dismissed the Troups' demand for rescission under the TILA, concluding that "there was conspicuous notice given" of the right to rescind.

I.

The Troups and amicus contend that the trial court erred in dismissing the Troups' claim of predatory/discriminatory lending practices against Associates, claiming that genuine fact issues exist precluding summary judgment. Amicus contends that at the very least the dismissal of the claim was premature because the Troups did not have the opportunity to develop it by way of meaningful discovery. We agree with amicus.[2]

The Troups and amicus claim that Associates engaged in a predatory lending practice by actively discriminating against them in consort with ECM by treating the Troups, African-Americans, less favorably than white borrowers in violation of the FHA, the CRA, and the LAD. Amicus adds that Associates may also be held accountable for ECM's discriminatory practice on the theory that Associates "controlled" ECM's conduct. The Troups do not seek money damages against Associates for any violation of these statutes.[3] Rather, they argue that Associates' discriminatory conduct supports the affirmative defense of equitable recoupment in these foreclosure proceedings. The trial court did not address this issue.

Predatory lending has been described as:

---

2. Amicus presented a certification to us by Elvin Wyly an Assistant Professor in the Department of Geography and the Center for Urban Research at Rutgers University. Because the certification was not presented below, we advised the parties that we would consider the certification only for the purpose of giving an overview concerning predatory lending practices in New Jersey. Professor Wyly states that it is evident from the data submitted pursuant to the Home Mortgage Disclosure Act of 1975 (HMDA), 12 U.S.C.A. §§ 2801 to 2810, that a "dual housing finance market exists in New Jersey for the refinance and home repair loans" market. Wyly reports that "urban areas of heavy minority concentration are being disproportionately serviced by subprime lenders...." The HMDA's data reveals that in predominately minority neighborhoods, subprime lenders control nearly two-thirds of the home improvement market. He concludes: "[i]n the home improvement market, African-Americans are almost four times as likely to be slotted into subprime/lenders as whites, even after accounting for income, loan amount, and differences between deposit-taking banks and nondepository independent mortgage companies."

3. We do not pass upon the legal viability of amicus' alternative claim. The cases cited by it stand for the proposition that the duty of a landlord or property owner under the FHA not to discriminate may not be delegated to an agent or employee. The question as to the applicability of this theory must be addressed by the trial court upon completion of discovery.

a mismatch between the needs and capacity of the borrower.... In essence, the loan does not fit the borrower, either because the borrower's underlying needs for the loan are not being met or the terms of the loan are so disadvantageous to that particular borrower that there is little likelihood that the borrower has the capability to repay the loan.

[Daniel S. Ehrenberg, If the Loan Don't Fit, Don't Take It: Applying the Suitability Doctrine to the Mortgage Industry to Eliminate Predatory Lending, 10 J. Affordable Housing & Community Dev. L. 117, 119–20 (Winter 2001).]

The Troups' expert, Calvin Bradford, summarized the concept of predatory lending as follows:

In using the term "predatory lending" I refer to lenders who target certain populations for onerous credit terms. The population generally targeted includes, among others, the elderly, minorities, and residents of neighborhoods that do not have ready access to mainstream credit. Credit terms *not* warranted by the objective facts regarding the creditworthiness of these individuals are imposed upon them because for various reasons the lenders feel they can take advantage of a borrower. Typically predatory lenders take advantage of borrowers due to their lack of sophistication in the lending market, due to their lack of perceived options for the loan based on discrimination or some other factor, or due to deceptive practices engaged in by the lender that mislead or fail to inform the borrower of the real terms and conditions of the loan. The record in this case indicates that this is consistent with what occurred in the Troup transaction.

Specifically, the Troups and amicus charge "reverse redlining" in this case. "Redlining is 'the practice of denying the extension of credit to specific geographic areas due to the income, race or ethnicity of its residents.' " Hargraves v. Capital City Mortgage Corp., 140 F.Supp.2d 7, 20 (D.D.C.2000). The term "redlining" is derived from the actual practice of drawing a red line around designated areas in which credit is to be denied. "Reverse redlining is the practice of extending credit on unfair terms to those same communities." Congress has reported that "reverse redlining ... [is] the targeting of residents of those same communities for credit on unfair terms. Considerable testimony before the committee indicates that the communities lacking access to traditional lending institutions are being victimized in this fashion by second mortgage lenders, home improvement contractors, and finance companies...." S.Rep. No. 103–169, U.S.Code Cong. & Admin.News 1994, 1881 at 1905. Reverse redlining has been held to violate the FHA and the CRA. Honorable [v. Easy Life Real Estate System], 100 F.Supp.2d 885, 892 (N.D.Ill.2000). We do not hesitate to conclude that the practice violates the LAD as well. See N.J.S.A. 10:5-12i(1) (it is unlawful for a mortgage company to "discriminate against any person ... because of race, ... in the granting, ... or in the fixing of the rates, terms, conditions or provisions" of a mortgage loan).

A plaintiff may establish a colorable claim of reverse redlining by demonstrating that "defendants' lending practices and loan terms were 'unfair' and 'predatory,' and that the defendants either intentionally targeted on the basis of race, or that there is a disparate impact on the basis of race." Hargraves v. Capital City Mortgage Corp., 140 F.Supp.2d 7, 20 (D.D.C.2000), at 20. See also United States v. Mitchell, 580 F.2d 789, 791 (5th Cir.1978) (the FHA prohibits "not only direct discrimination but practices with racially discouraging effects"); and see Jackson v. Okaloosa County, 21 F.3d 1531, 1543 (11th Cir.1994) (FHA violation can be demonstrated by a showing of either direct discrimination or discriminatory effects).

In this case the Troups' predatory lending claim was dismissed without permitting them to conduct meaningful discovery on the issue. The Troups laid the foundation for a reverse redlining case by establishing that they are African Americans living in a predominately African-American neighborhood in Newark. Their expert stated that the 11.65 percent interest rate and other terms of the loan were unjustified from an objective viewpoint, given the Troups' credit history and favorable debt-to-income ratio. Moreover, an Associates' representative testified during deposition that Associates paid a premium of $2,325 to ECM for securing the Troups' loan. He explained that "[w]e [Associates] pay a premium for the loan ... [which] increase[s] as the interest rate of the loan increased," a practice recognized in the lending community as "yield spread premium."

Also significant is the fact that Associates gave ECM a "pre-approval determination" on February 23, 1996, two months before the Troups executed their loan application with ECM and ECM assigned the loan to Associates nine days after the loan was closed. The Troups argue that a fair inference can be drawn from these facts that Associates participated in inflating the interest rate and imposed the terms of the loan characterized by the Troups' expert as "onerous." These facts at the very least are supportive of the Troups' claim that Associates participated in the targeting of inner-city borrowers who lack access to traditional lending institutions, charged them a discriminatory interest rate, and imposed unreasonable terms.

With this showing, we agree with the Troups and amicus that the Troups were entitled to additional discovery in order to bolster their predatory-lending assertion. See Wilson v. Amerada Hess Corp., 168 N.J. 236, 253, 773 A.2d 1121 (2001) (slip op. at 22) (denial of discovery was abuse of discretion because "we cannot dismiss the possibility that the information plaintiffs sought would raise a jury question on the issue of breach of the implied covenant"). They understandably seek additional information from Associates respecting any guidelines it followed in fixing the rate and terms of the Troups' loan, and whether in fact those guidelines are facially, or as applied, discriminatory against borrowers based on their place of residence, income, race or ethnicity.

Further, we agree with the Troups that they are entitled to be informed concerning loans made by ECM and Associates to other New Jersey borrowers during the time period when the loan was made to the Troups. This information may or may not disclose a pattern of discriminatory lending practice in New Jersey's inner cities. If it does, the trial court should consider the Troups' request for further information about the loans, such as the location of the property, and race and income of the borrowers. The discovery order must not, of course, be overly burdensome and should be made subject to any legitimate claim of confidentiality, appropriate protective orders and redaction.

We agree with the trial court that the Troups' affirmative claims for damages against Associates under the FHA, the CRA and the LAD are barred by the governing statutes of limitations. The alleged discriminatory conduct on the part of ECM and Associates occurred from September 1995 through April 27, 1996, when the Troups closed on their loan. The Troups filed their counterclaim and third-party complaint on August 9, 1999. The Troups' claims under the CRA, the FHA and the LAD are governed by a two-year statute of limitations.

However, the Troups' claims under the pertinent federal and state statutes are cognizable under the theory of equitable recoupment as an affirmative defense to Associates' foreclosure complaint. "[T]he fundamental purpose of recoupment ... is the examination of a transaction in all its aspects to achieve a just result." Beneficial Fin. Co. of Atlantic City v. Swaggerty, 86 N.J. 602, 612, 432 A.2d 512 (1981). A successful recoupment defense acts to reduce the amount the plaintiff can recover on the claim for the debt when the counterclaim arises from the same transaction.

Further, it has been observed that:

> any claim of recoupment must arise out of the *identical* transaction that provided plaintiff with a cause of action, and no affirmative relief may be granted independent of plaintiff's claim. As an equitable concept, judges invented the doctrine of equitable recoupment in order to avoid an unusually harsh or egregious result from a strict application of a statute of limitations.

[Midlantic Nat'l Bank v. Georgian Ltd., 233 N.J.Super. 621, 625–26, 559 A.2d 872 (Law Div.1989).

Consequently, "the defense of recoupment 'is never barred by the statute of limitations so long as the main action itself is timely.' " Nester v. O'Donnell, 301 N.J.Super. 198, 208, 693 A.2d 1214 (App.Div.1997).

Consequently, the Troups may assert their recoupment defense under both New Jersey and federal law notwithstanding expiration of the controlling statutes of limitations. See Beneficial Fin. Co. Of Atlanta City v. Swaggerty, 86 N.J. 602, 612, 432 A.2d 512 (1981), at 608, (borrowers have the right to assert recoupment in a counterclaim against lender under the TILA, despite expiration of the one-year statute of limitations). The recoupment defense in this case arises out of the same transaction as the claim for the debt. The underlying loan transaction was the common source of both the Troups' liability to pay the debt and their correlative rights under the fair housing and civil rights statutes. The Troups' recoupment defense is not intended to invalidate the debt; it is asserted to reduce the amount that Associates may recover on its claim.

Associates argue that the underlying premise of recoupment is inapplicable here because its complaint is for foreclosure, rather than for collection of a debt. In support of that proposition, it cites New York Guardian Mortgage Corp. v. Dietzel, 362 Pa.Super. 426, 524 A.2d 951, 953 (1986), which concluded that "a judgment in foreclosure is not a judgment for money damages" under the TILA, observing that:

> An action in mortgage foreclosure is strictly an *in rem* proceeding, and the purpose of a judgment in mortgage foreclosure is solely to effect a judicial sale of the mortgaged property. A judgment in a mortgage foreclosure action is not a judgment for money damages and therefore cannot be "an action to collect amounts owed" or "an action to collect the debt" as required under § 1640(h) and (e) of the Truth-In-Lending Act.

The Bankruptcy Court in Dangler v. Central Mortgage Co., 75 B.R. 931, 935 (Bkrtcy.E.D.Pa.1987), expressly disagreed with New York Guardian, holding that "[o]n its own terms, the [New York Guardian] decision is plainly incorrect." Id. at 935.

Further, a foreclosure action is not strictly an *in rem* proceeding. It is a quasi *in rem* procedure, to determine not only the right to foreclose, but also the amount due on the mortgage. As stated, what the Troups seek is a diminution of the amount due based on Associates' violation of statutory fair housing and civil rights laws. In our view, it would be fundamentally unfair and contrary to the remedial goals expressed by these statutes to preclude the recoupment remedy simply because it is invoked in a foreclosure proceeding. Without the defense, the mortgagee could simply take the mortgaged premises, leaving the borrower without a remedy. We therefore, reverse the summary judgment order dismissing the Troups' claim against Associates, and direct that an appropriate discovery order be entered.

II.

The Troups and amicus argue that the trial court erred in dismissing the Troups' claims against ECM and Ahrens based on the so-called "Holder Rule."

16 C.F.R. §433.2 (2001) provides that, in connection with any sale of goods or services to consumers, affecting commerce, it is an unfair or deceptive act or practice within the meaning of §5 of the Federal Trade Commission Act for a seller to accept as full or partial payment for the services rendered:

> the proceeds of any purchase money loan (as purchase money loan is defined herein), unless any consumer credit contract made in connection with such purchase money loan contains the following provision in at least ten point, bold face, type:
>
> NOTICE
>
> ANY HOLDER OF THIS CONSUMER CREDIT CONTRACT IS SUBJECT TO ALL CLAIMS AND DEFENSES WHICH THE DEBTOR COULD ASSERT AGAINST THE SELLER OF GOODS OR SERVICES OBTAINED WITH THE PROCEEDS HEREOF. RECOVERY HEREUNDER BY THE DEBTOR SHALL NOT EXCEED AMOUNTS PAID BY THE DEBTOR HEREUNDER.

A "[c]onsumer credit contract" is defined as "[a]ny instrument which evidences or embodies a debt arising from a 'Purchase Money Loan' transaction or a 'financed sale'...."16 C.F.R. at §431.1(i) (2001). 16 C.F.R. §433.1(e) defines "[f]inancing a sale" as "[e]xtending credit to a consumer in connection with a 'Credit Sale' within the meaning of the TILA and Regulation Z." The TILA, specifically 15 U.S.C.A. §1602(g) defines "credit sale" as:

> any sale in which the seller is a creditor. The term includes any contract in the form of bailment or lease if the bailee or lessee *contracts to pay as compensation for use a sum substantially equivalent to or in excess of the aggregate value of the property and services involved* and it is agreed that the bailee or lessee will become, or for no other nominal consideration has the option to become, the owner of the property upon full compliance with his obligations under the contract.

[Ibid. (emphasis added).]

Further, Regulation Z defines "credit sale" as "any sale in which the seller is a creditor."

12 C.F.R. §226.2(a)(16).

Essentially, the Holder Rule strips the ultimate holder of the paper of its traditional status as a holder-in-due-course and subjects it to any potential defenses which the purchaser might have against the seller. The Federal Trade Commission has included within the reach of the Holder Rule those sellers and creditors who "employ procedures in the course of arranging the financing of a consumer sale which separate the buyer's duty to pay for goods or services rendered from the seller's reciprocal duty to perform as promised." 40 F.Reg. 53,506, 53,522 (1975). The agency has recognized this practice as "dragging the body," wherein:

> a merchant, desiring to circumvent restrictions upon the holder in due course doctrine, arranges for a consumer purchase to be financed by a cooperating financing agency. The resultant financial transaction has the appearance of a direct cash loan, payment of which can be enforced by the loan company without reference to the underlying transaction.

[40 F.Reg., supra, at 53,514.]

Consequently, the Holder Rule expressly incorporates "purchase money loan[s]" within the scope of the rule. See 16 C.F.R. § 433.2(b). A "[p]urchase money loan" is defined as "[a] cash advance which is received by a consumer" which is applied "in whole or substantial part, to a purchase of goods or services from a seller who (1) refers consumers to the creditor or (2) is affiliated with the creditor by common control, contract or business arrangement." 16 C.F.R. § 431.1(d).

Here, there is at the very least a fact issue concerning whether ECM's note constituted a "purchase money loan." ECM's financing provided the Troups with a "cash advance" totaling $49,990 which was applied in "substantial part" to pay for the improvements made to the home by Wishnia. There is also evidence that Wishnia "refers consumers" to ECM. Indeed, in this case Wishnia made all the arrangements for the loan and had the Troups chauffeured to ECM's offices to close. A reasonable jury could also conclude that Wishnia was "affiliated with" ECM by "business arrangement." The Troups presented evidence that Wishnia and ECM had mutually arranged at least six other home improvement or equity loans to other customers living in the City of Newark or the Newark area.

Nevertheless, ECM argues that the Holder Rule is inapplicable for three reasons. First, it claims that it did not "purchase" a "consumer credit contract" because initially the Troups paid Wishnia's affiliated companies monthly payments on the home repair contracts before the loan was made by ECM. This argument ignores the undisputed evidence that, before the Troups signed the first contract, Wishnia told Beatrice "not to worry, he would get [her] financing." Further, the second contract provides that "[payments] are to be made beginning January 1, 1996 payable to Property Redevelopment Center, Inc. until permanent financing is obtained." (Emphasis added). Indeed, after the contract was executed, Wishnia promptly arranged the loan with ECM, with whom he had placed other home repair contracts on behalf of other borrowers. In our view, reasonable minds could conclude that Wishnia and ECM contemplated from the outset that the loan to finance Wishnia's contracting work would be placed by ECM. We agree with the Troups that, under these circumstances, Wishnia and ECM should not be permitted to circumvent the consequences of the Holder Rule simply because Wishnia arranged for temporary financing with his affiliated companies.

Second, ECM argues that the Holder Rule is inapplicable because the bold-typed notice required by 16 C.F.R. 433.2 was never placed on the relevant documents. We reject that argument. Although it is true that the documents did not contain the requisite notice, it is inconceivable to us that ECM and Ahrens may evade the remedial reach of the Holder Rule simply because of that omission. It was their responsibility to insert the notice. Indeed, as a financing institution, ECM must be charged with notice of the requirement. Moreover, the bold-typed notice is required by New Jersey law. N.J.A.C. 13:45A-16.2(a)(13)ii, states:

> No home improvement contract shall require or entail the execution of any note, unless such note shall have conspicuously printed thereon the disclosures required by ... Federal law (16 C.F.R. section 433.2) concerning the preservation of buyers' claims and defenses.

"[T]he law is a silent factor in every contract." Moreover, equity looks to substance rather than form. These well-settled maxims should apply here to effectuate New Jersey's regulatory goal by "reading into" the pertinent documents the notice required by 16 C.F.R. § 433.2 and N.J.A.C. 13:45A-16.2(a)(13)ii.

Third, ECM claims that the Holder Rule is inapplicable because it has assigned the note to Associates.[8] We reject that argument as well. The clear and unambiguous language of the Rule "notifies *all potential holders* that, if they accept an assignment of the contract, they will be 'stepping into the seller's shoes.' " Thus, the creditor-assignee becomes " 'subject to' *any* claims or defenses the debtor can assert against the seller." See Simpson v. Anthony Auto Sales, Inc., 32 F.Supp.2d 405, 409 n. 10 (W.D.La.1998) (holding that the Holder Rule permits consumers to bring claims against assignee without regard to whether damages warranted rescission). Here, ECM, as "a potential holder" had notice that if it procured the purchase money loan arranged by Wishnia, it may be stepping into Wishnia's shoes. We cannot accept the proposition that the FTC contemplated that such result would not attach simply because of a subsequent assignment of the loan, especially when, as here, it is claimed that ECM actively participated with Wishnia, the seller, in placing the loan with the Troups.[9]

We conclude that fact issues exist respecting ECM's liability under the Holder Rule. Summary judgment dismissing the Troups' claims is therefore reversed. Ahrens' argument that there is no basis to hold him personally liable may be revisited after conclusion of all discovery concerning application of the Holder Rule.

III.

The Troups argue that the trial court erred in dismissing their consumer fraud claims against Associates and third-party defendants.

[24] N.J.S.A. 56:8-2 prohibits:

> [t]he act, use or employment by any person of *any unconscionable commercial practice*, deception, fraud, false pretense, false promise, misrepresentation, or the knowing, concealment, suppression, or omission of any material fact with intent that others rely upon [it] … in connection with the sale or advertisement of … merchandise.…
>
> [Ibid. (emphasis added).]

Loans are included in the definition of "advertisement," N.J.S.A. 56:8-1(a), and the definition of "merchandise," see N.J.S.A. 56:8-1(c), has been held to include "the offering, sale, or provision of consumer credit."

The word "unconscionable" must be interpreted liberally so as to effectuate the public purpose of the CFA. It is not intended to "erase the doctrine of freedom of contract, but to make realistic the assumption of the law that the agreement has resulted from real bargaining between parties who had freedom of choice and understanding and ability to negotiate in a meaningful fashion." The standard of conduct contemplated by the unconscionability clause is "good faith, honesty in fact and observance of fair dealing[,]" and the need for application of that standard "is most acute when the professional seller is seeking the trade of those most subject to exploitation—the uneducated, the inexperienced and the people of low incomes." Whether a particular practice is un-

---

8. The Troups do not argue that the Holder Rule applies to Associates.

9. There is some debate respecting the level of recovery under the Holder Rule when the consumer asserts an affirmative claim against the creditor. In this appeal, we are called upon only to decide whether the Holder Rule applies, not to define the extent of the Troups' remedy, if it applies. Suffice it to say that, as we understand the Troups' claim, they seek to assert their rights under the Holder Rule by compelling ECM to pay their debt owed to Associates, in the event the Troups do not prevail against Associates. In addition, the Troups seek an award of counsel fees under the CFA.

conscionable must be determined on a case-by-case basis. In this case, whether the acts of Associates and third-party defendants were unconscionable was for the jury to decide.

As noted, the trial court concluded that the rate charged and terms of the loan were not unconscionable. The trial court's assessment of the terms of the loan ignored the opinion of the Troups' expert, Calvin Bradford. Bradford stated that "[t]he average initial rate on a one year adjustable rate mortgage in April 1996 was 5.73[%]" (the Troups received a rate of 11.65%). Moreover, Bradford stated that the "[a]verage points in April 1996 on one year adjustable mortgages was 1.4" (the Troups were charged four points). Bradford observed that ECM's credit report listed no negatives on Beatrice's credit history, while Curtis Troup's credit history revealed only a $75 "charge off" and a DMV liability of $250. The expert also claimed that the Troups' debt-to-income ratio was favorable. In sum, Bradford opined that "the income, credit history and other factors ... [did] not warrant the credit terms given to the Troups."

Conversely, third-party defendants assert that the Troups received higher loan terms because of their "derogatory" credit history. However, the "derogatory history" offered mainly concerns the Troups' sketchy credit after the loan was obtained. Further, the trial court's finding that ECM's conduct regarding the procurement of the loan, specifically, that the Troups did not lack bargaining power, is at best conclusory. The trial court stated:

> This Court is not satisfied that the terms were unfavorable nor that there was any disproportionate bargaining power between the Troups and the lending institution. While it does appear that the Troups did not bargain with the lending institution, that does not in and of itself mean they had no bargaining power.

It is well established, however, that " '[t]he effect of the unconscionability rule is not designed to upset the terms of a contract resulting from superior bargaining strength, but to prevent oppression and unfair surprise.' " The Troups stated in their answers to interrogatories that they spoke to no one from ECM until they were brought to ECM's offices to sign the loan papers on April 27, 1996. Beatrice was confused because of the number and complexity of the documents. When she asked ECM's attorney if the principal balance will be due in fifteen years, the attorney told her not to worry about it. We are satisfied that, considering all of the evidentiary material in a light most favorable to the Troups, a reasonable jury could conclude that Associates and third-party defendants engaged in an unconscionable business practice. Therefore, we reverse the summary judgment order dismissing the consumer fraud claim.

IV.

We affirm the trial court's dismissal of the Troups' demand for rescission under the TILA. 15 U.S.C.A. § 1635(a) relevantly states:

> in the case of any consumer credit transaction ... the obligor shall have the right to rescind the transaction until midnight of the third business day following the consummation of the transaction or the delivery of the information and rescission forms.... The creditor shall clearly and conspicuously disclose ... to any obligor in a transaction subject to this section the rights of the obligor under this section.

Further, 15 U.S.C.A. § 1635(f) provides:

> An obligor's right of rescission shall expire three years after the date of con-
> summation of the transaction or upon the sale of the property ... notwith-
> standing the fact that the information and forms required under this section or
> any other disclosures required under this part have not been delivered to the
> obligor....

12 C.F.R. § 226.23 (2001) provides that the notice of right to rescind shall clearly and
conspicuously disclose: (1) the consumer's right to rescind the transaction; (2) how to
exercise the right to rescind with a form for that purpose, which must include the address of the creditor's place of business; (3) the effect of rescission; and (4) the date the
rescission period expires.

The purpose of the three-day waiting period under § 1635(a) is to give the consumer
the opportunity to reconsider any transaction which would have the serious consequence of encumbering title to his or her home. If a lender's notice of the right to rescind is deficient, a mortgagor's rescission rights are extended to three years. 15
U.S.C.A. § 1635(f). If the creditor fails to comply with the written requirements of the
notice to rescind, or if a "material" disclosure is not correctly made, the rescission period is extended for three years. 12 C.F.R. § 226.23(a)(3).

We agree with the trial court's determination that the notice of right to cancel in this
case complied with the mandates of the TILA. The "date of the loan" is "4/27/1996." The
form signed by the Troups is clearly identified as the "Notice of Right to Cancel" and
contains ECM's address. Further, the notice provides a subtitle "How to Cancel," which
informed the Troups as to the manner, date and method of cancellation. The Troups
argue that the notice is confusing because under the subtitle "I Wish to Cancel" is the
date "4/27/1996." They argue that the insertion of the date had the effect of causing
them to believe that their right to cancel expired on that date. We disagree. On the same
page as this notation, the Notice of Right to Cancel expressly states: "[y]ou have a legal
right under federal law to cancel this transaction, without cost, within three business
days from ... the date of the loan shown above...." The "date of the loan" is "4/27/1996."
We are satisfied that the notice of right to cancel is clear and unambiguous. Indeed, the
notice is substantially similar, if not identical, to the form suggested in the Federal Regulations. 13 C.F.R., Pt. 226, App. H.

The Troups further argue that the three-year time for rescission is applicable because
ECM failed to disclose as a "finance charge," a $50 disbursement fee imposed by ECM's
attorney. Notably, the Troups' counterclaim alleges that ECM failed to properly disclose
a $25 recording fee and a $360 fee for the payoff of a judgment lien. It makes no mention of the $50 fee imposed by ECM's attorney.

15 U.S.C.A. § 1635(i)(2) provides that "any finance charge shall be treated as being
accurate for the purposes of this section if the amount disclosed as the finance charge
does not vary from the actual finance charge by more than $35...." The Troups argue
that the fee charged by ECM's attorney, being in excess of $35, constitutes an undis-
closed "finance charge." However, 15 U.S.C.A. § 1605(a) expressly states that the "finance charge shall not include fees and amounts imposed by third party closing agents
(including settlement agents, attorneys ...) if the creditor does not require the imposition of the charges or the services provided and does not retain the charges." (Emphasis
added). The $50 fee complained of was payable to a third party closing agent. It was not
a disbursement fee required by ECM or retained by it.

Affirmed in part, reversed and remanded in part.

U.S. Bank National Association v. Ibañez

941 N.E.2d 40, 458 Mass. 637 (2011), 2011 WL 3807 (Mass.)

Civil actions commenced in the Land Court Department. Motions for entry of default judgment and to vacate judgment were heard by Keith C. Long, J.

R. Bruce Allensworth (Phoebe S. Winder and Robert W. Sparkes, III, with him) for U.S. Bank National Association and another.

Paul R. Collier, III (Max W. Weinstein with him) for Antonio Ibañez.

Glenn F. Russell, Jr., for Mark A. LaRace and another.*

Present: Marshall, C.J.; Ireland, Spina, Cordy, Botsford, & Gants, JJ.

Gants, J:

After foreclosing on two properties and purchasing the properties back at the foreclosure sales, U.S. Bank National Association (U.S. Bank), as trustee for the Structured Asset Securities Corporation Mortgage Pass-Through Certificates, Series 2006-Z, and Wells Fargo Bank, N.A. (Wells Fargo), as trustee for ABFC 2005-OPT 1 Trust, ABFC Asset Backed Certificates, Series 2005-OPT 1 (plaintiffs), filed separate complaints in the Land Court asking a judge to declare that they held clear title to the properties in fee simple. We agree with the judge that the plaintiffs, who were not the original mortgagees, failed to make the required showing that they were the holders of the mortgages at the time of foreclosure. As a result, they did not demonstrate that the foreclosure sales were valid to convey title to the subject properties, and their requests for a declaration of clear title were properly denied.

Procedural history. On July 5, 2007, U.S. Bank, as trustee, foreclosed on the mortgage of Antonio Ibañez, and purchased the Ibañez property at the foreclosure sale. On the same day, Wells Fargo, as trustee, foreclosed on the mortgage of Mark and Tammy LaRace, and purchased the LaRace property at that foreclosure sale.

In September and October of 2008, U.S. Bank and Wells Fargo brought separate actions in the Land Court under G.L. c. 240, § 6, which authorizes actions "to quiet or establish the title to land situated in the commonwealth or to remove a cloud from the title thereto." The two complaints sought identical relief: (1) a judgment that the right, title, and interest of the mortgagor (Ibañez or the LaRaces) in the property was extinguished by the foreclosure; (2) a declaration that there was no cloud on title arising from publication of the notice of sale in the Boston Globe; and (3) a declaration that title was vested in the plaintiff trustee in fee simple. U.S. Bank and Wells Fargo each asserted in its complaint that it had become the holder of the respective mortgage through an assignment made *after* the foreclosure sale.

In both cases, the mortgagors—Ibañez and the LaRaces—did not initially answer the complaints, and the plaintiffs moved for entry of default judgment. In their motions for entry of default judgment, the plaintiffs addressed two issues: (1) whether the Boston Globe, in which the required notices of the foreclosure sales were published, is a

---

* The following submitted briefs for amici curiae:
   Martha Coakley, Attorney General, and John M. Stephan, Assistant Attorney General, for
   the Commonwealth. Kevin Costello, Gary Klein, Shennan Kavanagh, and Stuart Rossman
   for National Consumer Law Center and others. Ward P. Graham & Robert J. Moriarty, Jr.,
   for Real Estate Bar Association for Massachusetts, Inc. Marie McDonnell, pro se.

newspaper of "general circulation" in Springfield, the town where the foreclosed properties lay. See G.L. c. 244, § 14 (requiring publication every week for three weeks in
newspaper published in town where foreclosed property lies, or of general circulation in
that town); and (2) whether the plaintiffs were legally entitled to foreclose on the properties where the assignments of the mortgages to the plaintiffs were neither executed
nor recorded in the registry of deeds until after the foreclosure sales.[6] The two cases
were heard together by the Land Court, along with a third case that raised the same issues.

On March 26, 2009, judgment was entered against the plaintiffs. The judge ruled
that the foreclosure sales were invalid because, in violation of G.L. c. 244, § 14, the notices of the foreclosure sales named U.S. Bank (in the Ibañez foreclosure) and Wells
Fargo (in the LaRace foreclosure) as the mortgage holders where [sic] they had not yet
been assigned the mortgages.[7] The judge found, based on each plaintiff's assertions in
its complaint, that the plaintiffs acquired the mortgages by assignment only after the
foreclosure sales and thus had no interest in the mortgages being foreclosed at the time
of the publication of the notices of sale or at the time of the foreclosure sales.[8]

The plaintiffs then moved to vacate the judgments. At a hearing on the motions, the
plaintiffs conceded that each complaint alleged a postnotice, postforeclosure sale assignment of the mortgage at issue, but they now represented to the judge that documents might exist that could show a prenotice, preforeclosure sale assignment of the
mortgages. The judge granted the plaintiffs leave to produce such documents, provided
they were produced in the form they existed in at the time the foreclosure sale was noticed and conducted. In response, the plaintiffs submitted hundreds of pages of documents to the judge, which they claimed established that the mortgages had been assigned to them before the foreclosures. Many of these documents related to the creation
of the securitized mortgage pools in which the Ibañez and LaRace mortgages were purportedly included.

The judge denied the plaintiffs' motions to vacate judgment, concluding that the
newly submitted documents did not alter the conclusion that the plaintiffs were not the
holders of the respective mortgages at the time of foreclosure. We granted the parties'
applications for direct appellate review.

Factual background. We discuss each mortgage separately, describing when appropriate what the plaintiffs allege to have happened and what the documents in the record
demonstrate.[10]

---

6. The uncertainty surrounding the first issue was the reason the plaintiffs sought a declaration
of clear title in order to obtain title insurance for these properties. The second issue was raised by
the judge in the LaRace case at a January 5, 2009 case management conference.

7. The judge also concluded that the Boston Globe was a newspaper of general circulation in
Springfield, so the foreclosures were not rendered invalid on that ground because notice was published in that newspaper.

8. In the third case, LaSalle Bank National Association, trustee for the certificate holders of
Bear Stearns Asset Backed Securities I, LLC Asset-Backed Certificates, Series 2007-HE2 vs. Freddy
Rosario, the judge concluded that the mortgage foreclosure "was not rendered invalid by [the
trustee's] failure to record the assignment reflecting its status as holder of the mortgage prior to the
foreclosure since it was, in fact, the holder by assignment at the time of the foreclosure, it truthfully
claimed that status in the notice, and it could have produced proof of that status (the unrecorded
assignment) if asked."

10. The LaRace defendants allege that the documents submitted to the judge following the
plaintiffs' motions to vacate judgment are not properly in the record before us. They also allege that
several of these documents are not properly authenticated. Because we affirm the judgment on

The Ibañez mortgage. On December 1, 2005, Antonio Ibañez took out a $103,500 loan for the purchase of property at 20 Crosby Street in Springfield, secured by a mortgage to the lender, Rose Mortgage, Inc. (Rose Mortgage). The mortgage was recorded the following day. Several days later, Rose Mortgage executed an assignment of this mortgage in blank, that is, an assignment that did not specify the name of the assignee.[11] The blank space in the assignment was at some point stamped with the name of Option One Mortgage Corporation (Option One) as the assignee, and that assignment was recorded on June 7, 2006. Before the recording, on January 23, 2006, Option One executed an assignment of the Ibañez mortgage in blank.

According to U.S. Bank, Option One assigned the Ibañez mortgage to Lehman Brothers Bank, FSB, which assigned it to Lehman Brothers Holdings Inc., which then assigned it to the Structured Asset Securities Corporation,[12] which then assigned the mortgage, pooled with approximately 1,220 other mortgage loans, to U.S. Bank, as trustee for the Structured Asset Securities Corporation Mortgage Pass-Through Certificates, Series 2006-Z. With this last assignment, the Ibañez and other loans were pooled into a trust and converted into mortgage-backed securities that can be bought and sold by investors—a process known as securitization.

For ease of reference, the chain of entities through which the Ibañez mortgage allegedly passed before the foreclosure sale is:

> Rose Mortgage, Inc. (originator)
> Option One Mortgage Corporation (record holder)
> Lehman Brothers Bank, FSB
> Lehman Brothers Holdings Inc. (seller)
> Structured Asset Securities Corporation (depositor)
> U.S. Bank National Association, as trustee for the Structured Asset Securities
> Corporation Mortgage Pass-Through Certificates, Series 2006-Z

According to U.S. Bank the assignment of the Ibañez mortgage to U.S. Bank occurred pursuant to a December 1, 2006 trust agreement, which is not in the record. What is in the record is the private placement memorandum (PPM), dated December 26, 2006, a 273-page, unsigned offer of mortgage-backed securities to potential investors. The PPM describes the mortgage pools and the entities involved, and summarizes the provisions of the trust agreement, including the representation that mortgages "will be" assigned into the trust. According to the PPM, "[e]ach transfer of a Mortgage Loan from the Seller [Lehman Brothers Holdings Inc.] to the Depositor [Structured Asset Securities Corporation] and from the Depositor to the Trustee [U.S. Bank] will be intended to be a sale of that Mortgage Loan and will be reflected as such in the Sale and Assignment Agreement and the Trust Agreement, respectively." The PPM also specifies that "[e]ach Mortgage Loan will be identified in a schedule appearing as an exhibit to

---

other grounds, we do not address these concerns, and assume that these documents are properly before us and were adequately authenticated.

11. This signed and notarized document states: "FOR VALUE RECEIVED, the undersigned hereby grants, assigns and transfers to _____ all beneficial interest under that certain Mortgage dated December 1, 2005 executed by Antonio Ibañez...."

12. The Structured Asset Securities Corporation is a wholly owned, direct subsidiary of Lehman Commercial Paper[,] Inc., which is in turn a wholly owned, direct subsidiary of Lehman Brothers Holdings[,] Inc.

the Trust Agreement." However, U.S. Bank did not provide the judge with any mortgage schedule identifying the Ibañez loan as among the mortgages that were assigned in the trust agreement.

On April 17, 2007, U.S. Bank filed a complaint to foreclose on the Ibañez mortgage in the Land Court under the Servicemembers Civil Relief Act (Servicemembers Act), which restricts foreclosures against active duty members of the uniformed services. See 50 U.S.C. Appendix §§ 501, 511, 533 (2006 & Supp. II 2008).[13] In the complaint, U.S. Bank represented that it was the "owner (or assignee) and holder" of the mortgage given by Ibañez for the property. A judgment issued on behalf of U.S. Bank on June 26, 2007, declaring that the mortgagor was not entitled to protection from foreclosure under the Servicemembers Act. In June 2007, U.S. Bank also caused to be published in the Boston Globe the notice of the foreclosure sale required by G.L. c. 244, § 14. The notice identified U.S. Bank as the "present holder" of the mortgage.

At the foreclosure sale on July 5, 2007, the Ibañez property was purchased by U.S. Bank, as trustee for the securitization trust, for $94,350, a value significantly less than the outstanding debt and the estimated market value of the property. The foreclosure deed (from U.S. Bank, trustee, as the purported holder of the mortgage, to U.S. Bank, trustee, as the purchaser) and the statutory foreclosure affidavit were recorded on May 23, 2008. On September 2, 2008, more than one year after the sale, and more than five months after recording of the sale, American Home Mortgage Servicing, Inc., "as successor-in-interest" to Option One, which was until then the record holder of the Ibañez mortgage, executed a written assignment of that mortgage to U.S. Bank, as trustee for the securitization trust.[14] This assignment was recorded on September 11, 2008.

The LaRace mortgage. On May 19, 2005, Mark and Tammy LaRace gave a mortgage for the property at 6 Brookburn Street in Springfield to Option One as security for a $103,200 loan; the mortgage was recorded that same day. On May 26, 2005, Option One executed an assignment of this mortgage in blank.

According to Wells Fargo, Option One later assigned the LaRace mortgage to Bank of America in a July 28, 2005 flow sale and servicing agreement. Bank of America then assigned it to Asset Backed Funding Corporation (ABFC) in an October 1, 2005 mortgage loan purchase agreement. Finally, ABFC pooled the mortgage with others and assigned it to Wells Fargo, as trustee for the ABFC 2005-OPT 1 Trust, ABFC Asset-Backed Certificates, Series 2005-OPT 1, pursuant to a pooling and servicing agreement (PSA).

---

13. As implemented in Massachusetts, a mortgage holder is required to go to court to obtain a judgment declaring that the mortgagor is not a beneficiary of the Servicemembers Act before proceeding to foreclosure.

14. The Land Court judge questioned whether American Home Mortgage Servicing, Inc., was in fact a successor in interest to Option One. Given our affirmance of the judgment on other grounds, we need not address this question.

For ease of reference, the chain of entities through which the LaRace mortgage allegedly passed before the foreclosure sale is:

Option One Mortgage Corporation (originator and record holder)
Bank of America
Asset Backed Funding Corporation (depositor)
Wells Fargo, as trustee for the ABFC 2005-OPT 1
ABFC Asset-Backed Certificates, Series 2005-OPT 1

Wells Fargo did not provide the judge with a copy of the flow sale and servicing agreement, so there is no document in the record reflecting an assignment of the LaRace mortgage by Option One to Bank of America. The plaintiff did produce an unexecuted copy of the mortgage loan purchase agreement, which was an exhibit to the PSA. The mortgage loan purchase agreement provides that Bank of America, as seller, "does hereby agree to and does hereby sell, assign, set over, and otherwise convey to the Purchaser [ABFC], without recourse, on the Closing Date … all of its right, title and interest in and to each Mortgage Loan." The agreement makes reference to a schedule listing the assigned mortgage loans, but this schedule is not in the record, so there was no document before the judge showing that the LaRace mortgage was among the mortgage loans assigned to the ABFC.

Wells Fargo did provide the judge with a copy of the PSA, which is an agreement between the ABFC (as depositor), Option One (as servicer), and Wells Fargo (as trustee), but this copy was downloaded from the Securities and Exchange Commission Web site and was not signed. The PSA provides that the depositor "does hereby transfer, assign, set over and otherwise convey to the Trustee, on behalf of the Trust … [,] all the right, title and interest of the Depositor … in and to … each Mortgage Loan identified on the Mortgage Loan Schedules," and "does hereby deliver" to the trustee the original mortgage note, an original mortgage assignment "in form and substance acceptable for recording," and other documents pertaining to each mortgage.

The copy of the PSA provided to the judge did not contain the loan schedules referenced in the agreement. Instead, Wells Fargo submitted a schedule that it represented identified the loans assigned in the PSA, which did not include property addresses, names of mortgagors, or any number that corresponds to the loan number or servicing number on the LaRace mortgage. Wells Fargo contends that a loan with the LaRace property's zip code and city is the LaRace mortgage loan because the payment history and loan amount matches the LaRace loan.

On April 27, 2007, Wells Fargo filed a complaint under the Servicemembers Act in the Land Court to foreclose on the LaRace mortgage. The complaint represented Wells Fargo as the "owner (or assignee) and holder" of the mortgage given by the LaRaces for the property. A judgment issued on behalf of Wells Fargo on July 3, 2007, indicating that the LaRaces were not beneficiaries of the Servicemembers Act and that foreclosure could proceed in accordance with the terms of the power of sale. In June 2007, Wells Fargo caused to be published in the Boston Globe the statutory notice of sale, identifying itself as the "present holder" of the mortgage.

At the foreclosure sale on July 5, 2007, Wells Fargo, as trustee, purchased the LaRace property for $120,397.03, a value significantly below its estimated market value. Wells Fargo did not execute a statutory foreclosure affidavit or foreclosure deed until May 7, 2008. That same day, Option One, which was still the record holder of the LaRace mortgage, executed an assignment of the mortgage to Wells Fargo as trustee; the assignment was recorded on May 12, 2008. Although executed ten months after the foreclosure sale, the assignment declared an effective date of April 18, 2007, a date that preceded the publication of the notice of sale and the foreclosure sale.

Discussion. The plaintiffs brought actions seeking declarations that the defendant mortgagors' titles had been extinguished and that the plaintiffs were the fee simple owners of the foreclosed properties. As such, the plaintiffs bore the burden of establishing their entitlement to the relief sought. To meet this burden, they were required "not merely to demonstrate better title ... than the defendants possess, but ... to prove sufficient title to succeed in [the] action." There is no question that the relief the plaintiffs sought required them to establish the validity of the foreclosure sales on which their claim to clear title rested.

Massachusetts does not require a mortgage holder to obtain judicial authorization to foreclose on a mortgaged property. With the exception of the limited judicial procedure aimed at certifying that the mortgagor is not a beneficiary of the Servicemembers Act, a mortgage holder can foreclose on a property, as the plaintiffs did here, by exercise of the statutory power of sale, if such a power is granted by the mortgage itself.

Where a mortgage grants a mortgage holder the power of sale, as did both the Ibañez and LaRace mortgages, it includes by reference the power of sale set out in G.L. c. 183, §21, and further regulated by G.L. c. 244, §§11–17C. Under G.L. c. 183, §21, after a mortgagor defaults in the performance of the underlying note, the mortgage holder may sell the property at a public auction and convey the property to the purchaser in fee simple, "and such sale shall forever bar the mortgagor and all persons claiming under him from all right and interest in the mortgaged premises, whether at law or in equity." Even where there is a dispute as to whether the mortgagor was in default or whether the party claiming to be the mortgage holder is the true mortgage holder, the foreclosure goes forward unless the mortgagor files an action and obtains a court order enjoining the foreclosure.[15]

Recognizing the substantial power that the statutory scheme affords to a mortgage holder to foreclose without immediate judicial oversight, we adhere to the familiar rule that "one who sells under a power [of sale] must follow strictly its terms. If he fails to do so there is no valid execution of the power, and the sale is wholly void." See Roche v. Farnsworth, 106 Mass. 509, 513 (1871) (power of sale contained in mortgage "must be executed in strict compliance with its terms").[16]

One of the terms of the power of sale that must be strictly adhered to is the restriction on who is entitled to foreclose. The "statutory power of sale" can be exercised by "the mortgagee or his executors, administrators, successors or assigns." G.L. c. 183, §21. Under G.L. c. 244, §14, "[t]he mortgagee or person having his estate in the land mortgaged, or a person authorized by the power of sale, or the attorney duly authorized by a writing under seal, or the legal guardian or conservator of such mortgagee or per-

---

15. An alternative to foreclosure through the right of statutory sale is foreclosure by entry, by which a mortgage holder who peaceably enters a property and remains for three years after recording a certificate or memorandum of entry forecloses the mortgagor's right of redemption. A foreclosure by entry may provide a separate ground for a claim of clear title apart from the foreclosure by execution of the power of sale. Because the plaintiffs do not claim clear title based on foreclosure by entry, we do not discuss it further.

16. We recognize that a mortgage holder must not only act in strict compliance with its power of sale but must also "act in good faith and ... use reasonable diligence to protect the interests of the mortgagor," and this responsibility is "more exacting" where the mortgage holder becomes the buyer at the foreclosure sale, as occurred here. Because the issue was not raised by the defendant mortgagors or the judge, we do not consider whether the plaintiffs committed a breach of this obligation.

son acting in the name of such mortgagee or person" is empowered to exercise the statutory power of sale. Any effort to foreclose by a party lacking "jurisdiction and authority" to carry out a foreclosure under these statutes is void. Chace v. Morse, 189 Mass. 559, 561, 76 N.E. 142 (1905), citing Moore v. Dick, supra. See Davenport v. HSBC Bank USA, 275 Mich.App. 344, 347–348, 739 N.W.2d 383 (2007) (attempt to foreclose by party that had not yet been assigned mortgage results in "structural defect that goes to the very heart of defendant's ability to foreclose by advertisement," and renders foreclosure sale void).

A related statutory requirement that must be strictly adhered to in a foreclosure by power of sale is the notice requirement articulated in G.L. c. 244, § 14. That statute provides that "no sale under such power shall be effectual to foreclose a mortgage, unless, previous to such sale," advance notice of the foreclosure sale has been provided to the mortgagor, to other interested parties, and by publication in a newspaper published in the town where the mortgaged land lies or of general circulation in that town. "The manner in which the notice of the proposed sale shall be given is one of the important terms of the power, and a strict compliance with it is essential to the valid exercise of the power." See Chace v. Morse, supra ("where a certain notice is prescribed, a sale without any notice, or upon a notice lacking the essential requirements of the written power, would be void as a proceeding for foreclosure"). Because only a present holder of the mortgage is authorized to foreclose on the mortgaged property, and because the mortgagor is entitled to know who is foreclosing and selling the property, the failure to identify the holder of the mortgage in the notice of sale may render the notice defective and the foreclosure sale void.[17] See Roche v. Farnsworth, supra (mortgage sale void where notice of sale identified original mortgagee but not mortgage holder at time of notice and sale). See also Bottomly v. Kabachnick, 13 Mass. App. Ct. 480, 483–484, 434 N.E.2d 667 (1982) (foreclosure void where holder of mortgage not identified in notice of sale).

For the plaintiffs to obtain the judicial declaration of clear title that they seek, they had to prove their authority to foreclose under the power of sale and show their compliance with the requirements on which this authority rests. Here, the plaintiffs were not the original mortgagees to whom the power of sale was granted; rather, they claimed the authority to foreclose as the eventual assignees of the original mortgagees. Under the plain language of G.L. c. 183, § 21 and G.L. c. 244, § 14, the plaintiffs had the authority to exercise the power of sale contained in the Ibañez and LaRace mortgages only if they were the assignees of the mortgages at the time of the notice of sale and the subsequent foreclosure sale. See In re Schwartz, 366 B.R. 265, 269 (Bankr. D. Mass.2007) ("Acquiring the mortgage after the entry and foreclosure sale does not satisfy the Massachusetts statute").[18] See also Jeff-Ray Corp. v. Jacobson, 566 So.2d 885, 886 (Fla.Dist.Ct.App.1990) (per curiam) (foreclosure action could not be based on assignment of mortgage dated four months after commencement of foreclosure proceeding).

The plaintiffs claim that the securitization documents they submitted establish valid assignments that made them the holders of the Ibañez and LaRace mortgages before the

---

17. The form of foreclosure notice provided in G.L. c. 244, § 14, calls for the present holder of the mortgage to identify itself and sign the notice. While the statute permits other forms to be used and allows the statutory form to be "altered as circumstances require," we do not interpret this flexibility to suggest that the present holder of the mortgage need not identify itself in the notice.

18. The plaintiffs were not authorized to foreclose by virtue of any of the other provisions of G.L. c. 244, § 14: they were not the guardian or conservator, or acting in the name of, a person so authorized; nor were they the attorney duly authorized by a writing under seal.

notice of sale and the foreclosure sale. We turn, then, to the documentation submitted by the plaintiffs to determine whether it met the requirements of a valid assignment.

Like a sale of land itself, the assignment of a mortgage is a conveyance of an interest in land that requires a writing signed by the grantor. In a "title theory state" like Massachusetts, a mortgage is a transfer of legal title in a property to secure a debt. Therefore, when a person borrows money to purchase a home and gives the lender a mortgage, the homeowner-mortgagor retains only equitable title in the home; the legal title is held by the mortgagee. See Vee Jay Realty Trust Co. v. DiCroce, 360 Mass. 751, 753, 277 N.E.2d 690 (1972), quoting Dolliver v. St. Joseph Fire & Marine Ins. Co., 128 Mass. 315, 316 (1880) (although "as to all the world except the mortgagee, a mortgagor is the owner of the mortgaged lands," mortgagee has legal title to property). Where, as here, mortgage loans are pooled together in a trust and converted into mortgage-backed securities, the underlying promissory notes serve as financial instruments generating a potential income stream for investors, but the mortgages securing these notes are still legal title to someone's home or farm and must be treated as such.

Focusing first on the Ibañez mortgage, U.S. Bank argues that it was assigned the mortgage under the trust agreement described in the PPM, but it did not submit a copy of this trust agreement to the judge. The PPM, however, described the trust agreement as an agreement to be executed in the future, so it only furnished evidence of an intent to assign mortgages to U.S. Bank, not proof of their actual assignment. Even if there were an executed trust agreement with language of present assignment, U.S. Bank did not produce the schedule of loans and mortgages that was an exhibit to that agreement, so it failed to show that the Ibañez mortgage was among the mortgages to be assigned by that agreement. Finally, even if there were an executed trust agreement with the required schedule, U.S. Bank failed to furnish any evidence that the entity assigning the mortgage — Structured Asset Securities Corporation — ever held the mortgage to be assigned. The last assignment of the mortgage on record was from Rose Mortgage to Option One; nothing was submitted to the judge indicating that Option One ever assigned the mortgage to anyone before the foreclosure sale.[19] Thus, based on the documents submitted to the judge, Option One, not U.S. Bank, was the mortgage holder at the time of the foreclosure, and U.S. Bank did not have the authority to foreclose the mortgage.

Turning to the LaRace mortgage, Wells Fargo claims that, before it issued the foreclosure notice, it was assigned the LaRace mortgage under the PSA. The PSA, in contrast with U.S. Bank's PPM, uses the language of a present assignment ("does hereby ... assign" and "does hereby deliver") rather than an intent to assign in the future. But the mortgage loan schedule Wells Fargo submitted failed to identify with adequate specificity the LaRace mortgage as one of the mortgages assigned in the PSA. Moreover, Wells Fargo provided the judge with no document that reflected that the ABFC (depositor) held the LaRace mortgage that it was purportedly assigning in the PSA. As with the Ibañez loan, the record holder of the LaRace loan was Option One, and nothing was submitted to the judge which demonstrated that the LaRace loan was ever assigned by Option One to another entity before the publication of the notice and the sale.

Where a plaintiff files a complaint asking for a declaration of clear title after a mortgage foreclosure, a judge is entitled to ask for proof that the foreclosing entity was the

---

19. Ibañez challenges the validity of this assignment to Option One. Because of the failure of U.S. Bank to document any preforeclosure sale assignment or chain of assignments by which it obtained the Ibañez mortgage from Option One, it is unnecessary to address the validity of the assignment from Rose Mortgage to Option One.

mortgage holder at the time of the notice of sale and foreclosure, or was one of the parties authorized to foreclose under G.L. c. 183, § 21, and G.L. c. 244, § 14. A plaintiff that cannot make this modest showing cannot justly proclaim that it was unfairly denied a declaration of clear title.

We do not suggest that an assignment must be in recordable form at the time of the notice of sale or the subsequent foreclosure sale, although recording is likely the better practice.* Where a pool of mortgages is assigned to a securitized trust, the executed agreement that assigns the pool of mortgages, with a schedule of the pooled mortgage loans that clearly and specifically identifies the mortgage at issue as among those assigned, may suffice to establish the trustee as the mortgage holder. However, there must be proof that the assignment was made by a party that itself held the mortgage. A foreclosing entity may provide a complete chain of assignments linking it to the record holder of the mortgage, or a single assignment from the record holder of the mortgage. The key in either case is that the foreclosing entity must hold the mortgage at the time of the notice and sale in order accurately to identify itself as the present holder in the notice and in order to have the authority to foreclose under the power of sale (or the foreclosing entity must be one of the parties authorized to foreclose under G.L. c. 183, § 21, and G.L. c. 244, § 14).

The judge did not err in concluding that the securitization documents submitted by the plaintiffs failed to demonstrate that they were the holders of the Ibañez and LaRace mortgages, respectively, at the time of the publication of the notices and the sales. The judge, therefore, did not err in rendering judgments against the plaintiffs and in denying the plaintiffs' motions to vacate the judgments.

We now turn briefly to three other arguments raised by the plaintiffs on appeal. First, the plaintiffs initially contended that the assignments in blank executed by Option One, identifying the assignor but not the assignee, not only "evidence[ ] and confirm[ ] the assignments that occurred by virtue of the securitization agreements," but "are effective assignments in their own right." But in their reply briefs they conceded that the assignments in blank did not constitute a lawful assignment of the mortgages. Their concession is appropriate. We have long held that a conveyance of real property, such as a mortgage, that does not name the assignee conveys nothing and is void; we do not regard an assignment of land in blank as giving legal title in land to the bearer of the assignment.

Second, the plaintiffs contend that, because they held the mortgage note, they had a sufficient financial interest in the mortgage to allow them to foreclose. In Massachusetts, where a note has been assigned but there is no written assignment of the mortgage underlying the note, the assignment of the note does not carry with it the assignment of the mortgage. Rather, the holder of the mortgage holds the mortgage in trust for the purchaser of the note, who has an equitable right to obtain an assignment of the mortgage, which may be accomplished by filing an action in court and obtaining an equitable order of assignment. ("In some jurisdictions it is held that the mere transfer of the debt, without any assignment or even mention of the mortgage, carries the mortgage with it, so as to enable the assignee to assert his title in an action at law.... This doctrine has not prevailed in Massachusetts, and the tendency of the decisions here has been, that in such cases the mortgagee would hold the legal title in trust for the purchaser of the debt, and that the latter might obtain a conveyance by a bill in equity"). In the absence of a valid written assignment of a mortgage or a court order of assignment, the

---

* Editor's Note: The lower court had held that both Massachusetts law and the lenders' contracts required that assignments be in recordable form. U.S. Nat'l Bank Ass'n v. Ibañez, 2009 WL 3297551, *6 (MA Land Ct. 2009).

mortgage holder remains unchanged. This common-law principle was later incorporated in the statute enacted in 1912 establishing the statutory power of sale, which grants such a power to "the mortgagee or his executors, administrators, successors or assigns," but not to a party that is the equitable beneficiary of a mortgage held by another.

Third, the plaintiffs initially argued that postsale assignments were sufficient to establish their authority to foreclose, and now argue that these assignments are sufficient when taken in conjunction with the evidence of a presale assignment. They argue that the use of postsale assignments was customary in the industry, and point to Title Standard No. 58(3) issued by the Real Estate Bar Association for Massachusetts, which declares: "A title is not defective by reason of … [t]he recording of an Assignment of Mortgage executed either prior, or subsequent, to foreclosure where said Mortgage has been foreclosed, of record, by the Assignee."[21] To the extent that the plaintiffs rely on this title standard for the proposition that an entity that does not hold a mortgage may foreclose on a property, and then cure the cloud on title by a later assignment of a mortgage, their reliance is misplaced, because this proposition is contrary to G.L. c. 183, § 21, and G.L. c. 244, § 14. If the plaintiffs did not have their assignments to the Ibañez and LaRace mortgages at the time of the publication of the notices and the sales, they lacked authority to foreclose under G.L. c. 183, § 21, and G.L. c. 244, § 14, and their published claims to be the present holders of the mortgages were false. Nor may a postforeclosure assignment be treated as a preforeclosure assignment simply by declaring an "effective date" that precedes the notice of sale and foreclosure, as did Option One's assignment of the LaRace mortgage to Wells Fargo. Because an assignment of a mortgage is a transfer of legal title, it becomes effective with respect to the power of sale only on the transfer; it cannot become effective before the transfer.

However, we do not disagree with Title Standard No. 58(3) that, where an assignment is confirmatory of an earlier, valid assignment made prior to the publication of notice and execution of the sale, that confirmatory assignment may be executed and recorded after the foreclosure, and doing so will not make the title defective. A valid assignment of a mortgage gives the holder of that mortgage the statutory power to sell after a default regardless whether the assignment has been recorded. Where the earlier assignment is not in recordable form or bears some defect, a written assignment executed after foreclosure that confirms the earlier assignment may be properly recorded. A confirmatory assignment, however, cannot confirm an assignment that was not validly made earlier or backdate an assignment being made for the first time. Where there is no prior valid assignment, a subsequent assignment by the mortgage holder to the note holder is not a confirmatory assignment because there is no earlier written assignment to confirm. In this case, based on the record before the judge, the plaintiffs failed to prove that they obtained valid written assignments of the Ibañez and LaRace mortgages before their foreclosures, so the postforeclosure assignments were not confirmatory of earlier valid assignments.

Finally, we reject the plaintiffs' request that our ruling be prospective in its application. A prospective ruling is only appropriate, in limited circumstances, when we make a significant change in the common law. We have not done so here. The legal principles and requirements we set forth are well established in our case law and our statutes. All that has changed is the plaintiffs' apparent failure to abide by those principles and requirements in the rush to sell mortgage-backed securities.

---

21. Title Standard No. 58(3) issued by the Real Estate Bar Association for Massachusetts continues: "However, if the Assignment is not dated prior, or stated to be effective prior, to the commencement of a foreclosure, then a foreclosure sale after April 19, 2007 may be subject to challenge in the Bankruptcy Court," citing In re Schwartz, 366 B.R. 265 (Bankr. D. Mass.2007).

Conclusion. For the reasons stated, we agree with the judge that the plaintiffs did not demonstrate that they were the holders of the Ibañez and LaRace mortgages at the time that they foreclosed these properties, and therefore failed to demonstrate that they acquired fee simple title to these properties by purchasing them at the foreclosure sale.

Cordy, J. (concurring, with whom Botsford, J., joins).

I concur fully in the opinion of the court, and write separately only to underscore that what is surprising about these cases is not the statement of principles articulated by the court regarding title law and the law of foreclosure in Massachusetts, but rather the utter carelessness with which the plaintiff banks documented the titles to their assets. There is no dispute that the mortgagors of the properties in question had defaulted on their obligations, and that the mortgaged properties were subject to foreclosure. Before commencing such an action, however, the holder of an assigned mortgage needs to take care to ensure that his legal paperwork is in order. Although there was no apparent actual unfairness here to the mortgagors, that is not the point. Foreclosure is a powerful act with significant consequences, and Massachusetts law has always required that it proceed strictly in accord with the statutes that govern it. As the opinion of the court notes, such strict compliance is necessary because Massachusetts both is a title theory State and allows for extrajudicial foreclosure.

The type of sophisticated transactions leading up to the accumulation of the notes and mortgages in question in these cases and their securitization, and, ultimately[,] the sale of mortgaged-backed securities, are not barred nor even burdened by the requirements of Massachusetts law. The plaintiff banks, who brought these cases to clear the titles that they acquired at their own foreclosure sales, have simply failed to prove that the underlying assignments of the mortgages that they allege (and would have) entitled them to foreclose ever existed in any legally cognizable form before they exercised the power of sale that accompanies those assignments. The court's opinion clearly states that such assignments do not need to be in recordable form or recorded before the foreclosure, but they do have to have been effectuated.

What is more complicated, and not addressed in this opinion, because the issue was not before us, is the effect of the conduct of banks such as the plaintiffs here on a bona fide third-party purchaser who may have relied on the foreclosure title of the bank and the confirmative assignment and affidavit of foreclosure recorded by the bank subsequent to that foreclosure but prior to the purchase by the third party, especially where the party whose property was foreclosed was in fact in violation of the mortgage covenants, had notice of the foreclosure, and took no action to contest it.

The Bank of New York Mellon v. De Meo
227 Ariz. 192, 254 P.3d 1138
(AZ Ct. App. 2011)

Patricia De Meo, Appellant, *In Propria Persona.*

Perry and Shapiro, LLP, by Christopher R. Perry [and] Jason P. Sherman, Attorneys for Appellee.

Community Legal Services, by Jeffrey Kastner, Attorneys for Amici Curiae.

Weisberg, J.; Kessler, P.J. and Johnsen, J. concur.

Appellant, Patricia De Meo, appeals from a judgment finding her guilty of forcible entry and detainer and ordering her to surrender her leased premises to Appellee, The

Bank of New York, as Trustee for the Structured Asset Securities Corporation Mortgage Pass-Through Certificates Series 1998-8, its assignees and/or successors-in-interest ("the Bank"). For reasons that follow, we reverse the judgment.

Procedural History

The Bank held a note secured by a deed of trust on real property ("the property") owned by J.S. J.S. had leased the property to De Meo pursuant to a written lease agreement for one year commencing on August 31, 2005, with an option to purchase that expired on August 31, 2006. After not exercising her option to purchase, De Meo continued to lease the property on a month-to-month basis.

J.S. later defaulted on the note and the Bank acquired the property at a trustee's sale. The trustee's deed was recorded on August 18, 2009. On August 19, 2009, the Bank, through its attorneys, sent a letter to J.S. and/or Occupants giving notice to vacate the property within five days of the date of the letter pursuant to Arizona Revised Statutes) ("A.R.S.") 12-1173 and 12-1173.01 (2003).[1]

On November 24, 2009, the Bank filed a forcible entry and detainer ("FED") complaint against J.S. and "Occupants and Parties-in-Possession." De Meo was personally served on December 1, 2009. De Meo filed an answer on January 6, 2010 and raised several defenses, including that the Bank did not serve her with the 90-day notice required by the Protecting Tenants at Foreclosure Act of 2009 ("PTFA") § 702, 12 U.S.C. § 5220 (2009).

Regarding the 90-day notice requirement under the PTFA, the Bank's attorney told the court that the Bank did not file the FED action until 97 days after the August 19, 2009 letter, and that he did not "find anything here that would require us to provide any additional notice or any additional time." The court noted that the PTFA was a new law and that "all of us had a little bit of problem[] trying to figure out what it required, but the one thing that is certain that it requires is 90 days before an individual is going to be subject to a writ of restitution on a piece of property that they're renting." The court continued, "You had a valid lease. Once the term of the original written lease expired, it became a month-to-month tenancy. You're entitled to at least 90 days' notice from the date of the trustee's sale." However, the court reasoned that because the bank was the rightful owner, there was "no theory" that precluded the court from granting immediate possession of the property to the Bank.

The court granted judgment in the Bank's favor. The court denied De Meo's motion for the court to set bond and for a stay pending the outcome of the appeal. De Meo timely appealed.

DISCUSSION

De Meo claims the Bank violated the PTFA by failing to give her a 90-day written notice to vacate and that the court therefore erred in granting judgment in the Bank's favor. The Bank responds that this appeal should be dismissed because De Meo no longer resides on the property, rendering the appeal moot. The Bank also argues that the court did not err in entering judgment in its favor because the PTFA does not re-

---

1. Under A.R.S. § 12-1173, there is a forcible detainer when a month-to-month tenant refuses to surrender possession of property "for five days after written demand." Under A.R.S. § 12-1173.01(A)(2), a person who retains possession of property after receiving "written demand of possession" may be removed through an action for forcible detainer "[i]f the property has been sold through a trustee's sale under a deed of trust."

quire a written 90-day notice, and because the Bank waited more than 90 days after giving De Meo a written five-day notice to institute the FED action.

Mootness

"A decision becomes moot for purposes of appeal where as a result of a change of circumstances before the appellate decision, action by the reviewing court would have no effect on the parties." We may, however, consider an issue that has become moot "if there is either an issue of great public importance or an issue capable of repetition yet evading review." Even accepting arguendo the Bank's argument, the issue of notice under the PTFA and its application to the FED statutes falls within both exceptions to the mootness rule, and we therefore decline to dismiss this appeal on that basis.

90-Day Notice under the PTFA

The PTFA, effective May 20, 2009, is a federal law protecting tenants who reside in certain foreclosed properties. It provides in pertinent part,

(a) In General—In the case of any foreclosure on a federally-related mortgage loan or on any dwelling or residential real property after the date of enactment of this title, any immediate successor in interest in such property pursuant to the foreclosure shall assume such interest subject to—

(1) the provision, by such successor in interest of a notice to vacate to any bona fide tenant *at least 90 days before the effective date of such notice*; and

(2) the rights of any bona fide tenant—

(A) under any bona fide lease entered into before the notice of foreclosure to occupy the premises until the end of the remaining term of the lease, except that a successor in interest may terminate a lease effective on the date of sale of the unit to a purchaser who will occupy the unit as a primary residence, subject to the receipt by the tenant of the 90 day notice under subsection (1); or

(B) without a lease or with a lease terminable at will under state law, subject to the receipt by the tenant of *the 90 day notice* under subsection (1),

except that nothing under this section shall affect the requirements for termination of any Federal- or State-subsidized tenancy or of any State or local law that provides longer time periods or other additional protections for tenants.

(Emphasis added).

The Bank did not dispute below that the PTFA applies in this case. The Bank argues, however, that the PTFA does not require a written 90-day notice to vacate. Instead, it claims, the tenant need only receive "some notice" and that in this case, the five-day written notice was sufficient.

The interpretation and application of statutes are questions of law, which we review *de novo*. In statutory construction, we first look to the plain language of the statute to determine its meaning and to discern the intent of Congress. We consider the words or phrases in their statutory context. Also, if there is an ambiguity in a statute, we may consider its legislative history.

Section 702(a)(1) of PTFA provides that a successor property owner assumes an interest in the property subject to its provision of "a notice to vacate to any bona fide tenant *at least 90 days before the effective date of such notice."* (Emphasis added). Section 702(a)(2)(B) specifies that a successor property owner acquires its property interest subject to the right of a bona fide tenant who is "without a lease or a lease terminable at will under state law" to receive *"the 90 day notice* under subsection (1)." (Emphasis added.) Accordingly, by its express terms, §702 (a) requires that a successor property owner provide a bona fide month-to-month tenant with a 90-day notice to vacate *before* terminating the tenancy, and the 90-day period must be completed *before* the notice's effective date.

The Bank nonetheless argues that the phrase "effective date of such notice" in §702(a)(1) refers to the date the owner "takes action to force the tenant to vacate." Because the FED hearing did not take place until 97 days after the notice, the Bank asserts that De Meo "received the notice required by the PTFA." However, that interpretation is not consistent with the language of §702(a) within the context of the entire provision. As explained above, §702(a) requires that the effective date *provided in the notice* to vacate be not less than 90 days after service of the notice upon the tenant. Our reading of this section is supported by the opinions of courts in other jurisdictions.

In *Nativi v. Deutsche Bank National Trust Co.*, 2010 WL 2179885 at *3 (N.D. Cal. May 26, 2010), the court opined that "[t]he PTFA protects tenants who are the victims of the foreclosure crisis. Included in the Act is a right for the tenant to occupy the premises until the end of the lease, as well as a right to receive a notice to vacate 90 days before the effective date." *See also Bank of America, N.A. v. Owens,* 903 N.Y.S.2d 667, 671–72 (City Ct. 2010) (the PTFA's advance notice provisions cannot be construed to permit owners to take measures to circumvent or "short-circuit" the 90-day notice requirement). Obviously, a five-day notice, even when followed by an unannounced 90-day delay, is at best misleading. The noticed tenant could reasonably conclude that all arrangements to vacate the property and relocate must be concluded within the five-day notice period. Such misleading information would not be consistent with the PTFA's requirement.

Moreover, the Bank's interpretation is contrary to the legislative intent expressed in support of the PTFA. As noted by Senator Christopher Dodd, one of the drafters of the PTFA, "all bona fide tenants who began renting prior to transfer of title by foreclosure ... must be given at least 90 days' notice before being required to vacate the property." He added that [t]his new law protects tenants facing evictions due to foreclosure by ensuring that they ... at the least, receive sufficient notice and time to relocate their families and lives to a new home." 155 Cong. Rec. S8978-01 (August 6, 2009).[4] Our holding is consistent with this legislative intent.

Because the Bank failed to comply with the PTFA's 90-day notice requirement, the trial court erred in finding De Meo guilty of forcible entry and detainer and in entering judgment in the Bank's favor. The trial court further erred in failing to dismiss the FED action.

Landmark National Bank v. Kesler

216 P.3d 158 (KS 2009)

Tyson C. Langhofer and Court T. Kennedy, of Stinson Morrison Hecker, L.L.P., of Wichita, for appellants/cross-appellees.

---

4. The Bank also asserts that a written 90-day notice to vacate is not required and that oral notice is sufficient to satisfy the PTFA. But the Bank has not cited any authority for this assertion and such an interpretation would be contrary to the express language of the law.

Ted E. Knopp, of Ted E. Knopp, Chartered, of Wichita, for appellee Boyd A. Kesler.

David A. Schatz, of Husch Blackwell Sanders L.L.P., of Kansas City, Missouri, for amicus curiae American Land Title Association.

The opinion of the court was delivered by Rosen, J.:

Mortgage Electronic Registration Systems, Inc. (MERS) and Sovereign Bank seek review of an opinion by our Court of Appeals holding that a nonlender is not a contingently necessary party in a mortgage foreclosure action and that due process does not require that a nonlender be allowed to intervene in a mortgage foreclosure action.

The facts underlying this appeal are not in dispute. On March 19, 2004, Boyd Kesler secured a loan of $50,000 from Landmark National Bank (Landmark) with a mortgage registered in Ford County, Kansas. On March 15, 2005, he secured an additional loan of $93,100 from Millennia Mortgage Corp. (Millennia) through a second mortgage registered in Ford County. Both mortgages were secured by the same real property located in Ford County.

The second mortgage lies at the core of this appeal. That mortgage document stated that the mortgage was made between Kesler—the "Mortgagor" and "Borrower"—and MERS, which was acting "solely as nominee for Lender, as hereinafter defined, and Lender's successors and assigns." The document then identified Millennia as the "Lender." At some subsequent time, the mortgage may have been assigned to Sovereign and Sovereign may have taken physical possession of the note, but that assignment was not registered in Ford County.

On April 13, 2006, Kesler filed for bankruptcy in the United States Bankruptcy Court for the District of Kansas, Wichita Division. He named Sovereign as a creditor; although he claimed the secured property as exempt, he filed an intention to surrender the property. The bankruptcy court discharged his personal liability on November 16, 2006. The record contains little documentation or evidence explaining the interplay of the bankruptcy and the foreclosure action, except to suggest that the bankruptcy action may have given Sovereign constructive notice of a possible default on payments.

On July 27, 2006, Landmark filed a petition to foreclose on its mortgage, serving and naming as defendants Kesler and Millennia. It did not serve notice of the litigation on MERS or Sovereign. In the absence of answers from either defendant, the trial court entered default judgment against Kesler and Millennia on September 6, 2006. The trial court then filed an order of sale on September 29, 2006. Notice of the sale was initially published in the Dodge City Daily Globe on October 4, 2006. On October 26, 2006, Dennis Bristow and Tony Woydziak purchased the secured property at a sheriff's sale for $87,000, and on November 14, 2006, Landmark filed a motion to confirm sale of the secured property.

Also on November 14, 2006, Sovereign filed an answer to the foreclosure petition, asserting an interest in the real property as the successor in interest to Millennia's second mortgage. A week later, on November 21, 2006, Sovereign filed a motion to set aside or vacate the default judgment and an objection to confirmation of sale. The motion asserted that MERS was a K.S.A. 60-219(a) contingently necessary party and, because Landmark failed to name MERS as a defendant, Sovereign did not receive notice of the proceedings. The motion asked the court to vacate the default judgment under K.S.A. 60-260(b). The motion further asked the court to set aside the surplus from the sale, holding it to later to be paid to Sovereign if the court elected not to grant the motion to vacate.

On November 27, 2006, Kesler filed a motion seeking distribution of surplus funds from the sheriff's sale, and on January 3, 2007, Kesler filed a motion joining Landmark's earlier motion to confirm the sheriff's sale. The trial court conducted a hearing on the various motions on January 8, 2007, at which counsel for Landmark, Kesler, Sovereign, and Bristow appeared and presented their cases.

On January 16, 2007, MERS filed a motion joining Sovereign's motion to vacate the journal entry of default judgment and objecting to confirmation of the sheriff's sale, followed on January 18, 2007, by a motion to intervene under K.S.A. 60-224. MERS proffered an answer and a cross-claim to the original foreclosure petition.

On that same date, the trial court filed an order finding that MERS was not a real party in interest and Landmark was not required to name it as a party to the foreclosure action. The court found that MERS served only as an agent or representative for Millennia. The court also found that Sovereign's failure to register its interest with the Ford County Register of Deeds precluded it from asserting rights to the mortgage after judgment had been entered. The court denied the motions to set aside judgment and to intervene and granted the motions to confirm the sale and to distribute the surplus.

MERS and Sovereign filed motions to reconsider. [These were denied.]

I. Did The District Court Abuse Its Discretion In Denying MERS's Motion To Set Aside Default Judgment And Motion To Intervene As A Contingently Necessary Party?

At the heart of this issue is whether the district court abused its discretion in refusing to set aside the default judgment and in refusing to join MERS as a contingently necessary party.

The statutory provision for setting aside a default judgment is K.S.A. 60-255(b), which refers to K.S.A. 60-260(b), relating to relief from judgment, in a manner similar to the correlation between the corresponding federal rules, Fed. R. Civ. Proc. 55(c) and 60(b). K.S.A. 60-260(b) allows relief from a judgment based on mistake, inadvertence, surprise, or excusable neglect; newly discovered evidence that could not have been timely discovered with due diligence; fraud or misrepresentation; a void judgment; a judgment that has been satisfied, released, discharged, or is no longer equitable; or any other reason justifying relief from the operation of the judgment. K.S.A. 60-260(b) requires that the motion be made by a party or by a representative who is in privity with a party, thus precluding a nonparty of standing to file such a motion. K.S.A. 60-255(b) does not, however, require that the movant be a party to the action.

It is appropriate—and probably necessary—for a trial court to consider evidence beyond the bare pleadings to determine whether it should set aside a default judgment. In a motion to set aside default, a trial court should consider a variety of factors to determine whether the defendant (or would-be defendant) had a meritorious defense, and the burden of establishing a meritorious defense rests with the moving party.

We accordingly find that it was incumbent on the trial court, when ruling on the motion to set aside default judgment, to consider whether MERS would have had a meritorious defense if it had been named as a defendant and whether there was some reasonable possibility MERS would have enjoyed a different outcome from the trial if its participation had precluded default judgment....

The law relating to a contingently necessary party closely resembles the law relating to vacating a default judgment, in that both require the party asserting the interest to demonstrate a meritorious defense or an interest that may be impaired. In order to prevail on appeal, MERS must demonstrate that the trial court abused its discretion when it found, based on the testimony, evidence, and pleadings before the court at the time when it considered the motion to set aside default judgment, that MERS lacked a meritorious defense to the foreclosure proceeding or had an interest that could be impaired. We will accordingly examine the nature of the interest in the mortgage that MERS has demonstrated.

Sovereign is a financial institution that putatively purchased the Kesler mortgage from Millennia but did not register the transaction in Ford County. The relationship of MERS to the transaction is not subject to an easy description. One court has described MERS as follows:

> MERS is a private corporation that administers the MERS System, a national electronic registry that tracks the transfer of ownership interests and servicing rights in mortgage loans. Through the MERS System, MERS becomes the mortgagee of record for participating members through assignment of the members' interests to MERS. MERS is listed as the grantee in the official records maintained at county register of deeds offices. The lenders retain the promissory notes, as well as the servicing rights to the mortgages. The lenders can then sell these interests to investors without having to record the transaction in the public record. MERS is compensated for its services through fees charged to participating MERS members. Mortgage Elec. Reg. Sys., Inc. v. Nebraska Depart. of Banking, 270 Neb. 529, 530, 704 N.W.2d 784 (2005).

The second mortgage designated the relationships of Kesler, MERS, and Millennia and established payment and notice obligations. That document purported to define the role played by MERS in the transaction and the contractual rights of the parties.

The document began by identifying the parties:

> THIS MORTGAGE is made this 15th day of March 2005, between the Mortgagor, BOYD A. KESLER, (herein 'Borrower'), and the Mortgagee, Mortgage Electronic Registration Systems, Inc. ('MERS'), (solely as nominee for Lender, as hereinafter defined, and Lender's successors and assigns). MERS is organized and existing under the laws of Delaware, and has an address and telephone number of P.O. Box 2026, Flint, MI 48501-2026, tel. (888) 679-MERS. MILLENNIA MORTGAGE CORP., A CALIFORNIA CORPORATION is organized and existing under the laws of CALIFORNIA and has an address of 23046 AVENIDA DE LA CARLOTA # 100, LAGUNA HILLS, CALIFORNIA 92653 (herein 'Lender').

The third paragraph of the first page of the mortgage document conveyed a security interest in real estate:

> TO SECURE to Lender the repayment of the indebtedness evidenced by the Note, with interest thereon; the payment of all other sums, with interest thereon, advanced in accordance herewith to protect the security of this Mortgage; and the performance of the covenants and agreements of Borrower herein contained, Borrower does hereby mortgage, grant and convey to MERS (solely as nominee for Lender and Lender's successors and assigns) and to the successors and assigns of MERS the following described property located in the County of FORD, State of Kansas.

The first paragraph of the second page of the mortgage document contains the following language that apparently both limits and expands MERS's rights:

> "Borrower understands and agrees that MERS holds only legal title to the interests granted by Borrower in this Mortgage; but, if necessary to comply with

law or custom, MERS, (as nominee for Lender and Lender's successors and assigns), has the right: to exercise any and all of those interests, including, but not limited to, the right to foreclose and sell the Property; and to take any action required of Lender including, but not limited to, releasing or cancelling this Mortgage.

Paragraph 7 of the mortgage document provides the lender with the right to protect the security:

If Borrower fails to perform the covenants and agreements contained in this Mortgage, or if any action or proceeding is commenced which materially affects Lender's interest in the Property, then Lender, at Lender's option, upon notice to Borrower, may make such appearances, disburse such sums, including reasonable attorneys' fees, and take such action as is necessary to protect Lender's interest.

Paragraph 9 of the mortgage document provides the lender with rights in the event of a condemnation:

Condemnation. The proceeds of any award or claim for damages, direct or consequential, in connection with any condemnation or other taking of the Property, or part thereof, or for conveyance in lieu of condemnation, are hereby assigned and shall be paid to Lender, subject to the terms of any mortgage, deed of trust or other security agreement with a lien which has priority over this mortgage.

Paragraph 12 of the mortgage document addresses notice:

Notice. Except for any notice required under applicable law to be given in another manner, (a) any notice to Borrower provided for in this Mortgage shall be given by delivering it or by mailing such notice by certified mail addressed to Borrower at the Property Address or at such other address as Borrower may designate by notice to Lender as provided herein, and (b) *any notice to Lender* shall be given by certified mail *to Lender's address stated herein* or to such other address as Lender may designate by notice to Borrower as provided herein. Any notice provided for in this Mortgage shall be deemed to have been given to Borrower or Lender when given in the manner designated herein. (Emphasis added.)

The signature page of the mortgage document contains language relating to notice in the event of default:

Borrower and Lender request the holder of any mortgage, deed of trust or other encumbrance with a lien which has priority over this Mortgage *to give Notice to Lender, at Lender's address* set forth on page one of this Mortgage, *of any default* under the superior encumbrance and of any sale or other foreclosure action. (Emphasis added.)

The mortgage instrument states that MERS functions "solely as nominee" for the lender and lender's successors and assigns. The word "nominee" is defined nowhere in the mortgage document, and the functional relationship between MERS and the lender is likewise not defined. In the absence of a contractual definition, the parties leave the definition to judicial interpretation.

What meaning is this court to attach to MERS's designation as nominee for Millennia? The parties appear to have defined the word in much the same way that the blind men of Indian legend described an elephant—their description depended on which part they were touching at any given time. Counsel for Sovereign stated to the trial court that MERS holds the mortgage "in street name, if you will, and our client the bank and other banks transfer these mortgages and rely on MERS to provide them with notice of foreclosures and what not." He later stated that the nominee "is the mortgagee and is holding that mortgage for somebody else." At another time he declared on the record that the nominee

> "is more like a trustee or more like a corporation, a trustee that has multiple beneficiaries. Now a nominee's relationship is not a trust but if you have multiple beneficiaries you don't serve one of the beneficiaries you serve the trustee of the trust. You serve the agent of the corporation."

Counsel for the auction property purchasers stated that a nominee is "one designated to act for another as his representative in a rather limited sense." He later deemed a nominee to be "like a power of attorney."

Black's Law Dictionary defines a nominee as "[a] person designated to act in place of another, usu. in a very limited way" and as "[a] party who holds bare legal title for the benefit of others or who receives and distributes funds for the benefit of others." Black's Law Dictionary 1076 (8th ed.2004). This definition suggests that a nominee possesses few or no legally enforceable rights beyond those of a principal whom the nominee serves.

In its opinion below, the Court of Appeals cited *Thompson v. Meyers*, 211 Kan. 26, 30, 505 P.2d 680 (1973), which provides the only discussion in Kansas of the legal significance of a nominee:

> In common parlance the word 'nominee' has more than one meaning. Much depends on the frame of reference in which it is used. In Webster's Third New International Dictionary, unabridged, one of the definitions given is 'a person named as the recipient in an annuity or grant.' We view a 'nominee', as the term was used by the parties here, not simply in the sense of a straw man or limited agent…, but in the larger sense of a person designated by them to purchase the real estate, who would possess all the rights given a buyer…."

The legal status of a nominee, then, depends on the context of the relationship of the nominee to its principal. Various courts have interpreted the relationship of MERS and the lender as an agency relationship. See In re Sheridan, 2009 WL 631355, at *4 (Bankr.D.Idaho March 12, 2009) (MERS "acts not on its own account. Its capacity is representative."); Mortgage Elec. Registration System, Inc. v. Southwest, 2009 Ark. 152, 301 S.W.3d 1 (Ark. 2009) ("MERS, by the terms of the deed of trust, and its own stated purposes, was the lender's agent"); LaSalle Bank Nat. Ass'n v. Lamy, 12 Misc.3d 1191, 824 N.Y.S.2d 769, 2006 WL 2251721, at *2 (Sup.2006) (unpublished opinion) ("A nominee of the owner of a note and mortgage may not effectively assign the note and mortgage to another for want of an ownership interest in said note and mortgage by the nominee.")

The relationship that MERS has to Sovereign is more akin to that of a straw man than to a party possessing all the rights given a buyer. A mortgagee and a lender have intertwined rights that defy a clear separation of interests, especially when such a purported separation relies on ambiguous contractual language. The law generally understands that a mortgagee is not distinct from a lender: a mortgagee is "[o]ne to whom property is mortgaged: the mortgage creditor, or lender." Black's Law Dictionary 1034 (8th ed.2004). By statute, assignment of the mortgage carries with it the assignment of the debt. K.S.A. 58-2323. Although MERS asserts that, under some situations, the mortgage document purports to give it the same rights as the lender, the document consistently refers only to rights of the lender, including rights to receive notice of litigation, to collect payments, and to enforce the debt obligation. The document consistently limits MERS to acting "solely" as the nominee of the lender.

Indeed, in the event that a mortgage loan somehow separates interests of the note and the deed of trust, with the deed of trust lying with some independent entity, the mortgage may become unenforceable.

> The practical effect of splitting the deed of trust from the promissory note is to make it impossible for the holder of the note to foreclose, unless the holder of the deed of trust is the agent of the holder of the note. [Citation omitted.] Without the agency relationship, the person holding only the note lacks the power to foreclose in the event of default. The person holding only the deed of trust will never experience default because only the holder of the note is entitled to payment of the underlying obligation. [Citation omitted.] The mortgage loan becomes ineffectual when the note holder did not also hold the deed of trust. Bellistri v. Ocwen Loan Servicing, LLC, 284 S.W.3d 619, 623 (Mo.App.2009).

The Missouri court found that, because MERS was not the original holder of the promissory note and because the record contained no evidence that the original holder of the note authorized MERS to transfer the note, the language of the assignment purporting to transfer the promissory note was ineffective. "MERS never held the promissory note, thus its assignment of the deed of trust to Ocwen separate from the note had no force." 284 S.W.3d at 624; see also In re Wilhelm, 407 B.R. 392 (Bankr.D.Idaho 2009) (standard mortgage note language does not expressly or implicitly authorize MERS to transfer the note); In re Vargas, 396 B.R. 511, 517 (Bankr.C.D.Cal.2008) ("[I]f FHM has transferred the note, MERS is no longer an authorized agent of the holder unless it has a separate agency contract with the new undisclosed principal. MERS presents no evidence as to who owns the note, or of any authorization to act on behalf of the present owner."); Saxon Mortgage Services, Inc. v. Hillery, 2008 WL 5170180 (N.D.Cal.2008) (unpublished opinion) ("[F]or there to be a valid assignment, there must be more than just assignment of the deed alone; the note must also be assigned.... MERS purportedly assigned both the deed of trust and the promissory note.... However, there is no evidence of record that establishes that MERS either held the promissory note or was given the authority ... to assign the note.").

What stake in the outcome of an independent action for foreclosure could MERS have? It did not lend the money to Kesler or to anyone else involved in this case. Neither Kesler nor anyone else involved in the case was required by statute or contract to pay money to MERS on the mortgage. See Sheridan, 2009 WL 631355, at *4 ("MERS is not an economic 'beneficiary' under the Deed of Trust. It is owed and will collect no money from Debtors under the Note, nor will it realize the value of the Property through foreclosure of the Deed of Trust in the event the Note is not paid."). If MERS is only the mortgagee, without ownership of the mortgage instrument, it does not have an enforceable right. See Vargas, 396 B.R. at 517 ("[w]hile the note is 'essential,' the mortgage is only 'an incident' to the note" [quoting Carpenter v. Longan, 83 U.S. 271, 275 (1872)]).

When it found that MERS did not have an interest in the property that was impaired by the default judgment, the trial court properly considered four factors: (1) that the written pleadings and oral arguments by MERS and Sovereign identified MERS as acting only as a digital mortgage tracking service; (2) that counsel for MERS insisted that no evidence of a financial or property interest was necessary and its argument rested solely on its identity as the mortgagee on the mortgage document, when counsel was directly challenged to produce evidence of a financial or property interest; (3) that evidence showed that Sovereign was on notice that Landmark had leave of the bankruptcy court to proceed with foreclosure and that MERS did not attempt to intervene in the action until after its alleged principal, Sovereign, had already had its motion to intervene and to set aside judgment denied; and (4) that the case law submitted by the parties weighed more in favor of denying the motion. These factors were properly before the trial court and were consistent with the evidence and supported the court's legal reasoning.

Counsel for MERS explicitly declined to demonstrate to the trial court a tangible interest in the mortgage. Parties are bound by the formal admissions of their counsel in an action. Dick v. Drainage District No. 2, 187 Kan. 520, 525, 358 P.2d 744 (1961). Counsel for MERS made no attempt to show any injury to MERS resulting from the lack of service; in fact, counsel insisted that it did not have to show a financial or property interest.

MERS argued in another forum that it is *not* authorized to engage in the practices that would make it a party to either the enforcement of mortgages or the transfer of mortgages. In Mortgage Elec. Reg. Sys. v. Nebraska Dept. of Banking, 270 Neb. 529, 704 N.W.2d 784 (2005), MERS challenged an administrative finding that it was a mortgage banker subject to license and registration requirements.

The Nebraska Supreme Court found in favor of MERS, noting that "MERS has no independent right to collect on any debt because MERS itself has not extended credit, and none of the mortgage debtors owe MERS any money." 270 Neb. at 535, 704 N.W.2d 784. The Nebraska court reached this conclusion based on the submissions by counsel for MERS that

> MERS does not take applications, underwrite loans, make decisions on whether to extend credit, collect mortgage payments, hold escrows for taxes and insurance, or provide any loan servicing functions whatsoever. MERS merely tracks the ownership of the lien and is paid for its services through membership fees charged to its members. MERS does not receive compensation from consumers. 270 Neb. at 534, 704 N.W.2d 784.

Even if MERS was technically entitled to notice and service in the initial foreclosure action—an issue that we do not decide at this time—we are not compelled to conclude that the trial court abused its discretion in denying the motions to vacate default judgment and require joinder of MERS and Sovereign. The record lacks evidence supporting a claim that MERS suffered prejudice and would have had a meritorious defense had it been joined as a defendant to the foreclosure action. We find that the trial court did not abuse its discretion and did not commit reversible error in ruling on the postdefault motions.

We note that various arguments were presented suggesting that economic policy provides independent grounds for reversing the trial court. MERS and the *amicus curiae* American Land Title Association argue that MERS provides a cost-efficient method of tracking mortgage transactions without the complications of county-by-county registration and title searches. The *amicus* suggests the statutory recording system is grounded in seventeenth-century property law that is entirely unsuited to twentieth-century financial transactions. While this may be true, the MERS system introduces its own problems and complications.

One such problem is that having a single front man, or nominee, for various financial institutions makes it difficult for mortgagors and other institutions to determine the identity of the current note holder.

> [I]t is not uncommon for notes and mortgages to be assigned, often more than once. When the role of a servicing agent acting on behalf of a mortgagee is thrown into the mix, it is no wonder that it is often difficult for unsophisticated borrowers to be certain of the identity of their lenders and mortgagees. In re Schwartz, 366 B.R. 265, 266 (Bankr.D.Mass.2007).

> [T]he practices of the various MERS members, including both [the original lender] and [the mortgage purchaser], in obscuring from the public the actual ownership of a mortgage, thereby creating the opportunity for substantial abuses and prejudice to mortgagors…, should not be permitted to insulate [the mortgage purchaser] from the consequences of its actions in accepting a mortgage from [the original lender] that was already the subject of litigation in which [the original lender] erroneously represented that it had authority to act as mortgagee. Johnson v. Melnikoff, 20 Misc.3d 1142, 873 N.Y.S.2d 234, 2008 WL 4182397, at *4 (Sup.1008).

The *amicus* argues that "[a] critical function performed by MERS as the mortgagee is the receipt of service of all legal process related to the property." The *amicus* makes this argument despite the mortgage clause that specifically calls for notice to be given to the *lender,* not the putative mortgagee. In attempting to circumvent the statutory registration requirement for notice, MERS creates a system in which the public has no notice of who holds the obligation on a mortgage.

The Arkansas Supreme Court has noted:

> The only recorded document provides notice that [the original lender] is the lender and, therefore, MERS's principal. MERS asserts [the original lender] is not its principal. Yet no other lender recorded its interest as an assignee of [the original lender]. Permitting an agent such as MERS purports to be to step in and act without a recorded lender directing its action would wreak havoc on notice in this state. Southwest Homes v. Carmen Price, ___ Ark. at ___.

In any event, the legislature has established a registration requirement for parties that desire service of notice of litigation involving real property interests. It is not the duty of this court to criticize the legislature or to substitute its view on economic or social policy. Samsel v. Wheeler Transport Services, Inc., 246 Kan. 336, 348, 789 P.2d 541 (1990).

II. Did The Trial Court's Refusal To Join MERS As A Party Violate MERS's Right To Due Process?

MERS contends that the Fourteenth Amendment and § 18 of the Kansas Constitution Bill of Rights guarantees of due process were violated when the foreclosure action was consummated without MERS receiving notice of the proceeding and without MERS having the opportunity to intervene in the action.

The Due Process Clause does not protect entitlements where the identity of the alleged entitlement is vague. Castle Rock v. Gonzales, 545 U.S. 748, 763 (2005). A protected property right must have some ascertainable monetary value. 545 U.S. at 766. Indirect monetary benefits do not establish protection under the Fourteenth Amendment. 545 U.S. at. An entitlement to a procedure does not constitute a protected property interest. 545 U.S. at 764.

MERS's contention that it was deprived of due process in violation of constitutional protections runs aground in the shallows of its property interest. As noted in the discussion of the first issue above, MERS did not demonstrate, in fact, did not attempt to demonstrate, that it possessed any tangible interest in the mortgage beyond a nominal designation as the mortgagor. It lent no money and received no payments from the borrower. It suffered no direct, ascertainable monetary loss as a consequence of the litigation. Having suffered no injury, it does not qualify for protection under the Due Process Clause of either the United States or the Kansas Constitutions.

Furthermore, MERS received the full opportunity to present arguments and evidence to the trial court. Only after Sovereign clearly had notice of the litigation, had filed a motion to intervene, and had participated in a hearing on the motion did MERS-Sovereign's nominee-elect to file for joinder. Despite its late decision to enter an appearance in the case, the trial court allowed MERS the opportunity to present arguments and evidence. It cannot be said that MERS was prejudicially denied notice and the opportunity to be heard.

We find that the district court did not abuse its discretion in denying the motions to vacate and for joinder and in holding that MERS was not denied due process. We accordingly affirm the district court and the Court of Appeals.

Coleman v. Hoffman

115 Wash. App. 853, 64 P.3d 65 (2003)

Bradley Rowland Marshall, The Marshall Firm, Seattle, WA, for Appellant.

Stephen Michael Hansen, Attorney at Law, Tacoma, WA, James Anthony Santucci, Bernard G. Lanz, The Lanz Firm PS, Seattle, WA, R. McCluskey, Attorney at Law, Tacoma, WA, for Respondents.

Bridgewater, J.

Roberta Lynn Coleman appeals the trial court's grant of summary judgment on her common law premises liability claims against Anderson Hunter, Hoffman, and Olympic Coast Investment, Inc. (OCI). We reverse in part, holding that genuine issues of material fact exist regarding possession of the Sound View II complex by Anderson Hunter and Hoffman. Also, we recognize that mere collection of rents does not establish possession and therefore affirm that portion of the trial court's order granting summary judgment to OCI.

Facts

In July 1997, Roberta Coleman lived with her six-month-old daughter, Makaliah Paige, at the Sound View II apartment complex in Pierce County. On July 4, as Coleman prepared food for the evening's celebration, an unrelated child named Paris, age 9 years, walked Makaliah in a stroller along the balcony. The offending balcony was located outside of Coleman's apartment and was thus part of a common area. As Paris pushed Makaliah, the stroller's wheel caught in a rotten portion of carpet, causing the stroller to lurch forward into the balcony's rotten railing. Makaliah fell through the broken railing and onto the ground one story below. She sustained a broken arm, fractured skull and other injuries.

OCI brokers secured real estate investments. In late 1996, OCI arranged a loan to David Brown and Steve Clem, who owned and were refinancing Sound View II. The loan was secured by a deed of trust, of which OCI was beneficiary, which carried a standard assignment of rents provision. Anderson Hunter, a law firm, funded the loan.

In early April, after Brown and Clem's default, Anderson Hunter commenced judicial foreclosure proceedings and directed that OCI begin collecting and forwarding rents (OCI remained as beneficiary under the deed of trust). To comply, OCI instructed Sound View II tenants to begin making payments to OCI rather than Brown and Clem. And, to protect its investment, Anderson Hunter began paying utility and repair costs.

Sometime before Makaliah's injury, although disputed, Anderson Hunter hired Craig Hoffman to make repairs and manage the apartment complex. Hoffman previously tried to purchase the complex from Brown and Clem, but the transaction never closed. When Anderson Hunter hired Hoffman, which apparently occurred after the failed transaction, Hoffman expected to purchase the complex at the foreclosure sale.

On July 22, 1997, deciding against judicial foreclosure, Anderson Hunter sent a notice of default and of trustee's sale to Brown and Clem. The sale occurred on October 31, 1997. Hoffman was the purchaser.

Coleman, individually and as parent and guardian of Paige, sued Anderson Hunter, Hoffman, and OCI. She alleged several causes of action, including a common law premises liability claim. The trial court granted the defendants' summary judgment motions on all claims. Coleman appeals only the trial court's order dismissing her common law premises liability claim.

Analysis

…

I. Possession Liability

Coleman appeals only the summary dismissal of her common law premises liability claim. Her theory is that the various respondents were mortgagees in possession and therefore can be held liable for the condition of the premises.

In an action for negligence, a plaintiff must prove four basic elements: (1) the existence of a duty, (2) breach of that duty, (3) resulting injury, and (4) proximate cause. The threshold determination of whether a duty exists is a question of law.

Although no Washington case is directly on point, other jurisdictions impose a duty of care on mortgagees in possession. See Mollino v. Ogden & Clarkson Corp., 243 N.Y. 450, 154 N.E. 307 (1926). Various treatises also support mortgagee liability:

> A mortgagee who properly acquires 'mortgagee in possession' status is held accountable for that possession … to third parties. In general, the mortgagee in possession is held to the standard of the provident owner to use reasonable diligence to keep the property … in a good state of repair.

Restatement of Property (Third), Mortgages, §4.1, at 189 (1997).

In order for a mortgagee to be responsible for damages to

> third parties caused by unsafe conditions on the property, the mortgagee must exercise dominion and control over the property; a mortgagee out of possession of the mortgaged premises, with no management or control, is not liable for defects therein. Constructive possession is not sufficient to constitute control.

62 AM.JUR.2D Premises Liability, §8, 356 (1990).

Although the cases and treatises cited throughout our opinion refer to "mortgagee in possession" liability, the determinative issue is not whether each respondent is properly titled a "mortgagee in possession," but whether each respondent actually possessed the premises. This inquiry is proper because the common law duty of care existing in premises liability law is incumbent on the *possessor* of land ... [S]ee also 62 AM.JUR.2D §6, at 354 ("Anyone who assumes control over premises, no matter under what guise, assumes the duty to keep them in repair"); Fitchett v. Buchanan, 2 Wash.App. 965, 972, 472 P.2d 623 (1970) ("It is a general rule that one who assumes to be the owner of real property, and who, as such, assumes to control and manage it, cannot escape liability for injuries resulting from its defective condition by showing want of title in himself"), *review denied*, 78 Wash.2d 995 (1970). As such, whether someone is a mortgagee is not critical. The critical point is the possession itself. Nonetheless, as certain cited cases deal with "mortgagees in possession," and because the parties use the phrase, we employ the "mortgagee in possession" and "possession" language interchangeably.

"A possessor of land is (a) a person who is in occupation of the land with intent to control it or (b) a person who has been in occupation of land with intent to control it, if no other person has subsequently occupied it with intent to control it, or (c) a person who is entitled to immediate occupation of the land, if no other person is in possession under Clauses (a) and (b)."

A. Anderson Hunter

By its affidavits, Anderson Hunter established that it collected rents from the tenants after Brown and Clem's default. Clise v. Burns involved a trustee who, under a deed of trust, received rents, issues, and profits from mortgaged property. Clise v. Burns, 175 Wash. 133, 26 P.2d 627 (1933). The Clise court stated that the trustee's actions did not constitute possession and control for mortgagee in possession purposes.

However, Coleman produced two relevant letters and the deposition testimony of an Anderson Hunter attorney that, together, weigh heavily in our analysis. First, a May 24, 1999 letter prepared by Paul Carpenter, a member of the Anderson Hunter firm and Hoffman's attorney, states, "at the time of the alleged accident (7/4/97) we, together with [OCI], had, for all practical purposes *taken over control of* [*the premises*] in that we could not locate and/or communicate with [Brown and Clem]." (Emphasis added). Although conclusory as to control, the letter is in the nature of an admission by Anderson Hunter and therefore factors into our analysis. Second, an October 1997 letter from OCI's senior vice-president to Carpenter states "that Craig Hoffman had been heading the 'facelift' since last April and Anderson Hunter pool was advancing funds to him for that purpose." Finally, Carpenter indicated at his deposition that Anderson Hunter began paying utility bills on June 11 and paid repair costs to a plumbing company in May or June 1997.

B. Hoffman

In his affidavit, Hoffman stated that he did not own the premises until November 1997, that he did not make any repairs or collect rents at the premises until August 1997, and that he did not fire the apartment manager until September 1997.

But Coleman produced several other documents that bear on our analysis of Hoffman's possession. First, the October 1997 letter stated that Hoffman had been making repairs since April 1997, which was before the accident. Second, in her declaration in opposition to summary judgment, Coleman states that, in May or June 1997, "Mr. Hoffman and Billy began tearing up the floorboard in front of my apartment. The work lasted for about two days. By the time they ended, the sinkhole was repaired[.]" Third, in his deposition, Carpenter stated that "[m]y recollection is Craig Hoffman terminated [the apartment manager's] service." Although the record does not reflect the specific date of termination, the line of questioning at the deposition indicates that Hoffman fired the manager sometime in May, June, or July 1997.

C. OCI

OCI carried its burden of establishing the absence of an issue of material fact regarding its possession. In its summary judgment motion, OCI stated that it has never had an ownership interest in the premises; that it had no involvement in the repair, maintenance, control, or operation of the premises; and that, in servicing Anderson Hunter's loan to Brown and Clem, it activated the assignment of rents provision contained in the deed of trust and collected those rents during May, June, and July 1997. Coleman establishes no other issue of fact as to OCI's possession.

The mortgagee possession issue was addressed in two cases from other jurisdictions that involved facts similar to those presented here. Scott v. Hoboken Bank for Sav. in City of Hoboken, 126 N.J.L. 294, 19 A.2d 327 (1941), was a premises liability case where the plaintiff sued the mortgagee bank for injuries received in a fall on an ill-maintained stairway. The court stated that the bank "had in fact assumed complete control over the premises not alone as to the collection of rents and payment of bills but also as to the making of repairs … and … the owner, in the position of a rent paying tenant, had no control."

Scott aligns perfectly with Pantano v. Erie County Sav. Bank of Buffalo, 257 A.D. 451, 13 N.Y.S.2d 932 (N.Y.App.Div.1939), which was also a personal injury suit against a mortgagee bank. In Pantano, the bank had "the exclusive right to lease the property, to bring, prosecute and settle summary proceedings for the removal of tenants, or actions at law for the recovery of rents or of any damage done premises or for the abatement of any nuisance thereon, [and] to make necessary repairs and alterations to the building." Pantano, The court allowed suit against the bank, holding that the bank possessed and controlled the premises.

In an apartment building, factors indicating a mortgagee's possession include the indicia of control that landlords normally exhibit. *Scott* and *Pantano* demonstrate certain such factors: leasing, making repairs, and paying bills. Additional factors could include making management decisions and receiving and responding to tenant complaints.

Hoffman performed two acts that show possession and control: he made repairs and a managerial decision. Similarly, Anderson Hunter performed acts indicating possession and control: it paid utility bills and repair costs, collected rents, and hired Hoffman. But the facts show that OCI only collected rents; under *Clise,* this action alone does not establish possession and control. Thus, as to Hoffman and Anderson Hunter, Coleman carried her burden in establishing genuine issues of fact regarding possession of the Sound View II. On her claim against OCI, Coleman has failed to establish an issue of fact. Therefore, the trial court erred in granting summary judgment in favor of Hoffman and Anderson Hunter, but it did not err in granting summary judgment to OCI.

II. Inapplicable Defenses

Other than disputing possession, the respondents have several different theories as to why summary judgment was proper. First, Anderson Hunter and OCI claim that they owed no duty because RCW 7.28.230 prevents a mortgagee from obtaining possession of a mortgaged premises; and, if a mortgagee was in possession here, the possession was not rightful. Second, Hoffman contends that he was merely a prospective purchaser, and, therefore, he owed no duty to Coleman or her daughter. Finally, Hoffman claims that the rotten railing was a patent defect for which he cannot be liable.

A. Lien Theory Jurisdiction Defense

Anderson Hunter and OCI assert that, because RCW 7.28.230 prohibits a mortgagee from recovering possession without a foreclosure and sale, they could not have been mortgagees in possession. This argument would preclude premises liability for any mortgagee unless and until the mortgagee purchases the premises at a foreclosure sale and then takes possession.

RCW 7.28.230 guarantees a mortgagor his right to possession of the mortgaged property until foreclosure and sale. A mortgagor does not lose his right to possession by failing to make payments on the mortgage, by moving out of the community, or by abandonment. Although RCW 7.28.230 effectively precludes a mortgagee from obtaining possession of property to the mortgagor's exclusion, the statute does not bear on the question of whether a mortgagee actually possesses the property. Actual possession, not a right to possession, is the critical inquiry in premises liability cases.

To illustrate, in Howard v. Edgren, after the mortgagor defaulted but prior to foreclosure, the mortgagee *took possession* of the mortgaged property and ran his business there for 19 months. The court forced the mortgagee to pay a reasonable rental value to the mortgagor, who had abandoned, because of that possession. The important point in *Howard* is not that the mortgagor was owed rent for the mortgagee's possession, but that the mortgagee in fact possessed the property during a time when RCW 7.28.230 gave the mortgagor the sole right to possession.

A similar point is illustrated by a trespasser seeking title by adverse possession. Before the statutory period has run, the person has no right to possession, but it would be untenable to say that the person, assuming he meets the requirements for adverse possession, is not actually in possession.

Case law in other jurisdictions is directly on point and supportive:

> The [mortgagee] asserts that because it was not entitled to immediate occupation of the land under our mortgage law, it could not have been a "possessor" of the property in question for purposes of premises liability. Although we agree that the [mortgagee] had no legal right of possession before May 3, 1990, possession for purposes of premises liability does not turn on a theoretical or impending right of possession, but instead depends on the actual exercise of dominion and control over the property.

Kubczak v. Chem. Bank & Trust Co., 456 Mich. 653, 575 N.W.2d 745, 748 (1998). Because premises liability depends on actual possession rather than a right of possession, the Anderson Hunter-OCI argument fails.

The second prong of the Anderson Hunter-OCI argument is that, if they possessed the premises, that possession was not rightful; and, because rightful possession is required for mortgagee in possession status, Anderson Hunter and OCI could not have been mortgagees in possession. Whether Anderson Hunter's or OCI's possession, if any, was rightful is not important. As stated previously, premises liability depends on actual possession, not on whether a possessor is titled a "mortgagee in possession." Thus, we need not decide whether Anderson Hunter and/or OCI rightfully possessed the premises.

B. Prospective Purchaser Defense

Hoffman claims that he cannot be liable for the condition of the premises because he was merely a prospective purchaser when the injury occurred. Hoffman's theory hinges premises liability on ownership or title. But as possession and control, not title, is the threshold inquiry in common law premises liability, Hoffman's argument fails. Despite his status as a prospective purchaser, Hoffman may be liable if Coleman establishes that he possessed the premises.

C. Patent Defect Defense

Finally, Hoffman claims that he cannot be liable to Coleman because the rotten railing was a patent defect. The rule in Washington is that a landlord is not liable for injuries caused by patent defects. But this rule only applies where a tenant is injured on the demised premises. It does not apply to injuries that occur in a common area. As to common area injuries, a landlord is liable if his negligent maintenance or negligent act causes an injury.[1] Although certain defenses, i.e., assumption of risk or comparative fault, may preclude or otherwise affect Hoffman's liability, the patent defect defense does not apply here because the injury occurred in a common area.

The trial court's order of summary judgment on Coleman's common law premises liability claim is reversed as to Hoffman and Anderson Hunter but affirmed as to OCI.

We concur: Houghton, P.J., and Armstrong, J.

---

1. Because a landlord's ultimate liability for common area injuries depends on an issue of fact, i.e., whether he exercised reasonable care, we limit our review to deciding whether the respondents owed the plaintiffs a duty.

Table of Authorities

Broussard, K., Social Consequences of Eminent Domain: Urban Revitalization Againstthe Backdrop of the Takings Clause, 24 Law & Psychol. Rev. 99 (2000), 441

Cahan, R., Home is No Haven: An Analysis of Sexual Harassment in Housing, 1987 Wis. L. Rev. 1061 (1987)

Calmore, J.O., Race/ism Lost and Found: The Fair Housing Act at Thirty, 52 U. Miami L. Rev. 1067 (1998)

Calmore, J.O., Spacial Equality and the Kerner Commission Report: A Back-to-the-Future Essay, 71 N.C. L. Rev. 1487 (1993)

Clark, I.G., Water in New Mexico, A History of Its Management and Use (1987)

Cohen, C.E., Eminent Domain after *Kelo v. City of New London*: An Argument for Banning Economic Development Takings, 29 Harv. J.L. & Pub. Pol'y 491 (2006)

Collins, C., et al., Shifting Fortunes: The Perils of the Growing American Wealth Gap (1999)

Connelly, M., Who Voted: A Portrait of American Politics, 1976–2000, N.Y. Times, §4 (Nov. 12, 2000)

Cook, A.E., King and the Beloved Community: A Communitarian Defense of Black Reparations, 68 Geo. Wash. L. Rev. 959 (2000)

Corbin, A., Jural Relations and Their Classification, 30 Yale L.J. 226 (1921), 14

Corbin, A.L., Taxation of Seats on the Stock Exchange, 31 Yale L.J. 429 (1922), 14

Crenshaw, K.W., Race, Reform, and Retrenchment: Transformation and Legitimation in Antidiscrimination Law, 101 Harv. L. Rev. 1331 (1988)

Delgado, R., First Amendment Formalism Is Giving Way to First Amendment Legal Realism, 29 Harv. C.R.-C.L. L. Rev. 169 (1994)

Delgado, R., Toward a Legal Realist View of the First Amendment, 113 Harv. L. Rev. 778 (2000)

Derricotte, T., The Black Notebooks: An Interior Journey (1997)

Developments in the Law: Legal Responses to Domestic Violence, 106 Harv. L. Rev. 1528 (1993)

DuBois, W.E.B., The Souls of Black Folk 36–51 (1989 ed.)

_____, Enforcement of Municipal Housing Codes, 78 Harv. L. Rev. 801 (1965)

Entin, J.L., Defeasible Fees, State Action, and the Legacy of Massive Resistance, 34 Wm. & Mary L. Rev. 769 (1993)

Epstein, R.A., Takings: Private Property and the Power of Eminent Domain (1985)

Farber, D.A., Afterword: Property and Free Speech, 93 Nw. U. L. Rev. 1239 (1999)

Fehrenbacher, D.E., The Dred Scott Case: Its Significance in American Law and Politics (1978), 11-12

Foscarinis, M., et al., The Human Right to Housing, Making the Case in U.S. Advocacy, 38 Clearinghouse Rev. 97 (2004)

Foscarinis, M., Homelessness and Human Rights: Towards an Integrated Strategy, 19 St. Louis U. Pub. L. Rev. 317 (2000)

Friedman, L.M., Government and Slum Housing: A Century of Frustration (1968)

Ginsburg, Justice Ruth Bader: Remarks for the American Constitution Society, Looking Beyond Our Borders: The Value of a Comparative Perspective in Constitutional Adjudication (Aug. 2, 2003)

Gribetz and Grad, Housing Code Enforcement: Sanctions and Remedies, 66 Colum. L. Rev. 1254 (1966)

Hafen,L.R. and Hafen, A.W., Colorado: A Story of the State and its People 130 (1947)

Harper and James, The Law of Torts (1986)

Harris, C., Whiteness as Property, 106 Harv. L. Rev. 1707 (1993)

Heifetz and Heinz, Separating the Objective, the Subjective and the Speculative: Assessing Compensatory Damages in Fair Housing Adjudications, 26 J. Marshall L. Rev. 3 (1992)

Hernandez-Truyol & Day, Wealth, Inequality and Human Rights: A Formula for Reform, 34 Ind. L. Rev. 1213 (2001)

Heybach, L. and Nix-Hodes, P., Is Housing a Human Right?, Homeward Bound (Chicago Coalition for the Homeless 2003)

Hirsch, A.R., Searching for a 'Sound Negro Policy': A Racial Agenda for the Housing Acts of 1949 and 1954, 11 Housing Pol'y Debate 393 (2000)

Hoerder, D., Crowd Action in Revolutionary Massachusetts, 1765–1780 (1977)

Hohfeld, W., Some Fundamental Legal Conceptions as Applied in Judicial Reasoning, 23 Yale L.J. 16 (1913)

Holdsworth, A History of English Law 122–123 (6th ed. 1934)

Horwitz, M.J., The Transformation of American Law: 1870–1960 (1992), 14

Issacharoff, S., et al., The Law of Democracy: Legal Structure of the Political Process 1–2 (2d ed. 2001)

Jaffe, E.S., "She's Got Bette Davis['s] Eyes": Assessing the Nonconsensual Removal of Cadaver Organs Under the Takings and Due Process Clauses, 90 Colum. L.Rev. 528 (1990), 18-19

Jolin, M., Good Cause Eviction and the Low Income Housing Tax Credit, 67 U. Chi. L. Rev. 521 (2000)

Joyce, J., Treatise on the Law Governing Nuisances (1906)

Kessler, F., The Protection of the Consumer Under Modern Sales Law, 74 Yale L. J. 262 (1964)

Kurland, Foreword: Equal in Origin and Equal in Title to the Legislative and Executive Branches of the Government, 78 Harv. L. Rev. 143 (1964)

Lamb, C.M., Housing Segregation in Suburban America since 1960: Presidential and Judicial Politics (2005)

Lawrence III, C.R., If He Hollers Let Him Go: Regulating Racist Speech on Campus, 1990 Duke L.J. 431 (1990)

Leavitt, N., International Human Rights Violations Here in the U.S.: A U.N. Visit to Chicago's Cabrini-Green Housing Project, available at http://writ.corporate.findlaw.com/leavitt/20040506.html (Thursday, May. 06, 2004)

Levi, J., et al., Model Residential Landlord-Tenant Code 6–7 (Tent. Drft. 1969)

Lewis, A., Make No Law: The Sullivan Case and the First Amendment (1991)

Lincoln-Douglas Debates: The First Complete, Unexpurgated Text (H. Holzer, ed. 1993), 11

Luce, H.H., The Meaning of Blight: A Survey of Statutory and Case Law, 35 Real Prop. Prob. & Tr. J. 389 (2000)

Maier, P., American Scripture: Making the Declaration of Independence (1997), 11

Mandela, N. Foreword: National Perspectives on Housing Rights xvii (Scott Leckie ed., 2003)

Marcuse, P., Housing Policy and the Myth of the Benevolent State, in Critical Perspectives on Housing 148 (Bratt, Hartman, and Meyerson, eds., 1986)

Marcuse, P., The Myth of the Benevolent State: Notes Toward a Theory of Housing Conflict (Discussion paper, Division of Urban Planning, Columbia University, 1978)

Marden, C.F., et al., Minorities in American Society (1992)

Marger, M.N., Race and Ethnic Relations (2000)

Matsuda, M.J., et al., Words that Wound: Critical Race Theory, Assaultive Speech, and the First Amendment (1993)

McClain, C.J., In Search of Equality: The Chinese Struggle Against Discrimination in Nineteenth-Century America 229 (1994)

Meltz, R., at al., The Takings Issue: Constitutional Limits on Land Use Control and Environmental Regulation (1999)

Merrill, T.W., The Economics of Public Use, 72 Cornell L. Rev. 61 (1968)

Merrill, T.W., The Landscape of Constitutional Property, 86 Va. L. Rev. 885 (2000)

Michelman, F.I., Mr. Justice Brennan: A Property Teacher's Appreciation, 15 Harv. C.R.-C.L. L. Rev. 296 (1980)

Michelman, F.I., Liberties, Fair Values, and Constitutional Method, 59 U. Chi. L. Rev. 91 (1992)

Michelman, F.I., Process and Property in Constitutional Theory, 30 Clev. St. L. Rev. 577 (1982)

Miller, W. L., Arguing About Slavery: The Great Battle in the United States Congress (1996)

Mureinik, E., A Bridge to Where? Introducing the Interim Bill of Rights, 10 S. Afr. J. Hum. Rts. 31 (1994), 23

Murphy, L. and Nagel, T. , The Myth of Ownership: Taxes and Justice (2002)

National Law Center on Homelessness & Poverty, Homeless in the United States and the Human Right to Housing (2004)

O'Connor, Justice Sandra Day: Keynote Address, American Society of International Law, Proceedings of the Ninety-Sixth Annual Meeting of the American Society of International Law (March 16, 2002)

Ortiz, D.R., The Democratic Paradox of Campaign Finance Reform, 50 Stan. L. Rev. 893 (1998)

Overton, S., But Some Are More Equal: Race, Exclusion, and Campaign Finance, 80 Tex L. Rev. 987 (2002)

Pearce, E. and Meston, Handbook on the Law Relating to Nuisances 2 (1926)

Polikoff, A., Waiting for Gautreaux: A Story of Segregation, Housing, and The Black Ghetto (2006)

Pollak, L.H., Racial Discrimination and Judicial Integrity: A Reply to Professor Wechsler, 108 U. Pa. L. Rev. 1 (1959)

Pollock and Maitland, The History of English Law 131 (2nd ed. 1923)

_____, President's Committee on Urban Housing, A Decent Home 96 (1968)

Pritchett, W.E., The "Public Menace" of Blight: Urban Renewal and the Private Uses of Eminent Domain, 21 Yale L. & Policy Rev. 1 (Spring 2002)

Prosser, Private Action for Public Nuisance, 52 Va. L. Rev. 997 (1966)

Prosser, W. and Keeton, Handbook on the Law of Torts (5th ed. 1984)

Public Campaign, The Color of Money: Campaign Contributions and Race (1998)

Rabin, E.H., The Revolution in Residential Landlord-Tenant Law: Causes and Consequences, 69 Cornell L. Rev. 517 (1984)

Radin, M.J., The Liberal Conception of Property: Cross Currents in the Jurisprudence of Takings, 88 Colum. L. Rev. 1667 (1988)

Ralph, Jr., J.R., Northern Protest: Martin Luther King, Jr., Chicago, and the Civil Rights Movement 1 (1993)

Rao, R., Property, Privacy, and the Human Body, 80 B.U. L. Rev. 359 (2000), 18

Rawls, J., A Theory of Justice (rev. ed. 1999)

Reich, C.A., Individual Rights and Social Welfare: The Emerging Legal Issues, 74 Yale L.J. 1245, (1965)

Reich, C.A., The New Property, 73 Yale L.J. 733 (1964)

Reynolds, Foreword: The Legal History of the Great Sit-In Case of Bell v. Maryland, 61 Md. L. Rev. 761 (2002)

Rich, M., Restrictive Covenants Stubbornly Stay on the Books, New York Times, April 20, 2005, at D1

Robinson, R., The Debt: What America Owes to Blacks (2000)

Rustin, B., From Protest to Politics: The Future of the Civil Rights Movement, Commentary (Feb. 1965)

Sack, E.J., Battered Women and the State: The Struggle for the Future of Domestic Violence Policy, 2004 Wis. L. Rev. 1657 (2004)

Sax and Hiestant, Slumlordism as a Tort, 65 Mich. L. Rev. 869 (1967)

Schorr, A., Slums and Social Insecurity (1963)

Scott, C., Reaching Beyond (Without Abandoning) the Category of "Economic, Social and Cultural rights." 21 Hum. Rts. Q. 633 (1999)

Selected Speeches of Booker T. Washington 32–36 (E. Davidson Washington ed., 1932)

Sidney, M.J., Images of Race, Class, and Markets: Rethinking the Origin of U.S. Fair Housing Policy, 13 J. of Pol'y Hist. 191 (2001)

Siegan, B.H., Property and Freedom: The Constitution, the Courts, and Land-Use Regulation (1997)

Simes, L.M. and Smith, A.F., The Law of Future Interests (2d ed. 1956)

Singer, J.W., No right to exclude: Public accommodations and private property. 90 Nw. U. L. Rev. 1283 (Summer 1996)

Singer, J.W., The Continuing Conquest: American Indian Nations, Property Law, and Gunsmoke, 1 Reconstruction 97 (1991)

Singer, J.W., The Legal Rights Debate in Analytical Jurisprudence from Bentham to Hohfeld, 1982 Wis. L.Rev. 975 (1982), 15

Singh, R., The Congressional Black Caucus: Racial Politics in the U.S. Congress (1998)

Smith, R.C., Financing Black Politics: A Study of Congressional Elections, 17 Rev. of Black Pol. Econ. 5 (1988)

Stephen, General View of the Criminal Law in England 105 (1890)

Stoebuck, W.B., A General Theory of Eminent Domain, 47 Wash. L. Rev. 553 (1972)

Suggs, R.E., Bringing Small Business Development to Urban Neighborhoods, 30 Harv. C.R.-C.L. L. Rev. 487 (1995)

TenBroek, J., Equal Under Law 179 (1965 ed.)

The Private Use of Public Power: The Private University and the Power of Eminent Domain, 27 Vand. L. Rev. 681 (1974)

Theilmann and Wilhite, Discrimination and Congressional Campaign Contributions (1991)

U.S. Bureau of the Census, Money Income in the United States: 1995 (1996)

Verba, S., et. al., Voice and Equality: Civil Voluntarism in American Politics (1995)

Walsh, K., The Mandatory Arrest Law: Police Reaction, 16 Pace L. Rev. 97 (1995)

Waldron, J., Homelessness and the Issue of Freedom, in Jeremy Waldron, Liberal Rights: Collected Papers 1981–1991 (1993)

Wanless, M., Mandatory Arrest: A Step Toward Eradicating Domestic Violence, But is It Enough? 1996 U. Ill. L. Rev. 533 (1996)

Wasby, S.L., Harry Andrew Blackmun, in The Oxford Companion to the Supreme Court of the United States (Kermit L. Hall ed. 1992)

Washington, B.T., Opening of the Cotton States' Exposition in Atlanta, Ga., (September, 1895)

Wharton, E., The Descent of Man, 35 Scribner's Magazine (March 1904)

Wimmer, K.A., The Future of Minority Advocacy Before the FCC: Using Marketplace Rhetoric To Urge Policy Change, 41 Fed. Comm. L.J. 133 (1989)

Zorza, J., The Criminal Law of Misdemeanor Domestic Violence, 1970–1990, 83 J. Crim. L. & C. 46 (1992)

Table of Cases

Table of Statutes

Code of Federal Regulations

Acts of Congress

Uniform Acts

Foreign Laws

International Conventions and Treaties

Index